D1613434

International Corporate Governance After Sarbanes-Oxley

Founded in 1807, John Wiley & Sons is the oldest independent publishing company in the United States. With offices in North America, Europe, Australia, and Asia, Wiley is globally committed to developing and marketing print and electronic products and services for our customers' professional and personal knowledge and understanding.

The Wiley Finance series contains books written specifically for finance and investment professionals as well as sophisticated individual investors and their financial advisors. Book topics range from portfolio management to e-commerce, risk management, financial engineering, valuation, and financial instrument analysis, as well as much more.

For a list of available titles, please visit our Web site at www.Wiley Finance.com.

International Corporate Governance After Sarbanes-Oxley

Edited by PAUL U. ALI and
GREG N. GREGORIOU

John Wiley & Sons, Inc.

Published by John Wiley & Sons, Inc., Hoboken, New Jersey.
Published simultaneously in Canada.

For general information on our other products and services or for technical support, please contact our Customer Care Department within the United States at (800) 762-2974, outside the United States at (317) 572-3993 or fax (317) 572-4002.

Wiley also publishes its books in a variety of electronic formats. Some content that appears in print may not be available in electronic books. For more information about Wiley products, visit our web site at www.wiley.com.

Library of Congress Cataloging-in-Publication Data:

International corporate governance after Sarbanes-Oxley / edited by Paul U. Ali and Greg N. Gregoriou.
    p.   cm.—(Wiley finance series)
    Published simultaneously in Canada.
    Includes bibliographical references and index.
    ISBN-13: 978-0-471-77592-8 (cloth)
    ISBN-10: 0-471-77592-4 (cloth)
    1. Corporate governance.   2. United States. Sarbanes-Oxley Act of 2002.
    3. Corporate governance—Law and legislation.   I. Ali, Paul U.   II.
Gregoriou, Greg N., 1956-   III. Series.
    HD2741.I589   2006
    658.4—dc22
                                                                            2005026054

Printed in the United States of America.

10   9   8   7   6   5   4   3   2   1

For my parents.
PUA

*In loving memory of my father, Nicholas,
and to my mom, Evangelia.*
GNG

Contents

Preface

This reader comprises an edited series of papers on the latest developments in corporate governance worldwide following the introduction of the Sarbanes-Oxley Act in the United States. That Act has transformed corporate governance practices in the United States and has strongly influenced the development of corporate governance in the Asia-Pacific and European markets discussed in the reader. Corporate governance remains a topic of keen interest not only for the accounting, financial, and legal sectors but also for the broader business and investor communities due to the measures taken by regulators around the world in response to the highly publicized collapses of Enron, Parmalat, and WorldCom and other accounting scandals and corporate fraud at Adelphia, Global Crossing, Merck, and Tyco. This is evident in the recent development of corporate governance standards by professional organizations and societies, the growing trend for institutional investors to involve themselves in the governance of the corporations that they invest in, and the increased regulatory scrutiny of risk management regimes and other internal controls implemented by corporations.

This reader brings together experts on corporate governance who have each contributed papers on the impact of the Sarbanes-Oxley Act and legislation influenced by it on corporate governance worldwide. The reader is divided into five parts. Part One provides the context for the current debate on corporate governance. It discusses the ethical and political underpinnings of corporate governance and examines the relationship between corporate governance and economic performance and stock markets. Part Two looks at the corporate governance aspects of transactions in the global financial markets, including the governance of hedge funds, and the role of institutional and other investors in corporate governance. Part Three deals with shareholder empowerment and the corporate governance implications of different ownership structures and the balance of power between shareholders, and the use of the control rights vested in shareholders to influence corporate governance. Part Four investigates issues relating to executive power and corporate governance measures directed at the board level. Finally, in Part Five, the book discusses the future of corporate governance, in terms of corporations and their internal/external stakeholders, family-dominated corporations, and the seeming ubiquity of corporate governance codes, and concludes with a discussion of corporate governance assessments.

The editors believe that this reader can assist directors and officers, institutional and professional investors, and their respective accounting, audit, and legal advisers, in navigating the complex field of international corporate governance.

Acknowledgments

The editors wish to thank Bill Falloon, senior finance editor, for his enthusiastic support of this reader, and Laura Walsh, assistant editor, for her outstanding assistance during the publication process. It has been a pleasure working with John Wiley & Sons on the production of this reader. In addition, the editors would like to express their gratitude to the contributors, without whom it would not have been possible to create this reader.

Paul Ali would like to thank Martin Gold, Sydney Business School, for providing invaluable information and insights in relation to the Australian equity market and Australian mutual funds. Paul also wishes to thank Geof Stapledon, Managing Director of ISS Australia and Professor of Law, Faculty of Law, University of Melbourne, for his ongoing and generous support of corporate governance research initiatives within Australia. Thanks are, in addition, due to the Australian Research Council for their funding of Paul's corporate governance research.

About the Editors

Paul U. Ali is an Associate Professor in the Faculty of Law, University of Melbourne, Australia. Paul was previously a lawyer in Sydney, specializing in corporate finance, securitization, and structured finance. He was part of the corporate advisory team that advised the Australian Mutual Provident Society, the largest Australian life company, on its demutualization and the reconstruction of its group, and the IPO of a new holding company, AMP Limited, on the Australian and New Zealand Stock Exchanges in 1998 (the then-largest IPO ever in Australia). Paul has published several books and articles, including articles on finance law in the *Banking and Finance Law Review, Company and Securities Law Journal, Derivatives Use, Trading and Regulation, Journal of Alternative Investments, Journal of Banking and Finance Law and Practice, Journal of Banking Regulation*, and *Journal of International Banking Law and Regulation*, and most recently, has co-edited a book on innovative securitizations (*Securitisation of Derivatives and Alternative Asset Classes*, 2005). He holds an SJD from the University of Sydney.

Greg N. Gregoriou is Associate Professor of Finance and coordinator of faculty research in the School of Business and Economics at State University of New York, College at Plattsburgh. He obtained his PhD (Finance) from the University of Quebec at Montreal and is the hedge fund editor for the peer-reviewed journal *Derivatives Use, Trading and Regulation*, published by Henry Stewart Publications, based in the U.K. He has authored over 40 articles on hedge funds, and managed futures in various U.S. and U.K. peer-reviewed publications, including the *Journal of Futures Markets, European Journal of Finance, Journal of Asset Management, European Journal of Operational Research*, and *Annals of Operations Research*. This is his fourth book with John Wiley & Sons.

About the Authors

Andrea Beretta Zanoni is a Professor of Business Economics and Strategic Management in the Milan State University, Faculty of Economics. His research focuses on Strategic Management behavior, value, and corporate governance. He earned his *Laurea, magna cum laude*, in Business Economics from Bocconi University, where he received the Gold Medal for Academic Honor. He is a member of the National University Evaluation Council (NUEC), an institutional body of the Ministry for Universities and Scientific and Technological Research and a Fellow of the Italian Academy of Business Economist (*AIDEA*) and member of Strategic Management Society. He has published extensively on corporate governance, including the books *Strategia e politica aziendale negli studi italiani ed internazionali* (*Business Policy and Strategy in Italian and International Studies*) and *Pianificazione, controllo e bilancio del valore* (*Planning and Statement of Economic Value*), and numerous articles in the leading Italian business and finance journals.

Øyvind Bøhren is a Professor in the Department of Financial Economics at the Norwegian School of Management. His primary interests are corporate finance, corporate governance, and the philosophy of science, and he has published extensively in the *Journal of Financial Economics, European Finance Review, Journal of Banking and Finance, Scandinavian Journal of Economics, Economics Letters, Decision Sciences, Journal of Business Ethics, Journal of Economic Psychology*, and *Energy Economics*. He has co-authored two recent textbooks in corporate finance. His current consulting is on minority freezeouts in listed firms and the redesign of ownership and organizational structures in large, private family firms. He has recently served as an expert witness in a corporate governance case at the Norwegian Supreme Court. He holds a PhD in Management from the Norwegian School of Economics and Business Administration.

Alain-Xavier Briatte is *avocat au Barreau de Paris* with Haarmann Hemmelrath. He graduated from the University of Law of Paris II, and Paris X. He studied at Reims Management School and teaches corporate law there. His practice as an *avocat* includes corporate law, corporate governance, corporate litigation, and banking activities in France. He has represented major pension funds in the context of securities offerings in France and engaged several corporate governance-related judicial actions when counseling employee shareholders in the context of the merger of multi-billion-euro pension funds. He also represented the U.S.-based rating agency, Governance Metrics International, in 2003, covering the CAC 40 listed companies' governance issues. He served on the OECD Corporate Governance Task Force, participated in drafting the Director's Charter of the French Institute of Directors (*Institut Français des Administrateurs*), served on the United Nations Economic Commission for Europe's Round Table on Corporate Governance in 2005, and founded the French Corporate Governance Association.

Darrell Brown is currently senior legal adviser on the USAID-funded Macedonian Corporate Governance and Company Law Project. He has 16 years of experience in financial services, securities and investment, pension, insurance, corporate governance, and commercial law reform as a legal adviser and government relations consultant. He has worked in nine countries across North America, Asia, and Europe, including three former republics of the Soviet Union. He was the editor and contributing author to the multivolume loose-leaf reference *Mercer Pension Manual*, covering tax, trust, investment, and securities law as it relates to the provision of capital accumulation and retirement plans. He was a contributing author to the International Foundation's *Employee Benefits in Canada*.

Robert Christopherson is a Professor of Economics and Finance at the State University of New York (Plattsburgh). He holds a BS degree in both Economics and Psychology from Central Michigan University, a MA degree in Economics from Central Michigan University, and a PhD in Economics from Wayne State University. He has taught Economics and Finance since 1980, and his research interests include corporate governance of hedge funds, local/regional pricing, and the economics of journal pricing. He has numerous journal publications, edited books, book chapters, and articles to his credit.

Marijan Cingula is a Professor at the University of Zagreb, Faculty for Organization and Informatics in Varazdin and teaches Strategic Management, Organizational Design, and Capital Markets. He also acquired extensive business experience during the transition period in Croatia, including managing the reengineering process of operations at the Varazdin OTC Market from pink-sheet and fax-based trading to computer-supported on-time order-driven operations. He organized the Market and adjusted the operations to Croatian laws and international standards, evaluated by the ABA. He also managed 38 broker/dealers to establish the first Croatian capital market, now the Varazdin Stock Exchange. He is the author of the first book on entrepreneurship for secondary schools in Croatia and the co-author of several books on management and organizational change.

Blanaid Clarke is a senior lecturer in Law in the Law Faculty, University College Dublin, where she teaches at both the undergraduate and postgraduate levels in Corporate Governance, Corporate Finance Law, Contract Law, and Financial Services Law. She is a founding member of the Institute of Directors' Centre for Corporate Governance at University College Dublin. She also works with the Irish Takeover Panel. She holds a PhD in Law from the University of Manchester. She has published several texts including *Contract Cases and Materials* and *Takeovers and Mergers Law in Ireland*, and numerous articles and papers, including in the *Journal of Corporate Studies*.

Albert Corhay is Professor of Accounting and Finance at the HEC Management School of the University of Liège, Belgium, and Associate Professor of Finance at the University of Maastricht, the Netherlands. He was Dean of the Faculty of Economics, Management, and Social Sciences of the University of Liège and was Chairman of the Management School of that University for four years. He holds a BA and an MA degree in Management from the University of Liège and a PhD in Financial Economics from the University of Cambridge. During his doctoral research, he was a fellow of the Intercollegiate Centre for Management Sciences, Brussels. His research centers on portfolio management, asset pricing models, market efficiency, stock price modeling, and estimation of risk. He has written over 40 articles published in journals such as the *Journal of Finance, Journal of Banking and Finance, Applied Financial Economics, Journal of Business Finance and Accounting, Review of Financial Economics, Quarterly Review of Economics and Finance* and the *International Review of Economics and Finance*.

Andree Dighaye is a research and teaching assistant in Accounting and Finance at the HEC Management School of the University of Liège, Belgium. She holds a BA and an MA degree in Management from the University of Liège, Belgium, and is doing a PhD in Financial Economics at the University of Liège. Her doctoral research deals with the success of stock option plans.

Irene Lynch Fannon is a Professor in the Faculty and Department of Law, University of Cork. She holds a BCL from University College Dublin, a BCL from Oxford University, where she was a Senior Scholar of Somerville College, and a Doctor of Juridical Science from the University of Virginia. She is qualified as a solicitor and has practiced law in London. She was a member of the Audit Review Group established by the Irish Government following the Public Accounts Committee Enquiry into DIRT and other irregularities. She was head of the Department of Law at UCC and was also Dean of the Faculty of Law. She is currently on leave of absence at Cleveland Marshall College of Law, where she has been appointed to the Baker Hostetler Chair for distinguished visiting academics. She is the author of *Working within Two Kinds of Capitalism*.

Björn Fasterling is the head of EDHEC's Department of Law. In this position he directs academic programs and administers the school's law faculty. He teaches European law, company law and international legal risk management. His research and publications focus on comparative aspects of company, financial, and liability law. Prior to joining EDHEC, he worked as a German lawyer in the Berlin office of the law firm Wilmer, Cutler & Pickering, and practiced in the fields of corporate law and international arbitration. He holds German law degrees (1 state exam, 2 state exam), a PhD in Law from the University of Osnabrück, and an LLM degree from the University of Stockholm. He is a member of various academic associations, including the European Corporate Governance Institute and the Max Planck Institute for Foreign Private and Private International Law.

Martin Gold lectures in the postgraduate programs of the Sydney Business School, Australia. Martin is an experienced funds manager and investment analyst who worked for several institutional investment firms before becoming an academic in 2003. He publishes in the areas of innovative financial products and the fiduciary responsibilities of fund managers.

Silvia Gómez-Ansón is an Associate Professor of Finance in the Department of Business Administration and Accountancy, Faculty of Economics and Business Administration, University of Oviedo, Spain. She holds a PhD in Economics from the University of Oviedo. She is currently undertaking a major research project on the corporate governance of Spanish listed companies in conjunction with the Financial Studies Foundation and the Spanish Association of Financial Analysts, and has published extensively on corporate governance, including numerous books and book chapters. She is a member of the European Corporate Governance Institute, the International Family Enterprise Research Academy, the Centre for Corporate Governance Research at the University of Birmingham, and the Working Group on Corporate Social Responsibility of the Spanish Civil Sector.

Michael Julian is a member of the New York and Paris Bars and practices with the Paris office of Haarmann Hemmelrath. He advises European and American companies on a variety of corporate governance and M&A issues. In addition to his extensive work in the field of international mergers and acquisitions, he has significant experience in the development and implementation of corporate governance compliance programs within listed and privately held companies. He earned his JD from the West Virginia University College of Law and holds a postgraduate degree (*Diplôme d'Etudes Spécialisées*) from the Institute for European Studies at the Free University of Brussels, Belgium. In addition to his legal practice, Michael lectures and regularly speaks at conferences on corporate governance and legal compliance issues.

Sven Kehren holds a diploma in economics from University of Hamburg. He started his research in corporate governance in 2001. Currently, he is preparing his dissertation on the economic impact of the second largest shareholder for publication.

William R. Kelting is Associate Professor of Accounting at the State University of New York (Plattsburgh). He obtained his PhD from the University of Arkansas and his MBA from Rutgers. He is also a CPA. His research interests include auditing, governmental and nonprofit accounting, and accounting history. He has published in *The Accounting Educators Journal, Pensions: An International Journal* and in the *Journal of Financial Crime*.

Hubert de La Bruslerie is Professor of Finance at the University of Paris I Sorbonne and is currently Dean of the Management and Business Department of that University. His areas of interest are corporate governance and corporate finance. He has recently published a book on bond management and he is a regular contributor to French finance academic reviews. He is also the official financial expert to the Court of Appeal of Paris.

Richard Leblanc is an Assistant Professor, Corporate Governance, Law and Ethics, at the Atkinson Faculty of Liberal and Professional Studies, York University, Toronto, Canada. He was recently chosen as one of Canada's "Top 40 Under 40,"™ and is an award-winning teacher, certified management consultant, professional speaker, professor, lawyer, and independent adviser and specialist in boards of directors and effective corporate governance. As an educator, he was the recipient of the first Schulich Teaching Award from York University's Schulich School of Business, as selected by his students. He also holds a PhD from the Schulich School of Business. His PhD was adjudicated as the winner of the Best Dissertation Award by the Administrative Sciences Association of Canada, as assessed by independent peer-review (June 2004). In addition, he provides advisory assistance to boards of directors and has advised directors and executives from the United States, U.K., Australia, New Zealand, Europe, Russia, China, and Mexico. He is the co-author of *Inside the Boardroom: How Boards Really Work and the Coming Revolution in Corporate Governance* (2005), published by John Wiley & Sons.

Gregory F. Maassen (a Fulbright scholar) specializes in the management and implementation of technical assistance projects (USAID, World Bank, OECD, EBRD) in the fields of economic law reform, private sector development, and corporate governance. He is an Assistant Professor at the Rotterdam School of Management, Erasmus University in the Netherlands, where he regularly publishes articles in international journals and where he teaches MBA courses on corporate governance and strategic management. He is also Chief of Party (Project Manager) and Technical Expert of a three-year USAID Corporate Governance and Company Law Project implemented by Emerging Markets Group, previously Deloitte Touche Tohmatsu in Macedonia. He was Head of Office and Project Manager for the International Finance Corporation (IFC) of the World Bank Group in Armenia and senior specialist in Russia. Other work experience with the IFC included assignments in Georgia, Uzbekistan, Azerbaijan, Mongolia, Kazakhstan, and Ukraine. He holds a PhD from Erasmus University, and his doctoral dissertation on international corporate governance models was published by Spencer Stuart.

Pierre A. Michel is Professor of Investment Analysis at the HEC Management School of the University of Liège, Belgium, and Affiliate Professor of Financial Accounting at the Solvay Business School of the Free University of Brussels. He is the Academic Director of the Luxembourg School of Finance (University of Luxembourg). He served as Chairman of the Management School of the University of Liège for six years. He holds both an MBA and a PhD in Finance from the Stern School of Business of New York University. He has published seven books in finance and accounting and has written over 40 book chapters and articles, which have appeared mostly in international journals, on a variety of topics that include asset valuation, risk estimation, market efficiency, corporate finance, and financial statements analysis. He also is President of the Economics and Management Commission of the National Fund of Scientific Research (Belgium).

Timothy J. Nichol is Associate Dean of Newcastle Business School, University of Northumbria. He holds a degree in Jurisprudence from Oxford University, and is a Qualified Chartered Accountant and Fellow of the Chartered Institute of Taxation. In 1997, he was seconded to the Know How Fund and worked as a Resident Advisor at the Ukrainian Central Bank as part of a multiagency team advising on the implementation of banking reform measures.

Justin O'Brien runs the corporate governance program at the School of Law, Queen's University, Belfast. He is the author of *Wall Street on Trial* (2003), and the editor of *Governing the Corporation: Corporate Governance and Regulation in Global Markets* (2005). Dr. O'Brien's main research interests lie in the intersection between Market Regulation and Public Policy; Corporate Crime; International Comparative Corporate Governance, and Business Ethics. He has recently received a major grant from the Economic and Social Research Council in the United Kingdom to examine the international implications of the U.S. Sarbanes-Oxley legislation. A former investigative journalist and television editor, he has worked for a range of national and international broadcasters, including three divisions of the BBC. He holds a doctorate in Political Science and a Masters of Philosophy in Law from Queen's University, Belfast.

Bernt Arne Ødegaard is an Associate Professor in Finance at the Norwegian School of Management. He holds a PhD in Finance from Carnegie Mellon University. He has published in leading journals, including the *Journal of Finance* and *Nordic Journal of Political Economy*, and has recently co-authored a book on corporate finance.

Stefan Prigge holds a doctoral degree in Economics from the University of Hamburg. He has undertaken research into corporate governance since 1995 at the University of Hamburg and Max Planck Institute for Foreign Private and Private International Law, Hamburg (1996–1998). Among other publications, he edited, in cooperation with Hideki Kanda, Klaus J. Hopt, Mark J. Roe, and Eddy Wymeersch, *Comparative Corporate Governance: The State of the Art and Emerging Research* (1998). Additional research areas include competition in financial markets and regulation of the financial sector.

Colin Read is interested in the interplay between public and tax policy, economic efficiency, and ethics. He holds a PhD in Economics, a JD in Law, and a Master of Accountancy in Taxation. His publications are primarily in the areas of the economics of information and in law and economics. He is currently the Dean of the School of Business and Economics at Plattsburgh State University.

María Sacristán-Navarro is a Professor in the Department of Business Administration, Rey Juan Carlos University, Spain.

Geof Stapledon is Managing Director of ISS Australia and a Professor of Law at Melbourne University. He has published widely in the areas of corporate governance, institutional investment, and corporate law. His book, *Institutional Shareholders and Corporate Governance*, was published by Oxford University Press in 1996. Geof has degrees in Economics and Law from the University of Adelaide, and obtained his doctorate from the University of Oxford. He has practiced as a solicitor with the Adelaide commercial law firm, Finlaysons, and with Minter Ellison in Sydney.

Clemens Völkl studied law at the University of Vienna, Stockholms Universitet, and the London School of Economics. After working as a lawyer's associate in Vienna, he became a research assistant at the University of Vienna's Department of Civil Law, earning a PhD in Corporate and Commercial Law. His dissertation concerned corporate governance enforcement in Austria. He currently works as a lawyer's associate in Vienna and is an Assistant Professor at the University of Vienna's Department of Civil Law. His research is focused on tort, corporate and capital markets law, and corporate governance. His publications include a book, and various articles on corporate governance enforcement, the *Societas Europaea*, liability for false information under civil law, capital markets law, and reporting requirements and alternative dispute resolution.

Margaret Wang is a lecturer in the School of Law, and an Associate of the Centre for International Corporate Governance Research, Victoria University, Melbourne, Australia. Before taking up her position with Victoria University, she worked in law firms in Taiwan and Hong Kong where she specialized in corporate advisory matters and capital market transactions. She is also admitted to practice in Australia. Margaret has published extensively on corporate governance in Asia, with a particular focus on the operation of Chinese businesses within the Greater China region. She is currently undertaking research on the challenges confronted by the introduction of western standards of corporate governance in Asia. She has published a number of articles on corporate governance and independent directors, including in the *European Business Law Review*.

Framework of Corporate Governance

The Ethics of Corporate Governance: What Would the Political Philosophers Say?

Colin Read

INTRODUCTION

Ethics involves a determination of what is right and what is wrong; or in the words of the Greek philosopher, Epicurus, ethics "deals with things to be sought and things to be avoided, with ways of life and the (end of life)" (Laertius 1925). Ethics extends beyond the individual and invokes a permanent rather than a situational perspective. (However, the existential theory of Jean Paul Sartre would argue otherwise.) Ethics invokes the management of the environment within which we function from a perspective broader than, but obviously inclusive of, the current cohort. Again borrowing from the Greek, the terms *ecology* and *economics* share a root in the Greek word *oikos*, literally meaning *house*, but interpreted as meaning the environment within which we live. While ecology is the logical study of the environment, economics is the management of the environment within which we operate. Since the corporate environment is in theory an infinitely lived entity owned by finitely lived shareholders, a governance ethic must represent a system that serves the needs of the current ownership while preserving the ability of the corporation to sustain itself and benefit future cohorts.

Before engaging in the techniques one could use to frame governance problems within an ethical foundation, let us bound the argument by two extremes, and from there gain confidence that the ethical solution lies somewhere in between. The first argument states that the corporation is here only to serve the current cohort. That argument cannot serve as a truly corporate ethic because the argument could have been made generations ago and generations hence with equal conviction but without equal correctness. It would instead create a series of mutually exclusive governance prescriptions without regard for the costs imposed upon any future cohort wishing to invoke the same situationally convenient argument.

Alternately, we can dispense with the second argument, that the corporation should perpetuate itself in its current form. The market forces thrust upon a corporation are in constant flux, and hence preservation of its current state is impossible. Instead, this latter argument might be to try to manage the corporation for maximum preservation. Such a preservationist argument would preserve all corporate capital for future generations. Of course, we should anticipate using capital at some point since, by doing so, one cohort can benefit and no other cohort would suffer. (This notion of an ethical decision is also an efficient decision. It is named the Pareto Principle, after the Italian economist who originated the notion.) The ethical quandary would then be the determination of which generation should be permitted to benefit from the value of the corporation. Should we delay paying out dividends indefinitely by constantly retaining earnings, even if the capital is depreciated through obsolescence? If such were the case, and hence no single cohort benefits, we would violate the premise that decisions are to be made for things sought and to be avoided in life.

The corporate ethic must then lie somewhere between these two extremes. It must necessarily promote efficiency in coexisting with the environment to generate the quality of life for a current cohort and yet also provide an equity that does not disadvantage a future cohort by the decisions of a current cohort. Our test for a corporate ethic must establish a balance between these two competing views.

As an example to further explore this balance, consider corporate perks, bestowed on the current cohort of principals or agents, always at the expense of future cohorts, or even some current cohorts deluded by accounting practices that mask such perks. While such violations by agents of principals' interests impose inefficiencies, we shall next see that they also impose intertemporal inequities. Negotiations over improvements in current accounting can mitigate the delay in costing such practices. However, the decisions of mortals will always favor benefits that come with delayed costs. The insights of Robert Solow question this ethic.

THE THEORY OF SOLOW IN A CORPORATE CONTEXT

Let us begin by offering up contributions from some eminent social and economic philosophers. I begin with Robert Solow, a contemporary economist who won the Nobel Prize in economics for his study of optimal economic growth. In determining the level of optimal growth, Solow observed that we can accelerate current growth simply by "eating the seed," or growing presently by detracting from the wellbeing of those that follow. Indeed, even we as individuals are familiar with that concept. In the cartoon *Popeye*, Wimpy was always willing to pay you Tuesday for a hamburger today. Economic theory deduces all of us would rather consume a certain amount today than trade it for the same amount a year from now. This universal discount for the future is a mere expression of our mortality rather than a flaw in our individual ethic. However, it would be a flaw in the corporate ethic. Society is infinitely lived and cannot say that one cohort is more important than another. Hence, Solow argues that the only ethical discount rate is a zero discount rate—in other words, no decision, benefit, or cost ought to be more highly valued in one generation than another. As a consequence of this governance ethic, we must include in our theory an intergenerational benchmark, with all generations weighted identically. This is not to say that a decision should not be made that would benefit one generation. Rather it states that benefits incurred by one generation be balanced against, and indeed should bear, the costs to others that follow.

THE THEORY OF KANT IN AN ENVIRONMENTAL CONTEXT

Immanuel Kant provides us with the notion of universal law. Kant states, "If we now attend to ourselves in any transgression of a duty, we find that we actually do not will that our maxim should become a universal law—because this is impossible for us—but rather that the opposite of this maxim should remain a law universally. We only take the liberty of making an exception to the law for ourselves (or just for this one time) to the advantage of our inclination" (Kant 1993). In this argument, my current generation could not determine it correct to irreversibly consume corporate capital to the detriment of any other (now or in the future) that would also like to consume that resource but cannot because of my decision. In other words, I cannot rationalize my decision to consume and deprive others simply because I am fortunate enough to be in the circumstance that allows me to make such a decision. (This circumstance-specific decision making is often called a *situational ethic*.)

THE THEORY OF RAWLS IN AN ENVIRONMENTAL CONTEXT

Finally, let us have the (up to very recently) contemporary economic philosopher John Rawls weigh into the discussion (Rawls 1999). Rawls argues for distributive justice. He acknowledges that our decisions are al-most fatally influenced by the self-serving benefits and less influenced by the costs of our decision borne by others. As a consequence, a wealthy person finds herself believing in low taxes and a poor person believes in a highly progressive tax structure. As an environmental ethic analogy, those living today naturally believe in dividend payouts today with less regard for the consequences tomorrow, and those living tomorrow would prefer dividend payouts tomorrow without regard for the sacrifices we make to-day to allow their greater consumption tomorrow. Rawls' resolution to this dilemma was to impose a *veil of ignorance* on the decision-maker. Under this technique, a decision is made without regard (or perhaps with equal regard) to which class (of those that benefit or those that pay the cost of the decision) the decision-maker may find herself in.

To some degree, we all go through a Rawlsian veil. For instance, I may make self-sacrificing decisions for the benefit of my daughter, as may a grandmother for her grandchild. The philosophical biologist Hamilton formulated what has become known as Hamilton's Rule to explain such a phenomenon (Hamilton 1964). Within the parlance of economics, he recognizes that an externality exists when a decision is made that confers the benefits b on one agent, while imposing the costs c on another. One makes the correct decision only if an agent enjoys the positive externality he generates on another. Of course, if he is so positively related to the other (a relatedness coefficient r equal to one), then the other's benefit is like his own, and he is willing to incur the costs to obtain benefit for another. Indeed, he will make the decision if:

$$rb > c$$

(Actually, Hamilton's Rule is most often expressed as $rb - c > 0$, but has been modified to more closely conform with the economic rule for efficient decision making that $MB = MC$, where MB is the marginal benefit earned by making an incremental decision and MC is the marginal cost incurred for such a decision.)

In a Rawlsian world, correct decisions would be made if the relatedness coefficient would be equal to one for all decisions and all decision-makers. Perhaps the most useful implication of this notion in our context would be to have all decision-makers feel equally wed to all future generations as their current generation, a notion consistent with Solow's notion of a zero social discount rate. Yet this is at odds with most mortals' and markets' natural inclination to adopt a positive discount rate approximated by the prevailing return to capital.

TOWARD AN INTEGRATION AND AN EMERGING GOVERNANCE ETHIC

Let us again frame the governance problem. Decision-makers make decisions based on their perception of the benefits and costs flowing to them and perhaps their current cohort. These benefits are in the form of a consumer's surplus, the amount gained through the decision in excess of the amount given up. When there is a simultaneous benefit conferred or cost incurred upon the current cohort in a market-based decision, we can use the political process to correct the self-serving nature of a marketplace populated by finite-lived individuals who collectively determine the value for infinitely lived corporations.

This complementarity between market and individual decisions can work well in theory if transactions costs are low and information is good. However, the marketplace is decidedly oriented toward current market participants, while corporate politics caters primarily to current corporate executives, directors, and shareholders. Neither mechanism can be expected to make decisions based on a universal governance ethic unless at least a majority of the political constituents desire decisions based on that ethic, or unless almost all market participants act consistently with the ethic.

CONCLUSION

Given the unrealism of an emerging corporate ethic through the actions of mortal cohorts, it is difficult to develop an institution that creates the appropriate incentive for ethical corporate decisions. There emerges no single theory of a corporate ethic. Indeed, the marketplace is at odds with the principle of a zero social discount rate. Nonetheless, these theories all suggest a corporate ethic that recognizes the relationship between intergenerational decision making.

CHAPTER 2

The Politics of Symbolism: Sarbanes-Oxley in Context

Justin O'Brien

INTRODUCTION

The passage by the United States Congress of the Public Company Accounting Reform and Investor Protection Act 2002 (Sarbanes-Oxley) functions as the theoretical and practical lynchpin of a domestic policy response to corporate malfeasance and misfeasance. The legislation serves four interlinked purposes. It creates new structures to regulate both the audit process and the profession; increases the responsibilities and liabilities of corporate boards for failure to insure against future malefaction; provides protection for internal whistleblowers; and enhances the authority of the Securities and Exchange Commission (SEC) to police the market. Given the depth and liquidity of U.S. capital markets and the increased securitization of the global economy, the legislation and its underlying normative assumptions that enhanced disclosure obligations will provide for greater transparency and accountability have implications far beyond the country's geographical contours.

Heralded (and since denigrated) as the most far-reaching change to the governance of corporations and the markets in which they operate since the 1930s (Walker 2005; Romano 2004; Skeel 2005), does the contested claim withstand forensic investigation? This chapter deconstructs the policy response to ascertain its underlying function. First the rationale and main

Note: This research was facilitated by a grant from the Economic and Social Research Council, which is gratefully acknowledged (Grant Number: RES-156-22-0033).

provisions of the legislation are traced and then critiqued. In the following two sections, drawing from the work of Murray Edelman (1960, 1964, 1988) to critique the history of financial regulation, I argue that despite its ostensibly stringent provisions, Sarbanes-Oxley should be viewed primarily as an exercise in symbolism. Next, I assess how the reforms address the role of the gatekeepers and the implications of efforts to place the responsibility for detecting corporate crime on the shoulders of boards of directors and the audit profession alone. In the final section, I demonstrate how the contours of the contemporary debate over the internal control provisions of Sarbanes-Oxley are linked directly to the relative and contingent power of associational actors in the corporate governance paradigm.

THE RATIONALE AND PROVISIONS OF SARBANES-OXLEY

The pricking of the overblown equity markets in 2000 and the related question of who was ultimately responsible for the erosion of regulatory oversight placed inexorable pressure on the political system. Congress was forced to move quickly to address the corporate malfeasance crisis exposed as the bubble deflated. Hearings were convened and executives called to partial account. In the main they asserted their constitutional right to plead the fifth amendment to avoid the risk of self-incrimination (Senate 2002; GAO 2003). The passage of Sarbanes-Oxley within weeks of the collapse of the telecommunications giant WorldCom is testament to the political imperatives at work. The political establishment asserted through the Securities and Exchange Commission and the newly established Public Company Accounting Oversight Board a public degree of power and authority over corporate bodies, self-regulatory organizations, and professions not seen since the New Deal era. In so doing it reconstituted the boundaries of state–federal relations. Through an intensification of partial preemption constitutional arrangements governing the incorporation of entities long accepted as the preserve of the states were transferred to federal jurisdiction with as-yet unknown consequences (Romano 2002; Strine 2002; Chandler and Strine 2003; Clarke 2004, 389).

While the events leading to the passage of Sarbanes-Oxley indicate a remarkable degree of consensus, it is also the case that the political establishment had much to gain from curtailing partisan mudslinging. By adopting a robust legislative response predicated primarily on a discourse that posited the blame on corrupted individuals, attention was deflected from the underlying structural conditions. The result was that salience was dissipated at precisely the moment when it had the most potential to impinge on the political environment. As Romano (2004, 144) has pointed out,

"Electoral concerns were thereby aided at the cost of a comprehensive consideration of the implications of the legislation." With mid-term elections scheduled for the following November, there was a common determination that if corporate failure could not be eradicated, an effective political firewall could and should be erected (see Figure 2.1 for a diagrammatic representation of the drivers for regulatory change).

In many ways events followed a script outlined in 1978 by the then-chairman of the Securities and Exchange Commission, Harold Williams. Referring to the scandals that led to the passage of the Foreign Corrupt Practices Act, Williams likened the dynamics governing corporate America to a dismal three-act play, in which isolated malfeasance is replaced with flagrant abuse followed by legislative fiat (Harris and Kraemer 2003, 51). In an acute observation, Williams suggested that unless voluntary action was taken to improve the ethical foundation of the model, the performance would be reprised in a much more intrusive form as "federal legislation on corporate accountability."

Far from taking the warning seriously, corporate America made an advance payment on its own defenestration. The accountancy profession, which played a key enfranchised role in the policing of the markets, found its previous privileged position thoroughly undermined by its startling abdication of responsibility. The systemic nature of the scandal and the hubris subsequently put on display in courthouses from Houston to New York forced a temporary realignment that curtailed the capacity of those facing oversight from mounting an effective counterattack. (See Figure 2.1.) The regulatory elite was unexpectedly and temporarily empowered to force through the best practice guidelines it had advocated throughout the 1990s (MacAvoy and Millstein 2003; Levitt 2004; Romano 2004).

The Creation of the Public Company Accounting Oversight Board and Auditor Independence

The most important innovation in the legislation is the creation of the Public Company Accounting Oversight Board (Sections 101, 102, 104, 107), which is charged with establishing enhanced quality control mechanisms. The PCAOB is further mandated to conduct inspections, launch disciplinary proceedings and apply sanctions when warranted. Auditors are prohibited from the provision of non-audit services without the explicit approval of the audit committee (Section 202). The audit firm is mandated to provide the audit committee with a report that explicitly examines the impact of accounting treatment and what impact alternative interpretations would have on financial projections (Sections 204, 301). While there is not to be a mandatory rotation of audit firms, the lead partner must

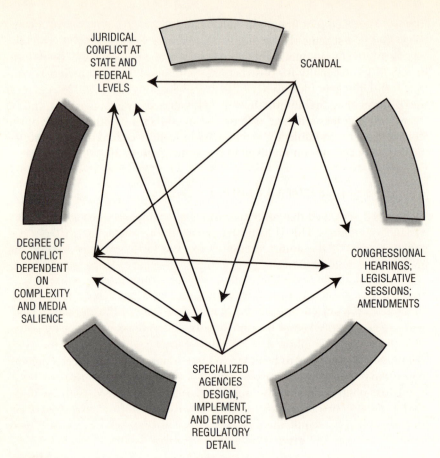

FIGURE 2.1   The Drivers of Regulatory Change

change every five years (Section 203). The revolving door between the corporation and the profession is temporarily jammed with the ban on a firm carrying out an audit if a senior executive at the corporation to be examined had participated in the exercise for the accounting firm in the preceding 12 months (Section 206).

Increased Corporate Liabilities

Chief Executive and Chief Financial Officers are mandated to attest to the truthfulness of corporate accounts in order to minimize any future defense based on ignorance (Section 906; Section 302). Penalties for failure to certify are increased to a fine of $5 million and up to 20 years imprisonment. Engaging in a scheme that fraudulently misrepresents material facts to the marketplace is now punishable with a prison term of up to 25 years (Section 807). The penalty for obstruction, including, but not limited to, document shredding is increased to 20 years (Sections 802, 1102). There is recognition that the auditor may be pressurized by management and it, therefore, becomes a federal offense for any director or other officer of the corporation to fraudulently attempt to influence, coerce, manipulate, or mislead any accountant involved in the audit (Section 303).

Strengthening the Internal Control Procedure

Congress determined that all corporations must improve their internal governance structures. This is achieved primarily by buttressing the role and independence of the audit committee (Section 301). At least one of the members of the committee must be a financial expert (Section 407). Senior management is further mandated to disclose to the audit committee any deficiency in internal controls or material weaknesses (Section 302). The audit committee is given the right to hire auditors and has the ultimate responsibility as to whether a firm can provide non-audit services (Sections 201–202), which, if allowed, must be disclosed. Each member of the audit committee is mandated to be independent and is barred from accepting any consultancy fees from the corporation or any of its key suppliers.

Most controversially, the audit committee is charged with ensuring that internal controls are commensurate with levels of operating risk (Section 404). These include the maintenance of records that reflect particular transactions and the attestation of management that the controls are robust enough to ensure early reporting of any material fact whose disclosure could impact on the financial statements.

While the SEC has not prescribed a model, it does argue that it "must be based on a recognized control framework established by a body or group that has followed due process procedures including a broad distribution of the framework for public comment" (Cohen and Brodsky 2004, 318). Not only has the framework to be tested, but the evidence on which evaluation is based must be capable of retrieval.

Increased Disclosure

The Act calls for the disclosure of all off-balance-sheet transactions and mandates increased internal financial control mechanisms (Section 404). Corporations are mandated to promptly disclose to the SEC any material changes in financial condition or operation (Section 409). The need to place a copy of a corporate ethics program with the SEC (Section 406) and report any derogation from it offers a way to ensure that internal controls are ethically grounded. Some of the most egregious examples of unethical behavior revealed in the governance crisis are explicitly proscribed. No executive may sell stock at a time when the pension fund holders are precluded (Section 306) and the extension of loans to senior executives or directors is severely curtailed (Section 402). Stock options and bonuses paid as a consequence of earnings that have subsequently to be restated are liable to disgorgement (Section 304).

While this provision applies when the perpetrator is brought to justice, it fails to tackle the issue of how stock options create the dynamic for aggressive financial engineering in the first instance. Coffee (2004a, 346) argues cogently that there remains a public policy imperative to increase further the *legal threat* necessary to ensure gatekeeper quiescence, to reduce the *perverse incentives* created by stock options, and to ensure that structural defects in what he terms "an excessive market bias" toward optimism.

It was initially proposed that lawyers should noisily withdraw by reporting to the SEC if they become aware that their clients are attempting to engage in financial misrepresentation. In the final Act this was watered down to the reporting of any concerns about potential breaches to the Chief Legal Counsel or Chief Executive Officer (Section 307). Protection of whistleblowers is not only mandated (Section 806) but there is an obligation on the audit committee to proactively create procedures to receive and retain complaints (Section 301).

THE POLITICS OF SYMBOLISM

While problematic across all aspects of public policy, governance has had the most emasculating effect on the policing of corporations, the markets in which they operate, and the professions that provide intermediating services of a fiduciary nature. The inherent complexity of the sector renders effective accountability difficult (Moran 1991, 2003). The emphasis on self-regulatory structures designed and policed by communities of enfranchised professional groupings effectively privatizes and thus emasculates enforcement capacity (McBarnet 2005). Salience for the general public is low, making the degree of traction required for constant political oversight difficult to obtain in the absence of catastrophic failure. It is for this reason that disclosure regimens, even one as detailed as that now implemented in the United States, are best understood as symbolic statements of intent.

The importance of symbols as weapons in the management of contemporary regulatory warfare can be traced to the early work of the political sociologist Murray Edelman. The explanatory power of the *symbolic* lens is linked directly to its capacity to frame both the process through which the initial legislation is enacted but also the management of its subsequent implementation. Edelman sought to understand two competing and conflating imperatives evident in the operation of the American regulatory arena: first, why policies tend to be pursued only if they are in the ultimate interests of those regulated; and second, what factors govern the dissipation of initial fervor even when enforcement deficiencies fail to meet expectation. In a seminal article, Edelman (1960) argued that public quiescence is correlated to one of two factors: indifference, or the degree to which stated policy objectives satisfy the preferred choices of constituent groups.

Regulatory capacity, according to Edelman, is conditioned by the fact that "the interests of organized groups in tangible resources or in substantive power are less easily satiable than are interests in symbolic reassurance" (Edelman 1960, 695). He concluded that "the most intensive dissemination of symbols commonly attends the enactment of legislation that is most meaningless in its effects upon resource allocation" (Edelman 1960, 697). This is not to denigrate their importance.

> *The laws may be repealed in effect by administrative policy, budgetary starvation, or other little publicized means; but the laws as symbols must stand because they satisfy interests that politicians fear will be expressed actively if a large number of voters are led to believe that their shield against a threat has been removed.*
>
> *More than that, it is only as symbols that these statutes have utility to most of the voters. If they function as reassurances that threats in the economic environment are under control, their indirect effect is to permit greater exploitation of tangible resources by the organized groups concerned than would be possible if the legal symbols were absent. (Edelman 1960, 702)*

The efficacy of the mechanism has increased dramatically because the transformation from *governing to governance* (Kooiman 2003) mediated through the ideational power of *associational democracy* (Streeck and Schmitter 1985) has further overtly constrained the independent capacity of the state to create or enforce regulatory instruments (Jessop 2003; Demirag and O'Brien 2004). Nowhere is this more apparent than in the constant battles over the structure of financial markets that have defined regulatory policy since the 1930s.

THE STRUCTURE OF AUTHORITY IN
FINANCIAL GOVERNANCE

The securities architecture created in the 1930s was predicated on the premise that enhanced disclosure would result in increased transparency and accountability (Seligman 2003a). Despite initial quiescence, as the reform process gathered pace both the rationale and provisions became exceptionally contested. Castigated as unnecessary and burdensome (McCraw 1984; Merino 2003; Seligman 2003a; Fraser 2005), the increased animosity evident then mirrors the contours of the contemporary debate over Sarbanes-Oxley three years after its enactment. The processes by which the reporting regimen was introduced and calibrated in response to a nexus of endogenous and exogenous factors, however, provide a remarkably clear example of how the shifting balance of power and differing self-interests of the corporations, market, and nascent regulators can influence the dynamics if not the underlying structure of the financial markets in the United States.

While the balance shifted over time, it was not until the 1990s that the paradigm itself came under sustained assault. The symbolic importance of the New Deal reforms were either hollowed out or repealed as the securitization of the economy deepened (Nofsinger and Kim 2003, 250). The conflation of the tripartite relationship between the market, the corporations, and the regulated into a false dichotomous battle between regulators and the regulated was underpinned by the ideational rhetoric of New Federalism (O'Brien 2005b), the individuated nature of congressional politics (Drew 2000), and the growing importance of financial services as the underwriter of the wider political and economic system.

This heady mix inflated an equity bubble already dangerously overblown by the capital flight into the United States as a consequence of the Asian financial crisis. The alchemy required to guarantee the surpassing of Wall Street metrics faced little critical questioning. Individual reporting failures were dismissed as outliers, irrelevant to the plot. The boom created a spectacle skillfully exploited by the development and needs of business cable television that positioned growth over analysis (Dyck and Zingales 2003). A conception of the United States as a shareholder nation that was privileged approximated reality only when viewed through a miasmic lens (Fraser 2005, 506). The inexorable rise of equity markets as a source of guaranteed wealth impeded any serious traction developing. The importation into the executive of former investment bankers, including Robert Rubin as Treasury Secretary, completed the transformation of government into a facilitator of securitization (O'Brien 2004b). In the judgment of a second former chairman of the Securities and Exchange Commission, "Despite a belated lurch towards reform . . . the Congress that enacted the Securities Act of 1933 bears little resemblance to recent legislatures that have short-changed the SEC" (Levitt 2002, 14).

Levitt had played a pivotal role in highlighting the dangers inherent in the manipulation of financial reporting. In a speech at New York University (SEC 1998, 95), 20 years after his predecessor had alerted his audience of the inevitable ending, Levitt warned that the legitimacy of the market system was at stake. Levitt lacked, however, the institutional muscularity necessary to compete with interest groups given voice by the mechanisms of associational democracy, and legitimacy through the gravity-defying success of the securities market on the cusp of the millennium (O'Brien 2003; McDonough 2005; Walker 2005).

Both piecemeal and radical change were deemed necessary to retain American competitiveness. The inordinate caution and bureaucratic overreach of a cumbersome regulatory framework was deemed the most significant brake on the development of the new economy. Senior executives in the banking and accountancy profession regarded Levitt as an irritant and obstacle, suggesting his concern about financial reporting displayed histrionic paranoia (Levitt 2002, 221). Private disputes within the Clinton administration about the efficacy of internal controls advanced by the investment houses as a cogent and effective alternative with cabinet-level approval remained hidden from public view (Stiglitz 2003, 159–162).

It was indicative of the increased power of the securities industry that the Financial Modernization Act of 1999, allowing for the recombination of investment and commercial banking (and a major contributing force to the scandal), could repeal the Glass-Steagall Act of 1933 without major principled rather than partisan dissension in any branch of federal government (O'Brien 2003, 102; Lowenstein 2004, 97). Even more remarkable was the shortened timeframe operated by Congress in adjudicating the wisdom of allowing more power to seep into Lower Manhattan without a concomitant recalibration of enforcement capacity to take into account a much more complex domestic and international marketplace. The passage of the FMA graphically demonstrated the capacity of The Street to reinvent itself as a model of probity a decade after the excesses that led to the disintegration of Drexel Burnham Lambert, one of its most venerable institutions (Stewart 1992; Bruck 1989). The legislative changes were also indicative of the Congressional calculation that "the determinants of future political disaffection and political sanctions" (Edelman 1960, 701) could be managed without significant cost.

The collapse of Enron in late 2001 and the fall of WorldCom the following year temporarily stymied the inexorable advance of the ideational power of self-regulation (Kirshner 2004). Congress retreated to a tired political discourse that trumpeted the protection of the metaphorical *small investor*. This in turn explains the inordinate emphasis on disclosure in Sarbanes-Oxley. The underlying imperative for stability can be traced back to the public policy efficacy of the theory and practice of Louis Brandeis and his acolytes, Felix Frankfurter and John Landis, the primary architects of American securities regulation.

If, as Edelman suggests, each political goal is at once a name and a metaphor to create reassurance (Edelman 1964, 157–158), the official title of the contemporary return to basics—the Public Company Accounting Reform and Investor Protection Act of 2002—demonstrates its central purpose. Its ostensibly stringent provisions reassure the investing public that policymakers are just as shocked by the scale of the malfeasance. There were substantial self-interested grounds for making swift decisions. Corporate America contributes strategically according to degree of individual political influence rather than affiliation across a system that is a weak facsimile of European party politics (McChesney 1997). At a national level, the Democrats could argue that the legislation owed its strength to its Senate sponsor, Paul Sarbanes. Opposition to its extended mandates risked allegations of complicity. For Republicans, there was also recognition that opposition for opposition's sake would serve only to keep the spotlight on Congress as part of the problem, an uncomfortable position when control of both houses of the legislature was finely balanced. Corporate governance slipped down the agenda. Business lobbying groups, particularly those associated with the accountancy profession, were not in a position to contest the need for greater oversight.

The charge by critics that Sarbanes-Oxley can be dismissed as a mere exercise in political grandstanding (Perino 2002, 673) represents a profound misunderstanding of the dynamics of American regulatory politics. Sarbanes-Oxley is underpinned by the six crucial symbolic criteria identified by scholars using the Edelman lens (e.g., Marion 1997, cited in Stolz 2002, 271–272). It enhanced the popularity of the officeholder (or more accurately arrested a precipitous decline); provided reassurance that significant action was being taken; simplified a complex problem (Edelman 1964, 40); provided a normative improvement in corporate governance with applicability across the states that was difficult to contest; provided an identifiable class of perpetrator, in this case the accountancy profession; and provided an educative function in how to restore an ethical basis to corporate governance.

To be effective, an exercise in symbolism requires a diffusion mechanism. Crucially, the underlying message must not be diluted by the capacity of elite groups to distort or taint the underlying message (Hart 1995, 397). Those circumstances held firm during the passage of Sarbanes-Oxley and its immediate aftermath. The adroit use of television cameras to record once-deified executives arriving in federal and state courthouses in handcuffs to face indictments reinforced the perception of zero-tolerance (O'Brien 2004a). The recalibration of federal sentencing guidelines served a supporting role in providing legitimacy for the muscular approach to corporate responsibility mandated in Sarbanes-Oxley. Its symbolic value has been increasingly tainted by a concerted attack on its provisions as a costly impediment to business efficiency. Whether the critics can gather sufficient support for a wholesale reform or be content with an administrative hollowing out remains to be seen. After three years of relative quiescence a concerted counterattack has begun, emboldened by spectacular court failures, including the acquittal of Richard Scrushy of HealthSouth, the first chief executive charged under the legislation with orchestrating financial reporting fraud.

The outgoing chairman of the SEC, William Donaldson, pointedly chose a meeting of the industry-funded U.S. Conference Board to launch a coruscating attack on the dangers of continued sharp practice:

> *This erosion of trust in business is a serious and worrying development, and there's no guarantee the problem will automatically get resolved. While regulators such as the SEC can enact bright, redline rules about what is and is not permissible behaviour, we know from the course of history that human nature will push aggressive managers and organizations to continue to test new laws. . . . The SEC and others like us can set the rules and define independence— but legal definitions can only go so far. And our free market, democratic system will gradually erode, and inevitably suffer grievous harm, if remedial efforts are not undertaken and endorsed by a broad cross-section of our business and financial communities. (Donaldson 2004)*

Despite the fact that the SEC has been empowered and its capacity enhanced by the creation of the PCAOB, much of the policing function remains in the hands of the accountancy profession. This remains an acute cause for concern, particularly now that the immediate pressure for change has been satiated and the details of regulatory instruments mandated by Congress rest in the hands of a changing commission. The direction of SEC policy is heavily dependent on the composition of the five commissioners. The departure of Donaldson and the return to academic life of Harvey Goldschmidt have changed the balance of power dramatically toward the philosophical disposition of ranking member Paul Atkins. Atkins (2005) has publicly criticized the robust stance adopted by the Enforcement Division as publicity seeking and counterproductive. Just weeks after the speech, the long-term Director of Enforcement, Steve Cutler, resigned, acknowledging philosophical differences in a politicized SEC (Interview, Washington DC, 10 May 2005). It is therefore necessary to investigate further whether the external oversight over the accountancy profession will, on its own, act as a sufficient break to misfeasance.

QUIS CUSTODIET IPSOS CUSTODES: GUARDING THE GATEKEEPERS

The Roman philosopher Juvenal identified a defining question for the study of regulatory politics: *Quis custodiet ipsos custodies:* Who will guard the guardians themselves? As the centerpiece of the legislation, the PCAOB marks a significant, if partial, retraction from the self-regulatory basis of associational governance in the United States. The gradual disintegration of the profession into *highly skilled technicians* who misunderstood the "unforgiving nature of equity markets" was highlighted by its own leadership (Zeff 2003, 267), long before Levitt took to the podium at NYU to warn: "Today, American markets enjoy the confidence of the world. How many half-truths and how much accounting sleight of hand will it take to tarnish the faith?" (SEC 1998, 95). Despite these calls for restraint, the balance of power within the profession had changed and with it the capacity of engineering self-restraint until the tipping point to scandal had been reached. As Colin Scott (2000, 39) has argued, "Trust in mechanisms of accountability is a central precondition for the legitimate delegation of authority." The accountancy profession forfeited that trust, making it a convenient scapegoat for wider systemic failures.

Given the involvement of Arthur Andersen (and later KPMG) in the unfolding scandal, it was not unexpected that the media and political discourses would simplify the crisis to a corrupt alliance between the accountancy profession and morally bereft executives. When Andersen was further implicated in the collapse of WorldCom, no amount of lobbying could stave off public and political perception that the entire audit process was the weakest link in the corporate system. Following two major audit failures at Waste Management and Sunbeam, Arthur Andersen was already operating under a cloud. The shredding of documents in London and Houston exacerbated its ensnarement in the off-balance-sheet aggressive financial engineering at Enron.

David Duncan, the Andersen partner running the Enron account, admitted overseeing the destruction of documents but claimed in court that this should not be confused with the underlying issue: The auditors had disagreed with and disapproved of the off-balance-sheet transactions. Duncan testified that as a partnership Andersen reasoned that "this was an area of corporate governance, and as long as it had been thoroughly vented through the corporation, that was a business determination by Enron" (McLean and Elkind 2003, 407). Following its conviction in June 2002, Andersen continued to maintain that it should not be punished by guilt by association. The partnership released a statement saying "the reality here is that this verdict represents only a technical conviction" (McLean and Elkind 2003, 406). The argument received partial backing from the Supreme Court, which overturned the conviction on the grounds that pursuing Andersen on the basis of alleged tampering of evidence in the absence of a federal investigation represented prosecutorial overreach. If the conviction was technical it is arguable that a similar rationale can be applied to the acquittal.

Andersen viewed its responsibility in the design and execution of the aggressive accounting in strict legal terms. Each transaction was individually audited and accepted. At no stage did Andersen take into consideration how the aggregate fundamentally distorted the overall picture. Like the other major institutional players, Andersen complained that it was an unwitting victim of Enron's deceptions, a charge dismissed by congressional and academic researchers (GAO 2003; McBarnet 2005). While the partnership had an arguable case in law, for the future of the firm the argument was academic. The shredding of documents represented a mortal blow for a firm that traded on its reputation for probity.

The remit of the Public Company Accounting Oversight Board is explicitly designed to recalibrate this baleful influence on the accountancy profession, which Braithwaite and Drahos (2001, 159) term the "model mercenaries in the globalization of U.S. regulatory and corporate governance practice." There are sound structural reasons for this partial privileging. For capital markets to function effectively it is imperative that they are underpinned by a sound legal and accounting foundation (Spencer 2000). The Chair of the PCAOB, William McDonough (2005), accepts that while it is debatable whether the primary emphasis on the accountancy profession can provide a panacea, the failure by auditors to internalize ethical restraint mandated an exceptional degree of stringent oversight that far exceeds the peer review system of piecemeal technical compliance.

> At the PCAOB, we begin by looking at the business context in which audits are performed. We focus on the influences—both good and bad—on firm practices. These include firm culture and the relationships between a firm's audit practice and its other

practices and between engagement personnel in field and affiliate offices and a firm's national office. By doing so, we believe that we will gain a much better appreciation for the practices and problems that led to the most serious financial reporting and auditing failures of the last few years. (McDonough 2005, 56)

Critics argue that the creation of the PCAOB merely replicates existing enforcement capacity within both the SEC and the Financial Accounting Standards Board (Nofsinger and Kim 2003, 212–213) and that it introduces an unnecessary new layer of complexity for little demonstrable return. Other scholars maintain that there is no empirical evidence to back up assertions that splitting the audit and consultancy functions makes any discernible difference on either board performance or propensity toward a weakened audit (e.g., Romano 2004, 166–169).

An alternative reading, however, following the Hood, Rothstein, and Baldwin (2004) model of regulatory regime dynamics, suggests that the PCAOB offers a potentially significant qualitative improvement in regulatory oversight. This occurs not only because of the probity and drive of McDonough, nor indeed its lack of financial dependence on the profession. The innovation centers on how it widens how information is gathered, enhances the degree of separation between those setting the rules and those bound by them, and is predicated, for now, on a behavior-modification strategy. Through its inspection regimen the PCAOB has the capacity to ensure that the tone at the top of the organization both filters downward throughout the firm and is reinforced by recalibrated standards.

The efficacy of the PCAOB approach will not be clear until next year because firms have a year to fix any structural problems identified by the PCAOB before the findings can be made public. This is a drawback, which McDonough ascribes to "the will of Congress" (Interview, Washington, DC, 10 May 2005). The kind of questions raised, however, does give an indication of how moral concerns, linked directly to a reinvigorated conception of the profession as a profession rather than business agents, inform his agenda. According to McDonough, auditors are not only asked whether they lost any business because of inordinate pressure, but more importantly, what happened to the audit partner involved, and to what extent the loss of an audit or the failure to be retained has impacted on payments of bonuses.

Just as important, the information-gathering component of the exercise extends down "to the least experienced members of the audit teams" (*Accountancy Ireland* 2004, 22). These reforms are to be welcomed, but it remains very much open to question whether this reliance on a reinvigorated accountancy profession alone can achieve the necessary goals given the propensity of corporate America to rely on an emasculated conception of compliance as a strict legal rather than ethical consideration.

RECONFIGURING THE BATTLEFIELD

The unrelenting focus on the punishment of individual malefactors and the creation of new stringent legislation focused on boards and auditors, but not the wider financial arena in which they operate, risks obscuring fundamental systemic flaws in the wider corporate governance model in the United States (GAO 2003). Without tackling the other associational actors responsible, there remains a profound risk that the problem is displaced rather than eradicated. It is the failure to deal with this complex reality that undermines the effectiveness of the legislation. The fact that Congress was well aware of the problem makes the oversight more troubling. As Sarbanes-Oxley was making its way through Congress, significant evidence was being presented that demonstrated conclusively the complicity of leading investment banks. Major players, including JP Morgan Chase, Citigroup, and Merrill Lynch, were intricately involved in the design and execution of many of the structured finance deals that so exercised Andersen before consultancy fees of $53 million assuaged its concern about the legality if not the probity of the transactions. In hearings in July 2002, investment bankers maintained that they too were unwitting victims (O'Brien 2003, 84–95).

The complaint by Donaldson (2004) that "some managers will pursue questionable activity right up to technical conformity with the letter of the law, and some will step over the red line either directly or with crafty schemes and modern financial technology that facilitates deception" (Donaldson 2004) suggests that leaving enforcement within the private sector without credible oversight is of questionable value. As Steve Cutler, outgoing Director of Enforcement at the SEC, explained in a recent interview: "[In the past] there was a general reluctance on the part of federal prosecutors to take on complicated accounting fraud cases. These are very difficult cases and require lots of resources, lots of time, [are] difficult to explain to juries and that makes for a less than ideal track record as far as a prosecutor is concerned. When you have got limited resources as every prosecutor does, you begin to wonder to yourself: 'Boy, is it worth spending all of these resources going after this case when I only have an X percent of success, when with the same resources I can bring six narcotic cases and take five drug dealers off the street?'" (Interview, Washington DC, 10 May 2005).

The situation is further complicated because the vast majority of economic crime is not reported. This can be traced to "the incommensurability of the public model of justice with their own needs and interests, and the costs and liabilities associated with invoking a public solution to what is often defined, first and foremost, as a private problem" (Williams 2004, 10). This ordering also has the effect of privileging crimes against the corporation to the detriment of corporate defects. More insidiously, it serves another key dynamic. It delineates the realm of acceptable debate to an endogenous conception of the limits of external legal oversight by privileging internal control systems that serve truncated and symbolic purposes, which are then given political and media validation.

The capacity to critically determine juridical norms is based on the degree of clarity and political salience underpinning the legal framework. If laws and regulations are vague, or the details left to regulatory bodies to negotiate with institutional actors given equal voice by the *heterarchy* of governance (Jessop 2003), particular intractable problems emerge. The dichotomy between appearance and reality in regulatory politics and the wider symbolic nature of law as a rhetorical device that is capable of manipulation through creative interpretation is particularly problematic. In the United States, this is a critical unresolved issue. Evidence of legislative effectiveness in instilling ethical restraint is already in question because of high-profile corporate governance failures within Citigroup, Hollinger, and HealthSouth (O'Brien 2005b). The debate on how internal controls should be viewed by regulators further demonstrates the inordinate endogenous pressures at the national level to construct a hollow shell that provides symbolic reassurance. There is a profound risk of reduced legal liability because of judicial or agency deference to an organizational response based on the institutionalization of *rational myth* (Edelman, Uggen, and Erlanger 1999, 447–448) that in turn subverts stated policy imperatives.

CONCLUSION

The corporate governance reforms advanced in response to the crisis serve a palliative purpose, treating the symptoms but not the cause. The primary emphasis on only one part of the associational matrix—the audit profession and corporate boards—merely displaces the risk. There is considerable merit in the argument by two of the most senior judges in the Delaware Chancery Court that many of the provisions in the act "appear to have been taken off the shelf and put into the mix, not so much because they would have helped to prevent the scandals, but because they filled the perceived need for far-reaching reform and were less controversial than other measures more clearly aimed at preventing similar scandals" (Chandler and Strine 2003, 6).

Even before the passage of Sarbanes-Oxley, the securities market in the United States was one of the most codified in the world. Yet its regulatory structures were incapable of instilling credible ethical restraints. While the investigative process—legal, legislative, and corporate—has proved instrumental in revealing what went wrong, there is little appetite for a more thorough examination into how to ensure the maintenance of muscular enforcement after the spotlight of media interest dims. The analysis of corporate failure must also take into account the wider structural architecture and the environmental impact on that structure of specific cultural and behavioral mores. In order to assess the consequences of any political action, it is necessary to strip away rhetorical justifications and assess just who benefits from the application or stymieing of particular policy directions. This analysis must take place at a number of levels: within the corporation, within the market, within the regulatory bodies, and ultimately, within the political system itself, which legislates and therefore legitimizes both the terms of the debate and the realm of acceptable conduct. It is only through a more granular understanding of corporate governance dynamics that we can begin the process of inculcating the cultural change that has the capacity to subordinate value to values.

CHAPTER 3

Governance and Performance Revisited

Øyvind Bøhren and Bernt Arne Ødegaard

INTRODUCTION

The fundamental question in finance-based corporate governance research is whether economic value is driven by governance mechanisms, such as the legal protection of capitalists, the firm's competitive environment, its ownership structure, board composition, and financial policy. Research on the interaction between governance and economic performance has been rather limited, however, and the empirical evidence is mixed and inconclusive. This is both because corporate governance is a novel academic field and because high-quality data are hard to obtain. Not surprisingly, therefore, we cannot yet specify what the best governance system looks like, neither in a normative nor a positive sense.

There are four different ways in which our chapter may contribute to a better understanding of how governance and performance interact. First, unlike most existing research, we include a wide set of mechanisms, such as

Note: The authors are grateful for input from seminar participants at the University of Cambridge, Norwegian School of Economics and Business Administration, Norwegian School of Management BI, University of Oslo, Universitat Autònoma de Barcelona, the meetings of the European Finance Association in Glasgow, and the European Corporate Governance Symposium of the European Financial Management Association in Leeds. The chapter has also benefited from the comments by Miguel Garcia-Cestona, Bruno Gerard, Ulrich Hege, Jarle Møen, and Richard Priestley. Financial support from the Research Council of Norway (Grant 124550/510) is acknowledged.

the identity of outside owners (for example, institutional, international, and individual), the use of voting and nonvoting shares, board size, and dividend policy. This approach brings us closer to capturing the full picture and allows us to explore the validity of more partial approaches (for example, Demsetz and Lehn 1985; Morck et al. 1988; McConnell and Servaes 1990; Gugler 2001). Due to limited data availability in most countries, such partial approaches will also have to be used in the future.

Second, we help clarify how the existing evidence depends on its specific context. Most extant research deals with large U.S. firms operating in a common-law regime with an active market for corporate control, where outside ownership concentration is very low, strong incentive contracts for management are the rule, and inside directors are common. In contrast, our Norwegian sample firms are much smaller, the legal regime is the Scandinavian version of civil law, hostile takeovers are practically nonexistent, firms are more closely held, performance-related pay is less common, and boards have at most one inside director, who by law is never the chairperson. Principal agent theory predicts that all these governance mechanisms matter for performance. By testing these predictions on firms with quite different mechanism profiles, we can better judge their general validity.

Third, the quality of our data may produce more reliable evidence. Anderson and Lee (1997), who replicate three U.S. studies using four alternative data sources, find that changes in data quality distort conclusions, and that poor data quality reduces the power of the tests. Existing analyses of ownership structure in the United States, Japan, the U.K., and continental Europe are based on large holdings (blocks) only, as there is no legal obligation to report other stakes (Barca and Becht 2001). This means holdings below a minimum reporting threshold cannot be observed, typically implying that the owners of roughly one third to one half of outstanding equity are ignored. As changes in large holdings are only registered at certain discrete thresholds, any stake between these discrete points is estimated with error, and every stake above the highest reporting threshold is underestimated. Also, except for the U.K. and the United States, the available international evidence refers to just one or two years in the mid-1990s. In contrast, our data include every single stake in all firms listed on the Oslo Stock Exchange over the period 1989–1997. They involve a relatively long time series and suffer from neither the large holdings bias nor the discrete thresholds problem.

The fourth contribution concerns endogeneity and reverse causality, which is underexplored theoretically and empirically. Endogeneity occurs when mechanisms are internally related, for example, when agency theory argues that outside concentration and insider holdings are substitute governance tools. Reverse causation occurs when performance drives governance; an example would be privately informed insiders asking for stock bonus plans before unexpectedly high earnings are reported. Our simultaneous equation approach, which has the potential of capturing both mechanism endogeneity and reverse causation, has been used earlier in a governance-performance setting (Agrawal and Knoeber 1996; Loderer and Martin 1997; Cho 1998; Demsetz and Villalonga 2002; Bhagat and Jefferis 2002). The typical findings using this approach, which Becht et al. (2003) call third-generation studies due to what they consider "vastly improved econometrics," differ markedly from those of single-equation methods. In particular, the significant relationships between governance and performance in single-equation models often disappear under third-generation approaches. We explore whether this is due to the nature of the corporate governance problem or to the methodological difficulty of using a simultaneous system when the theory cannot specify how mechanisms interact.

Using the traditional single-equation approach, we find a highly significant inverse relationship between outside concentration and economic performance as measured by Tobin's Q. In contrast, insider holdings are value creating up to roughly 60%, which is far above the insider fraction in most sample firms. Individual (direct) owners are associated with higher performance than multiple-agent intermediaries, small boards create more value than large, and firms issuing shares with unequal voting rights lose market value. Practically all these results survive across a wide range of single-equation models, suggesting that governance mechanisms are rarely substitutes or complements. Thus, studying a comprehensive set of mechanisms is unnecessary for capturing the true effect of any single one of them. In contrast, the choice of performance measure in governance-performance research does matter, as very few of the results based on Tobin's Q hold up under other proxies used in the literature, such as book return on assets and market return on equity. Moreover, most relationships are sensitive to the choice of instruments when we use simultaneous equations to handle endogeneity and two-way causation. Because the theory of corporate governance cannot rank alternative instruments, simultaneous system modeling is not necessarily superior to single-equation models when exploring the relationship between governance and performance.

Existing research is discussed in the first section below, and the second section presents descriptive statistics of our governance and performance data. The third section analyzes the interaction between governance and performance in a single-equation setting, whereas the fourth section uses a simultaneous equation framework. We conclude in the final section.

THEORETICAL FRAMEWORK AND EXISTING EVIDENCE

Corporate governance mechanisms are vehicles for reducing agency costs, that is, tools for minimizing the destruction of market value caused by conflicts of interest between the firm's stakeholders (Shleifer and Vishny 1997; Tirole 2001; Becht et al. 2003). Focusing on the principal-agent problem between managers and owners and between subgroups of owners, we start by briefly outlining the major theoretical ideas behind the mechanisms we will analyze empirically, which are the large outside owners, the identity of outside owners, inside owners, board composition, security design, and financial policy.

Predictions

When products, labor, and takeover markets are fully competitive, self-serving managers will maximize their welfare by maximizing the market value of equity (Fama 1980; Fama and Jensen 1985; Stulz 1988). Outside such a world, agency problems may still be solved with complete contracts, but such contracts can in practice not be written without excessive costs (Hart 1995; Vives 2000). Therefore, market discipline alone is insufficient, and other governance mechanisms must be called upon to reduce agency costs. Our theoretical framework assumes imperfect markets and incomplete contracts.

The expected effect of outside ownership concentration on performance is unclear, as it reflects the net impact of several benefits and costs which are difficult to rank a priori. The benefits are the principal's monitoring of his agents (Jensen and Meckling 1976; Demsetz and Lehn 1985; Shleifer and Vishny 1986), higher takeover premia (Burkart 1995), and less free riding by small shareholders (Shleifer and Vishny 1986). The costs are reduced market liquidity (Holmstrom and Tirole 1993; Brennan and Subrahmanyam 1996; Chordia et al. 2001), lower diversification benefits (Demsetz and Lehn 1985), increased majority–minority conflicts (Shleifer and Vishny 1997; Johnson et al. 2000), and reduced management initiative (Burkart et al. 1997).Since theory cannot specify the relative importance of these costs and benefits, the shape of the relation between concentration and performance must be determined empirically.

Agency theory argues that owner type matters. Direct principal–agent relationships represented by personal investors is considered better than indirect ownership, where widely held private corporations or the state invest on others' behalf (Jensen and Meckling 1976). Pound (1988), however, argues that institutions may still outperform personal owners, provided the institutions' lower monitoring costs are not offset by the negative incentive effect of delegated monitoring. The net impact of replacing personal investors by institutions is therefore unclear. Furthermore, since international (foreign) investors may be at an informational disadvantage, they bias their portfolio toward domestic firms and invest abroad only to capture diversification benefits rather than to improve governance (Kang and Stulz 1994; Brennan and Cao 1997). Thus, we would expect that because increased holdings by international investors reduces monitoring, firm performance is adversely affected.

Whereas the primary governance function of outside owners is to monitor management, a larger insider stake reduces the need for such control. The convergence-of-interest hypothesis predicts that insider holdings and economic performance are positively related. In contrast, Morck et al. (1988) argue that powerful insiders may entrench themselves and expropriate wealth from outside owners. Also, because there are other sources of insider power than insider ownership, such as tenure and charisma, one cannot predict at what fraction the insider stake diminishing returns sets in. Finally, as insiders carry a larger fraction of the destructed market value the higher their stake, the negative entrenchment effect may diminish as the insider stake becomes sufficiently large. Consequently, governance theory cannot specify the relation between insider ownership and performance unless we put a priori restrictions on the component costs and benefits.

Because groups communicate less effectively beyond a certain size, there is pressure from self-serving managers or entrenched owners to expand board size beyond its value-maximizing level (Jensen 1993). Agency theory predicts that board size will be larger than optimal from the owners' point of view. The security design mechanisms of voting/nonvoting shares represent a deviation from one share–one vote, creating a stockholder conflict resembling the one between majority and minority voting owners. Since most theories of price differences between dual class shares assume a potential extraction of private benefits by voting shareholders, we expect firms to have lower market value the higher the fraction of nonvoting shares outstanding (Grossman and Hart 1988; Harris and Raviv 1988b).

Financing policy can be used to limit management discretion over free cash flow by financing with debt rather than equity and paying out earnings as dividends or stock repurchase (Jensen 1986). Also, higher payout forces the firm more frequently to the new issue market and exposes it to more monitoring (Easterbrook 1984). Thus, owners may reduce agency costs through high leverage and high payout.

The equilibrium hypothesis of Demsetz (1983) argues that if optimally installed, every mechanism satisfies a zero marginal value condition, such that a small change in any mechanism leaves firm value practically unaltered. Since two firms may have different sets of optimal mechanisms, the equilibrium condition implies that no mechanism will be significantly related to performance in a cross-sectional regression. Conversely, a significant relationship reflects a disequilibrium and a source of improved performance. Coles et al. (2003) questions this simple idea by showing that when managerial ownership is optimally tailored to managerial and capital productivity in every firm, reasonable parameter values produce a roughly quadratic cross-sectional relationship between managerial ownership and Tobin's Q.

Empirics

Our chapter compares the performance of firms with given governance mechanisms in place. The analytical tool used by existing research in this field is regressions, the sample is a cross section, and the vast majority of papers analyze one or a few ownership characteristics, which is most often outside concentration. Most studies use just one performance measure, which is either Tobin's Q, book return on assets, or market return on equity.

Among the 33 empirical ownership performance papers from 1932 through 1998 surveyed by Gugler (2001), 27 deal with outside and 6 with inside concentration. The papers mostly find either a positive or no link between outside concentration and performance, except Lehmann and Weigand (2000), which estimates a negative relationship for a sample of German firms. Four of the six insider papers (Morck et al. 1988; McConnell and Servaes 1990; Belkaoui and Pavlik 1992; Holderness et al. 1999) find a nonmonotone relationship between insider holdings and firm performance. The curve increases with insider holdings at low insider stakes, then decreases, then either still decreases, slightly increases, or stays constant. The two other studies (Agrawal and Knoeber 1996; Cho 1998), which both use simultaneous equations, cannot detect a significant link.

The evidence on owner identity is mixed, and according to Gugler (2001) "remarkably unexplored." Some find a positive performance effect of family control (Jacquemin and de Ghellinck 1980; Mishra et al. 2000), of founder-insiders in young firms (Morck et al. 1988), of private ownership (Boardman and Vining 1989), and of institutional investors (McConnell and Servaes 1990). Others cannot detect any pattern, like Kole and Mulherin (1997) for state owners and Smith (1996) for institutional shareholder activism.

Security design, financial policy, and market competition are the mechanisms that have been studied the least. The governance effect of product market competition is analyzed by Palmer (1973) and Crespi et al. (2004), and the findings are consistent with the notion that outside owner monitoring and product market competition are substitute mechanisms. We are unaware of any paper on security design and economic performance in a corporate governance setting. Except for Agrawal and Knoeber (1996), who model the debt-to-equity ratio as one of seven governance mechanisms, existing research only includes financial policy as a control variable reflecting governance-independent determinants of performance, such as the interest tax shield (Demsetz and Lehn 1985; Morck et al. 1988; McConnell and Servaes 1990; Cho 1998). Finally, although research on board characteristics and economic performance has produced mixed results (Bhagat and Black 1998; Becht et al. 2003), the finding that performance decreases with increasing board size is quite robust, suggesting that boards are on average too large.

Three Problems in Governance-Performance Research

Partial Theories Corporate governance theory very often deals with univariate rather than multivariate relationships. For instance, Demsetz and Lehn (1985) model the performance effect of outside ownership concentration, whereas Morck et al. (1988) and Stulz (1988) focus on insiders. Not surprisingly, more formal models are even more restrictive. For instance, Burkart et al. (1997) derive optimal concentration under one benefit (improved monitoring) and one cost (reduced management initiative).

Testing such predictions is problematic if real-world mechanisms are substitute or complementary ways of reducing agency costs. For instance, although McConnell and Servaes (1990) consider ownership concentration, insider holdings, and institutional owners, they present no theory of interrelations and use a multivariate approach that cannot capture mechanism endogeneity. In contrast, the pioneering paper by Agrawal and Knoeber (1996) establishes a system of endogenous, multiple governance mechanisms, arguing theoretically (although rather incompletely) why the mechanisms are modeled as functions of each other and of exogenous firm characteristics.

The second partiality problem concerns the order of causation between governance and performance. Since causation may run either way, the relationship should be modeled accordingly. Although the issue has been raised earlier (for example, McConnell and Servaes 1990), it has only recently been analyzed empirically (Agrawal and Knoeber 1996; Loderer and Martin 1997; Cho 1998; Demsetz and Villalonga 2002). The only paper that addresses the problem both theoretically and empirically is Cho (1998).

Biased Samples   The data used in the empirical tests are dominated by U.S. firms, where the firms are very large, the ownership structure variables only reflect block-holders, insider holdings are often biased toward board members, the set of owner types is narrow, and most of the evidence is based on a single year. Among the 28 studies surveyed by Gugler (2001), 18 use U.S. data, 5 are British, 2 are German, and the remaining 3 use data from respectively Australia, France, and Japan. The 6 insider papers are all from the United States. Morck et al. (1988), Agrawal and Knoeber (1996), and Cho (1998), among whose are the most sophisticated and influential papers, all sample from the Fortune 500 list. McConnell and Servaes (1990) are less restrictive, as they randomly sample NYSE and Amex firms. Ownership concentration per firm is always based on the aggregate fraction across all reported blocks, that is, stakes above a certain limit (normally 5%). As the most common insider proxy is the aggregate director stake, ownership by non-board insiders like non-director officers is ignored. Most studies ignore owner identity altogether, and the others use two categories only, such as institutional versus noninstitutional, state versus private, and personal versus nonpersonal. Finally McConnell and Servaes (1990) and Holderness et al. (1999) are exceptions to the single-year approach, sampling from two different years and testing the predictions on both sets.

   This sample bias creates several generalization problems. If the regulatory environment drives the governance mechanisms, the U.S. evidence may be insufficient to judge the general validity of any theory. The overrepresentation of large firms is problematic if the link between governance and performance depends on firm size. The current focus on block-holdings is not dictated by theory, but by an arbitrary cutoff point for mandatory reporting. If the ratio of board to non-board insider holdings differs systematically across firms, the focus on directors rather than all insiders or other insider subgroups like the management team may fail to detect the true relationship between insider ownership and performance. Since different owner types have different roles to play when ownership is separated from control, a data set with a richer classification of types has a better chance of capturing the relevance of owner identity for economic performance. Finally, the snapshot approach, which is due to limited data availability, cannot tell whether relationships between governance and performance persist over time, or are due to the specific period chosen.

Weak Simultaneous Equations   Table 3.1 classifies the methodologies used in existing empirical research into four groups. Almost without exception, existing research belongs in cell 1, where the econometric approach takes the mechanisms as externally given, causation is supposed to run from gov-

TABLE 3.1 Mechanism Interaction and
Mechanism Performance Causality

	Causation	
Mechanisms	One-way	Two-way
Exogenous	1	3
Endogenous	2	4

ernance to performance, and where the single-equation regression typically contains one or two mechanisms.

Himmelberg et al. (1999) come close to cell 2. Although they ignore mechanism interaction and analyze one-way causation running from insider ownership to performance only, they do estimate insider ownership from firm characteristics. Cell 3 is infeasible, as two-way causation cannot be modeled without letting at least one mechanism be endogenously related to performance.

Starting with a cell 1 approach and then moving to cell 4 by estimating the governance mechanisms and performance as a system of simultaneous equations, Agrawal and Knoeber (1996) and Cho (1998) find that most of the significant results disappear. This evidence brings the authors close to concluding that the equilibrium condition prevails. For instance, Agrawal and Knoeber (1996) find that if each of their seven governance mechanisms are considered exogenous and related to Q one by one, four of them are significant. Keeping the exogeneity assumption, but allowing for all the exogenous mechanisms in one multivariate regression, one more mechanism drops out. Finally, when allowing for two-way causality, board independence is the only significant mechanism in their simultaneous system. Whereas Agrawal and Knoeber (1996) do not report their findings on causation, Cho (1998) concludes that causation is reversed, running from performance to insider holdings (which is their only governance mechanism) rather than the opposite way.

Endogeneity and reverse causation favor simultaneous system equations, which is a cell 4 methodology. However, successful implementation of this method depends on whether corporate governance theory can offer well-founded restrictions on the equation system. Such a theory does not yet exist. The theoretical literature addresses neither how a wide set of mechanisms interact, nor what exogenous variables are driving two-way causation, nor the nature of the equilibrium in terms of an optimal combination of governance mechanisms for a given set of exogenous variables. Since the findings of Agrawal and Knoeber (1996) and Cho (1998) strongly depend on whether cell 1 or cell 4 approaches are used, an important unresolved issue is whether cell 4 methodologies provide reliable evidence on the interaction between governance and performance. The findings reported in the fourth section suggest the answer is no.

DESCRIPTIVE STATISTICS

Our sample is all the nonfinancial firms listed on the Oslo Stock Exchange (OSE) in 1989–1997. The OSE is medium-sized by European standards, plays a modest but increasingly important role in the national economy, and became considerably more liquid over the sample period. The 217 firms listed in 1997 had an aggregate market cap equivalent of 67 billion U.S. dollars, which ranks the OSE twelfth among the 21 European stock exchanges for which comparable data are available. The number of firms listed rose from 129 to 217 over the sample period, market cap grew by 7% per year, and turnover increased from 52% to 97%. Market capitalization per unit GDP grew steadily to 43% in 1997, when the European median was 49% (www.fibv.com).

Although Norway has a civil law regime, the protection of shareholder rights is better than in the average common-law country (La Porta et al. 2000). This may be one reason why OSE firms have less concentrated ownership than any other European country except the U.K. For instance, the typical holding of the largest owner in a listed firm in the mid-1990s was 3% in the United States, 14% in the U.K., 45% in continental Europe (Barca and Becht 2001), and 30% in Norway (Bøhren and Ødegaard 2001).

Table 3.2 presents descriptive statistics for governance mechanisms, controls, and performance measures. Except when we study security design, every conclusion in this chapter is based on direct holdings of cash flow rights. However, no result changes materially if we alternatively use voting rights.

A common concentration measure in the literature is the Herfindahl index, which is the sum of all squared ownership fractions. It has a maximum of one when one investor owns everything and approaches its minimum of zero as ownership gets increasingly diffuse. Another measure often used is the fraction of outstanding equity owned by the nth or the n largest shareholders, n mostly varying between 1 and 5. The table reports the Herfindahl index and large owner fractions for n up to 20, the number of owners, the median and mean fraction, and the average stake of the largest outside (that is, non-insider) owner. The median owner is minuscule, the largest holds 29%, the two largest are a blocking minority against charter

TABLE 3.2 Descriptive Statistics

Panel A

	Mean	StDev	Q1	Median	Q3	n
Ownership concentration						
Herfindahl index	0.2	(0.2)	0.0	0.1	0.2	1069
Median owner	0.0	(0.0)	0.0	0.0	0.0	1069
Mean owner	0.2	(0.3)	0.0	0.1	0.1	1069
Largest owner	29.0	(19.2)	14.3	23.2	40.6	1069
1–2 largest owners	40.1	(20.2)	23.6	36.3	53.8	1069
1–3 largest owners	47.0	(20.0)	30.3	44.2	62.6	1069
1–4 largest owners	52.0	(19.6)	35.8	50.5	66.9	1069
1–5 largest owners	55.9	(19.1)	40.6	55.0	70.4	1069
1–10 largest owners	67.5	(16.9)	54.7	68.4	80.9	1069
1–20 largest owners	77.4	(14.0)	67.6	79.5	88.4	1069
Number of owners	4392.5	(9578.5)	691.0	1245.0	2938.0	1069
2nd largest owner	11.1	(6.1)	6.9	9.7	13.8	1069
3rd largest owner	7.0	(3.6)	4.7	6.3	8.8	1069
4th largest owner	5.0	(2.3)	3.5	4.7	6.3	1069
5th largest owner	3.9	(1.8)	2.7	3.7	4.9	1069
Largest outside owner	25.7	(19.3)	11.0	19.1	35.6	1069
Insider ownership						
Directors	7.8	(20.7)	0.0	0.1	2.5	1069
Officers	4.2	(14.7)	0.0	0.0	0.7	1069
Insiders	8.2	(19.0)	0.0	0.4	4.5	1069
Largest insider	5.5	(12.1)	0.0	0.4	4.5	1062
Owner type						
Aggregate state holdings	5.1	(13.8)	0.0	0.0	3.8	1069
Aggregate international holdings	22.1	(22.3)	4.6	14.8	32.8	1069
Aggregate individual holdings	17.8	(15.6)	6.5	12.4	25.2	1069
Aggregate financial holdings	16.6	(14.0)	5.5	14.2	23.7	1069
Aggregate nonfinancial holdings	39.0	(24.0)	17.5	37.5	58.7	1069
Aggregate intercorporate holdings	9.0	(14.9)	0.3	3.0	10.7	1067
Board characteristics						
Board size	6.6	(2.5)	5.0	6.0	8.0	964
Security design						
Fraction voting shares	96.8	(9.3)	100.0	100.0	100.0	1054

(Continued)

TABLE 3.2 *(Continued)*

Panel A

	Mean	StDev	Q1	Median	Q3	n
Financial policy						
Debt to assets	57.1	(19.4)	46.2	60.2	70.0	1058
Dividends to earnings	26.5	(68.1)	0.0	0.0	33.0	1040
Controls						
Investments to income	60.2	(283.7)	3.2	8.1	30.4	1006
Stock volatility	54.2	(28.7)	33.7	46.3	65.3	949
Stock turnover	59.4	(65.3)	13.4	40.3	79.0	1034
Stock beta	0.9	(0.6)	0.5	0.8	1.2	947
Equity value	1995.4	(6062.9)	168.6	480.8	1429.9	1069
Performance measures						
Q	1.5	(1.0)	1.0	1.2	1.6	1068
RoA	5.0	(14.8)	3.2	7.3	10.9	1061
RoS	33.1	(92.4)	−16.7	13.0	49.0	894

Panel B

Type of Largest Owner	Percentage of Sample
State	8.6
International	13.2
Individual	10.4
Nonfinancial	54.9
Financial company	7.8
Listed company	12.9

Panel A shows equally weighted averages across firms and years. Equity value is in millions of constant 1997 NOK. The other variables are in percent except for the Herfindahl index, board size, stock beta, and Q, which are in their natural units. The listed companies in panel B are either nonfinancial or financial owners. Data for all nonfinancial firms listed on the Oslo Stock Exchange, 1989–1997.

amendments (1/3 of the votes required), the four largest produce a simple majority, and the 10 largest can force a charter amendment. Considering only firms where the largest owner holds less than two-thirds of the shares, the average (median) firm needs the 15 (7) owners next in line to block a charter amendment. The largest outside owner holds 26% on average.

We classify investors into five types: state, individuals (persons), financials (institutions), nonfinancials, and international. To capture a case of pure indirect holdings in firms with many owners, we also consider inter-corporate holdings between OSE firms (cross holdings). The equally weighted averages show that national corporations are the largest type by aggregates and also the most frequent largest owner. However, value-weighted averages not shown in the table reveal that international investors hold the largest and personal investors the smallest fraction of the market portfolio. International investors hold almost one third of OSE market cap, nonfinancial domestic firms about one fourth, the state and financial investors both own roughly one fifth, and individuals about one tenth. Financial investors increase and individuals decrease their share almost every year. By 1997, individuals owned a smaller fraction of market cap than in any other European country (Bøhren and Ødegaard 2001).

Due to the overlap between directors (8%) and officers (4%), who together constitute the insiders, the average insider fraction (officers and directors) is 8%. Since the CEO is the only inside director of OSE firms, these figures reflect that officer holdings are mostly CEO holdings. Unfortunately, no reliable data exist on performance-dependent pay other than stock ownership.

Norwegian boards are outsider dominated and small by international standards. The average number of directors is seven, and 75% of the boards have eight members or less. Nonvoting shares are issued by 14% of the firms; international investors hold 54% of these shares and are heavily overrepresented. The average debt to total assets is 57%; dividends are 27% of earnings for all firms and 52% for the dividend payers, which is half the firms. Regulation made stock repurchases practically nonexistent in the sample period.

Our controls are investments (measured as accounting investments over sales), stock volatility, stock liquidity (annual turnover), stock beta, and equity value (the log of market value of equity). Asset pricing theory predicts that equity value is negatively related to beta and positively to liquidity. Demsetz and Lehn (1985) argue that the value of owner monitoring increases with increasing uncertainty in the firm's environment, making concentration and volatility positively related. Investments are supposed to control for noise in accounting-based performance measures (Demsetz and Lehn 1985), and equity value is used to capture the association between size and performance (Hawawini and Keim 2000). The average value of our sample firms in 1997 is roughly one-fifth the average NYSE firm and twice the average NASDAQ firm.

The performance proxies used in the literature are Tobin's Q, the accounting rate of return on assets (RoA), and the market return on the stock (RoS). Because we miss data on replacement values, Q is operationalized as the market value to book value of assets. The mean (median) estimate is

1.5 (1.2) for Q, 5.0% (7.3%) for RoA, and 33.1% (13.0%) for RoS. The consistency between these performance measures is generally low. A typical rank correlation is 0.25; pairwise consistency is higher when Q is one of the performance measures and stronger when RoA and RoS are based on five-year returns rather than annual.

SINGLE EQUATION ESTIMATES

This section tests and compares a wide range of models that all belong in cell 1 of Table 3.1. We start with the simplest univariate approach, switch to the opposite extreme of a full multivariate model, and finally compare both approaches to the findings from several partial multivariate models.

Univariate Analysis

Table 3.3 summarizes the findings of univariate regressions under five alternative performance measures. For each model, where we regress a performance measure on either a governance mechanism or a control variable, the table shows the sign and the significance level of the coefficient estimate. We use both annual and five-year average returns, and we measure outside concentration by single investor stakes (for example, fraction held by largest owner), aggregate stakes (for example, fraction held by five largest), and a proxy that reflects the entire ownership structure (the Herfindahl index). We do not report the R^2 values, which all vary between 0 and 4%.

Two distinct patterns in the table suggest that the choice of performance measure matters. First, the strength of a relationship differs across performance measures. In particular, the covariation is more often significant with Q, more often with the five-year averages RoA_5 and RoS_5 than with their annual counterparts, and, for a given averaging period, more often when performance reflects total assets than equity. Second, consistency across performance measures is higher when the return on assets and equity are five-year averages than annual. This is particularly true for the relationship between Q and RoA_5, which both measure value creation for the firm as a whole.

Although both Q and RoA_5 produce the cleanest relationships, we use Q as our base case in the remainder of the chapter. Since it is the most commonly used measure in the recent literature, using Q facilitates the comparison with extant research. RoA_5 is constructed from overlapping observations, which will induce autocorrelation in pooled panel–time series regressions. Also, since RoA_5 is accounting based, it may deviate from market returns and be biased by earnings management.

TABLE 3.3 Summary of the Univariate Regressions

	Dependent Variable (Performance Measure)				
	Q	RoA$_5$	RoS$_5$	RoA	RoS
Ownership concentration					
Herfindal index	−***	−***	−	−	−
Largest owner	−***	−***	−	−	−
1–3 largest owners	−***	−***	−*	−	−
1–5 largest owners	−***	−***	−**	−	−
2nd largest owner	−	−	−**	+	−
3rd largest owner	+	−	−	−	−
4th largest owner	+	+	−	−	−
5th largest owner	+	+	−	−	−**
Owner type					
Aggregate state holdings	−***	−	−*	−	−
Aggregate international holdings	+	−	+	−	−
Aggregate individual holdings	+***	+***	+***	−***	+***
Aggregate financial holdings	+	+	−*	+***	+
Aggregate nonfinancial holdings	−***	−*	−	+	−
Aggregate intercorporate holdings	−***	−**	−	+***	+
Largest owner is state	−***	−	−*	+	−
Largest owner is international	−	+	+	−	+
Largest owner is individual	+***	+**	+***	−*	+
Largest owner is financial	−	−	−	+	+
Largest owner is nonfinancial	−***	−	−	+***	−
Largest owner is listed	−*	−**	−	+	+
Insider ownership					
Directors	+***	+***	−	+	+
Officers	+	+**	+***	−	+
Insiders	+***	+***	+*	−	+
Board characteristics					
ln(Board size)	−	−	−***	+	−
Security design					
Fraction voting shares	+*	−	+*	−	+
Financial policy					
Debt to assets	−***	−***	−***	+***	−
Dividends to earnings	−	+	−	+***	+
Market competition					
Industrial	+	−	+	+	+
Transport/shipping	−***	−***	−**	+	−
Offshore	−*	−***	+	−	+

(Continued)

TABLE 3.3   *(Continued)*

	Dependent Variable (Performance Measure)				
	Q	RoA$_5$	RoS$_5$	RoA	RoS
Controls					
ln(Equity value)	+***	–	–	+***	+*
Investments to income	–	–	–	+	–
Stock volatility	–***	–**	+***	–***	+
Stock turnover	+***	+	+***	–	+***
Stock beta	+	–	+***	–	+

The table summarizes univariate regressions relating five alternative performance measures to one independent variable (a governance mechanism or control) by showing the estimated sign and its significance. The univariate relationship is estimated with an OLS regression:

$$\text{Performance} = a + b \text{ Independent variable} + \varepsilon$$

We report the estimated sign of b and indicate statistical significance with *, **, and ***, which means the relationship is significant at the 5%, 2.5% and 1% level, respectively. The performance measures are Tobin's Q (Q, operationalized as the market value of the firm divided by its book value), the book return on total assets (RoA), and the market return on stock (RoS). Variables subscripted with a 5 are five-year averages. Data for all nonfinancial firms listed on the Oslo Stock Exchange, 1989–1997.

Focusing on Q, the univariate models in Table 3.3 show that outside ownership concentration is inversely related to performance when concentration is measured by the Herfindahl index, the largest stake, and by alliances of large owners, such as the three or five largest as a group rather than the third or fifth largest alone. The covariation with performance is positive for individual investors and negative for the state and nonfinancials, regardless of whether we measure owner identity by aggregate holdings per type or type of the largest owner. Directors and insiders as a group both have large stakes when performance is high, and performance is lower for firms that finance heavily with debt.

The Full Multivariate Model

Based on the theory and evidence discussed in the first section, we specify a full multivariate model relating Q to ownership concentration, insider holdings, owner type, board characteristics, security design, financial policy, and controls. The estimates are presented in Table 3.4,

TABLE 3.4 The Full Multivariate Model

	coe	(stdev)	pvalue	mean
Constant	−1.04	(0.69)	0.13	
Ownership concentration	−0.63	(0.19)	0.00	0.28
Insiders	1.64	(0.47)	0.00	0.08
Squared (Insiders)	−1.34	(0.58)	0.02	0.04
Aggregate state holdings	−0.37	(0.34)	0.29	0.06
Aggregate international holdings	0.15	(0.25)	0.54	0.21
Aggregate individual holdings	1.04	(0.30)	0.00	0.18
Aggregate non-financial holdings	−0.17	(0.26)	0.52	0.38
ln(Board size)	−0.19	(0.09)	0.03	1.83
Fraction voting shares	1.19	(0.36)	0.00	0.97
Debt to assets	−1.51	(0.18)	0.00	0.59
Dividends to earnings	−0.10	(0.05)	0.05	0.27
Industrial	−0.20	(0.08)	0.01	0.37
Transport/shipping	−0.47	(0.09)	0.00	0.22
Offshore	−0.56	(0.14)	0.00	0.06
Investments to income	−0.00	(0.01)	0.98	0.59
ln(Equity value)	0.14	(0.02)	0.00	20.06
n	868			
R^2	0.29			
Average Q	1.52			

The table reports estimates for a OLS regression relating performance (Q) to ownership concentration (measured as the fraction of equity held by the largest owner), insider ownership (the fraction held by officers and directors), the squared value of the insider ownership measure, the fraction held by respectively state, international, individual, and nonfinancial owners, the natural logarithm of board size, the fraction of equity which is nonvoting (B) shares, debt to assets, dividends to earnings, dummy variables for whether the firm is an industrial, transport/shipping or offshore company, investments as a fraction of income, and the natural logarithm of the firm's equity value. Q is the dependent variable, and the independent variables are listed in the first column. The column labeled "coe" contains the regression coefficient, "(stdev)" holds the estimated standard deviation, the "pvalue" column shows the probability that the coefficient differs from zero under a normal distribution, and the "mean" column holds the average of the explanatory variable. n is the number of observations, and R^2 is the adjusted R-squared for the regression. Equity value is in terms of the 1997 general price level. The regression pools data for all nonfinancial firms listed on the OSE from 1989 to 1997.

which also reports sample means of the dependent and independent variables. It turns out that the results are insensitive to whether we measure concentration by the holdings of the largest owner as used in Table 3.4, the two largest, three largest, four largest, five largest, or by the Herfindahl index. Also, since our results are robust to whether we proxy for owner identity by aggregate holding per type or by the identity of the largest owner, we use aggregate holding per type. Because the five aggregate fractions sum to unity per firm by construction, we avoid econometric problems by excluding one type and interpreting it as the reference case. We arbitrarily choose financial owners as the base type.

The table shows that outside ownership concentration and economic performance are inversely related, that individual owners are associated with higher performance than others, that performance increases with insider ownership up to roughly 60% and then decreases, and that performance is inversely related to board size, to the fraction of nonvoting shares outstanding, and to financial leverage. Also, performance varies systematically with industry and firm size.

The finding that performance and outside concentration are inversely related supports the idea that outside monitoring by powerful owners either does not occur or does not benefit all owners if carried out. If the primary function of the outside owner is to hold on to a big stake, the typical firm would do better with small owners who vote with their feet. This finding differs from the mostly positive or neutral effects reported in the literature, but is consistent with evidence from Germany (Lehmann and Weigand 2000). The superior performance of individual owners supports the hypothesis that owner identity matters and that delegated monitoring destroys value. Thus, although performance is inversely related to outside concentration in general, the negative effect is less pronounced when the outside ownership is direct rather than indirect. The third ownership structure result suggests that although ownership concentration in general destroys value, this may be driven by unique costs of outside as opposed to inside concentration. It highlights the difference between inside incentives and outside control, supports the notion that minority shareholder protection is value creating, and is consistent with most earlier findings. Since the average insider fraction in the sample is 8%, and only 3% of the firms have insider holdings above 60%, many firms are on the steep, increasing part of the curve, and almost all are on the increasing part. Thus, although there are universally decreasing returns to insider holdings, the marginal return is typically positive.

The negative link between board size and performance is consistent with earlier evidence that small groups are more efficient than large, and that the efficiency loss sets in at a rather small group size. The security design hypothesis that nonvoting equity enables voting shareholders to extract wealth from others may explain why issuing such securities reduces market value. The inverse link between leverage and performance does not support the agency argument that debt disciplines management. The significant industry effects are difficult to interpret because we do not know whether our rather crude industry index reflects a governance mechanism (market competition) or a governance-independent industry effect. Anyway, the evidence does reflect some source of industrywide performance differences that are not picked up by other variables in the model, and which would otherwise have ended up in the error term. The positive association between firm size and Q reflects a governance independent value source, possibly market power and economies of scale and scope. Finally, since several mechanisms covary significantly with performance, the full multivariate model rejects the equilibrium hypothesis. Performance is inferior because the average firm has suboptimal governance.

Even if two governance mechanisms have coefficients that both differ significantly from zero, their importance for performance may still be widely different. We may quantify this performance sensitivity by the impact on Q of a modified mechanism, focusing on ownership concentration, insider holdings, individual investors, board size, and security design. Table 3.4 shows directly that Q decreases by 0.63 units when outside concentration increases with one unit, and that performance sensitivity is roughly twice as strong to aggregate individual holdings (1.04) and to voting shares (1.19). These effects may also be expressed as valuation effects for the average firm. Due to the two nonlinear terms, we cannot estimate such effects by simply plugging in the mean values from the rightmost column, but instead insert the square of the mean insider stake and the log of average board size. Similarly, the estimated Q for the average firm is not the average Q (1.520), but the Q of a firm where every governance and control variable equals the sample mean (1.558).

Following this procedure, we find that the ownership characteristic with the strongest impact on firm value is insider holdings, where a percentage point higher stake increases firm value by 1% for the average firm. The performance effect of a corresponding growth in the other governance mechanisms is 0.8% for individuals' holdings, –0.4% for outside ownership concentration, and 0.8% for the fraction of voting shares. Firm value will grow by approximately 2% if board size is reduced by one member. Since equity is on average 40% of total assets, the relative impact on equity will be higher, and more so the less debt is influenced by modified governance mechanisms. If debt value is unaffected, the relative equity value effect will be 2.5 times the relative firm value effect.

Robustness of the Full Multivariate Model

Table 3.4 was estimated using OLS and pooled data. Disregarding simultaneity and reverse causation, which we address in the fourth section, this approach means that the same firm may appear numerous times in the sample (autocorrelation), that the independent variables be related (multicollinearity), and that a time-independent model is misspecified if the underlying structure changes over the nine years (instability). We address these problems by first running year-by-year OLS regressions, which have no time series correlation, and where structural shifts will show up in the time series of estimated coefficients. Since these regressions only have roughly 100 rather than 900 observations, we expect less significant coefficients, and hence a bias toward accepting the equilibrium hypothesis. To avoid the small sample problem and also address autocorrelation and instability, we use two other approaches with the pooled data. In GMM regressions, error term dependency is picked up by the estimated standard errors and hence reflected in the p-values. We also add annual indicator variables to the pooled OLS model, such that the resulting fixed effects regression may capture certain types of instability by allowing the constant term to change over time. Finally, since multicollinearity inflates standard errors in all three approaches and also in our base case model in Table 3.4, it biases our tests toward keeping the equilibrium hypothesis.

Table 3.5 shows that the overall pattern from Table 3.4 mainly persists. The inverse relation between performance and concentration shows up everywhere, is highly significant in the GMM and fixed effects regressions (panel B), but is only significant at the 1% level in two of the nine years in the year-by-year regressions (panel A). Although both methods in panel B estimate the usual positive and significant coefficient for the linear insider term and a negative coefficient for the quadratic insider term, the p-value of the latter is 10% with GMM and 4% with fixed effects. The fixed effects model produces a significantly positive coefficient for international investors, and the structural relationship changes in the two final sample years, when the marketwide Q moves strongly upward.

Because Table 3.3 showed that the univariate relationships are sensitive to the choice of performance measure, Table 3.6 reestimates the full multivariate model with five alternative performance measures. To simplify the comparison, we repeat the findings for Q in the second column.

Just as in the univariate case, consistency across performance measures is low, particularly for the market return on stock. For instance, outside concentration is only significant using Q. Thus, our findings on the interaction between governance and performance based on Q cannot be generalized to other performance measures.

TABLE 3.5 Robustness of the Full Multivariate Model

Panel A: Year-by-Year OLS Regressions

	Year								
	1989	1990	1991	1992	1993	1994	1995	1996	1997
Constant	+	+	−	−	+	−	−*	+	−
Ownership concentration	−***	−*	−*	−	−	−***	−	−	−
Insiders	+	−	+	+	+	+	+	+	+
Squared (Insiders)	+	+	+	−	−	−	+	−	−
Aggregate state holdings	+	+	+	+	+	+	+*	+	−
Aggregate international holdings	+	+	+	−	+	+*	+***	+**	+
Aggregate individual holdings	+	+	+	+	+	+	+	+	+
Aggregate nonfinancial holdings	+	+	+	−	−	+	+	+	−
ln(Board size)	−***	−	−	−	−	−	+*	−	−
Fraction voting shares	+	+	+	−	+	+	+***	+	+
Debt to assets	−	−	−*	+	−	−*	−**	−***	−***
Dividends to earnings	+	+	+	−	−	+	−	−	−
Industrial	−	−	+	−	−	+	−	−	−
Transport/shipping	−	−*	−*	−	−**	−***	−	−	−
Offshore	−	−	−*	−	−	−*	−	−	−
Investments to income	+	−	−	−	−	−	−	−	−
ln(Equity value)	+***	+*	+	+***	+	+*	+	+	+*
n	81	73	64	83	90	98	108	118	153
R²	0.35	0.30	0.37	0.34	0.34	0.43	0.53	0.40	0.36
Average Q	1.32	1.18	1.13	1.07	1.41	1.34	1.51	2.04	2.00

(Continued)

TABLE 3.5 *(Continued)*

Panel B: Pooled GMM and Fixed Annual Effects Regressions

	coe	pvalue	coe	pvalue
Constant	-0.94	0.10	-0.42	0.54
Ownership concentration	-0.68	0.00	-0.82	0.00
Insiders	1.64	0.01	1.43	0.00
Squared (Insiders)	-1.37	0.10	-1.15	0.04
Aggregate state holdings	-0.43	0.10	0.01	0.99
Aggregate international holdings	0.12	0.63	0.61	0.01
Aggregate individual holdings	1.02	0.00	1.10	0.00
Aggregate nonfinancial holdings	-0.23	0.25	0.10	0.68
ln(Board size)	-0.19	0.01	-0.23	0.01
Fraction voting shares	1.14	0.00	0.93	0.01
Debt to assets	-1.54	0.00	-1.36	0.00
Dividends to earnings	-0.11	0.00	-0.08	0.13
Industrial	-0.19	0.02	-0.16	0.03
Transport/shipping	-0.46	0.00	-0.45	0.00
Offshore	-0.57	0.00	-0.60	0.00
Investments to income	-0.00	0.95	-0.00	0.86
ln(Equity value)	0.14	0.00	0.10	0.00
1990			-0.20	0.15
1991			-0.20	0.17
1992			-0.11	0.42
1993			0.11	0.41
1994			-0.05	0.68
1995			0.06	0.64
n	868			
Average Q	1.52			

TABLE 3.5 *(Continued)*

Panel B: Pooled GMM and Fixed Annual Effects Regressions

	coe	pvalue
1996	0.52	0.00
1997	0.49	0.00
n	868	
R^2	0.35	
Average Q	1.52	

The table explores the robustness of the full multivariate model by redoing the regression in Table 3.4 with OLS on annual data, GMM on pooled data, and OLS on pooled data with fixed annual effects. Panel A shows OLS estimates on a year-by-year basis. The left table in panel B uses GMM and pooled data. The table to the right in panel B shows results of a pooled OLS regression where dummy variables for each year capture fixed effects, using 1989 as the base year. Each regression relates performance (Q) to ownership concentration (measured as the fraction held by the largest owner), insider ownership (the fraction owned by officers and directors), the squared insider holding, the equity fraction held by respectively state, international, individual and nonfinancial owners, the natural logarithm of board size, the fraction of equity which is nonvoting (B) shares, debt to assets, dividends to earnings, dummy variables for whether the firm is an industrial, transport/shipping or offshore company, investments as a fraction of income, and the natural logarithm of the firm's equity value. Q is the dependent variable. The independent variables are listed in the first column. The column labeled "coe" in panel B contains the regression coefficient, the "pvalue" column shows the probability that the coefficient differs from zero under a normal distribution. *n* is the number of observations, and R^2 is the adjusted R-squared. Equity value is in terms of the 1997 general price level. The regressions include data for all nonfinancial OSE firms from 1989 to 1997.

TABLE 3.6 The Full Multivariate Model under Five Alternative Performance Measures

	Dependent Variable (Performance Measure)				
Independent variable	Q	RoA$_5$	RoS$_5$	RoA	RoS
Ownership concentration	−***	−	+	+	+
Insiders	+***	+***	−	+**	+
Squared (Insiders)	−**	−**	+	−***	−
Aggregate state holdings	−	+	−	−***	−
Aggregate international holdings	+	+	+	−***	−
Aggregate individual holdings	+***	+	+***	−	+***
Aggregate nonfinancial holdings	−	−	−	−	−
ln(Board size)	−*	−	−**	+	−
Fraction voting shares	+***	−	+*	−	+
Debt to assets	−***	−***	−***	+*	−
Dividends to earnings	−*	+	−	+**	−
Industrial	−**	−***	+**	−	+
Transport/shipping	−***	−**	+	−	+
Offshore	−***	−***	+	−	+
Investments to income	−	−	−	+	+
ln(Equity value)	+***	−	+	+	+***
n	868	851	621	869	743
R^2	0.27	0.12	0.12	0.11	0.05

The table summarizes results from estimating the full multivariate model of Table 3.4 using five alternative performance measures. The performance measures are Q (the market value of the firm divided by its book value) RoA (the book return on total assets), and RoS (the market return on stock). Performance variables subscripted with a 5 are five-year averages. The independent variables are listed in the first column. Each regression relates a performance measure to ownership concentration (measured as the fraction held by the largest owner), insider ownership (the fraction owned by officers and directors), the squared insider holding, the equity fraction held by respectively state, international, individual and nonfinancial owners, the natural logarithm of board size, the fraction of equity which is nonvoting (B) shares, debt to assets, dividends to earnings, dummy variables for whether the firm is an industrial, transport/shipping or offshore company, investments as a fraction of income, and the natural logarithm of the firm's equity value. The regression summarized in the first column corresponds to the one in Table 3.4. We report the sign of the regression coefficients, and indicate statistical significance with *, **, and ***, which means the relationship is significant at the 5%, 2.5% and 1% level, respectively. Data for all nonfinancial firms listed on the Oslo Stock Exchange, 1989–1997.

One may wonder whether the use of equity market capitalization as a control for size matters for the estimated relationship, since the dependent variable Q is partially determined by the same market cap. Using instead sales as the size proxy, we find that although no estimated sign is reversed for any governance mechanism, the coefficient is no longer significant at the 5% level for the quadratic insider term, individual owners, board size, and the fraction of voting shares. The negative impact of indirect ownership through nonfinancial firms becomes significant at the 1% level.

Partial Multivariate Models

After having used the simplest univariate relationships and the opposite extreme of a full multivariate model, we compare both approaches to the findings from several partial multivariate models in Table 3.7, where our estimates of the full multivariate model from Table 3.4 are reported as model (8) in the rightmost column. First, we briefly relate (1) through (7) to the existing international evidence, which is mostly based on these models.

Demsetz and Lehn (1985) (hereafter DL) relate Q to the holdings of the five largest owners in large U.S. corporations. Their estimated relationship is insignificant at conventional levels, which is inconsistent with Berle and Means (1932), but supportive of the equilibrium argument of Demsetz (1983). Model (1) in Table 3.7 shows the results of a replication of the DL approach with our data. Unlike DL, we find that ownership concentration and performance are significantly related. The DL controls are industry dummies for utilities and financials, investments in real assets, R&D, advertising, firm size, and stock price volatility. Because our sample contains no financials and very few utilities, we use the industry classification from Table 3.2. Since Norwegian firms do not specify R&D and advertising, these items must be ignored. We use investment intensity (investment over sales) as a substitute, and we log transform the holding of the five largest owners in order to be consistent with DL. DL's assumption of a linear concentration performance relationship was criticized by Morck et al. (1988), stating that "the failure of Demsetz and Lehn to find a significant relationship between ownership concentration and profitability is probably due to their use of a linear specification that does not capture an important non-monotonicity." Letting the five largest owners' stake enter both in a linear and a quadratic fashion, we still find a negative and significant linear term, but the quadratic term is insignificant. Thus, the simple linear specification of DL captures the essentials of the concentration-performance interaction in our sample.

TABLE 3.7 Alternative Multivariate Models

Independent Variables	Regression							
	(1)	(2)	(3)	(4)	(5)	(6)	(7)	(8)
lntrans(1–5 largest owners)	−***							
Largest owner			−***					
Ownership concentration				−***	−***	−***	−***	−***
Insiders (0 to 5)		+***						
Insiders (5 to 25)		+**						
Insiders (25 to 100)		−						
Insiders			+***	+***	+***	+***	+***	+***
Squared (Insiders)			−**	−***	−**	−**	−**	−**
Aggregate state holdings				−				−
Aggregate international holdings				+				+
Aggregate individual holdings				+***				+***
Aggregate nonfinancial holdings				−				−
ln(Board size)					−**			−*
Fraction voting shares						+**		+
Debt to assets		−***	−**	−***	−***	−**	−**	−***
Dividends to earnings						−	−	−
Industrial	−***	−***	−***	−***	−***	−***	−***	−***
Transport/shipping	−***	−***	−**	−**	−**	−**	−**	−***
Offshore	−***	−***	−*	−**	−*	−	−*	−**
Investments to income	−		+	−	+	+	−*	−
ln(Equity value)	+***	+***	+	+***	+*	+	+***	+***

52

Stock volatility	–							
n	905	1057	1057	1057	906	1042	1028	868
R^2	0.14	0.20	0.22	0.23	0.21	0.22	0.22	0.27

The table summarizes the estimated sign and significance levels in eight different multivariate models which all use performance measured by Q (market to book) as the dependent variable. Each column summarizes the results of a OLS regression relating Q as dependent variable to various permutations of explanatory variables. Model (1) is a pure concentration model, (2) is a pure insider model, (3) is a concentration-insider model, (4) is a concentration-insider-owner type model, (5) is a concentration-insider-board model, (6) is a concentration-insider-security design model, (7) is a concentration-insider financial policy model, and (8) corresponds to the full multivariate model in Table 3.4. The variable 1–5 largest owners is the fraction of equity held by the five largest owners, lntrans( ) is the logarithmic transformation used by Demsetz and Lehn (1985), Largest owner is the fraction of equity owned by the largest owner, and Ownership concentration is the Herfindahl index, which is the sum of squared ownership fractions, and insiders is the fraction of equity owned by directors and officers. The variables (0 to 5), (5 to 25) and (25 to 100) are dummy variables as used by Morck et al. (1988) to model a piecewise linear relationship with the stake of the largest owner being respectively less than 5%, between 5 and 25% and higher than 25%. Squared(Insiders) is the Insiders holdings squared. Aggregate holdings reflects the fraction of the company's equity held by the given type, Board size is the number of directors, ln() is the natural logarithm, and Fraction voting shares is the fraction of the company's equity with full voting rights. Industrial, Transport/Shipping and Offshore are industry dummy variables, Equity value is the market value of the company's equity, and Stock volatility is the standard deviation of the firm's daily stock returns. We report the sign of the regression coefficients and indicate statistical significance with *, **, and ***, which means the relationship is significant at the 5%, 2.5% and 1% level, respectively. R^2 is the adjusted R-squared for the regression, equity value is in terms of the 1997 general price level, and the sample is all nonfinancial firms on the OSE from 1989 to 1997.

53

Morck, Shleifer, and Vishny (1988) (MSV) analyze the relationship between Q and insider holdings, capturing nonmonotonicity through a piecewise linear function with prespecified steps that maximize the R^2. They find
that performance increases with insider holdings up to 5%, decreases as
the stake grows further to 25%, and increases again thereafter. Model (2)
estimates the MSV model in our sample. Our results are different, as the
relationship is positive through the first two intervals up to 25% and negative thereafter. Like in MSV, our p-values increase as we move upward in
the insider size intervals, p being below 1%, 3%, and 7%, respectively.

McConnell and Servaes (1990) (McS) expand the MSV approach by
roughly doubling the sample size, using more heterogeneous firms in
terms of size, and by including two years (1976 and 1986) instead of just
one (1980). They also consider outside concentration and institutional
ownership, their insiders are officers and directors, and they allow for a
less restrictive and more smooth relation between insider holdings and
performance by using a quadratic functional form. Their estimated in-
sider-performance relation has its maximum at 38% in 1986 and at 49%
in 1976.

Model (3) replicates McS by including outside concentration, a linear
and a quadratic insider term, and controls. We find a significant quadratic relationship between insiders and performance, and that the negative effect of outside concentration from (1) survives. One may perhaps
wonder whether this result is caused by an overlap between concentration and insider holdings, since some of the large owners may also be insiders. However, no conclusion changes if we account for this overlap by
removing the insiders from the concentration measure. Alternatively, if
we include an additional insider variable representing the stake of the
largest insider, its estimated coefficient is significantly negative, once
more suggesting that concentration per se is value destroying, also when
the large owner is an insider.

Model (4) expands further by adding not just institutional owners used
by McS, but all five owner types discussed earlier. The positive, significant
coefficient for individual holdings suggests that direct monitoring performs
better than delegated monitoring, regardless of whether the intermediary is
private or state, institutional or noninstitutional. According to Allen and
Phillips (2000), however, ownership by nonfinancials may still be better if
it acts as a sharing mechanism for jointly produced profits or an information channel in strategic alliances. Using intercorporate ownership between
OSE firms as a proxy for holdings between large firms with many owners,
we find a significantly negative link to performance. Thus, any positive
strategic effect of intercorporate investments seems more than offset by the
negative monitoring effect hypothesized by the agency model.

The multivariate regression of model (5), which includes outside concentration, linear and quadratic insider effects, board size, and controls, supports the international evidence that performance is negatively and significantly related to board size. Model (6) supports the security design prediction that since Q ignores the value of private, nonsecurity benefits, firms with dual-class shares will be less valuable than others by this measure, and more so the lower the fraction of voting outstanding. However, model (7) does not support an agency story for financial policy, as the estimated sign is negative for both debt and dividends. At conventional levels, the coefficient is significant for leverage and insignificant for payout.

Since most governance research has not tested for financial policy as a governance mechanism, (2) through (6) include the debt-to-assets ratio as a governance independent control.

Table 3.7 has one striking property. Notice by reading the table horizontally that most relationships survive all the way from the simplest models on the left to the most comprehensive models on the right. Performance is always significantly related to outside ownership concentration (–), direct ownership (+), the use of voting shares (+), and inside ownership (+) up to a certain point. The irrelevance of state, international, and nonfinancial owner identity occurs everywhere. In fact, these relationships also showed up in the univariate models in Table 3.3, except that univariate models cannot reflect nonmonotonicity. The only discrepancy is that although performance and board size are always inversely related in the univariate case, the link is only significant in the multivariate setting. Conversely, the negative univariate performance effect of state and nonfinancial owners disappears once we control for other governance mechanisms and controls.

This very persistent pattern suggests that the estimated interaction between governance and performance is relatively independent of what model specification we choose within cell 1 of Table 3.1. Because each mechanism has a separate, independent function, the performance effect of a given mechanism may not have to be estimated by complex, data intensive models. Our finding that signs and p-values persist when new variables are introduced suggests that governance mechanisms are not used as substitutes and complements.

SIMULTANEOUS EQUATION MODELS

We have so far taken the governance mechanisms as exogenously given by modeling neither their internal dependence nor the order of causation between governance and performance. Simultaneous equation models may in principle handle both aspects and bring us from cell 1 to cell 4 in Table 3.1. This section shows that because the estimates are sensitive to the choice of instruments (coefficient restrictions), and since governance theory cannot rank alternative instruments, the simultaneous equation approach is no panacea in cell 4 settings. This problem is evident in Agrawal and Knoeber (1996), who establish six equations to capture mechanism endogeneity. Any equation relates a mechanism linearly to the five others and to a set of exogenous variables. To model two-way causation, Q is included as an independent variable in each governance equation, and each mechanism is an independent variable in the Q equation.

The resulting system of 7 equations and 15 exogenous variables is to be estimated by 2SLS, which is infeasible unless the researcher restricts several coefficients, such as assuming independence between institutional ownership and board size. Because there is no theory yet providing such predictions, Agrawal and Knoeber (1996) must choose instruments in an ad-hoc fashion.

Because we cannot hope to validly restrict a system of equations that includes all the governance mechanisms analyzed in the third section, we choose to only endogenize outside ownership concentration and insider holdings. These two mechanisms have received the widest attention in the literature, and agency theory argues that they represent alternative vehicles for reducing agency costs (external monitoring versus internal incentives). Moreover, there is little theoretical guidance on how the two interact with the remaining mechanisms. This makes our setup well suited to explore how conclusions change when we alter the interaction assumptions by choosing alternative instruments for the two endogenous variables. The problems we encounter in this limited setting of two endogenous mechanisms and two-way causation should be sufficient to illustrate what would happen if more mechanisms were endogenized. We specify nine alternative models, each representing a particular set of instruments. The basic relationship is the full multivariate model from the third section except that we remove the quadratic term on insider ownership to avoid potential econometric problems in equation systems with nonlinear endogenous variables (Davidson and MacKinnon 1993, ch 18.7). In fact, the performance effect captured by the quadratic insider term in single-equation estimates may now instead be found directly in a system which allows for linear interaction.

Model (A) uses stock volatility and board size to identify the concentration and insider equations, respectively. Thus, higher stock volatility is assumed to increase concentration, but not insider ownership, using the Demsetz and Lehn (1985) idea that higher uncertainty increases the value of outside monitoring. Board size is assumed to affect insider ownership, but not concentration, by arguing that a larger board increases the number of insiders and hence the potential insider stake. One problem with this model is, however, that higher volatility increases the risk of an undiversified insider portfolio, the value of inside information, and also the power of incentive-based compensation. In fact, because the net benefit of holding insider shares may depend on total risk, Loderer and Martin (1997) assume that stock volatility and inside ownership are related. Therefore, our model (B) identifies the concentration equation not by the stock's volatility, but by its liquidity, which we operationalize as equity turnover. Because large owners may invest strategically and because block sales create price pressure, large owners hesitate to sell out. Thus, a smaller fraction of the equity will be traded under concentrated ownership. We assume no similar effect on insider holdings, which are normally much smaller. As in model (A), board size is supposed to identify the insider equation.

Model (C) introduces a new instrument for both mechanisms. The insider instrument is debt, arguing that more debt reduces the amount required to buy a given equity fraction. Although we cannot convincingly argue why this should not apply to outside concentration as well, it may be even more costly for insiders than for large outsiders to hold a large stake. We choose intercorporate shareholdings as the new instrument for ownership concentration, based on the evidence that when one firm owns nontrivial parts of another firm, the holding is relatively large. For instance, Bøhren and Ødegaard (2000) show that the mean intercorporate holding is 10% while the median is 3%. This reflects an ownership structure with a few large holdings and many small ones. We do not expect intercorporate investments and insider holdings to be related.

Stock beta is used to identify Q in all three models. Asset pricing theory predicts that systematic risk influences Q through the cost of capital, but we cannot convincingly argue why this instrument is unrelated to the other endogenous variables. One possibility is the order of magnitude argument that although beta drives all three variables, it has a stronger effect on firm value than on ownership concentration and insider holdings.

We consider two other methods for generating instruments. Models (D), (E), and (F) lag the instruments from models (A), (B), and (C) one period. Because most of these variables are persistent, the rationale for using time $t-1$ instruments is that they are strongly correlated with time t endogenous variables, but unrelated to time t error terms. The second class of alternative instruments, used in models (G) through (I), is lagged endogenous variables. Because these time $t-1$ variables are known data in the information set at t, they can be treated as constants in the time t regression.

The estimates shown in Table 3.8 leave three impressions. First, the estimated sign of the impact of an independent variable often differs across

TABLE 3.8 Summary of Simultaneous Equation Estimations

Panel A: The Performance Equation

Dependent Variable	Independent Variables	(A)	(B)	(C)	(D)	Instruments Lagged (E)	Instruments Lagged (F)	Dependent Variable Lagged (G)	Dependent Variable Lagged (H)	Dependent Variable Lagged (I)
Performance	Ownership concentration	+	−	−*	+	−	−*	−	−	−
	Insiders	−	+	−*	−	+	−	+	+	+
	Aggregate state holdings	−	+	+	−	+	+	−	+	−
	Aggregate international holdings	−	−	+**	−	−	+**	−**	+	−
	Aggregate individual holdings	+	−	+**	+	−	+	+**	−	−
	Aggregate nonfinancial holdings	−	−	+*	−	−	+	−	+	−
	ln(Board size)			−			−	−	−	−
	Fraction voting shares	−	+	−	−	+	+**	+**	+	+
	Debt to assets	−***	−	−	−	−	+**	−	+	+
	Dividends to earnings			+**			+	−	+	−
	Industrial	−	+	−**	−	+	−***	−	−	+
	Transport/shipping	−	+	−***	−	−	−***	−	+	+
	Offshore	−*	−		−	−	−**	−	+	+
	Investment to income	+	+	+	+	−	+	−	−	+
	ln(Equity value)	+	+	+	+	+	+**	+***	+	+
	Stock beta	−	+	−	−	+	−	−	−	+
	lag(-1) (Performance)							+***	+	+
	lag(-1) (Ownership concentration)							+***		+
	lag(-1) (Insiders)								+	+
	Constant	−	−	−	−	−	−	−***	+	−

Panel B: The Concentration Equation

Dependent Variable	Independent Variables	(A)	(B)	(C)	(D)	Instruments Lagged (E)	(F)	Dependent Variable Lagged (G)	(H)	(I)
Ownership concentration	Insiders	+	+	+	+	-	+***	+	+	+
	Performance	+	+***	-	+***	+	-*	-	-	-
	Aggregate state holdings	+***	+***	+***	+***	+***	+***	+***	-	-
	Aggregate international holdings	+***	+***	+***	+***	+***	+***	+***	-	-
	Aggregate individual holdings	-	-	+	-	-	+	+	-	+
	Aggregate nonfinancial holdings	+***	+***	+***	+***	+***	+***	+**	-	-
	Aggregate intercorporate holdings			+**			+*			
	ln(Board size)			-*			-**	-	+	-
	Fraction voting shares	+	+	+***	+	+	+***	+	+	+
	Debt to assets	+*	+		+	+	+	+	-	-
	Dividends to earnings	+	+	+	+	+	+	+	-	-
	Industrial	+	+	-*	+	+		+	+	-
	Transport/shipping	+	+	-*	+	+	-***	-	+	-
	Offshore	+	+	-	+	+	-*	+	+	-
	Investments to income	-	-	-	-	-	-*	-	+	-
	ln(Equity value)	-	-	-	-	-	+	-*	+	+
	Stock volatility	+	-***		+					
	Stock turnover					-*		+***		+
	lag(-1) (Performance)							+***		
	lag(-1) (Ownership concentration)									
	lag(-1) (Insiders)								-	-
	Constant	+	+	-	+	+	-	+	-	-

(Continued)

TABLE 3.8 *(Continued)*

Panel C: The Insider Equation

Dependent Variable	Independent Variables	(A)	(B)	(C)	(D)	Instruments Lagged (E)	(F)	Dependent Variable Lagged (G)	(H)	(I)
Insiders	Ownership concentration	+	+	+	+	+	+	+	+	+
	Performance	−	+	+	−	+	+***	+	+	+
	Aggregate state holdings	−	−	−	−	−	−	+	+	−
	Aggregate international holdings	−	−	−	−	−	−	+	+	−
	Aggregate individual holdings	+	−	−	+	+	−	+	−	+
	Aggregate nonfinancial holdings	−	−	−	−	−	−	+	+	+
	ln(Board size)	−	+	+	−	+	+	+	+	+
	Fraction voting shares	−	−	−	+	−	−***	−*	−	−
	Debt to assets	−	−	+		+	+	+	+	−
	Dividends to earnings	−	+	+		+	+***	+	+	−
	Industrial	−	+	+		+	+***	−	+	−
	Transport/shipping	−	+	+	+	+	+***	−	+	+
	Offshore	−	+	+	+	+	+***	−	+	−
	Investments to income	+	+	+	+	+	+	−**	+	+
	ln(Equity value)	+	+	+	−	+	−**	−**	−	+
	lag(−1) (Performance)		−							−
	lag(−1) (Ownership concentration)							+***		−
	lag(−1) (Insiders)							+***		−
	Constant	−	+	+	−	+	+**	+	+	−

The table explores the simultaneous determinants of performance, ownership concentration, and insider holdings, using nine alternative sets of instruments to estimate the equation system:

Performance = f(Concentration, Insiders, Other variables, Instruments)
Concentration = f(Performance, Insiders, Other variables, Instruments)
Insiders = f(Performance, Concentration, Other variables, Instruments)

The results for the performance equation, concentration equation, and insiders equation are reported in panels A, B, and C, respectively. Performance is measured as Q and ownership concentration by the Herfindahl index, which is the sum of squared ownership fractions. Insiders is the equity fraction owned by directors and officers, Aggregate holdings reflects the fraction held by the given type, Board size is the number of directors, ln() is the natural logarithm, and Fraction voting shares is the percentage of the company's equity which has voting rights. Industrial, Transport/Shipping and Offshore are industry dummy variables, Equity value is the market value of equity, Stock volatility is the standard deviation of daily stock returns, Stock turnover is annual trading volume of the stock divided by outstanding equity, Beta is the estimated beta of the company's stock, using daily returns over a 2 year period, and lag(-1) indicates that the variable equals the previous period's observation. The instruments for performance, ownership concentration, and insider holdings are stock beta, stock volatility, and board size in model (A), stock beta, stock turnover, and board size in model (B), and stock beta, intercorporate shareholdings, and debt to assets in model (C). Models (D)–(F) use the same instruments lagged one period, and the instruments in (G)–(I) are the endogenous variables lagged one period. We report the sign of the regression coefficients and indicate statistical significance with $*$, $**$, and $***$, which means the relationship is significant at the 5%, 2.5% and 1% level, respectively. We use 3SLS with Stata as the estimation engine. Data for all nonfinancial firms listed on the Oslo Stock Exchange, 1989–1997.

the nine instrument sets. For instance, the association between Q and insider holdings is positive in (B), (E), (G), (H), and (I), but negative in (A), (C), (D), and (F). Outside concentration is an exception, as the inverse relation to performance and the positive association with insiders is very robust to instrument choice. Second, compared to our earlier models in Tables 3.3 and 3.7, there is less significance. Still, the ability to produce significant coefficients in Table 3.8 differs considerably across models. For instance, five mechanisms in the performance equation are significant at the 5% level in (C), two mechanisms have this property in (G), and no variable is significant in (B). There is still some consistency in the sense that significant coefficients tend to have the same sign across models.

The third impression is that whereas significant coefficients are quite rare in the insider equation except in model (F), they are very common across the four owner types in the concentration equation. Judging from the interaction coefficients, there is no substitution between concentration and insider holdings, but rather independence. Since the insider coefficient is typically insignificant in the Q equation and Q is insignificant in the insider equation, we do not replicate the finding of Loderer and Martin (1997) and Cho (1998) that performance drives insider holdings and not vice versa.

Like us, Agrawal and Knoeber (1996), Cho (1998) and Demsetz and Villalonga (2002) conclude that the relationship between governance and performance is considerably less significant with a simultaneous equation system than with single-equation models. Unlike us, they do not consider different instruments, but interpret their mostly insignificant coefficients as supporting evidence of the equilibrium hypothesis of Demsetz (1983). We are not convinced by this conclusion, which implicitly assumes that the system is better specified than single-equation models. As illustrated by Table 3.8, the instability of qualitative results across instruments and the reduced significance in systems may be driven by the choice of instruments. Since there is no proper theoretical basis for choosing instruments, we cannot conclude that system estimates are better. Similar concerns have recently been expressed by others. Studying how takeover defense, performance, and takeover activity interact, Bhagat and Jefferis (2002) state that "from an econometric viewpoint, the proper way to study the relationship between any two of these variables would be to set up a system of simultaneous equations. . . . However, specification and estimation of such a system of simultaneous equations are nontrivial." To eliminate the problem of not knowing the underlying structural model, Coles et al. (2003) specify the true endogenous relationship between Q and managerial ownership, letting it be driven by the productivity of investment and management effort. They conclude: "The results in this section illustrate the difficulties associated with specifying a simultaneous equation system. First, we find that the inferences are quite sensitive to small changes in the regression specifications. . . . Second, the regressions using the modeled values of Q show that the simultaneous equations approach does not generally eliminate the relationships between the endogenous variables. Our speculation is that the specification errors and the difficulties in finding valid instruments to identify the system are the causes; however, more research is warranted on this issue."

CONCLUSION

Corporate governance is a young academic field characterized by partial theories, limited access to high-quality data, inconsistent empirics, and unresolved methodological problems. This chapter has tried to improve the empirical insight into the relationship between governance and performance by analyzing it in a different way in a new empirical setting. With better data for a wide range of governance mechanisms, a Scandinavian regulatory framework, and governance structures that differ considerably from those of most existing studies, we analyze how the interaction between governance and performance depends on the choice between simple and comprehensive single-equation models, on the instruments used in simultaneous equation models, and on how performance is measured. We have found that the estimated relationship depends critically on the performance measure used, on the choice between alternative instruments with weak theoretical backing, but not on whether single-equation models are simple or comprehensive.

Measuring performance by Tobin's Q and operationalizing it as market to book, most of our findings from single-equation models are consistent with agency theory. Large outside owners seem to destroy market value, inside owners to create it unless the stakes are unusually big, direct ownership seems more beneficial than indirect, small boards seem to produce more value than large, and firms issuing dual-class shares seem to lose market value. Although other performance measures generally produce more fuzzy relationships, Tobin's Q is usually consistent with long-term book return on assets, but not with stock returns.

The finding that most significant relationships in single-equation models survive all the way from the univariate analysis through partial to full multivariate models suggests that governance mechanisms are seldom complements or substitutes. When analyzing the performance relevance of any individual mechanism, it seems unnecessary to control for the others, which are often difficult to measure. Earlier findings that single-equation relationships change sign or become insignificant under simultaneous equation estimation have been used to support the idea that real-world governance mechanisms are optimally installed. Our analysis suggests the alternative hypothesis that this result is due to a misspecified model driven by ad-hoc instruments. Until corporate governance theory can capture how performance relates to a wider set of governance mechanisms instead of just to one at a time, we doubt whether simultaneous systems can offer deeper insight than single-equation models into how corporate governance and economic performance interact.

CHAPTER 4

Corporate Governance as a Process-Oriented Approach to Socially Responsible Organizations

Marijan Cingula

INTRODUCTION

Corporate governance is usually treated as a legal framework for decision making, or the set of financial regulations in modern organizations. It is possible, however, to highlight some other aspects of corporate governance within organizations or in their dynamic environment. According to the stakeholders' expectations, the concept of corporate governance, when being implemented, should facilitate the integration of strategic management and operating core of the organization structure, including its technostructure and supporting modules. Consequently, the proper definition of the dominant processes, building the corporate governance model in any organization, can significantly influence the organization's effectiveness. It is important to recognize at least two levels of the corporate governance influence: corporate level and board level. On the corporate level, the dominant processes are strategic planning, financial reporting, controlling, and public relations; while on the board level the most dominant are communicational aspects of enterprise functionality, such as board members' interaction and relationship between the board of directors and managing board. Collective dynamics in decision making and cooperation (that is, how separate entities in an enterprise function, both as teams and in interaction among each other) can also contribute to the proper definition of processes in corporate governance. The existence of two boards within a joint-stock company, representing owners and hired managers, opens many questions for monitoring diverse processes in corporate governance, and for development and use of the appropriate codes of behavior.

PROCESS-ORIENTED CORPORATE GOVERNANCE

A vast number of complex terms related to sophisticated concepts emerging in social sciences are easier to understand and interpret when decomposed. Namely, a detailed analysis of constituent parts of a new subject often makes it possible to recognize facts about that new concept that are not obvious at a glance. In research, the static structural approach is commonly used if the concept examined is to be deconstructed into objects. On the other hand, if the emphasis is on the activities or processes that can be identified within the given phenomenon, the structural dynamics approach will be employed. As much as corporate governance is a relatively new concept both in theory and in practice, one cannot expect its inherent processes to have been fully identified and analyzed.

Legal or financial aspects of an organization usually are based on a static structural approach, but organizational or managerial aspects have to respect more dynamic characteristics of the entity. If the organization is observed as a system, it is easy to understand that some processes are completely involved within the context of particular organization units (such as factories, divisions, sectors, or even smaller entities). However, there are also business processes, which cannot be distributed to a single organization unit; they are spread throughout the entire organization. Administrative processes or management, as well as the governance, should be treated this way.

Decomposition of management is necessary to achieve a dynamic approach in analysis and emphasizes the processes, not the objects, as its component. Planning, organizing, managing human resources, and controlling are processes that dominate in traditional management literature. These components of the entire process are very important for operative management in each organization, so it is understandable that they have been in the center of modern management theory for decades. The success stories of most of the world's well-known managers depend on their ability to coordinate these processes within their organizations. Regardless if he or she works in a business system or public organization, the successful manager is the one who coordinates the owner's wishes in the business plans with the efficiency of highly motivated associates and co-workers.

In Anglo-Saxon literature, management is usually accepted as a process integrating subprocesses or activities in planning, organizing, motivating, and controlling. The same meaning is expanded to the other areas so it is perfectly normal that the word *management* is nowadays common in all European languages as well as in most of the other world languages. Moreover, this term is used worldwide without any translation; but in spite of this, a need for a new word, *governance*, appeared in order to stress separately some other aspects of management process.

OECD Principles of Corporate Governance, based on the experience from leading companies in member countries, and introduced into practice at the end of the last century according to their national initiatives, are ready to extend to all other companies and countries in the world, from the beginning of the new century.

Establishing the new idea of governance implies that some other processes within management must be observed differently from those that establish the traditional ideas of organizations' success and development. The processes connected to the operative efficiency, so typical for general management, will be complemented with processes that are related to the owner's strategy, controlling operative processes as well as sophisticated public relations. This way management is more oriented toward operations while the governance is more oriented toward supervising operations management. Is it too soon to jump to this kind of conclusion? In every goal-oriented organization, starting activities are marked with a process of planning. This process coordinates wishes with possibilities, connects the present with the future, predicts the conditions of planning activities, and makes sure that the budget is big enough for the realization of the final object. The budgeting, operations structuring, and performance motivation are the processes at the core of operative management, a very demanding set of activities, and only the best can succeed in accomplishing them thoroughly.

Transforming owners' wishes and vision into precise tasks also belongs to management core activities, but professional managers can only make a suggestion to the owners of a business organization or to the high-ranking officials in the public institutions. Only after they accept the professional advice or if they express their wishes independently, operative managers have to see the possibility of realization and direct their demands to the real parameters, using all modern methods and techniques. These real parameters determine business process or process of public administration.

Monitoring the financial reports is the next step of a responsible manager and the biggest challenge to a director who wishes to see the efficiency of his best team players and conducts operative coordination in order to reach planned figures at the end of the fiscal year. Good financial report is basic for all relationships with investors and public as well. Responsibility toward customers, which is shown in the quality of the product or the service and post-sales activities, is only part of the general responsibility, which is defined by the OECD as a social responsibility toward all other subjects interested in the organization's results, such as the state or local community, employees, and professional unions. Can the owners of a business organization or selected high-ranking official of a state and public institution neglect the interests of all social groups that depend on the influence of their organization? Can they allow their managers, in their aspiration to please them and give them the most with minimal investment, or by following their own narrow and particular interests, to jeopardize any interested group? These questions dominate in subtle difference between two rather similar words: *management* and *governance*. One can say that respect for stakeholders makes the difference between management and governance.

If the analogy of decomposition of management is transmitted to the governance, its components could be defined as strategic planning, financial reporting, controlling, and public relations. Interaction of the board members as well as the interaction of the two boards in the organization, which function in dual system, requires separate attention.

CORPORATE-LEVEL PROCESSES

Similar to the business organization, other not-for-profit institutions that are related to public wellbeing can also express two types of processes, operating and administrative. Operations are the main part of an organization and can be observed as primary and supporting, while administration makes possible the establishment of a coordinating body in order to supervise the operations and conduct the core process to the final objective. Operations include production or service, logistic and marketing (primary processes), and purchase, development, accountancy, finances, and human resource management (supporting processes). Administration includes planning, coordinating, organizing, and supervising, which make up the complex management processes. Management also includes the processes that surpass the coordination of the operations and can be called governance. These processes supervise the administration, which operatively conducts the organization. Such decomposition of the business processes shows no difference between business and public organizations. There is also no difference between productive and service organizations. The core activity or its volume will influence particular processes, of course, but this is the subject of a structure or a process in each particular organization.

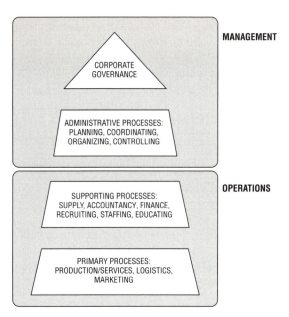

FIGURE 4.1 Processes in Business Organizations and Public Administration

It is important to note the need for observing the administration processes in all kinds of organizations. Therefore, owners' monitoring includes all techniques and controlling mechanisms aiming to protect their interests. This concept of universal connection of the processes in business organization and public administration is shown in Figure 4.1.

The figure presents operations (primary and supportive) as well as management processes (administration and governance) in which only the governing processes are not deconstructed. On the organization level, in both private and public organizations, processes related to corporate governance follow the logic of the owner's expectations. They expect from controlling as a business function to establish a permanent monitoring system in order to support effective managerial decisions.

What are the possible expectations of the owners of the business organization or high-ranking officials in public institutions regarding the operative efficiency of their organizations? The most important issue is to provide clients with the best quality products and services. The quality of the core activity has to be achieved with minimal investments to

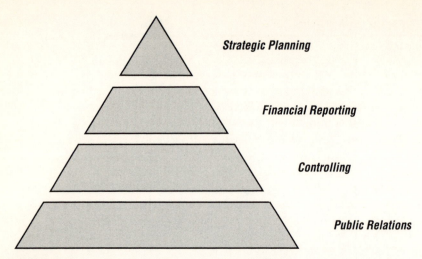

FIGURE 4.2   Corporate-Level Processes in Corporate Governance

provide all the other, mainly financial, objectives. If the main purpose of management is to realize particular economic objectives, such as making a profit or enlarging the assets as the result of operating activity, then the basic objective of governance is to achieve the same economic efficiency while considering the interests of all stakeholders, not only on the operating level but on the strategic top as well. This is why some of the controlling processes in governance, although identical to the ones in the management framework, will have a different importance and even a different position within the organizational structure. The traditional management processes pyramid, adjusted to a governance concept, is presented in Figure 4.2.

Processes selection in corporate governance, for building a corporate hierarchy pyramid, is compiled with the supposition that all the organization objectives are related to maximum effects and minimum expenses. It is important to note that operating efficiency is recognizable in business organizations as well as in those related to public well-being. If operating efficiency is observed as a technological factor in achieving the goals and the organization's activity purpose, all the other interests related to the organization's activities will be part of the strategic planning process while dissemination of these interests will be part of the public relations process. Financial reporting subprocesses, as well as controlling, form the link between the top and the bottom of the pyramid, showing the diversity of the constituent subactivities.

STRATEGIC PLANNING

Generally speaking, processes related to strategic planning have a long-term impact on the functioning of any organization (Weihrich and Koontz 1994). When it comes to any long-term arrangements, it is common for the purpose of the organization, as well as its mission and vision, to be defined prior to deciding upon a concrete strategy. Whereas the *mission* addresses the question of why we are engaging in particular endeavor, the *vision* refers to the kind of profile our organization should aspire to in the future; the *strategy*, on the other hand, provides the answer to the question of how these aspirations are to be accomplished. In an alternative approach to strategic planning, a detailed analysis of the current state of affairs is to be conducted, the development options assessed, and the terms of future activity forecast, before laying out any specific strategy. This explains why it is not easy to ascertain whether it is the owners or hired managers that are responsible for defining the strategy. While doing so, the owners are likely to have their abstract vision as the only guidance, whereas professional managers tend to base their choice of strategy on expert analyses and projections. In practice, there is a variety of options to choose from. However, while deciding which strategy to embark upon, the interests of all the stakeholders and other organizations involved in the activities of a particular organization are to be taken into consideration. A strategy ultimately arises from the mission in which the *raison d'être* of a particular organization is embodied, as well as the vision regarding the profile that the organization should aspire to in a given future period. It is to be assumed that the owner of a commercial organization and an appointed official in charge of a public institution have a vision concerning the character and structure of their respective organization, its scope of activity, and different ways of making an impact on their environment in the near future. It goes without saying that professional managers who, owing to their expertise and know-how, are hired to oversee an organization's business activity in the coming accounting period need to be aware of that as well. Additionally, it is to be assumed that all of them have insight into what resources they have at their disposal so as to be able to decide on the best way of harnessing them for achieving long-term results. Furthermore, whereas most of them are likely to be aware of the mission underlying their function, others may seek for that awareness in the program of their political party or in the religious organization they belong to. Similarly, they might draw on their nationality or simply on the customs of their local community. If strategic planning is viewed as a process within the broader term of corporate governance, it itself can be broken down into numerous activities and sub-processes, as shown in Figure 4.3.

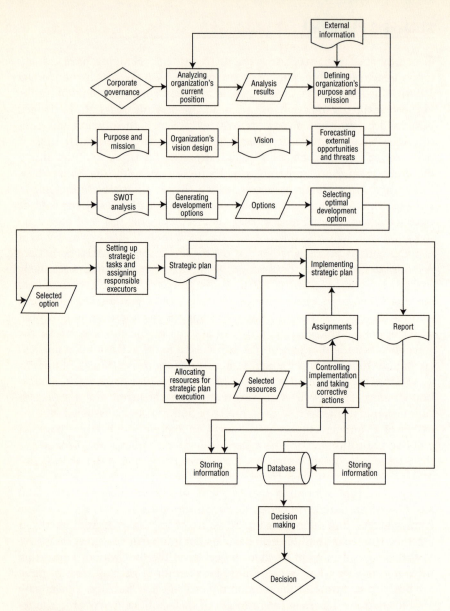

FIGURE 4.3 Activities and Subprocesses in Strategic Planning

It is evident from the flowchart that processes and subprocesses involved in strategic planning eventually lead to certain documents relevant to corporate governance. Each particular process is dealt with in more detail as follows:

■ *Analyzing the organization's current position.* True assessment of the initial position is critical to any activity, including strategic planning. Addressing the question *What is our position?* will contribute toward a better general orientation regarding one's potential. More than any other activity incorporated within strategic planning, this one should be based on judgment free from any subjectivity and sentimentality. Even in the case in which the owner is in sole charge of a corporation, a neutral analysis conducted by objective experts is recommended while assessing the initial positions; it is these experts that can best evaluate the organization's position in the market, the attractiveness of products or services for potential customers, relations with suppliers, as well as the organization's financial rating. In the context of corporate governance, these activities may be performed jointly by various stakeholders whose interests lie with the future of the organization, such as buyers and suppliers, stock exchanges and financiers, banks and insurance companies, the local community and state administration. Alternatively, the opinion about the organization's current position may be provided by professional associations, chambers of commerce, as well as independent analysts. The resources available for these particular activities should be focused on generating neutral opinion, rather than producing a biased attitude, which necessarily favors the sponsor.

■ *Defining the organization's long-term purpose and mission.* The point has already been made about who is responsible for defining the purpose of the overall business activity: It is either those who have undertaken a particular business enterprise themselves, or those who are entitled to make decisions regarding issues of public interest, provided they have acquired that right by democratic means. In both cases, the statement of mission needs to be presented to the general public, this being the very first activity an organization is inaugurated by, providing its potential stakeholders with the rationale concerning its values and underlying policies. Some of the key components of a well-articulated mission indicating a socially responsible organization include: achieving customer satisfaction, environmental awareness, promoting the wellbeing of the local community, compliance with law and business ethics, and so on. Obviously, the attempts at maximizing profit in commercial organizations and fully exploiting limited resources in public administration organizations explain why business objectives and social responsibility are often at odds. It is within the corporate governance domain that these delicate cases ought to be carefully resolved. It is hardly possible to anticipate conflicts and social tensions, but when they do occur, those in charge need to react promptly.

■ *Organization's vision design.* For one to have dreams, one does not need to be constantly asleep. Quite the contrary! If one's dreams are to be fulfilled, one should put a huge effort into realizing them. Vision refers to goals we aspire to accomplish and can thus be extremely motivating if it urges us to apply maximum energy toward seeing our strongest wishes come true. Designing a vision can prove to be a sensitive affair. Whereas goals lacking ambition may lead to lethargy and result in lagging behind the competitors, overly ambitious goals may ultimately produce a sense of frustration if not achieved. Knowing how to reconcile one's dreams in which apparently only the sky is the limit with the real circumstances arising from the objective analysis of the initial position is the exclusive privilege of hugely successful individuals. All the others have little option but to develop their vision according to their actual abilities and pursue a realistically designed mission aimed at establishing a viable socially responsible organization.

■ *Forecasting external opportunities and threats.* The SWOT analysis is commonly used by many organizations while laying out their strategy. The fact that in it both external and internal factors critical to the organization's success are intertwined makes it a convenient starting point for formulating an organization's strategy. This analysis is an invaluable tool for producing a realistic assessment of the current position, especially when internal weaknesses and strengths are considered. When it comes to external opportunities and threats, however, no direct influence can be exerted on the part of the organization; therefore, these factors cannot be perceived as a set value. Forecasts of external factors—both favorable and unfavorable—ought to be based on all available data processed by means of as many reliable methods and procedures as possible. All things considered, it is clear that the said activities call for engagement of neutral and objective experts. The owners' commitment, on the other hand, should lie within decision-making related to further activities within strategic planning. By definition, making decisions about the future is unlikely to be totally reliable and is scarcely determined by any previous experience. This is why variables arising from unreliability and risk should be kept to a minimum during the strategic planning process, especially while making decisions concerning future conditions. To the extent one is prepared for conditions likely to arise in future business activity, and even to anticipate negative developments, one is more apt to respond promptly and effectively if and when they eventually occur. We should bear in mind that even an uncertain future can provide opportunity for success, so it should not come as a surprise that many companies stick to this assumption as their steady determinant.

■ *Generating development options.* Once the conditions in which the organization is to sustain its future activity are forecast, plans can be formulated. Out of the interaction between the present weaknesses and strengths on the one hand, and external opportunities and threats on the other hand, a number of variations of projected results are likely to occur. Furthermore, finding numerous development options is closely related to both the availability of information and timely application thereof. In this context, *business intelligence*, used for generating development options, should be mentioned. It has been established as a scientific discipline dealing with gathering, processing, and dissemination of publicly available data. When it comes to the quality of the processed information, it has impact not only on the efficiency of business decision making but also on business results—financial results, among others—to be potentially formulated as a development option. Analytical performances, encompassing statistical calculations as well as trend and time analyses, rely on a number of procedures. These primarily include making a request for information, wherein the efficiency of the database search applications, such as SQL (Structured Query Language), is essential, and the data warehousing process (DWP). Regardless of whether sources of data are located within numerous databases or outside them, data first need to be recognized as relevant and subsequently extracted from their current location to a data transfer/transformation system through processes commonly referred to as ETL (*e*xtraction, *t*ransformation, *l*oad). The process can be reiterated, whereby the total cost of business intelligence implementation is significantly increased. Online analytical processing (OLAP) is an invaluable tool intended to support business intelligence. It allows for a multidimensional analysis of the warehoused data, which in turn results in extended metrics necessary for users' evaluation of data. In each particular dimension data are organized hierarchically, wherein both top-down and bottom-up extraction options are provided. Data mining, on the other hand, enables the user to elicit details previously inaccessible by means of conventional methods. All things considered, it should not come as a surprise that state-of-the-art IT support is considered to be one of the prerequisites for generating development options.

- *Selecting the optimal development option.* The current business intelligence technology can produce nearly reliable development options provided that contemporary analytical methods and procedures are successfully implemented. Whereas generating those options/varieties falls under the jurisdiction of neutral and objective experts, selecting a particular option is exclusively within the owner's authority. In view of the vision to be pursued, judgments can be made on the level of strategic planning in favor of massive expansion and acquisitions or, conversely, contraction in activity, which may eventually lead to putting the existing resources on sale, or even the organization's extinction. All these options are feasible since they all belong to inalienable ownership rights, although by any reduction of business activity the interests of the employees and the state are primarily jeopardized; it should be noted that these interests and ownership rights are equally legitimate. If business extension and extinction are perceived as two extreme developments within the present organization, there is presumably a whole range of possibilities in between, each of them resulting in a different business result. Socially responsible corporate governance will not only seek to satisfy the organization's needs, but will also attend to the needs of numerous stakeholders involved. It has been proven many times in practice that, in case an organization were to experience a crisis that would make it incapable of accomplishing its business goals, joint decision making between either the owner and the employees or the owner and the local community would indeed be feasible. It can be assumed, therefore, that even selecting the development option does not necessarily need to be under the sole jurisdiction of the owner.

- *Setting up strategic tasks and assigning responsible executors.* Once a development option has been agreed upon, the process of drafting strategic plans to be carried out in the future can be embarked upon. When we consider that the decision of the *managing board* is indeed the initial step in setting up strategic tasks, it does not come as a surprise that the destiny of an organization's top management is generally associated with its business strategy. Establishing the link between the tasks and responsible executors thereof makes sense since the setup tasks can provide parameters for performance assessment. For strategic tasks to be fulfilled, they can be conveniently organized into a series of subtasks referring to particular activities that constitute the process to be undertaken. Thus, upon defining the strategic task, all the requirements necessary for successful execution of that task need to be established. Consider a strategic task implying a 15% increase in the market share, for example: Whereas the fulfillment of the task may be the responsibility of the sales manager, its execution presumably depends on redesigning the product, assortment extension, changes in the pricing policy, providing various post-sale services, and so on. Although it is lower management that is in charge of this network of subtasks aimed at accomplishing the ultimate goal, in broader terms it ought to remain under the auspices of corporate governance. Controlling in turn implies constant monitoring of realization of tasks and deviation from projected figures. The information acquired in the process may initiate a change of behavior or call for an intervention in the performance of the activity.

- *Allocating resources for strategic plan execution.* Depending on the development option selected, resources for executing the strategic plan will be allocated. Provided there are sufficient resources within the organization itself, satisfactory results may be achieved by redistribution thereof. A decision to renounce the current way of allocating resources is likely to help the owners in creating conditions for the extension of future activities. On the other hand, if the company's present assets are insufficient, the lack of means will be made up for by redistributing its assets or incurring debts. For the latter to be achieved, the organization will rely on its cooperation with banks and other business associates, in compliance with the previous decisions made by authorized individuals. The extension of the ownership structure is achieved either by means of the initial issue of stock offered in the free market or through initial private offering. For most part, the issue of financing strategic projects is under the jurisdiction of the owner. However, all the other interested parties may have a say in it as well. In huge organizations, the activity of which, owing to its scope, may qualify as one of national interest, announcing changes in the ownership structure may mobilize domestic investors, especially if the initial offering is carried out through a public call.
- *Implementation.* It is generally considered that once a development option has been selected, related strategic goals assigned to responsible executors, and available resources for execution of these goals allocated, the strategic plan has been formally completed; that is, it has acquired a shape suitable for being stored in a database or disseminated as a hard copy. The implementation of a strategic plan refers to carrying out the intended activities and tasks, and this is where organization plays a major part. In other words, strategic plan implementation encompasses the accomplishment of corporate governance goals in both the management and the operations sphere.
- *Controlling implementation and taking corrective actions.* Controlling the implementation of the strategic plan is an important stage in the realization of planned activities. However, it constitutes only one segment within a more general concept of controlling, which in turn is

crucial for development of the concept of corporate governance. This aspect of controlling can be pursued as a regular activity of the *supervisory board* in their ordinary sessions convened several times a year. Generally speaking, this is sufficient for trends to be duly anticipated and for corrective actions to be taken, if necessary. However, the aspect of controlling related to operations needs to be addressed as well. This issue is permanently at the core of corporate governance.

These activities, extracted from strategic planning, have a major impact on the concept of corporate governance in business systems and public administration systems. It is in the process of defining the key components of a strategic plan, that is, in selecting a development option and overseeing its implementation, that the impact of these activities can be best perceived.

FINANCIAL REPORTING

Financial reporting is carried out in accordance with the International Financial Reporting Standards, which means that the processes incorporated within this field are widely recognized at the moment of introducing international regulations. Although in some countries different rules have been adopted—such as the American Financial Reporting Standards in the United States, for example—on the global level the tendency is toward harmonizing discordant regulations. On a larger scale, all these processes are aimed at establishing a unique corporate governance system within which the fair policy of safeguarding the interests of all participants will be promulgated. In view of this, it is necessary to be acquainted with the very assumptions underpinning financial reporting, which are commonly defined as:

- *Permanence.* It is generally assumed that no time limit concerning the organization's activity has been set nor intention made effectuating a significant reduction in the range of activity. Presumably, this principle is particularly important for gaining the trust of potential investors, maintaining business confidence of suppliers, as well as for the social security of the employees and the state depending on revenue inflow.
- *Consistency.* It is assumed that, once chosen, the accounting policies are bound to be permanently implemented, so there are no differences between particular periods. It is therefore possible to compare data from any given period against the corresponding data from any other period.

■ *Occurrence of the event.* Business events, primarily profits and expenses, are registered precisely as they occur and are entered into the records of the particular accounting period in which they arose.

Financial reporting is not only critical to the actual management of an organization's operations; it is closely associated with strategic oversight as well as various interests of a vast number of related individuals and groups, including shareholders, investors, the state, customers, suppliers, employees, analysts, and many others involved in financial affairs. Not only is reporting essential for keeping records and maintaining oversight, but it plays an important part in making decisions concerning future events. Consequently, within business reporting the processes shown in Figure 4.4 can be distinguished.

Processes involved in financial reporting eventually lead to certain documents relevant for presenting the organization in public and invaluable

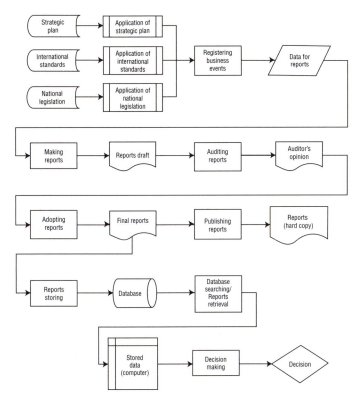

FIGURE 4.4 Financial Reporting Processes

while making decisions about all strategic and operational issues. Each particular process is dealt with in more detail as follows:

- *Application of standards.* Although the application of financial reporting standards can be imposed by national legislation, it can also be dictated by a stock market or a major business associate, including customers we rely on for acting as their certified suppliers, principals, or franchise providers. Standardization of reporting can also be carried out within the comprehensive process of applying standards to organizing overall business activity. An example of such standardization is the ISO standards, which lend themselves well to an integrated systems regime. In any case, from the investors' standpoint, the very existence of standards in business reporting is indicative of reliable and transparent procedures to be expected in the future in the highly sensitive area of disposing of a company's assets. A decision about standard application, whether prompted by a law, an external regulation, or an internal need, is by all means a strategic decision, the execution whereof will enable the advancement of corporate governance to a higher level. After all, the establishment of the principles of corporate governance is but another attempt of the international community to standardize the flow of managerial processes. This explains why the process of establishing the principles of standardization in business reporting stands out as one of the key processes within corporate governance in general.

- *Application of national legislation.* In business reporting, national legislation and international standards are equally important. Whereas in some countries International Financial Reporting Standards have been fully adopted as national standards, other countries adhere to their own national standards. In both cases, along with the standards themselves, national laws, government provisions, and professional organizations' codes ought to be applied if business reporting is to fulfill the requirements of all users.

- *Application of strategic plan.* Besides international and national regulations, business reporting is affected by regulations within the organization itself arising from the strategic plan as the document crucial for corporate governance implementation. It should be noted that the strategic plan is a business management document developed and adopted in strict accordance with the statute of an organization and its corporate governance code.

- *Registering business events.* Business reporting relies heavily on record keeping. The accountants' motto, according to which "Nothing has occurred as long as a business event has been registered," comes easily to mind. An analogy can be drawn with journalism, where it is assumed

that "There is no event as long as there is no written record about it."
After all, the ancient Romans expressed a similar sentiment on this matter by formulating the catchphrase *Verba volant, scripta manent.* ("The spoken word evaporates, the written word remains.") For today's businesspeople, it is probably not necessary to point out the importance of entering all events affecting a company's assets, or the relationship between particular organizational units or processes, into the company's records. Record keeping is of utmost importance when it comes to history: The current state cannot be fully grasped without the existence of past records. Nevertheless, this *history* component is just a lesser part of contemporary record keeping, which figures prominently in business decision making. Namely, it is through appropriate and resourceful use of past records that decisions regarding future are best formed. Bookkeeping is essentially based on keeping track of your business finances. Each business event ought to be tracked in compliance with the principles of bookkeeping and related policies, according to the place and time of occurrence of the event; in so-called double-entry bookkeeping it is possible to register the same business event as a debit entry in one account and a credit entry in another account, which assures better accuracy and control. Although within the company structure, a special operations service is in charge of bookkeeping procedures, it is considered to be a joint responsibility of those services and lower managers from concrete business units. Whereas taking care that business events are properly tracked lies within the domain of corporate governance, managing boards, being at the very top of an organization's hierarchy and thus entitled to strategic oversight, cannot focus on each and every detail of record keeping done at the operations level. For this reason, those boards are to be assisted by special professional bodies—(preferably permanent) internal audit committees.

- *Making reports.* This process is developed in compliance with international standards, national laws, as well as external and internal regulations. In drafting reports the focus must be on the user; thus, in multinational organizations several reports can be made concurrently in accordance with different users' needs (for example, national revenue audit, international stock exchange, and principal of another country). Making reports is carried out by the same services that are in charge of bookkeeping records, but the responsibility for reports lies with top operative management, namely the *chief financial officer.* The purpose of reports is to indisputably identify business events based on up-to-date records, and then display all relevant business events faithfully and fairly in a standardized form for all interested users to read and comprehend and then make decisions based on those reports. The concept of financial reports, regulated by standards, includes balance of accounts, profit and loss account, cash flow statement, notes on statements, capital changes statement, and other statements and explanations if marked as an integral part of financial reports. International standards on financial reporting apply to all business organizations with stock market quotations, while the term *small and medium enterprises* currently covers all entities free of public reporting commitment. Financial reports are made available to the public once a year at the shareholders' general assembly when they are subject to independent auditors' review. Stock exchanges may request that organizations included in their quotations present their business reports within shorter accounting periods, usually quarterly, but such reports need not be reviewed. Business reports are a vital part of regular monitoring carried out by the owners and the state, and all other stakeholders.

■ *Auditing reports.* Regarding the importance of business reports, they need checking. Competent checking of business reports by impartial experts is called a *commercial audit.* The audit includes examining accounting records and determining whether the accounting faithfully and honestly reflects the real state of the organization. Accounting records are done by internal services, while auditing is necessarily external. This is despite the possibility of there also being an internal audit in charge of monitoring bookkeeping records and preparing documents for external audit. The internal audit is responsible to the managing board or the owners. Auditing is done in compliance with national laws and international standards, so all of these subprocesses and activities are well structured. Annual financial reports presented at a regular shareholders' assembly are always accompanied by auditors' opinions, which might be unconditional (meaning that unreserved support is given to presented information) or conditional (meaning there are certain restrictions, for example: *We did not witness inventory control*; or *According to the information given by the management . . .*). In principle, the business public has complete confidence in auditing reports, since it is expected that auditing control is done by expert and incorruptible professionals. Occasional scandals, even in the most prestigious world markets, show that there still is a possibility of auditing errors and, when present, owners take the severest blows. Therefore, the concept of corporate governance is defined as a model of ownership control over the managing board. Auditing is helpful here, no doubt, but the current issue of *auditing the auditor* introduces a need for establishing an independent national control entity at the highest level to exert control over the performance of authorized auditors. Owners who exert strategic control within the organization can form special expert teams or subcommittees to carry out professional internal audits, which are delivered directly to the board of directors rather than the managing board.

■ *Adopting reports.* The process of adopting reports is not an easy one. It begins with the first version suggested to the managing board by professional services of the organization. This version is then examined by auditors. Auditing is not complete until agreement on reports between the managing board and the owners' management has been reached. The board of directors examines the reports, confident that the auditors have stated their opinion and that the managing board, cooperating with professional services, has correctly presented all business events. The reports can be prepared for adoption at a regular annual assembly only provided there are no remarks. In case there is the slightest doubt as to the truth or accuracy of reports in the chain of professional services–managing board–auditors–owners, the problem must to be dealt with through corporate governance. In legal terms: Professional services are professionally responsible to the managing board, the managing board is in turn professionally responsible to owners, auditors are independent, and owners are socially responsible to stakeholders. However, in case of disturbance, these authorities are not easily exerted, so it would be wise to seek new mechanisms of socially responsible monitoring of auditors, above all, and even above owners.

■ *Publishing reports.* Preparation of a business report in an accounting period is followed by its publishing in compliance with state laws and corporation regulations. Annual reports are usually issued at a regular annual shareholders' assembly, which means they are available from the moment of sending out invitations for the assembly. It is an opportunity for the general public to become acquainted with the main components of the business result, so sending out invitations for the assembly is usually accompanied by a press conference held by the managing board for the purpose of announcing business results. Since the assembly adopts reports, they can be formally published only after the assembly, when reports are officially delivered to users. Sending out regular annual reports to users is vital in creating an impression of successful business in the general public. It goes without saying that the stock exchange, brokerage houses, banks, insurance companies, as well as chambers and professional associations will be interested to get business organizations' reports. Business reports are the best means of communication with current and future investors. Nonprofit organizations also publish their reports in order to convince founders and sponsors of their successfully accomplished mission and achievement of goals within reasonable use of collected resources.

- *Storing reports.* Business reports must be stored in organizations and in a number of public databases. Storing reports must enable data preservation, but also their accessibility in the future. Modern information systems are built in such a way to enable both of these functions to be fulfilled. The conventional way of keeping data on hard copies in archives and libraries is also still in use. In this case, special care must be taken to physically protect data against possible damage.
- *Reports retrieval.* Searching data on a conventional medium (paper) may prove difficult due to inadequate archiving or physical distance. Retrieval of data by electronic means is easier and quicker, and information systems used for business research provide special ways of searching—so-called data mining. As with generating development possibilities, a number of methods and procedures are available here as well, based on computer support.
- *Decision making based on reports.* Business reporting is only one component in preparing a decision on the level of corporate governance. This means that other sources of information (business intelligence) must be taken into account, as well as forecasts of relevant future factors. However, all managers and potential investors agree that business decisions cannot be made without revised financial reports.

Financial reporting may be the most important process in corporate governance, if there could be any talk of hierarchy according to the importance of these processes. Reviews of all business events are written in accordance with international standards and national laws, which are then delivered to competent members of a wider group of stakeholders, after being examined by independent auditors. Financial reports provide a basis for communication between the organization and public and also a source of information for making decisions regarding future business activity. Since these reports are formally compiled after business events have been completed, it is necessary to ensure access to relevant information on business events also in the course of the accounting period. Controlling processes are established for this reason.

CONTROLLING

Controlling is a process present on both management levels: operative management and corporate governance. This process may be regarded as an all-inclusive managerial approach to leading and managing an organization, but also as a statistical process control (SPC). In both cases it is equally important for each management level. It is because of this importance that legitimate opinions are expressed as to each management level having its own control mechanism. In terms of organization it would mean that where there are two boards (the managing board and the board of directors/owners), there should also be two control systems, one for each board. The controlling subcommittee responsible to the managing board provides internal auditing and a basis for giving an opinion to authorized auditors. The subcommittee responsible to owners would be in charge of controlling business, but also evaluating auditors' reports, which means that the managing board could not exert any influence over this committee's operation. This would create the prerequisite for active decision making with auditing committee members who meet a few times a year and are not well acquainted with day-to-day business problems, but make decisions based solely on the information provided for them by the managing board. Regardless of the organization chart, basic processes that can be identified in the context of controlling are unique, as shown in Figure 4.5.

Subprocesses found within controlling are unique, but the division of controlling into strategic and operational is legitimate because it makes it

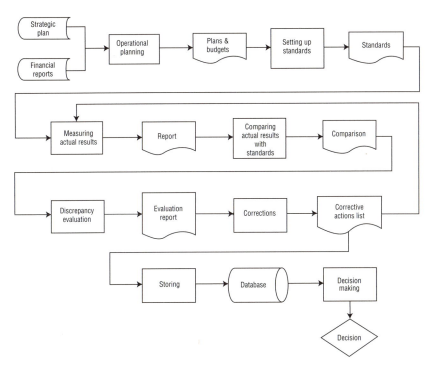

FIGURE 4.5 Controlling Processes

easier to decide within whose competence certain aspects of business events controlling reside. This must also meet owners' and all other stakeholders' expectations.

- *Operational planning.* This process relies on the strategic plan and financial reports. Based on strategic plan regulations and information available from the last accounting period, plans are made on the operational level directed toward accomplishing precise, easily measurable operational goals and tasks. Since these plans determine required material resources for their accomplishment and anticipate income from the realization of planned performance, this kind of operational plan is commonly referred to as a *budget.* Budgeting refers to a procedure of making and adjusting single operational plans to a planned annual balance of accounts and planned profit and loss account. Budgeting is crucial for preparing responsible executors in advance for accomplishment of those activities that will enable the goals of the whole organization to be achieved. In addition, a budget is a standard for monitoring and evaluating realization of planned activities and is therefore the most important instrument of effective operational controlling. The value is in the planning, not the plan itself (Bliss 1992).
- *Setting up standards.* In business monitoring it is important to know what the expectations are in order to evaluate efficiency. Owners present their expectations in the procedure of making and accepting a strategic plan, while executive managers suggest operational plans for formulating partial tasks intended to fulfill owners' expectations in the following accounting period. Therefore, operational plans are the best standards in evaluating efficiency of an organization and its executive manager. Many organizations pay a bonus to the management board if business performance within an accounting period exceeds the plan (Horngren, Foster, and Datar 2000). Therefore, it is vital for plans to be realistic, because if they are too modest, they will be easily reached, while unrealistic plans cause frustration when actual results are nowhere near the planned ones. Applying mechanisms contained in its code, corporate governance should satisfy not only the owner and manager, but also other stakeholders. Standards for evaluating business efficiency, done by the managing board and monitored by the owners, are usually defined as economic and financial indicators of frugality, profitability, returns from investment, and the like. As far as potential investors' expectations go, what counts is the rise in the organization's assets and efficient use of the same, reflected in customer and other stakeholders' satisfaction, and for business organizations, also the price-of-shares movements on the stock exchange.

■ *Measuring results.* Regular business activity produces effects recorded in accounting, and their comparison with projected figures shows positive or negative discrepancies. Measuring business results is done throughout the year in all instances within an organization where business changes occur, such as acquisition of raw materials, materials and external services, producing effects, selling products and services, providing logistics, human resources management, marketing, and public relations. These are only a few instances within the organization that result in certain costs or revenue. Measuring results is a simple count of quantities and values where up-to-date and impartial recording of the measuring in the accounting is vital for further analyses and evaluations.

■ *Comparing actual results with standards.* When the accounting period is over, results are compared with projected figures based on the bookkeeping records of organization's performance. At this stage, corporate governance has to perform twofold control: First, it is important to measure the difference between the actual result and one projected in the operational plan; second, it is vital to remove any doubt as to the authenticity of actual figures in the bookkeeping records. External audit confirms the bookkeeping records in terms of international standards and national laws, while internal audit, responsible to owners, should confirm the accuracy of documents submitted to auditors and the correctness of the auditing procedure itself.

■ *Discrepancy evaluation.* If there is a considerable discrepancy from projected figures, reasons should be found as to why this happened. The managing board must prepare expert analysis of internal and external events that had impact on the actual figures. This analysis must show what caused the discrepancy, and to what extent. Discrepancies may also be positive or beneficial for an organization, as in the case of higher income or lower costs. Regardless of what led to such discrepancies, the managing board is entitled to express their satisfaction with the result and expects to be rewarded by the owners. When discrepancies are negative for the organization, it must be determined whether they are consequences of external factors or internal weaknesses. The ultimate measure that stands at the owners' disposal is to dismiss the managing board. Corporate governance should enable other stakeholders to take part in evaluating discrepancies between actual and projected figures.

■ *Corrections.* Evaluating discrepancies at the end of an accounting period has a limited value for the organization because it offers only two possibilities: reward or punishment as the result. In the course of business process, it is of much greater importance to ascertain whether discrepancies from the plan are such as to jeopardize the accomplishment of goals set in the strategic plan. If that is ascertained, the managing board can undertake corrective actions, for example, reduce costs or invest in raising sales. In case unfavorable results not arising from internal weaknesses but objective external conditions are significant enough to cause serious damage, the managing board may require the owners to reassess and redefine goals in terms of the new situation. Here the importance of operational controlling for corporate governance in general can be best perceived because continuous monitoring enables corrective actions to be undertaken in time.

Controlling is an important process within corporate governance and no matter whether it is conducted on the strategic or operations level it always consists of identical subprocesses that enable its efficient use as an instrument of managerial monitoring. All stakeholders, who follow performance results of a business organization or an organization engaged in public well-being, must recognize the importance of controlling as an ongoing process of business monitoring, and not merely restricted to comparing bookkeeping records with operational plans.

PUBLIC RELATIONS

Public relations belong traditionally to the marketing process in the modern organization, or more accurately to customer relationship management (CRM), which includes unavoidable customers' support. In corporate governance, public relations has to keep its traditional role in searching for customers' needs, but must also expand to the fulfillment of the interests of all stakeholders. Although the customer is the most important client for executive managers, who tend to adopt all operations for satisfying his or her needs, there are also other clients in the modern CRM approach, and there is a need for satisfying their interests too. Perhaps the new approach to stakeholders' identification and satisfaction is not yet dominant in traditional companies, but many modern organizations treat their employees, contractors, and even the local community with the same responsibility and care as their most important customers. This shows the social responsibility of the organization, which is essential in developing the corporative governance concept. Subprocesses in public relations begin in previous corporative governance components—governance, business reporting, and controlling—as shown in Figure 4.6.

The public relations process starts with identifying clients and their

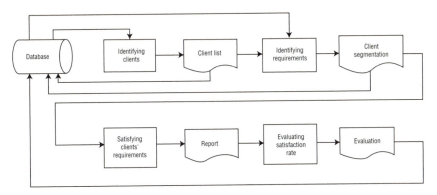

FIGURE 4.6   Activities and Subprocesses in Public Relations

needs and finishes with the evaluation of clients' satisfaction rate. In this cycle, the most important subprocesses can be identified as follows:

- *Identifying clients.* This is a very complex subprocess with the priority of establishing the client list—those whose needs are being satisfied—and only then identifying their requirements. In the corporate governance context, the clients are all subjects interested in result of the organization: their owners and/or their founders, executive managers, employees, contractors, buyers and consumers, distributors, local community, state government, professional alliances (unions), present and future financiers, insurance companies, and others. Each of them has the right to establish particular and original requirements, while corporate governance has to include these requirements into the strategic plan. From the strategic plan, the requirements are transmitted to operative plans and budgets before being accomplished by business operations.

- *Identifying requirements.* Different clients' requirements can sometimes be in conflict. When the owners wish to achieve higher profit, they usually tend to decrease expenses, while the employees object to reduction in their wages, and customers object to shrinking the products' or services' quality. The priority of corporate governance is harmonization of stakeholders' interests and avoiding any conflicts. The organization's subjectivity must also be observed and protected, especially in the sense of maintaining continuous operations and organizational development. Many stakeholders usually have the same interests, but they also can generate specific expectations: The owners need the increase and refund of the invested assets, executive management is interested in bonuses and affirmation, employees in working conditions, buyers in satisfying their needs even after they have paid for the product or service, contractors are interested in better payment conditions, the state in regular tax payment, the local community in taking care of the environment and support for general local needs, professional organizations in sponsoring their work, and so on. The proper identification of the needs and expectations is not possible without permanent communication with the clients. Modern computer support makes this communication easier and helps preserve the information of every client's needs.

■ *Satisfying the client's requirements.* The client's interests are fulfilled by providing operations according to the strategic plan, operating plans, and budgets. If the organization meets the expectations of only a limited number of stakeholders, there can be short-term benefits, but long-term goals can be seriously jeopardized. If the stakeholders feel insecure, they have other options. Buyers are attracted by other products and services, executive management and employees can seek other employers, investors are ready to move into other markets, while the state can even use force in collecting taxes. Information technology can help in both identification and fulfillment of different expectations by supporting the operating activities, according to the budgets. Fulfillment of needs usually means dissemination of standardized goods at a fair price and on time.

■ *Evaluating satisfaction rate.* Satisfaction with the product or service can be expressed objectively or in the form of subjective feelings, but executive management must take care of both aspects. Quality, measured by reliability, safety, and durability, will contribute to the objective satisfaction. The kind of sale, design, or level of maintenance will influence the subjective feeling of satisfaction. Stakeholders who are not consumers will express their objective satisfaction on the level of standard relationships, for instance, establishing the wages according to the contract with trade unions, or paying the supplier according to the standard contract. Their subjective satisfaction will appear if the additional attention is recognized, such as pleasant working climate or a long-term contract with the supplier. Measuring the objective and subjective satisfaction with the business is possible by using different methods like statistics, surveys, and interviews or balanced scorecard (BSC).

In the process of corporate governance, public relations consist of more components than in a traditional marketing approach, because the wider range of clients is included. Beside consumers, there are other interested subjects as well. Modern customer relationship management is very close to what corporate governance wants to accomplish: satisfying the interests of all interested subjects—stakeholders. This can be reached by reinstatement of corporate culture. The new approach stresses ethical values and the social responsibility of the organization. Awareness of the need for strengthening social responsibility puts most responsible owners and executive managers in the position where they care for both financial effectiveness and public wellbeing.

INTEGRATIVE ROLE OF CORPORATE GOVERNANCE IN ORGANIZATIONS

Corporate governance principles influence the functioning of each organization independently, but national economic systems as well as general democracy and the political and judicial environment provide strong feedback to the governance implementation in a particular country. In addition to the corporate level, governance influences the internal level of board functioning, mostly in these economies where the two-board system is implemented. The board of directors, elected at the regular shareholders' meeting, in many countries is known as the *supervisory board*. Owners, who delegate executive prerogatives on the basis of expected professional authority of executive or managing board members, elect the other board. The hired members of the managerial board or executive board act on the basis of a contract with owners from the board of directors or supervisory board.

Is it possible to identify conflict of interest among the highest institution of executive management, such as the managerial board or chief executive officer (CEO), and the highest institution of governance or owner's management, such as the board of directors or supervisory board? If these two boards are acting as one, there is no confrontation, but if they are separated, conflict is possible.

If the one-board system is implemented, it means that owners' responsibility and the executive management function are completely integrated and there is no possibility for a conflict between these two management groups. In some countries, this is a legal option. On the other hand, there may be some legal obstacles in other countries that do not support integration of executive and supervisory management functions. In these situations, the owners sometimes take over the executive role by themselves. They are not formally involved in governance, but acting as the executive managers the owners are sure to take good care of their assets. Other stakeholders may be suspicious, and there is a good reason for monitoring how the main interest of the company is protected. If everything is working well, especially when the owner's ability of managing the operations is on an acceptable level, the organization can reach very good results. In this case, family members or very reliable friends enter the supervising board. Independent experts are not very often in owners' boards. This kind of corporative governance is typical for transitive countries when the new owners of the great companies want to gain and keep complete control over the organization's business. Most of the time this is possible because of their domination from an earlier period, so the main question of corporate governance is how to shape social supervising over the manager-owners. It is not unusual that newly fledged owners consider the corporation as their individual property, neglecting its legal personality and other stakeholders' interests. Sometimes the owners misuse their domination and sell the company's property as real estate, and take no care for business continuance, social security of the workers, or tax obligations toward the state. Some transitive countries have many examples of devastation of business organizations with complete lack of any legal sanctions.

Another large problem of corporate governance, specifically in transitional countries, is diversification of the ownership among a great number of so-called small stockholders, usually with a great part of the state ownership in a particular company's structure. Supervisory board functioning is limited and executive managers take over both roles—administrative and supervising, though without any higher participation in ownership and owner's risk. Monitoring is done only formally, without direct responsibility of board members, even without their interest in the business future of the organization. Executive managers, because of their well-established authority, and without serious supervision, can easily misuse their position and completely neglect the interests of all the other subjects. To avoid this situation it is necessary to reestablish an efficient mechanism of permanent supervision of executive management and owners who neglect the subjectivity of business organization.

Even though two management bodies, highly ranked in the organization's hierarchy, establish contractual relationship, conflict among them arises because executive management takes care of operations on a daily basis, while owners have insight into operations only from time to time, and exclusively based on the information provided by the executive managers. When the board of directors negotiates contracts with executive managers, their relationship is unambiguous and clear: the contract is the proof of mutual trust and conformity in collaboration. Hopefully, the future should confirm this reestablished harmony. A closer look, however, shows the area of clear responsibility for each of the boards:

Supervisory Board:
- Election and dismissing of executive management
- Vision and mission defining
- Strategy defining

- Supervision of operations and executive management
- Evaluation of results
- Reporting to shareholders' meeting

Managing Board or Chief Executive Officer:

- Managing the operations
- Generating strategy options
- Modeling, executing, and supervising operative plans and budgets
- Selecting, motivating, and leading people
- Monitoring and managing expenses
- Managing clients' relationships

Obviously, there is intensive interaction between the two boards in processes of defining the organization's vision and mission, generating development options and selecting development strategy, operations and customer relationship management, and supervising operations and executive management as well. These areas of intensive interaction introduced by the concept of the social responsibility within corporate governance are shown in Figure 4.7.

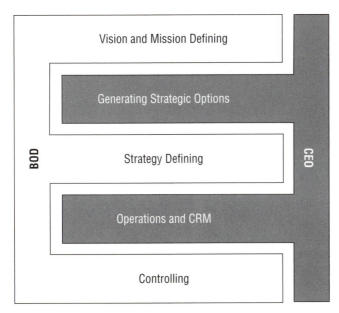

FIGURE 4.7 BOD/CEO Responsibilities Interaction

Different processes in which each particular board takes responsibility can be shown as black-and-white contrasts, symbolizing their specific separation, but if they are shown in grayscale, that would point to cooperation and responsibility for all specified processes. Corporate governance aims to establish mutual responsibility not by questioning the owners' identity or their right of supervision, but by reestablishing cooperation among the most responsible persons and institutions interested in the organization's success and social prosperity.

CHAPTER 5

The Impact of the New Corporate Governance Code on the Belgian Stock Market

Albert Corhay, Andree Dighaye, and Pierre-Armand Michel

INTRODUCTION

Corporate governance, the way by which companies are controlled and governed, is nowadays an increasingly important component of the firm's environment (Belgian Banking & Finance Commission, 1998). The debate on corporate governance has mostly emerged in the European Union (EU) following recent scandals such as Enron. Thus, it has principally been since 1998 that several countries have worked out their own codes of best practice.

In Belgium, the Federation of Enterprises in Belgium, the Belgian Banking & Finance Commission, and the Belgian Stock Exchange Commission set up recommendations in 1998. The Directors' Belgian Association also elaborated a set of recommendations in 2000. In January 2004, following the invitation by the European Union to issue codes of best practice, a Belgian Commission—called Corporate Governance Committee—was created to elaborate a new code, which is partly based on the previous recommendations. This Committee published the code project on June 18, 2004. The final version of this code was issued at the end of that year.

The purpose of this chapter is to evaluate the impact of the creation of the Corporate Governance Committee and of the appearance of the code project on the domestic stocks of the Brussels Stock Exchange and to analyze the volatility of Belgian stocks. We also test the reaction of the Belgian market to the invitation by the European Union to issue a corporate governance code. Finally, we divide our sample according to the size of the firms and their activity sector. We then test the reaction of these announcements on the new samples.

This chapter is organized as follows. The next section is devoted to the notion of corporate governance. In the third section, we discuss the recommendations in force in three countries: Belgium, France, and the United Kingdom. We then describe the contents of the Belgian recommendations. In the fourth section, we analyze the new Belgian corporate governance project and its contents. The objectives and methodology of the chapter are explored in the fifth and sixth sections. We present empirical results and analysis in the penultimate section, followed by a summary and conclusions in the final section.

THE CONCEPT OF CORPORATE GOVERNANCE

Control over conflicts of interest is an essential dimension of corporate governance concerns (Cobbaut 1997). Separation between ownership (the shareholders) and control (the managers) in a firm gives rise to an agency situation (Berle and Means 1932). This separation mostly appears in managerial firms, where the shareholding is very dispersed. The ideal situation arises where managers act in the best interests of the shareholders. Agency conflicts can exist between shareholders and managers, but also between shareholders and debtholders. The nature of the conflict can vary according to the culture and the characteristics of the firms. In Anglo-Saxon countries, we principally have manager–shareholder relationships, whereas in Belgium the conflicts between majority and minority shareholders are more pronounced. Because communication between the parties is imperfect, the reality is, however, different. Agency theory deals with agency problems that emerge because of divergence of interests. "We define an agency relationship as a contract under which one or more persons (the principal) engage another person (the agent) to perform some service on their behalf which involves delegating some decision making authority to the agent. If both parties to the relationships are utility maximizers, there is a good reason to believe that the agent will not always act in the best interests of the principal" (Jensen and Meckling 1976). Agency costs tend to limit opportunistic behaviors by the agent.

Corporate governance is based on the idea that it is fundamental to implement systems in firms that allow the reduction of conflict (Bancel 1997). Appropriate incentives linked to remuneration can reduce divergence of interests and induce managers to act in the interests of the principal (Cobbaut 1997; De Fusco, Johnson, and Zorn 1990). Stock option plans can help to align interests because the managers become potential shareholders and are thus interested in increasing the value of the shares. Boards of directors are another solution to align interests because they allow the direction and control of the company.

The interest in corporate governance has grown during the past decade, mostly in European countries. It "[. . .] reflects an understanding that equity investors [. . .] are considering the quality of corporate governance along with financial performance and other factors when deciding whether to invest in a company. [. . .] They are willing to pay more for a company that is well-governed [. . .]" (European Commission 2002). Thus, a key reason for the development of *best practice* is the ability of a firm to attract capital across borders, something that is directly related to the quality of corporate governance.

The main objective of corporate governance is indeed to increase the transparency of financial information, as well as the transparency of the managers' and the boards of directors' responsibility (Weynand and Lemaire 2004); another important objective is to maintain investor confidence. It is also important to distinguish countries where equity markets are liquid and shareholders dispersed (like in the United States and United Kingdom) from countries where shareholding is not dispersed. In this last case, corporate governance also aims to protect minority shareholders by ensuring their fair treatment (European Commission, Comparative Study of Corporate Governance Codes Relevant to the European Union and Its Member States 2002; hereafter, European Commission, Comparative Study 2002). Finally, corporate governance is also a way of aligning the interests of different stakeholders. In summary, the basic corporate governance principles may be defined in terms of transparency, accountability, responsibility and fair treatment of shareholders.

Nowadays, nearly all EU Member States have issued their own corporate governance code, which is a set of principles, standards, best practice and/or recommendations, either legal or contractually binding, linked to the internal governance of corporations (European Commission, Comparative Study 2002). However, corporate governance systems appear to be defined in a variety of ways, according to corporate culture, national priorities and legislation. "Corporate governance, in the sense of a set of rules according to which firms are managed and controlled, is the result of norms, traditions and patterns of behavior developed by each economic and legal system and is certainly not based on a single model that can be exported and imitated everywhere" (Preda Report 1999). A comparative study of corporate governance codes relevant to the EU and its Member States (European Commission, Comparative Study 2002) states that "the greatest distinctions in corporate governance practices among EU Member States appear to result from differences in law rather than from differences in recommendations that emanate from the types of codes analyzed [. . .]." Despite national culture, international capital markets are leading to convergence of corporate governance practices, so that the different recommendations serve as a converging force.

On the other hand, international codes also exist, such as codes from the OECD (May 1999) and from the International Corporate Governance Network (July 1999), which are relevant to EU Members, and Pan-European codes from the European Association of Securities Dealers (EASD) (May 2000) and from the Euroshareholders (February 2000). The recommendations included in these codes are expressed for listed companies. The objectives of the first two codes are to improve the performance of firms, their competitiveness and access to capital. The EASD has the same objectives but also aims to improve the quality of information available to equity markets. Finally, the Euroshareholders' guidelines aim to improve accountability to shareholders and to maximize shareholder value (European Commission, Comparative Study 2002).

The approach advocated by the different corporate governance codes can be voluntary, which means that firms can decide for themselves whether they want to follow the recommendations. On the other hand, disclosure is sometimes required by some codes. Finally, an approach of *comply or explain* is also followed by some codes. It means that companies that do not comply to the best practice recommendations are required to explain why.

THE GROWING INTEREST IN CORPORATE GOVERNANCE

Even though our objective is not to compare and detail codes issued in different countries, it is still interesting to analyze the evolution of corporate governance in Belgium, France, and the United Kingdom. In this way, we can judge that this new environment is of great interest to companies and see that, in the European Union, the largest development of corporate governance was made in 1998.

We will therefore mention the codes existing in France and in the United Kingdom. France is a frontier country and the U.K. has been chosen because Belgian recommendations are based on their principles. We close this section by describing the three Belgian recommendations because our study is directly linked to the situation in Belgium.

Before the new code issued at the end of 2004, Belgium had three kinds of recommendations. In January 1998, the Federation of Enterprises in Belgium (FEB), the Belgian Banking and Finance Commission, and the Belgian Commission for Corporate governance (called the Cardon Commission) separately issued recommendations that were set up in the Cadbury Report (UK). At the end of the same year, the *Dual Code* (which is a combination of the Cardon Report and the Banking and Finance Commission) was published. In 2000, an association of Belgian corporate directors (called *La Fondation des Administrateurs*) also published the Directors' Charter.

In France, different recommendations are already well established. A first report was made public in 1995. It was called *Vienot I Report* and was initiated by the AEFP (Association Française des Entreprises Privées) and the CNPF (Conseil National du Patronat Français). In 1998, the investors association AFG-ASFFI (Association Française de la Gestion Financière and Association des Sociétés et Fonds Français d'Investissement) issued the *Hellenbuyck Commission Recommendations*. An update of the first Vienot Report was made in 1999 by the AEFP and MEDEF (Mouvement des Entreprises de France). A law was then voted in 2001, called the *Loi Relative aux Nouvelles Régulations Economiques*. Other efforts have been made in the last few years to further improve corporate governance.

In the United Kingdom, the Financial Reporting Council and the London Stock Exchange established a first code of best practice in 1992. It was called the *Cadbury Report* and was the first worldwide code. Three years later, the *Greenbury Report* was issued. Several reports subsequently followed: the *Hampel Report* in 1998 and a *Combined Report* (a combination of the Cadbury Report, the Greenbury Report, and the Hampel Report), the *Turnbull Report* in 2001, the *Higgs Report* and the *Smith Report* in 2002, and a *New Combined Code* in 2003 (a combination of the Higgs Report and the Smith Report).

The enumeration of all these codes of best practice thus gives evidence of the growing importance of corporate governance in EU countries. We will now study and detail the content of the three Belgian recommendations in force since 1998.

Three reasons explain the development of these recommendations in Belgium (Snoy 2001). First, because the shareholder structure is concentrated, we find mostly dominant shareholders. Because shareholding is not dispersed, corporate governance aims to protect minority shareholders by ensuring their fair treatment and is also a way of aligning the interests of different stakeholders. The second reason for the development of these recommendations is the interest in reading more easily the financial accounts of Belgian listed companies. The third reason is that a well-structured company performs better.

The three kinds of recommendations are based on a voluntary approach (soft law), but disclosure is encouraged. Autoregulation allows easier adaptation in reaction to an evolving environment and, thus, flexibility. The Federation of Enterprises in Belgium (FEB) explains that its recommendations must be adapted to the specific needs of individual companies and should not be followed without adaptation.

Moreover, although these recommendations have evident similarities, each of them follows a particular aspect. For example, the Belgian Banking and Finance Commission recommendations are principally devoted to financial information and to listed companies. Indeed, they aim to improve the quality of information available to equity markets. The recommendations of the Federation of Enterprises in Belgium and the Cardon Report aim to improve company performance, competitiveness, and access to capital. Indeed, the Cardon Commission's objective is to reinforce the competition of companies on the equity markets, to make a clear separation of competencies between the different committees concerned by corporate governance, and also to reinforce financial reporting rules (Keutgen and Darville 1998). FEB recommendations are expressed for all companies, whereas Cardon recommendations are expressed for listed companies. Finally, the objective of the Directors' Charter, also expressed for all companies, is to improve the quality of board governance (European Commission, Comparative Study 2002).

As we have already explained in the previous section, corporate governance is defined differently according to the codes. We can read in the OECD principles that "corporate governance involves a set of relationships between management, the board and the stakeholders of a company and also provides the structure through which the objectives of the company are set, and the means of attaining those objectives and monitoring performance." In the U.K. Cadbury Report, corporate governance is defined as the system by which businesses are directed and controlled. In Belgium, the Cardon Report describes corporate governance as "the set of rules applicable to the direction and control of a company," whereas the FEB defines it as "the organization of the administration and management of companies."

The Dual Code explains that "the board of directors is responsible for all strategic decisions, for ensuring that the necessary resources are available to achieve the objectives, for appointing and supervising the executive management and, lastly, for reporting to the shareholders on the performance of its duties" (European Commission, Comparative Study 2002). Indeed, the Cardon Commission explains that the board is the supreme management body. Its role is to control the company and its direction. According to the FEB, the board must decide on strategic objectives and implement procedures to reach them. Moreover, it must monitor the company and give necessary information to the stakeholders. The board also checks financial accounts and presents them to the General Assembly. Concerning the dissemination of information, the board must establish a management report on the company situation (FEB and Cardon Commission).

Regarding remuneration, the FEB recommendations and those in the Dual Code state that the way in which directors are paid has to be disclosed. The Cardon Commission mentions that a remuneration committee (composed of a majority of nonexecutives) must fix recommendations regarding remuneration. If such a committee does not exist, the board is responsible for the determination of the senior executives' compensation. The Cardon Commission advocates that a part of the remuneration of the directors' committee be linked to company performance. It also recommends that nonexecutive members should not receive stock options or other incentives. For the FEB, this is crucial in order for nonexecutive members to maintain their independence.

The board is responsible for nominating directors (Dual Code). The Belgian Corporate Governance Commission (Cardon Commission) takes the view that, in most cases, the board of directors should consist of no more than 12 members. The board of directors should decide on the number of directors necessary to govern the company in the best possible manner. The FEB explains that the separation of responsibilities between the board and the directors' committee must be clearly established. If the same person is president of the board and of the directors' committee, members may be present on the board to mitigate the president's influence.

In a one-tier system, attention has to be paid to the representation of internal and external members. The latter can be executive or nonexecutive members. The aim is to ensure objective judgment and a diversity of opinions about the strategy and results of the company. In Belgium, the Dual Code requires that the board includes a majority of nonexecutives and some independent outsiders. Some nonexecutives must be independent. Nonexecutive members are those who do not have a directorial function in the company. On the other hand, the concept of independence is defined differently according to recommendations in different countries. It is for the board to decide whether a particular independent satisfies the definition of independence (European Commission, Comparative Study 2002).

The functions of the board can be delegated to committees, such as audit, nomination, and remuneration committees. Creating an audit committee with nonexecutive members is a way to reduce conflicts of interest. The role of this kind of committee is to prepare the decisions that the board have to take and its creation is recommended in companies with a large number of administrators. The board determines its roles. According to the Dual Code, an audit committee must check the reliability of annual accounts. Regarding its composition, the Cardon Commission recommends at least three nonexecutives in this committee. In fact, all members should be nonexecutives, with a majority being independent. The FEB advocates, for its part, that this committee be composed of nonexecutives and independent members, but executives can take part in this committee. As for the nomination committee, it makes propositions on the nomination of nonexecutives to the board. For the Cardon Commission, it also can make propositions for the nomination of executive members and, for the FEB, it can make propositions regarding some key people.

THE BELGIAN CODE PROJECT: OBJECTIVES AND CONTENTS

The three kinds of Belgian recommendations do not in themselves constitute a code. Due to economic globalization and growing interest in corporate governance, a commission—called Corporate Governance Committee—created in January 2004 was charged with issuing a new unique code of best practice to replace the three previous recommendations. This code project is based on some key references: OECD principles, the European Commission study, and its propositions and different corporate governance codes. The final version of this new code was issued on December 9, 2004. The code is applicable on and after January 1, 2005.

The main objective of this new code is to create value in the long term, to reinforce investors' confidence, and to attract foreign investors. In its terms, the commission explains that corporate governance incites both the board and the management to pursue objectives consistent with corporate and shareholders' interests. Corporate governance also increases efficiency and economic growth and allows efficient monitoring. Corporate governance thus has an impact not only on the company, but also on society in general, which requires more accountability and transparency.

The code is based on a comply-or-explain approach, to allow flexibility for companies. The code is based on principles defining essential aspects of good corporate governance. In this way, companies can adapt these principles to develop their own corporate governance model, by taking into account their size, their shareholding structure and their life cycle. Moreover, each principle is explained by a disposition. If a firm does not disseminate information, as set out in the code, the Belgian Banking & Finance Commission can ask the firm why it has not done so and can also refer back to the comply-or-explain approach.

As we have seen in the previous section, in a one-tier system, attention has to be paid to the representation of internal and external members. Indeed, it is of great importance to have a well-balanced board, which includes both executives and nonexecutives. This internal monitoring is therefore practiced by administrators, who must be objective and independent in their judgment. We have also seen that the shareholding structure in Belgium is not dispersed. Thus, we find majority shareholders who are influential and who have the role of internal and external monitoring. Attention can nevertheless be reserved for minority shareholders' interests. External monitoring is also experienced by shareholders. Finally, because transparency is a form of external control, the code devotes attention to the publication of information.

The role of the board is to contribute to long-term performance of the firm, by favoring entrepreneurial spirit and controlling the risks linked to the activity of the company. In this way, the board defines the values and strategies of the firm and evaluates its management performance. Regarding its composition, we have just seen that the Commission insists on a balance between executive and nonexecutive members being included on the board and requires that some nonexecutives be independent, to ensure that no one group of administrators has the dominant decision-making power. More precisely, the Commission recommends that at least half the board be nonexecutives. It also recommends the separation of the CEO function and the board's president function.

Concerning the organization of the board, the Belgian code does not require the following of strict rules, but explains that the company is free to institute the best functioning of government for the company. So, the Commission only *proposes* rules. Regarding the nomination of its members, the board insists on objectivity and transparency. The code institutes a mechanism by which administrators are to be kept well informed about the firm's activities and competitive environment. The board of directors evaluates itself, but also its administrators and the different committees.

As far as remuneration is concerned, the board affirms that nonexecutive members must have a fixed remuneration linked to their responsibilities and executives must have a level of remuneration linked to the benefits. The objective is to attract qualified professionals. The annual report contains information about remuneration. The Commission recommends that the rules devoted to each committee be included in the section relating to corporate governance in the financial accounts of the firm.

Finally, the code recommends that special committees be created to help the board in different important tasks. Audit, nomination and remuneration committees are therefore set up. Members of these committees should be composed of nonexecutive and independent members. The board's president cannot be on the audit committee. The board defines the roles of this committee. These roles are linked to financial reporting, internal control implemented by senior management, and risk management.

The audit committee has to report internally to the board and, in the same way, the internal auditor has to report to the audit committee. Internal reporting is, thus, a really important part of the code's recommendations. The nomination committee is responsible for the composition of the board. Its role is to check that the nomination procedure is organized with objectivity. The remuneration committee is in charge of the remuneration of the administrators and senior management.

The code recommends an efficient interaction between the senior management and the board, which requires a clear definition of the responsibilities of each of them. Each firm determines the composition of its senior management. The Belgian code only recommends, on the one hand, that executives be included in it and, on the other hand, that the board take part in the discussion about remuneration and that this discussion be transparent. A part of the senior management remuneration has to be linked to company performance, so that the interests of senior management and shareholders are convergent. Information on CEO remuneration and senior management remuneration has to be published in the firm's annual report.

The third part of the Belgian code concerns the shareholders. The Commission recommends interaction between shareholders and the firm. Information must be thus diffused to enable shareholders to be informed about financial accounts and corporate governance practices. For example, online access to information should be available. Moreover, the board encourages the presence of shareholders at the General Assembly. The firm also informs the shareholders of its control structures and its main shareholders in order to be transparent. Finally, the board checks that majority shareholders do not have too much influence. In this way, it aims to protect minority shareholder interests.

The last point is linked to the divulging of information. The information published about corporate governance is divided into two points: the declaration on corporate governance and the chapter on corporate governance issued in the annual report. The first point aims to define the firm's corporate governance practices and the derogations of the code. The second point aims to show the application of the principles included in the code.

We have just considered the contents of the three previous recommendations in force in Belgium since 1998 and the new corporate governance code project issued in June 2004. This code project became definitive by the end of 2004 but before this, it was submitted to public scrutiny in order to make improvements. This public consultative phase lasted three months, beginning on June 21 and ending on September 15, 2004. The Commission received some comments, mostly from professionals. The last phase consisted of examining these different comments in order to adapt the code project and to publish the final version of the code, which happened on December 9, 2004.

RESEARCH QUESTIONS AND HYPOTHESES

This chapter aims to study the impact of the appearance of the Belgian Corporate Governance Commission on the stock prices and volatility of Belgian listed companies. The announcement of the creation of this Commission in charge of the elaboration of the code project was made public on January 22, 2004 and constitutes the first test. The second test is related to the announcement date of the code project realization, on June 18, 2004. We also test the announcement date of the European Commission to invite Member States to issue codes of best practice. As we have already mentioned, this invitation was made on May 21, 2003.

We predicted that the announcement of these different events would have an impact on the stock prices and on the volatility of Belgian companies. In order to examine the possibility that impact intensity might vary according to different characteristics of the companies, we also create several subsamples. These were formed on the basis of the size of the listed companies, represented by the market value and the number of workers in the firms, and on the basis of the sector of activity, represented by the NACE codes. We then completed our study by comparing the evolution of different indices to be sure that our results were not simply due to a market trend.

METHODOLOGY

Data

Stock prices and market values were collected for the Belgian market, which initially gave a total of 228 listed domestic stocks. In order to be included in the sample, stocks had to be quoted during the period January 3, 2000 to August 26, 2004, representing 1,214 trading days, and needed a minimum of 300 daily prices available during the whole period of study. In addition, strips were also deleted from the sample. Finally, a sample of 157 listed stocks was used in the study.

The daily prices and market values of these firms were collected from Datastream International (a U.K.-based data service company). The number of full-time workers, interim workers, and NACE codes were collected from BEL FIRST, a database provided by the Belgian Van Dijck company. Returns were calculated as the difference in natural logarithm of the prices and dividends for two consecutive trading days:

$$R_t = \ln(P_t + D_t) - \ln(P_{t-1})$$

We also collected the proxies of five different market indices: the BEL20, the CAC40, the FTSE100, the S&P500, and the NASDAQ. Data for the five indices were collected during the same period, that is, from the beginning of 2000 to August 2004.

Methodology

Our first objective is to examine the influence of the announcement of the Belgian corporate governance code project on stock returns and volatility. So we first use event study methodology, which consists of examining the behavior of stock returns for an event period surrounding the event date, and determining the presence of systematic abnormal returns during that period. These abnormal returns are obtained as the difference between the observed returns and those one could expect from an estimation or reference period preceding the event period. At this level we consider that there are three event dates. The first is the invitation made by the EU to Member States to issue a code of corporate governance (on May 21, 2004), the second date is the announcement of the Commission's creation (on January 22, 2004), and the third is the date of the code project issuance (on June 18, 2004). Therefore, the reference period we use starts on January 3, 2000 and ends on March 20, 2003. As for the three event periods, they include 20 days before and after the events, that is, respectively from April 23, 2003 to June 18, 2003 for the first, from December 25, 2003 to February 19, 2004 for the second, and from May 21, 2004 to July 16, 2004 for the third period.

The same methodology is applied to subsamples. The 157 companies are ranked according to their market values. The size of a stock is the market value of that stock on January 1, 2004. Stocks are then split into five subsamples of equal size, that is, 31 stocks per subsample, except for the fifth one, which includes 33 stocks. The subsample, called MV1, includes the 31 largest stocks and MV5 includes the smallest stocks.

For subsamples related to the number of full-time workers, interim workers, and activity sector, only 105 listed companies were kept.

As for the activity sectors, NACE codes are initially ranked from 1 to 9, and their description is reported in Table 5.1. The ranking of the codes and the number of firms are also described.

Concerning full-time workers, the subsample CETP1 includes 33 companies employing fewer than 10 workers, CETP2 20 companies with 11 to 50 workers, CETP3 20 companies with 51 to 200 workers, and CETP4 32 companies with more than 200 workers. As for interim workers, we divide our sample as follows: INT1 includes 56 companies where there are no interim workers, INT 2 contains 27 companies with 1 to 10 interim workers,

TABLE 5.1   Activity Sectors

Class	Activity Sector	Ranking	Number of Firms
1	Primary sector	CNACE 1	23
2	Energy and water		
3	Chemical industry and minerals	CNACE 2	25
4	Metals transformation		
5	Other manufacturing industries		
6	Construction sector	CNACE 3	24
7	Commerce, lodging, and catering		28
8	Transportation sector	CNACE 4	
9	Leasing, finance, and insurance		

and INT3 contains 22 companies with more than 10 interim workers. Tables for these subsamples are not represented in the chapter.

In order to determine whether any impact revealed by the event studies might be related to a general trend in the financial markets, we also applied event study methodology to the rates of returns of BEL20 and four other countries. In addition, we applied the methodology to the differences between the Belgian rates of return of our whole sample and the BEL20, and those of each foreign index.

The event study is complemented by a time series analysis with dummy variables relating to the three event periods previously defined. More precisely, a Generalized AutoRegressive Conditional Heteroscedastic GARCH(1,1) model will be used in order to take into account the presence of heteroskedasticity, volatility clustering, and asymmetric volatility. The dummy variables will be integrated in both mean and variance equations in order to point out the impacts of the three events on the rates of returns and volatility. This analysis will be conducted on the average rates of return of the whole sample and all subsamples, as well as on the BEL20. We also apply this model to the differences between the Belgian rates of return of our whole sample and the BEL20, and those of each foreign index.

Event Study

In an event study, abnormal returns on day t (A_{it}) are calculated for a test or event period surrounding the event date of firm i. We use in this study the Mean Adjusted Return method (MAR), as well as the Risk Adjusted Return method (RAR), which are both traditional parametric tests developed by

Brown and Warner (1985). As far as the index rates of return are concerned, only the MAR method will be applied.

According to the MAR method, abnormal returns on day t are obtained as the difference between the observed returns on that day and the mean return calculated on the estimation or reference period:

$$A_{it} = R_{it} - \bar{R}_i \tag{5.1}$$

This method assumes that the expected return of a firm is constant, which is only conceivable if the risk of the firm and the risk premium are constant across time. Therefore we also applied the RAR method allowing the testing of a change in the level of systematic risk during the event period.

In the case of the RAR method, abnormal returns on day t are obtained as the difference between the observed returns and those predicted by the market model, the parameters of the market model being calculated on the estimation period using the *least squares* estimation procedure. However, as this study deals with events occurring on the same day, we calculated an autocorrelated and heteroscedastic consistent estimate of the covariance matrix:

$$A_{it} = R_{it} - \hat{\alpha}_i - \hat{\beta}_i R_{mt} \tag{5.2}$$

The impact of an event on the returns is measured by the magnitude of the average abnormal return (AR_t) for each day t of the test period, as well as by the magnitude of the cumulative abnormal return (CAR_p) for any specified subperiod:

$$AR_t = \left(\sum_{i=1}^{N} A_{it} \right) \bigg/ N$$

$$CAR_p = \sum_{p=t_1}^{t_2} AR_p \tag{5.3}$$

where p determines a subperiod inside the test period.

Then, the student t-tests of abnormal returns on day t and cumulated abnormal returns from t_1 to t_2 are:

$$t(AR_t) = \frac{AR_t}{s_t} \quad \text{for day } t$$

$$t(CAR_{t_1,t_2}) = \frac{CAR_{t_1,t_2}}{s\sqrt{t_2 - t_1 + 1}} \quad \text{for subperiod } t_1 \text{ to } t_2 \tag{5.4}$$

where s_t is the standard deviation of the abnormal returns on the reference period.

In order to examine the behavior of the abnormal returns inside the event periods, t-tests are calculated for the three whole test periods, as well as for subperiods of 20 days before and after the event day. The t-test of the abnormal return on each event day is also reported.

Since the event is regulatory, one can expect some cross-correlations in the returns, due to calendar clustering. Therefore, we also apply the Seemingly Unrelated Regression (SUR) technique developed by Zellner (1962) on the average returns of the subsamples. That is, we estimate a system of equations, one for each subsample, using dummy variables to identify the three event periods.

Time Series Study

The use of dummy variables in a GARCH model allows joint testing of the impact of the events on both rates of return and the volatility of the indices and all subsamples, as well as on the differences in returns between the Belgian indices and the foreign ones. GARCH models, developed by Bollerslev (1986), allow the avoidance of statistical problems relating to the presence of heteroskedasticity and nonnormality in the rates of return. The model used in this study is the Glosten, Jagannathan, and Runkle (1993) model. This is a GARCH(1,1) model with asymmetric effects. It takes into account the fact that negative shocks can have a greater impact on volatility than positive ones, which is usually the case in stock returns and is quite consistent with the risk aversion assumption:

$$
\begin{aligned}
&\varepsilon_{it}|\Psi_{it-1} \sim N\left(0, h_{it}\right) \\
&\varepsilon_{it} = R_{it} - \phi_i - \lambda_{i1}D_{1t} - \lambda_{i2}D_{2t} - \lambda_{i3}D_{3t} \\
&h_{it} = \nu_i + \alpha_i \varepsilon^2_{it-1} + \beta_i h_{it-1} + \gamma_i \varepsilon^2_{it-1} I_{t-1} + \delta_{i1}D_{1t} + \delta_{i2}D_{2t} + \delta_{i3}D_{3t}
\end{aligned}
\tag{5.5}
$$

where I_{t-1} = 1 if $\varepsilon_{t-1} > 0$
I_{t-1} = 0 otherwise

where Ψ_{it} represents the information available in t and h_{it} is the conditional variance of the rates of return of stock i, with ν_i, α_i, $\beta_i \geq 0$.

If γ_i is negative, it means that negative residuals tend to increase the variance more than positive residuals. The coefficient λ_{i1} measures the impact of the first event on the rates of return, while λ_{i2} and λ_{i3} measure the additional return due to the other two events. As for the estimated coefficients δ_{i1}, δ_{i2} and δ_{i3} in the variance equation, these can be interpreted in the same manner, but for volatility.

EMPIRICAL RESULTS

The cumulated average abnormal returns for the total sample obtained by the MAR and RAR methods are presented in Figure 5.1, as well as in Table 5.2. This table also reports their t-tests, and in addition the Cumulated Abnormal Returns (CARs) and t-tests for the subperiods corresponding to each event and for the abnormal returns on the event days. The CAR for the total period of 376 days reaches respectively 56% and 39%, according to the MAR and the RAR methods, both being statistically significant. The same observation can be made for the 41-day period of the first and the second events. Returns appear, therefore, to have increased during the period relative to the first two events. However, examining the detail, one can notice that the increase is concentrated between the day of the first announcement and 20 days after the second one. These results suggest that the first event, the announcement by the European Union, generates some positive and significant impact only after the day of the announcement, while the second announcement, the creation of the Belgian Commission, has a significant influence on stock returns before and after the event day. Yet, the third event, the publication of the code project, does not have any impact on the returns.

The same conclusions can be derived from the results obtained for the subsamples relating to market values in Table 5.3. The CARs are significant for MV2 and MV3 for the 41-day period of the first and the second event. It appears, however, that the impact is less pronounced for the subsamples MV1, MV4, and MV5, which is consistent with the hypothesis that bigger firms were no longer concerned by the code project because

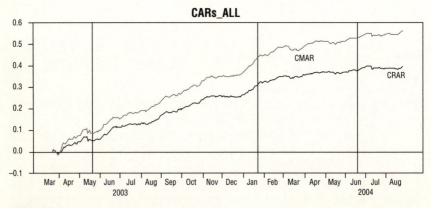

FIGURE 5.1 Cumulated Average Returns

TABLE 5.2 Cumulated Average Returns and Student t-tests of the CARs

Sample	Subperiod		Days	Mean Adjusted Rates of Return (MAR)		Risk Adjusted Rates of Return (RAR)	
				Cumulated Abnormal Returns (Cars)	t-test	Cumulated Abnormal Returns (Cars)	t-test
	2003:03:21	2004:08:26	376	0.56390	5.74	0.39550	5.39
	2003:04:23	2003:06:18	41	0.09160	2.82	0.07255	2.99
	2003:04:23	2003:05:21	21	0.02201	0.95	0.01940	1.12
ALL	2003:05:21	2003:05:21	1	-0.00457	-0.90	-0.00093	-0.25
n=157	2003:05:21	2003:06:18	21	0.06501	2.80	0.05221	3.01
	2003:12:25	2004:02:19	41	0.12199	3.75	0.08639	3.56
	2003:12:25	2004:01:22	21	0.07862	3.38	0.05682	3.27
	2004:01:22	2004:01:22	1	0.00624	1.23	0.00576	1.52
	2004:01:22	2004:02:19	21	0.04960	2.13	0.03534	2.04
	2004:05:21	2004:07:16	41	0.03412	1.05	0.02251	0.93
	2004:05:21	2004:06:18	21	0.02124	0.91	0.01184	0.68
	2004:06:18	2004:06:18	1	0.00257	0.51	0.00111	0.29
	2004:06:18	2004:07:16	21	0.01544	0.66	0.01179	0.68

TABLE 5.3 Cumulated Average Returns and Student t-tests of the CARs—Market Value

		Mean Adjusted Return Model (MAR)									
Subperiod		MV1 CAR	31 t-test	MV2 CAR	31 t-test	MV3 CAR	31 t-test	MV4 CAR	31 t-test	MV5 CAR	33 t-test
2003:03:21	376	0.65164	3.00	0.684	5.45	0.48604	4.07	0.39764	3.18	0.59797	2.90
2003:04:23	41	0.0927	1.29	0.18294	4.41	0.09328	2.37	0.07058	1.71	0.02292	0.34
2003:04:23	21	0.0412	0.80	0.06774	2.28	0.02608	0.92	0.01068	0.36	-0.03214	-0.66
2003:05:21	1	-0.00982	-0.88	-4.77E-04	-0.07	-0.00322	-0.52	-0.01147	-1.78	0.00171	0.16
2003:06:18	21	0.04168	0.81	0.11472	3.86	0.06398	2.27	0.04843	1.64	0.05678	1.16
2004:02:19	41	0.11883	1.65	0.13506	3.25	0.099	2.51	0.12473	3.02	0.13169	1.93
2004:01:22	21	0.07638	1.49	0.09852	3.32	0.05732	2.03	0.08506	2.88	0.07599	1.56
2004:01:22	1	0.00214	0.19	0.00665	1.03	0.00512	0.83	0.00775	1.20	0.00932	0.88
2004:02:19	21	0.04459	0.87	0.04318	1.45	0.0468	1.66	0.04743	1.60	0.06502	1.33
2004:05:21	41	0.06185	0.86	0.03882	0.94	0.04077	1.03	-0.0165	-0.40	0.04494	0.66
2004:06:18	21	0.03612	0.70	0.019	0.64	0.02163	0.77	0.03123	1.06	-3.62E-04	-0.01
2004:06:18	1	0.00291	0.26	1.92E-04	0.03	-0.00128	-0.21	0.00877	1.36	0.00229	0.21
2004:07:16	21	0.02864	0.56	0.02001	0.67	0.01786	0.63	-0.03896	-1.32	0.04759	0.98

Risk Adjusted Rates of Return (RAR)

Subperiod			MV1 CAR	31 t-test	MV2 CAR	31 t-test	MV3 CAR	31 t-test	MV4 CAR	31 t-test	MV5 CAR	33 t-test
2003:03:21	2004:08:26	376	0.21033	2.08	0.50667	4.75	0.3808	3.48	0.31517	2.63	0.5543	2.69
2003:04:23	2003:06:18	41	0.04275	1.28	0.16291	4.62	0.08138	2.25	0.06125	1.54	0.01798	0.26
2003:04:23	2003:05:21	21	0.03458	1.44	0.0647	2.56	0.02448	0.94	0.00942	0.33	-0.0328	-0.67
2003:05:21	2003:05:21	1	-1.52E-04	-0.03	0.00318	0.58	-9.27E-04	-0.16	-0.00967	-1.56	0.00267	0.25
2003:05:21	2003:06:18	21	0.00802	0.33	0.10139	4.02	0.05597	2.16	0.04215	1.48	0.05345	1.10
2003:12:25	2004:02:19	41	0.025	0.75	0.09832	2.79	0.07669	2.12	0.10725	2.70	0.1224	1.80
2003:12:25	2004:01:22	21	0.01885	0.79	0.07609	3.01	0.04364	1.68	0.07434	2.62	0.07029	1.44
2004:01:22	2004:01:22	1	8.95E-04	0.17	0.00615	1.12	0.00483	0.85	0.00752	1.21	0.0092	0.87
2004:01:22	2004:02:19	21	0.00705	0.29	0.02837	1.12	0.03787	1.46	0.04043	1.42	0.0613	1.26
2004:05:21	2004:07:16	41	0.03166	0.94	0.02631	0.75	0.03354	0.93	-0.02216	-0.56	0.04195	0.62
2004:05:21	2004:06:18	21	0.01147	0.48	0.00909	0.36	0.01575	0.61	0.02662	0.94	-0.0028	-0.06
2004:06:18	2004:06:18	1	-9.43E-04	-0.18	-0.0013	-0.24	-0.0022	-0.39	0.00805	1.30	0.00191	0.18
2004:06:18	2004:07:16	21	0.01924	0.80	0.01592	0.63	0.01559	0.60	-0.04073	-1.43	0.04666	0.96

they had been applying the recommendations since 1998, while small firms were less concerned by the concept of corporate governance per se. Concerning full-time workers, the CAR for the total period of 376 days is statistically significant for all subsamples. Moreover, the impact is again less pronounced for small firms, measured in terms of workers, but the CAR is significant for the 41-day period of the first and the second event for nearly all subsamples. As for the size of companies measured by the number of interim workers, the same conclusion appears, that is, that the CAR is significant for the whole period of 376 days and that the impact is more pronounced for the 41-day period relative to the first and the second event.

The results related to the activity sector are reported in Table 5.4. It again appears that the CAR is significant for the total period of 376 days. Subsamples CNACE 2 to 4 are significant in the 41-day period relative to the second event, according to both the MAR and the RAR methods. The impact is still more pronounced for CNACE 3 and 4 because results are also statistically significant for the 41-day period of the first event. The results of the SUR technique, which are not reported in this chapter, are consistent with the results of the OLS estimation method.

We complete our study by examining the impact of the three events on the BEL20 and the foreign indices. Normally the index rates of return of the other countries should be less affected by the events than the Belgian ones. Only the first announcement, the European one, could have an impact. Table 5.5, which reports the results of the same event study for these index returns, using the MAR method only, shows that the behavior of the CARs of these indices is very similar to that of the Belgian one. Nevertheless, none of the t-tests is statistically significant in Table 5.5. This suggests that the results we observed for the Belgian data are not due to a general trend in the financial markets. In conclusion, the results for the BEL20, which represents the biggest Belgian companies, are not significant, and the conclusions for the indices are the same. On the other hand, we have just shown that the CARs are significant in the first two events concerning the whole sample of 157 listed companies. This suggests that the impact of the first two events is more pronounced for small and medium-sized firms, but less pronounced for the biggest firms. This conclusion was also revealed by the results of subsamples relating to company size and measured by the market values.

In order to determine whether the behavior of Belgian stock returns is different from that of foreign countries, the event study is also applied to the differences in mean returns between the Belgian sample and the mean returns of country indices, as well as between the BEL20 and the indices of other countries. Results are presented in Tables 5.6 and 5.7.

TABLE 5.4 Cumulated Average Returns and Student t-tests of the CARs—Activity Sectors

			Mean Adjusted Return Model (MAR)							
Subperiod			CNACE1 CAR	23 t-test	CNACE2 CAR	25 t-test	CNACE3 CAR	24 t-test	CNACE4 CAR	28 t-test
2003:03:21	2004:08:26	376	0.42712	2.612	0.77599	4.181	0.56687	4.015	0.72087	4.291
2003:04:23	2003:06:18	41	0.05793	1.071	0.08462	1.379	0.12949	2.774	0.16803	3.025
2003:04:23	2003:05:21	21	0.02718	0.702	0.02099	0.478	0.06878	2.058	0.03861	0.971
2003:05:21	2003:05:21	1	-0.00695	-0.82	-0.00263	-0.27	-0.00377	-0.52	-0.0089	-1.03
2003:05:21	2003:06:18	21	0.0238	0.615	0.06099	1.389	0.05694	1.704	0.12052	3.032
2003:12:25	2004:02:19	41	0.07629	1.411	0.17433	2.841	0.1143	2.448	0.20311	3.657
2004:01:22	2004:01:22	21	0.04471	1.155	0.12128	2.761	0.08343	2.497	0.1251	3.147
2004:01:22	2004:01:22	1	4.89E-04	0.058	0.00924	0.964	0.00699	0.959	0.01256	1.448
2004:01:22	2004:02:19	21	0.03208	0.829	0.06229	1.418	0.03787	1.133	0.09057	2.278
2004:05:21	2004:07:16	41	0.01929	0.357	0.08096	1.319	0.03129	0.67	0.06072	1.093
2004:05:21	2004:06:18	21	2.66E-04	0.007	0.04238	0.965	0.00427	0.128	0.03149	0.792
2004:06:18	2004:06:18	1	0.00744	0.881	0.00211	0.22	-1.07E-04	-0.01	0.00519	0.598
2004:06:18	2004:07:16	21	0.02647	0.684	0.04069	0.926	0.02691	0.805	0.03442	0.866

(Continued)

TABLE 5.4 *(Continued)*

Subperiod			CNACE1 CAR	23 t-test	CNACE2 CAR	25 t-test	CNACE3 CAR	24 t-test	CNACE4 CAR	28 t-test
					Risk Adjusted Rates of Return (RAR)					
2003:03:21	2004:08:26	376	0.23756	1.642	0.57873	3.518	0.33281	3.161	0.51397	3.43
2003:04:23	2003:06:18	41	0.03647	0.762	0.06231	1.145	0.103	2.958	0.14464	2.919
2003:04:23	2003:05:21	21	0.02437	0.712	0.01785	0.459	0.06531	2.621	0.03516	0.992
2003:05:21	2003:05:21	1	-0.00278	-0.37	0.00158	0.186	0.00138	0.254	-0.00457	-0.59
2003:05:21	2003:06:18	21	0.00933	0.272	0.04604	1.183	0.03907	1.568	0.10491	2.959
2003:12:25	2004:02:19	41	0.03589	0.75	0.13284	2.442	0.06442	1.85	0.15998	3.229
2003:12:25	2004:01:22	21	0.01992	0.582	0.09589	2.463	0.05283	2.12	0.09875	2.785
2004:01:22	2004:01:22	1	-4.40E-05	-0.01	0.00868	1.022	0.00633	1.164	0.01198	1.549
2004:01:22	2004:02:19	21	0.01593	0.465	0.04564	1.172	0.01793	0.719	0.07322	2.065
2004:05:21	2004:07:16	41	0.00636	0.133	0.06729	1.237	0.01532	0.44	0.04623	0.933
2004:05:21	2004:06:18	21	-0.01032	-0.3	0.03136	0.806	-0.0088	-0.35	0.01993	0.562
2004:06:18	2004:06:18	1	0.00578	0.774	4.12E-04	0.049	-0.00216	-0.4	0.00343	0.443
2004:06:18	2004:07:16	21	0.02246	0.656	0.03634	0.933	0.02196	0.881	0.02972	0.838

TABLE 5.5 Student t-tests of the CARs—Mean Adjusted Rates of Return (MAR)

Subperiod			IND20		CAC40		FTSE100		NASDAQ		SP	
			CAR	t-test	CAR	t-test	CAR	t-test	CAR	t-test	CAR	t-test
2003:03:21	2004:08:26	376	0.70707	2.488	0.60456	1.717	0.42504	1.522	0.76108	1.529	0.45943	1.649
2003:04:23	2003:06:18	41	0.08004	0.852	0.13442	1.155	0.09936	1.076	0.19737	1.199	0.12766	1.386
2003:04:23	2003:05:21	21	0.01047	0.156	0.00725	0.087	0.01916	0.29	0.05322	0.452	0.02584	0.392
2003:05:21	2003:05:21	1	-0.01557	-1.06	0.00226	0.124	-0.00822	-0.57	0.00047	0.018	0.00461	0.32
2003:05:21	2003:06:18	21	0.054	0.803	0.12943	1.553	0.07198	1.089	0.14462	1.228	0.10642	1.614
2003:12:25	2004:02:19	41	0.15068	1.604	0.11306	0.971	0.04395	0.476	0.09101	0.553	0.07214	0.783
2003:12:25	2004:01:22	21	0.09243	1.375	0.07808	0.937	0.0216	0.327	0.10034	0.852	0.05731	0.869
2004:01:22	2004:01:22	1	0.00199	0.136	0.00611	0.336	-0.00697	-0.48	-0.00971	-0.38	-0.00261	-0.18
2004:01:22	2004:02:19	21	0.06024	0.896	0.04108	0.493	0.01538	0.233	-0.01905	-0.16	0.01222	0.185
2004:05:21	2004:07:16	41	0.04824	0.513	0.03678	0.316	0.0077	0.083	0.04567	0.277	0.03595	0.39
2004:05:21	2004:06:18	21	0.03949	0.587	0.0544	0.653	0.03166	0.479	0.07347	0.624	0.05392	0.818
2004:06:18	2004:06:18	1	0.00619	0.422	0.00701	0.386	0.00346	0.24	0.00283	0.11	0.00323	0.224
2004:06:18	2004:07:16	21	0.01494	0.222	-0.01061	-0.13	-0.02049	-0.31	-0.02497	-0.21	-0.01475	-0.22

TABLE 5.6 Student t-tests of the CARs – Mean Adjusted Rates of Return (MAR)

Subperiod			IND20 CAR	t-test	ALLCAC40 CAR	t-test	ALLFTSE100 CAR	t-test	ALLNASDAQ CAR	t-test	ALLSP CAR	t-test
2003:03:21	2004:08:26	376	0.70707	2.488	-0.04636	-0.15	0.13793	0.554	-0.20288	-0.41	0.09876	0.362
2003:04:23	2003:06:18	41	0.08004	0.852	-0.04344	-0.42	-0.00787	-0.1	-0.10639	-0.65	-0.03668	-0.41
2003:04:23	2003:05:21	21	0.01047	0.156	0.01445	0.196	0.0028	0.048	-0.03153	-0.27	-0.00415	-0.06
2003:05:21	2003:05:21	1	-0.01557	-1.06	-0.00685	-0.43	0.00364	0.283	-0.00506	-0.2	-0.0092	-0.65
2003:05:21	2003:06:18	21	0.054	0.803	-0.06474	-0.88	-0.00702	-0.12	-0.07992	-0.68	-0.04173	-0.65
2003:12:25	2004:02:19	41	0.15068	1.604	0.0083	0.081	0.07794	0.947	0.03036	0.186	0.04923	0.546
2003:12:25	2004:01:22	21	0.09243	1.375	2.17E-04	0.003	0.05697	0.967	-0.02204	-0.19	0.02099	0.325
2004:01:22	2004:01:22	1	0.00199	0.136	1.12E-04	0.007	0.0132	1.027	0.01593	0.626	0.00883	0.627
2004:01:22	2004:02:19	21	0.06024	0.896	0.0082	0.111	0.03417	0.58	0.06833	0.586	0.03706	0.575
2004:05:21	2004:07:16	41	0.04824	0.513	-0.00328	-0.03	0.02631	0.32	-0.01218	-0.07	-0.00246	-0.03
2004:05:21	2004:06:18	21	0.03949	0.587	-0.03348	-0.45	-0.01047	-0.18	-0.05254	-0.45	-0.033	-0.51
2004:06:18	2004:06:18	1	0.00619	0.422	-0.00446	-0.28	-8.95E-04	-0.07	-2.73E-04	-0.01	-6.69E-04	-0.05
2004:06:18	2004:07:16	21	0.01494	0.222	0.02574	0.349	0.03589	0.609	0.04009	0.344	0.02987	0.463

TABLE 5.7 Student t-tests of the CARs—Mean Adjusted Rates of Return (MAR)—Difference in the Mean Returns

Subperiod		IND20 CAR	t-test	BELCAC40 CAR	t-test	BELFTSE100 CAR	t-test	BELNASDAQ CAR	t-test	BELSP CAR	t-test
2003:03:21	376	0.70707	2.488	0.10251	0.41	0.28247	1.192	-0.05401	-0.11	0.24763	0.806
2003:04:23	41	0.08004	0.852	-0.05438	-0.66	-0.01927	-0.25	-0.11733	-0.7	-0.04762	-0.47
2003:04:23	21	0.01047	0.156	0.00322	0.054	-0.00867	-0.15	-0.04275	-0.36	-0.01537	-0.21
2003:05:21	1	-0.01557	-1.06	-0.01784	-1.38	-0.00736	-0.6	-0.01604	-0.61	-0.02018	-1.27
2003:06:18	21	0.054	0.803	-0.07543	-1.28	-0.01796	-0.32	-0.09062	-0.75	-0.05242	-0.72
2003:12:25	41	0.15068	1.604	0.03762	0.456	0.10679	1.363	0.05968	0.355	0.07855	0.773
2003:12:25	21	0.09243	1.375	0.01435	0.243	0.07086	1.264	-0.00791	-0.07	0.03513	0.483
2004:01:22	1	0.00199	0.136	-0.00412	-0.32	0.00896	0.732	0.0117	0.446	0.0046	0.29
2004:01:22	21	0.06024	0.896	0.01915	0.324	0.04488	0.801	0.07929	0.659	0.04802	0.661
2004:05:21	41	0.04824	0.513	0.01147	0.139	0.04059	0.518	0.00257	0.015	0.01229	0.121
2004:06:18	21	0.03949	0.587	-0.01491	-0.25	0.00785	0.14	-0.03398	-0.28	-0.01443	-0.2
2004:06:18	1	0.00619	0.422	-8.21E-04	-0.06	0.00273	0.223	0.00336	0.128	0.00297	0.187
2004:07:16	21	0.01494	0.222	0.02556	0.432	0.03546	0.632	0.03991	0.332	0.02969	0.408

One can observe that none of the CARs for the differences in returns is statistically significant, which suggests that there is no effect. However, this is perhaps due to the size of our total sample.

Estimates of the GARCH(1,1) model, with asymmetric effects and dummy variables identifying the event periods for the total sample and all subsamples, are presented in Table 5.8. Concerning the mean equation, the results are consistent with previous ones obtained in the event studies. Apart from a few exceptions, coefficients (λ_2 and λ_3) for the dummy variables D_2 and D_3, which measure the differences in returns specifically due to each of the last two events, are not statistically significant, while all but one coefficient λ_1 are positive and statistically significant. This indicates again the existence of higher returns during the first event period. Concerning the variance equation, one can notice that the coefficients γ, the asymmetry coefficients, are generally negative and statistically significant, except for small firm portfolios, MV4 and MV5, and for RCNACE2. This confirms the fact that negative shocks have a greater impact on volatility than positive shocks, at least when stocks are sufficiently liquid. The lack of liquidity of small stocks impedes such observations, since it generates some serial correlation in the returns and delays any impact. As for the coefficients of the dummy variables, which measure the impact of the three announcements on volatility, these are generally not at all significant. We can therefore conclude that there is no impact of the three events on the volatility of stocks.

Finally, we apply a GARCH model to the differences between the Belgian sample and the country indices, as well as between the BEL20 and the other country indices (Table 5.9). It seems that the results for the FTSE are not conclusive because there is a convergence problem. It appears that coefficients λ_1, λ_2, and λ_3 are not significant. Thus, concerning the mean equation, results are not significant, except for ALLNASDAQ. However, concerning the variance equation, results are interesting. The variance γ_i is statistically significant, except for BELSP. Finally, we can see that the coefficient δ_{i1} is always significant. It reveals that the first event has an impact on volatility.

TABLE 5.8 GARCH Model

		ϕ_i	Mean λ_{i1}	λ_{i2}	λ_{i3}
IND20	Coefficient	-0.000328	0.001468	-0.000907	0.000086
	Probability	0.19	0.00	0.24	0.92
RALL	Coefficient	-0.000460	0.001262	-0.000545	-0.000441
	Probability	0.00	0.00	0.28	0.42
RMV1	Coefficient	-0.000106	0.001199	-0.000729	0.000336
	Probability	0.68	0.00	0.23	0.61
RMV2	Coefficient	-0.000365	0.001789	-0.001598	0.000187
	Probability	0.04	0.00	0.00	0.72
RMV3	Coefficient	-0.000315	0.001159	-0.000236	-0.000615
	Probability	0.00	0.00	0.00	0.00
RMV4	Coefficient	-0.000746	0.001140	-0.000633	-0.000302
	Probability	0.00	0.01	0.31	0.77
RMV5	Coefficient	-0.000979	0.001465	-0.000608	-0.000263
	Probability	0.02	0.31	0.66	0.74
RCNACE1	Coefficient	-0.000422	0.001281	-0.000736	-0.000009
	Probability	0.00	0.00	0.00	0.00
RCNACE2	Coefficient	-0.000497	0.001660	-0.000603	-0.000378
	Probability	0.18	0.01	0.64	0.81
RCNACE3	Coefficient	-0.000380	0.001016	-0.000699	0.000071
	Probability	0.07	0.01	0.17	0.90
RCNACE4	Coefficient	-0.000866	0.001637	-0.001130	0.000090
	Probability	0.00	0.00	0.16	0.91

(Continued)

TABLE 5.8 (Continued)

		Variance						
		ν_i	α_i	β_i	γ_i	δ_{i1}	δ_{i2}	δ_{i3}
IND20	Coefficient	0.000002	0.202300	0.858900	-0.150500	-0.000001	0.000001	-0.000002
	Probability	0.00	0.00	0.00	0.00	0.34	0.29	0.13
RALL	Coefficient	0.000002	0.147100	0.833300	-0.094900	0.000000	0.000000	0.000000
	Probability	0.06	0.01	0.00	0.06	0.28	0.58	0.76
RMV1	Coefficient	0.000002	0.199200	0.856500	-0.166200	-0.000001	0.000000	-0.000001
	Probability	0.01	0.00	0.00	0.00	0.43	0.75	0.12
RMV2	Coefficient	0.000002	0.181300	0.815400	-0.107600	0.000000	0.000000	-0.000001
	Probability	0.00	0.00	0.00	0.00	0.79	0.82	0.13
RMV3	Coefficient	0.000002	0.129800	0.840400	-0.085700	-0.000001	0.000000	0.000000
	Probability	0.00	0.03	0.02	0.01	0.00	0.00	0.00
RMV4	Coefficient	0.000001	0.017900	0.950600	0.012900	0.000000	-0.000001	0.000006
	Probability	0.07	0.29	0.00	0.56	0.77	0.19	0.28
RMV5	Coefficient	0.000008	0.025200	0.895500	0.051500	-0.000003	-0.000002	-0.000001
	Probability	0.04	0.37	0.00	0.30	0.21	0.47	0.44
RCNACE1	Coefficient	0.000020	0.124600	0.630300	-0.078300	-0.000012	0.000003	-0.000004
	Probability	0.00	0.04	0.12	0.05	0.00	0.00	0.00
RCNACE2	Coefficient	0.000005	0.140300	0.831800	-0.116900	0.000001	-0.000004	-0.000001
	Probability	0.49	0.26	0.00	0.20	0.70	0.45	0.69
RCNACE3	Coefficient	0.000002	0.131900	0.880300	-0.105200	0.000000	-0.000001	0.000000
	Probability	0.17	0.02	0.00	0.02	0.87	0.50	0.63
RCNACE4	Coefficient	0.000001	0.098800	0.920700	-0.083100	0.000000	0.000000	-0.000001
	Probability	0.08	0.00	0.00	0.00	0.96	0.87	0.26

TABLE 5.9 GARCH Model on the Differences

				Mean	
		ϕ_i	λ_{i1}	λ_{i2}	λ_{i3}
ALLCAC40	Coefficient	5.0801e-04	-5.3212e-04	8.6551e-04	-4.7961e-04
	Probability	1.06	-0.66	0.754	-0.34
ALLFTSE100	Coefficient	0.00000	0.00000	0.00000	0.00000
	Probability	0.00000	0.00000	0.00000	0.00000
ALLNASDAQ	Coefficient	5.8184e-04	-1.1604e-03	2.6466e-03	-1.3602e-03
	Probability	0.78	-1.06	1.79	-0.75
ALLSP	Coefficient	4.3368e-04	-2.8033e-04	1.0472e-03	-9.0985e-04
	Probability	0.99	-0.42	1.13	-0.82
BELCAC40	Coefficient	3.0895e-04	-3.3756e-04	3.3833e-04	3.9388e-04
	Probability	0.76	-0.57	0.49	0.48
BELFTSE100	Coefficient	NA	NA	NA	NA
	Probability	0.00000	0.00000	0.00000	0.00000
BELNASDAQ	Coefficient	3.5972e-04	-7.4442e-04	2.3423e-03	-6.3470e-04
	Probability	0.48	-0.68	1.53	-0.31
BELSP	Coefficient	2.3156e-04	-5.5880e-05	7.2665e-04	-8.9787e-05
	Probability	0.49	-0.07	0.63	-0.06

(Continued)

TABLE 5.9 *(Continued)*

					Variance			
		v_i	α_i	β_i	γ_i	δ_{i1}	δ_{i2}	δ_{i3}
ALLCAC40	Coefficient	3.2063e-06	0.0130	0.9346	0.0802	-2.3906e-06	8.8878e-07	-7.1394e-07
	Probability	2.01	0.98	60.71	3.41	-1.97	0.81	-0.59
ALLFTSE100	Coefficient	1.30871e-04	0.05000	0.05000	0.00000	0.00000	0.00000	0.00000
	Probability	0.00000	0.00000	0.00000	0.00000	0.00000	0.00000	0.00000
ALLNASDAQ	Coefficient	1.0292e-05	1.9613e-03	0.9278	0.1033	-7.1158e-06	1.0233e-06	-1.3458e-06
	Probability	2.14	0.15	53.31	4.43	-1.89	0.39	-0.39
ALLSP	Coefficient	4.9448e-06	-0.0160	0.9233	0.1495	-3.2017e-06	5.0891e-08	-4.2069e-07
	Probability	2.38	-1.40	47.27	5.67	-1.99	0.05	-0.34
BELCAC40	Coefficient	4.0404e-06	0.0643	0.9255	-0.0325	-3.0175e-06	-3.4108e-07	2.5210e-08
	Probability	2.01	4.37	43.71	-2.16	-2.14	-0.64	0.04
BELFTSE100	Coefficient	NA	NA	NA	NA	NA	NA	NA
	Probability	0.00000	0.00000	0.00000	0.00000	0.00000	0.00000	0.00000
BELNASDAQ	Coefficient	1.2953e-05	0.0447	0.9089	0.0471	-9.1094e-06	1.1516e-06	-5.0749e-07
	Probability	2.24	2.86	48.89	2.16	-2.08	0.55	-0.14
BELSP	Coefficient	7.7859e-06	0.0785	0.8759	0.0270	-5.1694e-06	2.0082e-06	-1.6137e-06
	Probability	3.49	4.37	46.578	0.97	-2.89	1.30	-0.87

CONCLUSION

Corporate governance is of a growing interest for companies. Belgium had three recommendations relating to this in force from 1998 to 2004. In 2003, the European Union invited Member States to issue codes of best practice. A Belgian Commission was therefore created in January 2004 to discuss a code of corporate governance. In June 2004, the Commission issued the new code project and its final version became available in December 2004.

It seemed interesting to study the impact of these three events on Belgian listed companies. So, the announcement of the European Union, the announcement of the creation of a Belgian Commission, and the appearance of the code project were the events we decided to test. An event study was thus applied to Belgian listed companies. According to our results, it appears that the invitation date of the European Union to issue a code and the appearance of the Belgian Commission both had a positive impact on Belgian stock returns. As a consequence, investors seemed to react positively to these different events and we can deduce that the issuing of a corporate governance code was viewed positively by the market. Other event studies were also carried out on subsamples relating to company size and their activity sector. We finally completed our study by applying the event study methodology to several foreign indices to analyze whether the results we had observed in the Belgian market were due to a general trend in the financial markets. Finally, the impact of these events on the volatility of Belgian stocks was tested on the whole market, the BEL20 and the different subsamples, as well as on the differences between the Belgian sample and the indices of different countries.

In conclusion, it seems that the first and the second events had an impact on the returns of the whole sample of 157 listed companies. On the other hand, results concerning the BEL20 and the four other indices were not significant. This suggests that the impact of these events was more pronounced for small and medium-sized firms. Using the GARCH(1,1), we found that the impact on returns was statistically significant around the first event. However, there was no impact of the three events on the volatility of stocks.

Corporate Governance and the Global Financial Markets

Improving the Corporate Governance of Hedge Funds

Greg N. Gregoriou, William R. Kelting, and Robert Christopherson

INTRODUCTION

Corporate governance has recently drawn a good deal of public interest because of its apparent significance for the economic health and well-being of corporations and the general public. However, the concept of corporate governance is improperly defined because it potentially covers a great number of different economic actions. Throughout the last decade corporate governance has been defined as the relationship between a corporation and its shareholders or investors, and requires the corporation to be fair and transparent.

When examining the corporate governance of hedge funds one immediately thinks of the Russian ruble crisis and the collapse of Long-Term Capital Management in August 1998. This incident occurred due to the great amount of asymmetrical information between owners and investors. Investors did not know the positions LTCM held or the amount of leverage used, which later resulted in its demise. Hedge funds have not been required to disclose their holdings to the Securities and Exchange Commission in the United States and thus agency theory and corporate governance are violated. However, hedge fund managers will argue they must protect their trading strategies and the stock selection process and positions so as to maintain their proprietary standing. Hedge fund managers have also argued that if the positions of their funds were fully known, a domino effect could transpire on Wall Street, resulting in a dramatic selloff.

Many hedge funds provide little or no detail of their positions to investors. In fact, a great majority of funds are still nontransparent and many newly created startup funds use past work experience as the sole criterion for manager selection. This can be misleading, since institutional investors prefer that hedge fund managers have at least a five-year track record before investing any funds. Some hedge funds provide a partial list of their positions to investors that usually include their top-10 holdings. Forcing hedge funds to disclose their entire operations may merely cause them to relocate offshore. With more than half of all hedge funds in existence today based offshore, it is difficult to establish proper corporate governance due to the unregulated status of those havens. Offshore jurisdictions or tax havens popular with hedge funds and funds of hedge funds include the Bahamas, Isle of Man, Cayman Islands, the Channel Islands, Switzerland, Austria, and others.

LITERATURE REVIEW

Corporate governance aims to improve the performance of a firm or, in our case, a hedge fund, and to ensure that owners offer an appropriate rate of return to their investors (Mathiesen 2002). Corporate governance usually assumes that managers behave as rational individuals who will not attempt to exploit their authority of power for self-serving fulfillment (Shleifer and Vishny 1997). Furthermore, corporate governance is a structure by which funds are controlled and monitored. The formulation of decisions enables a structure to be created, in which the aims and objectives of a hedge fund are laid down as a foundation. Thus, Cadbury suggests we can evaluate the aims and objectives as well as performance and return on investment for investors at the outset (Cadbury 1992).

Hedge fund managers are paid an incentive fee for above-average performance or *absolute performance*. In many cases, this practice became excessive when funds in the mid-1990s charged premiums of up to 70% to invest in a fund having triple-digit returns. Studies have concluded that only a small number of hedge fund managers keep a significant amount of their personal wealth invested in their own fund, which allows them to maintain an alignment between managers and investors. However, these funds do not perform better than ones where managers invest their own money (Boyson 2002). Additionally, recent studies demonstrate that a hedge fund with a high-incentive fee structure is likely to maintain the interest of both its managers and investors.

If hedge funds are suspected of fraud (i.e., the Manhattan Fund, the Berger fund and others), this will surely lead to a downfall of a hedge fund manager's career or even the closing of the fund. The more hedge fund managers take on risk, the greater the chances of mortality according to Gregoriou (2002). In fact, the author concludes that global macro funds have a quick death, whereby 50% of funds die within 3.72 years (median survival time). However, funds of hedge funds have the highest median survival time, among hedge fund classifications, with 7.50 years. The 25% survival time was calculated for both global macro and fund of hedge funds classifications, and was found to be 1.83 and 3.42 years, respectively.

AGENCY THEORY

Agency theory addresses the divergence of interest between managers and investors (or stakeholders). Managers operate as agents of the owners and are rewarded with incentives. In the hedge fund industry, bonuses can be very lucrative ranging from 1% to 2% of management fees and a minimum of 20% of performance fees, both based on gross returns. Many funds also employ high watermarks and hurdle rates to convey confidence to investors that they will attain their objectives (Liang 1999). In a vast majority of cases, performance fees are calculated after a hedge fund outperforms a hurdle rate, such as the 30-day U.S. Treasury-bill rate. A high watermark demands that hedge fund managers recover any losses before receiving performance fees. Investors in pension funds, endowments and others have accepted these high management fees for many years.

Agency theory examines how companies can be governed to persuade employees (the *agents*) to pursue the goals of the owners (stockholders), rather than their individual agendas. Investors purchase hedge funds to diversify traditional investment portfolios, and the selling feature of this alternative asset class is the low correlation when compared to stock and bond markets. Coupled with the lack of offshore regulation, hedge fund managers have a multitude of strategies, derivative instruments, and leverage, creating for them an advantage over typical fund managers.

Many star hedge fund managers create hedge funds to line their pockets with high performance fees and neglect their providers of capital (the investors), as witnessed with the LTCM incident. That is, intelligence, skills, and experience of managers tend not to be used to realize the goals of the organization (Gadhoum 1998). Approximately 14% of American corporations are controlled by private trusts, many of which are domiciled in offshore jurisdictions (Gadhoum, Lang, and Young 2005). This can have a serious detrimental effect on the American economy in light of the recent Enron and WorldCom frauds, which may have weakened the optimism of corporate governance in the United States. The argument is that because of the added value a hedge fund provides, the manager wants to maximize his or her personal gain. Using the TASS and Zurich hedge fund databases, the median or 50% survival times of hedge funds is 30 months, 40 months during the 1993–2000 period and 66 months during the 1990–2001 period, according to Brown, Goetzmann, and Park (2001), Amin and Kat (2002), and Gregoriou (2002), respectively. Given this limited survival time, hedge fund managers must act fast to maximize their performance fees.

A classic example of the agency theory problem is the case of Long-Term Capital Management, where information asymmetry was present and the fund was not transparent. Neither the investors nor the banks knew the underlying positions of LTCM and the excessive leverage that existed, which led to continuous inadequate management of the fund. Investors knew very little about the internal workings of the firm and since the interest of the principals (investors) and agents were not aligned this led to the demise of LTCM.

Investors do not have complete information on how a hedge fund trades, nor how much effort the manager is providing to the hedge fund. Therefore, investors are not able to accurately measure the performance of the manager and to observe if they are actually putting forth their best performance and ethically trying to maximize the value of investor's assets rather than their own.

PERFORMANCE FEES

According to Brown, Goetzmann, and Park (2001), hedge fund managers with poor returns during the first part of a calendar year are forced to take on additional risk in the second half of the year, to obtain their performance fees. This entails taking a more aggressive investment position to ensure a significant positive return to keep the fund going, as well as to line their own pockets. Although many hedge fund managers claim they invest most of their money into their own fund, this remains to be seen and is difficult to prove due to offshore accounts and secrecy laws protecting client and manager accounts.

The trouble with the existing performance fees is that potential returns for hedge fund managers and investors might still be too far apart. For example, a manager investing 5% of his personal money in his hedge fund, with a 2% management fee and a 20% performance fee, will make a gross return of about 140% if the fund returns 20%. On the other hand, the manager will receive a 16% gross return if the fund posts a 20% loss. Investors however, will either obtain an 18% return or a 20% loss according to Nagy (2002). Even after adjusting for professional investment management compensation, costs, and trading expenses, the compensation structures are too high. These fees produce an imbalance between hedge fund managers and investors, whereby managers are rewarded more when there are large positive returns but still profit even when the fund suffers a loss.

BETTER REGULATION OF HEDGE FUNDS

The massive losses of LTCM in August 1998 confirmed the risk that materializes from hedge funds and how these funds affect the stability of global markets. The danger of high performance fees is that they can produce conflicts of interest, since hedge fund managers receive performance fees when returns are positive but are not affected when returns are negative.

The SEC could attempt to address these risks through improved supervision of hedge funds and by requiring them to provide transparency in terms of their various types of risk (hedge funds usually have operational, credit, liquidity, and market risk). This could limit the amount of leverage and improve the creditors' risk management position. Pension funds and endowments must also insist on tight examination of hedge fund operations to ensure these funds adhere to their investment strategy. Due diligence is of the utmost importance when selecting hedge fund managers, as well as careful analysis of financial reports. Further, one should attempt to make peer comparisons with other funds in the same classification. As a final point, the risk of moral hazard (moral hazard is the possibility that a contract will alter the risk-taking behavior of one or both parties and can be diminished by putting the responsibility on each party of the contract) would be diminished, if hedge fund managers were required to have a large personal investment position in their own fund. These procedures would allow for markets to function properly and would minimize hedge fund collapses in the future.

In fact, the SEC has adopted rules whereby hedge fund advisers with 15 or more investors and $25 million or more in assets will have to register under the Investment Advisers Act of 1940 (Advisers Act). Advisers who will be required to register under the new rules must comply by February 1, 2006. Registered advisers are required to develop procedures ensuring compliance with securities laws and to have someone designated as a chief compliance officer. Registration also subjects the books and records of the adviser to inspection by the SEC. Registered advisers must also develop a written code of ethics. Interestingly, many advisers have registered voluntarily under the Advisers Act. This could be attributed to the due diligence requirements of some institutional investors or may be a result of the advisers, as agents, attempting to mitigate the perception of investors or potential investors that the adviser may pursue goals inconsistent with the objectives of the investors. It is important to note that a significant number of advisers will not meet the thresholds established by the new requirements and thus not be subject to SEC scrutiny under the Advisers Act.

Thus far, the SEC has not proposed changes to the Investment Company Act of 1940 under which an investment company must register if either offering securities to the public or its securities are owned by more than 100 persons. Most hedge funds have been set up so that regulation under this Act is avoided. Funds subject to the Investment Company Act would also be subject to provisions of the Sarbanes-Oxley Act of 2002, including Section 302, which requires the investment company's chief executive and chief financial officer to certify information provided in reports filed with the SEC.

As in the case of investment advisers, some hedge funds chose to register as investment companies under the Investment Company Act, thus becoming subject to the filing requirements of that Act. Here again, this may be an example of an attempt to signal investors that the fund managers, or agents, would pursue objectives consistent with those of the principals.

IS CORPORATE GOVERNANCE NECESSARY FOR HEDGE FUNDS?

For the average institutional investor and pension fund manager who has increased her investment in hedge funds, the issue of corporate governance is becoming increasingly important. Due to recent hedge fund scandals, the SEC is now trying to keep an observant eye on these notoriously speculative vehicles or, as Warren Buffett calls them, "financial weapons of mass destruction." Can hedge funds continue to provide superior returns to investors if more restrictive forms of corporate governance exist? Most hedge fund managers and traders of stocks, bonds, and derivatives, have no financial incentive to enhance the management practices within a fund. Traders are more interested in taking advantage of market instabilities to earn bonuses at the end of the year than they are with the long-term profit trends of their firm as a result of their trading activities.

Hedge funds on average possess little incentive to participate in corporate governance. Success here is defined by the fund's ability to meet the expectations of investors while maintaining its investment strategies, guiding ethics, and principles. Since hedge funds can vary their exposure, this is seen as a powerful tool in changing market and economic conditions, However, good corporate governance must be in place to correctly assess the manager's ability to control risk. Whether or not recent SEC actions will ensure improvements in corporate governance remains to be seen. However, investors will still be at risk in cases involving unregistered advisers or funds.

A rational bubble implies that agents have imperfect information concerning the approximate time a bubble might burst, but are aware of the probability of an imminent crash (Blanchard and Watson 1982). Allen and Gorton (1993) present a model of the emergence of rational bubbles resulting from agency theory, stating that bubbles develop through asymmetric information among investors. This neglects the problem of poorly aligned interests between managers and investors, which arise when the risk controls of the firm do not reveal the complexity of the instruments, or when employees are not properly trained to handle complex derivative instruments.

A last concern is the increasing existence of fraud occurring in hedge funds. How can potential investors detect and avoid it? Is the hedge fund manager's past experience and resume enough? Recently, many funds of hedge fund managers have hired detectives to investigate hedge funds they invest in (Gregoriou and Kelting 2003).

CONCLUSION

A possible solution to the agency theory problem and corporate governance is to provide a structure that will attain a good balance between investors and managers. Perhaps an industrywide incentive scale for performance fees is a solution. For example, outperforming the high watermark of the hedge fund would result in a predetermined compensation amount. Using predetermined levels of performance fees for achievement above the watermark would eliminate excessive returns and risk-taking behavior. Another possibility is to force the hedge fund manager to lock in his or her money, like the investors, until the closure of the fund. Creating a best practices report for the hedge fund industry to set corporate governance guidelines might also be a partial solution. That is, hedge funds would be carefully monitored by a regulator in the industry, and the names of the funds would be published on a monthly basis.

Finally, a possible new structure would be to calculate performance fees based on a risk-adjusted performance ratio such as the modified Sharpe ratio (Favre and Galeano 2002). This ratio is preferred over the traditional Sharpe ratio because the latter overestimates risk-adjusted returns, when hedge funds have nonnormal returns. Therefore, the modified Sharpe ratio would precisely reflect the risk-adjusted performance, and would encourage hedge fund managers to benefit from the funds' return, given risk, yielding the maximum return for the manager.

CHAPTER 7

Corporate Governance Reform in Australia: The Intersection of Investment Fiduciaries and Issuers

Martin Gold

INTRODUCTION

Concerns about standards of corporate governance have typically arisen in the aftermath of corporate failures and executive misdemeanors, not during periods of prosperity and investor euphoria. The infrequent incidence of corporate failures is therefore problematic for empirical analysis purposes: In many recent cases, the underlying causes of these failures can be more accurately attributed to fraud and negligence, and investor gullibility, rather than systemic defects in corporate governance or ethical standards *per se*. Further, Coffee (2004) argues that recent corporate debacles can be blamed on *good* governance measures that have encouraged earnings management (notably premature accruals of income) and introduced *perverse* managerial incentive structures (originally intended to mitigate agency costs), and the passivity of institutional investors and financial analysts who ignored valuation concerns due to their fixation on relative performance and commercial self-interests.

By virtue of their substantial shareholdings in those companies, and their ability to act more effectively than other shareholders, investment fiduciaries are expected to more actively exercise power over the boards of investee firms. Whereas investment fiduciaries traditionally became involved in corporate governance matters reactively, more recent trends in corporate governance reveal an increasing externalization of internal processes, and the recasting of the corporation's responsibilities to include a broader range of constituents. Hawley and Williams (1997) argue that fiduciaries owe a significantly broader responsibility of economic guardianship: As *universal owners* the authors argue that fiduciaries should be active in proxy matters and have concerns for the welfare of stakeholders beyond their traditional shareholder constituency. Camara (2005) notes that institutional investors are most likely to use voting powers effectively and can overcome the significant disincentives faced by other shareholders; however, they risk compromising the economic (and fiduciary) rationale for activism if their voting is motivated by sociopolitical rationales rather than maximizing investment returns for their beneficiaries. Against this background, the existence of financially successful firms displaying nonconformance with corporate governance best practices may suggest that financial performance determines corporate governance structures rather than vice-versa (MacNeil and Li 2005).

The first part of this chapter briefly describes the origins and functional application of Australia's best practice corporate governance standards, and the methods used by investment fiduciaries to incorporate corporate governance standards into the portfolio management. It discusses the theoretical origins of the corporate governance problem and best practice measures, and the matrix of fiduciary obligations owed by different actors. Boards and corporate officers are entrusted to maximize shareholders' returns but owe fiduciary duties to the firm, while trustees and institutional investors charged with the responsibility of maximizing the investment returns owe fiduciary duties to the beneficiaries. This analysis reinforces the need to confirm the economic efficacy of corporate governance standards, especially in light of the direct and indirect corporate resources they consume. In the second part of this chapter, we examine the investment thesis of common *good* corporate governance measures using a unique research methodology. In contrast to existing literature that has sought to validate the premise that these measures make a positive contribution to the investor returns and the financial performance of the firm, we examine the reverse: Do *poor*-governance firms—those not fully adopting promulgated corporate governance best practices and subject to substantial *insider* influence—*outperform*? This is the first study to employ this methodology. Finally, we draw some conclusions from our empirical findings, particularly in the context of the fiduciary duties owed by investment fiduciaries (such as superannuation trustees and funds managers) and corporate officers.

FUNCTIONAL APPLICATION OF AUSTRALIAN CORPORATE GOVERNANCE MEASURES

Background

Australia has adopted a market-based response rather than a regulatory regime to address corporate governance concerns. The principal best practice corporate governance measures are exemplified by market-based guidelines that apply to entities listed on the Australian Stock Exchange (ASX). The development of corporate governance best practices was initiated by institutional fund managers acting on behalf of superannuation trustees, and the industry lobbies for professional trustees. Australia's first efforts to formalize corporate governance practices were developed in 1985 by the Investment and Financial Services Association (IFSA), an industry association of fund managers. These guidelines followed from a public campaign by fund managers that successfully forced a large retailing firm, Coles Myer, to disclose its related-party transactions with directors who were also significant shareholders and suppliers, and to restructure its board in recognition of the potential conflicts of interest that arose from the firm's commercial relationships with those directors. Following high-profile corporate collapses (One.Tel in 2000 and HIH Insurance in 2001), and a number of corporate debacles in offshore jurisdictions, increased political pressure was exerted on regulators to move onto a more proactive footing. In August 2002, the ASX announced proposals to formalize its guidance on corporate governance best practice. The ASX convened a broadly representative forum—the ASX Corporate Governance Council (ASX CGC)—including institutional and personal investor groups, and corporate and professional lobbies, to address concerns about corporate behavior and to restore investor confidence in the proper functioning of financial markets.

In March 2003, the ASX CGC enunciated its best practice corporate governance guidelines (*ASX Principles of Good Corporate Governance and Best Practice Recommendations*). The effect of these guidelines was to introduce a regime of comprehensive disclosures for corporate governance practices within Australia's 500 largest listed firms. In common with the development of corporate governance codes in the United Kingdom, the Australian system is based on the *comply-or-explain* principle: Adoption of the guidelines by issuers was voluntary; however, disclosures of nonconformance and explanations were mandated under the ASX listing rules, commencing in the 2004 annual reports to shareholders. Following a postimplementation review, the ASX CGC revised its guidelines with respect to the composition of audit committees scaling this back to the 300 largest entities. This change was made as smaller firms, which on average had fewer than five directors, were unable to attract suitable candidates or found it was impractical to expand their boards. The corporate law has also been reformed, making the requirement that CEO/CFO sign off financial statements showing conformance with accounting standards (the *true and fair view*) mandatory effective from 1 July 2004. The industry association representing trustees of large superannuation funds, the Australian Council of Superannuation Investors (ACSI), also released its best practice corporate governance guidelines for issuers in March 2003.

While the ASX CGC guidelines represent a consensus of corporate governance best practices, there have been concerns expressed by the business community, which has queried the economic value of these structures and the increased compliance burden for firms, and expanded the potential liability of corporate officers (Coulton and Taylor 2004). Following the introduction of the ASX CGC guidelines, a survey of 1,500 company directors drawn from firms both inside and outside the top 500 instigated by the Institute of Company Directors (AICD) revealed that the majority of professional directors were concerned about government regulation if the ASX CGC guidelines were not adopted; however, few believed they would enhance returns or investor confidence (AICD 2003). Analysis of early reporting trends has revealed considerable diversity in the form and quality of disclosures, attributable to the absence of explicit materiality criteria, suggesting that more prescriptive reporting of corporate governance practices may be necessary (KPMG 2004; 2005).

Functional Specification and Application of Internal Governance Structures

Australian issuers are subjected to three main prescriptions of corporate governance best practice. There is considerable unanimity in the composition and functional application of corporate governance structures, as shown in Tables 7.1 and 7.2. These guidelines reinforce the primacy of board control over the firm, the necessity of independence in board leadership and composition, and the use of separate board committees to promote effective monitoring of executive discretion and decision making.

From an issuer's perspective, although the IFSA and ACSI guidelines have been well publicized, the ASX CGC guidelines are the primary corporate governance standards because they apply to all listed firms in the Top 500 irrespective of the composition of their shareholder registers. For example, firms that have no significant institutional shareholders would not

TABLE 7.1 Key Governance Structures—Issuers

Corporate Control, Board Leadership & Structure, Executive Power		ASX CGC	IFSA	ACSI
Effective board control of the corporation		1.1	12	2
Majority of independent directors		2.1	3	3.1
Independent chairperson		2.2, 2.3	5	10.1
Separation of chief executive and chairperson (nonduality)		2.2, 2.3	5	10.1
Board committees with independence of decision making	Nomination	2.4	6, 7	11.3
	Audit	4.2	6, 7	11.1
	Remuneration	9.2	6, 7	11.2
Remuneration & Accountability of Corporate Officers				
Responsible remuneration of directors and executives and timely disclosure		9	13	13
Performance evaluation for the board and senior executives		2.4, 8.1	10	7, 12.1
Financial Integrity				
CEO and CFO signoffs for financial integrity		4.1, 7.2		16
Auditor independence		4.4	7	17
Responsibility to Shareholders and Stakeholders				
Codes of ethics/ethical decision making		3	17	
Submit major corporate changes to shareholders' vote			16	6
Shareholders' rights and communication		6		6, 14
Respect for stakeholders		10		

be required to respond to the ACSI and IFSA guidelines that represent the trustees of superannuation funds and fund managers, respectively.

While the IFSA and ACSI guidelines outline the preferred corporate governance practices from the investment fiduciary's perspective, only IFSA explicitly prescribes the exercise of voting power arising from portfolio investments. Although ACSI represents trustees of large superannuation

TABLE 7.2   Key Governance Structures—Investment Fiduciaries

	ASX CGC	IFSA	ACSI
Direct communication with investee companies		1	
Obligation to vote on all resolutions/disclosure		2	
Formal corporate governance policy		3	
Reporting to clients		4	

funds, its guidelines do not provide direction in relation to the exercise of proxy powers or corporate governance actions generally.

In Australia, the capacity of investment fiduciaries to influence corporate governance practices resides in their exercise of voting power, and dialogue with issuers (IFSA 2004). Australian institutional investors have taken a high profile in initiating change and exercising power over boards. It is notable that Australian institutions control approximately 25% of the equity market, while it is offshore institutional investors (with 41%), which hold the balance of power in many corporations, although the extent to which offshore institutional investors vote their proxies, and thus drive corporate governance change, remains unclear.

In Australia, the capacity of trustees as institutional equity owners to influence investee firms to adopt best practice corporate governance is subject to a range of legal considerations. Ali, Stapledon, and Gold (2003) note that under Australian superannuation regulations, trustees are not obligated to exercise their proxies; rather they must be able to demonstrate that adequate consideration has been given to the issues to be voted. Trustees, and more frequently, their appointed fund managers who instigate corporate governance actions, must ensure that *free-rider* benefits do not arise that undermine the fiduciary's obligation to exclusively maximize the returns of their clients (as distinct from any other shareholders), in light of any costs involved in those actions. Fiduciaries who engage in private discussions with directors and management also must be mindful of breaching the insider-trading provisions of the corporate law. While concerted efforts to organize actions on corporate governance matters with other significant investors may be laudable, the *shadow director* provisions of the corporate law can operate to deem trustees to be directors with all of the attaching responsibilities and personal liability—but not the perquisites—of formal office.

The exercise of proxy voting is further complicated because large superannuation funds, pooled superannuation funds, and other collective investment funds generally use custodians to record the underlying holdings of fund managers within omnibus accounts. These arrangements make it impossible for custodians to accept multiple instructions from fund managers for the purposes of attendance at company meetings where voting is by show of hands. This drawback has been ameliorated to some extent by IFSA Guideline 11.15.4, which directs firms to ensure that all proxies are counted for contentious resolutions prior to company meetings and a poll used where the outcome of those resolutions is different if the decision was carried by a show of hands.

In the face of more recent concerns regarding corporate governance and managerial excesses, Australian superannuation trustees have needed to resolve a practical concern: how to demonstrate prudent exercise of voting powers that address broader beneficiary concerns regarding the management of investee firms, while providing defensible, competitive returns. Since most trustees employ fund managers rather than investing in markets directly, it has become increasingly common for trustees to direct their fund managers to vote proxies and to report these activities to beneficiaries. In response to demand from trustees, corporate governance engagement and proxy voting advisory services have also been developed. ACSI has introduced a Voting Alert Service on the corporate governance practices of Australia's largest companies to aid trustees with voting and engagement decisions. The investment management arm of the Westpac Banking Corporation (itself an ASX-listed firm) offers a Governance Advisory Service. Trustees use this service to communicate views on corporate governance and other topical matters with investee firms, in addition to the activities of fund managers that manage the underlying portfolio holdings, and have more routine interaction with investee firms. Finally, given the latent power residing in offshore institutions, the recent acquisition of proxy advisory services firm Proxy Australia by Institutional Shareholder Services (ISS) suggests that issuers will require an increasing awareness of corporate governance actions by institutional shareholders.

LITERATURE REVIEW

Agency Concerns and Sociolegal Features Underlying Corporate Governance

The essential concern of corporate governance arises from the separation of ownership and control in modern public corporations. Early legal scholars and financial economists (Berle and Means 1932; Jensen and Meckling

1976) have argued that agency problems are expected to arise between shareholders and managers due to the separation of ownership and control, especially in the context of diffuse corporate ownership. Under this theoretical prescription, managers will generally exercise full control and are expected to pursue self-serving activities to the detriment of shareholders' interests. La Porta et al (1998) hypothesize that legal protections enforcing shareholder rights are critical to effective corporate governance. Shleifer and Vishny (1997) argue that legal protections of investors' rights alone are not sufficient to mitigate agency concerns. Bebchuk (2005) proposes shareholders be empowered to intervene in major corporate decisions (rather than merely approving board-initiated proposals on an ad hoc basis) providing shareholders with an increased latent power to induce management to act in their best interests. Fama and Jensen (1983) argue that agency costs are reduced by institutional arrangements that separate decision management from decision control. The board of directors is therefore proposed as a primary corporate governance structure because it acts as an oversight of managerial and firm performance, and limits the discretion of managers.

Ownership Structure and Corporate Governance

Ownership structure is also considered to be an important corporate governance structure. With the increasing institutional ownership of equities, the research literature shows that large shareholders who have sufficient incentives to monitor and control managerial activities, may limit agency problems and provide shared benefits of control for all shareholders. Demsetz and Lehn (1985) note that combining ownership and control is likely to mitigate managerial expropriation. The research literature exploring the influence of ownership concentration blockholders on firm value generally reveals benign effects. Ownership concentration itself has little impact on firm value and there is little discernible evidence that blockholders have deleterious effects on small or diffuse shareholders, especially where a large shareholder is active in firm management (Holderness 2003).

While institutional investors have become more prominent as blockholders and brought popular expectations of corporate governance reform and performance improvements, the research literature also notes increasing ownership by insider blockholders such as family founders, directors, and executives. Holderness et al. (1999) note that the prevalence of insider block ownership in U.S. companies rose on average from 13% to 21% between 1935 and 1995 and estimate insider ownership of public U.S. firms to be 20%. Anderson and Reeb (2003b) find that founder and family-controlled firms constitute over 35% of the S&P 500 Industrials, and approximately 18% of outstanding equity of these firms.

Insider blockholder ownership is most likely to trigger agency concerns given that insiders have close proximity to decision-making processes and have the greatest capacity to extract private benefits at the cost of remaining stockholders or to make suboptimal corporate investments (Demsetz 1983; Fama and Jensen 1983; Shleifer and Vishny 1997). Burkart et al. (2003) suggest that founder-family control is less desirable where adequate safeguards exist to limit minority shareholder wealth expropriation. In this context, it is particularly interesting that a positive association between insider ownership and control and firm performance is found in the literature. Jensen and Meckling (1976), Fama and Jensen (1983), Morck, Shleifer, and Vishny (1988) find insider ownership tends to be accompanied by increases in firm value (measured by Tobin's Q, the ratio of market value of equity plus book value of debt over total assets); however, this relationship is not linear across ownership levels. McConnell and Servaes (1990) find firm value (also measured by Q) increases as share ownership becomes concentrated in the hands of corporate officers, and a significant positive relation between firm value and the proportion of shares held by institutional investors, but do not rule out management entrenchment effects. Craswell et al. (1997) examine ownership structure and find weak support for a relationship between insider ownership and corporate performance for 349 Australian firms in the late 1980s. Anderson and Reeb (2003a) find that the financial performance and stock returns of 141 large U.S. founder/family-controlled firms are superior to firms with diffuse ownership structures, suggesting that founder shareholders and insider management reduce agency costs and improve corporate efficiency, rather than adversely affecting the rights of minority owners. Their study also concludes that the financial markets reward more highly firms that appoint a CEO who is unaffiliated with founder-family; however, accounting measures of financial performance are higher where an insider CEO affiliated with the family-founder shareholders is appointed.

Empirical Evidence on the Value Added by Corporate Governance Measures

Given that common corporate governance measures incorporated into industry guidelines create an expectation of issuer conformance, a number of studies have attempted to complete the logical first step: to validate the premise that *good governance* translates into economic value-added. At the outset, therefore, it is somewhat troubling that the available empirical research literature does not support any nexus between common corporate governance structures and improved financial performance and/or share-holder returns.

Bhagat and Black (2002) examine 934 large U.S. firms and find an inverse correlation between board independence and financial performance, suggesting that the conventional wisdom of mandating independence may actually impair firm performance. Lawrence and Stapledon (1999) also find no correlation between board composition and firm performance in Australia. Regarding the concerns arising from the concentration of executive power and excessive board influence of CEO/chairperson duality, Brickley et al. (1997) studied 661 U.S. firms in 1988 that combined the roles of CEO and chairperson and found that these firms outperformed those that divided these roles. Yermack (1996) had earlier analyzed board structure and firm performance and found an inverse correlation between boards size and firm value, and some evidence that firms were more highly valued when the CEO and chair positions are separated. More recently, an event study of U.K. firms announcing the separation of these previously combined roles, in compliance with the Cadbury Code of corporate governance, did not find any positive share price reaction associated with the announcement (Dedman and Lin, 2002). Vafeas and Theodorou (1998) fail to find any association between the composition of audit committees and firm performance in the United Kingdom.

Modes of Corporate Governance Activism by Institutional Investors

Hirschman (1970) provides a broad framework for activism by institutional investors who are dissatisfied with investee firm performance (exiting their investment, voicing their concerns and seeking change, or retaining investments on expectations of consequential performance improvements). Drucker (1976) stipulates that institutional investors should sell stocks of firms if they are dissatisfied with performance. Corporate governance concerns, however, are not necessarily correlated with performance, and pressures to reform corporate governance structures are clearly a relatively recent phenomenon.

Nonetheless, the continuing trend to institutionalization of equity ownership has provided investment fiduciaries with the capacity to influence the corporate governance structures of investee corporations. By virtue of this ownership, the question appears to become not *if*, but rather *how*, investment fiduciaries can be involved in corporate governance actions and reform efforts. There has been considerable debate regarding the appropriate role of superannuation trustees and their fund managers as monitors of corporate officers and the operations of investee firms. Monks and Minow (1996) assert that trustees possess no specific expertise as owners, much less as monitors of the performance of corporate managers and directors, and advocate the appointment of specialized professionals to undertake the monitoring task.

While undertaking corporate governance reform actions is often suggested as an essential part of the institutional investment process in both practitioner literature and popular forums, perhaps the most significant obstacle to activism is presented by the precepts of modern financial theory, which underpins generally accepted standards of fiduciary investment and has seemingly created an inexorable trend toward index-tracking strategies. In the process of *modernizing* the prudential investor standards in most jurisdictions, a key theoretical paradigm of financial economics—*informationally efficient* markets—has been codified. Under this paradigm, the notion of *trusting the market* has achieved increasing legal acceptance, and an index-tracking strategy offering low operating costs is expected to provide optimal investor outcomes. This paradigm has the effect of reversing the traditional onus on trustees to undertake active management and to exercise judgment in portfolio selections. Several authors (Porter 1997; Carleton et al. 1998; Short and Keasey 1997) note the increasing proclivity of institutional investors adopting index-tracking strategies that constrain their willingness to sell securities from their portfolios, and that these investors are unable to dispose large portfolio positions due to execution costs and indirect market impacts. The reality that many institutional investors are largely *captives* has seen modes of activism evolve that emphasize the voicing of concerns regarding performance and corporate governance issues, rather than an exit strategy. In context of indexing strategies, Koppes and Reilly (1995) suggest that trustees use corporate governance screening in order to discharge their fiduciary duty to monitor the performance of index portfolio constituents.

The consensus of empirical evidence indicates that institutional shareholders are effective in targeting poorly performing firms and sponsoring changes to corporate governance structures; however, the evidence linking these changes to economic outcomes is equivocal. Consequently this undermines the economic efficacy of institutional investor activism in both the United States and United Kingdom (Karpoff 1998; Gillan and Starks 2003; Dedman 2002). Karpoff et al. (1996) find that proposals initiated by institutional investors are successful in changing corporate governance structures; however, this has little effect on the target firm's long-term share values, profitability, or top management turnover. Gillan and Starks (2000) also find that coordinated proposals sponsored by institutional investors are more likely to gain support than those of individual active shareholders; however, the impact on share prices of these changes is minimal. Wahal

(1996) finds no evidence of significant long-term improvements in either stock prices or accounting measures of financial performance after firms are targeted by large *activist* pension funds on governance-related proxy proposals in the late 1980s and 1990s. Song and Szewczyk (2003) examine the performance impacts on firms that are publicly targeted in a coordinated manner by major U.S. pension funds (via the Council of Institutional Investors *Focus List*) but are unable to attribute any incremental performance effects to this institutional activism. Faccio and Lasfer (2000) note that while U.K. pension funds actively promote corporate governance measures, they are ineffective monitors: The firms in which they own large stakes are not more likely to conform with best practice internal corporate governance structures including board composition and removal of chairperson/CEO duality.

Evidence of the Efficacy of Good Governance as an Investment Strategy

While a multitude of modes of corporate governance activism exist, fund managers have created investment strategies constructed using corporate governance ratings. These financial products satisfy demands from trustees who wish to be active in improving corporate governance standards in portfolio investments, or to offer beneficiaries increased investment choices. As discussed above, since the empirical justification of corporate governance measures is equivocal, it is not surprising that research examining the linkages between corporate governance ratings (which form the basis of good-governance investment strategies) and economic outcomes is similarly inconclusive. More recent studies have bypassed the more fundamental question of the efficacy of corporate governance measures to examine if good governance used as the basis of an investment strategy provides economic value-added compared to a market portfolio or peer firms.

Gompers et al. (2003) analyze the relationship between corporate governance provisions, shareholder returns, and firm value for 1,500 U.S. firms throughout the 1990s. The authors construct a *long-short strategy* (which purchases the stocks of firms with the strongest shareholder rights and sells those that have weakest shareholder rights) based on corporate governance ratings. They find this strategy generates significant abnormal shareholder returns, affirming the benefits of good-governance firms. Using a similar methodology, albeit over a shorter time frame, Bauer, Guenster, and Otten (2004) examine the performance characteristics of European and U.K. firms and find a positive relationship exists among good governance measures, firm value, and shareholder returns; however, in contrast to Gompers et al., the authors find a negative relationship with profitability. Linden and Matolcsy (2004) examine the financial performance and shareholder returns of the largest 250 Australian companies stratified according to corporate governance ratings. The authors do not find any relationship with value-added and corporate governance ratings, but note that corporate governance ratings are related to firm size and are not reliable predictors of future performance.

Like all active investment strategies, the empirical validation of corporate governance investment strategies is not expected to surmount the charge leveled by proponents of efficient markets: Active strategies are not expected to be economically viable (Gold 2004). Aside from this more technical hurdle, corporate governance indices (and index-tracking products) would not be expected to deliver material incremental performance because these indices typically use only marginal up or down weightings of constituents compared to the conventional market index.

Corporate Governance and Modern Pension Economics

The willingness of investment fiduciaries to participate in corporate governance actions and reforms can be affected by the competitive pressures operating in the contemporary financial services environment. Whether undertaking investment selections internally or employing external fund managers, pension fund trustees are concerned with demonstrating a prudent investment process; however, increasingly it is the performance outcomes that provide the point of differentiation between largely fungible financial products. From a commercial, rather than theoretical perspective, therefore, significant pressure is exerted upon trustees (many of whom are commercial entities in business for themselves) to ensure that their portfolio returns are commensurate with market indices and peer funds, in order to maximize scale of funds under management and profitability (Ali, Stapledon, and Gold 2003). Investment fiduciaries must therefore give careful consideration to any costs associated with corporate governance actions because these have the potential to add overhead costs (and thus adversely affect profitability) or reduce the beneficiaries' returns. It is important to note that the existence of these considerations does not necessarily create significant agency conflicts between beneficiaries and trustees and/or between trustees and their appointed fund managers, however, because the structure of their investment mandates usually emphasizes relative rather than absolute targets for returns and volatility, and thus agency concerns are also contracted out, relying on the premise of market efficiency.

EMPIRICAL ANALYSIS—POOR-GOVERNANCE FIRMS

Sample Construction and Definition of Proxy Variables

In contrast to prior studies that have sought to validate a nexus between good corporate governance structures and improved economic returns, we examine the good corporate governance investment thesis using a principle of mutual exclusion. By specifying *poor* corporate governance and selecting a cohort of firms, we measure their security returns and financial performance. If poor corporate governance firms deliver superior investor returns and financial performance relative to market averages, then this would undermine the validity of conventional corporate governance practices.

For the purposes of this study, we seek to incorporate popular perceptions that both minority and dispersed shareholders are likely to face diminished corporate governance standards, where insiders (founders, families, and executives founders and other related parties) hold substantial ownership positions and/or managerial control (Australian Financial Review 2005a; 2005b). As discussed above, agency concerns are expected to arise due to the capacity of management and other insiders to extract benefits not available to other shareholders and financial stakeholders.

The construction of our sample for poor-governance firms therefore requires two separate filtering stages. In the first stage, we use a positive screen that includes the constituents of the leading institutional Australian equity benchmark—the S&P/ASX200 index—which display nonconformance with key best practice corporate governance standards. In the second stage of sample construction, we use a positive screen that includes only those firms that exhibit substantial insider ownership. The combination of these screens is intended to identify a representative sample of firms which exemplify heightened corporate governance risks and are most susceptible to agency costs.

The first stage of filtering involves identifying firms disclosing nonconformance with the ASX CGC guidelines. The requirement for firms to disclose their corporate governance practices (including nonconformance and explanatory commentary) on an exception basis became mandatory under the ASX Listing Rules from 1 January 2003. Using the ISS Proxy Australia (ISSPA) corporate governance analytics database we analyze nonconformance with the ASX CGC guidelines, using the first full year of mandatory disclosures for all firms in the 2004 annual reporting season. As shown in Table 7.3, the results of this analysis confirm the high level of conformance with the best practice corporate governance standards within a large sample of firms that are considered to be the largest and most liquid stocks in the Australian share market.

TABLE 7.3   Issuer Conformance with ASX CGC Guidelines

Overall Conformance with ASX CGC Guidelines	Full Conformance	Partial Nonconformance
No. of firms	93	97
Ratio of total	49%	51%
Most Frequent Areas of Nonconformance (According to Corporate Governance Structure)	**ASX CGC Recommendation**	**No. of Firms Disclosing Nonconformance**
Board independence (majority of nonexec)	2.1	44
Independent chair	2.2	30
CEO/chair duality	2.3	12
Board nomination committee	2.4	32
Executive remuneration	8.1	19

For the purposes of our sample construction (and in accordance with the agency theoretic perspective), we select firms not adopting the recommended internal corporate governance structures directly associated with the apex of corporate power and control (as shown in Table 7.3), namely, separation of board control and executive decision-making, board leadership and board independence. Nonconformance with these structures is expected to impede the effective functioning of the board, to introduce potential (or actual) interference between decision management and control, and provide greatest potential for entrenchment by directors and/or executives. Most significantly, nonconformance with these key structures is likely to result in low ratings provided by corporate governance consultants. We apply an additive screen (shown schematically in Table 7.4) from which we identify 36 firms (a statistically significant number given that the market benchmark comprises 200 securities).

The second phase of screening specifically identifies firms that have substantial shareholdings held by founders, their families, executives, and related parties (including trusts). Under Australian securities regulations, *substantial* shareholdings are deemed to be holdings greater than 5% of issued capital that must be disclosed. Using ISSPA's database, which provides a *look-through* analysis of substantial shareholding disclosures based on beneficial rather than legal ownership (as noted earlier, legal ownership of substantial shareholdings is often recorded by legal nominees and custodians), we collect information on substantial insider ownership to identify insider firms. As shown in Table 7.5, consistent with trends previously

TABLE 7.4 Poor Governance Screening Factors

Corporate control, board leadership & executive power	Nonindependent chair *and/or* CEO/chair duality *plus*
Board independence and entrenchment	Lack of majority of independent directors *and/or* Lack of an independent nomination committee *equals* Poor Corporate Governance

identified in offshore markets (Anderson and Reeb 2003a; Holderness 2003), our analysis reveals a significant level of insider block ownership in Australia. We find substantial insider ownership in 48 of Australia's largest publicly listed entities (approximately one quarter of the market benchmark by number) representing approximately 16% of the market, and 17% of the S&P/ASX200 index capitalization, respectively.

TABLE 7.5 Insider Blockholder Firms in the Australian Equity Market

		Shareholding Ranges		
Distribution of substantial insider ownership (as proportion of issued capital)	Total	5–20%	20–49%	50%+
Number of insider firms	48	19	20	9
Percentage of total		40%	42%	18%
Median inside ownership level in S&P/ASX200 (%)	28.9			
Market value of firms with insider influence ($ billion)	147.8			
Total market capitalization ($ billion)	951.8			
Insider firms as proportion of market capitalization (%)	15.5			
Insider firms as proportion of S&P/ASX200 Index capitalization (%)	16.6			

Notes:
Insider ownership is defined as shareholdings held by founders, family, or managers. All shareholding data sourced from ISS Proxy Australia based on most recent annual report data (2004).
Market capitalization and index capitalization data provided by ITG Australia; data as at 30 June 2005.

After applying the second positive screen for insider influence, we refine our sample of poor-governance firms (shown in Table 7.6), excluding firms that have been in operation for less than three years and are therefore likely to affect the robustness of our results. Since the ASX CGC guidelines were introduced relatively recently, we confirm that none of our poor-governance firms had previously adopted good corporate governance structures or undergone significant changes with respect to insider influence.

Market Performance Study

Using the cohort of poor-governance firms (shown in Table 7.5), we compute a Poor-Governance Index, which measures the performance of an equally weighted portfolio of these stocks. The index is rebalanced at the end of each month to mitigate distortionary effects on the overall performance results from individual firms. For the purposes of this analysis, we use the performance variable that is most relevant from an investment fiduciary's perspective—total returns (i.e., returns that include price appreciation and dividends). We compare the performance of the Poor-Governance Index with the leading institutional Australian equity benchmark (the S&P/ASX200) using monthly data for the five years ended 30 June 2005. This extended analysis period is selected for its statistical robustness and because it incorporates a period of heightened corporate governance concerns. As shown in Figure 7.1 and Table 7.7, the Poor-Governance Index demonstrates substantial outperformance of the market over the long term, with high persistence levels and lower systematic risk.

The market performance study using an extended time series reveals that a statistically significant sample of poor-governance firms significantly outperforms the broad equity market. Poor-governance firms also show reduced market risk although the variability of the (higher) returns is greater. Bearing in mind that our sample selection process accords with industry corporate governance ratings assessments, these firms would typically be excluded from a typical good corporate governance investment portfolio or index-tracking product. Our analysis indicates that the exclusion of these firms to construct a good-governance portfolio is likely to result in significant opportunity costs for investment fiduciaries in terms of forgone returns and portfolio diversification. Using a methodological principle of *mutual exclusion*, it can be posited that the good-governance investment thesis is not validated by these empirical results.

TABLE 7.6 Descriptive Statistics for Australian Poor-Corporate-Governance Firms

Stock Code	Firm Name	Industry (GICS Classification)	Market Capitalization ($ million)	Operating Revenue ($ million)	Assets ($ million)	Reported Net Profit after Tax ($ million)	3 yr EPS Growth (%)	Beta	Top 20 Shareholders (%)
AEO	Austereo Group Ltd.	Media	608.8	240.4	1,039.0	41.9	50.1	0.96	94.7
APN	APN News & Media	Media	2,484.8	1,257.0	2,801.3	128.3	14.0	0.77	62.5
CPU	Computershare Ltd	Software & Services	1,738.7	872.4	1,187.1	79.9	12.8	1.60	65.3
FWD	Fleetwood Corp	Automobiles & Components	348.2	251.2	165.8	20.2	50.8	0.14	60.8
GNS	Gunns Limited	Materials	1,111.7	649.7	951.4	105.3	43.8	0.71	72.2
HIL	Hills Industries Ltd	Capital Goods	540.6	717.0	428.1	31.1	5.7	0.50	38.9
HVN	Harvey Norman	Retailing	2,980.3	1,735.6	2,369.0	176.1	17.6	1.10	82.7
HWI	Housewares Internat.	Retailing	252.2	457.6	278.8	22.9	25.5	0.99	71.3
IFM	Infomedia Ltd	Software & Services	240.3	69.9	69.4	20.7	16.7	1.16	88.5
JBM	Jubilee Mines NL	Materials	499.8	235.4	224.0	95.1	74.0	0.99	58.3
MTS	Metcash Limited	Food & Staples Retailing	1,579.2	7,201.2	1,488.7	101.8	27.4	1.14	86.1
NWS	News Corp	Media	26,627.0	29,428.0	73,738.0	2,312.0	17.0	2.30	91.1
PBL	Publishing & Broad	Media	8,505.7	2,894.3	7,541.5	668.2	15.6	1.20	80.2
RHC	Ramsay Health Care	Health Care Equipment & Services	701.4	767.6	690.2	38.4	31.0	0.77	85.4
SEV	Seven Network	Media	1,111.6	1,141.5	2,067.9	93.3	27.9	1.45	82.2
SPT	Spotless Group Ltd	Commercial Services & Supplies	991.7	2,455.0	1,346.7	22.7	-22.7	0.62	61.7
THG	Thakral Holdings Grp	Property Trusts	386.7	-	763.2	35.0	-7.4	0.40	82.6
WDC	Westfield Group	Property Trusts	27,653.3	1,612.9	34,821.0	832.9	—	0.52	72.1
	Median		1,051.7	872.4	1,113.1	86.6	17.6		76.2
	Market average (n=305)		481.8	404.5	455.4	23.6	14.9		

All data are reported according to latest company balance dates.

Beta values are estimated from 5 years of monthly return data to 30 June 2005; reference index is the S&P/ASX200 Index.

The market average is a median of all firms with operating revenue exceeding $100 million and excludes financial and real estate sectors.

Source: Aspect Financial *Fin Analysis* database.

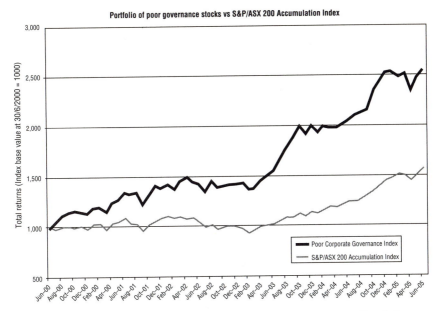

FIGURE 7.1 Cumulative Gains from a Poor-Corporate-Governance Portfolio

TABLE 7.7 Performance Analysis of the Poor-Governance Index

(Panel A) Total Returns (to 30 June 2005)	1 Year	3 Years	5 Years	10 Years
Poor-Governance Index	26.2%	20.4%	22.5%	21.3%
S&P/ASX200 Index	26.4%	14.7%	9.4%	12.2%
Outperformance margin	–0.1%	5.6%	13.1%	9.1%
Persistence ratio (outperformance versus market)	50%	64%	68%	
No. of index constituents	18	18	16	15

(Panel B) Comparative Risk Measures (Five years to 30 June 2005)	Poor Governance Index	S&P/ ASX200 Index	Relative
Annualized standard deviation of returns	29.2%	10.2%	2.9X
Downside risk (ratio of negative returns)		30%	37%	0.82X
Beta	0.96	1.00	0.96X
Skewness of returns	(0.28)	(0.46)	0.62X

Data source: Iress.

Analysis of Financial Performance

We undertake an analysis of the financial performance of our cohort of poor corporate governance firms focusing on metrics that exclude the distorting effects of market valuation (Demsetz and Villalonga 2001). In contrast to other recent studies (Gompers et al. 2003; Bauer, Otten, and Rad 2004; Anderson and Reeb 2003a), therefore, we do not rely upon Tobin's Q to proxy firm value. Instead, we calculate financial performance metrics (shown in Table 7.8) that are considered to be most insulated from accounting adjustments and are largely independent of financial structure.

In accordance with market practice, we use earnings before interest, taxes, depreciation and amortization (EBITDA) as the main proxy for operating performance. As with our market performance study, we apply a *mutual exclusion* methodology: We compare the performance of poor gov-

TABLE 7.8   Financial Performance Variables

Key Variables for Operating and Financial Efficiency	Poor Corporate Governance Firms		Market Average	
	Median	Mean	Median	Mean
EBITDA growth—3yr average (%)	19.3	23.5	15.7	21.6
EBITDA growth—5yr average (%)	19.2	27.2	14.5	17.8
Core earnings per share growth—3yr average (%)	12.6	22.1	13.4	15.5
Core earnings per share growth—5yr average (%)	14.3	19.1	6.4	8.8
EBITDA margin (%)	21.0	26.5	14.9	19.1
EBIT margin (%)	16.1	22.1	9.4	13.0
Return on assets (%)	7.5	10.2	7.0	7.9
Return on capital invested (%)	15.3	43.2	15.2	26.7
Dividends per share growth—5yr average (%)	15.8	24.0	8.5	9.8
Dividend payout ratio (%)	59.8	71.2	62.1	67.4
Price to Gross Cash Flow (X)	8.9	11.1	7.8	8.9
Enterprise value/EBITDA (X)	8.7	9.1	7.5	8.6

Notes:
All data are reported according to latest company balance dates.
    Core earnings are reported earnings pre-abnormal items and adjusted for dilution from corporate actions. Growth shown over 5 years unless shown otherwise.
    Market sample excludes financial and real estate firms (*n* = 308).
Source: Aspect Financial *Fin Analysis* database.

ernance with the market median and average to examine if this cohort provides stronger financial performance. As financial aggregates are not published for the market, we create market aggregates based on a large sample of publicly listed Australian firms with reported revenue exceeding $100 million and positive earnings before interest and taxes (EBIT). This is a stringent sample for comparison purposes because it excludes smaller firms and those with poor underlying profitability.

As shown in Figure 7.2 and Table 7.8, our analysis of financial performance reveals that poor-governance firms exhibit operational and financial efficiency superior to the market. Over an extended analysis period incorporating five years of annual financial returns, poor-governance firms show stronger growth in underlying cash flow (EBITDA), normalized earnings per share, and dividends. Significantly, the poor-governance firms have significantly higher operating profit margins (EBITDA margin), while their capital efficiency (ROA and ROIC) is also higher than the market overall.

Interestingly, from an agency perspective, poor-governance firms generated far higher rates of growth in dividends than the market average; however, this appears to have been achieved as a function of superior

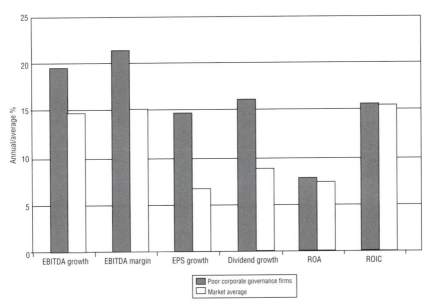

FIGURE 7.2 Comparative Financial Performance Ratios

earnings rather than dividend policy (payout ratio). Finally, as an expected corollary of our market performance survey results, the market valuation of poor-governance firms (Gross Cash per Share/Price and Enterprise Value/EBITDA multiples) shows investors' willingness to pay a premium for these firms versus the broader equity market. This suggests from the shareholder perspective that excluding poor-governance firms from a portfolio would result in lower economic value-added. In summary, our empirical analysis of financial performance does not support the good-governance investment thesis.

CONCLUSION

Australia's best practice corporate governance standards exemplify a high standard of formalization. Our analysis of early reporting trends reveals a high level of conformance with these market-based structures by Australian firms; however, there is a significant number of firms, especially those exhibiting substantial insider influence, that have chosen to adopt alternative structures of corporate governance.

Consistent with trends in other jurisdictions, despite several significant practical and legal obstacles, Australian investment fiduciaries have shown an increased willingness to engage proactively with issuers and to encourage issuer conformance with corporate governance best practice. The presumption that appears to be made is that poor corporate governance is economically undesirable; however, the body of available empirical evidence does not support any association between good corporate governance and economic value-added, nor does it support the economic efficacy of activism by institutional investors to reform corporate governance structures within investee firms.

Researching the performance of good corporate governance as an investment strategy (as distinct from broad tests of association between good corporate governance and improved financial performance) provides the most direct and relevant test of its economic efficacy for both investment fiduciaries and corporate officers. In this context, this study deliberately selects firms with poor corporate governance structures and finds that they provide superior investment returns for portfolio investors and financial performance. On the basis of these results, we conclude that the good corporate governance investment thesis is not validated in Australian firms.

The results of this study therefore add to the overall consensus of research that questions the economic value of common corporate governance measures. From the issuers' perspective, this has significant implications for corporate officers who must justify the economic rationale of any expenditure incurred adopting these measures in the context of their fiduciary duties to the firm. A remaining empirical issue is to quantify the direct costs and indirect effects associated with conformance with best practice corporate governance guidelines. In contrast to earlier portfolio studies which have relied upon good governance ratings, these findings have not been significantly assisted by so-called *survivorship* and *hindsight* biases.

Our findings also call into question the efforts by investment fiduciaries (professional superannuation trustees, fund managers, and other institutional shareholders) and other stakeholders to exert pressure on firms to adopt best practice corporate governance measures, given that they are not proven to increase firm value or enhance portfolio returns. In the context of creating active investment strategies (whose economic value already faces direct challenges under financial theory), using corporate governance as a basis of security selection may result in suboptimal portfolio returns—an important consideration for investment fiduciaries under the prevailing regulations.

CHAPTER 8

Corporate Social Responsibility and Fiduciary Investment in Australia

Paul U. Ali

INTRODUCTION

Corporate governance, as it is conventionally understood, can be described as a system of principles governing the interactions between a company's managers, directors, shareholders, and other financial stakeholders that has as its objectives the reduction of agency costs and assuring shareholders and other providers of finance of a return on their investment in the company (Shleifer and Vishny 1997; Standard & Poor's Governance Services 2002). In recent years, the debate on corporate governance has expanded beyond its traditional concerns with the protection of shareholders and other financial stakeholders to address what is perceived as the broader social responsibility of companies, as the principal instruments and expressions of capitalism.

Companies are now being enjoined to implement a disparate range of ethically informed or socially oriented measures, ranging from the promotion of racial and gender diversity in their boardrooms and senior executive ranks, the improvement of human rights, labor, and environmental standards in the less-developed countries in which the companies operate or source materials from, to the greater use of renewable energy sources and recyclable materials, and an increased support of charitable causes. In

Note: This research was supported by a grant from the Australian Research Council (DP0557673).

Australia, companies listed on the Australian Stock Exchange are required to take into consideration the interests of their nonfinancial stakeholders (namely, employees, customers, and the community as a whole) and publicly disclose how they intend to comply with their social responsibilities (Australian Stock Exchange Corporate Governance Council 2003).

This emphasis on modifying the conduct of companies has, in Australia, been accompanied by a rapid growth in fiduciary investment funds, in particular, mutual funds, designed to reward companies viewed as socially responsible by investing in their securities and to punish unethical or socially irresponsible companies by shunning their securities. An estimated AUD3.3 billion has been invested in these funds by Australian retail investors and pension funds (Deni Green Consulting Services 2004).

The emergence of these socially responsible investment (SRI) funds is a corollary of the more general professionalization of the supply and management of investment capital, where decisions as to the use of capital have been delegated by the ultimate suppliers of capital (retail investors in mutual funds, contributors to pension funds, and customers of life insurance companies) to trustees, fund managers, and other professional fiduciaries (Clark 1981; Hawley and Williams 2003). More specifically, the increasing popularity of SRI funds in Australia reflects heightened concerns in the community with ethical standards, environmental issues, and occupational health and safety. This is well exemplified by the broad-based public support within Australia for the Kyoto Protocol to the United Nations Framework Convention on Climate Change and public perceptions of dereliction of duty by corporate office-bearers in the wake of the recent collapse of several large Australian companies, in particular HIH Insurance and OneTel. These concerns have been specifically catered to by the proponents of SRI funds.

This chapter focuses on SRI funds in Australia. It explains the investment strategies adopted by SRI funds in the furtherance of corporate social responsibility. It also discusses the legal framework for SRI funds, in particular the difficulty with accommodating them within the *prudent investor rule* that governs the management of all fiduciary investment products. Although this chapter is concerned with Australian law, the conclusions articulated in respect of the prudent investor rule are relevant to all jurisdictions whose investment management laws are based upon English law (for instance, the United States and Canada).

INVESTMENT STRATEGIES OF SRI FUNDS

While the profile of SRI funds has been greatly enhanced by the current discourse on corporate social responsibility, they are not new products.

The origins of SRI funds can be traced to the Quaker and Methodist religious movements in the nineteenth century and the anti-apartheid investment policies adopted by many mutual funds in the 1970s (Kroll 1999). In Australia, the first SRI fund, the Friends Provident Ethical Fund, was launched in 1986. The SRI funds now available to Australian investors have moved beyond their religious and political origins and display a diversity of investment strategies. In addition, these funds and their counterparts in other markets such as the United States and the United Kingdom are open to the entire spectrum of investors; in contrast, SRI funds when originally developed were largely the province of wealthy individuals and religious and charitable foundations.

SRI funds employ the same legal structures as conventional mutual funds. An SRI fund is structured as a company or trust, and investors purchase shares in the company or fractional, beneficial interests (units) in the trust. The consideration provided by the investors for the acquisition of the shares or units is pooled by the company or trustee of the trust, and is used to acquire a range of securities (including shares or units in other mutual funds), for the purpose of generating a financial return for the investors. Decisions as to security selection are made on behalf of the investors by the company or trustee, or a fund manager to whom the investment management function has been delegated (Ali, Stapledon, and Gold 2003).

SRI Portfolio Construction Using Screens

The portfolios of contemporary SRI funds are typically constructed using targeted security screens. These screens filter potential investments in or out of a portfolio based on a wide range of nonfinancial criteria. This screening process, like the funds that employ them, is not a new phenomenon. A similar process of security screening is used in the creation of sector-specific or country-specific mutual funds, such as mutual funds that specialize in biotechnology or Internet investments and mutual funds that specialize in certain markets. However, the screens employed by SRI funds are designed to capture selected nonfinancial criteria across the entire universe of investable securities as opposed to sector funds that are limited to the securities issued by companies in a specific sector or country (Hallerbach, Ning, Soppe, and Spronk 2004). There are basically two types of screens: negative and positive screens.

Negative screens are the way in which the portfolios for the majority of Australian and overseas SRI products are constructed (Ali, Stapledon, and Gold 2003). While the particular screening criteria employed may vary considerably from negative screen to negative screen, all of these screens operate by limiting the securities that the SRI fund may invest in. Securities are excluded primarily based on the industries in which the companies that have issued the securities operate. The most common criteria used to reject securities relate to companies in the alcohol, armaments, gaming, nuclear energy, pornography, and tobacco sectors. More recently, negative screens have been used to exclude the securities of companies considered to have failed to meet *best practices* requirements in relation to affirmative action, environmental standards, gender diversity, human rights, labor standards, occupational health and safety, product safety, and racial diversity.

In contrast, positive screens are used to select securities for inclusion in the portfolio based, again, on the industries in which the companies operate and also the business practices of companies. Securities may be selected due, for example, to the fact that their issuers are involved in the development or manufacture of pharmaceuticals or renewable energy technology, or operate in aged-care or health-care sectors. Alternatively, the selection of securities may be determined by the extent to which a particular company is judged to have conformed to best practices in relation to affirmative action, and so on, or by reference to the environmental impact of a company's business activities.

A recent development in relation to positive screens is their use in creating *best-in-class* portfolios (O'Rourke 2003). Here the securities issued by companies are judged suitable for inclusion in a portfolio by reference to relative, rather than absolute, criteria. A company's securities will be selected for the portfolio on the basis that that company is the leader in a particular industry in relation to certain socially oriented policies. Accordingly, companies such as BP Amoco or Royal Dutch Shell whose securities might otherwise be rejected by conventional negative screens or fail the criteria for selection in the case of conventional positive screens might nonetheless be invested in by an SRI fund using a best-in-class screen due to the innovative steps taken by those companies to reduce their greenhouse gas emissions.

Legal Context of Security Screening

The employment of a negative or positive screen incorporating the features discussed above is not, however, the exclusive arbiter of the investment strategy of an SRI fund.

An SRI fund, regardless of the criteria used by it to construct a screen, must possess a more fundamental attribute, one that is common to all mutual funds and fiduciary investment products. In short, the use to which the screen is put must legally constitute *investing*; that is, the overarching objective of the SRI fund must be to allocate the assets under management for the substantial purpose of generating a financial return. There is little guidance as to what constitutes an investment under Australian law beyond the recognition that investing denotes the acquisition of an asset capable of generating income. A court is now, however, likely to take a broader view of financial return, given that modern mutual funds and other fiduciary investment products (other than cash management trusts) seek to derive financial returns for their investors from the capital appreciation of securities, rather than solely or predominantly dividends or interest distributions on securities.

The rejection or selection of securities based on nonfinancial criteria for an exclusive or predominant nonfinancial goal cannot be viewed as investing, for example, where the securities are acquired to enable the fund to propose socially oriented resolutions at the meetings of the issuer's shareholders and to solicit proxies in support of such resolutions. Such corporate activism is not investing, and the trustee or fund manager of an SRI fund that conducts itself in that manner, without reference to the derivation of a financial return on the securities acquired by it, will be held by a court to have acted beyond the scope of its legal powers.

The consequences for the operator of the SRI fund are severe. The investors in the fund will, in relation to the securities acquired, be legally entitled to disclaim the acquisition and can pursue the operator personally for any loss incurred on those securities (O'Dell 2000).

Legal Character of SRI Investment Strategies

To ascertain the legal character of the investment strategies followed by SRI funds, it is helpful to contrast those strategies with the socially-neutral strategies followed by conventional mutual funds.

A *socially neutral* investment strategy is one in which the operator of the mutual fund seeks to optimize the returns of the fund, as measured against the investment objectives of the fund (for instance, the fund may adopt a relative benchmark for investment performance and seek to generate returns of at least a designated margin above a benchmark index), for an acceptable level of risk within the parameters dictated by the fund's investment mandate (for instance, the mandate may state that no more than a prescribed proportion of the assets under management can be allocated to the securities of a single issuer or issuers in a single industry) (Ali, Stapledon, and Gold 2003).

The critical criterion for consideration by the operator of the mutual fund is the risk and return profile of a particular security and the likely impact of the inclusion of that security in the fund's portfolio on the overall risk and return profile of the portfolio. Despite that, it is common practice for the operators of a mutual fund in designing or implementing a socially neutral investment strategy to take account of nonfinancial criteria that may impact on the risk and return profile of securities. The operator may legitimately reject a security on the grounds that the issuer is in breach of environmental standards and that such breach may have a material, negative impact on the profitability or financial stability of the issuer. Nonetheless, while nonfinancial criteria may play a material or even decisive role in the selection of securities for a portfolio, that role is secondary and is subordinate to the overarching, financial return objectives of mutual funds that adopt socially neutral investment strategies. All mutual funds in Australia, not only SRI funds, must publicly disclose to prospective investors how labor standards and environmental, social, and ethical factors are taken into account in security selection (Australian Securities and Investments Commission 2003).

The investment strategies of SRI funds can be characterized as *socially sensitive* or *socially dictated* (Hutchinson and Cole 1980). As regards such strategies, nonfinancial criteria are of primary importance. A socially sensitive investment strategy is one in which the operator of the SRI fund selects securities from an investable universe of securities with comparable risk and return profiles, by having regard to nonfinancial criteria. Nonfinancial criteria play an even more important role in the case of socially dictated investment strategies; the operator of the SRI fund seeks to generate financial returns for the fund while also undertaking a nonfinancial objective. In both cases, however, the securities selected by the SRI fund must be consistent with the financial objectives of the fund and also satisfy the nonfinancial criteria of the fund as incorporated in the fund's security screen. A security will therefore be rejected if it fails the screening process, regardless of its risk and return profile vis-à-vis the fund's financial objectives.

The investment strategies of SRI funds can therefore be defined as *dual-objective* strategies (Ali, Stapledon, and Gold 2003). In selecting securities for the SRI fund's portfolio, the operator of the fund takes into account both the risk and return profile of the security and whether the company that has issued the security passes the screening process for the fund that has been established using nonfinancial criteria. In contrast to socially neutral mutual funds where the nonfinancial criteria employed are subordinate to the financial objectives of the fund, the nonfinancial criteria used to construct security screens for an SRI fund, whether the fund is socially sensitive or socially dictated, operate at the same level as the fund's financial objectives. In neither case, however, are the financial objectives of the fund subordinated to these nonfinancial criteria (to do so would be to eliminate the investment character of the fund and expose the operator to consequences mentioned above).

SRI FUNDS AND THE PRUDENT INVESTOR RULE

Prudent Investor Rule and Modern Portfolio Theory

The construction of a security screen for an SRI fund and the selection of securities using a combination of financial criteria and the nonfinancial criteria embodied in that screen are, under Australian law, subject to the strictures imposed by the so-called prudent investor rule. This rule applies to all fiduciary investors, such as the operators of SRI funds, and requires them to act prudently when using the consideration entrusted to them by investors to select securities (Ali, Stapledon, and Gold 2003).

The clearest statement of the strictures of the prudent investor rule may be found in the Uniform Prudent Investor Act of 1994, which has been adopted in the majority of the U.S. states. Equivalent principles govern mutual funds in the U.K. and, arguably, also Australia.

The 1994 Act explains the prudent investor rule in the following terms:

- The operator of a mutual fund or other fiduciary investor must, in investing and managing the assets of the fund, consider the purposes, terms, distribution requirements, and other material circumstances of the fund.
- Decisions made by the fiduciary investor concerning individual assets must be "evaluated not in isolation but in the context of the trust portfolio as a whole and as a part of an overall investment strategy having risk and return objectives reasonably suited to the [fund]."
- Among the factors that the fiduciary investor must consider when making an investment decision are "the role that each investment or course of action plays within the overall [fund] portfolio," "the expected total return from income and the appreciation of capital," and "needs for liquidity, regularity of income, and preservation or appreciation of capital."
- The fiduciary investor must "diversify the investments of the [fund]."

The above expression of the prudent investor rule is consistent with the provisions of the Trustee Act 2000 that govern U.K. mutual funds and also with earlier judicial comments on the prudent investor rule in the U.K. (Ali, Stapledon, and Gold 2003).

In contrast, in Australia, it remains uncertain whether the above expression of the prudent investor rule applies to SRI funds and other mutual funds in Australia, or whether fiduciary investors are bound by a stricter version of the rule that requires them to give primacy to the preservation of the capital and income of the fund and avoid all risky investments. Judicial opinion on this issue is divided, and a study of the Trustee Acts yields no better answer, due to the contradictory provisions of that legislation (Ali, Stapledon, and Gold 2003). Nonetheless, it is arguable that were the issue of the interpretation of the prudent investor rule to come now before an Australian court, that court would be guided by the version of the prudent investor rule that applies in the U.K. (which, in turn, has been influenced by the earlier U.S. articulation of the rule).

The content of the prudent investor rule recognized in the U.K. and arguably also in Australia is informed by modern portfolio theory. Modern portfolio theory assesses securities not in isolation but in terms of the likely impact of their selection on the return objectives and risk profile of the entire portfolio of the fund (Gordon 1997; Bines and Thel 2004). This whole-of-portfolio approach toward security selection is concerned with the relationship between the risk and rates of return of securities and how different combinations of securities can be used to construct efficient portfolios (a portfolio is efficient, if there are no other portfolios with the same level of return that can provide the investor with a lower level of risk).

The return on a portfolio and its overall riskiness is dependent upon the correlation of returns between the various constituent securities of the portfolio (Bines and Thel 2004). In order to maximize returns for a given level of risk (or, in other words, minimize the portfolio's overall risk exposure for a given rate of return), the fiduciary investor must diversify its portfolio. This involves devising a mix of securities for a portfolio that has a collective risk profile consistent with the fiduciary investor's financial objectives and which is expected to generate the maximum aggregate returns for the portfolio for the particular level of risk assumed. This can be achieved by combining securities that are negatively correlated, lowly correlated or uncorrelated to each other. The lower or weaker the correlation between different securities, the greater their collective potential to reduce the overall risk profile of a portfolio or generate a greater aggregate return for the same overall level of risk. Hence, even where two securities have the same risk and return profiles, modern portfolio theory favors the selection of the security that is negatively correlated to the securities already held in the fund's portfolio because the inclusion of that security would lower the overall risk of the portfolio.

Implications for SRI Funds

The investment strategies of SRI funds described in this chapter involve the narrowing of the securities that the operator of an SRI fund can invest in (through the application of negative or positive screens) or widening the stated objectives of the fund to include nonfinancial objectives (through the use of positive screens). However, the whole-of-portfolio approach embodied in the prudent investor rule has important ramifications for the interaction of the screening process with the financial objectives contemplated by the prudent investor rule.

The prudent investor rule is concerned with the optimization of financial returns to the investors in an SRI fund or other mutual fund. For SRI funds, this return objective is paramount and the pursuit of nonfinancial objectives, in case of socially dictated SRI funds, will expose the operator of the fund to personal liability for losses incurred by the fund, if that return objective is disregarded or subordinated to the fund's nonfinancial objectives (Ali, Stapledon, and Gold 2003; Bines and Thel 2004).

In addition, the use of security screens by an SRI fund to create an investable universe of securities leads to the operator of the fund selecting securities from a pool that is necessarily smaller than the universe of securities available to a socially neutral mutual fund with comparable financial return objectives. This reduction in investment opportunities may impact negatively upon the ability of the operator of both socially sensitive and socially dictated SRI funds to diversify the funds' portfolios and thus optimize their financial returns. The sacrifice of portfolio diversification by the operator of the fund may, again, depending on the lower returns or increased riskiness of the fund's portfolio compared to the efficient portfolios available to socially-neutral mutual funds, expose the operator to personal liability (Ali, Stapledon, and Gold 2003).

This means that care must be taken when managing an SRI fund to ensure that the adoption of nonfinancial criteria for security selection or the pursuit of nonfinancial objectives does not undermine the operator's ability to optimize the fund's returns (Bobo 1984). In determining whether the operator of an SRI fund has improperly sacrificed financial returns and thus breached the prudent investor rule, it is likely that an Australian court would be guided by the returns that could be achieved by a socially neutral fund having comparable financial return objectives.

The above conclusions are based upon the application of the prudent investor rule in a form unmodified by the socially oriented objectives of SRI funds. This application, consequently, makes no distinction between socially neutral or conventional mutual funds, on the one hand, and SRI funds on the other.

This necessarily raises the issue of the extent to which the prudent investor rule that applies to socially neutral funds is capable of modification via contract in the context of SRI funds.

A contractual view of the nature of the duties of the operator of an SRI fund would lead to the conclusion that those duties should reflect the expectations of the investors in the fund (Djurasovic 1997). In circumstances where the nonfinancial criteria employed by, and the nonfinancial objectives of, an SRI fund have been clearly disclosed to investors and the investors in purchasing shares or units in that fund have expressed their acceptance of those criteria and objectives, the contractual view states that such criteria and objectives must be given effect to, even where they conflict with the financial objectives of the fund. Extrapolating this, the investors should be able to require that the operator of an SRI fund prioritize the fund's nonfinancial objectives over its financial objectives and refrain from pursuing financial objectives at the expense of the nonfinancial objectives.

However, as Australian law now stands this is an open question. Balanced against the contractual view of the fiduciary investor's duties to the investors in an SRI fund are two principles of equity that an Australian court may well find compelling.

First, a fiduciary investor that is a trustee of an investment trust or the donee of an investment power cannot fetter the exercise of its investment powers (Thomas 1998) and must retain the flexibility accorded to it by the unmodified version of the prudent investor rule. This would prevent the operator of an SRI fund from entering into a contractual arrangement or adopting an inflexible investment policy that would be determinative of the future exercise of its investment powers and that would derogate from the flexibility conferred by the prudent investor rule.

Second, the investors in an SRI fund as the beneficiaries of the trust or the power cannot dictate to the operator of the SRI fund as to how that power should be exercised (Thomas 1998). The investors cannot interfere in the day-to-day management of the fund or more generally dictate the terms on which the operator is to exercise its powers; instead, their ability to involve themselves in the management of the fund is limited to right of such beneficiaries, under the well-known *Rule in Saunders v Vautier*, to requisition the dissolution of the fund and the distribution of its assets to the investors.

Accordingly, it would seem that, regardless of the socially oriented goals of an SRI fund that have been bargained for between the operator of that fund and the fund's investors, the operator, as a fiduciary investor, cannot sacrifice the achievement of optimum returns to the pursuit of the fund's socially oriented goals (Lord Nicholls of Birkenhead 1995).

This legal constraint would be of little practical consequence if it were the case that SRI funds could fulfill their socially oriented goals without sacrificing financial returns. The application of a contractually modified prudent investor rule would, in that event, be able to deliver the same financial returns to investors in SRI funds as they could have obtained had they instead invested in a socially neutral mutual fund with comparable financial return objectives. However, two recent empirical studies of Australian SRI funds have revealed that there may be a financial cost to the pursuit of socially oriented goals, thus raising doubts as to whether a fiduciary investor that prioritizes nonfinancial objectives can be said to have discharged its duty to invest prudently. Ali and Gold (2002) identified a material financial cost to excluding unethical securities from an Australian investment portfolio over the period 1994–2001. This is partially supported by Bauer, Otten, and Rad (2004), who found that Australian SRI funds significantly underperformed their socially neutral counterparts over the period 1992–1996 but that there was no discernible difference in performance from 1996 to 2003.

CONCLUSION

In Australia, the increased public scrutiny of corporate conduct and demands for companies to behave in a more socially responsible fashion have been accompanied by the rapid growth in the assets managed by SRI funds.

These SRI funds use two general screening techniques to select securities for their portfolios. Negative and positive screens are used to create an investable universe of securities from the pool of securities available to a conventional mutual fund with comparable financial return objectives, with securities being selected from that pool on the basis of disparate nonfinancial criteria. Alternatively, positive screens are employed to extend the investment objectives of an SRI fund beyond the derivation of financial returns to include nonfinancial objectives.

Australian law, however, has not kept pace with these developments. The prudent investor rule, while eminently suitable for conventional mutual funds, does not, in the form that it is currently recognized in Australia, fully accommodate the needs of SRI funds. Investors and operators of Australian SRI funds, despite having agreed on the use of nonfinancial criteria to select investments or the pursuit of socially oriented goals, may find that the law demands instead that they give primacy to optimizing financial returns.

Given the rapid growth of SRI funds in the Australian market and the fact that investor demand shows no sign of abating, there would seem to be good grounds for legislative intervention to clarify the duties of the operators of these funds. Reform is a feasible option. The Australian Securities and Investments Commission already requires all Australian mutual funds, including socially neutral funds, to disclose the extent to which nonfinancial, socially oriented criteria have been used in selecting investments.

CHAPTER 9

Issuers' Liability for Financial Information as an Instrument of Corporate Governance Enforcement

Clemens Völkl

INTRODUCTION

Corporate governance regulation and enforcement, disclosure requirements, and their enforcement on capital markets by corporate and tort law are often neglected in the European corporate governance debate. The role of investors is frequently ignored or underestimated. When analyzing the potential of investors and their role in corporate monitoring, the legal framework cannot be ignored. On the basis of this assessment specific alterations in tort law can be designed to empower investors, allowing them to become an efficient and cost-effective monitoring authority supplementing and relieving public monitoring regimes. However, a balanced litigation environment needs to be guaranteed between the parties.

The object of the international corporate governance debate is the improvement of the organization and governance standards of corporations in various ways and by various means. Still, the general focus lies rather with the ways than with the means. The means to improve governance standards are generally referred to as *enforcement*, while the ways to advance the standards can be referred to as *regulation-theories*. There have been a number of different approaches to corporate governance enforcement in continental Europe but it seems that these approaches have been rather unreflective and certainly lack a systematic classification. Simultaneously, the governance development has lost momentum as the debate has been fanned out toward an innumerable number of other topics, sometimes closely linked to the original notion of corporate governance (such as *corporate sustainability reporting*) and sometimes concerning completely different matters (such as *corporate social responsibility*).

The resulting delay naturally is beneficial for those eyeing the development of corporate governance with suspicion. In response the debate should be brought back to its original focus: Approaches to corporate governance enforcement originally aim at stakeholder protection (Hertig et al. 2004). The corporations' stakeholders are to be protected from directors' misconduct by making processes inside the corporation more transparent to persons outside and thus improving governance standards by elevating stakeholders to become a monitoring authority.

The underlying problem is known as the principal–agent conflict (Hansmann and Kraakman 2004; for a comparative analysis, see Barca and Becht 2001). The management only acts as the stakeholders' agent and the agent naturally possesses more knowledge about the company than his principal while working with the principal's assets (and not his own). An information asymmetry results from the agency-relationship between management and owner. The objective of good corporate governance is widely understood to be the improvement of this information gradient. This, it is generally accepted, can only be achieved by imposing reporting duties on the corporation's management (Fox 1998), thus leveling the playing-field between principal and agent.

From a legal point of view one crucial aspect apart from this information gradient has to be pointed out within the relationship between principal and agent—fiduciary duties: As the agent acts on his principal's behalf, he has to act in the shareholder's best interest and can be held liable for breach in this quasicontractual relation or can be forced to act in some way or another by shareholders. Generally it is undisputed that, where a party is placed in a position of trust, he or she will be expected to act in good faith and protect the interests of the other party. Such duties may arise in a number of circumstances, for example, where the very nature of the relationship implies trust, such as a solicitor/client or doctor/patient relationship, or where the relationship between the parties as a matter of fact has given rise to fiduciary obligations. Such relationships will include that of principal and agent partnerships, and companies and their promoters (for the case-law approach in company law see, for example, *Armstrong v. Jackson* [1917] 2 KB 822). The management's duties resulting out of this relationship can be widely extended to include investors' interests at large, as it lies in the shareholders' interest that management acts properly on the capital market.

Still, this way only actual shareholders are entitled to take legal steps;

duties directly enforceable by investors can arise out of *precontractual* information duties that the management directly has toward the market (for an analysis under Austrian law, see Völkl 2004). Both pre- and quasicontractual information duties establish a general duty of care (or in this context *fair reporting*) toward shareholders and investors (see Martin 2001) while also constituting the dogmatic base for concrete reporting duties under corporate or capital markets law. Most of the following remarks are based on the legal consequences arising from this special relationship between principal and agent.

REGULATION

The principal questions arising from this insight are how these duties are to be imposed on the management and how much disclosure is actually needed. There are two commonly quoted theories on how to solve the problem: Reporting duties can be imposed either by new legislation and/or state authorities (public regulation) or by the market itself (self-regulation; Merkt 2001). The discussion is often mixed with the issue of enforcing regulation, and indeed they are closely linked to each other. Still, they are not the same. The first problem concerns who is to impose the rules; the second deals with the question of who is to sanction a breach of the rules imposed.

European legislators have already answered the first question by imposing rules regarding publication duties for mandatory corporate information. There are countless national acts and proposals to this end (see Macey 1998; Haberer 2003) and the EU has passed its Prospectus (Directive 2003/71/EC [L 345/64]), Market Abuse (Directive 2003/06/EC [L 96/16]) and recently Transparency Directives (Directive 2004/109/EG). Generally this is a beneficial development (Hopt and Wymeersch 2003).

At the same time it is a rather one-sided solution: The trend in the European arena is following only those voices asking for the state to set standards and exercise control. This view neglects the dynamics of market forces completely. In an integrated financial market issuers need to publish information on their ventures in order to acquire capital (in this direction, see Macey 1998). It does not, as has been argued by those favoring the self-regulation approach, suffice to call for no regulation at all because of the capital markets' immune system. For certain types of information, market pressure can never be an adequate medium to entice issuers to disclose. It should therefore be noted that legal reporting duties should only be imposed for critical information and where issuers are not subject to market pressure and thus would not publish information at all were it not for such a reporting duty. In this context it would be advisable for European legislators to impose publication duties only where necessary because of a lack of market pressure.

The problems at present often enough do not lie with mandatory but with voluntary disclosure (see also Hopt 2001), published in response to market pressure. The EU directives on disclosure requirements, for instance, do not concern voluntary information at all. This leaves a crucial gap in many national legal systems as defaulted information is not covered by their framework often enough, and a general duty for corporations to provide a true and fair picture of their own situation is generally amiss. In consequence, the European legislator should provide for a general requirement to update or adjust information provided by issuers mandatorily or voluntarily when the information later turns out to be wrong. The issuer should be obliged to correct the information or at least withdraw it as soon as its falsity becomes or should have become apparent to him. This shortcoming of timely duties to adjust information specifically concerns reports on future prospects or assessments given by an issuer that might have been absolutely accurate at the time of their publication but later turn out to be wrong, such as strategic assessments, anticipated profits, and so on. Thereby issuers at present are often able to manipulate share value by freely choosing when to publish the appropriate updates, thereby abusing market confidence and often causing panic reactions in the market.

The explicit implementation of such a duty on a European level could, for example, be compared with the broad concept of misrepresentation under British contract law: Liability for misrepresentation will arise where the defendant has made a false statement of existing or past fact that is addressed to the claimant and on which the claimant has reasonably relied. Liability is confined, however, to false statements of fact. Mere silence or inactivity will not give rise to liability unless the claimant can identify a preexisting relationship in contract or tort with the defendant in which an obligation to disclose may arise. Regarding financial information, this relationship can be deduced from the agency-function of the management as pointed out above, establishing liability because of a breach of either pre- or quasi-contractual obligations.

This broad understanding of the concept of misrepresentation is also in accordance with English legal practice, which under certain circumstances will extend liability to a duty to communicate the change of circumstances and to adjust information previously stated that is now known to be incorrect (see *With v. O'Flanagan* [1936] Ch 575; *Edington v. Fitzmaurice* [1885] 29 Ch D 459). This concept is even stretched so far as to hold somebody liable for his or her opinion when they possess superior knowledge or skill and should therefore be aware of facts that reasonably justify the opinion if the statement turns out to be wrong. The backdrop of these duties is common to most European legal systems, comparable to the Austrian and German figure of *Redlicher Verkehr* for example; irreproducibly it is seldom put to use in the context of financial information. In essence, information given by an issuer of shares must not be of such a nature (from an investor's angle) as to create a misleading or even fraudulent picture of the issuer's state of affairs. This holds true for mandatory as well as voluntary information. Regulation in this text will therefore be understood as concerning both types of information.

An adjustment duty such as the one proposed in combination with mandatory reporting requirements would acknowledge and integrate market pressure, thereby balancing out parts of the agency relationship. However, disclosure requirements need to be enforced in order for them to be effective.

ENFORCEMENT

The application of market pressure theories has not only led to the self-regulation approach but also to the self-enforcement approach. As has been said, regulation and enforcement theories should not be mixed, as enforcement can only be the consequence either of regulation or voluntary publication of information. Comparable to the field of corporate governance regulation there are two major theories of enforcement as well: On the one hand there is (again) the public-enforcement side of the discussion arguing that there has to be a (public) monitoring authority competent to control the nature of companies' information policies and enforce publication duties by imposing sanctions of either penal or administrative law, mostly (petty) fines. On the other side stand the proponents of self-enforcement. As with regulation they argue that market forces would suffice to enforce publication duties as investors are likely to abstain from investments in a company or sell their shares of that company if it does not abide by reporting requirements, either not publishing at all, not promptly, or publishing false information.

Both theories possess their own virtues and both have a crucial deficiency: Both fail to realize the capabilities of investors in their own way. Public enforcement proponents underestimate investors and shareholders and overestimate public authorities. To solely entrust authorities with the monitoring and sanctioning of corporate misconduct overburdens them in a way that they cannot fulfill the objective set for them, and it also creates a situation similar to the one it is supposed to solve. This is because, as is the case with agent and principal, an entity is entrusted with the vital function of control and protection of assets of which it is not the owner.

The public enforcement approach also neglects another important aspect: One objective of most laws and regulations is to prevent damage or loss. Concerning information duties this is exceedingly the case as the timely publication of information can prevent investors from losses and builds trust in the capital market at large. Balancing loss is one of the most prominent principles of private law. The problem with theories of public enforcement is that they usually fail to include any notions of compensation, either rejecting them as nonessential or (wrongly) anticipating them to be drawn from general tort law (for Austria, see Völkl 2004).

The neglect of compensation considerations—and therefore the neglect of one of the principles of private law—not only applies to the public enforcement proponents, it also holds true for the theories of self-enforcement.

The fundamental idea of self-enforcement lies in the pressure of market forces. If corporations misbehave in the market their misbehavior will be sanctioned by investors. The only sanction needed in a self-enforced system is the prospect of financial disadvantages. This conclusion is based on an overestimation of investors' power: It leaves out first of all those cases where huge profits can be reaped through information-misconduct by individuals who naturally have no interest or fear of later sanctions by other market participants. And it also completely neglects the need for compensation and the existing possibilities for investors to receive compensation for their losses. Would the financial market function on the basis of market players' logic assumptions it would be in the issuers' own best interest to publish accurate, timely and sufficient information. Sadly, the fact is that the market does not work that way, insofar as proponents of self-enforcement critically overestimate investors' leverage and ability to enforce corporations' publication duties. Often they have called for the empowering of investors and abolishing of mandatory information. In reality, shareholders and investors are powerless in this respect, as the law (often) does not provide for the appropriate means to facilitate enforcement.

THE POWERLESS INVESTORS

The lack of regulations concerning investors' compensation for losses resulting from breaches of information duties is where the true deficits in the field of corporate governance and market transparency lie today. And indeed empowering investors in connection with the already existing regulatory framework of mandatory information can provide a key element in solving a large portion of the remaining problems in corporate governance: A functioning monitoring system can be created only if investors are integrated into it by enabling them to successfully sue a corporation.

This is also the most efficient and cost-effective monitoring system, as it lies in the investors' best interest to receive compensation for their losses. Another advantage of this approach is that the trust placed in the European capital market by international investors would be boosted because of the compensation they could reasonably expect in case of breaches of information duties.

In this context, compensation by way of tort works as a kind of insurance for investors as they can expect to balance their loss if it was inflicted upon them unlawfully, because they could not base their investment decisions on proper information. Thereby the long-standing claim for a higher level of investor protection and corporate transparency in the Euro-Zone could be met. Without empowering investors in this sense, corporate governance regulation remains toothless and incomplete in many ways, as it constitutes only imperatives but not consequences.

Therefore an important question to bring up for discussion should be how to empower investors. Empowering investors must not, as has been argued (for example, Romano 1998), be understood as taking away authority from legislators and institutions but as an attempt to integrate investors into the monitoring and sanctioning regime governing the disclosure of information.

With regard to compensation claims, this is where the real problems start: To successfully claim for damages under continental European tort law it is necessary for the claimant to provide evidence for the illegality, the default, the adequacy, and the causality of the defendant's breach of an information duty and the loss suffered because of this action (for a comparative summary, see Koziol and Steininger 2004). To prove illegality, default, and adequacy will not pose a greater challenge for the claimant than in any other area of tort law. The problems lie with causality and the size of the loss suffered (loss adjustment).

To prove the causality of an action or default for a consequence generally means to prove that without the action the consequence would not have occurred. The aggrieved investor needs to bring forward evidence that the corporation's violation of reporting requirements led to a decline in the market value of the shares if she owns shares or bought shares because of the violation. This can be achieved comparatively easily, as it can be assumed that faulty information of a certain persuasive character will most certainly influence the value of shares in either a negative way or—more likely—the publication of positive information has boosted the share price only to have it collapse after the correct information has been made public. The same goes for defaulted information when share prices collapse after publication at a later date and when investors did not buy shares because of the corporation's misconduct. In both cases it can reasonably—

meaning: to the standards of civil procedural law—be assumed that the violation causally influenced the share value (problems of reflexive loss and share value recovery cannot be addressed in this chapter in detail; see Kowalski 1990). The truly problematic part is for the investor to provide objective evidence for the violation's causal influence on her investment decision, meaning that there is no possible other cause for her to have taken this particular decision at this particular moment. This, of course, is nearly impossible for the investor to prove.

The second problem lies with the proof of the amount of loss causally generated by the violation of a reporting requirement. Accurately assessing the loss is simply impossible as the defendant's violation cannot be isolated. During the time between violation and claim, other factors play their part to influence the shares' value. Furthermore, it is completely unclear what the time span for this assessment should be.

Under Austrian and German law some of these problems can be bypassed by accurately interpreting the law and by making use of the entire instrument of facilitations of proof. However, the situation remains insecure and investors are deterred from taking legal action as the outcome of proceedings cannot be anticipated. Therefore, investors in their current situation cannot be counted on as a monitoring authority. This deficiency is not unknown to issuers of shares and their managers, either, which is not quite the ideal basis for the financial market.

EMPOWERING INVESTORS

Only the legislator can provide a solution to this dilemma, and the European Commission at least starts to become aware of the problem when it calls for the member states to "ensure that their laws, regulations and administrative provisions on liability apply to the issuers, the bodies referred to above [that is, administrative, management or supervisory bodies] or persons within the issuer" in its recent Transparency Directive (Art. 7 Directive 2004/109/EG). Moving the responsibility to national legislators is not a very commendable way, either. The important step to take would be to introduce the issues of enforcement into the discussion on a European level to find a solution, as national legislators are too much under the influence of either investors' or—mostly—corporations' interest groups. Likewise the Austrian and German legislators have been proposing an act explicitly governing directors' personal liability for false financial information just recently (§ 82a BörseG idF, GesRÄG 2005 in Austria and Kapitalmarktinformations-HaftungsG in Germany). Both the Austrian and the German draft had to be withdrawn due to industry pressure.

One possible solution to start a discussion with could be the implementation of a relief of evidence for the claimant in order to overcome his incapability of proof. This of course would have to be balanced against the issuers' interest in not being overcharged with claims by any person. One way to do this would be to give both sides the opportunity to furnish facts indicating their position with regard to the investment decision. The facts furnished by either side would not have to reach the degree of certainty demanded for evidence in general. It would rather lie with the judge or arbitrator and external experts involved in the trial to assess the relevance of the material brought forward. If the facts furnished by the claimant are considered to have most likely led to his investment decision, all other preconditions of the claim are met, and the defendant cannot provide material making his position seem more convincing than the claimant's, it can be consequently assumed that the defendant's violation has actually caused a loss. Therefore, the facts required from the claimant still need to meet a certain level of persuasiveness to convince the court.

In this state of the trial the only remaining duty for the investor would be to attempt to prove the accurate amount of the loss incurred. The advantage of this—under Austrian procedural law—is that the investor would already at this level of proceedings be freed of the risk of bearing the actions' costs, as he would have won a substantial part of the proceedings (*Stufenklage*). In consequence the claimant would then have to attempt to adjust the loss and the judge could then—with the help of experts—under Austrian and German procedural law estimate the loss. As long as the investor does not unreasonably overestimate the amount of loss to be compensated in the claim he will be awarded his costs of the proceedings by the court, as well. Otherwise, he has to pay for the costs proportionately. Thereby, the most crucial element hindering investors in becoming an effective monitoring authority for corporate governance standards and disclosure policies would be removed, as they no longer would have to bear the risk of an action's cost and as it would also be less likely for investors to lose an action. This fact would in itself constitute a deterrent for corporate misinformation as corporations and corporate directors would have to fear their behavior becoming the subject of such claims.

CREATING A BALANCED LITIGATION ENVIRONMENT

However, the competence of courts of law to decide upon claims of compensation and the use of reliefs of evidence—apart from lengthy proceedings—bears the risk of creating a litigation environment hostile either toward investors or toward issuers. At present, continental European legal systems tend to discriminate against investors, while the U.S. litigation environment is just as hostile toward issuers of shares. A litigation environment similar to that of the United States has to be avoided in all events. Therefore a solution has to be found balancing the interests of investors against the interests of issuers (the problem is also related to the definition of the circle of potential claimants in the area of information liability and questions of compensation of pure economic loss; see von Bar and Drobnig 2004; van Boom, Koziol, and Witting 2004).

One deficiency of the U.S. system is its failure to award the costs of litigation to the prevailing party. In consequence corporations, having to bear their own costs for legal advice, often prefer settlements to litigation. This environment is burdening companies with huge and unfair risks and makes the directors' and officers' positions increasingly uninsurable and hazardous (for attempts to resolve this situation in the United States, compare the recent Class Action Fairness Act of 2005).

The present continental European framework leads to the opposite result. By imposing systematic barriers for claimants to take legal action regarding causality and loss adjustment investors are completely powerless. In no other area of the law is it so prohibitively difficult for the aggrieved party to claim compensation as in capital markets law. This situation not only is unjustifiable but it also hinders the preventive aspect of tort law from coming into effect (for a comparative analysis of this aspect, see van Boom 2004). Due to this loophole, violations of capital markets law are in many regions of Europe still looked upon as a gentleman's crime or slight misdemeanor.

In essence, the two major global capital markets have chosen approaches on either end of the spectrum, both of which are inadequate. Creating a balanced litigation environment implies setting the standards of entry into proceedings high enough to deter claimants from simply trying their luck or even blackmailing corporations by taking legal action. The above proposed solution of a combination of relaxation of evidence requirements and the requirement to furnish accurate evidence with regard to loss adjustment features the merit that taking legal action does not automatically promise any financial success at all when the still-complicated proof of the size of the loss cannot be furnished by the claimant; therefore improper use of claims against issuers is limited. Of course, having proven the violation of a disclosure requirement, a limited danger remains for persons initially not interested in the capital market to see proceedings as a *minimum risk lottery*. Therefore an additional barrier of entry has to be introduced.

Compensation claims for violation of disclosure requirements belong to a high-risk field of litigation for both parties. German and Austrian Stock Corporation Acts have already responded to a similar situation:

When minority shareholders plan to take legal action against incorporators, other shareholders, directors, or members of the board according to §§ 122 and 123 of the Austrian Stock Corporation Act, the court is entitled to require them to provide adequate fiduciary securities for counterclaims of the defendant that arise out of the proceedings or have arisen against the claimant in the past.

Implementing a similar duty for claimants to provide security before they are entitled to take legal action against issuers because of violations of reporting requirements would reduce the risk of abuse of the simplified procedure of taking evidence vitally. Investors could only hope to get compensation in cases where the violation of a disclosure requirement is evident, their investment decision was comprehensibly influenced by the violation, and they can afford to provide adequate security for the defendant. This regime would benefit institutional investors most, although it is likely that small investors might bundle their interests to form litigation syndicates (comparable to U.S. class actions; for an analysis of the role of institutional investors in corporate governance enforcement, see Macey 1998). Focusing efforts on empowering institutional investors seems most relevant insofar as they possess adequate resources and consequently show the most promise to effectively act as a monitoring authority and a deterrent for corporations' financial information misconduct.

CONCLUSION

Incorporating adjustment duty and empowered investors into the legal framework governing the marketplace is likely to resolve major parts of the agency dilemma purely by its preventive character. Combined with a public control authority furnished with executive powers it should ensure a functioning corporate governance environment and result in a considerable step forward in advancing confidence in the European capital markets.

CHAPTER 10

Investing in Death/Speculating on Mortality: Some Thoughts on Life Insurance Securitization

Paul U. Ali

INTRODUCTION

The extension of the corporate governance debate that has traditionally been concerned with the internal management of corporations to normative issues such as whether a corporation's business practices are environmentally sound or sustainable and whether the very business in which a corporation is involved is of an ethical character, also raises the question of whether similar constraints are relevant to financial innovation. Institutional investors have, in recent years, found that their suppliers of capital—the contributors to pension funds and the investors in mutual funds—have increasingly begun to demand that a consideration of these normative issues be incorporated into the investment selection process. This trend has been directly manifested in the rapidly growing number of pension funds, mutual funds, and other collective investment vehicles that are now being marketed as explicitly taking into account the environmental, labor, and even gender/racial diversity and human rights practices of the corporations they invest in.

The focus of this ethically or socially responsible investment has to date been primarily or even exclusively upon the issuers of the securities as opposed to the securities themselves. What industrial or business sectors does the issuer derive its revenues from? What is the environmental impact of

Note: This research was supported by a grant from the Australian Research Council (DP0557673).

the issuer's business activities? How does the issuer treat its employees? Does the issuer have in place affirmative action policies? How well represented are female employees and employees from racial minorities in the upper echelons of the issuer's management? Does the issuer take into account the needs of the broader community in which it operates? Is the issuer a responsible corporate citizen? And so on.

The collapse of Enron and the resultant disclosure of its extensive use of special-purpose vehicles brought the term *securitization* into the public lexicon, a term that previously was largely unfamiliar to persons outside the corporate and banking sectors. The opprobrium with which that term has been greeted, although largely misconceived (at least from the perspective of prudential financial and risk management), has nonetheless served to highlight a more fundamental issue. Are there any ethical constraints on the progress of securitization?

This is of considerable significance to institutional investors on two counts. First, institutional investors are the largest investors in the securities that are issued in securitization transactions and as such are the *natural consumers* of securitizations. Second, securitization is routinely used by corporations and commercial banks to raise funds, manage their balance sheets and capital requirements and layoff risks, and is a major source of fee revenue for the investment banks involved in designing and executing securitizations. Institutional investors are, again, typically the largest investors in publicly listed corporations and banks.

Although the vast majority of securitization transactions worldwide are concerned with the repackaging of the cash flows from conventional or plain-vanilla financial assets (for instance, residential mortgages, commercial mortgages, auto loans, credit card receivables, student loans, and corporate loans), the broad range of transactions that have been closed successfully to date suggests that virtually any financial asset is capable of being securitized. Some of the more novel financial assets that have been securitized include aircraft, champagne, designer clothes, diamonds, films, hedge funds, life insurance policies, music CDs, perfumes, ships, sports stadiums, and wine (de Vries Robbé and Ali 2005).

In the above list, one type of transaction deserves further scrutiny in terms of the potential ethical constraints on securitization, namely the securitization of life insurance policies.

LIFE INSURANCE SECURITIZATION

Securitization has typically been used by life insurance companies to release the profits embedded in a block of life insurance business (open block securitization), or to raise funds to meet the reserve requirements for a specified block of life insurance business that is being run off (closed block securitization), or to meet regulatory capital requirements generally (IAIS 2003; Cowley and Cummins 2005). Open block securitizations, which are the most common form of this emerging class of securitization transactions, are structurally similar to conventional securitizations in that the profits generated over the term of the life insurance policies in the securitized block of business are used to service principal and interest payments on the securities issued to investors (Ali and de Vries Robbé 2003). In this manner, the life insurance company is able to release up front the present value of the profits expected to be achieved on those policies, thus raising capital that can be used to write new business or boost its reserve requirements.

However, what all of these securitizations have in common is that there is no transfer or *true sale* of the underlying life insurance policies, as is the case in a conventional securitization of financial assets; instead, it is the cash flows received from the assumption of liability by the life insurance company under those policies that are securitized, either wholly or in part. It is not the life insurance company, but the policyholders (the persons who, under life insurance policies, have agreed to pay premiums to the life insurance company against the termination or survival of the insured life) who own the policies issued by the life insurance company.

Now, a new category of transactions has emerged in which the benefit of life insurance policies (as opposed to the surplus derived from the assumption of liability under such policies) has been securitized, with mortality risk being explicitly transferred to institutional investors and other investors in the capital markets. These transactions, in contrast to those described above that have been undertaken by life insurance companies, involve the raising of funds via securitization to acquire life insurance policies from policyholders generally (life settlement securitization) or policyholders who are terminally ill (viatical settlement securitization) (Ali and de Vries Robbé 2003; Lin and Cox 2005).

In both life settlement and viatical settlement securitizations, a special-purpose vehicle is established to issue debt securities to investors, with the proceeds of issuance being used to purchase individual life insurance policies. The additional amounts required to maintain those policies can be sourced from the investors either up front (as part of the subscription amount for the securities) or periodically; this is necessary to ensure that the purchased policies remain in force and, accordingly, the life insurance company remains obligated to pay to the special-purpose vehicle, as the holder of the policies, the contracted amount on the occurrence of the insured event, such as the death of the person insured (usually, the original policyholder). The return to the investors is derived from the positive difference between the cost of acquiring and maintaining the life insurance policies and the monetary benefits received on the occurrence of the insured event.

ETHICAL CONCERNS

The chief ethical objection to life insurance securitization is that the investors are speculating on mortality, on the death of the insured person or the insured person surviving to a specified age, depending on the type of policy that has been securitized. The most common types of life insurance policies are *whole of life* policies (which pay out on the death of the insured), *term life* policies (which insure against dying during a specified period), and *endowment* policies (which pay out on the death of the insured or on the insured reaching a specified age). The return to the investors will, consequently, be impacted by the timing of the death of the persons insured in respect of the securitized life insurance policies. All things being equal, the early death of the insured persons should contribute positively to the returns enjoyed by the investors.

Other ethical concerns for investors relate to whether a fair price has been paid to the policyholder (profiteering is a particular concern where the policyholder is terminally ill and is in need of cash for medical treatment) and whether the policyholder has freely consented to the sale (the need for cash, particularly in the emotionally charged situation of being diagnosed with a terminal illness, may operate as a vitiating factor) (Crites-Leoni and Chen 1997; Albert 1999; Badreshia et al. 2002). On the other hand, the availability of a secondary market in life insurance policies may considerably benefit policyholders, in particular as the secondary purchasers of policies often purchase policies for a price higher than that at which the life insurance company that has issued the policies is prepared to buy them back (Doherty and Singer, 2003). While a further consideration of these matters is outside the scope of this chapter, it should be noted that some jurisdictions (for example, Ontario) have responded by prohibiting sales of life insurance policies while others (for example, New York) have responded by regulating such sales by restricting the purchase of life insurance policies to licensed parties, imposing disclosure requirements, and regulating advertising for the purchase of policies (Perez 2002).

INSURABLE INTERESTS

As a matter of law, however, the chief obstacle—the requirement for an *insurable interest* in the life being insured—to the securitization of life insurance policies has, in jurisdictions such as Australia, been abolished. In fact, not only is it now possible for special-purpose vehicles to raise funds to buy life insurance policies, they can even, in principle, use those funds to establish new life insurance policies.

The validity of contracts of life insurance has traditionally been dependent on the person entering into such a contract with an insurer—and thus, on the payment of the insurance premiums, being entitled to receive a payment on the occurrence of the insured event (typically, the termination of the life being insured)—having an insurable interest in the life being insured (Swisher 2005).

This was designed specifically to differentiate contracts of life insurance (so that they would continue to enjoy enforceability) from contracts of gaming or wagering (which were, in general, unenforceable as a matter of public policy) and, by so doing, address the public policy concerns with persons speculating on the life (or, more precisely, the time of death) of third parties with whom they had no familial connection, an activity that was rife in the main center of life insurance, London, in the seventeenth and eighteenth centuries (Clark 1999). The requirement of an insurable interest was also designed to address the issue of moral hazard, where a person having no familial connection with the insured person or not at risk of suffering financially on the death of the insured person might seek to benefit financially by bringing about the occurrence of the insured event, namely by murdering the insured person.

In Australia, this requirement was abandoned in 1995. While the requirement did serve the purpose of differentiating life insurance policies from gambling (in that a person had to have some interest in the contract beyond the money that might be lost in entering into and maintaining the policy or gained from the occurrence of the events satisfying the conditions for a payout under the policy), it did not fully resolve the issue of moral hazard (ALRC 1982, 145–146). Murderers often are persons who have a familial relationship, or are in a domestic relationship, with their victims.

Accordingly, the validity of contracts of life insurance, under Australian law, is no longer dependent upon the policyholder having an insurable interest in the subject matter of the contract, namely the life of the insured (Insurance Contracts Act 1984, Commonwealth of Australia, § 18). Nor, in contrast to contracts of general insurance, is it necessary under Australian law for the policyholder to have a pecuniary or economic interest in the subject matter of the contract. This is in marked contrast to the position that prevailed in Australia under the predecessor of the current life insurance act, the Life Insurance Act 1945 (Commonwealth of Australia).

The 1945 Act (§ 86(1)) recognized the following interests as satisfying the requirement for an insurable interest in the life of an insured:

- The interest of a parent in the life of his or her child while that child is a minor.
- The interest of a spouse in the life of his or her spouse.
- The interest of a person in the life of a person on whom the former is financially dependent for support or education.
- The interest of a corporation in the life of an officer or employee.
- The pecuniary interest of a person in the life of another person. (That is, the policyholder must be able to establish that he or she would suffer financially as a result of the death of the insured person.)

The requirement for an insurable interest was dispensed with by the Insurance Contracts Act 1984. This was effected by the Life Insurance (Consequential Amendments and Repeals) Act 1995 (Commonwealth of Australia). Curiously, while the Australian Federal Parliament adopted the Australian Law Reform Commission's recommendations in relation to the modification of the requirement for an insurable interest in relation to contracts of nonmarine, general insurance, it subsequently departed, in 1995, from the Commission's recommendation that the corresponding requirement be retained in relation to contracts of life insurance. The current life insurance act, the Life Insurance Act 1995 (Commonwealth of Australia), the successor to the 1945 Act, makes no mention of insurable interests. Under the latter act, a contract of life insurance is defined, in general, simply as a contract that provides for the payment of money by reference to the mortality or disability of the insured.

Anonymous Investors

One argument that has been advanced in support of this change is that the consent of the person insured should be an adequate substitute for the requirement for an insurable interest. It has been contended that the moral hazard created by a person insuring the life of another is capable of being resolved by the participation of the latter in the life insurance policy, through the giving of consent to formation of the policy: "If a person has consented to the taking out of insurance on his life by a third party, he is at

least put on notice that a motive for murder has been created . . . a requirement of consent would bring to the attention of the life insured the economic interest of the policyholder in the life insured's death" (ALRC 1982,
139 and 140). While neither the Life Insurance Act 1995 nor the Insurance
Contracts Act 1984 explicitly requires the insured person to give his or her
consent to a third party taking out insurance on that person's life, the consensual participation of the insured person (through the provision of personal details to the life insurance company and the undertaking of a
medical examination for the purposes of obtaining the insurance cover)
will nonetheless be necessary.

This presupposes, in terms of the consent of the insured being obtained, that the policyholder—and thus, the party with an economic interest in the mortality of the insured—is known to the insured. This
comfortable premise is entirely absent in a life insurance securitization
where the economic interest in the life of the insured constituted by the life
insurance policy has been divided up and distributed among a group of investors who, in turn, are free to sell or subdivide further their fractional
economic interests. Here, the ownership and economic benefit of the life
insurance policy have been segregated, and the investors who collectively
hold the economic benefit are anonymous to the insured.

The converse may, however, not be the case; depending upon the level
of disclosure and the type of life insurance policy, the investors may have
sufficient information to ascertain the likely identity of the insured. The
risk of identification should be minimal for a typical securitization of life
insurance policies. The investors will typically receive only portfolio-level
information about the entire pool of securitized policies (for example, the
proportion of males and females insured, the average age and distribution
of ages of the insured persons, the average level and distribution of cover,
and a generalized breakdown of the different types of policies). However,
the risk of identification is much greater where only a single policy or a
small number of select high-value policies is being securitized.

Assignment of Life Insurance Policies

A second argument that has been advanced for doing away with insurable
interest is that its abolition would correct a legal anomaly. The policyholder
was required by the Life Insurance Act 1945 to have an insurable interest in
the life of the insured only at the inception of the life insurance policy but
there was no substantive restriction (putting aside the formalities for transfer) under that Act on a person not having such an interest later acquiring
the policy from the initial policyholder. Equally, under the 1995 Act, a policyholder may freely transfer a policy to a third party, provided that the

transfer complies with certain formalities stipulated by that Act (§ 200). Apart from these formalities, there is no bar on the purchase of life insurance policies for the purpose of securitization or otherwise.

Accordingly, while a person could not, as a general rule, enter into a contract to insure the life of a person with whom he or she had no familial or pecuniary relationship, there was nothing to stop the former from later acquiring the benefit of that contract (ALRC 1982, 145).

The decision not to require an insurable interest for the term of the life insurance policy or even at the time of the occurrence of the event triggering payment under the life insurance policy (the death of the insured person or the insured person reaching a certain age) seems to have been motivated by two factors (ALRC 1982, 144).

The first is that a policyholder, despite satisfying the requirement for an insurable interest when entering into a contract of life insurance, might later lose that interest due to a change in the relationship between the policyholder and the insured person (a divorce, for instance, would extinguish the insurable interest of a spouse in the life of his or her spouse).

The second factor concerns the use of life insurance policies to raise funds; the willingness of a lender to advance funds on the security of a life insurance policy depends on the lender being able to assume for itself the benefit of the policy, on the policyholder's default or insolvency. This would be jeopardized by limiting recoveries under life insurance policies to only those persons with an insurable interest in the life of the insured.

It is not clear that the anomaly identified is of itself a sufficient basis to dispense with the requirement for an insurable interest entirely. The retention of this requirement would not affect those persons whose insurable interest was subsequently eliminated by their change in status. Nor would creditors be affected if the original policyholder had an insurable interest in the life of the insured on the inception of the contract. In any case, a creditor that advances funds to an individual has an insurable interest, on the basis of the creditor's pecuniary interest in the continued life of that person. Moreover, as the Australian Law Reform Commission pointed out, retention of the requirement would "avoid an increase in the risk of hoped-for-gain from a life policy forming the motive for murder" (ALRC 1982, 145).

CONCLUSION

The securitization of life insurance policies is both a logical consequence and a facilitator of the secondary market in policies that exists in Australia and other jurisdictions. Both the sale and securitization of life insurance policies raise serious ethical questions and, in the case of the latter, whether there should be any ethical constraints on financial innovation. These matters are—or, arguably, should be—of interest to institutional investors, which are among the largest investors in securitization transactions generally as well as being the largest investors in the other participants in securitization transactions.

One could argue that there is no material difference between investing in a life insurance company and investing in securitized life insurance policies. Life insurance companies generate returns through their assumption of liability under the life insurance policies issued by them. In a securitization of life insurance policies, the returns to investors are derived from the amounts paid out under those policies. An investment in securitized life insurance policies, in common with an investment in life insurance companies, entails an assumption of mortality risk in respect of the insured persons.

Nonetheless, those institutional investors whose mandates require them to invest only in ethically or socially responsible issuers or take into account ethical issues when selecting securities, may wish to pay attention to the issues that arise in the securitization of life insurance policies. This not only relates to the circumstances in which the policies have been acquired but also involves a consideration of a key difference between life insurance companies (which assume liability under life insurance policies) and the special-purpose vehicles in a life insurance securitization (which hold the benefit of life insurance policies): In the case of the latter, but not the former, the earlier-than-expected deaths of the insured persons are likely to impact positively on the returns to the investors. This is precisely why the persons entitled to payment under life insurance policies have traditionally been required to hold an insurable interest in the life being insured, a requirement that has now been abandoned in Australia.

Share Ownership and Shareholder Control Rights

Ownership Structure Metrics

Stefan Prigge and Sven Kehren

INTRODUCTION

Blair (2001, 2797) defines corporate governance as follows: "The term 'corporate governance' refers to the legal rules, institutional arrangements, and practices that determine who controls business corporations, and who gets the benefits that flow from them. Corporate governance issues include how major policy decisions are made in business corporations, how various stakeholders can influence the process, who is held accountable for performance, and what performance standards are applied." In a nutshell: Power and influence are crucial aspects in corporate governance.

Shareholders belong to the most important stakeholders. Accordingly, ownership structure analysis is one of the major fields in corporate governance research. Ownership structure metrics is an important area of ownership structure analysis. It is the task of ownership structure metrics to describe the balance of power among shareholders. Power and influence among shareholders have to be transformed into figures. Operationalizing power and influence of shareholders is a precondition to conducting more advanced studies in ownership structure analysis such as a regression of corporate performance on the ownership structure. There, the ownership structure variables should be numerical representatives of the shareholder power structure.

Ownership structure is multidimensional. It has a horizontal and a vertical dimension. Direct shareholders are a good starting point to demonstrate this. We start our investigation with the following shareholder structure. See Figure 11.1.

Shareholders A, B, C, and D hold larger direct blocs, the size of which is not important for this introductory example. The remaining shares are widely held. Figure 11.1 displays the horizontal shareholder structure on

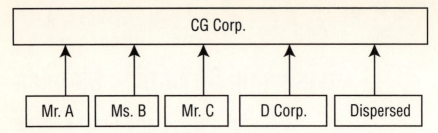

FIGURE 11.1   Direct Shareholders of the CG Corp.

the first, that is, the direct level. A, B, and C are natural persons. Thus, they are also ultimate shareholders. With respect to the dispersed shares we have no further information. But shareholder structure analysis should not end here for the D Corp. A closer look reveals the following. See Figure 11.2.

D Corp. is a good case in point to introduce the vertical dimension of the ownership structure. D Corp. is a legal entity. Beneath D Corp. there is a chain of shareholders, which has to be considered. D Corp. has three shareholders, among which F Corp. holds a majority of 60% and is thus able to determine the business policy of D Corp. When we continue our analysis with the F Corp. we discover two shareholders. Since both Mr. H

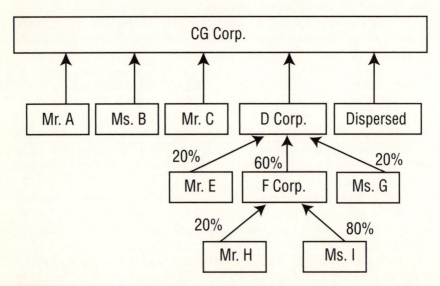

FIGURE 11.2   Complete Voting Rights Structure of the CG Corp.

and Ms. I are natural persons, we have found the end of this chain of shareholders. Ms. I holds a bloc of 80% in F Corp. She controls F Corp.; as a consequence, she indirectly controls D Corp. and is thus by means of this chain an ultimate shareholder of CG Corp. This simple example only serves to present a first demonstration of shareholder chain analysis. To be sure, real-life cases usually are more complex than this one where we have a majority shareholder on each level. We will come back to this issue in the subsection on vertical ownership structure metrics.

Our analysis enables us to depict the ultimate shareholder structure of CG Corp. See Figure 11.3.

The purpose of the introductory example was to provide a first impression of this chapter's topic: The shareholder structure is the subject of ownership structure metrics. It is multidimensional. Of the horizontal levels two are of major interest: the first level of direct shareholders and the final level with ultimate shareholders. First and ultimate level may be the same, as was the case for shareholders A, B, and C in the example. But there could be a chain of shareholders between first and ultimate level as well. The analyses of a shareholder chain and of a horizontal stage have to answer the same question: What are the power structures at that particular chain link and on this specific horizontal level respectively like? It is the task of ownership structure metrics to transform a shareholder structure like that in the example into figures that represent the power structure among the shareholders.

The remainder of this chapter consists of two parts. In the section on horizontal ownership structure metrics, we first substantiate the requirements the transformation of the shareholder structure into numbers should achieve. Then we present and recognize the concepts that can be found in the literature. Early empirical studies relied mainly on the formation of categories. Contemporary research rests on the largest voting rights bloc. We pay a great deal of attention to the comparatively new instrument of power

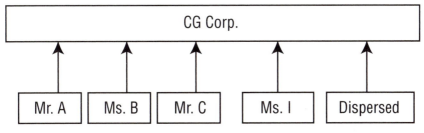

FIGURE 11.3 Ultimate Shareholders of the CG Corp.

indices. The second section of this chapter on vertical ownership structure metrics can be shorter because the problems and solutions in this area resemble very much those on the horizontal level.

HORIZONTAL OWNERSHIP STRUCTURE METRICS

The Problem

In the context of the stock corporation, Leech and Manjón (2003, 848) define power as "the a priori capacity of a large shareholder to influence a vote in a hypothetical company meeting." Instead of power, the notion of control can be found quite often in the context of shareholder structure analysis. Leech and Leahy (1991, 1418) define control as "the power to exercise discretion over major decision making, including specifically the choice of directors." Usually, this requires 50% of the votes. There may be agenda points in the general meeting of a stock corporation that require a larger majority, but we ignore them here. The majority threshold of 50% is by far the most important one.

If the principal shareholder, that is the largest shareholder, holds more than 50% of the votes, ownership structure metrics is a trivial task. The majority shareholder controls the corporation; his regency cannot be terminated against his will.

But what is the control situation like, if the principal shareholder owns less than 50% of the votes? Assume, for instance, the principal owner holds 30% of the votes and the second largest shareholder 25%. In this case, the principal owner cannot take the continuity of his control as granted, because the second largest shareholder may form a coalition with other bloc holders or he may purchase additional shares with voting rights at the stock exchange to take over the dominating position in the corporation. The situation is completely different, if there is only one bloc holder in the corporation disposing of 30% of the votes and the remaining shares being widely held. In this case, the principal owner will take up a position of power that is similar to but somewhat weaker than that of a majority owner because the small shareholders would behave rationally passive. This suggests that the power of the principal shareholder is not so much a question of the pure size of his voting bloc but of the contestability of his leading position (see the model by Bloch and Hege (2001) on this issue). The contestability is determined by the absolute and relative voting shares of the bloc holders, the free float, and the majority rule. Methods of ownership structure metrics should consider all of these factors as much as possible.

Former and Current Measures

"Most of the earlier empirical studies differentiate between owner-controlled firms and management-controlled firms, based on a percentage ownership criteria" (Short 1994, 207). This kind of classification goes back to the influential study of Berle and Means from 1932. Berle and Means read press articles and collected information from capital market insiders to investigate a corporation's control situation. They concluded that a share of voting rights of 20% is sufficient to supply a shareholder with the dominating position. In those corporations where there was no voting bloc of at least 20%, Berle and Means inferred that the employed managers controlled the corporation (Leech 2002b, 8). Although Berle and Means (1939, 70) actually differentiated between five control categories, it became a custom in empirical research to distinguish only two categories of stock corporations: owner-controlled versus managerially controlled (surveys in table form of these studies can be found in Cubbin and Leech (1983, 352) and Short (1994, 208–215). The classification is mainly based on the share of votes at the disposition of the principal shareholder. If the share of votes of the principal shareholder exceeds a certain threshold, he is deemed to be a dominating principal shareholder and, accordingly, the corporation is owner-controlled, unless the dominant shareholder is also a manager of that corporation. The cutoff points vary from 10% to 50%.

This dichotomy is simple, even trivial, if the principal shareholder owns more than 50% of the votes. This procedure becomes problematic if the principal owner disposes of 50% or less of the voting rights. But it is particularly critical that the remaining shareholder structure is completely ignored. As already noted in the introductory example, the power of the principal shareholder is determined not only by his share of votes, but also by the absolute and relative shares of votes held by the remaining bloc holders, the free float, and the majority rule. Assigning a certain constant cutoff point is to a certain degree arbitrary. Choosing a high threshold close to 50% raises the possibility that the principal shareholder actually does have a dominating position, but increasing the threshold makes it less probable to identify dominating minority principal shareholders correctly. Instead, these corporations are wrongly deemed to be managerially controlled. Two types of mistakes can be made in the classification of dominating and nondominating shareholders:

- Assigning a dominating position to a principal shareholder who does not have a dominating position (type I error)
- Not assigning a dominating position to a principal shareholder who actually does have a dominating position (type II error)

A discrete variable, which can only have the values of an owner- or managerially dominated corporation, can be easily overstrained with the description of shareholder structures, which are more complex due to the absence of a majority owner.

One option to improve this kind of measure is to take into account the remaining shareholder structure in the classification rules. For instance, Elston and Goldberg (2003, 1401) consider a corporation to be dominated by a certain type of shareholder if this shareholder owns more than 50% of the votes or if he controls at least 25% of the voting rights and no other shareholder owns more than 25% of the votes.

More recent studies mainly do not use the dichotomy of owner- and managerially controlled corporations. Instead they employ the direct share of votes (first level) of the principal shareholder as a measure of his power. The main weakness of the discrete classification scheme, that it ignores the consequences of the remaining shareholder structure for the position of the principal shareholder, is not solved by the continuous variable, either. Moreover, this measure assumes a linear relationship between the share of votes and the influence of the principal shareholder. This is not convincing. There are good reasons to doubt that the increase of the principal owner's share of votes from, say, 48% to 52% exerts the same effect on his influence in the corporation as an increase from 90% to 94% (or from 90% to 97.5%, if a comparison of two increases by 8.33% is preferred to two increases by 4 percentage points). In this respect even a step backward compared with the categories has to be stated. Categories allow for the possibility to assign a particular importance to certain bloc sizes by using them as thresholds for the categories. Contrary to that, the size of the largest voting bloc neglects the majority rule and the remaining shareholder structure.

In some corporate governance studies other measures of concentration such as the cumulated shares of votes of all bloc holders or the Herfindahl index can be found. The Herfindahl index is the sum of the squared voting rights blocs. If there are two voting rights blocs known for a corporation, which have a size of 30% and 15% respectively, this yields a Herfindahl index of $0.3^2 + 0.15^2 = 0.225$. The value of the index ranges from zero to one; a higher value indicates a more concentrated ownership structure. The Herfindahl index includes the complete shareholder structure.

At the root of these concentration variables is the idea to measure that part of the shareholders that most probably do not suffer from rational passivity and from which therefore some monitoring activities of the management can be expected. The cumulated shares of votes of all bloc holders includes a larger fraction of the shareholder structure than the voting bloc of the principal shareholder, but, depending on the shareholder structure, a significant sector of the shareholder structure might still be ignored, leading to the difficulties described above. The Herfindahl index does even include the complete shareholder structure. But both concentration measures implicitly assume that all bloc holders share identical goals and are willing to form coalitions. Moreover, different constellations of the power structure are not considered. Again, there is no distinction whether a majority owner exists or not. And the majority rule does not play a role, either.

Since the currently used measures are unsatisfactory, two power measures, developed in game theory, the Banzhaf index and the Shapley-Shubik index, meet with increasing attention in corporate governance research. Both power indices account for the complete shareholder structure and the majority rule, and they supply a continuous variable. These features make them quite attractive for corporate governance research.

Emerging Measures: Power Indices

Generally, a power index measures the relative power of each player in a decision-making process. (The terms *player* and *game* reflect the origins of power indices in game theory. In the context of ownership structure metrics, the shareholders are the players and the ballot in the general meeting is the game.) It is based on the extent a certain player contributes to the success of a coalition, that is, his ability to change a winning coalition into a losing coalition by leaving it and turn a losing coalition into a winning coalition by joining it. Each player's a priori voting strength is measured in view of a given distribution of the votes and a given majority rule. Several power indices have been developed for this purpose. The most familiar ones are the Shapley-Shubik index (Shapley 1953; Shapley and Shubik 1954) and the Banzhaf index (Banzhaf 1965).

The Shapley-Shubik Index   We start with a theoretical explanation how to calculate the Shapley value and turn then to a less technical example. Point of departure for the Shapley-Shubik index is the following situation: Coalitions C and the values of coalitions $v(C)$ are being examined. Coalitions consist of several players. Each player receives the increase in the coalition value caused by his entry. For example, if player i leaves coalition C and causes a drop in coalition value from $v(C)$ to $v(C - \{i\})$, this yields a value of player i of $[v(C) - v(C - \{i\})]$. This value is incorporated into the Shapley value of player i.

To simplify the calculation of the Shapley value, a simple game may be assumed. In a simple game a value of one is ascribed to the winning coalition and a value of zero to the losing coalition. If player i is the crucial player, that is, the so-called pivotal player for the success of a coalition, then the coalition value of $[v(C) - v(C - \{i\})] = 1$ is ascribed to him. If player i is not the pivotal player for the coalition under investigation, then the coalition value is zero.

The assumption about the distribution of the coalition value stems from the idea that the players join a coalition one after another and that each sequence of joining has the same probability. Therefore, the set of players N is ordered; for example, for the set of players N = (A, B, C, D, E, F) there is a sequence of joining r = (A, B, F, C, D, E). If, for instance, coalition C = (A, B, F) is a winning coalition and the coalition without player F K − {F} = (A, B) is a losing coalition, then player F is the pivotal player and the marginal coalition return is ascribed to him. Thus, in the simple game, he receives the value of one.

The crucial question then is how often player i is at the pivotal position k in the sequence. Since there are n! permutations with that set of players, the probability of a certain sequence of joining equals 1/n! (if n = 6, then n! = 1 * 2 * 3 * 4 * 5 * 6= 720). If we consider all permutations of the set of players N (for example, the six players A, B, C, D, E, F), then the probability that player i (for example, player F) can be found at position k in the sequence (for example, position 3) is equal to $(k - 1)!(n - k)!/n!$ (in this case 2!3!/6! = 1/60). The term $(k - 1)!$ indicates the number of permutations, in which player i is the pivotal player of a winning coalition because he can be found at position k, which is in our example the crucial position in the sequence. Besides, there are $(n - k)!$ permutations, which differ from the joining sequence r with respect to the order of the n − k players following player i, but which share with sequence r the order of the first k players, that is, from player 1 to player i.

In order to calculate the Shapley value of each player i the products of marginal coalition gain $[v(C) - v(C - \{i\})]$ and the probability $(k - 1)!(n - k)!/n!$ that player i receives that gain are added up. But player i can be a pivotal player for other coalitions as well. For this reason, all coalitions for which player i is the pivotal player have to be added up (see Holler and Illing 2000, 299–305).

The Shapley value of player i can be calculated with the following equation:

$$SV_i = \sum_{K \ni i, K \subset N} \frac{(k-1)!\,(n-k)!}{n!} [v(C) - v(C - \{i\})]$$

The Shapley value falls into a range between zero and one. The higher the value the larger the a priori decision-making power of the shareholder.

Example 11.1 demonstrates the calculation of the Shapley value in a less abstract manner.

The Banzhaf Index   Contrary to the Shapley-Shubik index, the Banzhaf index is based on coalitions but not on permutations. In calculating the a priori decision-making power it ignores the order players join a coalition. Instead, it rests upon the size of a player's contribution to the success of a coalition. Thus, there can be several critical members in a winning coalition whose exit would turn the coalition into a losing coalition, that is, whose withdrawal would cause a swing. The frequency of the pivotal position, which was crucial for the Shapley value, is replaced by the frequency of the swing. As a measure of power in a weighted voting game, the normalized Banzhaf index relates the number of potential swings ascribed to player i to the total amount of swings of all players. The swings of all coalitions C in the power set P (N) enter the Banzhaf index with equal weights. This has the implication that all possible coalitions are assumed equally probable. The normalized Banzhaf value of player i is calculated as follows:

$$BV_i = \frac{\text{Number of swings of player i for all } C \in P(N)}{\text{Number of swings of all players i for all } C \in P(N)}$$

for all i ∈ N.

Example 11.1   The Shapley-Shubik Index

We assume that the votes of players A, B, and C amount to 50, 49, and 1 respectively. A simple majority, that is, 51 votes, is needed to get a resolution passed. Player B is the pivotal player in the permutation ABC, player C in the permutation ACB, and player A in the remaining permutations. Accordingly, the Shapley values are equal to 4/6 for A, 1/6 for B, and 1/6 for C. Note, that according to the Shapley value, player B is not more powerful than player C even though he can dispose of 49 times more votes than C.

| | | Player | |
Permutations	A	B	C
(A,B,C)	—	1	—
(A,C,B)	—	—	1
(B,A,C)	1	—	—
(B,C,A)	1	—	—
(C,A,B)	1	—	—
(C,B,A)	1	—	—
Number of pivots	**4**	**1**	**1**
Shapley value	0.67	0.17	0.17
Share of votes	0.50	0.49	0.01

The Banzhaf value falls into the range between zero and one as well. Again, a higher value indicates a larger a priori decision-making power of a shareholder. Next, in Example 11.2 we calculate the Banzhaf values for Example 11.1.

Obviously, Banzhaf and Shapley values may differ strongly from shares in votes. But the values of both power indices differ as well, which is often the case. See Table 11.1.

Coalitions between Shareholders   A major critique relates to the fact that both Shapley-Shubik index and Banzhaf index assume all possible permutations or coalitions equally probable, but that this assumption may not hold in reality. In contrast, Riker (1962) suggests that a winning coalition will emerge for which the surplus of the total member votes over the majority rule is minimized. Bennedsen and Wolfenzon (2000) come to the same result. But there are other approaches as well: Leiserson (1968) favors coalitions with the number of members as small as possible, that is, coalitions of members with larger voting weights. Preferences for coalitions exist in politics, which impairs the applicability of these power measures in that field. In corporate governance, some authors assume intrashareholder type preferences for a coalition, for example, Crespi-Cladera and Renneboog (2003, 8): "The reason why a coalition between shareholders of one particular type may be easier to forge, results from similarities in private benefits of control within shareholder classes." But these considera-

Example 11.2   The Banzhaf Index

As in Example 11.1 we assume that the votes of players A, B, and C amount to 50, 49, and 1 respectively and that there is still a simple majority rule. In this case, C_4, C_5, and C_N are winning coalitions. There are five swings overall. Three of them can be ascribed to player A, one to B, and one to C. The resulting Banzhaf values are 3/5 for A, 1/5 for B, and 1/5 for C.

Player	—	C_1	C_2	C_3	C_4	C_5	C_6	C_N
A	0	1	0	0	*1*	*1*	0	*1*
B	0	0	1	0	*1*	0	1	1
C	0	0	0	1	0	*1*	1	1
	L	L	L	L	W	W	L	W

Winning coalition: W
Losing coalition: L
Member of coalition: 1
Swing: *1*

TABLE 11.1 Comparison of the Shares in Votes, the Shapley Values, and the Benzhaf Values in the Example with Three Players

Player	A	B	C
Share in votes	0.5	0.49	0.01
Shapley value	0.67	0.17	0.17
Banzhaf value	0.6	0.2	0.2

tions are at their very beginnings. Shareholders of the same type should not be regarded as a homogeneous bloc, and intrashareholder type coalition preferences should not be taken for granted. For instance, some banks may only hold shares of a particular company while others are also lenders to that corporation, possibly differently collateralized. The assumption of intershareholder coalition preferences, for example, among nonfinancial companies and natural persons, is even more speculative.

As long as we do not have verified concepts of the formation of coalitions and provided we do not have specific information about the coalition preferences of the players, it is reasonable to use a neutral measure that weighs all possible coalitions equally. But if checked information about the coalition preferences among shareholders is available, then the Shapley-Shubik index and the Banzhaf index are less appropriate. But the difficulty is not that grave because it is possible to merge the votes of those shareholders forming a coalition into a single bloc. For example, until recently, this procedure would have been adequate for the often-cited core corporations of the financial sector in Germany. Due to mutual shareholdings, delegated voting rights and personal interlocking there was a large incentive to cooperate for these banks and insurances (compare, for example, Prigge (1998, 980–983) and Wenger and Kaserer (1998, 507)). Usually, separate voting rights of family members should be merged, too (see Rydqvist (1987, 109, 115) for an example).

Incomplete Data A serious problem when analyzing the power structure of a stock corporation is incomplete data. For example, in Germany, voting rights in a listed corporation must be notified when they amount to 5% or more. About the remaining shareholders nothing is known except that their share must be smaller than the notification threshold. But since power in a stock corporation is determined by the complete shareholder structure, concepts for the voting rights blocs below the notification threshold have to be developed. Two general procedures can be found in the literature: One procedure assumes that the unobserved votes are powerless, whereas the other procedure supposes that they might be influential.

Under the assumption of powerless dispersed unknown shareholdings, these shareholdings do not enter the calculation of the Banzhaf value (Dubey and Shapley 1979). Instead, the majority rule is modified. The same procedure can be applied to the calculation of the Shapley value (compare, for example, Crespi-Cladera and Renneboog (2003, 14)). The majority rule has to be modified as follows:

$$\text{Required majority} - \frac{1 - \text{Cumulated share in voting rights of all bloc holders}}{2}$$

An example may be useful to explain the modification of the majority rule. We look at a stock corporation with four known bloc holders. The shares in voting rights have the sizes of 10%, 20%, 25%, and 30% respectively. A simple majority is required, that is 50% and one vote. The cumulated share in voting rights of the four bloc holders adds up to 85%. Then, ignoring the single vote, the modified required majority is 42.5% (0.5 – (1 – 0.85)/2). This procedure stands in line with the usual assumption in corporate governance research that small shareholders remain rationally passive. The costs of forming a coalition would also be prohibitively expensive for them. Therefore, only bloc holders would actively use their voting rights.

But there are also good reasons not to rule out any influence of the dispersed shareholdings from the outset. Via the market for corporate control the unknown shareholdings may possess power and that should be considered when evaluating the decision-making power of the bloc holders. According to Manne (1965) the small shareholders initially leave corporate control completely to the bloc holders. Due to her small share in voting rights it would not be rational for a small shareholder to participate in corporate decision-making. Her influence is minor as would be her share of the benefits. Moreover, she would have to observe the costs of her intervention. But if the bloc holders decide in favor of value-decreasing investments or pocket private benefits to a greater extent, this should be reflected on an efficient stock market in a low market value. The low share price is then an incentive for a potential bidder to buy the shares from the dispersed shareholders until his stake is large enough to rule the corporation, to restructure it, and to benefit from the accompanying rise in the share price. The takeover threat has an effect on the decision-making power of the bloc holders and has therefore to be considered when the ownership structure is transformed into numbers (for this interpretation, see, for example, Rydqvist (1987, 61)). There are two options how to incorporate the potential influence of dispersed shareholders.

Under the assumption of concentrated unobserved ownership, it is presumed that the unknown shareholders own voting rights blocs of a size that ranges from almost zero to just below the notification threshold. For example, Guedes and Loureiro (2002, 11) state: "We assume that unidentified shareholders hold 1% of votes each, and we add unidentified shareholders to the shareholder list until the joint votes held by all shareholders add up to 100%." This procedure is applicable to the calculation of both Banzhaf and Shapley value.

Only the Shapley value allows for the additional option to ascribe a power value above zero to the entirety of the unknown shareholders. The unobserved voting rights are interpreted as an oceanic game. Rydqvist (1987, 32) defines an oceanic game as follows: "This is a model of the corporate meeting with a few major shareholders holding large blocks of shares and an ocean of infinite number of minor shareholders with infinitesimally small shareholdings." A potential effect of the entirety of the unknown shareholders on the bloc holders' power is considered (for the calculation of the Shapley-Shubik index for this kind of oceanic game, see Leech (2002a, 43–44)). So far, in the context of the Banzhaf index it is not possible to attach a power value exceeding zero to the collectivity of unknown shareholders. Figure 11.4 summarizes the alternative procedures to deal with unobserved voting rights.

The following two examples will highlight how important the assumptions for the unobserved voting rights are: We start with a corporation for which only a single voting rights bloc of 5% has been notified. Presuming for the Banzhaf value that the unknown voting rights are powerless, the modified majority rule will be applied. The modified required majority is equal to 2.5%. This leads to a Banzhaf value of one, which implies a dominating position of a principal shareholder only controlling 5% of the votes. This assessment is unsatisfactory because the dominating position of the principal shareholder can be easily terminated by means of share purchases at the stock market. If we assume instead, following Guedes and Loureiro (2002, 11), that the unknown shareholders own a 1% bloc of voting rights

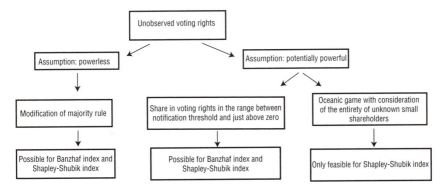

FIGURE 11.4 Consideration of Unobserved Voting Rights

each, we calculate a Banzhaf value of only 0.054. Obviously, this figure is a much better indicator for the power structure among the shareholders.

Another pitfall emerges in cases with two voting rights blocs that are of almost equal size. The principal shareholder A controls 17% of the votes and bloc holder B 15%. The modified majority requirement is at 16%. This yields a Banzhaf value of one for shareholder A. But if we assume again that the unknown shareholders own 1% voting rights blocs each, the Banzhaf value of the principal shareholder is equal to 0.142 and that of bloc holder B amounts to 0.097. Again, this seems to be a much more appropriate indicator of the control situation.

Applications of the Shapley-Shubik index with modified majority rule suffer from similar problems as the Banzhaf index. But for the Shapley-Shubik index we dispose of the option of the oceanic game with consideration of the unobserved voting rights, which does not yet exist for the Banzhaf index.

The impact of the assumptions about the unknown shareholders on the power values is the larger the higher the notification threshold, the larger the unknown shareholdings, and the smaller the number of known voting rights blocs. And it is larger if there is no principal shareholder owning a simple majority. Under these circumstances, it is of particular importance that the unknown shareholdings are not ignored in the calculation of the power indices. Only the Shapley-Shubik index provides the convenient feature that it is possible to ascribe a power value above zero to the unknown shareholdings via an oceanic game. Both power indices allow for assumptions about the distribution of the unknown voting rights by presuming, for example, that the unknown shareholders own 1% voting rights blocs each.

Which Index to Prefer?   Usually Shapley-Shubik index and Banzhaf index yield different results. This raises the question which index should be preferred. In science in general this issue is still highly controversial. For instance, Felsenthal et al. (1998, 84) state: "While papers have been written on the relative merits of these indices . . . it seems fair to say that no index has achieved general recognition as the one correct way to measure voting power. Authors have tended to use both the S-S and Bz indices [Shapley-Shubik index and Banzhaf index]." A similar situation can be stated for corporate governance research: So far, neither of the power indices is dominating, but the Shapley-Shubik index may have a small lead over the Banzhaf index. The Shapley-Shubik index is utilized, for example, by Rydqvist (1987), Wong (1989), Zingales (1994), Chung and Kim (1999), Guedes and Loureiro (2002), Gugler and Yurtoglu (2003), Crespi-Cladera and Renneboog (2003), and Nicodano and Sembenelli (2004). Both indices are applied by Leech (2002b), Leech and Manjón (2003), Edwards and Weichenrieder (2004), and Kehren

(2005). However, the subject of most of these studies is a comparison of both indices. Only the Banzhaf-Index is used by Leech (2000), Khatri et al. (2001), and Crama et al. (2003). In addition, the *degree of control*, which has been developed by Cubbin and Leech (1983), can be found in some studies, for example, Pohjola (1988), Leech and Leahy (1991), and Köke (2001, 2002).

Leech (2002b, 9) uses the study of Berle and Means and the Listing Rules of the London Stock Exchange to set up a catalogue of seven criteria to evaluate how appropriately a power index represents the power structure in a stock corporation:

1. The power value for the principal shareholder should vary as voting weights vary.
2. The power value for the principal shareholder should vary as the voting bloc sizes of the principal shareholder and the second largest bloc holder vary between companies.
3. The power value of the principal shareholder should increase with his voting rights bloc and decrease with an increase in the voting rights bloc of the second largest shareholder.
4. The power value of the principal shareholder should almost always be close to one whenever his voting rights bloc exceeds 30%.
5. The power value of the principal shareholder should often be close to one whenever his voting rights bloc is between 20% and 30%.
6. The power value of the principal shareholder should sometimes be close to one whenever his voting rights bloc is between 15% and 20%.
7. The power value of the principal shareholder should virtually never be close to one whenever his voting right bloc is less than 15%.

Despite the general quality of the appraisal criteria, some details could be questioned. For example, Leech's threshold values comply with concepts of power prevalent in corporate governance research, but still it can be doubted that a principal shareholder controlling 30% of the votes should have the same power value as a principal shareholder owning a simple majority. The regency of the latter cannot be contested, but this contrast cannot be seen from their power values.

A Concluding Application of Power Indices   In this subsection we use the example of British stock corporations to demonstrate how different variants of the power indices represent the ownership structure. British corporations are particularly suitable for this purpose because in the U.K. the principal shareholder usually disposes of less than 50% of the votes. As a consequence, a comprehensive variety of shareholder structures can be found and analyzed. The data in Table 11.2 are taken from Leech (2002b). A similar study for Spanish corporations is conducted by Leech and Manjón (2003).

TABLE 11.2 Comparison of the Shapley-Shubik Index and the Banzhaf Index for Selected Large U.K. Stock Corporations

Stock Corporation	Shares in Votes and Power Index Variant Resp.	Largest Shareholder		Second Largest Shareholder		Third Largest Shareholder		Fifth Largest Shareholder	
		Shapley Value	Banzhaf Value	Shapley Value	Banzhaf Value	Shapley Value	Banzhaf Value	Shapley Value	Banzhaf Value
Plessey	Voting Rights	0.019		0.015		0.013		0.011	
	Variant C	0.020	0.020	0.015	0.015	0.013	0.013	0.011	0.011
	Variant D	0.020	0.087	0.015	0.065	0.013	0.055	0.011	0.045
Berisford	Voting Rights	0.058		0.020		0.016		0.009	
	Variant C	0.061	0.080	0.020	0.019	0.016	0.016	0.009	0.009
	Variant D	0.061	0.528	0.020	0.059	0.016	0.055	0.009	0.036
United Spring & Steel	Voting Rights	0.123		0.109		0.098		0.037	
	Variant C	0.134	0.143	0.117	0.124	0.103	0.112	0.036	0.033
	Variant D	0.135	0.233	0.118	0.202	0.104	0.183	0.036	0.052
Suter	Voting Rights	0.128		0.065		0.053		0.031	
	Variant C	0.143	0.169	0.067	0.060	0.054	0.051	0.031	0.029
	Variant D	0.144	0.270	0.067	0.093	0.055	0.080	0.031	0.046
Sun Life	Voting Rights	0.222		0.035		0.019		0.013	
	Variant C	0.283	0.981	0.033	0.000	0.017	0.000	0.012	0.000
	Variant D	0.284	1.000	0.033	0.000	0.017	0.000	0.012	0.000

Company		Shareholder 1		Shareholder 2		Shareholder 3		Shareholder 4	
Liberty	Voting Rights	0.226		0.226		0.089		0.050	
	Variant C	0.248	0.203	0.247	0.201	0.089	0.112	0.046	0.053
	Variant D	0.249	0.235	0.248	0.233	0.092	0.131	0.046	0.062
Securicor	Voting Rights	0.316		0.073		0.053		0.029	
	Variant C	0.448	0.930	0.059	0.003	0.043	0.003	0.023	0.003
	Variant D	0.451	0.971	0.059	0.002	0.043	0.002	0.023	0.002
Bulgin	Voting Rights	0.310		0.222		0.045		0.028	
	Variant C	0.356	0.372	0.174	0.059	0.049	0.053	0.028	0.034
	Variant D	0.355	0.546	0.172	0.079	0.049	0.075	0.029	0.051
Ropner	Voting Rights	0.410		0.060		0.050		0.020	
	Variant C	0.676	1.000	0.029	0.000	0.025	0.000	0.011	0.000
	Variant D	0.680	1.000	0.028	0.000	0.025	0.000	0.011	0.000
Steel Brothers	Voting Rights	0.425		0.213		0.038		0.030	
	Variant C	0.616	0.991	0.055	0.000	0.035	0.000	0.028	0.000
	Variant D	0.618	0.999	0.052	0.000	0.035	0.000	0.028	0.000
Associated Newspapers	Voting Rights	0.500		0.026		0.021		0.021	
	Variant C	0.984	1.000	0.000	0.000	0.000	0.000	0.000	0.000
	Variant D	0.998	1.000	0.000	0.000	0.000	0.000	0.000	0.000

Source: Leech (2002b, 14f). Ownership structure data of large U.K. stock corporations in 1985 and 1986 respectively. The table displays Banzhaf and Shapley values under the assumptions of both concentrated and dispersed unobserved voting rights. In the case of concentrated unobserved voting rights (Variant C) it is assumed for both power indices that the unknown shareholders own voting rights blocs of 0.25%. In the case of dispersed unknown shareholders (Variant D), the Banzhaf value is calculated with a modified majority rule, that is, powerless dispersed shareholdings are assumed, and the Shapley value is computed with an oceanic game that ascribes a power value to the unobserved voting rights.

Table 11.2 depicts power values for selected corporations from Leech (2002b). Different power values for the same shareholder can easily be compared. In addition, Table 11.2 reveals the difference between power values and the corresponding shares in voting rights, which are currently the dominating measure in corporate governance research. The sample taken from Leech is characterized by a particularly large variation in the voting rights bloc sizes of the two largest shareholders.

Table 11.2 demonstrates that the Shapley value is more closely related to the share in voting rights than the Banzhaf value, but it reacts quite insensitively to varying shareholder structures. For instance, the principal shareholders in Sun Life and Liberty control about 22% of the votes. However, the size of the second largest shareholder differs substantially. He holds only about 3.5% in Sun Life, but is almost as large as the principal shareholder in Liberty. Surprisingly, the Shapley values—assuming concentrated unobserved voting rights, index (C)—for both principal shareholders are almost identical: 28.3% in Sun Life and 24.75% in Liberty. In contrast to that, the Banzhaf index yields considerably different power values for the two principal shareholders: 98.1% in Sun Life and 20.25% in Liberty. The Shapley value hardly indicates the differences in the shareholder structures beyond the principal shareholders, whereas the Banzhaf index tends to underestimate the contestability of the principal shareholder's position and delivers too high a score.

A look at the complete sample of Leech reveals that the Shapley-Shubik index does not comply with his appraisal criteria very well. These results cannot be found in Table 11.2, but in Leech (2002b, 16–17). Only in three out of 19 cases with a principal shareholder controlling more than 40% of the votes, the Shapley value exceeds 90%, whereas the Banzhaf index falls below 95% only once. All things considered, it seems that for this sample the Banzhaf index meets Leech's criteria better.

So far, none of the power indices and their variants dominates in the corporate governance literature. And it can be doubted whether that should be expected. The power values of a variant depend very much on the height of the notification threshold, the size of the unobserved voting rights, and the number of known voting rights blocs. It can easily be imagined that not one variant fits all data sets best. Rather, the current state of the research strongly suggests the following procedure for the analysis of a data set: Some neuralgic cases should be selected, for example, two corporations with principal shareholders of similar sizes without a simple majority, where there exist additional bloc holders in one corporation whereas for the other corporation no further bloc holders are known. At the outset, the power structure in neuralgic cases could be analyzed qualitatively. After that, in a kind of calibration process, it could be searched for that power index variant that comes closest to the qualitative results.

Conclusion

Using the Banzhaf index and the Shapley-Shubik index to measure the power structure in stock corporations may be criticized for some reasons. Nevertheless, it seems that these power indices yield more adequate representations of the power structure than shares in voting rights or the classification of shareholder structures. They incorporate the complete shareholder structure in their power values. Moreover, they do not assume a linear relationship between the share in voting rights and power. This characteristic becomes particularly obvious when the share in voting rights of the principal shareholder exceeds 50%. Both Banzhaf index and Shapley-Shubik index yield power values of one regardless of whether the principal shareholder controls 51% or 99% of the votes. This represents a clear advantage over the usual procedure in corporate governance research, which equates the size of the voting bloc with power and thus presumes a linear relationship. An internationally accepted standard for the operationalization of the power structure has not yet emerged. At the moment, it is recommended to select a power index variant and to calibrate it for each data set separately.

VERTICAL OWNERSHIP STRUCTURE METRICS

The Problem

Describing the shareholder structure on the basis of the directly held votes will not deliver an adequate result, unless the direct shareholders are also the ultimate shareholders. This distinction is of particular importance for corporations in Continental Europe and Asia (see the examples in La Porta et al. (1999a, 480–491)). In Europe, the investigation of shareholder chains—and the analysis of voting rights instead of cash flow rights—gained momentum by the implementation of the Large Holdings Directive of the European Union. Moreover, the divergence of cash flow and voting rights attracted increasing research interest. In his empirical study of German corporations, Köke (2002, 139) concludes that direct and ultimate shareholdings are not perfectly correlated, and he can only confirm for ultimate shareholdings a relationship with performance, measured with productivity growth, but not for direct shareholdings.

The task of vertical ownership structure metrics is to determine the ultimate shareholder for each directly held share. As a result, a corporation may have more than one ultimate shareholder. Using the methods of the horizontal ownership structure metrics, it is then possible to specify the dominating ultimate shareholder. There is a minor part of the literature that uses the technical terms differently: There, only a single ultimate shareholder is identified who is then, necessarily, also the dominating ultimate shareholder (compare, for example, Gugler and Yurtoglu (2003, 754–756)).

Figure 11.5 displays the fictitious shareholder structure of the CG Corp. (2). This example illustrates the following explanations.

It is remarkable that two direct shareholders are the starting point of vertical chains of shareholders and two direct shareholders are not. Besides the four direct shareholders, there is only dispersed ownership for which no additional information is available. If a shareholder is a natural person or is a part of the public sector, then the vertical analysis can be terminated at this stage because it is impossible to hold a share in a natural person or in the state. The ultimate shareholder is certain. The situation is different when a corporation holds a stake in another corporation. In Figure 11.5, the B Corp. holds a stake in CG Corp. (2), and C Corp. holds a majority stake in B Corp. In this case it is hard to believe that B Corp. would use its votes in CG Corp. (2) against the will of C Corp. If we only had information about the direct level of shareholdings, then C Corp. would not appear. The crucial shareholder is that one who actually controls the votes: the ultimate shareholder.

It has to be decided how far and according to which rules the shareholder chain should be analyzed. For instance, if a natural person or a part

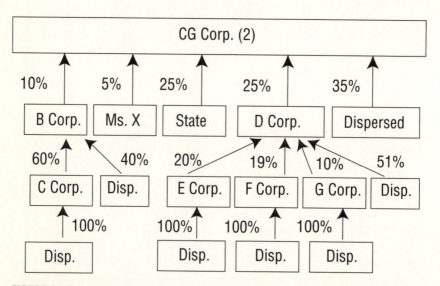

FIGURE 11.5   Voting Rights Structure of the CG Corp. (2)

of the public sector held the majority in C Corp., the chain of shareholders would end there. If another corporation was principal shareholder in C Corp., the analysis would continue with an inspection of the principal shareholder's ownership structure. In case the principal shareholder of that company is still another corporation, the procedure repeats until the state or a natural person is principal owner, there is not enough information for thorough investigation, or none of the owners is powerful enough to dominate. Turning back to our vertical chain starting with B Corp., we declare C Corp. the ultimate shareholder because shareholdings in C Corp. are completely dispersed.

But things are not always that easy with a shareholder owning a simple majority on each level in the vertical chain. The situation gets more complex when we have stages in the chain without simple majority. A case in point is the D Corp. in our example in Figure 11.5. E Corp., F Corp., and G Corp. hold 20%, 19%, and 10% of the votes respectively, and the remaining shareholdings are dispersed. Here we are in need of a criterion to determine whether the principal shareholder E Corp. is dominating this part of the chain. Otherwise, there would be no dominating shareholder in D Corp. Hence, D Corp. would be an ultimate shareholder in CG Corp. (2) and the analysis of this vertical chain could be terminated. It becomes obvious that we have to solve similar problems in the analysis of the vertical chain as we had to on the horizontal dimension. So it comes as no surprise that the literature discusses similar solutions for the vertical dimension.

Concepts to Determine Ultimate Owners

Several concepts are used in corporate governance research to assign the ultimate shareholder. Most of them are based on a constant threshold that only considers the share of the principal owner. The thresholds fall in a range between 10% and 50%. If the share in voting rights of the principal owner exceeds that threshold, he is assumed to dominate the corporation, that is he is able to push through his business policy. In their study, La Porta et al. (1999a, 476) choose a threshold of 20%. La Porta et al. (1999a, 477) state: "The idea behind using 20 percent of the votes is that this is usually enough to have effective control of a firm." In addition, La Porta et al. also use a 10% criterion. Claessens et al. (2000) and Faccio and Lang (2002) also utilize both the 10% criterion and the 20% criterion; Claessens et al. (2002) use additionally a 40% threshold.

As we saw above for the horizontal ownership structure metrics, the weak point of a constant threshold whose only criterion is the share in voting rights of the principal shareholder is the almost complete ignorance of the remaining shareholder structure with the only exception being the recognition that the principal shareholder disposes of more votes than any other shareholder. In Figure 11.5, D Corp. is a direct shareholder in CG Corp. (2), and E Corp., F Corp., and G Corp. are direct shareholders in D Corp., holding 20%, 19%, and 10% of the votes respectively. Following the proposal of La Porta et al. (1999a), E Corp. would be an ultimate shareholder in CG Corp (2). Accepting this for the moment, the next question emerges: How large is the voting bloc ascribed to E Corp. in CG Corp. (2)? If one declares D Corp. to be controlled by E Corp. it seems natural to ascribe all of the voting rights of D Corp. in CG Corp. (2) to E Corp. Thus, E Corp. would control 25% of the voting rights in CG Corp. (2). Figure 11.6 displays the resulting ultimate shareholder structure. Some authors utilize an alternative method for the calculation of stake sizes. It is called the *weakest link principle* (compare Claessens et al. (2000), Gorton and Schmid (2000), Claessens et al. (2002), and Faccio and Lang (2002)). According to the weakest link principle the share in voting rights of an ultimate owner amounts to "the weakest link in the chain of voting rights" (Claessens et al. (2000, 91)). Thus, E Corp. would control 20% of the votes in CG Corp. (2), which is the minimum of 20% and 25%.

But the declaration of E Corp. the dominating minority shareholder in D Corp. does not take into account that F Corp. controls almost as many votes as E Corp., or that a coalition of F Corp. and G Corp. or a concentration of dispersed shares could overrule E Corp. A higher threshold value would diminish that problem. For example, Köke (2001) uses a threshold of 50% (*strong ownership rule*). Such a high threshold guarantees an incontestable position of the principal shareholder but it also rules out any dominating position of a minority principal shareholder. We are already aware of this dilemma of type I error versus type II error from the section on horizontal ownership structure metrics. Its emergence here stresses the similarity of the problems when analyzing the two dimensions of the shareholder structure. Again, the threshold has to be found that minimizes the sum of type I and type II error.

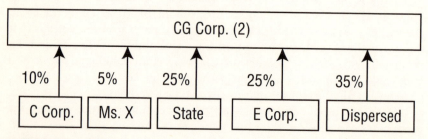

FIGURE 11.6 Ultimate Voting Rights Structure of the CG Corp. (2) Using the 20% Cutoff Criterion

As before with the horizontal ownership structure metrics, one option is to integrate the remaining shareholder structure in the definition of categories. For instance, Köke utilizes not only the strong ownership rule, but also a *weak ownership rule* (Köke 2002: 53). This rule considers further voting rights blocs besides the votes held by the principal shareholder. The principal shareholder is declared dominating if he owns at least 25% of the votes and no other owner holds more than 25% of the votes.

In what follows, we propose a refined concept for the determination of the ultimate shareholder that is inspired by Köke's (2002) procedure. On the one hand, a principal shareholder is declared dominant if she controls a simple majority. However, relying solely on this criterion would be very susceptible to type II error because any dominating minority bloc holder would be ignored. Therefore, on the other hand, a principal shareholder is assumed to be dominating if her share in votes amounts at least to 25% and the total of the votes of all other bloc holders is smaller than her bloc.

The second part of our criterion needs some explanation: Empirical studies of the shareholder structures of German corporations find a significant concentration of voting blocs in the area of 25% (see, for example, Köke (2001, 270) and Bott (2002, 257)). The concentration around 25% seems to be caused by the stock corporation act: A share in votes of 25% grants the shareholder several blocking rights, which makes the dominating position of the principal shareholder less contestable because potential bidders are discouraged. Moreover, the 25% threshold is supported by the fact the average attendance rate in the general meetings of the DAX-30 corporations decreased to 50% in 1999 and 2000 (see the press release "HV-Präsenzen der DAX 30-Unternehmen (1998–2004)," available under: http://www.dsw-info.de/uploads/media/HVPraesenz2004_01.pdf). Therefore, the principal shareholder often needs no more than 25% of the votes to select supervisory board members, and thus the management board, which meet her preferences. It seems plausible to assume that a principal shareholder controlling at least 25% of the votes could be dominating. The constant threshold of 25% is augmented with a variable component. As an additional requirement, the share in votes of the principal shareholder must exceed the aggregated votes of all remaining bloc holders. Otherwise, contestability of the principal shareholder's position would be too large. To illustrate our concept, we analyze the ownership structure of the Thüga AG, a German utility, in Figure 11.7.

There are three direct bloc holders in Thüga AG: Preussen Elektra AG holds 56.3% of the votes, Bayerische Landesbank 29.7%, and Ruhrgas Energie Beteiligungs-AG 10.02%. The remaining votes are dispersed.

Next we determine the ultimate shareholders. For each directly held voting bloc the ultimate shareholder has to be found. Preussen Elektra

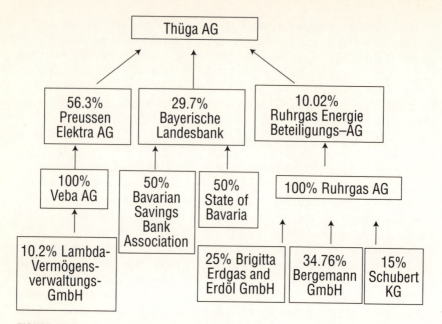

FIGURE 11.7 Voting Rights Structure of the Thüga AG as of 30 Sept. 1996

AG is fully owned by Veba AG. In turn, Lambda-Vermögensverwaltungs-gesellschaft mbH is the principal shareholder of Veba AG with a share of voting rights of 10.02%. Thus, Lambda's share does not exceed the 25% threshold and Lambda is not the dominating shareholder in Veba. Therefore, Veba is the ultimate shareholder of Preussen Elektra's votes in Thüga.

There are two shareholders in Bayerische Landesbank, each holding a 50% stake. Under the assumption that the Bavarian Savings Bank Association is not so close to the state to justify the merging of its stake with that of the State of Bavaria, none of them has a dominating position. As a consequence, Bayerische Landesbank, the direct shareholder, is the ultimate shareholder as well.

Ruhrgas AG is the 100% owner of Ruhrgas Energie Beteiligungs-AG. Bergemann GmbH holds 34.76% of the votes in Ruhrgas AG and is the principal shareholder. It exceeds the 25% threshold, our first criterion. But the voting rights of Schubert KG and Brigitta Erdgas und Erdöl GmbH in Ruhrgas AG add up to 40%. If they form a coalition they could terminate the leading position of Bergemann AG. Our second criterion is not complied with. None of the shareholders on the third level disposes of a dominating position in Ruhrgas AG. Figure 11.8 summarizes the ultimate ownership structure.

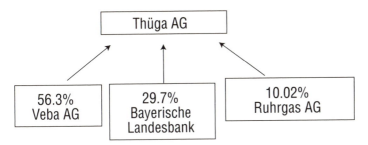

FIGURE 11.8 Ultimate Voting Rights Structure of the Thüga AG as of 30 Sept. 1996

Of course, power indices are a further option to analyze a chain of shareholders (for early applications, see Gugler and Yurtoglu (2003, 735) and Edwards and Weichenrieder (2004)). The far-reaching similarity of problems and concepts of both the horizontal and the vertical dimension of the shareholder structure analysis should have become sufficiently evident by now. But there is one crucial distinction: On the horizontal level, a continuous variable such as a power value seems to be superior. But when analyzing a chain of shareholders, the gray delivered by a continuous variable must be transformed into the black and white of a discrete variable—shareholder X is dominating: true or false. Thus, a threshold is needed for this transformation. For this reason, the power index variant applied to this task has to be extremely carefully selected and calibrated. Contrary to the horizontal shareholder structure analysis, we cannot yet observe an advantage of power indices over advanced classification schemes, because the vertical shareholder structure analysis requires a discrete power variable.

CONCLUSION

Only those shareholder structure analyses that consider *ultimate* ownership can claim to be state of the art. Therefore, vertical ownership structure metrics is of eminent importance. On the road from direct to ultimate shareholders as well as for the analysis of the horizontal structure of ultimate shareholders, measures for the representation of the corporation's power structure are needed. This is the subject of ownership structure metrics.

This chapter has demonstrated the ability of power indices to express the power position of a certain shareholder subject to the remaining entirety of the shareholder structure in a single value. This feature lends power indices the potential to advance the field of ownership structure metrics, with an emphasis on vertical ownership structure metrics. But still a lot of theoretical and empirical work has to be done before power indices become a common tool in corporate governance research. For empirical analyses, the power index variant applied to the investigation of a horizontal shareholder structure should be selected and calibrated on the basis of the particular dataset to be analyzed. As to vertical analyses, the advantage of power indices over their traditional competitors is—contrary to horizontal analyses—not yet clear.

CHAPTER 12

The Effectiveness of Shareholders' Meetings: An Overview of Recent Developments

Gregory F. Maassen and Darrell Brown

INTRODUCTION

The foundations of modern corporate law and corporate governance standards are based on principal/agency relationships. Directors act as shareholders' agents and oversee the management of the corporation. They enter into arm's-length agreements with management respecting management's compensation and, ideally independent of management, they nominate the people who will serve shareholders' interests. Shareholders, as the principals of the agents, have a bundle of rights in relation to the corporation through their ownership of shares. Shareholders, however, following a strict legal definition of property rights, do not own the business carried on by the corporation or the property belonging to that corporation. The rights and obligations of managers and those with interests represented by shares of the corporation are legally distinct. As an independent legal entity, a corporation carries on business, owns property, possesses rights, and incurs liabilities with property rights that are separate from shareholders' cash flow and voting rights. Generally, shareholders are supposed not to manage the corporation but to rely on the board and the appointed officers to direct day-to-day company activities. However, to exercise their franchise, shareholders must be privy to sufficient information on a timely basis in order to assess the efficacy of the directors' actions.

The fundamental underpinning that is supposedly the foundation of corporate democracy is the ability of shareholders to exercise these rights. In addition to financial compensation as residual claimants, a fundamental right of shareholders is to elect the board of directors and, when necessary, to take remedial action in the form of board dismissals and election of new directors. While there are other formalities dealt with at shareholders meetings, including shareholder approval of significant transactions, appointment of auditors, and approval of financial statements, the pivotal power of the shareholders is the ability to control management through control of a board's composition at shareholders' meetings.

In a company that has only a few shareholders, the need for formal accountability mechanisms may be minimal. With widely dispersed share ownership, minimum standards for formal communication and disclosure must be regulated through corporate law and self-regulation such as voluntary corporate governance codes (Maassen et al. 2004). However, such communication, disclosure, and governance mechanisms will be of value only if the shareholders are empowered to act on such information.

THE LIMITATIONS OF SHAREHOLDER ACTIVISM AND SHAREHOLDERS' MEETINGS

Dispersed ownership exacerbates the agency problem and the ability of shareholders to exercise their rights. Typically, a corporation's thousands of retail shareholders are scattered over large geographic areas and operate in international financial markets with restrictions and often incompatible legislation and regulations. In addition, with each having only a relatively small proportional interest in the company, they are often not able to monitor, much less control management. This may be partially offset by institutional ownership. Significant shareholdings may lead to access and negotiation with management on particular issues, if not direct shareholder activism through proxy solicitation contests.

However, the composition of institutional owners and their voting predispositions vary widely and the effectiveness of institutional investors' ability to protect shareholders' rights is widely debated in the literature. While some significant institutional investors such as major mutual funds have tended to align with management and be passive, public pension systems appear to be more active in corporate governance reform. In the absence of effective shareholder advocacy, the door is open for entrenched management to develop self-preservation or self-enhancement policies that run contrary to shareholder interest and maximization of share value.

Types of Institutional Shareholder Activism

Institutional shareholder activism comes in several forms (Karpoff 2001) or is based on distinctive *corporate engagement strategies* (Hebb 2003). First, shareholders and their representatives can submit proposals that fall within their legal competence at shareholders' meetings. They also can engage in private negotiations with the company and/or launch offenses against the firm and its management through the media. According to Hebb (2003), U.S. pension funds were valued at $7.4 trillion in 2003 representing enormous financial pools of concentrated shareholder capital and associated shareholders' rights. CalPERS, the large Californian pension fund, has been among the more active institutional investors in corporate governance reform and shareholder activism. An early study of CalPERS' shareholder activism (Smith 1996) is often used to support the thesis that institutional investors are well positioned to offset agency problems associated with dispersed share-ownership. The study found evidence that CalPERS' activities resulted in "significant positive stock price reactions" for corporations that were successfully targeted by the institutional investor. The study also indicated that CalPERS was largely successful in changing governance structures of targeted corporations.

Although the study demonstrated the effectiveness of institutional shareholder activism, the financial impact for CalPERS appeared to be limited. The increase of shareholder value resulted in an increase of $19 million of share capital of the 34 corporations that were investigated between 1987 and 1993. In the same period, CalPERS invested approximately $3.5 million in its corporate engagement activities and managed some $72 billion in assets in 1993. In addition, the study found no significant statistical relationship between shareholder activism and financial operating performance of targeted companies. In order words, the study failed to reveal a direct link between the improved corporate governance standards of targeted firms and their financial performance.

A weak link between institutional shareholder activism and firm performance was also found by Daily et al. (1996). The study investigated institutional shareholder activism targeted at 200 Fortune 500 companies by 975 institutional investors. The authors concluded that institutional shareholders activism had no appreciable effect on firm performance. Moreover, the results of the study indicated that, on average, firms with higher proportions of their equity held by institutional investors did not enjoy higher performance.

Misdirected Shareholder Activism

Romano (2000) found that shareholder activism has little or no effect on
targeted firm's performance since much of the activism appears to be mis-
directed. The ineffectiveness of shareholder activism can be explained by
the nature of shareholder proposals at shareholders' meetings. Traditionally, these focus on changes to the target firm's board composition, board
leadership structures (CEO duality), board remuneration, and voting systems (cumulative voting and confidential voting). Contrariwise to the conventional wisdom of corporate governance reformers, an indisputable
relationship between these traditional corporate governance interventions
and firm performance appears not to exist (Donaldson and Davis 1994).
For example, Baliga et al. (1996, 51) report in a study on the relationship
among firm performance, board leadership, and CEO-duality: "Our findings stand in sharp contrast to the recommendations of those who call for
the abolition of duality as a primary way to improve firm governance and
performance." Related to the independence and the composition of the
board, Donaldson and Davis (1994) stated: "'We believe that it would be
unwise at the present time to go along with calls to require boards of corporations to be dominated by non-executives." Agrawal and Knoeber
(1996) even found a negative relationship between board independence
and firm performance.

Institutional Shareholder Activism and
Populist Sentiment

Voting guidelines of institutional investors nevertheless are often based on
the popular belief that corporate governance interventions have a direct
impact on the performance of corporations. While the impact can be contested, voting guidelines and institutional shareholder activism appear to
serve an additional purpose. As noted by Romano (2000), private benefits
of fund managers and other sponsors of shareholder proposals at shareholders meetings appear to coincide with popular beliefs or political preferences. Pressured by financial markets and corporate governance reforms,
institutional investors undoubtedly have an incentive to focus on shareholder proposals that attract greater media publicity and that are believed
to have a greater positive impact on the performance of targeted firms. According to Romano (2000, 80–81): "Proposals to limit executive compensation and increase board diversity, appealing to populist sentiment or the
political preferences of some constituents, are more likely to enhance political reputations for fund managers than confidential voting or takeover defense rescission proposals. There is far greater media publicity surrounding

executive compensation and minority representation issues, and these proposals implicate the kinds of social issues on which political reputations can be furthered, in contrast to more mundane corporate governance devices." As such, institutional investors' ability to represent retail shareholders at shareholders' meetings not only may be less effective due to the conventional wisdom of financial markets and corporate governance reformers, but may be hampered as well by fund managers' desire to attract publicity and build reputations. In addition, recent lawsuits (see case study below) against the actions of activist investors and the free-rider problem tend to discourage active intervention on the part of institutional investors.

CASE STUDY: The Cintas Corp. Shareholder Defamation Lawsuit

Although the shareholders' meeting is advocated as a forum for free speech and debate among shareholders and their company, a recent lawsuit alarmed corporate governance observers because it could have set unprecedented limitations on shareholders' ability to freely speak at shareholders' meetings in the United States.

Cintas Corp., an American firm, filed a defamation lawsuit against socially responsible investment firm Walden Asset Management and its senior vice president, Tim Smith, in December 2003. The $75 million lawsuit apparently focused on a speech made by the CSR firm's representative during the shareholders' meeting that was held in October 2003. The representative asked Cintas to "assess the efficacy of its code of conduct preventing sweatshop labor in countries where it sources," while he referred to a report of a labor union allegedly stating that Cintas was violating its own code of conduct (www.sri-advisor.com). The result was an international outcry of violations of shareholders' constitutional free speech rights in the United States by civil rights organizations, corporate governance experts, and the media.

The parties settled the suit in September 2004 directly after the board of directors of Cintas recommended voting for a resolution requesting a report on adherence to the Code of Conduct for Vendors (which was strongly opposed a year earlier) and after the CSR firm openly apologized for allegedly incorrectly phrasing facts (www.institutional shareowner.com).

Beneficial Shareholder Representation

Latham (2005) suggests unbundling voting from investment management as a means of addressing the representation issue. Only 41% of stock, for example, is now held by individuals in the United States. Latham suggests passing through the voting rights to the beneficial owners. In written submissions to the Select Committee on Trade and Industry (United Kingdom), Brewin Dolphin Securities (BDS) described, in a similar vein, their system of enabling any client holding shares in a portfolio, whether from a pooled fund or elsewhere. They describe their system as follows (House of Commons 2002, 1):

- Clients log onto a secure extranet using own password.
- Notices of meetings and all resolutions will be posted on the site as soon as they are published, provided the company allows for electronic proxy appointment via the CREST system.
- Clients will be able to tick boxes indicating their voting intentions on each resolution and return their instructions to BDS online.
- BDS will verify the instructions and cast all votes received both for and against resolutions accordingly, including any positive abstentions.
- If some clients choose not to vote their shares, BDS reserves the right to cast the unused votes in line with the views of the majority of its clients, or alternatively as it so thinks (but is not obliged to do so).
- The results of clients' votes will be published within the site.
- A request facility for other company information such as Annual Reports will also be provided.

BDS provides the facility at no charge to their clients and casts votes using an electronic proxy voting service.

THE FUNCTION OF SHAREHOLDERS' MEETINGS

Regardless of the disputed effectiveness of institutional shareholder activism to offset agency problems, shareholders' meetings are a legal necessity and an economic reality. Modern company laws oblige companies with a widely dispersed ownership to organize and invest in a meeting at least once a year while extraordinary meetings are called when unusual circumstances arise and particular decisions need to be ratified by shareholders.

According to Strätling (2003), shareholders' meetings service three legal functions: The first function is to approve corporate decisions that fall within the authority of the shareholders' meeting. These typically include the approval of the annual accounts and the election of the accountant, the election and dismissal of board members, the approval of large and related party transactions, and the distribution of annual dividends. Second, shareholders are informed by management and directors during the meeting and through materials that are distributed prior to the meeting such as the annual report, voting guidelines, proxy statements, and so on. A third function of shareholders' meetings is to serve as a discussion forum for shareholders and representatives of the company.

The Ceremonial Function of Shareholders' Meetings

A few academic studies and an overwhelmingly large body of anecdotal evidence seem to support that shareholders' meetings perform a ceremonial function as well. Some observers characterize shareholders' meetings as the "least useful rituals in business" and "a monumental waste of time and money" (Lochner and Koppes 1994, quoted in Lane 1999), while others see the meeting as a "grand public relations event" (Lane 1999). Companies are using the annual meeting as an opportunity to communicate with shareholders and the public. Some companies, such as Berkshire Hathaway Inc., organize annual meetings that attract over 16,000 shareholders with three-day programs, while car manufacturers see the meetings as an opportunity to display the latest products (see the case study below).

CASE STUDY: The Ceremonial Function of Shareholders' Meetings

To attract shareholders, some companies organize shareholders meetings as mega events. Warren Buffett's Berkshire Hathaway Inc. attracted some 16,000 individual shareholders to its annual meeting on April 30, 2005. The meeting was organized in the Arena of the Quest Center, a convention center that can host up to some 18,000 guests. Buffett's annual meeting is an important ingredient of a three-day event that includes BBQs, discount shopping trips during an "exclusive shareholder shopping day," and meet-and-greet sessions with Warren himself. The meeting itself lasts for 45 minutes preceded by a company movie in the morning and a question-and-answer session between 9:30 A.M. and 3 P.M.

General Motors organizes regional events (stockholder forums) prior to its annual meeting in which shareholders can learn more about the company and discuss issues with GM management. Meanwhile, they can participate in auto shows to experience first hand the quality of the company's products. Volkswagen AG, the German car manufacturer, combines a motor show with its annual meeting that is attended by some 4,000 retail shareholders.

In their quest to understand the function of shareholders meetings, Maug and Rydqvist (2001) documented 6,000 shareholder proposals of large U.S. corporations between 1993 and 1997. The authors concluded that management proposals always passed and shareholder proposals always failed. De Jong et al. (2004) show a similar observation within a European context. An analysis of 245 minutes of shareholders meetings in the period 1998–2002 held by 54 Dutch listed companies indicated that 9 out of 1,538 items on the agenda of the shareholders' meetings were rejected or withdrawn.

Limitations of Shareholders' Meetings

Only recently has the international corporate governance discussion begun to focus on the limitations of shareholders' meetings. Baum (2000) identifies three reasons for the shareholders' meetings' appearance on the reform agenda. First, institutional shareholders have emerged as watchdogs for retail shareholders, which could mitigate problems associated with shareholders' collective actions. Second, new information technology is an important factor to lower the costs of shareholder voting and to improve shareholders' ability to communicate and vote. And third, the internationalization of shareholdings appears to complicate the communication with shareholders, the casting of votes, and the enforcement of shareholders' rights. So while new technology and increasing shareholder activism may positively affect the functioning of shareholders' meetings, the internationalization of share ownership emerges as an additional complicating factor. Cross-border proxy voting, for example, is currently fiercely debated in the European Union as part of an elaborate consultation process in preparation of a new EU Directive on shareholders' rights. Other factors that seem to challenge the effectiveness of shareholders' meetings include the manipulation by outsiders, shareholder disinterest, agency problems, procedural flaws, and other legal limitations.

CASE STUDY: Distortion of Shareholders' Meetings by Outsiders

---

The *sokaiya* (meeting men) in Japan are a prime example of the manipulation of shareholders meetings instigated by outsiders combined with agency problems and legal limitations. In the late 1990s, these "corporate racketeers" or "extortionists" affiliated with the Jakuza *en masse* threatened to disrupt the annual shareholders meetings of Japanese companies while they preyed upon the desire of Japanese managers and directors to maintain at least "the outward appearance of harmony and avoid public humiliation" (CNNfn, 1997). The *sokaiya* would generally threaten management with embarrassing questions or they would otherwise try to disrupt a company's meeting unless they were paid off. Managers and directors apparently did find such disruptions so distasteful that they usually acquiesced to the extortionists' demands (Choy 2000).

   To overwhelm the *sokaiya* and to make it physically impossible for the scam artists to attend all annual meetings of shareholders, Japanese companies hold their annual shareholders' meetings the same day and at roughly the same time. According to the Commercial Law Center in Japan, 1,766 of 1,884 publicly traded companies held their shareholders' meetings on a single day in June in 1996 (some 94% of the companies). The average meeting lasted 26 minutes and shareholders did not ask questions at 86% of the listed companies' meetings (Morishita 1997:4). The latest figures do not indicate any major changes in the organization of shareholders' meetings in Japan. According to Institutional Shareholder Services (ISS), 90% of June 2004 meetings were squeezed into a three-day period. Of the

2,100 Japanese shareholders' meetings in June covered by ISS in 2004, 1,300 of them fell on the peak date of June 29, although ISS commented that this was a lower proportion of meetings than at any time in recent memory in Japan (Goldstein 2004a).

CHALLENGES FACING SHAREHOLDER ACCESS AND SHAREHOLDERS' MEETINGS IN THE EUROPEAN UNION

In the European Union (EU), the shareholders' meeting is seen by lawmakers as a one-way process that urgently needs an overhaul to meet modern standards. While individual member states of the EU seem to have overcome the first legal and technological barriers to the introduction of proxy solicitation, cross-border proxy voting and other issues remain obstacles for shareholders to exercise their rights across the EU. As part of its Corporate Governance Action Plan, the European Commission began a consultation process in 2004 in preparation of a new Shareholder Rights Directive. The Directive, along with the new Transparency Directive and amendments to existing Company Law Directives, would remove legal obstacles for shareholders to exercise their right to (1) ask questions, (2) table resolutions, (3) vote in absentia, and (4) participate in shareholders' meetings via electronic means across the EU (European Commission 2004a, 3). The new 2004 Transparency Directive already gives listed companies the opportunity to provide shareholders information on the place, time, and agenda of meetings, introduces the timely disclosure of information, and enables the usage of electronic means to inform shareholders. In addition, the Market Abuse Directive basically requires companies to have a web site to post inside information they are required to disclose publicly. This web site could also be used to disseminate other information as well, such as an annual corporate governance statement of listed companies that will be required once the fourth and seventh Company Law Directives are amended.

Problems Associated with Cross-Border Proxy Voting

According to the European Commission (2005b, 4), 30% of the share capital of listed companies is held by non-resident shareholders in the UK, Spain, Italy, France, or Germany (30 DAX companies). In Luxembourg, Latvia, Hungary, Belgium, and the Netherlands, nonresident shareholdings may be as high as 50% to 70–80%. These shares are typically held through chains of intermediaries that make it difficult to identify the person who is entitled to vote. As a result, nonresident shareholders, intermediaries, and listed companies across the EU face obstacles such as the authentication of the ultimate investor through the chain of intermediaries and whether depositary receipts holders can be recognized as shareholders. According to the Winter Report, a report that was commissioned by the European Commission prior to the implementation of its Corporate Governance Action Plan, "Cross-border voting is often almost impossible in practice, and the integration of financial markets calls for an urgent solution" (European Commission 2002b, 8).

The EU action plan calls for solutions that will enable nonresident shareholders to exercise their voting rights across the European Union. Proposed solutions mainly focus on the usage of modern technology. Notices, annual reports, and agendas of meetings could be made available through dedicated investor relations segments of the web sites. Proxy and voting instructions could be downloaded and submitted electronically. This would not only considerably increase the involvement of shareholders in the process, but would also lead to huge reductions in communications costs.

In the United States, for example, where proxy solicitation through the Internet and phone is more common, considerable cost savings have been achieved by specialized firms to whom companies can outsource the entire proxy process. ADP, the largest proxy processing company in the United States, processed more than 152 million proxy pieces covering more than 299 billion shares in 2005 (ADP 2005). A total of 168.2 billion votes were cast electronically—by phone, Internet, and ProxyEdge (84.5% of all shares voted)—in 2005. The usage of modern technology reduced the issuing companies' total costs reaching out to shareholders by more than $370 million due to savings on postage and paper during the proxy season and over $600 million during the last 12 months (including the 2005 proxy season). The new technology also has resulted in greater quorum results (an average of 87.7% of total shares processed).

Problems Associated with Electronic Voting

While electronic voting is commonplace in the United States, European financial markets are just recently embarking on electronic voting. In the Netherlands, shareholders can vote through the Internet since 2004 after the law was amended. Shareholders can now vote through a specialized web site for a total of 12 listed companies after they have registered with their broker. Out of a total of 119,002,679 shares of the 12 participating companies, 22.03% of the shares were used to vote through the Internet (www.communicatiekanaal.nl). As of 2005, approximately 200,000 Dutch shareholders have registered with the new voting system. In a similar vein,

German shareholders could cast their vote electronically after the law was amended in 2000. Although figures were not present on the usage of the Internet, turnout at annual meetings of shareholders of the top 30 German listed companies continues to decrease. In 2002, an average of 60.95% of the voting capital was present at the annual shareholders' meetings of the DAX 30 companies. In 2004, only 47% registered for the meetings of these companies (DSW 2004), a trend that could be reversed by modern technology.

CASE STUDY: The Manipulation of Voting Equipment in Europe

Vivendi Universal, the French media conglomerate, issued a statement in April 2002 describing that hackers using radio transmitters allegedly tampered with shareholders' voting that would have granted a new stock option plan for executives of the company during its annual meeting on April 24, 2004. The Commercial Court of Paris appointed in May 2002 an expert to examine the voting equipment and the possibility of fraud. Although the report was submitted on December 10, 2002 and "the Court's expert accepted that there may have been radio interference with, or a malfunction of, the voting equipment used at the general shareholders' meeting," Vivendi determined that "the resolutions at issue" were "no longer pertinent to Vivendi Universal in 2003" and the company submitted a request for dismissal of this suit which was granted by the French Court on February 4, 2003 (Vivendi Universal, Form 20-F—2002, 2003, 131).

Interestingly, the hackers were never found, the independent report was never used to pursue further litigation, IT experts questioned the allegations (Wired News 2002), the CEO was ousted in July 2002, and the investor relations department did not respond to enquiries. Whether this was an attempt by a CEO of a distressed company to reconvene the shareholders' meeting to have shareholders vote on his remuneration package, or whether the manipulation of absentee votes was a reality will possibly never be known.

Record Dates and the Problem of Share Blocking

A particular problem across the European Union is share blocking. Shareholders have to deposit their shares for a few days prior to the shareholders' meeting. As a result, ". . . many institutional investors will not choose to vote rather than be prevented from selling their shares any time. Voting is often considered as not being worth the financial risk associated with the immobilization of shares" (European Commission 2005b, 11). The solution is found in the introduction of a compulsory record date to determine whether shareholders are eligible to participate in a meeting.

CHALLENGES FACING SHAREHOLDER ACCESS AND SHAREHOLDERS' MEETINGS IN THE UNITED STATES

Shareholder Access in the United States

Similar to shareholder access limitations in the EU, challenges associated with the representation of shareholder interests and the exercise of shareholders' rights can be attributed to differences in state legislation in the United States. The evolution of corporate law in the United States has run tandem with longstanding debates on the relative roles that should be accorded shareholders and management. While in the EU, internal competition is a relatively new phenomenon, states in the United States have competed to attract corporate domicile since the nineteenth century. Those states that have chosen to relax corporate legal restrictions attract a greater number of corporate registrants. Delaware was an early actor in relaxing key restrictions. In the 1890s, rules were repealed that required businesses to incorporate for defined purposes, for limited durations, and in particular locations. Restrictions on mergers and acquisitions were substantially relaxed and ownership by one corporation of another's stock was eliminated (Bakan 2004). These early changes led to a consolidation blitz between 1898 and 1904 that resulted in a reduction from over 1,800 corporations to 157 large corporate entities in the United States. This set the stage for modern-day corporate America. By the early twentieth century, large corporation shareholders had little, if any, power and control (Bakan 2004, 13–15).

Concern over management's dominance became an issue in Washington. A congressional committee established in 1913 to investigate *money trusts* reported:

> *None of the witnesses called was able to name an instance in the history of the country in which the stockholders had succeeded in overthrowing an existing management in any large corporation, nor does it appear that stockholders have ever even succeeded in so far as to secure the investigation of an existing management of a corporation to ascertain whether it has been well or honestly managed. . . . [In] all great corporations with numerous and widely scattered stockholders . . . the management is virtually self-perpetuating and is able through the power of patronage, the indifference of stockholders and other influences to control a majority of stock. (Bakan 2004, 15)*

Despite the concern over governance, corporations were increasingly viewed as the engine of economic growth and prosperity. After the depression of 1920–1921, a period of boundless optimism ensued. A number of reputable economists expounded on the likelihood of continued stock appreciation for years to come. Many of these same economists were later employed by managers of investment trust companies to add to the image of such companies as providing scientific expertise in the area of investment. Lending on margin grew exponentially to finance ever-increasing trade volumes in common stock. By the summer of 1929, there was worry that there might not be enough common stocks available to the broadening base of purchasers. One answer to the supply problem was the proliferation of investment trusts (companies).

The Role of Investment Trusts

The investment trust was the mechanism lauded as enabling a small shareholder to hold an interest in many companies. The shareholder purchased the shares of the trust. From the proceeds of the sale of such shares, the managers of the trust invested in hundreds of companies thereby spreading the risk in a manner that would otherwise be unavailable to the small investor. The trusts of the 1920s, however, brought "an almost complete divorce of the volume of securities outstanding from the volume of [underlying] corporate assets in existence" (Galbraith 1997, 47).

In nearly all cases, trust companies were founded by other companies including other investment trusts. In the late twenties, the exposure these funds created was compounded by the use of leverage. Galbraith (1997, 57) explains leverage as follows:

> *Consider, by way of illustration, the case of an investment trust organized in early 1929 with a capital of $150 million—a plausible sum by then. Let it be assumed, further, that a third of the capital was realized from the sale of bonds, a third from preferred stock, and the rest from the sale of common stock. If this $150 million were invested, and if the securities so purchased showed a normal appreciation, the portfolio value would have increased by midsummer by about 50 percent. The assets would be worth $225 million. The bonds and preferred stock would still be worth only $100 million; their earnings would not have increased, and they claim no greater share of the assets in the hypothetical event of a liquidation of the company. The remaining $125 million, therefore, would underlie the value of the common stock of the trust. The latter, in other words, would have increased in asset value from $50 million to $125 million, or by 150 per cent, and*

> *as a result of the increase of only 50 per cent in the value of the assets of the trust as a whole. . . . [B]ut this was not all of it. Were the common stock of the trust, which had so miraculously increased in value, held by still another trust with similar leverage, the common stock of that trust would get an increase of between 700 and 800 per cent from the original 50 per cent advance.*

Massive amounts of money accumulated in these trust companies, particularly in 1928 and 1929. By way of example, in less than one month in 1929, Goldman Sachs had issued more than a quarter of a billion dollars' worth of securities through the Shenandoah and Blue Ridge Corporations. The latter provided the option to investors to exchange shares of routine securities such as stock held in the American Telephone & Telegraph Company for preferred and common shares of the investment trusts. Managers had limitless discretion as to the investment of shareholder dollars. Shareholder intervention in management was prevented by selling nonvoting stock or requiring the assignment of voting rights to a management-controlled voting trust.

Although detractors were few and far between during the height of the twenties' speculation frenzy, the sobering results of the crash and the Great Depression prompted further discussion respecting the disclosure requirements that should attach to share issuances and ultimately led to the passage of the Securities Act of 1933. While federal authority asserted its influence on disclosure matters, the core elements of corporate law including the authorities granted to shareholders and managers have remained firmly within the jurisdiction of the state legislatures and have tended to evolve to support further management entrenchment both through subsequent legislative activity and through judicial precedent.

Limited Shareholder Power to Initiate

With few exceptions, U.S. corporate law has insulated management from shareholder interference. All major corporate decisions must be made, or at least initiated, by the board. In the United States, shareholders cannot take the initiative in a procedure that would be legally binding on management. Using Delaware as an example:

- Charter amendments require shareholder approval by a majority of the outstanding stock, but voting can take place only on proposals brought by the board of directors. Shareholders cannot initiate charter amendment proposals and bring them to a vote. (Delaware General Corporation Law: § 242(b)).

- Shareholders are not empowered to initiate merger or termination decisions. A decision made by the board on a merger or consolidation must be approved by a majority of the outstanding stock (a veto power). However, even when majority approval has been obtained via a shareholders' meeting, the board has the discretion to abandon the shareholder-approved sale of assets or merger (Delaware General Corporation Law: § 271(b)).
- The power to declare dividends is granted exclusively to the board. No shareholder approval is required (Delaware General Corporation Law: § 170).
- Shareholders have no veto power on scaling down decisions. Management is granted full discretion to approve and implement such measures (Delaware General Corporation Law: § 170).

Although rules under federal legislation provide a mechanism for shareholder proposals, adoption of such proposals by a majority of shareholders at the annual meeting is not binding on the board. Consequently, these authorities can only be classified as advisory in nature.

Limitations of Proxy Solicitation Contests

Supporters of the status quo state that shareholders have a fundamental mechanism at their disposal—a proxy solicitation contest. Shareholder recourse is to replace an existing board with a new board. However, the shareholders' ability to replace an existing board is largely a myth in the United States. The proxy solicitation process is skewed to favor management. First, the initiator of the solicitation contest must bear the costs of such a contest. If successful, all shareholders will reap the benefits (or detriments) of the contest, but it is the initiator who will bear the disproportionate cost. Other shareholders can take a free ride at the initiator's expense. At the same time, management has the discretion to use the company's treasury to fund a campaign in support of the management slate of candidates. Management is within its authority to deplete company assets to battle shareholder initiatives that might otherwise be used to enhance firm value or provide increased investment returns to shareholders (Bebchuk 2004).

Opponents of the status quo state that a proxy solicitation contest is not a viable mode of shareholder access. Statistics from 1996 to 2002 show that proxy solicitation contests are used sparingly. There were 215 cases of contested solicitations—approximately 23 per year in U.S. public corporations. However, not all contested elections were initiated to replace the board. Only 77 of the 215 contests were over the appointment of an alternate management team—an average of 11 contests per year. The size of firms where there was a management replacement battle was small. Only 10 firms had a market capitalization in excess of $200 million—less than two per year on average (Bebchuk 2003a).

The Proposal Subsidy Issue

The U.S. Securities and Exchange Commission's Rule 14a-8 (the shareholder-proposal rule) allows any shareholder to submit a maximum of one proposal for the proxy statement with a 500-word supporting statement limit when he or she possesses at least 1% or $2,000 in market value of shares of the company for at least one year. However, the critical difference with shareholder proposal provisions in, for example, Canada, lies in whether the board is obligated to implement a proposal that is endorsed by the majority of the shareholders.

Critics of the SEC proposal rule state that the ease of access and company subsidy contribute to a growing number of spurious shareholder proposals that do little to increase the effectiveness of a firm's management. Under Rule 14a-8, the company incurs the costs of assessing the validity of proposals and distributing the proposals to shareholders prior to the meetings once it is included in the proxy statement. According to Hagaman (1995, 16), a new generation of "corporate gadflies is starting to appear at annual meetings [that] despite their love for their own voices" try to keep the company and its directors accountable to at least somebody. Since many retail investors are not in a position to privately negotiate terms with the company, the way forward is to submit a proposal to the company for the next annual meeting of shareholders.

Proxy proposals generally can be classified into two categories: corporate governance proposals and social policy proposals. They vary from providing new Oldsmobiles to directors of GM (see case study below) to the introduction of corporate governance and social responsibility standards by corporate governance activists, religious groups, and environmental organizations. Campbell et al. (1999) found for the 1997 U.S. proxy season, based on a sample of 394 large U.S. companies, that a large majority of the shareholder proposals were omitted by the company (26.2%) or withdrawn by the sponsors (17.7%) prior to the distribution of the proxy statement. Individual sponsors of shareholder proposals accounted for more than 85% of corporate governance proposals that were omitted while 71% of the social policy category that were sponsored by individuals were omitted. Overall, corporate governance proposals received support with a mean of 23.6% of the votes cast versus 6.6% for social policy proposals.

According to an estimate by the SEC (1998), the cost implications of proposal subsidy range from an average expenditure of approximately $50,000 on printing, distribution and tabulation costs of proposals that are included in the proxy statement to an average of $37,000 on determining whether a proposal should be accepted. According to Romano (2000), the estimated savings from eliminating subsidy for proposals that fail to receive at least 40 percent of the votes could be up to $1.9 billion.

CASE STUDY: The Negative Effect of Shareholder Proposal Subsidy— An Example of a Fortune 500 Company

ITEM NO. 9
John Lauve, 200 North Saginaw, Holly, MI 48442, owner of 412 shares of Common Stock, has given notice that he intends to present for action at the annual meeting the following resolution:

RESOLVED:
GM must have directors who can stop the decline.
The stock holders who know this will give them an incentive:
Double their pay to $240,000 any year the market share increases.
Also, this year, give each director the gift of a New Oldsmobile.

REASON: Market share reflects customer acceptance of our product. Below average cars, result in loss of market share. Find management that can change the record of decline.

The Board of Directors favors a vote AGAINST the adoption of this proposal for the following reasons:

General Motors strives to set director compensation at a level that will enable the Board to attract and provide adequate incentives for its members. GM's director compensation is regularly benchmarked against comparable corporations and advisors are consulted to ensure that the compensation is competitive. In recent years, GM has increased its emphasis on stock as an important element of director compensation in order to reinforce the alignment of the directors' interests with those of the stockholders. GM's current directors are significant owners of GM stock as disclosed on page 7 of the proxy statement. Changes in market share, like other elements of performance, are normally reflected in GM's share price, which directly impacts the value of a directors' holdings. GM's stockholders can be confident that the members of its Board are extremely attentive to all the elements that go into the Corporation's success, including net income, Return On Net Assets, market share, and quality, and also share the stockholders' determination to achieve significant improvements. The Board believes that the proposal would not enhance the effectiveness of the Board, however, and could impair the

Board's ability to attract, recruit, and secure the best qualified candidates for service on the Board.

The Board of Directors favors a vote AGAINST this stockholder proposal, Item No. 9. Proxies solicited by the Board of Directors will be so voted unless stockholders specify a different choice.

Source: GM Proxy Statement (2001).

SEC Proposed Rules Relating to Security Holder Director Nominations

With the advent of corporate scandals such as Enron and WorldCom, the SEC faced increasing pressure to provide greater shareholder access to the director nomination process. On October 14, 2003, it released a proposal regarding increased shareholder access and solicited comment (Exchange Act Release No. 34-48626). The proposal has resulted in heated debate that has clearly segregated proponents from opponents. Special-interest groups representing management have taken the unusual step of contracting for full-page advertisements in prominent papers such as the *New York Times* and the *Wall Street Journal* to advocate their position. Thousands of individuals and groups made representations to SEC regarding the proposals. Although some 20 months have passed since the release of the draft rules, as of July 2005 the SEC has yet to finalize rules that would accommodate greater shareholder access to the nomination process.

The access rules would apply to all companies subject to the SEC's proxy rules, including operating companies and investment companies. Once triggered by events set forth in the rules, shareholder access would apply for two years. For example, if shareholder access is triggered by a specified event at a company's 2005 annual meeting of shareholders, shareholder access would apply to that company's 2006 and 2007 annual meetings. A general right of shareholder access is not provided. Access is triggered by one or more triggering events. These events represent an attempt by SEC to establish objective criteria evidencing deficiencies in a company's proxy process. The deficiencies are considered to be of a nature such that shareholder views may not be adequately taken into account under the company's regular procedures. Consequently, a limited time access right is granted.

The shareholder nomination of director candidates in a company's proxy statement would be permitted where one or both of the following two triggers are present:

1. *The receipt of greater than 35% "withhold" votes in a director election.* Shareholder access would be triggered if a director receives

greater than 35% "withhold" votes in a director election based on the votes cast.

2. *Approval of a shareholder proposal to activate shareholder access.* Shareholder access would be triggered if a majority of the votes cast support a shareholder proposal to activate shareholder access. The shareholder access proposal must be submitted by a shareholder or group of shareholders beneficially owning at least 1% of a company's outstanding shares for at least the last one year, and these proponents must express intent to satisfy this ownership threshold through the date of a company's annual meeting.

The rules would permit only shareholders satisfying certain criteria to nominate a director in company proxy statements. More specifically, in order to nominate a director candidate under the proposed shareholder access rules:

- The nominating shareholder or shareholder group must have continuously held at least 5% of the company's outstanding shares of voting stock for at least the previous two years and express their intent to satisfy this minimum ownership threshold through the date of the annual meeting.
- A shareholder or group of shareholders nominating a candidate must be subject to the Section 13G, and not Section 13D, filing requirements (meaning that the nominating shareholder(s) must represent that they did not acquire the company's securities with the purpose or the effect of changing or influencing the control of the company).
- The nominating shareholder or shareholder group cannot have any direct or indirect agreement with the company regarding the director nomination.

Any director candidate nominated by a shareholder or group of shareholders using the shareholder access process must meet certain conditions:

- The nominee must satisfy the independence criteria of the applicable listing standard (NYSE/NASDAQ).
- The nominee must have no specified relationships with the nominating shareholder or group of shareholders (e.g., the nominee cannot be an employee of the nominating shareholder(s), an affiliate of the nominating shareholder(s), or receive fees from the nominating shareholder(s)).
- The candidacy and the election of a shareholder nominee must be consistent with applicable law.

A shareholder or group of shareholders may nominate a specified number of directors, which is determined by the number of directors serving on a company's board:

- One nominee if the board of directors has eight or fewer directors
- Up to two nominees if the board of directors has between nine and 19 directors
- Up to three nominees if the board of directors has 20 or more directors

If a company receives shareholder nominations in excess of the applicable number, the company must include those nominees from the shareholder or group of shareholders with the largest ownership stake.

In addition, the nominating shareholder or group of shareholders must file with the SEC all soliciting material distributed on behalf of such director nominee(s). This soliciting material would be subject to Rule 14a-9 (proxy antifraud rules). In order for a company's shareholders to use the shareholder access process, applicable state corporate law must provide shareholders with the right to nominate director candidates.

The Debate on the SEC Proposed Rules

The battle lines have been clearly drawn between investor and corporate/management interests regarding the SEC proposal. In the SEC's summary of submissions received, the respective positions and the identity of the advocates are painted as follows:

> *A significant majority of the commenters [sic], comprising virtually all of the unions; pension funds; social, environmental, and religious funds; a majority of institutional investors and institutional investor associations; a majority of investment advisers and managers; and a majority of individuals, supported the proposed rules. The exceptions were corporations, corporate executives, and corporate directors; law firms and attorneys; and most of the associations (primarily business associations), which were nearly unanimous in their opposition to the proposed rules. (SEC 2004:24)*

Management and their lobbyists presented several arguments against the imposition of the shareholder access rules. They can be roughly summarized as follows:

- Institutional investors are not the true owners of the securities issued and are not representative of the beneficial shareholders.

- The effect of recent changes in listing requirements imposing new corporate governance standards and the results of compliance with the Sarbanes-Oxley Act cannot be measured over such a short period. The results of these reforms should be measured prior to imposing further corporate governance revisions.
- Directors elected under this rule would be disruptive and representative of only special interests. Consequently, general investor and other stakeholder interests may be jeopardized.
- The SEC would be in violation of the states' legislative authority by imposing a shareholder access rule.

Failing an outright rejection of the proposal, the Business Roundtable, for example, proposed an increase in the opt-in threshold to 20% and an increase in the withheld-vote trigger to 50%.

The Wait-and-See Approach

The Business Roundtable also suggested that SEC's actions are premature. The recent changes in listing requirements, mutual fund disclosure, and compliance with Sarbanes-Oxley should be given time to take effect. SEC Commissioner Campos describes the application of Sarbanes-Oxley in this manner:

The enactment of the Sarbanes-Oxley Act has led to a number of reforms in corporate governance. It required that the SEC direct SROs to make changes to their listing standards to require that audit committees be comprised entirely of independent directors, who will manage the outside auditor. In addition, in response to Sarbanes-Oxley, the NYSE and the NASD imposed listing requirements under which an issuer's nominating and compensation committees must be composed entirely of independent directors. The SEC also adopted rules aimed at improving communications by the nominating committee. Among other requirements, these rules require that an issuer disclose its nomination procedures and whether it considers candidates for director nominees put forward by shareholders. . . . Through Sarbanes-Oxley, Congress has focused on independent directors as the vehicle for making management more accountable and for having boards of directors that truly discharge their oversight duties. The frank truth is that the jury is out on whether directors who are on the surface "independent" can actually stand up and hold managers accountable. I believe that even independent directors still can possibly be

compliant and controlled by management. . . . Unlike director in-
dependence reforms, the shareholder access rule is not a part of
Sarbanes-Oxley reforms. It is an aspect of proxy reform that has
its own unique history of consideration by the Agency dating back
to the 1970s. All along the way, the Agency's view has been that if
the proxy system is "broken," then it should be fixed. The current
access proposal is just the latest edition of these efforts, and should
be viewed separately and apart from Sarbanes-Oxley inspired re-
forms. (Campos 2005, 5)

Supporters of the access rules note that Sarbanes-Oxley does not provide the tools for investors to take preventive action against "bad actors"
(Bebchuk 2003b). As Commissioner Campos emphasized, it relies on the
independent director to act on behalf of investors in ensuring that nominations to the board are made on an appropriate basis.

Disruption and Division at the Board Level

Opponents of the access rule claim that the rule will be divisive as it will
lead to representation of special interests in board deliberations. This argument has been used to lobby against the implementation of cumulative voting, but it has less credibility when attacking a general investor access rule.
Although institutional investors now represent 59% of all investors in the
United States, huge blocks of voting shares in large cap companies are not
controlled by a single institutional investor, especially a single institutional
investor that is inclined to be an activist. Public pension and union funds are
compelled to use a diversified, risk limiting portfolio. Few institutions hold
even 1% of the outstanding shares in major public companies. The Council
of Institutional Investors (2004) estimates that public pension funds, one of
the most active groups of institutional investors, hold less than 8% of the
total U.S. equity market (Campos 2005, 4). Data gathered by the Commission during the comment gathering process indicate that among firms trading on the NYSE, AMEX, or NASDAQ, 58% have no single shareholder
that exceeds 5% of voting stock. Fifty percent of the companies have less
than two institutional shareholders with more than a 2% holding. In 50%
of the considered firms, the two largest institutional shareholders together
could not meet a 5% holding threshold (Bebchuk 2005).

A director that is elected after having been nominated using the access
rule should not be considered a *special-interest director*. The director is
elected by a plurality as with any other elected director. Another way of
stating this is that the director is elected by a majority of votes cast (excluding withheld votes). Consequently, the mandate must be sourced from

a significant and representative group of shareholders. It will be impossible for the special interests from a narrow group of institutional investors to dominate the balloting (Bebchuk 2003a, 14–15; 2003b).

The argument that increased shareholder access could jeopardize stakeholder interests has long been put forward as a rationale to minimize investor intervention. In 1932, Professor Edwin Dodd wrote, "Modern large-scale industry has given to the managers of our principal corporations enormous power. Desire to retain their present powers accordingly encourages [them] to adopt and disseminate the view that they are guardians of all the interests which the corporation affects and not merely servants of its absentee owners" (Bakan 2004, 20). Typically, corporations represent stakeholder interests only in so much as this is required by contractual relations and mandated by legislation. There is no formal process of accountability to stakeholders. With respect to a shareholder access rule, failure to adopt the rule does not increase the accountability and responsibility of corporations to other stakeholders. It merely ensures that there will not be enhanced accountability to shareholders.

No Resolution in Sight

On June 1, 2005, Mr. William Donaldson, Chairman of the SEC, announced his intention to resign. Mr. Donaldson was one of the most activist chairs of the Commission in its history but he drew the ire of the business community by supporting several regulatory initiatives of an interventionist nature. In a speech delivered at the Seventh Annual Corporate Breakfast at Yale Law School Center for the Study of Corporate Law, Commissioner Campos noted possible future compromises to the access rule including dropping the 1% opt-in rule and raising the withhold vote trigger to 50% (excluding broker nonvotes and abstentions). This is in line with the Business Roundtable's recommendations but in stark contrast to the majority of investors who support the introduction of the access rules.

Supporters of the access rules argue that the trigger methodology is flawed in that it delays effective action until after the holding of at least two annual meetings. They have emphasized the difficulty in orchestrating an effective proxy battle against large cap companies noting that even the largest of institutional investors, standing alone, may not muster the 1% of share ownership required for the opt-in. While the nominee for Chairman of the SEC, Christopher Cox, is on record as supporting the further study of proposals to give investors more power to propose directors (Johnson 2005), the lack of a clear statement of intent implies that the shareholder access proposal is destined to flounder, at least in the near term.

SHAREHOLDER ACCESS IN COMMON LAW JURISDICTIONS

The United States differs from other countries with a common law heritage with respect to the level of access and degree of authority accorded the shareholders. While directors in the United States have the discretion not to comply with precatory resolutions passed at a shareholders' meeting, shareholders in other common law jurisdictions have the right to make fundamental changes in the corporation by way of special resolution. In effect, this enables shareholders to direct management to take certain actions.

Shareholder Access in Canada

In Canada, under the Canada Business Corporations Act (CBCA), shareholders holding not less than 5% of shares that carry the right to vote at a shareholders' meeting may require the directors to call a special meeting (CBCA: § 143). If the directors fail to call a meeting within 21 days of any such requisition by a shareholder, he or she may call a meeting and the corporation must reimburse the shareholder for the expenses of doing so. Also, any director or shareholder entitled to vote may apply to a court to have a shareholders' meeting called if it is impracticable to call a meeting in the ways mentioned above, or to have a meeting conducted as prescribed in the bylaws or the CBCA (§ 144).

As in the United States, public companies are required to send out proxy circulars. The contents of the management proxy circular (CBCA Regulations: §§ 35–36) include the following categories of information:

- A description of shareholders' rights to appoint a proxy and how this appointment must be done
- Disclosure of transactions with insiders of the corporation (e.g., affiliated corporations, significant shareholders, directors, and officers)
- Disclosure of shareholders holding more than 5% of the issued shares of the corporation
- Details about the directors who are proposed for election
- Details about any special business to be dealt with at the shareholders' meeting

Similar to rules in the United States, shareholders who disagree with management proposals also may solicit the votes of their fellow shareholders. Dissident shareholders are entitled to obtain a list of shareholders, the shares they hold, and their addresses from the corporation and to contact other shareholders for the purpose of influencing their voting (CBCA: § 21(3) & (9)). A dissident shareholder solicitation must be sent to shareholders in the form of a dissident proxy circular. Recourse to a dissident proxy circular has rarely been used in Canada.

Proposal Subsidy in Canada

Typically, the agenda for shareholders' meetings is set by the directors. However, the CBCA provides a limited right for shareholders to add items to the agenda (CBCA: §137), including the amendment of bylaws and articles (CBCA: §§ 103(5) & 175(1)). Any shareholder entitled to vote may submit to the corporation a notice—called a *proposal*—of any matter he or she proposes to discuss. As in the United States, eligibility requirements to submit a proposal are modest. A shareholder may submit a proposal if he or she holds voting shares equal to 1% of the total number of the outstanding voting shares of the corporation, as of the day on which the shareholder submits a proposal, or holds shares whose fair market value, as determined at the close of business on the day before the shareholder submits the proposal to the corporation, is at least $2,000. In addition, the shares must have been held for at least six months prior to the submission of the proposal (CBCA: Regs. § 46).

Corporations that are required to send out a management proxy circular must include the shareholder proposal along with a supporting statement of up to 200 words from the proposing shareholder (CBCA: § 150). As a result, shareholders avoid the expense of having to send out a separate communication to other shareholders for consideration of shareholder proposals. While a similar right to propose is provided by federal rules in the United States, there are critical differences (see below).

A proposal under the CBCA may include nominations for the election of directors if the proposal is signed by the holders of not less than 5% of the shares entitled to vote. It may also include amendments to the articles and/or bylaws of the corporation (CBCA: § 175). These special resolutions, required for amendments to articles and certain other fundamental changes, must be passed by two-thirds of the votes cast at the meeting (CBCA: §§ 140, 173, 183, and 189). Unless the bylaws provide otherwise, voting is by a show of hands, but any shareholder may require that a ballot be taken—meaning that each vote is recorded on a ballot, which is collected and counted.

The corporation does not have to circulate a proposal in any of five circumstances:

1. The proposal is not received at least 90 days before the anniversary date of the last annual meeting.

2. It clearly appears that the proposal is primarily for the purpose of:
   - Enforcing a personal claim or redressing a personal grievance against the corporation, the directors, officers, or security holders; or
   - Promoting general economic, political, racial, religious, social, or similar causes
3. The proposing shareholder made a proposal within the last two years, then failed to show up, in person or by proxy, to speak to it at the meeting.
4. Substantially the same proposal was submitted to a meeting of shareholders and defeated.
5. The right to make a proposal is being abused to secure publicity.

The limits on what may be subject to a proposal apply equally to what may be the subject of a shareholder-requisitioned special meeting (Van Duzer 2003).

The Agenda of Shareholders' Meetings in Other Common Law Jurisdictions

Other Commonwealth countries have adopted similar powers of intervention. In the United Kingdom, management by the board of directors is subject to any directions given by special resolution of the shareholders (U.K. Companies Act 1985: Article 70). Shareholders always have a residual right to amend the articles of association and to change corporate decisions. As in Canada, a special resolution requires a supermajority. In the U.K. this supermajority is slightly higher, set at 75% of votes cast as opposed to the two-thirds standard prescribed in Canada.

Australia provides similar provisions. All powers are given to the board subject to the corporate charter (Australia Corporations Act 2001: § 198A). However, shareholders have the right to amend the charter by special resolution thereby retaining residual power (Australia Corporations Act 2001: § 252L).

THE RISE AND FALL OF CUMULATIVE VOTING

Cumulative voting is seen by corporate governance reformers as a mechanism to improve shareholder representation on boards. The system originates in the United States as an outgrowth of a political reform. When Illinois revised its constitution in 1870, it introduced cumulative voting for the Illinois House of Representatives. This revision was also applied to the election of directors of private corporations. The objective was to protect minority interests against overreaching by a majority, particularly in circumstances in which representation on the board would give the minority the information necessary to police against fraud (Gordon 1994).

Seven states adopted mandatory cumulative voting provisions by 1880. This increased to 18 by 1900 with all but six introduced under state constitutional provisions. Several states adopted permissive cumulative voting provisions, including New York (1892), New Jersey (1900), and Delaware (1917). By 1945, 22 states had mandatory cumulative voting provisions, and 15 had permissive. There was additional legislative and regulatory support for cumulative voting including under the Banking Act of 1933, with respect to reorganization cases overseen by the Securities and Exchange Commission and under the first Model Business Corporations Act published in 1950.

From the 1950s onward, there was a steady decline in the percentage of jurisdictions requiring mandatory cumulative voting. Those jurisdictions that introduced cumulative voting introduced it on a permissive basis. From the 1960s onward, states began switching from mandatory cumulative voting to voluntary. By 1992, only six states maintained mandatory cumulative voting, 44 provided for voluntary inclusion while one state, Massachusetts, prohibited cumulative voting (Gordon 1994, 143–146).

Gordon (1994) postulates that there were significant managerial motives that prompted the two most sweeping periods of legislative change moving from mandatory to permissive cumulative voting regimes, during the 1950s and 1980s. Empirical evidence supports that there was a greater incidence of proxy battles in companies subject to cumulative voting, a greater likelihood of voluntary inclusion of minority nominees, and a virtual one-to-one relationship between insurgent victory in representation battles and the presence of cumulative voting. In the 1950s these proxy battles related to board representation; in the 1980s they were also coupled with hostile takeover actions. Although not high in number, the proxy contests were high profile with cumulative voting figuring prominently.

In general, management opposed cumulative voting. The American Bar Association, in the 1955 revision to the Model Business Corporations Act, reversed its recommendation on mandatory cumulative voting. States having mandatory cumulative voting recognized that companies were inclined to move to jurisdictions where cumulative voting was voluntary. Each aspect had its influence, but the timing of the most dramatic shifts in legislative policy implies that the management lobby played a significant role. Of the many examples discussed in Gordon's examination, the California motivation for legislative change is particularly interesting:

> . . . *The actual political impetus for passage of the legislation was apparently supplied not by the small high-tech firms, but by California public utilities that could not exit from the California corporate law regime. At its 1989 annual meeting, Pacific Enterprises, parent of Pacific Gas & Electric as well as Thrifty Stores, a drug store chain, was surprised by the near success of a labor union leader at winning a board seat. Marshalling support from employees under an ESOP with pass-through voting, a regional director of the Utility Workers Union obtained 75 percent of the votes necessary (7 percent) to win a board seat. In shocked reaction to the possibility of a union representative on the board, the public utilities' managements, which are tied to a California corporate domicile by the Public Utility Commission, began pushing for the repeal of mandatory cumulative voting. The repeal measure, which was obtained at the very next legislative session, was not high-profile legislation. Most of the legislative actors believed it to be anti-takeover legislation designed to retain California corporations, and the unions, completely unaware of the proposal, made no move to oppose it. It was only in 1990, when Pacific Enterprises proposed to eliminate cumulative voting from its charter, that unions were alerted to the change. The California State Association of Electrical Workers strenuously sought to reverse the change in the next legislative session but was unsuccessful; a legal change that could easily have been blocked was impossible to undo. In 1990, all three investor-owned electric utilities in California eliminated cumulative voting from their charters. (Gordon 1994, 158–159)*

Cumulative Voting Fundamentals

Cumulative voting has been promoted by shareholder activists as a remedy to solve the inability of minority shareholders to elect representatives to the board of directors. Under a normal voting arrangement, each director is elected separately normally by a simple majority vote of shareholders present at and registered for the shareholders' meeting. In contrast, cumulative voting is designed to ensure that minority shareholders can elect a representative to the board of directors.

A few jurisdictions provide a definition of cumulative voting. Under Canadian law, cumulative voting provisions read as follows:

107. Where the articles provide for cumulative voting,

> *(a) the articles shall require a fixed number and not a minimum and maximum number of directors;*
>
> *(b) each shareholder entitled to vote at an election of directors has the right to cast a number of votes equal to the number of votes attached to the shares held by the shareholder multiplied by the number of directors to be elected, and may cast all of those votes in favour of one candidate or distribute them among the candidates in any manner;*
>
> *(c) a separate vote of shareholders shall be taken with respect to each candidate nominated for director unless a resolution is passed unanimously permitting two or more persons to be elected by a single resolution;*
>
> *(d) if a shareholder has voted for more than one candidate without specifying the distribution of votes, the shareholder is deemed to have distributed the votes equally among those candidates;*
>
> *(e) if the number of candidates nominated for director exceeds the number of positions to be filled, the candidates who receive the least number of votes shall be eliminated until the number of candidates remaining equals the number of positions to be filled;*
>
> *(f) each director ceases to hold office at the close of the first annual meeting of shareholders following the director's election;*
>
> *(g) a director may be removed from office only if the number of votes cast in favour of the director's removal is greater than the product of the number of directors required by the articles and the number of votes cast against the motion; and*
>
> *(h) the number of directors required by the articles may be decreased only if the votes cast in favour of the motion to decrease the number of directors is greater than the product of the number of directors required by the articles and the number of votes cast against the motion. (R.S. 1985, c. C-44: § 107; 2001, c. 14: §§ 39(E) and 135(E))*

In the Russian Law on Joint Stock Companies (article 66, clause 4), cumulative voting is defined as a system in which the number of votes to which a shareholder is entitled is multiplied by the number of persons to be elected to the board of directors. The shareholder may cast all such votes for a single candidate or distribute such votes between or among two or more candidates. The candidates who have received the greatest number of votes shall be deemed to be elected to the board of directors.

Cumulative Voting Requirements

Regardless of the definition of the system, a relatively simple calculation can be used by shareholders to determine how many shares they will need to elect one or more directors to the Board of Directors.

Although cumulative voting may improve shareholder democracy and as such the functioning of shareholders meetings, the system only seems to work when shareholders:

- Have been educated about the system, when they have a good understanding of the company law, and when they are able to strategically use cumulative voting
- Have the resources and skills to campaign for candidates for the board of directors
- Have the willingness to be actively engaged in contacting other shareholders prior to and during the shareholders' meeting
- Have the explicit right to nominate candidates

Cumulative voting must be coupled with the shareholders' ability to nominate directors. If management controls the nomination process, pooling of votes will not affect management entrenchment. Assuming that management would fully understand the system and would be able to implement cumulative voting, it means in practice that shareholders need to contact each other, discuss their voting plans, nominate candidates, and in the end agree to vote together for a candidate. These assumptions may be valid in theory, but too often seem not to work in practice. The access of shareholders to a company's shareholders' list has been a major issue, for example, in developing countries where managers often have manipulated the records of shareholders. The education of shareholders and cultural differences appear to be other obstacles to the implementation of the system.

By 2003, only 9.2% of the Standard & Poor's Super 1500 have cumulative voting, according to the Investor Responsibility Research Center (IRRC 2003). Outside the United States, where contained in legislation, the trend is for cumulative voting to be permitted but not mandatory such as in Canada, Australia, and the U.K. (Baum 2000). Remarkable therefore has been the insistence of some corporate governance experts to oblige

The agenda of the general Meeting of Shareholders indicates that shareholders will elect 9 members to the Board of Directors. The company has 2,500 shareholders who collectively own a minority of 20 percent of the shares with voting rights (3,000 shares). The company also has one majority shareholder who owns 80 percent of the shares of the company (12,000 shares). The company has issued in total 15,000 common shares with voting rights. The company does not have preferred shares. 12 candidates have been proposed for a seat on the board of directors.

$$\frac{nS}{D+1} + 1 = \frac{9 * 15,000}{9+1} + 1 = 13,501 \text{ shares}$$

Where D = the number of directors to be elected, S = number of outstanding voting shares and n = the total number of directors the shareholder wants to elect (n = 9 directors in this example).
Source: Maassen and Brown (2005).

Russian shareholders by law to always elect their board of directors with cumulative voting. Under the old 1995 Russian Law on Joint Stock Companies, cumulative voting was required if the number of a company's voting shareholders exceeded 1,000. A recent amendment to the Russian Law on Joint Stock Companies in March 2004 has made cumulative voting mandatory for all companies with a board of directors. A Russian company is required to have a supervisory board if it has 50 or more shareholders with voting rights.

This amendment possibly can be attributed to Black's *self-enforcement doctrine* that apparently has been advocated in Russia. As stated by Black et al. (1998, 50–51), "Our approach to voting for directors, relies on a less common solution: mandatory cumulative voting, together with related requirements for minimum board size and annual election of directors . . . it is a central element of a self-enforcing company law. We are not so sanguine as to rely on the board of directors as a whole . . . but cumulative voting can strengthen the boards of many companies."

Companies that have cumulative voting and have the discretion to remove it, continue to find ways to justify its removal thereby reducing the overall incidence of companies using cumulative voting. Telus Corporation is a Canadian corporation that recently amended its articles to remove cumulative voting. The rationale presented in its Information

Circular is typical of the arguments usually presented by management against cumulative voting. The explanation is presented in the case study below.

CASE STUDY: Special Resolutions Removing Cumulative Voting Rights

The Articles of the Company currently provide that holders of common shares elect directors through cumulative voting. See "Election of Directors." The cumulative voting provisions were included in the Articles when the Company was first created from the merger of BC TELECOM Inc. and the predecessor Alberta based, TELUS Corporation.

Cumulative voting rights are often found in companies with a significant shareholder, and may afford minority shareholders a greater ability to elect directors to the board. The Company no longer has a significant shareholder and the candidates for election to the Board are assessed and recommended by an all-independent Corporate Governance Committee and approved by an independent Board of Directors. The Board believes that cumulative voting rights are not necessary to protect the interests of shareholders. Rather, its continuation may serve to enable the election of persons who represent the interests of particular or small shareholder groups. The Board believes that the interests of shareholders are better served by having a well-balanced Board of Directors that represents the interests of all shareholders on an equal basis and not the special interests of any particular or small group of shareholders. The Board further believes that its process for selecting candidates for nomination results in a group of directors with the breadth and diversity of experience and skills to work effectively together and provide all shareholders with effective representation on an equal basis.

It is the responsibility of the Corporate Governance Committee of the Board, which is comprised entirely of independent directors, to recommend to the Board of Directors all candidates being proposed for nomination as directors. Accordingly, the selection of director candidates is completely outside the control of management. The Corporate Governance Committee annually reviews the composition of the Board to ensure it is comprised of persons having the skills and experience necessary to allow it to supervise the business and affairs of the Company, assesses the skills and performance of each director, and identifies any skill gaps that should be filled through new directors. These procedures ensure the optimal mix of skills and talents required for overall Board effectiveness.

For these reasons the Board of Directors is recommending that the holders of common shares approve a special resolution deleting Article 27.4.2, to remove cumulative voting and adding Article 14.10 to the Articles to permit holders of common shares to vote by a separate resolution for each director rather than by a slate. This will ensure that holders of common shares can vote or withhold their votes on any particular candidate for director.

Source: Telus Corporation (2005, 14).

SUPPORT FOR ANTI-TAKEOVER MEASURES

Anti-Takeover Measures in the United States

As stated above, it appears that the move to reject cumulative voting in the United States was, in part, an act to strengthen management's defense against takeover. With the blitz of hostile takeovers in the 1980s, management pressed states for legislative change that would permit management to engage in a variety of anti-takeover strategies. The U.S. Supreme Court decision in *CTS Corp. v. Dynamics Corp. of America* (481 US 69 (1987)), which confirmed the jurisdictional authority of Indiana's state legislature respecting anti-takeover legislation, paved the way for the rapid introduction of a variety of anti-takeover acts leaving only a handful of states without new legislation on the subject into the 1990s. There are five types of anti-takeover statutes in common use today. These types of statutes are as follows:

- *Control Share Acquisition Statutes.* Legislation that prevents a bidder from voting its shares beyond a specified threshold (typically between 20% and 50%) unless a majority of disinterested shareholders vote to allow the bidder to exercise the voting rights of its control stake.
- *Business Combination (Freeze-Out) Statutes.* Legislation that prevents a bidder from engaging in a wide range of transactions with an acquired company (i.e., merger, liquidation, sale of assets, etc.) for a specified period of time, typically three or five years, after the bidder acquires its controlling stake, unless the target board approves the acquisition.
- *Fair Price Statutes.* These statutes are often combined with business combination statutes. It sets procedural criteria for the determination of a fair price in takeover contests. Some state statutes eliminate business combination restrictions if fair price criteria are met, and fair price criteria in turn can often be avoided if the bidder gains approval from a supermajority of disinterested shares (typically 80%).
- *Other Constituency Statutes.* These statutes allow the board to consider the welfare of nonshareholder constituencies (such as employees or the local community), either in the particular context of a takeover contest or more generally.
- *Poison Pill Statutes.* These statutes endorse the use of a poison pill against a hostile bidder.

By 2000, 27 states in the United States had control share acquisition statutes, 33 had freeze-out statutes, 27 had fair price statutes, 31 had constituency statutes, and 25 had poison pill validation statutes (Subramanian 2001).

There has been great debate as to whether the proliferation of anti-takeover legislation and the resulting charter-shopping behavior of management serve to increase or decrease shareholder value. There is empirical evidence that these statutes decrease shareholder wealth (Bebchuk, Coates, and Subramanian 2001) and managerial agency costs (Garvey and Hanka 1999). Executive pay increases in firms that have switched domicile for greater anti-takeover protection (Bertrand and Mullainathan 1999a) and one study indicate a decrease in plant-level efficiency tied to the shift (Bertrand and Mullainathan 2000).

Subramanian (2001) examined the migration patterns of companies and concluded that managers migrate to jurisdictions with anti-takeover statutes. In so doing, he also described jurisdictional case studies. The case study below presents an extract from his description of California's experience and presents a recent case of a firm, ESS Technology Inc., that has followed the pattern described by switching domicile from California to Delaware.

CASE STUDY: Switching Domicile from California to Delaware

. . . California is the headquarters of more corporations than any other state (16% by number and 11% by sales), yet it has only 4% of the corporate charter market by number and 1% by sales. Mostly it has lost these companies to Delaware: during the 1990s, 114 companies shifted their state of incorporation from California to Delaware (and only 7 went the other way), so that by 2000 a full two-thirds of companies headquartered in California are incorporated in Delaware [this data excludes financial firms]. This is one of the highest Delaware incorporation rates among all the states, and much higher than the national average of 50%.

California is not only losing to Delaware: in 2000, 130 companies headquartered in California were not incorporated in California or Delaware, but in some third state. In contrast only 18 companies choose California incorporation over their own home state and Delaware. California's market share of the corporate charter market has declined from 5% to 4% in the 1990s and will likely continue to decline in the foreseeable future.

Why is California such a poor player in this market? As described by the Investor Responsibility Research Center, "California has long been known for its shareholder rights stance and its unwillingness to bend to corporate interests." . . . California has no anti-takeover statutes, a feature that it shares with only six other states—Alabama, Alaska, Arkansas, Montana, New Hampshire, and West Virginia—which collectively are home to 124 companies but state of incorporation for only 39 of them. In 1988, the California Senate Commission on Corporate

Governance, Shareholder Rights, and Securities Transactions reviewed the state's takeover regime and made a number of pro-shareholder recommendations. The California legislature quickly acted on these recommendations and approved bills that provided for disclosure of proxy voting records, restricted the use of super-majority voting requirements, required an independent fairness opinion in management buyouts, and restricted the payment of greenmail. Governor Deukmejian signed all into law except the anti-greenmail provision, on the view that greenmail was "essentially an interstate market phenomenon" and thus better regulated at the federal level.

In 1989, California went further by amending its corporate code to require directors to act not only in "the best interest of the corporation" but also (explicitly) in the best interest of "its shareholders." (Cal. Code. Ann: § 190). The additional language, essentially amounting to an "anti-constituency" provision, received substantial attention from California business lawyers at the time and illustrates the extent of California's pro-shareholder leanings. Finally, and perhaps most importantly, California has not validated the "flip-over" poison pill, which is the most common version of the pill today. . . . The leading treatise on California corporate law suggests that such a pill "appears to be violative" of Section 203 of the California Corporate Code, which prohibits distinctions among shareholders. . . . 128 companies have migrated away from California and 9 companies have migrated into California since these laws were enacted [as of the study date in 2001].

Source: Subramanian (2001, 52–53).

Illustrative of this trend is the agenda presented and subsequent action taken at ESS Technology, Inc.'s 2005 annual shareholders meeting held on June 16, 2005. One of the agenda items was to "approve changing the Company's state of incorporation from California to Delaware." The summary reasons presented for the move were:

- The greater predictability, flexibility, and responsiveness of Delaware law to corporate needs
- Enhanced ability of Delaware corporations to attract and retain qualified independent directors
- More certainty regarding indemnification and limitation of liability for directors (ESST Proxy Statement 2005)

In the explanation of the first bullet point, emphasis was placed on anti-takeover measures as follows:

[W]hile the Company is currently unaware of any hostile attempts to acquire control of the Company, it believes that Delaware law is

better suited than California law to protect shareholders' interests in the event of an unsolicited takeover attempt. (ESS Technology 2005, 10)

This was elaborated upon further in the proxy circular as follows:

The Board of Directors believes that unsolicited takeover attempts can seriously disrupt the business and management of a corporation and may be unfair or disadvantageous to the corporation and its shareholders because:

- *A non-negotiated takeover bid may be timed to take advantage of temporarily depressed stock prices;*
- *A non-negotiated takeover bid may be designed to foreclose or minimize the possibility of more favorable competing bids; and*
- *A non-negotiated takeover bid may involve the acquisition of only a controlling interest in the corporation's stock, without affording all shareholders the opportunity to receive the same economic benefits. (ESS Technology 2005, 13)*

Under the heading *Possible Disadvantages*, the board acknowledges a possible diminution of minority shareholder rights as follows:

Despite the unanimous belief of the Board of Directors that the Reincorporation Proposal is in the best interests of ESS California and its shareholders, it should be noted that Delaware law has been criticized by some commentators on the grounds that it does not afford minority stockholders the same substantive rights and protections as are available in a number of other states. Reincorporation of the Company in Delaware may make it more difficult for minority stockholders to elect directors and influence Company policies. It should also be noted that the interests of the Board of Directors, management and affiliated shareholders in voting on the Reincorporation Proposal may not be the same as those of unaffiliated shareholders. . . . (ESS Technology 2005,14)

A clear reading of the proxy circular lends support for Subramanian's findings that a prime motivator in the migration of companies' domicile is the ability to implement anti-takeover measures. The ESST example also lends support for a move away from jurisdictions that promote shareholder intervention.

The European Response to Anti-Takeover Measures

The European Union has long grappled with the issue of takeover and its implications for shareholders. Beginning in 1974, Robert Pennington was assigned to review takeover legislation in Europe and to draw up a first draft directive for takeover bids. Eleven years later, a Takeover Directive was included in the medium-term objectives of the 1985 White Paper. In 1989/1990 the first draft proposal was prepared. These early attempts were more focused on "achieving detailed harmonisation in the field of takeover bids . . ." (European Commission 2002a).

In 1996, a framework directive was prepared that marked a shift toward providing greater flexibility on the part of member states as to what would be included in national law. This proposal was the subject of protracted negotiation and amendment. During these negotiations, the Commission announced the Financial Services Action Plan (European Commission 1999), in which it made it quite clear that the Takeover Directive was of immediate importance for the further integration of the European single market and the development of a consistent corporate governance policy (European Commission 1999). In 2001, a draft proposal was submitted to the European Parliament but was rejected by a tied vote.

There were several reasons for the 2001 defeat. Some Members of the European Parliament (MEPs) felt that there was no level playing field for takeover bids due to the diversity of company and securities law structures in Europe. This objection was particularly coming from German MEPs— 99% of them voted against the proposal. But there were other issues. MEPs protested the lack of employee protection. The draft Directive also required the Board to remain neutral during a takeover bid. In other words, it would prohibit the Board from taking anti-takeover actions. This is in stark contrast to the U.S. approach. MEPs worried that without harmonization with U.S. law, European corporations would be placed at a competitive disadvantage.

With the failure of the 2001 initiative, the Commission appointed a High Level Working Group of Company Law Experts. With respect to takeovers, the Group was asked to investigate three questions: how to ensure the existence of a level playing field in the EU concerning the equal treatment of shareholders across member states; what should be defined as the *equitable price* to be paid to minority shareholders; and what right a majority shareholder should have to buy out minority shareholders (European Commission, 2002a). The Working Group followed two defining principles: Takeover decisions are shareholder decisions, and risk-bearing capital should exercise control.

With respect to the issue of ensuring a level playing field the Working Group recommended:

- *Full Disclosure.* Listed companies should be required to disclose complete information about their capital and control structures (except for those deriving from general applicable law), for instance in their annual reports, listing particulars and prospectuses. If important changes occur in this information, listed companies should be under a continuous obligation to disclose such changes. Disclosure of some of these elements is already required under existing Directives: The Group recommends that these elements be disclosed and presented in a combined, coherent way.
- *Board Neutrality.* After announcement of a bid, the board of the offeree company should not be permitted to take actions frustrating a takeover bid on the basis of a shareholders' meeting authorization given prior to the bid. Only when a bid is actually announced and the shareholders can assess all relevant information, can they in fairness be asked to decide whether a takeover bid should be frustrated by the board.
- *Breakthrough Rule.* A rule should be introduced that allows the bidder to break through mechanisms and structures that are defined in the articles of association and related constitutional documents with the intent to frustrate a bid. The rule should be applied after completion of a takeover bid for all the risk-bearing shares of the company which achieves such a measure of success as clearly to justify the breakthrough.

These issues were transposed into a Directive that focused on shareholder protection, board neutrality, and the establishment of a level playing field (Directive 2004/25/EC, adopted April 24, 2004). The Directive prescribed the basic principles underlying a mandatory bid rule (Article 5), the establishment of an equitable price (Article 5), board neutrality (Article 9), a breakthrough rule (Article 11), and squeeze-out and sell-out rights (Article 15 and 16). To elaborate on key provisions:

- Board neutrality means that a board must obtain shareholder approval before taking actions to frustrate a bid or, where there was a prior authorization, obtain shareholder confirmation that a previously approved action may still be taken.
- The breakthrough rule provides protection during a bid and afterward:
    - During the time of the bid, any restrictions on voting rights do not apply (and dual or multiple voting shares are also subject to the

one-share-one-vote principle) at a shareholders' meeting where defensive measures mentioned in Article 9 are decided upon.

- Once a bidder has reached 75% of the capital carrying voting rights, no restrictions on voting rights (e.g., voting caps) or any other extraordinary rights of shareholders (for example, to appoint or remove a board member) apply. Dual and multiple voting rights are subject to a one-share-one-vote principle at the first shareholders' meeting held after reaching the threshold. At this meeting, the successful bidder has the right to amend the company's articles of association and to remove or appoint board members.
- *Sell-Out/Squeeze-Out Rights.* If an offeror obtains or has the contractual right to obtain 90% or more of the voting securities, minority shareholders can demand that the offeror purchase their shares (Article 16). Likewise, the offeror can squeeze out minority shareholders by forcing the sale of the minority shareholders' securities (Article 15).

The Directive did not mirror the recommendations of the High Level Working Group. Three notable variations from the Takeover Report's recommendations (European Commission 2002a) found their way into the Directive:

- In addition to anti-takeover provisions contained in the charter and bylaws of a company, the Directive also covers contractual arrangements. Any restrictions on the transfer of securities provided for in contractual agreements between the offeree company and holders of its securities, or in contractual agreements between holders of the offeree company's securities entered into after the adoption of the Directive, do not apply vis-à-vis the offeror during the time allowed for acceptance of a bid. In this respect, the coverage of the Directive is more sweeping than envisaged by the High Level Working Group.
- Where shareholder rights are restricted pursuant to the Directive, compensation must be paid to the affected shareholders for any loss they suffered as a result of the restriction of their rights.
- Golden shares held by member states in offeree companies are exempt from the rights restrictions contemplated in the Directive.

Inclusion of contractual arrangements is a positive step as it places constitutional and contractual provisions targeting the same result on an equal footing. However, the latter two changes must be viewed as negative. The Directive sets out a right to compensation but leaves it to member states to determine the nature of the compensation. The High Level Working Group had recommended that there be no compensation paid in respect of the temporary restriction on shareholder rights so as not to undermine the goal of establishing a level playing field throughout the bidding process. Establishing an equitable basis for compensation will be elusive and may lead to widely disparate member state provisions. Likewise, exempting golden shares from rights restrictions creates inequity amongst shareholders and places state ownership of shares in a privileged category. This violates the principle that shareholders should be treated equally.

By far the most damning move away from the High Level Working Group recommendations was to make the board neutrality and breakthrough provisions subject to an opt-out by member states. If a member state decides not to opt in, however, it still has to grant any company which has its registered office within it the option of applying the board neutrality and breakthrough rules. This decision is made by the shareholders' meeting and can be revoked in the same way. If a member state decides to opt in, these provisions apply all to companies that have their registered office in that member state. Companies that apply these provisions can be exempted from the provisions if they are subject to a bid from a bidder who does not apply the same articles they do (commonly referred to as the reciprocity rule).

The High Level Working Group Report was decidedly in favor of shareholder decision-making when presented with a takeover offer. In the United States, in contrast, considerable deference is given to management. While the decision to accept an offer is put to shareholders, the board can subsequently step back from this decision. Further, the considerable latitude granted to the board to take measures to obstruct the efforts of a *bona fide* bidder prior to and during the extension of an offer would be in direct contravention of the principles underlying the Directive. This said, the end result between Europe and the United States may not differ significantly. The Directive defers to member states with respect to the opting in of key Directive provisions. This may give rise to radically different implementation strategies by member states and thereby present the opportunity for companies to engage in jurisdiction shopping much in the same way as has occurred in the United States.

Entrenching Management: The Staggered Board

A board may be removed in one of two ways: through a contested proxy solicitation or through a hostile takeover. In the United States, corporations have either a board that is elected each year or a staggered board where directors are grouped into classes and one class stands for election at each year's annual meeting. The most common form of a staggered board has three classes of directors thereby requiring three annual meetings for a wholesale change in board composition. Based on information extracted from the Investor Responsibility Research Center during the period from 1995 through 2002, approximately 60% of companies in the dataset have staggered boards. Of the 60%, roughly 50% had established the staggered board structure under the charter thereby ensuring that the structure could not be amended by a subsequent shareholder initiative (Bebchuk and Cohen 2004).

The staggered board structure is viewed as a reasonable defensive strategy to counter an outright and wholesale change in board membership resulting from a takeover battle. U.S. anti-takeover legislation has provided strong support for the imposition of indefinite poison pill defense strategies and a willingness on the part of the judiciary to support the management prerogative to just say no. In light of these developments, the success of a hostile bid may lie in the bidder's ability to replace incumbent directors. A staggered board ensures that such an effort will be prolonged, at least covering two annual meetings. Bebchuk, Coates, and Subramanian (2003) assert that since 1996, and possibly before, no hostile bidder has ever persisted long enough to win two elections.

Even when there is a formal takeover bid, the existence of a staggered board has a significant influence on the likelihood of the bid's success. Staggered boards have been found to increase the possibility of the target company remaining independent 12 months after a bid has been proffered from 31% to 64% and have been found to demonstrate similar results 30 months after receiving the hostile bid (Bebchuk, Coates, and Subramanian 2002; 2003).

Gompers, Ishii, and Metrick (2003) reported a substantial correlation between firm value during the 1990s and a broad-based index of 24 management-favoring provisions. This index includes staggered boards as one of the 24 elements. A subsequent study attempted to isolate the staggered board factor and measure its influence on overall firm value. It concludes that staggered boards are associated with a lower firm value and that this lower value is economically meaningful (Bebchuk and Cohen 2004). However, there is an interesting dichotomy reported in the results. Firms with bylaws-based staggered boards do not exhibit the statistically significant negative correlation demonstrated by firms with charter-based staggered boards. While it may be an unwarranted leap in logic, the failure to demonstrate a statistically significant reduction in firm value for bylaws-based staggered boards implies that shareholders' authority to change the board structure matters in overall firm valuation.

CONCLUSION: THE COMPENSATION CONUNDRUM AND SHAREHOLDERS' RIGHTS

Progressively, U.S. companies have been able to insulate management from shareholder influence. As discussed above, firms tend to choose jurisdictions that provide favorable support for anti-takeover measures. The majority of firms employ a staggered board strategy and representative voices of business oppose shareholder intervention in the director nomination process, preferring to leave the nomination responsibilities to a nomination committee. Cumulative voting has been all but eliminated from the mainstream corporate culture.

A growing body of research supports the hypothesis that firm value decreases when companies shift to states supporting anti-takeover measures and that management agency costs increase. One measure that may indirectly support this hypothesis is to assess the level of executive compensation year over year. Managers of American companies owned, or had options on, 2% of the total of public company stock in 1992. In 2000, management owned or had options on 13% of public company stock, a staggering 11% increase. Robert Monks characterizes this shift as a 10% tax on shareholders per year (Bebchuk 2003b, 17). This has coincided with an increased ability for management to shelter itself from takeover attempts. Even with the scandals that have plagued the U.S. corporate environment over the past five years, reforms have focused on increased disclosure obligations and an increased role for independent directors. Shareholders' power to intervene remains unchanged.

Consequently, shareholders are dependent on management to support measures that will improve access in the absence of a regulatory mandate. There are rare examples of management-initiated access. For example, Apria Healthcare decided to provide a direct access policy. This U.S.-based company permits a shareholder or a group of shareholders possessing 5% or more of the voting stock to nominate a director. Apria Healthcare will put the nominee on the proxy on an equal basis as management-nominated candidates. The shareholder nominee must satisfy the same minimum qualifications as a management-nominated candidate. Once the qualifications are vetted, full access is provided (Bebchuk 2003b, 40–41).

The European Union is discussing measures to improve shareholder access. But the reality is that Europe lags behind the United States in the use of technology that would support improved shareholder access. There are significant obstacles preventing foreign shareholders from participating in shareholders' meetings. Investors are also reluctant to deposit their shares in order to establish their entitlement to attend and vote at the shareholders' meeting. While the European Commission's Takeover Report emphasized a shareholder-based decision-making paradigm respecting takeovers, the Takeover Directive fell short of this objective by allowing member states to opt out of the most fundamental protections against management interference. In addition, the requirement to compensate shareholders whose rights are restricted during a takeover bid makes it less likely that member states will opt into these requirements. The failure to stipulate a compensation methodology at the EU level will also contribute to disparate rulemaking among member states. Consequently, while the EU at the policy level appears to support a more significant shareholder role in the decisions affecting the fundamentals of the corporation, the member state flexibility granted under the Directive may translate into corporations engaging in member state shopping in similar fashion to the U.S. experience.

Studies have questioned the validity of the assumption that increased shareholder activism will result in increased firm value. However, proponents of increased access argue that event studies have examined a flawed system. Precatory resolutions carry no compulsory weight. Proxy contests place a heavy cost burden on the initiator and may generate legal challenges from other shareholders, other stakeholders, and/or the corporation subject to the contest. The costs, the free-rider problem, and the potential for litigation all contribute to the decision on the part of most institutional investors to avoid initiating proxy contests. Withholding votes against directors may convey a message but is of no legal consequence. In theory, 99.9% of the shareholders could withhold their votes for a particular director. If he holds the remaining 0.1% of the voting shares in the company and he votes for himself, he is elected by a plurality.

Supporters of increased access argue that firm value will increase if the field is leveled. What would constitute a level playing field? Shareholders should have the right to initiate and decide upon resolutions that address fundamental procedural, representative and substantive change in the corporation. This would include resolutions that

- Alter the charter and bylaws
- Decide upon mergers, acquisition, or downsizing decisions
- Relate to the nomination, election, and removal of directors

Supported by modern technology, such a regime would have to ensure that the costs of intervention are not borne by a disproportionately small percentage of shareholders and that the right to intervene is set at a threshold that will discourage frivolous proposals but at the same time enable legitimate shareholder activism.

CHAPTER 13

The Market for Corporate Control and the Implications of the Takeover Directive (2004/25)

Blanaid Clarke

INTRODUCTION

As early as 1932, Berle and Means emphasized that one of the implications of a diffuse ownership structure is the separation of ownership and control with its related agency problem. Since then, there has been substantial international debate, frequently fueled by financial scandals, as to how best to resolve this problem. Interestingly, the common theme in this debate is the position of management as villains of the piece. Even the European Commission has been blunt in its assertion that "shareholders own companies, not management—yet far too frequently their rights have been trampled on by shoddy, greedy and occasionally fraudulent corporate behaviour" (European Commission 2003a). Various solutions to the agency problem have been proposed including active institutional shareholders, nonexecutive directors, incentive pay, and an increased role for auditors. The proliferation of corporate governance codes both at a national and international level is testament to our optimism in the value of such internal controls in monitoring management. External market controls also exist that are said to operate as a stimulant to encourage directors to adopt an optimal governance structure (Jensen and Meckling 1976; Fama 1980). One mechanism that creates such an incentive is the "market for corporate control." This theory is based on the idea that inefficient management leads to share price decreases and shareholders seeking to exit these companies. Opportunities thus arise for other persons to acquire the companies cheaply, to install new management, and to achieve greater returns for the new shareholders. The theory suggests not only that takeovers lead to the removal of underperforming directors but also that the threat of such takeovers encourages directors to perform to the best of their abilities in order to avoid losing their jobs following such takeovers. All that regulators must do in such a scenario is to ensure that the takeover market operates freely and without hindrance from the directors themselves.

The 1990s were characterized by a large increase in mergers and takeovers in the Europe Union (EU). In 1999, the total deal volume, the average deal value, and the number of hostile takeovers almost reached U.S. levels (Goergen and Renneboog 2004). This latter statistic is all the more striking when one considers that while hostile takeovers are common in the U.K. and to a lesser extent Ireland, they are rare in continental Europe (McCahery, Renneboog, Ritter, and Haller 2003). Partly, this disparity between the U.K. and Continental Europe is attributable to the differences in ownership and control in these countries. In the U.K. and Ireland, the vast majority of shareholdings are dispersed (Franks, Mayer, and Rossi 2004). However, in most other EU countries, the majority of shares in listed companies are controlled by families or institutions closely linked to management. Reduced possibilities thus exist for takeovers. One of the features of the Directive 2004/25/EC on Takeover Bids ("the Directive"), which will be examined in the fourth section of the chapter, is a *breakthrough rule* that is intended to transform a bid for a company with a dominant blockholder into a bid for a company with dispersed ownership. A further explanation of the lack of takeover activity in the continental EU is the existence of cultural and structural barriers to takeovers (U.K. Department of Trade & Industry 1989). For example, the company law systems in certain countries permit or require effective legal obstacles to takeover such as unequal voting rights, poison pills, and other anti-takeover arrangements. As takeover bids cannot thus be undertaken with the same expectation of success in these Member States, there is said to be no level playing field in the EU. Both the breakthrough rule and the prohibition in the Directive on frustrating actions are designed to overcome the structural barriers to takeovers. This is consistent with the view that prevails in the European Commission that the availability of a mechanism that facilitates takeover bids is basically beneficial.

Despite the often conflicting evidence, the weight of empirical evidence tends to suggest that takeovers have on balance a positive economic effect (McCahery, Renneboog, Ritter, and Haller 2003). A number of reasons have been suggested as to why this might be the case. Takeovers are a means for bidders or *offerors* to create wealth by exploiting synergies between their existing business and the target company or *offeree*. Takeover bids also offer shareholders the opportunity to sell their shares to offerors who are willing to offer a price above the prevailing market price. Finally, as noted above, the market for corporate control, which is the subject of this chapter, suggests that actual and potential takeover bids are an important means to discipline the management of listed companies. The second section of the chapter considers the underlying assumptions and the ambiguities that threaten the acceptability of the market for corporate control as a rationale for takeovers and as a disciplinary force on management. Even if takeovers are encouraged, whether that be in order to facilitate the market for corporate control or otherwise, should such takeovers be capable of being frustrated by management in any circumstances? The third section examines the arguments that have been put forward suggesting that anti-takeover arrangements have a positive effect on shareholder wealth. It considers whether such arrangements can ever be consistent with the market for corporate control. The final part examines in detail the various provisions of the Directive that have been introduced in order to ensure a liberal EU marketplace where takeovers are facilitated and where, in theory at least, the market for corporate control can operate freely.

THE MARKET FOR CORPORATE CONTROL

The most renowned proponent of the market for corporate control was Henry Manne (1965), who argued that there is a high positive correlation between corporate managerial efficiency and the market price of shares. Even before Manne, however, Dewey (1961, 260) referred to a takeover as a "civilized alternative" to failures "that transfers assets from falling to rising firms." In his seminal article on the subject, Manne suggested that the control of companies may constitute a valuable asset that exists independently of any interest in either economies of scale or monopoly power. Manne pointed out that:

> the lower the stock price, relative to what it could be with more efficient management, the more attractive the takeover becomes to those who believe that they can manage the company more efficiently. (1965, 113).

Manne concluded that the potential return from the successful takeover and revitalization of a poorly run company could be enormous. While he admitted that the dissatisfied shareholders who sold their shares might suffer considerable losses, he suggested that even greater capital losses were prevented by the existence of a competitive market for corporate control. As a consequence of this market for corporate control, Manne advocated that the stock market provides the only objective standard of managerial efficiency.

At the same time as Manne was working on his theory in the United States, Robin Marris (1964) in the U.K. produced a theory of takeovers integrated into a comprehensive theory of the company. His theory of the company was based on the concept of *managerial capitalism*, which suggests that directors tend to maximize the rate of growth of the company. This growth is, however, subject to a constraint imposed by the security motive. In the event of financial failure or a takeover, directors' jobs are threatened. The constant presence of a potential raider is a theme in managerial capitalism suggesting that directors will operate within a valuation ratio constraint (Baumol 1959; Lintner 1954). According to Marris, the valuation ratio is the market value of the equity capital to the book value of the assets. The lower the valuation ratio of the company, the greater will be the probability that a raider will place a higher value on the company than the market does, and hence the greater the probability that the company will be taken over. Therefore, Marris suggested that takeover raids would be encouraged if directors did not act in a way consistent with maintaining an acceptable valuation ratio.

Coffee (1986) identified the principal contemporary function of takeovers as being to serve as a coercive measure by which directors are induced to accept risks that they would reject on their own. The threat of a takeover provides an external shock that deters managerial waste. As Easterbrook and Fischel (1981, 1173) explained:

> *All parties benefit from the process. The offeree's shareholders gain because they receive a premium over the market price. The offeror obtains the difference between the new value of the firm and the payment to the old shareholders.*

However, before one can unreservedly accept the legitimacy of the market for corporate control, a number of basic premises on which it depends must be considered.

Assumption I—Correlation between Share Price and Managerial Efficiency

Manne (1965, 112) himself acknowledged that a fundamental premise underlying the market for corporate control is the existence of a high positive correlation between corporate managerial efficiency and the market price of shares of that company. For the directors' inefficiency to lead to the undervaluation of the company's shares, share prices would have to reflect the relative expected profitability of the company. The efficient market theory suggests that a company's share price reflects all publicly available information and is based on the market's evaluation of its past performance, its present state, and the market's expectations of its future (Fama 1970). However, the efficient market theory also suggests that private information is not fully reflected in a company's share price. One conclusion therefore is that for poor management to be reflected in the share price, knowledge of this inefficiency would need to be made public. It is arguable that this knowledge may be communicated either directly or indirectly. For example, Manne (1966) was one of the few experts to advocate the advantages of insider dealing as an efficient method of increasing the speed and accuracy with which the market receives and integrates information about the company. Insiders who possess superior knowledge about corporate affairs are strongly motivated financially to perform a kind of arbitrage function for their company's shares. The effect of this reliable information is stronger than the ignorant information that, over a period of time, will be randomly distributed with an overall neutral effect. Thus, Manne argued, the average market price of a company's shares must be the correct one. In this context, insiders aware that the company is likely to report poor performance might sell their shares in advance, causing a decrease in the share price to a more appropriate level. An alternative explanation that seems more plausible is that the public becomes aware of the underperformance of the company but fails to attribute it specifically to the directors' inefficient management.

Studies by Conyon and Florou (2002), Huson, Parrino, and Starks (2001), and Warner, Watts, and Wruck (1988) indicate an inverse relationship between the probability of top management replacement and stock performance. Senior management are dismissed for poor performance. This relationship is consistent with the hypothesis that information about management performance is reflected in stock returns. However, it is also consistent with the hypothesis that such information is used in evaluating management performance. In other words, inefficient management are identified and replaced in advance of a takeover. This is considered further below.

Assumption II—Shareholders Will Exit an Inefficiently Managed Company and Offerors Will Buy

A second premise underlying the market for corporate control is that shareholders will sell their shares when they become unhappy about the manner in which the company is being operated. They will choose this course of action rather than attempting to control their directors' inefficiencies or to oust their directors and replace them with more efficient officers. There are two possible reasons why shareholders might do this.

First, as noted above, shareholders may not appreciate the inefficiencies involved and may not attribute poor performance to their directors' inefficiencies. Shareholders, Scharfstein (1988) maintained, simply cannot distinguish between low corporate value caused by mismanagement or caused by unfavorable environment. If a company's value is low because the director mismanaged, shareholders may sell their shares at low prices because they place a low value on the company. Where corporate value is low simply because the environment is unfavorable, the probability of a takeover is low because although the shareholders still tender their shares at a low price, potential offerors do not value the shares as highly. The market for corporate control theory is then dependent on the ability of the offeror to identify the cause of the low share price and to realize that the value of the company, if run properly, is high. Hirschey (1986, 320) suggested that "successful managers are especially well equipped to detect the failures of inefficient management and to seize the opportunity provided by that inefficiency." He noted that successful managers also possess strong economic incentives to spread their expertise over broader economic resources. Scharfstein argued that the takeover mechanism provides a means of penalizing the director precisely when he or she should be penalized—when corporate value is low because the director mismanaged and not because the environment was unfavorable. It is submitted that this attributes great foresight and expert knowledge to offerors and little insight to shareholders. It is not really a question of having good news before the market as in the private information theory, it is more a question of analyzing the performance and being able to attribute it to the management of the company rather than anything else. In a sense, however, both theories imply an informational advantage and the same difficulty therefore arises in accepting both. As Herman and Lowenstein (1988, 215) noted:

> the assumption that these buyers are well informed is . . . implausible as a general rule, given the frequent lack of familiarity of the acquirer with the offeree's business, the lack of access to sometimes crucial inside knowledge, the great speed with which major decisions are sometimes made, and the considerable evidence of unpleasant ex post surprises.

This emphasis also assumes that there will be sufficient companies in the market willing to act as offerors. In some industries, Coffee (1984) suggested, there might be too few offerors to generate sufficient deterrence.

A second and more plausible reason why shareholders choose to sell their shares is that they become aware of managerial inefficiencies but are unwilling to act upon them. They make the decision to sell their shares and exit the company rather than attempt to take action to remedy the situation. In *Exit, Voice and Loyalty* (1970), Hirschman identified a fundamental schism between the exit option, where shareholders choose to escape from an objectionable state of affairs, and the voice option, where shareholders express their dissatisfaction directly to directors in an attempt to change the objectionable state of affairs. Exit, Hirschman maintained, belongs to the realm of economics.

> *[Exit] is the sort of mechanism economics thrives on. It is neat . . . it is impersonal . . . and it is indirect . . .*

Voice, by contrast, belongs to the realm of politics.

> *In all these respects, voice is just the opposite of exit. It is a far more "messy" concept because it can be graduated, all the way from faint grumbling to violent protest; it implies articulation of one's critical opinions rather than a private "secret" vote in the anonymity of a supermarket; and finally, it is direct and straightforward rather than roundabout. Voice is political action par excellence. (Hirschman 1970, 16)*

A significant problem with exercising the voice option is that it is expensive. It requires that dispersed shareholders be informed and organized and that resolutions be presented. Easterbrook and Fischel (1981) pointed out that the majority of individual shareholders are passive investors seeking liquid holdings with no interest in managing the company. They are apathetic and have little incentive in incurring the expense and time necessary to make a change. The problem of free riding contributes to shareholders' difficulties.

> *No one shareholder can collect all or even a little of the gains available from monitoring the firm's managers. The benefits would be dispersed among all stockholders according to their investments, not according to their monitoring effects. (1981, 1171)*

A further problem identified by Hirschman is that: "voice is conditioned on the influence and bargaining power members can bring to bear within the firm." (1970, 40).

This aggravates the free riding problem as the shareholder who discovers the existence of excessive agency costs has no authority to compel the directors to change their ways or to induce his fellow shareholders to oust the directors and install new ones. Easterbrook and Fischel (1981) noted that successful campaigns against directors are rare because the other shareholders still find it in their own interests to be passive. The majority of these individual shareholders do not appear to believe that they can make a change. Warner, Watts, and Wruck (1988) concluded that performance must be extremely poor before the probability of management turnover increases significantly. Faced with the prospect of grievous managerial ineptitude, shareholders may opt for the exit option as the only course of action open to them. One of Hirschman's main contentions was that the presence of the exit alternative could tend to atrophy the development of the art of voice in that the propensity to resort to the voice option depends on past experience with the cost and effectiveness of voice.

This emphasis on the exit option overlooks the fact that many individual investors are simply not in a position to exit. Baysinger and Butler (1985) explained this by reference to transaction cost economics. Owners of large blocks of shares cannot make a quick exit without depressing the share price and precipitating a substantial loss. Because securities are unique commodities, institutional investors may not be able to duplicate their positions in the marketplace without considerable cost. In addition, as Lowenstein (1999) noted, liquidity has its costs. The frantic pace of trading on the markets has at times absorbed, by commissions and other expenses, much of the profits of the underlying enterprises.

In 1984 Coffee had suggested that internal monitoring should be designed to detect inefficiencies before outsiders and before the market discounts the shares by a sufficient amount. He suggested that internal monitoring should act thus as "an earlier trip-wire" and that a truly independent board would not tolerate suboptimal performance by directors resulting in a share discount large enough to elicit a premium. At the very least, he suggested independent boards would engage in crisis management. (Of course this may be too late to stem the flow of deserting shareholders and turn the company around.)

It is arguable that recent developments in corporate governance are encouraging and allowing shareholders to become more active participants in the running of companies. The prominence of nonexecutive directors on boards, greater disclosure obligations, media interest, and also the increasing pressure of institutional investors all arguably contribute to greater availability of information. Certainly, the empirical evidence indicates that shareholders are exercising the voice option to a greater extent. This is something not anticipated at the time Manne and Hirschman were writing and something that Lowenstein (1999) argues makes the traditional, Berle and Means separation-of-ownership and control model obsolete. The afore-mentioned studies (Conyon and Florou 2002; Huson, Parrino, and Starks 2001; Warner, Watts, and Wruck 1988) would appear to suggest that underperformance does lead to dismissals. Similarly in their study, Morck, Shleifer, and Vishny (1989) found that the company's board looks at other companies in the same industry to evaluate the performance of their management and replaces directors when the company underperforms its industry (i.e., when directors can be blamed with some confidence). However, Conyon and Florou (2002) indicated that performance must fall considerably to significantly increase the actual management dismissal rate.

Assumption III—Sufficient Reward for the Offerors

A third premise of the market for corporate control is that an offeror would be able to reap a sufficient reward from replacing the inefficient directors to be able to afford the acquisition. Recouping a sufficient reward depends first, on the cost of the company reflecting its underperformance and not being inflated in other ways. Transaction cost considerations will have to be taken into account in this respect. It has been argued that a high rate of executive turnover is often undesired by the offeror and is an example of a demoralization cost. One reason for this is the assimilation problems likely in the aftermath of the acquisition, which are often more serious than the offeror anticipated. Attempting to integrate new personnel from outside to a new corporate culture can also be difficult. Lawrence (1967) suggested that in many cases many failures to assimilate new acquisitions result in dissipating "the most important asset acquired—a strong, viable organisation" (p. 231). In addition, the offeror may not be able to capture all the benefit of the transaction as a result of defensive tactics aimed at increasing pre- or postacquisition costs. These tactics will be discussed further below.

The offeror's reward also depends on the directors' inefficiency being significant enough to be reflected in the share price. Most instances of self-dealing will not result in a significant enough discount in the company's share price to justify the substantial takeover premium that normally prevails. Thus the market for corporate control may not apply to small amounts of mismanagement. Coffee (1984) suggested that "no matter how venal or self-interested the management" it is unlikely that they could have misappropriated a sufficiently large proportion of the company's value to cause the market to discount the shares by more than half. He also argued that there is a timing problem that makes hostile takeovers largely irrelevant to the problem of self-dealing. The discount in the shares would only attract an offeror if it were reversible. However, substantial losses caused by a self-dealing management can seldom be restored. Consequently, the level of risk required to accept a financially distressed company is high. Extremely badly managed companies may thus become indigestible and survive. They are immune from attack precisely because of their pervasive inefficiency. This is consistent with Jensen's study of overvalued companies (2004). He argued that where a company's stocks become substantially overvalued, the market for corporate control is ineffective because "you cannot buy up an overvalued firm, eliminate the overvaluation and make money." For this reason, the discipline of the capital market may only be effective within a limited range. As Coffee explained (1984, 1204), companies where the level of inefficiency is either "not extreme enough to justify the necessary premium or so extreme as to surpass the offeror's level of risk aversion" fall outside the range and will not be considered as offerees. It has been argued thus that the market for corporate control is:

> *sufficiently limited that it can serve only as a remedy of last resort for massive managerial failures and not as the principal enforcer of corporate accountability. (Coffee 1984, 1153)*

Unresolved Issues

There are a number of issues still unresolved in the market for corporate control. First, the theory is not easily reconcilable with cyclical industry-specific takeovers as it would appear to suggest that offerors would search constantly and evenly throughout the marketplace to find mismanaged offerees (Coffee 1984, 1207). However, in many cases, takeovers tend to be cyclical and concentrate on first one industry and then another (Bradley and Sundaram 2004). A further factor not explained by the market for corporate control is why size is an important consideration. Galbraith (1967) maintained that "the danger of involuntary takeover is negligible in the management calculations of the large firm and diminishes with growth and dispersal of stock ownership." Studies by Singh (1971) suggested that offerees are selected on the basis of their size with smaller companies more likely to be acquired than large. This suggests that the market for corporate control may not have a significant disciplinary effect over directors' pursuit of growth. Directors may adopt growth strategies specifically to ensure that their companies do not become the subject of hostile offers. Against this Chiplin and Wright (1987) argue that the development of new innovative sources of finance has made the threat of acquisition more real for much larger companies than hitherto. In recent times, we have witnessed successful takeovers of corporate giants such as Mannesmann, Unocal, and Safeway.

Furthermore, the Market for Corporate Control theory does not explain why the search undertaken by offerors for potential offerees seems to be a restricted one that is strongly skewed by internal organizational considerations (Coffee 1984, 1207). A strong preference seems to be exhibited toward offerees whose organizational structure fits with that of the offerors. Jenkinson and Mayer (1994) in their study of hostile bids in the U.K. found that bids were made according to the strategic objectives of the offerors rather than to control poorly performing directors. This is in keeping with a recent study of large intra-European takeover bids (Goergen and Renneboog 2004), which suggested that synergies are the prime motivation for bids.

The available empirical evidence is ambiguous. A number of studies in the United States (Morck, Shleifer, and Vishny 1989; Palepu 1986; Firth 1980; Halpern 1973; Kummer and Hoffmeister 1978; Smiley 1976; Mandelker 1974) indicated that offerees have significantly worse share price performance in the pre-merger period than the average company in the market. However, contrary results indicating no evidence or only slight evidence of negative pre-offer performance compared to industry peers were reported in a number of other studies (Franks and Mayer 1996; Ravenscraft and Scherer 1987; Langetieg 1978; Dodd and Ruback 1977; Kuehn 1975; Singh 1971; Newbould 1970). Numerous studies also indicated that merged firms have no operating improvements and that the offeror's shareholders make no gain or incur a loss (Mueller and M. Sirower 1998; Gregory 1997; Berkovitch and Narayanan 1993; Bradley et al. 1988; Herman and Lowenstein 1988; Franks et al. 1988; Ravenscraft and Scherer 1987; Varaiya and Ferris 1987; Mueller 1985; Cowling 1980; Firth 1979; Meeks 1977). Goergen and Renneboog's (2004) study of price reactions to announcements of hostile bids confirmed this in its finding that offerors' shareholders disapprove of such takeovers. It would appear that the most that may be said is that the evidence indicates at best a weak version of the market for corporate control hypothesis, which may be valid at least in some countries.

POISON PILLS

There are two conflicting theories on the use of poison pills and anti-takeover actions. The *shareholders' welfare hypothesis* suggests that directors are acting in shareholders' best interests by frustrating offers they believe to be contrary to the interests of shareholders. For example, directors may consider the price offered to be inadequate and they may take actions to increase it to an acceptable level or to reject it outright. In part, this hypothesis is based on the management-knows-best premise. It is argued that shareholders will make the wrong decision if left to their own devices.

A number of reasons have been put forward to explain why this might be the case. Firstly, Bebchuk (1985) argued that the special dynamics of the takeover process might distort their choice. The *prisoner's dilemma* analogy is that shareholders will accept an offer, not because they truly believe that it is a good offer, but because they are afraid that if they do not accept it they will be left as an isolated minority when the other shareholders accept the offer. This could not happen in the U.K. as under the City Code (which is issued by the Panel on Takeovers and Mergers to provide an orderly framework within which takeovers are conducted), shareholders are given an opportunity to accept the offer after they have been informed of the other shareholders' reaction to it. This allows them to make a decision in the knowledge that the offer has been successful. However, Bebchuk argued that even within the current system, shareholders who prefer the offer to succeed may not bother to accept it, thus distorting the outcome of the offer against the offerors. He suggested that an offer might well fail even if a majority of the shareholders would prefer it to succeed. The shareholders may be too apathetic to accept or they may consider that if the offer is going to succeed anyway, their acceptance is irrelevant and that if it is going to fail they are helping to reduce transaction costs by ensuring less share certificates need be returned. Thus, the first round is likened to an *approval vote* because "a shareholder's decision whether to tender in that round matters only in the event that the decision proves pivotal for the bid's fate" (Bebchuk 1985, 1799). However, the City Code ensures that shareholders are kept informed of the levels of acceptance at all relevant stages of the process, particularly when the offer becomes unconditional as to acceptances. In practice, once an announcement is made to this effect, the majority of shareholders submit their acceptances promptly.

A second possible reason Lipton (1979) suggested as to why directors might argue that shareholders need protection is that they might lack the wisdom or skill to make an accurate assessment of an offer. In such cases, defensive actions are needed to allow the directors to ensure that only suitable offers are put to, or accepted by, shareholders. It is submitted that this is a particularly weak argument, particularly where the consideration offered is cash. The directors would have to argue, for example, that the offeror (and indeed the market) has undervalued the offeree and that the shareholders are not receiving a real premium. Even where the consideration offered is securities, the argument is potentially flawed. There is no reason why shareholders should not be able to evaluate the offer and to make their own decisions. Shareholders are provided with a large amount of information by the offerors and although the offeror is obviously biased, the City Code ensures that all information provided meets prospectus standards of accuracy and that profit forecasts and asset valuations are substantiated. In the case of institutional shareholders, it is submitted that they will be more familiar with the takeover process than the offeree's directors, who may have spent all their careers in the one company. In addition, the independent advisers involved during the offer in giving advice to shareholders will be familiar with the process and capable of giving good advice. The City Code ensures that such advisers are truly independent.

A more plausible argument is that defensive actions give directors stronger negotiating powers than they would otherwise have. They are therefore in a better position to negotiate better terms from the offeror for their shareholders and possibly to obtain a higher premium. If defensive tactics are prohibited, the offeror's bargaining position will be significantly strengthened relative to that of the directors. If defensive actions are allowed, instead of having to unite dispersed shareholders against an offer or potential offer, the directors may be able to take action independently. This gives them the added advantage of speed. From his analysis, Ruback (1988) concluded that directors' defensive actions may involve an attempt by the directors to get a higher price from the existing offeror or a competitor in order to benefit shareholders and thus may be described as "a fair gamble ex ante" (p. 138). This argument also has its detractors. For example, Coffee (1984) questioned why, if shareholder coordination was the rationale for defensive actions, institutional investors appear systematically to oppose them. A further means by which shareholders can benefit from poison pills such as golden handshakes is that they encourage the directors to pursue long-term strategies and investments in activities such as training. Without such incentives, directors might be less inclined to engage in activities that are ultimately in the best interests of the company.

The opposite side of the argument suggests that by increasing the cost of the acquisition, defensive measures such as poison pills may lead to a decrease in the number of hostile takeover offers and thus may harm shareholders. They may also prevent the efficient operation of the market for corporate control that Easterbrook and Fischel (1981) argued would increase agency costs. In addition, as Walking and Long (1984) noted, the offeree's directors may actually increase existing inequities by utilizing their company's resources in defense of their own position. The cost of adopting these actions is borne by the offeree itself. Directors may engage in such behavior despite these negative consequences for the company as they are guided by their own self-interest. The managerial welfare hypothesis asserts that directors are acting in their own best interests when they seek to frustrate a hostile offer. Offers that do not sufficiently cater to directors' interests are likely to be defended. Such a hypothesis views directors cynically as untrustworthy and unmotivated persons anxious to entrench themselves in their companies irrespective of the best interests of the shareholders. Certainly, such a view is not inconsistent with the description of directors by Berle and Means as a self-perpetuating body, with the power to divert profits into their own pockets, who do not share the interests of shareholders. This was the main argument used by the Commission-appointed High Level Group of Company Law Experts to criticize the use of defensive tactics. It noted that:

> *managers are faced with a significant conflict of interests if a takeover bid is made. Often their own performance and plans are brought into question and their own jobs are in jeopardy. Their interest is in saving their jobs and reputation instead of maximizing the value of the company for shareholders.*

It is argued that defensive tactics endow an already-strong management with excessive control leading to their entrenchment. Arguably, if one accepts that directors are sufficiently out of control to underperform until share price is reduced rendering their companies vulnerable to a takeover, one must accept that they will be out of control in other areas such as defensive tactics. Furthermore, in many cases shareholders are not involved in the decision to introduce defensive tactics. For example, the company's remuneration committee may take the decision to introduce a golden handshake agreement. Such an arrangement may only come to the attention of shareholders when it is disclosed subsequently in the annual report. Such an agreement could not truly be said to be consensual. A number of commentators argued that even if shareholders are afforded an opportunity to vote on the device, the process itself may not adequately protect their interests. While they maintained that the process of voting controls adverse terms to a degree, Easterbrook and Fischel (1991) noted that it is not perfect. First, where the actions pre-date the making of an offer, shareholders are not in a position to make an informed decision on an offer as no terms are available at this stage for them to consider. This, it is submitted, is a significant problem. Second, where individual shareholders with a relatively small stake in the company's internal affairs vote, they tend to vote in accordance with the directors' recommendations (Jarrell and Poulsen 1987). Indeed, the shareholders who consent to the tactics may not even be the shareholders affected by the tactic when implemented. However, this argument is less likely to apply to institutional investors, who clearly would have an incentive to become informed and to act on their own initiative (Gillan and Starks 2003; Noe 2002; Shleifer and Vishny 1996). Interestingly, Brickley, Lease, and Smith (1988) found that institutions vote more actively on anti-takeover amendments than other shareholders. This is important particularly in light of the fact that since the corporate scandals of 2001 and 2002, institutional investors have tended to become more active (Brent 2002). Indeed, it is reported that pressure from shareholder activism in the United States is responsible for the recent decline of anti-takeover structures. By the end of 2005, it is predicted that a majority of companies in the S&P will not have a poison pill or staggered board in place for the first time in 17 years (Costa 2005).

One means of frustrating specific bids that merits special treatment is the promotion of an auction. The crucial difference between this and other defensive actions is that while the promotion of an auction might lead to the frustration of a hostile offer, shareholders are afforded an opportunity to sell their shares. Bebchuk (1982) and Gilson (1982) agreed that auctions increase both shareholders' and society's wealth. Where an offeror discovers an offeree with synergistic potential, it will value it more highly than other potential offerors. Thus they argued auctions usually allocate resources to their highest-valuing prospective users. Easterbrook and Fischel (1982) on the other hand categorized auctions with all other forms of defensive action as a negative influence likely to expend the offeree's resources wastefully without producing gains for shareholders. As they believed that much of the gains the offeree's shareholders obtain in an auction come at the expense of the offeror's shareholders, they categorized them as mere trading gains that would not increase aggregate shareholders' wealth. Part of the difficulty in assessing auctions is that they may have two conflicting consequences—an increased premium for the offeree's shareholders but a reduced probability that an offer will be made in the first place. Easterbrook and Fischel thus maintained that on a more general level, all investors lose out from defensive action. They argued that while a buoyant market for corporate control leads to reduced agency costs and increased shareholder wealth, by contrast, a fall in demand and reduced takeover activity will lead to higher agency costs and a lack of takeover speculation price in the shares. As a result, shareholder wealth will be reduced. Easterbrook and Fischel concluded that shareholders' interests are better served by a system that increases the probability of offers being made. They thus recommended that auctioneering should be subject to the same treatment as directors' other responses to takeovers, because it needlessly reduces the efficacy of the takeover process. Bebchuk (1982) disagreed, stating:

> *From the perspective of targets' shareholders, abandonment of the rule of auctioneering to enhance further rewards for search is justified only if the resulting increase in offer frequency can be so large that it will outweigh the loss of the rule's significant positive effect on premiums. (p. 1038)*

He felt that the frequency effect is small and the premium effect large so that, on balance, auctions benefit the offeree's shareholders.

While the empirical evidence is often contradictory (Lipton and Rowe 2002), the majority of evidence would appear to support the hypothesis that defensive actions reduce shareholder value and are best explained as a device for management entrenchment (Bebchuk, Coates, and Subramanian 2002; Cotter and Zenner 1994; Dann and DeAngelo 1988; Easterbrook and Jarrell 1984; Asquith 1983; Dodd 1980). Interestingly, any gains to shareholders were found to be primarily associated with the contests in which the hostile offeror or a competing offeror prevailed. In the remaining cases, they found that shareholders typically lost large takeover premiums and experienced large share value declines when a sole offeror withdrew in the face of resistance by incumbents. The evidence would appear to suggest that insulation from the threat of a takeover, while it may lead to higher bids (Masulis, Wang, and Xie 2005) is associated with poorer operating performance and greater consumption of private benefits (Moeller 2004; Wulf 2004; Hartzell, Ofek, and Yermack 2004; Gompers, Ishii, and Metrick 2003; Bertrand and Mullainathan 1999b; Garvey and Hanka 1999; Borokhovich, Brunarski, and Parrino 1997). Recent studies suggest that when hostile bid costs, asymmetric information, and agency costs are considered, the bargaining power benefits of takeover defenses in negotiated acquisitions recede, and the costs of takeover defenses in the hostile bid context come to the fore (Subramanian 2001). Interestingly, despite all this, researchers have failed to find consistent evidence that antitakeover devices deter bids (Heron and Lie 2006; Coates 1999; Comment and Schwert 1995; Romano 1993; Karpoff and Malatesta 1989; Ryngaert 1988; Malatesta and Walking 1988; Dann and DeAngelo 1988; Jarrell and Poulsen 1987).

THE DIRECTIVE

A view emerged in Europe that since takeovers had an overall positive economic effect, European legislation to facilitate takeovers and to provide a level playing field for takeover bids was necessary. In 1974, the European Commission asked Professor Robert Pennington to produce a report on the European takeover marketplace. This eventually led to the announcement of an intention to propose a directive on the approximation of Member States' regulations governing takeover bids (White Paper on Completing the Internal Market 1985). The Commission's first proposal for a directive on Company Law concerning takeover bids was published in 1989. A further 15 years of debate then ensued. The process was beset with disagreement about the nature of the directive (detailed rules vs. framework), the viability of self-regulatory supervisory authorities, the necessity of mandatory general bids, and importantly the possibility of defensive actions. As late as 2001, the European Parliament rejected a compromise text proposed by the Commission on the basis of a number of political considerations, one of which was the rejection of the principle whereby, in order to take defensive measures in the face of a bid, the board of the offeree company must obtain the approval of shareholders once the bid has been made. The Rapporteur Klaus-Heiner Lehne had recommended that such a requirement could only be justified if a level playing field existed for European companies facing a takeover bid and that since this was not then the case the agreement should be rejected. This was an important acknowledgment given that initially both the Commission and the European Council denied the absence of such a playing field, arguing that the different anti-takeover measures existing in the economic and legal systems in each Member State neutralized each other (Dauner-Lieb and Lamandini 2002). The Council then placed the directive, which formed part of the Financial Services Action Plan, among the priorities as regards the integration of European financial markets by 2005. In October 2001, the Commission established a High Level Group of Company Law Experts, under the chairmanship of Professor Jaap Winter, to present suggestions for resolving the matters raised by the European Parliament. This Group's report in January 2002 ("the Winter Report") accepted the importance of the market for corporate control noting that "such discipline of management and reallocation of resources is in the long term in the best interests of all stakeholders and society at large" and that these views *inter alia* "form the basis for the Directive" (p. 19). A further proposal was introduced in October 2002 taking broad account of the Winter Report's recommendations. Agreement once again proved elusive and at the last minute a Portuguese compromise text was introduced to deal with the remaining contentious issues, notably Articles 9, 10, and 11. The compromise was eventually accepted and what became Directive 2004/25/EC on Takeover Bids ("the Directive") was accepted by Parliament in December 2003.

The Directive lays down measures coordinating the laws, regulations, administrative provisions, and codes of the Member States relating to takeover bids for companies the securities of which are traded on regulated markets. The stated aim of the Directive as set out in Recital 1 is to coordinate certain safeguards required by Member States in order to protect the interests of the offerees' shareholders. Recital 3 notes that the Directive is necessary to create EU-wide clarity and transparency in respect of legal issues to be settled in the event of a takeover and to prevent patterns of corporate restructuring within the EU from being distorted by arbitrary differences in governance and management cultures. Given the existing differences between legal systems in the Member States, the Directive takes the form of a framework of certain general principles (set out in Article 3(1)) and a number of general requirements that Member States will have to respect through detailed implementing rules. Article 3(2) expressly authorizes Member States to lay down additional conditions and provisions more onerous than those of the Directive. Thus the provisions of the Directive must be seen merely as minimum requirements for EU takeover regulation. While the Directive also allows Member States to provide in the rules introduced pursuant to the Directive for derogations from the rules, Article 4(5) clearly states that they may only do so where the general principles are respected.

In the debates on the Directive in the European Parliament in 2001, the argument was made that the introduction of a prohibition on frustrating action would create an unlevel playing field between the EU and the United States. The Winter Report acknowledged that boards of American companies generally have a broad discretion to put up defensive devices under the business judgment rule and that many individual states have enacted laws specifically permitting the board to consider other interests than shareholders' interests. However, it strongly argued that the American approach was likely to be less beneficial to the development of efficient integrated capital markets in Europe.

It cited three arguments to support this view. First, while American companies generally have a broad discretion to defend themselves under the business judgment rule, it argued that this discretion operates in a widely differing legal and capital market environment. It suggested that American boards are subject to greater pressure than their European counterparts to enhance shareholder value. This pressure comes from nonexecutive directors on the board, investment banks and advisers, and in particular from institutional investors. Board behavior is widely transparent under the legal transparency rules and the intense scrutiny of the media. In addition, proxy contests are more likely to ensue and liability suits against directors are more common as derivative actions are easier and the judicial system is better equipped.

Second, the Winter Report noted, while the relatively broad discretion of the board to defend against takeover bids has certainly led to a number of takeover bids not being successful or not being made at all, takeover activity in the American capital markets is intensive and forms an essential part of its financial and economical structure. It noted that European companies have benefited from this, and evidence gathered on mergers and acquisitions activity between 1990 and 2000 indicates that the existence of defensive mechanisms have not deterred European companies. By contrast, the existence of barriers in some Member States has resulted in control over listed companies being incontestable. The Winter Report concluded that this is undesirable in the European context, as an integrated capital market has to be built up in order for business to fully benefit from and make effective use of the integrating internal market in Europe.

Third, the Winter Report noted that certain defensive measures in the United States are prompted by the ability of bidders to obtain control through the making of a partial bid. Such bids are not possible under the mandatory bid provision in the Directive. Finally, it noted that a number of anti-takeover mechanisms applied in the United States are prompted by the ability of offerors to obtain control over a company by making a bid on only a part of the company's share capital. In order to prevent shareholders being pressured to tender, these mechanisms force the offeror to make a general takeover bid for all the shares in order to be able to exercise control. In Europe, however, the mandatory bid provision in the Directive would require an offeror to make a general bid to all shareholders for all their holdings at an equitable price, if it wished to acquire control of the company. In the system of the Directive, thus, specific anti-takeover mechanisms are not needed to achieve this goal. The Winter Report argued that it was not desirable that the American approach to defensive actions be followed in Europe. It concluded even if board resistance might in some circumstances be justified, "any regime which confers discretion on a board to impede or facilitate a bid inevitably involves unacceptable cost and risk." The cost factor was explained as the opportunity loss and the cost directly attributable to the introduction of the defensive mechanism.

Article 9

As a consequence of its deliberations, the Winter Report suggested that a guiding principle of any European company law regulation aimed at creating a level playing field should be the right of shareholders to make the ultimate decision in respect of whether to tender their shares and at what price. This is the view that appeared to find favor in the Directive. Recital 16 states that "in order to prevent operations which could frustrate a bid, the powers of the board of an offeree company to engage in operations of an exceptional nature should be limited, without unduly hindering the offeree company in carrying on its normal business activities." This theme is continued in Article 3(1)(c), which provides inter alia that "the board of an offeree company . . . must not deny the holders of securities the opportunity to decide on the merits of the bid." Article 9(2) giving effect to this principle requires the specific prior authorization of shareholders for "any action . . . which may result in the frustration of the bid other than seeking alternative bids" and specifically "before issuing any shares."

During negotiations on the Directive, a proposal was made to allow Member States to provide that the board could take actions frustrating a takeover bid if the general meeting of shareholders authorized such actions up to 18 months prior to the bid. The main justification for this was the lack of time to organize a vote during the offer period. The Winter Report explains that this proposal was refused on the basis that shareholders would not be able during this period to take into account and weigh all the circumstances that are relevant for their decision whether a takeover bid should be frustrated. Such circumstances would include the general market conditions prevailing at the time of a potential future bid, the performance of the company until that time, and the timing and attractiveness of any potential future bid. However, Article 9(4) was included to permit Member States to adopt rules allowing for the calling of such meetings at short notice.

Under Article 9(2), approval is required at least from the time the offeree is approached, but it may be earlier if Member States so choose. The U.K. would thus be entitled to and is likely to retain its more restrictive prohibition on such actions during the offer period or an earlier period during which the offeree board has reason to believe that "a bona fide offer might be imminent." While in practice this involves the Panel in making a determination as to whether there was reason to believe that a bid was imminent, practice has shown that more than mere press speculation or industry rumor is required.

Article 9(3) introduces a requirement for shareholder approval of "decisions taken . . . and not yet partly or fully implemented" before the beginning of the period during which Rule 9(2) applies where the decisions do not form part of the normal course of the company's business and where their implementation "may result in the frustration of the bid." The prohibition applies not only to contracts whose purpose is to frustrate the bid (as is currently the case, for example, under the Irish Takeover Rules), but to all decisions that have a chance of frustrating the bid. This appears extremely far reaching until one considers that Article 9(3) expressly excludes decisions that have been "partly or fully implemented." Transposing this particular provision will be challenging as no guidance is given as to what constitutes a decision or how one might be partly implemented. For example, if a decision to issue shares to a director was agreed and sanctioned by a board committee but not yet communicated to the relevant person, could it be said to be partly implemented? If a decision had been taken to buy property and preparatory due diligence had been undertaken but no contact made with the vendor, could this be said to be partly implemented? It is submitted that Article 9(3) makes a clumsy, if honest, attempt to prevent directors engaging in pre-bid activities that might jeopardize the market for corporate control. Under the City Code all contracts entered into prior to the offer period may be enforced. Concerns have thus been expressed in the U.K. that there needs to be a practical application of the stricter provision in the Directive in the implementing provisions in order to allow companies that are contractually committed to a course of action to be able to continue to be so and to ensure that bids are not used as a device to delay or frustrate perfectly reasonable commercial transactions (DTI 2005).

The Winter Report categorically stated, "If the board considers a particular bid not to be sufficiently attractive, it should be free and may sometimes be obliged to seek alternative bids from others." The prohibition in Article 9 expressly excludes the search for alternative bids. Such an exemption is also consistent with practice in the U.K. A further defense available to the offeree board is that of dissuading the offeree's shareholders from accepting the offer. The Winter Report advised that the Board's insight into, and responsibility for, the strategy and day-to-day affairs of the company enable and require it to advise the shareholders on the takeover bid. It thus opined that the board is best placed "to express its views on the consequences of the bid for the company and its business and on the attractiveness of the terms of the bid for the shareholders." Consistent with this view, Article 9(5) obliges the offeree board to draw up and make public a document setting out its opinion of the bid including its views on the effect of the implementation of the bid on all the company's interests.

Article 10—Disclosure

Article 10 requires companies admitted to trading on a regulated market to provide in their annual reports detailed information on: share capital structures; restrictions on the transfer of securities; significant shareholdings; shareholders with special control rights; systems of control of employee share schemes; restrictions on voting rights; agreements between shareholders that may restrict transfers of securities or voting rights; rules governing the appointment and replacement of board members and changes to the articles; powers of board members to issue or buy back shares; significant agreements to which the company is a party that take effect, alter, or terminate upon a change of control following a takeover; and agreements providing for compensation to board members or employees resulting from resignation or redundancy following a takeover bid. Boards are also required to present an explanatory report to shareholders on these issues at the AGM. An earlier version of the proposal required boards to obtain annual approval of such measures, but this was rejected as excessive.

The Winter Report advised that this disclosure requirement is essential for the protection of investors in order to enable them to assess the value of and risks related to their investment. It opined that markets could only judge the efficiency of companies with different capital and control structures on the basis of full disclosure. It is important to note that not all provisions relevant to Article 11 are included in Article 10. For example the reference in Article 10 is to agreements between shareholders that "are known to the company" and may restrict transfers of securities or voting rights. While clearly it would not be practical to impose any further obligation on the company in terms of disclosure, the breakthrough rule applies to all such contracts whether known to the company or not.

Article 11—Breakthrough

Article 11(2) and Article 11(3) disapply certain restrictions when a bid has been made public. During the acceptance period, Article 11(2) disapplies vis-à-vis the offeror restrictions on the transfer of securities provided for in the articles of association of the offeree and restrictions on the transfer of securities in contracts between the offeree and its shareholders or between shareholders entered after the adoption of the Directive. Article 11(3) provides that restrictions on voting rights provided for in the articles of association of the offeree and restrictions on voting rights in contracts between the offeree and its shareholders or between shareholders entered after the adoption of the Directive shall not have effect at the general meeting of shareholders "deciding on any defensive measures" in accordance with Article 9. In addition, Article 11(3) provides that multiple-vote securities will carry one vote each at the general meeting of shareholders which "decides on any defensive measures" in accordance with Article 9. Article 11(4) provides that where following a bid, the offeror holds 75% or more of the capital carrying voting rights, none of the above restrictions and none of the "extraordinary rights" of shareholders in the articles of association concerning the appointment/removal of board members shall apply. Furthermore, multiple-vote securities will carry one vote each at the first general meeting of shareholders following closure of the bid, called by the offeror to amend the articles or appoint/remove directors. The offeror is entitled to call such a meeting on short notice once at least 2 weeks' notice is given. Article 11(6) and 11(7) provides an exception to the application of Article 11(3) and 11(4) if the restriction on voting rights is compensated for by specific pecuniary advantages or if the rights are held by Member States.

The Winter Report argued that the presence of differentiated voting rights, voting caps, pyramid structures, and other such structures in Member States' company law was generally inconsistent with the principles of shareholder decision making and proportionality between risk-bearing capital and control. It argued that capital and control structures that grant disproportionate control rights to some shareholders should not operate to frustrate an otherwise successful bid. The breakthrough rule was designed thus to increase the number of takeovers in the EU by eliminating these corporate governance arrangements, which might otherwise impede takeovers. The desired effect is to transform a bid on a company where there is one dominant blockholder into a bid for a company with dispersed ownership. It allows the bidder thus to acquire control without necessarily persuading the dominant blockholder to sell. The Winter Report noted that the application of such a rule after a successful bid was designed to "strike a balance between, on the one hand, the need, at least for the time being, to allow differences in the capital and control structures of companies in view of the current differences between Member States, and on the other hand, the need to allow and stimulate successful takeover bids to take place in order to create an integrated securities market in Europe" (p. 30).

As a consequence of the rule, a blockholder who wishes to retain control must thus compete for the company. In the event that financing is thus available, the party with the higher valuation will prevail. Berglof and Burkart (2003) thus argued that, in the absence of wealth constraints, the breakthrough rule ensures an efficient allocation of corporate control. Interestingly the Winter Report also noted that in a fully integrated and well-developed securities market, the enforcement of the proportionality principle might be left to market forces. Such a market might be able to judge correctly the cost of capital of companies with capital and control structures that deviate from this principle and more efficient alternative investments would normally be available to investors in such a market. Thus structures deviating from this principle would wither and die out except to the extent that they are justified by the particular circumstances of a company. (The Winter Report stated that similar arguments might also be applied to the principle of shareholder decision making, though the conflict of interest of the board might well lead to market failure in this context.) However, as the securities markets differ and the markets in most Member States cannot efficiently judge companies that adhere to this principle, the Winter Report noted that the principle should be mandated.

This view is not without its critics and the Winter Report has been accused by Mulbert (2004) of dealing in a summary fashion with the question of whether such a rule is "necessary, justifiable or even advisable" (p. 718). The U.K. Company Law Review Group expressed the view that it was not objectionable to have shares with different proportions of control. It is also argued that the theoretical and empirical support for neutralizing the power of incumbent blockholders and boards is too weak to justify large-scale regulatory intervention. For example, Gugler (2001) found that companies with blockholders performed as well or better than widely held companies. Similarly, a study by Anderson and Reeb (2003c) determined that founder/family-controlled and -operated companies in the United States show better performance than those in the hands of outsiders, or those under their *de facto* control. Coates used economic theory of ownership structure; empirical research on ownership, value, and takeovers; and comparisons to U.S. law to argue that the breakthrough rule is not clearly better than the status quo, from either a political perspective or an economic perspective. Mulbert argued that there is no evidence to support the assertion that such structures would die in an efficient market and cited the Ford Motor Company as an example (2004, 718). Finally, the breakthrough rule may be avoided or its objective defeated by other means. It is possible that companies could avoid the rule by increasing ownership to more than 25% or reincorporating outside the EU. Alternatively they could introduce structures outside the scope of the rule such as crossholdings or pyramids. It is also relevant to note that the bulk of the massive concentration of voting control among public firms in the EU does not result from disproportionality but from the fact that owners retain a control block in an ordinary one-share/one-vote capital structure. A study by Bennedsen and Nielsen (2002) suggested that companies with these types of structures are relatively rare in the EU (circa 20%) and that only 4% of these are currently invulnerable to takeover but would be vulnerable under the Rule in that they would lose their veto power over a control transfer. This suggests that the breakthrough rule will do little in practice to achieve a level playing field.

On the contrary, the breakthrough rule has been characterized as a costly and inefficient measure. On the basis of economic theory, Khachaturyan (2005) argued that the rule violates the principles of shareholder democracy and decision making and freedom of contract. He argued further that it is capable of reducing the value of the offeree and eliminating any control premium after the bid has been announced. It has also been predicted that the breakthrough rule might induce firms—particularly new firms—to restructure specifically to avoid the rule. These new structures may be economically less desirable. Such a step may in turn give rise, among other things, to problems related to monitoring, managerial incentives, and liquidity (Bebchuk and Hart 2002; Hertig and McCahery 2003). For example, it may decrease the incentives for controlling shareholders to monitor. As the benefit of monitoring by institutional shareholders is constantly espoused, this may be a particularly counterproductive step. Furthermore, it may lead to the undermining of the very principles themselves. In its submission to the U.K. Department of Trade and Industry paper, the Australian Government noted that the implementation of Article 11 in the U.K. would nullify Australian/U.K. dual-listed company "joint electorate" shareholder structures, which currently ensure that all shareholders are treated equally in the event of a takeover bid.

A convincing argument can also be made that the breakthrough rule is unnecessary in that the mandatory bid rule ensures that the most efficient user will manage the company's assets. The latter rule also serves to protect minority shareholders by allowing them to share in the control premium. Berglof and Burkart (2003) argue that the breakthrough rule is inconsistent with it. For example, when faced with the option of acquiring control from a blockholder and thus triggering a mandatory bid, the bidder may circumvent the blockholder and directly make a bid for the company. Mandatory bids are less desirable from a bidder's perspective than voluntary bids in that under Article 5 there is a minimum consideration set out and depending on the circumstances a cash alternative may be required. In addition, under the City Code the number of conditions the offer may be subject to is severely restricted and the level of acceptances required cannot be more than 50%. Using the breakthrough rule may thus be perceived as a better option by the offeror. However, it may not necessarily be a better option for the small shareholders if the new owner chooses not to buy them out and no right to be bought out is triggered under Article 16. This in turn will lead to the problems associated with two-step offers where shareholders may feel pressurized into accepting unattractive general offers without sufficient opportunity to bargain with the offeror. The mandatory offer rule avoided these problems as the acquisition of control imposes an obligation on a party to make an offer to remaining shareholders at an equivalent price.

The issue of compensation for loss to shareholders may also cause difficulties. The Winter Report considered that no compensation should be payable in the situation envisaged under Article 11(4) as the loss would result from a public policy choice made by the EU and the Member State. "The holders of special rights lose them in a breakthrough situation basically because as a matter of public policy they should not be able to exercise those rights once a bidder has acquired 75% or more of risk bearing capital after a general takeover bid." However, it envisaged *exceptional cases* where specific damages could be proven. Recital 19 indicates a different approach. It states:

> *Where the holders of securities have suffered losses as a result of the removal of rights, equitable compensation should be provided for in accordance with the technical arrangements laid down by Member States.*

Thus Article 11(5) provides that where rights are removed on the basis of paragraphs 2, 3, or 4 and/or Article 12, "equitable compensation shall be provided for any loss suffered by the holders of those rights." Furthermore, "the terms for determining such compensation and the arrangements for its payment shall be set by Member States." Article 6(3) provides that the offer document must disclose "the compensation offered for the rights which might be removed as a result of the breakthrough rule laid down in Article 11(4)," "particulars of the way in which that compensation is to be paid," and "the method employed in determining it." A number of questions arise for Member States implementing this provision: Who pays the compensation? When do they pay? How is the quantum of pay determined? Who is entitled to be paid? Each decision has an implication for the effectiveness of the rule. For example, one might assume that the offeror pays. This is consistent with the requirement in Article 6(3) for disclosure in the offer document. The problem is that this makes the company more expensive for the offeror. How will different rights be valued? For example, how do you compensate someone for losing the right to appoint directors? How will the offeror identify all available contracts between shareholders of the offeree? If the compensation cannot be determined in advance on the basis of clearly accepted criteria, it will also create uncertainty for the offeror who will not be able to determine the exact cost of the acquisition. This appears consistent with the comment in the Winter Report that the compensation procedure should not prohibit the offeror from using the breakthrough rule to exercise control. In most cases the cost would be passed on to the offerees' shareholders as the offeror will be able to pay them less. In the event of compensation for Articles 11(2) and 11(3), will the offeror be expected to pay in circumstances where no takeover results? Where a restriction on voting is removed, should all other shareholders be compensated? Clearly, inappropriate implementation of Article 11 could give directors scope to deter hostile takeovers. A further factor in the determination is whether the breakthrough rule was imposed by the Member State or applied by the company opting-in pursuant to Article 12 discussed below. If the Member State opts out and the company itself opts back in, then an argument exists to suggest that no compensation is payable by the offeror as the offeree has made the decision itself to apply the rule (a view put forward by Skog 2004). In such a case, it is arguable that its shareholders have no right to complain as the majority-rule decision, which is one of the most basic tenets of company law, requires it to accept the decision taken. Yet it might be argued that such a view is inconsistent with the specific statement in Article 11(5) that "compensation shall be provided." It would seem that in most cases the Courts should be the best arbiters of these questions but some guidance must be given by Member States in the transposition process.

Article 12(1) and 12(2)—Opt In/Out

The main change made by the Council in relation to the Commission's 2002 proposal concerned the introduction of optional arrangements for the application of Articles 9 and 11. Article 12(1) provides that Member States may decide not to require companies registered in their jurisdiction to apply the prohibition on frustrating action in Article 9 and the break-through rule in Article 11. Article 12(2) provides that if Member States "make use of this option" they must still grant companies the reversible option of applying the Articles. This decision must be taken by the share-holders in general meeting in accordance with the rules applicable to the amendment of their articles of association. The "provisions applicable to the respective companies" must be disclosed without delay.

The Council viewed such a step as necessary in order to take into ac-count the existing differences in Member States' company law mechanisms and structures. In effect, thus, a Member State may choose not to require companies to apply these provisions, while allowing companies the oppor-tunity to opt in should they so choose. This compromise was welcomed by Nilsen (2004) as "a good solution which enables Member States with dif-ferent types of market economies to preserve their unique comparative ad-vantages, promoting a more competitive Europe as a whole" (p. 3). Winter (2004) noted that the Directive clearly sets the benchmark of Articles 9 and 11 being applied by Member States and the hope is that market pressure will provide incentives to adopt the benchmark (p. 18). However, the disin-centive to implementing Article 9 or more likely Article 11 is that compa-nies might change their listing from a Member State that does apply them into a Member State that does not. Commissioner Bolkestein strongly dis-agreed with the introduction of such optional measures, arguing that it would send the wrong message to the markets.

Article 12(3)—Reciprocity

The reciprocity clause in Article 12(3) introduces a new concept to EU company law. It allows Member States "to exempt companies which ap-ply" the articles "if they become the subject of an offer launched by a com-pany which does not apply the same Articles as they do" or a company controlled by such a company. To do so, however, Article 12(5) provides that they need the authorization of their shareholders at a meeting granted no more than 18 months before the bid.

The concept of reciprocity seeks to encourage companies to move to a more liberal regime voluntarily by allowing them the benefit of such a regime where they are the offeror in a takeover bid. It is also notable that the provision was introduced in the context of concerns that the Directive would not create a level playing field between the EU and the United States. It was felt that the Directive would restrict EU companies defending themselves against bids in circumstances where their U.S. counterparts might not be so limited. Ironically, a convincing argument can be made that the reciprocity provision may not apply to companies from third countries.

A strong view exists that the location or openness to takeover of the offeror is irrelevant and that what should be considered is the location of the offeree. It is argued that reciprocity in takeovers unduly restricts the group of potential offerors to listed companies that are themselves open to hostile bids and it reduces the potential benefits of contestable control (Becht 2003). From a theoretical perspective, this limitation is in conflict with the declared aim of protecting the minority shareholders of the offeree. As the empirical evidence suggests that multiple offerors are associated with higher premia for offeree shareholders, reciprocity is likely to hurt the minority shareholders the Directive seeks to protect in circumstances where it is not essential in addressing fairness concerns. In addition, it may be difficult to reconcile this provision with the freedom of establishment and free movement of capital, which do not impose any condition on the party wishing to enjoy rights under national company laws other than having the registered office or central administration in a Member State (Winter 2004). It seems likely that the majority of Member States will opt out of this Article.

CONCLUSION

As noted at the outset, both internal and external controls have been suggested as solutions to the agency problems that are endemic in any corporate structure. The market for corporate control as a form of external market force suffers from its reliance on disputable assumptions, limited application, and ambiguous empirical support. Even the U.K. Company Law Review Steering Group (2000, 4.56) concluded that "there may be an overdependence on takeovers as an instrument to secure managerial change." Yet, while the theory does not explain why all takeovers occur, its basic premise—that takeovers act as incentives to underperforming directors—is widely accepted. The Commission sought to take this conclusion to its next logical level. Having weighed up the arguments in favor of defensive actions and those against, it concluded that the risk was too great that directors would negate this disciplinary force and indeed the other positive effects of takeovers by engaging in actions that would frustrate hostile takeovers. Thus Article 9 prohibits defensive actions during a bid without shareholder approval. Unfortunately, the Commission failed to persuade all parliamentarians as to the correctness of such an approach. Those who feared that a liberal takeover market might threaten European companies and European jobs remained unconvinced. The ghost of the hard-fought hostile takeover of Mannesmann in Germany may have haunted the negotiating table in this respect. The ensuing optionalization of Article 9 seems to be the product of despair. It was reported that most Member States accepted the Rapporteur's view that "half a loaf is better than none" and sought to terminate "this never ending story" (The European Parliament—OEIL web site). It is submitted that this is a very poor justification indeed and that the optionalization of one of the core elements of the Directive must raise serious doubts about its ability to achieve its objective of coordinating the national measures designed to protect offeree shareholders. Certainly it is difficult to see how it might be reconciled with the acknowledged necessity to prevent patterns of corporate restructuring within the EU from being distorted by arbitrary differences in governance and management cultures (Recital 3). While one may be ambivalent about the need for a breakthrough rule, the optionalization of Article 9, which undermines one of the general principles of the Directive—allowing shareholders an opportunity to decide on the merits of an offer—must be regarded as a serious defect. Such apparent wearing down of Member States and their acceptance of a flawed proposal is not an appropriate response to the important issue of corporate control.

In relation to internal controls, it should be noted that there is substantial support at EU level for change that would lead to greater shareholder democracy. The European Commission in the *Company Law and Corporate Governance Action Plan* (2003) prioritized the improvement of shareholders' rights. The Transparency Directive (Directive 2004/109/EC), Market Abuse Directive (Directive 2003/6/EC), and Prospectuses Directive (Directive 2003/71/EC) will all facilitate greater public access to relevant information. In its consultation paper, *Fostering an Appropriate Regime for Shareholders' Rights* (2005a), the Commission advocated improvements in areas such as pre–general meeting communications, admissions to general meetings, electronic participation, asking questions, tabling resolutions, adding items to the agenda, and voting. These developments should have implications for the market for corporate control. In encouraging shareholders to choose the voice option rather than the exit option, a prerequisite for the market for corporate control will remain unsatisfied. Offerors will no longer be able to acquire cheap shares. However, if shareholder participation is proven to be an effective control, there may be less need to rely to such an extent on the disciplinary effects of hostile takeovers.

Four

Accountability
of Directors
and Executives

Board Power Relations and the Impact of the U.K.'s Combined Code on Corporate Governance

Timothy J. Nichol

INTRODUCTION

Corporate-based systems have never been free from failure or scandal. Anthony Trollope's novel, *The Way We Live Now*, published in the 1870s, recorded the dangers of a debased character prepared to use the corporate vehicle as a means to personal profit. The corrupting influence of Trollope's character, Augustus Melmotte, and his rise and subsequent fall prophetically anticipated some of the corporate scandals of the past 25 years. Many of these scandals centered on the character of leadership at the very apex of the companies concerned and have provided a clear message. Strong leadership, resulting in success, is both desirable and seductive. Dominant leadership, however, that both corrupts and defrauds is destructive to both personal wealth and market confidence.

Since the early 1990s it has been recognized by those responsible for regulating corporate activity in the U.K. that boards require guidance and regulation if they are to discharge their responsibilities effectively. The role of the board has been defined as being to provide entrepreneurial leadership within a framework of effective and prudent controls that enable risk to be assessed and managed (Financial Reporting Council 2003b). Creating a governance framework that provides a setting in which these responsibilities can be discharged has required policy makers to define board roles with greater certainty and examine the power relations between different groupings on the board. This chapter seeks to examine how those power relations have changed as a result of the governance framework created.

DEVELOPMENT OF THE CORPORATE GOVERNANCE FRAMEWORK IN THE U.K.

The development of the corporate governance framework in the U.K. has taken place outside of the legislative process. Since the publication of the Cadbury Report (1992) the development of a set of guiding principles underpinning the governance framework has been driven forward by the London Stock Exchange, the Confederation of British Industry, the accountancy profession, and other professional bodies. The Cadbury Report (1992) was concerned with the financial aspects of corporate governance but went beyond this in providing a basic framework around which subsequent principles have been developed. Between 1992 and the publication of the first Combined Code on Corporate Governance (2000), the debate about the nature of the U.K.'s framework was driven forward by the Greenbury Report (Confederation of British Industry 1995), the Hampel Report (1998), and the Turnbull Report (Institute of Chartered Accountants 1999).

The purpose of the first Combined Code (2000) was to draw together the conclusions drawn by the Cadbury Report (1992) and the subsequent committees and provide a set of principles around which companies could develop their governance structures and procedures. In keeping with the spirit of self-regulation that permeates the financial services in the U.K., the Code was adopted as part of the U.K. Stock Exchange Listing Rules and was issued on a comply-or-explain basis. Compliance with the Code was not mandatory, therefore, but disclosure of noncompliance was required in the annual financial statements.

Following the publication of the first Combined Code (2000), two further studies were conducted. The Smith Report (2003) considered the role of the audit committee and the Higgs Report (2003) reviewed the role and effectiveness of nonexecutive directors. The conclusions of both reports were incorporated into the current version of the Combined Code (2003), herein referred to as the *Code*. The framework created in 2003 is founded on the previous work but contains new provisions that have the potential to affect the power relations on the board.

NATURE OF POWER

Before examining the provisions of the Code it is necessary to ask what is meant by the term *power* in the context of the board. It can be said that we intuitively understand the notion of power, and daily both exercise various forms of it and are subject to the consequences of its exercise by others. Dahl (1957) has noted the difficulty encountered in formulating a concept of power that has universal acceptance. In the absence of any agreement over such a formulation researchers have sidestepped the task and have sought to isolate or describe either those elements that might constitute the notion of power or the conditions in which power can be evidenced. In doing so they have sought to describe its nature and the scope of its influence.

It is commonly accepted that power is evidenced by the ability of a person or a group of individuals to influence or control the behavior of others. (Dahl 1957; French and Raven 1959; Benfari et al. 1986). This statement contains no reference to motive but in the context of the business literature it has been argued that this can encapsulate the notion of self-interest (Berle and Means 1932; Pettigrew and McNulty 1998).

Power is a relation among people (Dahl 1957) and can be said to be situational, contextual, and dynamic (Pettigrew and McNulty 1998). In the context of business organizations there are two aspects to this relationship. First, the very structures created within an organization will create differing power relations between individuals and units. Second, there is an interpersonal dynamic to the actual exercise of power within such structures.

The normative and empirical works on the structural forms of power have sought to isolate the sources or bases of power within an organization. To Pfeffer (1981, 1992), power is a contest for resources in which those who do well succeed on the basis of the resources they control or acquire and the relationships they have with those who control resources. This resource dependency model identifies the potential bases of power as being the control of financial resources, rewards, sanctions, uncertainty expertise, status, prestige, information, and the ties with senior management. French and Raven (1959), considering power from the view of the reaction of the recipient to particular behavior, identify five bases: the power to reward, to coerce, referent power, legitimate power, and expert power. Such powers can influence the recipient at a psychological level. To Benfari et al. (1986) the effective use of power is linked to the enhancement of self-esteem, self-fulfillment, and competence. Building on the work of French and Raven (1959), they include within the bases of power not only reward, coercion, referent, and expert power, but also authority, information, affiliation, and group power. Units and individuals within an organization may possess some or all of these bases of power depending on their position within the organization's structure.

The power bestowed on a unit or individual through the hierarchy is, however, latent or potential. Dahl (1957) has analyzed four components of the power relation: the base or source of power, the means used to exert that power, the amount or extent of that power, and the range or scope of that power. Power bases or sources are inert or passive and need to be exploited if the behavior of others is to be influenced. The means provide the manner by which the power base can be exploited. For Benfari et al. (1986), the latent or potential power exists as a motive and is only manifested as a behavior when these motives are translated into action. To Pettigrew and McNulty (1998), the possession of these bases of power is a route to the potential power. They argue that the realization of the power possessed is dependent on the individuals' self-awareness of that power, their control over it, and their ability to employ the means by which to exercise it. These are the interpersonal skills or attributes necessary to influence the behavior of others.

In the context of power studies, the board of directors has received particular attention. Given the position of the board at the apex of an organization's structure, the bases of power available to specific board members noted by Pfeffer (1981, 1992), French and Raven (1959), or Benfari et al. (1986) have self-evident applicability. The way in which the potential power is exercised, however, is of particular interest because of the composition of the U.K. board itself. Whereas, at sub-board level, studies of power consider the position of full-time managers within an organization, any examination of the dynamics of the board must encompass the influence of the nonexecutive directors. The U.K. board is particular in the system of governance, sharing aspects of both the U.S. and continental systems but significantly differing from both. Like the U.S. system, it is founded on a unitary board. Whereas, however, the typical U.S. board is composed mainly of outside nonexecutive directors, the U.K. board is composed of a mixture of both executive and nonexecutive directors, all of whom have equal responsibility in law for the direction of the company. This sharing of responsibility between executive and nonexecutive directors reflects aspects of the composition of the two-tier continental systems, where both inside executives and outside stakeholder groups participate in the strategic direction of the organization. The U.K. board, however, is drawn from a narrower group of individuals, none of whom necessarily represent outside interests.

The position of the nonexecutive directors is unique in the context of the organization, for having no operational role they have no access to the structural bases of power other than to those arising in relation to other board members. It is possible to posit, therefore, that they have potentially little influence outside the board itself. As a result, empirical work into board power relations has focused on the means by which the nonexecutive directors have acquired power and exercised it within the confines of the boardroom. In the case of the U.K. board a study carried out by Pettigrew and McNulty (1995, 1998) has significantly informed our understanding of board dynamics. Their conclusions confirm previous studies but provide additional insights into the means by which nonexecutives can acquire and exercise power in and around the boardroom.

Confirming previous work, nonexecutives are seen to possess residual powers that have tended to be exercised only in times of crisis. Where power is exercised there is a tendency for the nonexecutives to negatively influence decisions rather than initiate and lead in the area of decision making. Where such positive influence is exercised the nonexecutives require a strong power base and considerable desire and expertise to exert that influence effectively.

The study provides further insights into the position of nonexecutives by identifying potential sources or bases of power. These include expertise and experience, power acquired through affiliation with other board members, power through participation on committees, and the individual's skill in creating effective networks in and around the boardroom. Structural and contextual factors highlighted include the accepted norms for board conduct, the attitude and behavior of the CEO and chairman, and the selection criteria for nonexecutives. The authors further posit that given the unstable nature of power relations, the nonexecutives' effectiveness and degree of influence may vary between companies and individuals and can change over time as the dynamics of the board change.

Pettigrew and McNulty's (1995, 1998) work is of importance to this chapter because it reflected conditions prior to the publication of the first Combined Code on Corporate Governance (2000). The Cadbury Report (1992) marked a significant step in the development of corporate governance regulation. The subsequent reports added to the development of the principles that formed the basis of the first Combined Code (2000). It is important to recognize that the findings of Pettigrew and McNulty's (1995, 1998) study were influenced by the changing attitudes reflected in the work of Cadbury (1992) and the subsequent committees that came to be summarized in the first Combined Code (2000). Since its publication, however, further significant revisions to the principles underpinning the governance framework have been made, these being reflected in the revised Code of 2003. It is these principles that will be examined in the context of board power relations.

THE 2003 COMBINED CODE PROVISIONS

It is argued that the Code significantly impacts on board power relations in the following manner:

- Three leaders are identified in the Board, each having different roles and spheres of influence. They are the Chairman, the CEO, and the Senior Independent Nonexecutive Director.

- The power position of the nonexecutive and executive directors has been structurally changed by providing that the independent nonexecutives should make up at least half of the board, excluding the chairman. This is a significant revision to board composition and represents a challenge to the previous dominant position of the executive directors.
- Without diminishing the existing framework of legal responsibility, the provisions have defined a particular role for nonexecutive directors in relation to specific areas of activity and more generally in relation to monitoring and controlling the activities of the board.
- The legitimacy of contact with the shareholders by board members other than the CEO has been promoted by the Code.

BOARD LEADERSHIP

A key area of discussion has been the appropriateness of chairman/CEO duality. It has long been accepted in the development of the U.K.'s corporate governance framework that these roles should be separated (Cadbury Report 1992). The Code requires, therefore, not only that the same person should not act as chairman and CEO but also further adds that the chairman should, on appointment to the board, be independent. Specifically, the chairman should not be the former CEO. Independence in this context is defined as having the same meaning as the test applied to nonexecutives and is discussed in greater detail below. The justification underpinning this separation is based on power considerations, the Code noting that "no one individual should have unfettered powers of decision" (para. A.2). The chairman's role is to run the board. This broad statement is expanded on to embrace the following responsibilities: to provide leadership to the board; to ensure its effectiveness through performance evaluation; to set the agenda for board discussions; to ensure the provision of accurate, timely, and clear information to all board members; to maintain effective communication with shareholders; to facilitate the effective contribution of the nonexecutive directors; and to ensure constructive relations between executive and nonexecutive directors.

As noted, the separation of the role of chairman and CEO was included in the Cadbury Report (1992) and formed part of the provisions of the first Combined Code (2000). The Higgs Report (2003) revealed that by the time it examined the structure of boards approximately 90% of listed companies in the U.K. had split the two roles. The Code can be seen to have addressed specific structural conditions, not just in terms of the separation of roles, but also in terms of the chairman's responsibility in relation to the provision of information and in the dialogue with shareholders. Taken as a whole, these provisions create a transfer of power from the CEO to the chairman by first creating an alternative leader and then providing exclusive power bases.

It is clear, however, that this structural solution to the question of leadership is not in itself sufficient. In a report commissioned as part of the Higgs review into nonexecutives, McNulty et al. (2003) noted that structure and composition could only provide the conditions in which a board could operate effectively but could not determine its effectiveness. In this respect the ability of chairmen to exploit the conditions created by the Code remains dependent on their ability to develop an effective relationship with the CEO and to bring the nonexecutive directors into the board to contribute effectively. Thus the interpersonal dynamics of power relations remain as the means by which the structural conditions can be converted into actual expressions of power.

It is interesting to note that the Code is silent as to the specific responsibilities of the CEO, or indeed the other executive board members, other than to refer to their role in running the operations of the company and commenting on their general responsibilities as board members. It is argued that this reflects an assumption implicit in the Code provisions that there is an existing power asymmetry that the Code is seeking to address.

On the basis of the findings of the Higgs Report (2003), the Code has promoted a new leadership figure in the senior independent nonexecutive director. The Code provides that the senior independent nonexecutive director should perform a number of key functions. These include leading the nonexecutive directors in the evaluation of the chairman's performance; leading meetings of the nonexecutive directors outside of the normal board meetings; and being an alternative source of communication with the shareholders. The latter role was particularly highlighted in the Higgs Report (2003), which regarded this as an important line of communication where shareholders had concerns that could not be resolved through dialogue with the chairman and the CEO. In terms of the analysis of power bases provided by French and Raven (1959) and Benfari et al. (1986), this can be seen as creating an authority or legitimate power base that provides for dialogue to take place with other nonexecutive directors and external shareholders without the involvement of the chairman or CEO. By making such actions legitimate they cannot be regarded as acts contrary to the values of board unity and responsibility. Nor can they be seen as actions that undermine the authority of the chairman or CEO. The Code, therefore, potentially invests the senior independent nonexecutive director with affiliation, group, and referent power in relation to the other nonexecutive directors.

BOARD COMPOSITION

The Code takes a radical position on board composition that directly addresses the power asymmetry between the executive directors and the independent nonexecutive directors. Since the Cadbury Report(1992), there has been an acceptance that the Board requires a group of directors who are independent of the executive function and independent in terms of their character and judgment. The motivation driving the Code principles regarding the balance of executives and nonexecutives is that "no one individual or small group of individuals can dominate the board's decision making" (para. A.3). The Code provides, therefore, that at least half of the board, excluding the chairman, should comprise nonexecutive directors determined by the board to be independent. The Code's provisions are radical in that they significantly depart from the previous accepted position. The Combined Code (2000) provided only that the nonexecutive directors should comprise at least one third of the board.

The meaning of independence must be explored, for this is a key aspect of the change in the position taken. The Higgs Report (2003) notes that independence had two aspects. First, independence is a question of character. In this respect individuals possessing independence of mind, a willingness to challenge constructively, to question and to speak up while at the same time being supportive, display those attributes possessed by one who may be regarded as being independent. The second aspect refers to the need for the individual to display dispassionate objectivity in exercising judgment. This is not so much a test of character but rather a description of the condition or circumstances of the individual when first joining the board. The same criteria are applied to determine the independence or otherwise of the chairman.

The conditions are as follows: the individual must not have been an employee of the company within the past five years; during the previous three years the individual must not have had a material relationship with the company; the individual must not receive remuneration from the company other than from the fees payable in respect of the directorship; the individual must not have close family ties with the company's directors, advisers, or senior employees; the individual must not hold cross directorships or have significant links with other directors through involvement in other companies or bodies; the individual must not represent a significant shareholder; and any director serving more than nine years on a board ceases to be regarded as an independent director.

The combination of the provisions relating to board balance and the need for half the board to be independent challenges the perceived dominance of the executive directors. The need to provide a counterbalance to the dominance of management, which in the case of the U.K. board is represented by the executive directors and potentially the senior executives at sub-board level, has been the subject of discussion among academics and practitioners alike. A major theory underpinning research into boards has been the managerial hegemony theory. This theory has taken its basis from the work of Berle and Means (1932) and their analysis of ownership structures and the motives driving the desire for control over corporations. This theory is centered on the power asymmetry that exists between the full-time managers of the corporation and the outside directors. Using their access to greater information, their experience and knowledge of the company, such directors can dominate and manipulate the board to achieve their ends, even though this may be to the detriment of the shareholders. The board is portrayed as a comfortable, passive, and unchallenging body that too readily acquiesces to the wishes of management.

The views of practitioners have reflected this theoretical position. Writing in the *Harvard Business Review*, George (2002) has noted, "Other boards are just complacent. They fail to challenge management about how earnings are generated, what the risks might be, whether investments are sound, or if the accounting numbers accurately reflect results. Or they're ignorant about these things" (p. 22).

The developments in the U.K. have sought to challenge this view of the operation of the board, and the provisions regarding board composition can be seen as a structural response to the potential dominance of management.

Further, the definition of independence in relation to the nonexecutives is of significance for it not only challenges companies to find individuals possessing the appropriate qualities and attributes but may also change the nature of individuals who may be willing to become nonexecutives in the future. The Higgs Report (2003) characterized the then-existing body of nonexecutive directors on U.K. boards in the following manner:

> My research shows that non-executive directors are typically white males nearing retirement age with previous PLC director experience. There are less than twenty non-executive directors on FTSE 100 boards under the age of 45. In the telephone survey for the review, seven per cent of non-executive directors were not British, and one per cent were from black and ethnic minority groups. The very low number of female non-executive directors is striking in comparison with other professions and with the population of managers in the UK companies overall. Across the corporate sector as a whole around thirty per cent of managers overall are female. Only six per cent of non-executive posts are held by women, and there are only two female chairmen in the FTSE 350. (2003, 10.21 and 10.22)

The Higgs Report (2003) findings were not surprising. The emphasis placed on the monitoring and control function of the nonexecutive directors can only be traced back to the Cadbury Report (1992). This report sought to emphasize, however, that the proposed monitoring and control role was not to detract from the main role of the nonexecutives, which was the contribution they could make to the strategic direction of the company. It was traditionally understood that nonexecutives were invited to join the board, usually through personal connections, on the basis of the experience or contacts they could provide. The practice of U.K. boards reflected the theoretical description of the board posited by the Power Coalitionist Theorists. In explaining board composition and functions, Dallas (1996), for example, has argued that companies seek to reduce the uncertainty of their environment by gaining access to resources such as information, contacts, and advice by forming relationships with other corporations and individuals through board membership. Nonexecutives have added value inter alia by providing the company with access to information and resources, enhancing the status of the corporation in the business community, and through generating support for the corporation through board members' identification with the corporation. Such a theory is helpful in explaining why nonexecutives are invariably successful current or retired executive directors of other companies, retired civil servants, and former Government Ministers or Members of Parliament.

Despite the 2003 Code's insistence that the board's overarching role remains the provision of entrepreneurial leadership, it is impossible not to acknowledge the increasing responsibility placed on the nonexecutive directors to perform a monitoring and control function. The definition of independence adopted in the Code potentially restricts the group of individuals companies can invite to the board, thus ensuring that new nonexecutives will not be captured by the executive grouping on the board. The Code further emphasizes this point by requiring companies to disclose in their annual reports when procedures for identifying new nonexecutive directors do not involve recruitment through professional search consultancies or open advertising. This not only safeguards the independent nature of the nonexecutives to be recruited but also seeks to break the traditional means by which such nonexecutives have been recruited.

ROLE OF THE NONEXECUTIVE DIRECTOR

As previously noted the Code is virtually silent as to the role of the executive directors other than to emphasize their general legal and operational responsibilities as board members. Since the Cadbury Report (1992) onward, however, there have been significant developments redefining the function of the nonexecutives. In developing the monitoring functions of the nonexecutives the Code has introduced structural changes to the board that have effected a shift in power from the executive directors to the nonexecutives.

The role of the nonexecutives has been summarized under four main headings: *strategy*, *performance*, *risk*, and *people*. The Code's guidance provisions note that the nonexecutives should constructively challenge management on its strategy. Pettigrew and McNulty (1995) found evidence that nonexecutives had an ability to negatively influence the board but had little ability to positively influence the strategy-making process. The Code reflects these findings by strongly emphasizing the need for the nonexecutives not only to constructively challenge the executive directors but also to help in developing proposals on strategy.

In respect of performance, the Code's guidance notes stress that the nonexecutives are responsible for scrutinizing the performance of the management team in meeting agreed objectives and goals and monitoring the reporting of performance by management. The Code provides that it is the responsibility of the chairman to lead on the evaluation of board performance and effectiveness although the evaluation of the chairman resides with the nonexecutives alone.

In structural terms, the Code contains no specific provisions designed to support the strategic and performance-monitoring role of the nonexecutives other than to create a board in which the composition provides group power (Benfari et al. 1986) through numerical equality. The same could not be said in respect of the two other responsibilities highlighted in the guidance notes.

In describing the responsibilities in relation to risk, the Code provides that the nonexecutives not only should concern themselves with the integrity of the financial information prepared for shareholders but should ensure that the risk management and financial controls systems are fit for the purpose. To fulfill this function the Code requires the board to establish an audit committee composed of at least three independent nonexecutive directors. The power base created by this requirement is substantial. The role of the audit committee is as follows: to monitor the integrity of the financial statements; to review the company's internal controls; to review the systems for internal control and risk management; to monitor and review the effectiveness of the company's internal audit function; to make recommendations on the selection and reappointment of the external auditors; and to review the external auditors' independence and the effectiveness of the audit process. In the absence of an internal audit function, the Code requires the committee to consider the need for such a function and report to the board should the need arise. Further, the audit committee must ensure that the concerns of whistleblowers in the company can be heard and their concerns independently investigated.

The audit committee was first proposed in the Cadbury Report (1992) and has been the subject of detailed consideration by the Smith Committee (2003). In power terms, the audit committee overtly challenges the power of the finance director in a number of ways. First, it provides a forum for the independent internal scrutiny of the financial statements prepared by management. The requirement that at least one of the members of this committee should possess recent and relevant financial experience means that the judgments underpinning the financial statements can be challenged and questioned. Second, the review function in respect of internal controls, risk management, and the effectiveness of the internal audit function takes this committee into the heart of the company's operations. The nature of all of these functions potentially extends the scope of the committee beyond those issues that might directly relate to the finance function. Most significantly, the committee is the prime point of contact for the external auditors. The audit function can only be effective if the auditors exercise their duties independent of the management of the company. The conditions necessary to maintain auditor independence remain subject to debate, although the impact of compromised independence has become apparent in recent corporate failures. Considerable debate has centered on how the provision of additional services may or may not impact on the independence of auditors, either in fact or in appearance. By transferring to the audit committee the responsibility for ensuring that the auditors' independence is not compromised, the Code provides that committee with an opportunity to review and intervene with operational decisions made in relation to the provision of non-audit services to the company. Such decisions will usually be within the ambit of the finance director.

The provisions of the Code relating to the nonexecutives' responsibilities in respect of people similarly transfer significant powers from the executive directors to the nonexecutive directors. The Code directs that the nonexecutive directors should be responsible for determining the remuneration of the executive directors, should have a prime role in appointing and removing directors, and should play a role in planning for succession. To perform these functions the Code requires boards to create a remuneration committee and a nomination committee.

The remuneration committee is composed of at least three independent nonexecutive directors. The scope of the committee encompasses not only the remuneration, pension provisions, and compensation payments payable to the chairman and executive directors, but also the levels and structure of the remuneration paid to the first layer of management below board level. Several studies have identified reward power as one of the main bases of power within an organization's structure (Pfeffer 1981; 1992; French and Raven 1959; Benfari et al. 1986). The provisions relating to the creation of the remuneration committee impact on the executive directors in two ways. First, it removes their power to determine their own levels of remuneration. The directions in the Code relating to the need to create remuneration policies containing significant elements that are performance related strengthen the power to monitor and control the behavior and rewards of the executives. Second, the extension of the remuneration committee's power to monitor the level and structure of the sub-board level of remuneration potentially removes from the executive directors a power base they formerly could exercise over that level of management.

The nomination committee is required to implement rigorous, transparent, and formal procedures for the appointment of new directors. Such procedures should reflect appointments based on merit judged against objectively set criteria. The majority on this committee should be independent nonexecutive directors but this committee can be chaired by the chairman. This committee, as with the other two committees, is not open to the executive directors. The criteria applicable to the appointment of independent nonexecutive directors have been set out above. These provisions directly challenge the executive board members' ability to introduce known individuals onto the board. They may also potentially impact upon the power the executives have over the non-board senior managers. Benfari et al. (1986) noted the impact of referent power. This base is developed through identification, and combined with reward and information power can lead to a reciprocal relationship. In effect, they note that in such a relationship each has IOUs that can be called in. One such IOU could be the promise of advancement. The removal of the power of nomination potentially reduces the referent power of the executives.

RELATIONS WITH SHAREHOLDERS

A continuing concern of governance policy makers in the U.K. has been the need to make explicit the nature of the dialogue required between shareholders and the board. The Code stresses the need for dialogue to take place between the major institutional shareholders and the board and it assumes an existing relationship between those shareholders and the executive directors. Specific provisions, however, draw into this dialogue both the chairman and the senior independent nonexecutive director. The inclusion of the senior independent nonexecutive director is provided as an alternative source of contact should relations with the chairman and CEO prove problematical.

The Code is silent as to the theory underpinning its view taken on shareholder/board dialogue, but agency theory may provide an insight into the motivation of the policy makers. As an alternative to the managerial hegemony theory and the coalition power theory, agency theory promotes the board as a monitoring device. The board's purpose is to ensure that the interests of shareholders (the principals) are promoted by the management (the agents). Effective boards will use the powers at their disposal to ensure that management does not abuse its position to promote its own self-interest to the detriment of the shareholders. It is implicit that the board understands the needs of shareholders. But how can those needs be communicated and judged in relation to the direction being taken by the board? Lines of communication between the executive directors and the major shareholders may not succeed in ensuring that the shareholders' objectives are communicated to the board. The Code provisions therefore formalize alternative channels of communication to the chairman and the nonexecutive directors.

DISCUSSION

In the context of highly publicized corporate failure and scandals involving fraud, the Code's provisions are directed at improving the effectiveness of the board and seek to protect the interests of the shareholder. Much of the Code's attention has focused on the disposition of power to ensure that individuals or groups cannot dominate the board's decision-making processes. In doing so, the Code has created a framework with the potential to change the composition of the board and has transferred specific areas of decision making from the executive directors to the nonexecutives. Through the provisions promoting the need for independent nonexecutive directors, the Code has also sought to influence the nature of the nonexecutives participating in board decisions. The question remains whether this approach will succeed in improving the effectiveness of U.K. boards.

The first point of potential weakness may be the standing of the Code itself. The Code forms part of the U.K. Stock Exchange Listing rules and is applicable to all listed companies. Although the provisions underpinning the Code are regarded as best practice they are not mandatory. There is an expectation that companies will generally comply with these provisions, and failure to comply requires a public explanation to be provided through the means of the Annual Report. Disclosure brings the matter to the attention of the shareholders, who must then decide whether to accept the company's position. A lack of subsequent action on the part of the majority of shareholders will provide tacit acceptance of the noncompliance.

More significant is the understanding provided by the previous studies on organizational power and, in particular, the work of Pettigrew and McNulty (1995, 1998) highlighting the importance played by context, as well as the structural conditions and interpersonal dynamics, in fashioning the nature of power in any individual company. They have characterized two types of boards. There is first the minimalist board. This is one in which conditions have been created to minimize the impact of the nonexecutive directors. The conditions include the size of the board and the attitude of the CEO or chairman. The second type of board has been characterized as the maximalist board. This board is proactive and inclusive and has created conditions in which power is more widely dispersed. The conditions contributing to this type of board include a relatively small board, a shared knowledge of the business among all board members, a high degree of participation of board members, usually facilitated by the chairman, and a culture promoting commitment and involvement created by the chairman.

The Code's response to the need to create effective, committed boards of the type defined as maximalist is essentially structural. Through the promotion of a strong, independent chairman, a balanced board containing a significant number of independent nonexecutives, the creation of committees staffed mainly or entirely by those nonexecutives, and in defining the nonexecutive role, the Code has sought to establish the structural conditions in which the board can operate effectively. The creation of such structures has provided the opportunity for the nonexecutives to gain access to new power bases not necessarily open to them in the past. The audit, remuneration, and nomination committees, for example, have defined areas of influence controlled by the nonexecutives. In terms of the French and Raven (1959) and Benfari et al. (1986) analysis, the power bases of reward, information, group, expert, and even coercive and affiliation power have potentially become available to the nonexecutives.

This form of analysis, however, suggests a unitary board composed of factions competing for power over certain areas of decision making. In reality, such an environment would seem to undermine the very reason for the unitary board structure and would add little to the development of responsible self-reflective and critical boards striving to perform in conditions of uncertainty. An alternative approach could be to regard the structural conditions created overall by the Code as a means of legitimizing the shift in power from the executives to the nonexecutives in order to enhance the contribution the nonexecutives can make not just in a monitoring and control context but also in terms of their contribution to the strategic direction of the company. For French and Raven

(1959), legitimate power is regarded as that power that stems from the internalized values of the recipient, which dictate that the actor has a legitimate right to influence the action of the recipient. Further, the notion of legitimacy involves some type of standard or value system that is accepted by the individual as a result of which the actor can assert power. Within this analysis, the Code can be seen as a legitimizing agent that seeks to transfer power over certain activities to the nonexecutives and it is necessary for the executives to recognize this legitimate authority if board effectiveness is to be improved.

Pettigrew and McNulty's (1995) empirical work would suggest, however, that this might not be enough. In particular, their work would suggest that the credibility of the nonexecutives in the eyes of the executives is an important factor in enabling the nonexecutive to influence the work of the board. Such credibility is established by the knowledge and experience of the nonexecutives, not just in relation to their background but also in relation to their specific understanding of the company's affairs. This credibility, combined with the personal attributes required to realize the potential of the bases of power, is necessary if the nonexecutive is to wield influence and power.

The importance perceived credibility plays in enabling the nonexecutive to participate in the board's processes further explains the pool of people who have traditionally occupied nonexecutive positions. As part of the evidence gathered to inform the findings of the Higgs Report (2003), Hemscott carried out an analysis of the profile of boards in the U.K. Excluding the 480 investment companies listed on the U.K. Stock Exchange, it was reported that among the remaining 1,702 companies there were 1,689 chairman posts, 5,172 executive posts, and 4,610 nonexecutive posts. The 4,610 nonexecutive posts were held by 3,908 individuals. Further, of those 3,908 individuals, 12 had executive and chairman roles in addition to the nonexecutive roles, 370 had both chairman and nonexecutive roles, 270 were both executive directors and nonexecutive directors, and 3,256 had nonexecutive roles only. Given the population of the U.K. and the international nature of the leading companies quoted on the London Stock Exchange, this was not seen by the Higgs Report (2003) to be a particularly representative or inclusive group of individuals.

This analysis could have added that in addition to the involvement of these nonexecutives in the corporate world, many additionally play prominent roles on government, professional, and charitable bodies, some will have had, or will continue to have significant roles in politics or the civil service, and many will have been honored with titles. These are individuals of considerable standing not just in the corporate sphere but also in the wider community.

The potential contribution such individuals can make to an organization would appear to further confirm the position taken by the Power Coalitionists such as Dallas (1996), namely, that these individuals are bringing to the board considerable experience, a knowledge of particular markets or geographical areas, and access to networks in the corporate, political, and even social sphere that would otherwise not be open to the board. The potential contribution such experience and knowledge can make to the strategic development of the company is self-evident.

The involvement of such individuals gives rise to a question not explicitly dealt with in the Code; namely, whether the nonexecutive role envisaged by the Code is one that the current cohort of nonexecutives could or would naturally wish to perform in the future. The combination of more onerous duties, focused essentially on what may be regarded as self-policing activities, and stricter conditions establishing independence have led to the recognition that the pool of suitable or willing candidates may diminish. This issue was addressed in the Higgs Report (2003).

This report, on examining the existing composition of boards, was critical of what it found, highlighting "a self-perpetuating tendency in the appointment process that militates against under representation in the boardroom. Previous PLC board experience is often seen to be the main, and sometimes only, competence demanded of potential candidates. Too often due consideration is not given to candidates with a broader mix of skills and experience" (2003, 10.18). The report also noted that "using personal contacts as a main source of candidates will tend to favour those with similar backgrounds to incumbent directors. A rigorous appointments process is important to offset this natural bias. The various criteria used for selection may also implicitly discriminate against women, such as requiring senior executive or PLC board experience" (2003, 10.24).

It went on to suggest that the pool of potential nonexecutives should be widened to include executive directors or talented individuals just below board level, executives from outside the U.K., lawyers, accountants and other consultants, executives of private companies, and those with a noncommercial background working in the public and charitable sector. The theme of this section of the report would appear to be the desire to create greater diversity on boards, drawing on skills and talents available from a wider group than has previously been called to perform the role of nonexecutive. The Higgs Report (2003) explicitly raises the question whether general business experience is a necessary qualification for the office of nonexecutive and notes that the qualities needed to contribute to the board can come from a range of backgrounds. It argues further that the bringing together of different and complementary perspectives among different board members can benefit overall board performance. It is difficult to reconcile this view with the empirical evidence provided by Pettigrew and McNulty (1995) on the need for nonexecutives to display specific and general business knowledge to establish their credibility.

Given such opinions it seems open to argue that what the Higgs Report (2003) and, by extension, the Code is signaling is the need for a significant change in board attitude and behavior if board effectiveness is to be improved. While retaining the unitary board structure and the formal composition of executive and nonexecutive membership, the Code provisions may be seen as a direct challenge to what could be regarded as the traditional board culture. Such a change is regarded as being necessary in order to improve the performance of the board, provide assurances as to the integrity of board processes, and thus retain the confidence of investors and the market generally. This change is to be brought about by having an independent chairman and by changing the nature and role of the nonexecutives. Outside, independent individuals, drawn from cultures and backgrounds other than those of the executives, are empowered by the Code to perform functions more directly related to the internal operations of the board itself. In such circumstances the credibility or otherwise of such individuals, and the power and influence they can wield, is drawn not from their personal knowledge and qualities but directly from the power bestowed on them by the Code provisions. In changing the power relations on the board the Code is also changing the context in which such power relations are played out.

Whether the Code will have such a radical impact on the nature and composition of the board remains open to question. The provisions regarding board tenure and the retirement and election of directors may delay the adoption of the Code provisions in full and only future empirical studies will establish whether the Code's potential to create new power relations has been realized.

CONCLUSION

The Combined Code on Corporate Governance (2003) has the potential to significantly affect board power relations in U.K. companies. The desire to improve board effectiveness by developing the self-monitoring and controlling function is promoted through structural changes. These changes seek to effect a transfer of power over specific functions from the executive grouping on the board to a grouping of independent nonexecutive directors free from any material relationships with the company and its executives and possibly from the traditional culture informing the thinking of those executives. Through performance evaluation, the control of rewards and nominations to the board, and the creation of lines of communication with external auditors and shareholders the nonexecutives have been given a variety of power bases through which they have the ability to monitor and control the behavior of the executive directors. Given the existing empirical evidence on board relations it remains open to question whether the structures created and the context in which the new responsibilities will be discharged will be sufficient in themselves to achieve the Code's objectives or whether the personal attributes of the different board members and their attitudes to the Code's imperatives will a remain a significant feature in determining the power relations on individual boards.

CHAPTER 15

CEO Compensation in Australia's Largest Companies

Geof Stapledon

INTRODUCTION

This chapter reports the results of a study of the compensation of the chief executive officer (CEO) of the 100 largest publicly traded Australian companies. It provides comparative data for the period 2000 to 2003. It includes analysis of the components of a typical compensation package—fixed, short-term incentive and long-term incentive. One major finding is that Australian CEOs are, on average, receiving a far smaller proportion of their total compensation in the form of long-term incentives than their United States counterparts. The long-term incentive component of pay for the average U.S. CEO is nearly double that of the average Australian CEO. However, the trend in Australia is clearly in favor of more at-risk pay. In 1987, on average the long-term incentive component accounted for 6.3% of total Australian CEO compensation. This rose to 13.3% by 1990, to 27.9% by 1995, and to 34% by 2002.

The second section of the chapter describes the sample and methodology used in the study. The third section deals with the fixed components of compensation. Key findings are that, across the Top 100 companies:

- The average fixed compensation increased by 38.6% between 2002 and 2003 (from A$1.03 million to A$1.42 million).
- The median fixed compensation was A$1,137,769. This is a 24.4% increase on the 2002 median (A$914,330), and a 45.5% increase on the 2001 median (A$781,788).

Note: This chapter is derived from a research paper prepared by the author for the Australian Council of Superannuation Investors.

- The largest fixed compensation was A$13,486,153 in 2003, compared to A$7,938,000 in 2002, A$8,543,137 in 2001, and A$7,205,688 in 2000.
- The smallest fixed compensation was A$345,056 in 2003, compared to A$50,575 in 2002, A$52,055 in 2001, and A$80,000 in 2000. (These small figures for earlier years reflect CEOs who had been in office for less than a full financial year.)

The fourth section addresses the short-term incentive component of pay. The short-term incentive is most commonly an annual bonus paid in cash. Key findings are that, across the Top 100 companies:

- The average short-term incentive increased by 36.9% between 2002 and 2003 (from A$937,347 to A$1,283,330).
- The median short-term incentive was A$735,129. This is a 54.7% increase on the 2002 median (A$475,000), and a 90.1% increase on the 2001 median (A$386,805).
- The largest short-term incentive was A$12,381,000 in 2003, compared to A$10,944,000 in 2002, A$6,239,739 in 2001, and A$13,808,000 in 2000.
- Twenty percent of CEOs did not receive a short-term incentive. Among those who did, the smallest short-term incentive was A$88,000 in 2003, compared to A$50,000 in 2002, A$73,000 in 2001, and A$50,000 in 2000.

The section following that deals with total compensation excluding long-term incentive (for example, options). The main findings are that, across the Top 100 companies:

- The average total compensation excluding long-term incentive increased by 2.6% between 2002 and 2003 (from A$2.38 million to A$2.44 million).
- The median total compensation excluding long-term incentive was A$1.77 million. This is a 22.5% increase on the 2002 median (A$1.45 million), and a 24.6% increase on the 2001 median (A$1.42 million).
- The largest compensation package, excluding long-term incentive, was A$25,793,845 in 2003, compared to A$16,294,620 in 2002, A$14,858,424 in 2001, and A$14,935,000 in 2000.
- The smallest compensation package, excluding long-term incentive, was A$387,472 in 2003, compared to A$50,575 in 2002, A$166,457 in 2001, and A$195,931 in 2000.

As mentioned above, average fixed compensation increased by 38.6% and average short-term incentive increased by 36.9%. The reason the average total compensation excluding long-term incentive increased by only 2.6% is that not all CEOs were paid a short-term incentive during the year (16 of the 78 CEOs did not receive a short-term incentive). If those CEOs who did not receive a short-term incentive are excluded, average (mean) pay, excluding long-term incentive, increased by 3.6% between 2002 and 2003 (from A$2.74 million to A$2.84 million).

The sixth section of this chapter examines total compensation including long-term incentive. The main findings are that, across the Top 100 companies:

- The average total compensation including long-term incentive decreased by 2% between 2002 and 2003 (from A$3.23 million to A$3.16 million).
- The median total compensation, including long-term incentive, was A$2.33 million. This is a 10.8% increase on the 2002 median (A$2.10 million), and a 9.7% increase on the 2001 median (A$2.12 million).
- The largest compensation package, including long-term incentive, was A$26,681,537 in 2003, compared to A$16,294,620 in 2002, A$14,858,823 in 2001, and A$69,098,875 in 2000.
- The smallest compensation package, including long-term incentive, was A$387,472 in 2003, compared to A$50,575 in 2002, A$166,457 in 2001, and A$348,338 in 2000.
- The long-term incentive component of pay accounted for, on average, 22.8% of total pay for the Top 100 CEOs in 2003. This was down from 34% in 2002 and 23.6% in 2001. This appears to have been driven by the increasing significance of the short-term incentive as a proportion of total CEO pay. The short-term incentive accounted for 32.3% of total pay in 2003, up from 23.2% in 2002 and 25.7% in 2001.

Combining the short-term incentive and long-term incentive, the proportion of CEO pay that was at risk in 2003 was 55.1%. It was 57.2% in 2002, and 53.7% in 2001.

Australian CEOs are, on average, receiving a far smaller proportion of their total compensation in the form of long-term incentives than their U.S. counterparts. The long-term incentive component of pay for the average U.S. CEO is nearly double that of the average Australian CEO. However, the average Australian CEO receives considerably more of her or his pay in the form of options and shares than the average British CEO. And the long-term incentive component of pay for Australian CEOs is now almost four times the level it was in the late 1980s.

The next section of the chapter provides greater detail on the various components of CEO compensation across the period 2001 to 2003.

The chapter also deals with a particularly topical issue in Australia—disclosure of the value of share options. Every sample company that granted options to a director or top-5 executive in 2003 disclosed a value for those options. At first blush, this appears to show that the tough stance of the Australian Securities and Investments Commission (ASIC) has led to 100% compliance with the relevant disclosure provision in the Corporations Act 2001 (Commonwealth of Australia). However, one company, which issued options in February 2002 (that is, in the previous financial year), did not allocate a portion of the value of those options in its 2003 annual report. This is inconsistent with the ASIC Guidelines. The same company also has a cash-based long-term incentive for senior executives. However, it did not disclose the amount that accrued under that plan for the CEO during the financial year.

Several companies use a loan-funded share plan as their long-term incentive. Invariably, these companies disclose either the "notional interest" that the company has forgone during the year (where the loan is interest-free), or details about the interest paid or payable (where the loan incurs interest). But is this really information about the *value* of the equity incentives being provided by the company? The ASIC Guidelines are not strictly relevant where a company has a loan-funded share plan rather than an options plan. However, going forward, for financial reporting purposes (rather than disclosure of pay purposes), these companies will need to recognize that Australian Accounting Standard AASB 2, "Share-based Payment," applies—as its title suggests—not only to options but also all other forms of equity incentives.

METHODOLOGY

The data described in this chapter are derived from the disclosed compensation of the most senior executive officer in a sample of S&P/ASX 100 companies. The research involved extracting the components of pay from the annual reports of the sample companies. This information has been disclosed by the companies under section 300A of the Corporations Act 2001.

The sample consisted of 78 companies. Not all the S&P/ASX 100 constituents were included because some are trusts (or managed investment schemes) rather than companies, and some are companies incorporated in another country that does not have compensation-disclosure rules analogous to section 300A.

For simplicity, the report refers to *CEO pay*. However, in relation to some companies the executive whose pay was analyzed is not the person carrying the formal title *CEO*. This could be, for example, because the company has an executive chairman and a separate chief executive officer, and the executive chairman's compensation is A$2 million higher than that of the CEO.

The study used data from annual reports *published* in 2003. For the majority of companies, this means the annual report relating to the financial year ended 30 June 2003. For a small number of companies (all of which are banks), it means the annual report relating to the financial year ended 30 September 2003. But for those companies that have a 31 December financial year-end, it means the annual report relating to the financial year ended 31 December 2002—which would typically have been published in early March 2003.

FIXED COMPENSATION

Fixed compensation comprises those components of a CEO's pay that do not vary with performance. These can include:

- Base (cash) salary
- Superannuation (pension) contributions
- Motor vehicle allowance
- Fringe benefits

Of these, base salary is almost always the most significant component. In 2003, it made up 83% of total fixed compensation for the average CEO.

Table 15.1 shows the fixed compensation statistics for the period 2000 to 2003. Between 2002 and 2003, average (mean) fixed compensation increased by 38.6% (from A$1.03 million to A$1.42 million). The average is skewed by the most highly paid CEOs, as indicated by the lower median figure: A$1,137,769 in 2003. However, even the median was up considerably from earlier years. It was 24.4% higher than the 2002 median (A$914,330) and 45.5% higher than the 2001 median (A$781,788).

Table 15.1 also shows the range of fixed pay: from A$345,769 to A$13.5 million. Although the smallest fixed pay package (A$345,056) is significantly higher than the minimum fixed pay for earlier years, this is driven by the fact that the small figures for earlier years were for CEOs who had been in office for less than a full financial year.

Figure 15.1 shows the distribution of CEO fixed compensation component. Thirty of the 78 sample CEOs had a fixed component of less than A$1 million. Thirty-nine CEOs had fixed compensation between

TABLE 15.1   Fixed Compensation: 2000–2003 Comparison

Yearly Comparison	2000	2001	2002	2003
Average	A$967,844	A$1,008,012	A$1,027,288	A$1,424,285
Minimum	A$80,000	A$52,055	A$50,575	A$345,056
Maximum	A$7,205,688	A$8,543,137	A$7,938,000	A$13,486,153
Median		A$781,788	A$914,330	A$1,137,769
Average Change . . .	*2000 to 2001*		*2001 to 2002*	*2002 to 2003*
for fixed pay . . .	+A$40,168		+ A$19,276	+A$396,997

A$1 million and A$2 million. Seven CEOs had fixed compensation between A$2 million and A$3 million. And then the there were the two outliers: A$6.7 million and A$13.5 million.

SHORT-TERM INCENTIVE

Most large Australian companies have a short-term incentive plan (STIP) for their senior executives. Of the 78 sample companies in this study, 62 (79.5%) made a payment to their CEO under a STIP.

As the word *incentive* suggests, a STIP is (or at least in theory is) de-

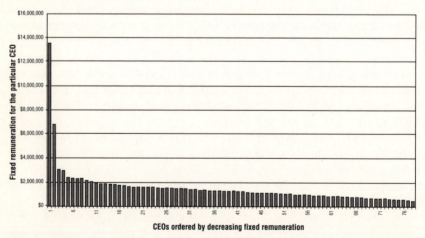

FIGURE 15.1   Distribution of Fixed Compensation Payments

TABLE 15.2 Short-Term Incentive: 2000–2003 Comparison

Yearly Comparison	2000	2001	2002	2003
Average	A$1,190,334	A$871,389	A$937,347	A$1,283,330
Minimum	A$50,000	A$73,000	A$50,000	A$88,000
Maximum	A$13,808,000	A$6,239,739	A$10,944,000	A$12,381,000
Median		A$386,805	A$475,000	A$735,129
Average Change . . .	*2000 to 2001*		*2001 to 2002*	*2002 to 2003*
for STI . . .	–A$318,945		+A$65,958	+A$345,983

signed to reward the executive if certain performance measures are met. However, unlike a long-term incentive plan (LTIP), it is not common for a STIP's performance measures to relate to the company's share price. Rather, it is common for performance indicators to relate to companywide accounting performance, business-division performance, successful completion of major projects, and so on.

By far the most common type of short-term incentive is an annual cash bonus. Sixty of the 62 sample companies that made a short-term incentive payment in 2003 made the payment entirely as a cash bonus. One delivered the incentive partly as a cash bonus and partly in the form of shares (which were required to be held for a specified number of years: "deferred shares"), and the other delivered the incentive wholly as deferred shares.

Table 15.2 shows the short-term incentive figures for 2000 to 2003. Sixteen of the 78 CEOs did not receive a cash bonus in 2003. For those CEOs who did receive a cash bonus, the average bonus payment rose by 36.9% (from A$937,347 in 2002 to A$1,283,330 in 2003). The average is again skewed by the largest figures, as indicated by the lower median figure: A$735,129 in 2003. However, as with the median for fixed pay, the median for short-term incentive was up considerably from earlier years. It was 54.7% higher than the 2002 median (A$475,000) and 90.1% higher than the 2001 median (A$386,805). Table 15.2 also shows the range of short-term incentive payments: from A$88,000 to A$12.38 million.

Figure 15.2 shows the distribution of bonus payments. Twenty-one payments were of less than A$500,000. Nineteen were between A$500,000 and A$1 million. Sixteen were between A$1 million and A$2 million. Four were between A$2 million and A$5 million. And the two outliers were A$12.3 million and A$12.4 million.

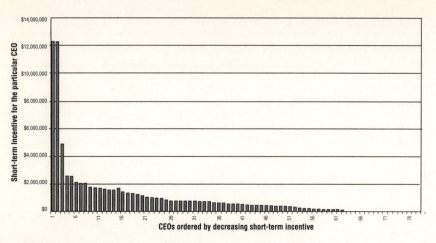

FIGURE 15.2 Distribution of Short-Term Incentive Payments

TOTAL COMPENSATION EXCLUDING LONG-TERM INCENTIVE

Background

Historically it has been important to consider total pay both *including* and *excluding* the long-term incentive. This is because the way companies have traditionally made long-term incentive awards, and recorded the value of them in the annual report, has led to significant fluctuations in total pay from year to year:

- In recent years, it has not been uncommon for companies to make "lumpy" grants of options (or another incentive instrument) under the LTIP. That is, they grant options to an executive only once every three or four years. (However, some companies have in recent years moved toward making more regular (annual), smaller, awards of options.)
- Until recently, when an Australian company disclosed the value of executive share options granted, it would typically allocate the entire value in the year of grant.

In combination, these two factors meant that a CEO's total compensation *including* long-term incentive could fluctuate considerably. It would appear to be relatively high in those years when options were granted, and relatively low in those years when options were not granted.

However, in June 2003, ASIC issued Guidelines stating that, for executive compensation disclosure purposes, the value of options granted during the financial year should be allocated equally over the period from grant date to vesting date. The following example illustrates the new approach. Assume a CEO was granted one million options on 1 July 2003, and the minimum time before the options could vest is four years. A valuation of the options is carried out by the company's compensation consultant and it is determined that each option's value is A$2.00 (giving a total options package value of A$2 million). In relation to this grant of options, the company should include A$500,000 as *value of options* in the directors' and executives' compensation section in each of the 2004, 2005, 2006, and 2007 annual reports.

Allocating the value across the vesting period will, in future, remove the lumpiness problem referred to above. However, for a transitional period of two years or so, a different problem will exist: ASIC's Guidelines state that no adjustments should be made to exclude amounts already disclosed in previous financial years. This means that, if a company made a grant of options to its CEO on 1 July 2002, with a four-year vesting period, and the company—under the previous practice—disclosed the full value in its annual report for the year ended 30 June 2003, the company will nevertheless need to include 25% of the options' value in the CEO's pay disclosure in the annual reports for years ending 30 June 2004, 2005, and 2006. So, some double-counting will occur for a transitional period due to ASIC's approach. However, ASIC's approach is consistent with that taken by the International Accounting Standards Board and the Australian Accounting Standards Board (Accounting Standard AASB 2, "Share-based Payment"), in relation to valuing options for the purposes of recognizing an expense in the financial statements.

Results

Table 15.3 compares total compensation (excluding long-term incentive) for the sample companies over the period 2000 to 2003. Average (mean) pay, excluding long-term incentive, increased by 2.6% between 2002 and 2003 (from A$2.38 million to A$2.44 million).

As mentioned above, during the year average fixed compensation increased by 38.6% and average short-term incentive increased by 36.9%. The reason the average total compensation excluding long-term incentive increased by only 2.6% is that not all CEOs were paid a short-term incentive during the year (16 of the 78 CEOs did not receive a short-term incentive). If those CEOs who did not receive a cash bonus are excluded, average (mean) pay, excluding long-term incentive, increased by 3.6% between 2002 and 2003 (from A$2.74 million to A$2.84 million).

TABLE 15.3   Total Compensation Excluding Long-Term Incentive:
2000–2003 Comparison

Yearly Comparison	2000	2001	2002	2003
Average	A$2,243,464	A$2,018,190	A$2,381,356	A$2,444,368
Minimum	A$195,931	A$166,457	A$50,575	A$387,472
Maximum	A$14,935,000	A$14,858,824	A$16,294,620	A$25,793,845
Median		A$1,422,662	A$1,447,111	A$1,773,180
Average Change . . .	*2000 to 2001*		*2001 to 2002*	*2002 to 2003*
for total compensation (excl LTI) . . .	–A$225,274		+A$363,166	+A$63,012

The median figure (A$1,773,180) was 22.5% higher than the 2002 median (A$1,447,111) and 24.6% higher than the 2001 median (A$1,422,662).

Table 15.3 also shows the range of total (non-LTIP) pay: from A$387,472 to A$25.8 million. The lowest figure is significantly higher than the minimum figure for earlier years, but again the small figures for earlier years reflect CEOs who had been in office for less than a full financial year. The highest figure (A$25.8 million) is noticeably higher than the highest figures recorded for 2000, 2001, and 2002.

Figure 15.3 shows the distribution of total (non-LTIP) pay. Seventeen

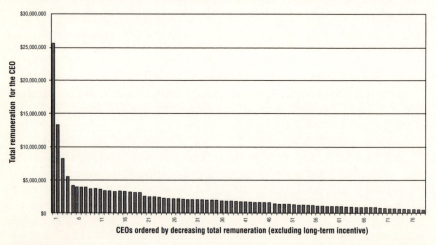

FIGURE 15.3   Distribution of Total Compensation (Excluding Long-Term Incentive)

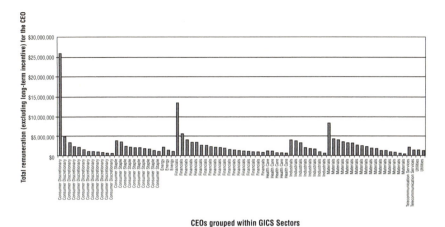

CEOs grouped within GICS Sectors

FIGURE 15.4 Total Compensation Excluding Long-Term Incentive, Ordered by GICS Sectors

of the 78 sample CEOs had a total package (excluding long-term incentive) of less than A$1 million. Twenty-six CEOs had a package between A$1 million and A$2 million. Sixteen CEOs had a package between A$2 million and A$3 million. Fourteen CEOs had a package between A$3 million and A$4 million. The remaining packages were A$4.2 million, A$5.5 million, A$8.3 million, A$13.4 million, and A$25.8 million.

Figure 15.4 shows total compensation (excluding long-term incentive) across industries. There are clear outliers in the Consumer Discretionary, Financials, and Materials sectors. When these outliers are disregarded, the spread of pay packets between CEOs in particular sectors is broadly similar. For instance, 13 out of 17 CEOs in the Materials sector were paid more than A$1 million during 2003, as were 16 out of 19 CEOs in the Financials sector.

TOTAL COMPENSATION INCLUDING LONG-TERM INCENTIVE

This section examines CEOs' total compensation packages, including the value of long-term incentives. The most common types of long-term incentives used by large Australian companies are traditional options and zero exercise price options (ZEPOs). ZEPOs are often called "performance rights" in Australia, and "restricted stock" in the United States. An executive who receives ZEPOs, unlike an executive who receives traditional op-

TABLE 15.4   Total Compensation Including Long-Term Incentive:
2000–2003 Comparison

Yearly Comparison	2000	2001	2002	2003
Average	A$4,190,660	A$2,644,393	A$3,228,695	A$3,163,769
Minimum	A$348,338	A$166,457	A$50,575	A$387,472
Maximum	A$69,098,875	A$14,858,823	A$16,294,620	A$26,681,537
Median	A$2,168,289	A$2,120,411	A$2,098,601	A$2,325,692
Average Change . . .	*2000 to 2001*		*2001 to 2002*	*2002 to 2003*
for total	−A$1,546,267		+ A$584,302	−A$64,926
compensation . . .				

tions, is not required to pay anything to the company at the time of exercising the instruments. The exercise price is zero—whereas the exercise
price for traditional options is normally whatever the company's share
price was back on the date the options were granted.

Table 15.4 compares total compensation from 2000 to 2003. Average
total pay, including long-term incentive, decreased by 2% between 2002
and 2003 (from A$3.23 million to A$3.16 million). The median figure
(A$2,325,692) was 10.8% higher than the 2002 median (A$2,098,601)
and 9.7% higher than the 2001 median (A$2,120,411). Table 15.4 also
shows the range of total pay: from A$387,472 to A$26.7 million.

Figure 15.5 shows the distribution of total pay. Ten of the 78 sample

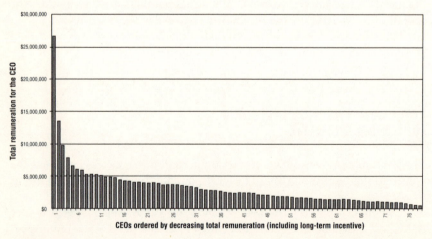

FIGURE 15.5   Distribution of Total Compensation (Including Long-Term Incentive)

CEOs had a total package (including long-term incentive) of less than A$1 million. Twenty-five CEOs had a package between A$1 million and A$2 million. Twelve CEOs had a package between A$2 million and A$3 million. Fourteen CEOs had a package between A$3 million and A$4 million. Six CEOs had a package between A$4 million and A$5 million. Six CEOs had a package between A$5 million and A$6 million. The remaining packages were A$6.5 million, A$7.8 million, A$9.8 million, A$13.4 million, and A$26.7 million.

COMPENSATION COMPONENTS IN DETAIL

This section is designed to allow analysis of the relative significance of base salary, annual bonus (short-term incentive), options/shares (long-term incentive), and other components of CEO compensation.

Australian companies have not adopted a standardized approach to disclosing the components of executive compensation. Investors would benefit if a standardized approach were to be adopted, because this would allow for much easier comparison between companies. There is a strong case for Australia to adopt the same approach as the United States—where SEC rules require companies to disclose the components of senior executives' compensation in standardized categories.

The problem is most pronounced in Australia in relation to amounts such as superannuation (pension), value of use of a motor vehicle, and other fringe benefits. Some companies itemize these elements of compensation, under their specific headings. But other companies use a general heading like "Noncash Benefits" to disclose the total of all these elements.

Some points to note about Table 15.5 are:

- For 2001 and 2002, the data on "Allowances," "Motor vehicle," and "Retirement benefits" were aggregated and included with "Other benefit"—for the reason outlined above. However, even though those three components of pay are itemized for 2003, the "Other benefit" figure will still include some motor vehicle allowances, retirement benefits and other allowances, even for 2003, because some companies continue not to provide separate figures. For the same reason, the "Other benefit" category also includes some superannuation for all three years.
- For 2003, the short-term incentive has been separated out as a cash bonus or a grant of shares. However, as the data show, the annual cash bonus is still by far the most popular form of short-term incentive.

TABLE 15.5 Components of Total Compensation

	2001 Total Amount	2002 Total Amount	2003 Total Amount	2001 Proportion of Total Pay	2002 Proportion of Total Pay	2003 Proportion of Total Pay	2001 Number Disclosing This Component	2002 Number Disclosing This Component	2003 Number Disclosing This Component
Base salary	A$64,512,799	A$80,211,417	A$92,421,433	38.1%	31.5%	37.5%	64	78	78
Bonus component (Cash)	A$43,569,466	A$59,128,151	A$78,209,362	25.7%	23.2%	31.7%	50	62	61
Bonus component (Shares)			A$1,357,121			0.6%			2
Other benefit	A$7,922,605	A$22,810,308	A$9,573,645	4.7%	9.0%	3.9%	48	56	51
Superannuation	A$2,414,713	A$5,869,570	A$3,041,119	1.4%	2.3%	1.2%	32	45	40
Allowances			A$841,986			0.3%			4
Motor vehicle			A$217,774			0.1%			4
Retirement benefits			A$4,998,265			2.0%			4
Cash long-term incentive payment	A$7,458,969	A$13,830,484	A$10,870,061	4.4%	5.4%	4.4%	11	7	5
Options	A$22,562,872	A$50,642,948	A$26,644,319	13.3%	19.9%	10.8%	19	39	36
Performance rights			A$10,488,984			4.3%			15
Deferred shares			A$6,143,166			2.5%			10
Loan-funded share scheme	A$17,514,110	A$22,076,408	A$1,966,764	10.3%	8.7%	0.8%	15	12	9
Free shares			A$0			0%			0
Total	A$169,241,163	A$251,838,210	A$246,773,999	100%	100%	100%			

- For 2003, the manner in which shares were provided as a long-term incentive is separately itemized: as either "Performance rights," "Deferred shares," "Loan-funded share scheme," or "Free Shares." Performance rights and deferred shares are both zero exercise price options (ZEPOs).
- The far-right column of Table 15.5 shows that the number of companies using performance rights and deferred shares was significantly higher in 2003 compared to 2001 and 2002. However, the value of those instruments awarded in 2003 does not appear to have been significantly different to 2001 and 2002 (although, due to aggregation in the earlier years, it is not possible to say with precision).
- The long-term incentive component of pay is detailed in the final six rows of Table 15.5. The data in these rows reveal that long-term incentives accounted for 28% of the average CEO's total compensation in 2001, 34% in 2002, and 22.8% in 2003. The dip in 2003 is interesting, given that the trend over the past two decades has been for long-term incentives to compose a greater proportion of total pay:
  - In 1987, on average long-term incentives accounted for 6.3% of total CEO pay.
  - In 1990, on average long-term incentives accounted for 13.3% of total CEO pay.
  - In 1995, on average long-term incentives accounted for 27.9% of total CEO pay.

An increase in the relative size of the *short-term* incentive (up from 23.2% in 2002 to 32.3% in 2003) appears to have driven the 2003 dip in comparative significance of the long-term incentive.

Table 15.6 shows that Australian CEOs are, on average, receiving a far smaller proportion of their total compensation in the form of long-term incentives than their U.S. counterparts. The long-term incentive component

TABLE 15.6 Components of Total Compensation: Australian, U.K., and U.S. CEOs

CEO of Company in . . .	Salary	Short-Term Incentive	Long-Term Incentive
Australia	38%	32%	23%
United Kingdom	59%	18%	10%
United States	29%	17%	42%

of pay for the average U.S. CEO is nearly double that of the average Australian CEO.

But, as Table 15.6 illustrates, the average Australian CEO in 2003 was receiving considerably more of her or his pay in the form of options and shares than the average British CEO in 1997 (source for U.K. and U.S. data: Conyon and Murphy 2000).

DISCLOSURE OF OPTIONS' VALUE

Background

Section 300A of the Corporations Act 2001 requires Australian publicly traded companies to disclose, in their annual report to shareholders, "details of the nature and amount of each element of the emolument of each director and each of the 5 named officers of the company receiving the highest emolument."

Until early 2003, a number of Australian companies had interpreted section 300A as not requiring them to disclose the value of share options granted to directors and senior executives.

However, in May 2003, ASIC announced—through a strongly worded media release and draft guidelines—that it interpreted section 300A as mandating disclosure of options' value. In the final version of its "Guidelines to Valuing Options in Annual Directors' Reports," released in June 2003, ASIC warned that it would "consider taking action against the directors" if a company did not disclose the value of options granted to directors or executives.

Also, in January 2004, the Australian Accounting Standards Board released AASB 1046, "Director and Executive Disclosures by Disclosing Entities." This new Accounting Standard requires the value of options (and other equity incentives) to be disclosed for reporting periods ending on or after 30 June 2004. Because it is an Accounting Standard, it has the force of law under the Corporations Act (section 296). So there is now no more uncertainty about the legal position where a company chooses not to disclose (or neglects to disclose) the value of options granted to directors and executives. Because the Corporations Act requires publicly traded companies to comply with all Accounting Standards, if a company does not disclose options' value for a reporting period ending on or after 30 June 2004, each of that company's directors will be subject to the civil penalty regime in the Act because the company's failure to comply with AASB 1046 will constitute a breach of section 296. That is, even if there is still some room for arguing about the meaning of section 300A, that will no longer be a valid basis on which not to disclose the value of options. AASB 1046 is a standalone disclosure requirement.

The study described in this chapter provides the first evidence of options' disclosure since ASIC adopted its hard-line stance. AASB 1046 did not apply to 2003 annual reports, although its requirements had been flagged to the market through an Exposure Draft standard (ED 106, released in May 2002).

Results

An earlier study with which the author was involved, which used 2002 annual reports, found that 75% of the sample companies disclosed the value of options or shares granted as at the grant date. This was a significantly higher incidence of disclosure than a year earlier, when only half the Top 100 companies disclosed this information.

Every sample company that granted options to a director or top-5 executive in 2003 disclosed a value for those options. At first blush, this appears to show that ASIC's tough stance has led to 100% compliance with section 300A. However, on closer inspection:

- One company, which issued options in February 2002 (that is, in the previous financial year), that remained unvested as at 30 June 2003, did not allocate a portion of the value of those options in its 2003 annual report. This is inconsistent with the ASIC Guidelines, which state that "these guidelines do not provide any exclusion for options granted before 7 November 2002." (In addition, the company had not disclosed any value for these options in its 2002 annual report.)
- The same company also has a cash-based long-term incentive for senior executives. However, it did not disclose the amount that accrued under that plan for the CEO during the financial year.
- Several companies use a loan-funded share plan as their long-term incentive. Invariably, these companies disclose either the *notional interest* that the company has forgone during the year (where the loan is interest-free), or details about the interest paid or payable (where the loan incurs interest). But is this really information about the *value* of the equity incentives being provided by the company? The ASIC Guidelines are not strictly relevant where a company has a loan-funded share plan rather than an options plan. However, going forward, for financial reporting purposes (rather than disclosure of pay purposes), these companies will need to recognize that Accounting Standard AASB 2, "Share-based Payment," applies—as its title suggests—not only to options but also all other forms of equity incentives.

- For another company, it is not possible to judge whether it complied with section 300A, or even whether the company issued options or other equity incentives during 2003, because the company appears not to have filed its full-length annual report with the ASX (the ASX announcements page contains only a copy of the concise annual report); and the company's web site does not contain a copy of its full-length annual report (again, there is only a copy of its concise annual report). The concise report does not contain the "Related Party" note to the financial statements.

CHAPTER 16

Directors' and Officers' Liability in France

Alain-Xavier Briatte and Michael Julian

INTRODUCTION

Though France has emerged relatively unscathed from the recent string of financial and governance scandals that have affected the major world markets, there have, nonetheless, been calls to modernize and open French corporate governance rules to conform to international standards and provide additional safeguards to investors. This movement has resulted in the adoption of significant reforms to the French regulatory framework, which will be analyzed in their historical legal context and with regard to financial disclosure rules. It is also important to trace the development of the newly created French market authority, the AMF, and explore the insurance regime available to directors and officers.

PRINCIPLES OF DIRECTORS' AND OFFICERS' CIVIL AND CRIMINAL LIABILITY

Directors' and officers' liability is but one aspect of the more general issue of power sharing and more precisely the key control rights within a company and the separation of ownership and control between management and shareholders. This separation should be considered as the crucial question in all legal systems due to the fact it automatically derives from the need to find a competent management team able to conduct the business and committed to providing value to shareholders (Berle and Means 1932, 68 and 196).

The liability regime of directors and officers is the necessary corollary to control issues within the company as it establishes the limits of management behavior and provides shareholders and third parties dealing with the company with legislative protection against management misconduct.

The importance of the liability regime has been highlighted by the recent scandals that have touched the world financial markets. In response to these events, the French legislature has adopted major legal reforms to reinforce the rules imposed on directors and officers. These new rules will be considered in their historical context, within the framework of the existing liability regime and the criminal liability rules for both individuals and legal entities.

History of Control Mechanisms in the Civil Corporate Law Countries

Civil law jurisdictions, such as France, have traditionally opted for an approach involving extensive regulation and oversight of business entities and their management. Historically, France has one of the most ancient, elaborate, and integrated corporate governance frameworks. This history dates back to the adoption of the first commercial code (*code de commerce*) in 1807, Code de Commerce (C. Com). This code is applicable to dealings between merchants and as such provides the fundamental rules governing legal entities having a commercial purpose. The French civil code, which was adopted three years before the commercial code, sets forth the rules for legal entities which do not engage in commerce and provides a collection of general rules which govern the inner workings of the legal entities, both commercial and civil.

The existence of the company as an independent corporate body, as well as the control of key stakeholders of the company, were recognized in the early stages of corporate law development in France. The important role of the legislature in this domain was formalized by the adoption of an extensive system of mandatory rules governing company activity.

Nowhere is this strict regime more evident than the rules governing the management of the company. Since 1867, comprehensive rules regarding the management of companies have been imposed by law (Art. 22 Law of July 24, 1867 amending the C. Com., Bull. Des Lois 11e S., B. 1513, n° 15, 328, p. 94). The articles of association, which are required by law to include detailed and often mandatory provisions regarding the decision-making process, shareholding and transfer of ownership and the activities of the company, form the basis of the *corporate contract* between the shareholders. As a general rule, any decision that affects or modifies the corporate contract must be made by the shareholders and may not be delegated by the shareholders to the board of directors.

For the purposes of our discussion, we will concentrate on the main form of legal entity that can be listed on a national market, the *société anonyme*, which may be set up either with a board of directors or with management and supervisory boards. Directors and officers that we refer to in the course of this chapter will include: the directors (*Administrateurs*), the chairman of the board of directors (*Président du conseil d'administration*), who can also be at the same time the chief executive officer (*Directeur Général*) when the company has not opted for management/supervisory board structure, the chairman of the management board (*Président du directoire*) in a *société anonyme* which has adopted this form, and the members of the management board (*membres du directoire*).

Principle of Civil Law Liability of Directors and Officers

Directors and officers are liable under French civil law to both the company and shareholders for their acts that cause damages to the company. Since there is no general text applicable to all company structures (C. civ., art. 1850: C. Com. art. L. 225-251, L. 225-256: directors, chief executive officer and member of the supervisory board of a *société anonyme*), the general principles of the civil liability (*responsabilité civile*) apply (C. Civ. Art. 1382).

A claim for damages based on the personal liability of directors and officers is conditioned on the showing of the existence of negligent or intentional acts or omissions (*faute*), damages (*dommage*) and a causal link (*lien de causalité*) between the conduct and the damages incurred by the company itself or its shareholders. The amount of damages allocated can be reduced depending on the existence of a fault or negligence of the victim.

The law enumerates three types of violations giving raise to possible liability: (1) the violation of any provision of law, (2) the violation of the articles of association, and (3) management misconduct.

Violation of law or the provisions of the company charter do not present many difficulties of interpretation. Violation of any provision of law is interpreted broadly and includes the commercial code as well as any provision of labor law, securities law, and criminal law. The violation of the articles of association will be obvious whenever the director or officer has breached one of the articles of association's limitation of power, for instance.

Management misconduct is based on the principle that a director or officer will only be considered in breach of his duty when he did not put in practice all possible means in order to act in the best interest of the company and to assure its prosperity. Thus, the management will not be found liable for failing to achieve the promised result. Within the French dichotomy of applicable duties of care, the management does not bear an obligation of attaining a desired result (*obligation de résultat* or strict liability), but a simple duty to use the best effort to achieve this result (*obligation de moyens*).

The standard of proof is objective. The judge will compare the questioned management activity to the standard of an average manager using the appropriate diligence and care. Other elements may be considered in assessing the management's duty, such as the fact the company is listed, the type of business carried out, or the size of the company, but no general definition of the misconduct is provided.

There are three types of management misconduct : (1) disloyalty of the directors and officers; (2) abstention from action when managing the company requires action to be taken; and (3) intentional management misconduct.

Generally, directors and officers will be sued separately and will only be responsible for the damages they personally caused. This is different for the liability of the board of directors, the supervisory board, or the members of the executive committee, who may generally be found jointly and severally liable.

Under French civil law, each individual engaging in management misconduct either by disloyalty or by omission may be found liable to indemnify the victim for all damages suffered, up to a proportion relating to the degree of their personal misconduct. The court will determine the responsibilities of each party and allocate the proper indemnification based on each one's misconduct.

Civil Actions

There are two different types of civil actions: either (1) the individual action, or (2) the derivative action (*action sociale* or *action ut singuli*) (C. Com., art. L. 223-22 and L. 225-252). The individual action is brought against the management by a shareholder who has suffered direct and personal damages, meaning damages different from those suffered by the company as a whole. Thus, for example, damages consisting of a sudden fall of the share prices will not be considered as direct and personal damages incurred by the shareholder as it affects the whole corporate body.

An action may also be brought on behalf of the company. France was one of the first countries to introduce the derivative action. This action may be brought by one or several shareholders of the company for the damages incurred by the company. The suit will be brought on behalf of the company against the management. The judge can order the management to indemnify the company. This claim is based on article C. Com. 225-251 and details three causes already mentioned above as the possible causes of the civil liability: (1) violation of laws and regulations—there are as many as 11,000 mandatory provisions imposed on the directors and officers under French Law; (2) violation of the articles of association; and (3) management misconduct.

Principle of Criminal Law Liability of Directors and Officers

Apart from the civil actions described above, the director or officer responsible for the violation of a regulation could alternatively be prosecuted under a criminal law offense provided that the judge succeeds in gathering the constitutive elements of the director's or officer's criminal activity; that is, (1) he is deemed responsible for an act or an abstention—this is a "material act"—and (2) he has had the intention to do so or, by default, he made a simple careless act or negligence. An example would be a chairman of the board publishing inaccurate financial statements with full knowledge of the facts, or negligently failing to verify their accuracy.

Criminal prosecutions are often favored by victims as they provide more possibilities to collect evidence against the management. This is due to the fact that the criminal courts and the public prosecutor have much more power to force the parties to produce the evidence necessary for the case. Also, the criminal judge has the power to allocate some civil damages when rendering its decision. It is important to note that under French law the victim of an alleged crime can, in most cases, force the public prosecutor to commence proceedings against the claimed perpetrator.

Most of the time the individual charged with committing the offense can be anyone in the company provided all the elements of the violation are proved. Yet in some cases the law precisely designates those who committed the offense. For example, in the bankruptcy context, individuals not quoted by the particular law on insolvency may not be found guilty for the offense.

Accomplices may also be prosecuted for contributing to the violation of law without personally committing the offense. One condition of the qualification of complicity remains the existence of a main punishable act to which the complicity is related. In the preceding example (publication of false accounts), the accountant will be deemed guilty to have published the false accounts in collusion with the chairman of the board once the false accounts have been printed, even if the chairman is no longer punishable or has been found guilty.

Perhaps the most common example of corporate crime is the misuse or abuse of the company's property and goods. Pursuant to articles C. Com. Art. L. 242-6-3° and L. 242-6-4°, the misuse or abuse covers any appropriation or disposal of the company's goods or assets. The use is qualified as *misuse* or *abuse* when the use is contrary to the company's general social interest, or contrary to any provision of the law in some extreme circumstances that can jeopardize the continuation of the business.

A director or officer may be found guilty of such an offense in the following circumstances:

- Transferring sums due to the company to a private bank account
- Having the company guarantee the director's or officer's debts and liabilities
- Having the company pay for personal expenditures (loan, life assurance premium, golf club fee, etc.)
- Bribing a public agent
- Organizing a serious and repeated fraud against the tax authorities (article L. 267 of the Tax Procedures Handbook (*Livre des procédures fiscales*))

Even if the activity is in the interest of the company, the director or officer may be found guilty when this situation has the company or its representatives run the risk of a criminal offense that may impair the business activity. The shareholders' assembly is barred from allowing the company to cover up such a misuse or abuse and thus may not prevent the management from incurring criminal liability.

Corporate Entities and their Criminal Liability

In a fairly recent development, corporate entities may also be found liable for criminal offenses. The offense must have been committed by its directors or officers, that is to say, its representatives including the shareholders as well. A key element of these offenses is that they must have been committed to serve the corporate interests, on the company's behalf. The corporate entity's prosecution is not exclusive of the suit brought at the same time against one or several individual directors or officers of the aforementioned company.

LIABILITIES INCURRED ON DISCLOSING FINANCIAL INFORMATION IN LISTED COMPANIES

Recent financial failures have highlighted the importance of accurate and timely disclosure of mandatory information. In the current business climate, violations of disclosure requirements have proven to be an expanding area for liability for the various corporate players. This is also amplified by the Sarbanes-Oxley Act—section 302 and section 404—which applies to approximately 70 French companies, either directly listed on a U.S. stock exchange or through ADRs. One must bear in mind that the U.S. Act imposes additional mandatory provisions in terms of financial information disclosure and internal procedures and risk management. Within the French legal framework, it is important to examine the liability regime of the issuer and the directors and officers regarding disclosure of financial information and then explore the additional obligations placed on directors and officers.

Liabilities Incurred by Issuers When Disclosing Financial Information in Listed Companies

Some commentators have argued that a number of liability cases against issuers may be entered into based on a contract, driven by the conclusion drawn from the analogy with French labor law (Letreguilly 2004). It is important to recall that in civil law jurisdictions the existence of a contract prevents the victim from having recourse to remedies in tort. Contractual liability is based on the same rules as the general liability regime and requires the existence of a contract, a contractual fault, damages, and causation. The contracts giving rise to this type of liability are, for example, subscription agreements, representations, and warranties included in syndicated loans or a prospectus. There remains some disagreement between commentators as to whether the contract forming the company itself could give rise to a liability in the context of the permanent duty of financial information disclosure imposed on the company.

With regard to the prospectus, the French market authority (art. 4 ter-1 of the ruling of French market regulator the *Commission des operations de bourse* (COB) n°98-01) has ruled that it should mention the names of the individuals responsible for preparing the document. According to instruction of COB of December 2001 applying ruling n°98-01, the information contained in the prospectus should be complete and accurate.

In line with the corporate governance history in France, most of these mandatory provisions are issued from the law or the market authority and may fall outside of the scope of the contract for various reasons—either such documents do not show an irrevocable commitment or the debt can be attached to another source of obligation than the documents.

Whether the liability cause of action is based on contract or tort, the civil liability regime will apply in all cases. When disclosing financial information in the listed companies, third parties may prefer suing the company itself rather than the directors and officers as it does not entail the strict condition pertaining to the necessary *separable fault (faute détachable)* carried out by the management. Indeed, French court decisions have established that directors' and officers' misconduct is only actionable if it is separable from the conduct of the normal business activity, that is to say, different from a *fault in service* as described below. Proving the existence of a separable fault often places an insurmountable barrier in the path of the potential plaintiff. Placing liability on the issuer has allowed the courts to award damages to plaintiffs when the separable fault cannot be proven.

In the Flammarion case (CA Paris, 25e Ch., sect. B, 26 sept. 2003, Soulier et a. c/ Flammarion et a. : Bull. Joly janv. 2004, p. 85, note J.-J. Daigre.), the Paris Court of Appeal (*Cour d'Appel de Paris*) ordered an issuer (Flammarion) to indemnify certain shareholders where the listed company had been sold at a high price six days after it announced catastrophic financial results. In reality, the information disclosed to the public was inaccurate and had been disclosed in circumstances that had misled the investors. The fault was certainly evident in the context of the disclosure and the damages suffered by certain shareholders were directly attributed to the issuer and its management.

Liabilities of Directors and Officers When Disclosing Financial Information in Listed Companies

Civil Liability of Directors and Officers vis-à-vis Third Parties   Third parties traditionally have limited success in claims against directors and officers. Article C. Com L. 225-252 provides that "the directors and the chief executive are liable . . . towards the company or towards third parties, for infringements to laws and regulations applying to commercial entities." It is important to mention that the Supreme Court (*Cour de Cassation*) has gradually exonerated directors and officers toward third parties with the theory of the separable fault.

It is now well-established case law that only directors' and officers' misconduct that is separable from the conduct of the normal business activity is subject to civil liability. Based on the principle developed in the legal representation and agency theory, whenever the misconduct falls within the normal course of the business activity, it should always be regarded as misconduct in the course of the service of the company (*faute de service*) and therefore bar any action aimed at questioning the directors and officers personally.

Thus, third parties are reluctant to sue directors and officers and prefer to sue the company itself. However, the characteristic of the separable fault, which some commentators have identified in the past as being the *unfindable fault* (D. Ohl, sous Cass. Com., 28 avril 1998 : JCP G 1998, II, 10177), has been modified as the fault may now be deemed to be carried out outside the course of the business activity if it is of a *particular seriousness* (Cass. 1ère civ, 6 oct 1998), as provided in a famous case where the chief executive officer had assigned twice the same receivables.

The intentional fault may give rise also to civil liability and is therefore considered a separable fault when such intention has been exercised in order to serve a personal interest (Cour d'Appel de Versailles, 17 janv. 2002).

Since the 1 August 2003 Law, allowing the beginnings of a type of class action suit, civil liability of directors and officers can also be triggered by shareholders associations, nonprofit legal entities set up for the purpose of defending their members' (i.e., groups of shareholders) interests, according to C. Com. L. 225-252 and L. 225-120, C. monét. Fin., art. L. 452-2, subject to their holding at least 5% of the capital of the company. This practice has become more common due to the fact that class action suits similar to the U.S. actions are not available in France.

Criminal Liability of Directors and Officers   Once again, the most efficient route open to third parties remains the criminal courts which prosecute directors and officers. Claims for civil damages may be brought at the same time as the criminal proceedings. Allowance for civil damages will be requested from the same criminal judge after such judge has found the existence of criminal acts. This avenue offers a better chance to the third parties to be indemnified (Cass. Com. 19 févr. 2003 : Dr. pén. juill.–août 2003, p. 17, note J.-H Robert) due to the fact that the liability of the directors and officers will be triggered even when the fault is the fault in service, that is to say exercised in the normal course of the business activity and is not necessarily separable.

Criminal courts, as well as the French Market Authority (*Autorité des Marchés Financiers*), which follows the same case law imposing damages, will allow damages in a situation where civil courts will bar any civil damages based on the theory of the separable fault.

Despite the advantages of the use of criminal courts, the current trend is toward diminishing the role of criminal liability in today's legal environment (Mattout 2004). This is due to an increase of the amount of civil damages awarded and the introduction of court-ordered fines to be paid by the management (C. Com., art. L 238-1 pertaining to the annual financial statement and consolidated financial statements and the management report, or an increase of causes of voidance in lieu of criminal offenses).

Nevertheless, criminal law still governs most questions of directors' and officers' liability such as:

- Disclosure of false or misleading information (C. monét. Fin., art. L. 465-1 al. 4 or règl. COB n° 98-07, art. 3)
- Market manipulation (*manipulation de cours*) (C. monét. Fin., art. L. 465-1, al. 1 and règl. COB n° 90-08)
- False financial accounts disclosure (C. Com., art. L. 242-6-2°)
- False information (C. pén, art. 441-1)

The Power of the French Market Authority A third means of sanctioning directors and officers is exercised by the French market authority (*Autorité des Marchés Financiers*) (AMF). As mentioned above, following the example of the criminal courts, the AMF does not require the existence of a separable fault in order to fine directors and officers as confirmed by the *Cour de Cassation* (Cass. Com., 31 mars 2004 : Bull. Joly juill. 2004, p. 982, note Gilles Auzero). It is, however, important to note that civil damages will not be granted to third parties by a civil judge (*tribunal de grande instance* or *cour d'appel*) based on the AMF's prior qualification of the facts presented thereafter to a civil jurisdiction unless, once again, a separable fault exists.

Additional Obligations of Directors and Officers

Recent laws and regulations have created additional duties of disclosure of information endorsed by the directors and officers. The 2003 Law has created a specific obligation on the chairman of the board or the executive director, pursuant to C. Com. Art. L. 225-35 al. 3, "to communicate to each individual director all documents and information necessary for the fulfillment of his mission." Moreover, in multinational groups of corporate entities, C. Com. Art. L. 225-100 provides that consolidated financial statements should be prepared in light of all financial information including the information disclosed by all consolidated entities.

The duty of information and disclosure is very large. A ruling of the French market authority (COB n° 98-07) compels the management to disclose any relevant and accurate information in due course. The market authority has also (Bull. COB n° 272, September 2003, 7) imposed some additional information disclosure duties in terms of permanent information and press releases. Other disclosure obligations include semiannual and annual filings, prospectus, information notices, reference documents, form 20F for U.S. listed companies, profit warnings, securities threshold crossing declarations, intention disclosures, shareholders agreements, disclosures and perspective of profit earning announcements.

Since 2003, the chairman of the board of directors or the chairman of the management board is required to render a report on risks and internal procedures and controls together with the management report (according to C. Com. Art. L. 225-37, al. 6 and L. 225-68, al. 3). Furthermore, based on the recommendations of the Securities and Exchange Commission, some French companies have decided to create financial information committees, working along with the audit committees, in charge of collecting, monitoring, and disclosing the company's financial information.

In addition to obligations imposed by law, French industry and market groups have embraced the recent development of corporate governance based on a *comply-or-explain* approach. Currently, French best practices include the application of corporate governance guidelines adopted by industry groups (the MEDEF and AFEP Corporate Governance Code of Listed Companies, October 2003, principles for corporate governance based on consolidation of the 1995, 1999, and 2002 AFEP and MEDEF's reports) (the "French Corporate Governance Code" or the "Code of Corporate Governance"), or explaining why they are not implemented. The Code of Corporate Governance indicates other practices which it considers as the industry norms. Directors are subject to additional responsibilities, especially as they relate to their general duty of disclosure to the financial markets.

As discussed previously, the civil, criminal, and commercial codes provide the mandatory provisions governing the conduct of the directors' and officers' activity and the liability regime. Therefore, the rules set forth by the Code of Corporate Governance, whose main features pertaining to the directors and officers are detailed below, will not be deemed as binding rules as such. Nevertheless, it is well established that these rules are becoming standard market practice that will clearly provide evidence to the civil or criminal judge to base his opinion upon when analyzing the facts relevant to a case. The plaintiffs may certainly use these rules in order to influence the court.

It is therefore important to note that the Code of Corporate Governance rules may be considered as sources of the law for the major listed companies on the Paris Stock Exchange and have been codified, in some cases as mandatory provisions in the recent laws of 2001 or 2003.

Pursuant to the Code of Corporate Governance, the board of directors is a collegial body representing all shareholders collectively and is required to act at all times in the interests of the company. In exercising its statutory prerogatives, the board of directors carries out a fourfold mission: it defines the corporation's strategy, appoints and monitors the corporate officers in charge of managing the corporation, selects the form of organization (separation of the offices of chairman and chief executive officer or combination of such offices), and secures the quality of information provided to shareholders and to the market.

At this stage it is important to remember that, according to the same code, "a director is independent when he or she has no relationship of any kind whatsoever with the corporation, its group or the management of either that is such as to color his or her judgment." According to the Code of Corporate Governance, an *independent* director is to be understood not only as a *nonexecutive director*, that is, one not performing management duties in the corporation or its group, but also as one devoid of any particular bonds of interest (for example, significant shareholder, employee). Moreover, it is stated that the criteria to be reviewed by the Board in order to have a director qualify as independent and to prevent risks of conflicts interests are the following:

- Not to be an employee or corporate officer of the corporation, or an employee or director of its parent or a company that it consolidates, and not having been in such a position for the previous five years
- Not to be a corporate officer of a company in which the director holds a directorship, directly or indirectly, or in which an employee appointed as such or a corporate officer of the corporation (currently in office or having held such office going back five years) is a director
- Not to be, or to be bound directly or indirectly to, a customer, supplier, investment banker, or commercial banker that is material for the corporation or its group, or for a significant part of whose business the corporation or its group accounts
- Not to be related by close family ties to a corporate officer
- Not to have been an auditor of the corporation within the previous five years
- Not to have been a director of the corporation for more than 12 years

The Code of Corporate Governance points out that as regards directors representing major shareholders of the corporation or its parent, these may be considered as being independent provided that the company is not in control of the corporation. Currently, the Board, upon a report from the appointments committee stating that a director has in excess of a 10% holding of stock or votes, should systematically review the qualification of a director as independent, having regard to the makeup of the corporation's capital and the existence of a potential conflict of interest.

Off-Balance-Sheet Items and Risk Disclosure in Listed Companies   According to the Code of Corporate Governance, each listed corporation should have reliable internal procedures to identify and evaluate its commitments and risks, and provide shareholders and investors with relevant information in this respect. For such purposes, the annual report should specify the internal procedures set up to identify and monitor off-balance-sheet commitments, and to evaluate the corporation's material risks. It is also stated that the report should specify the methods used for informing shareholders and investors regarding off-balance-sheet-commitments.

Furthermore, material risks should be identified and clarified through (1) provision of specific information on these matters in the annual report, presenting them in a clear and easily accessible manner; (2) bringing together under a separate heading the information relating to off-balance-sheet items provided in notes to the accounts; (3) gathering the information relating to market risks (interest rate, foreign exchange, equity, lending, commodity prices) under a specific heading in the notes to the accounts; (4) in the event of significant exposure to interest rate, foreign exchange or commodity price risks, publication of indicators for the earnings sensitivity to such risks, specifying the methods and assumptions used for the indicators selected; and (5) publication of the corporations' ratings by financial-rating agencies and changes having occurred during the financial year.

Remuneration of Individual Directors   According to the Code of Corporate Governance, the total remuneration and other benefits granted to individual directors over the relevant financial year should be disclosed in detail in the annual accounts or in the notes to the annual accounts or, where applicable, in the remuneration report. The annual accounts or the notes to the annual accounts or, where applicable, the remuneration report should show at least a minimum amount of information as listed in the document for each person who has served as a director of the listed company at any time during the relevant financial year. As regards the information disclosure pertaining to the remuneration and/or emoluments, which is now substantially incorporated in the mandatory provisions of the Law (C. Com L. 225-102 and L. 225-184), the following information should be presented:

- The total amount of salary paid or due to the director for the services performed during the relevant financial year, including, where appropriate, the attendance fees fixed by the annual general shareholders' meeting
- Remuneration and advantages received from any undertaking belonging to the same group
- Remuneration paid in the form of profit sharing and/or bonus payments and the reasons why such bonus payments and/or profit sharing were granted

- Where such payment is legally allowed, any significant additional remuneration paid to directors for special services outside the scope of the usual functions of a director
- Compensation paid to or receivable by each former executive director in connection with the termination of his activities during that financial year
- Total estimated value of non-cash benefits considered as remuneration, other than the items covered in the above points

If it is permissible under national law or under the Articles of Association of the listed company to make such payments, amounts should be shown which the company, or any subsidiary or company included in the company's consolidated annual accounts, has paid by way of loans, advance payments, and guarantees to each person who has served as a director at any time during the relevant financial year, including the amount outstanding and the interest rate.

Similar rules apply to supplementary pension schemes.

Share-Based Remuneration   According to the Code of Corporate Governance, the schemes under which directors are remunerated in shares, share options, or any other right to acquire shares or to be remunerated on the basis of share price movements should be subject to the prior approval of shareholders by way of a resolution at the annual general meeting prior to their adoption. The prior approval by the shareholders, which is now a condition precedent according to the Code de Commerce (article L. 225.45), should relate to the scheme in itself and not to the grant of such share-based benefits under that scheme to individual directors.

Approval by the shareholders at the annual general meeting should cover the following:

- Granting of share-based schemes, including share options, to directors
- Determining the maximum number and the main conditions of the granting process
- Setting the term within which options can be exercised
- Fixing the conditions for any subsequent change in the exercise price of the options, if this is appropriate and legally permissible
- Agreeing to any other long-term incentive schemes for which directors are eligible and which is not offered under similar terms to all other employees

The annual general meeting should also set the period during which the body responsible for directors' remuneration may award these types of compensation schemes to individual directors.

Any substantial change in the terms and conditions of the schemes should also be subject to the approval of shareholders by way of a resolution at the annual general meeting prior to their adoption. In those cases, shareholders should be informed of the full terms of the proposed changes and should be given an explanation of the effect of the proposed changes.

If such an arrangement is permissible under national law or under the articles of association of the listed company, any discounted option arrangement under which any rights are granted to subscribe to shares at a price lower than the market value of the shares on the date when the price is determined, or the average of the market values over a number of days preceding the date when the exercise price is determined, should also receive the approval of shareholders.

According to the Code of Corporate Governance, prior to the annual general meeting where a draft resolution is submitted in accordance with national law and/or the articles of association of the listed company, an information notice concerning the resolution should be made available to shareholders.

The notice should contain the full text of the share-based remuneration schemes or a description of their principal terms, and the names of the participants in the schemes. It should also set out the relationship of the schemes in the context of the overall directors' remuneration policy.

The draft resolution should clearly refer either to the scheme itself or to the summary of its principal terms. Information should also be made available to shareholders about how the company intends to provide for the shares needed to meet its obligations under incentive schemes. In particular it should be clearly stated whether the company intends to purchase the necessary shares in the market, whether it holds them in treasury, or whether it will issue new shares.

This information should also provide an overview of the costs of the scheme to the company in view of the intended application. Such information should be posted on the listed company's web site.

DEVELOPMENT OF ENFORCEMENT BY THE AMF

The recent consolidation of the various French market and banking authorities under the aegis of the newly formed market regulator, the *Autorité des marchés financiers* (AMF), has had a profound effect on the corporate governance landscape in France. The AMF was created in 2003, following the disappearance of the *Commission des operations de bourse* (COB), and has been very active in promoting its agenda. It is now the key player regarding financial information disclosure and market regulation. A novel feature of the AMF is that it consists of two bodies with collective responsibility: the Board and a commission (the Sanction Commission) with exclusive powers to impose penalties and sanctions.

This Sanction Commission has 12 members, none of whom are members of the Board:

- Two members of the French Administrative Supreme Court (the *Conseil d'Etat*) designated by the Vice-President of that body
- Two justices of the French Supreme Court designated by the Chief Justice of that court
- Six qualified persons with legal and financial expertise and experience in securities issuance and financial-instrument investments, designated by the finance minister after consultation with organizations representing securities-issuing industrial and commercial companies, fund management companies and other investors, investment services providers, market undertakings, clearing houses, operators of settlement systems, and central depositories
- Two representatives of the employees of investment service providers, fund management companies, market undertakings, clearing houses, settlement systems and central depositories, designated by the Finance Minister after consultation with representative labor unions and employee associations

Sanction Commission members serve a five-year term of office, renewable once. One-half of the Sanction Commission is renewed every 30 months. The creation of a Sanction Commission separate from the Board meets the French constitutional requirement that the prosecutorial and judgment functions be separated.

Four stages of an enforcement action can now be distinguished:

1. Supervision and investigations: initiated and conducted under the direction of the AMF General Secretary
2. Opening of an enforcement action: decided by the AMF Board, which serves notice of the charges and refers the case to the Sanction Commission after examining the report of the inspection or investigation
3. Evidentiary phase of the enforcement action: conducted by a member of the Sanction Commission serving as rapporteur
4. Imposition of sanctions or penalties: ordered by the Sanction Commission

Reports on the inspections and investigations ordered by the Secretary General are passed on to the Board. In the light of these findings, the Board may, at its discretion, decide to initiate an enforcement action. If the Board decides to initiate an enforcement action, it serves notice of alleged rule infringements to the person who is the subject of the complaint (the *respondent*) together with the inspection or investigation report.

The statement of alleged rule infringements is forwarded to the Chairman of the Sanction Commission. The respondent has one month in which to submit a written response to the Chairman of the Sanction Commission. If the respondent resides outside the European Economic Area, the deadline is extended to two months.

The statement of alleged rule infringements confirms the duration of the response period and informs the respondent that further information and copies of the evidence can be obtained from the Sanction Commission. Respondents can be assisted or represented by counsel.

The Chairman of the Sanction Commission assigns the case either to the full Commission or to one of its divisions, and appoints a member of the Sanction Commission to act as Rapporteur. The respondent may be heard at his own request or if the Rapporteur considers it expedient. The Rapporteur can also hear anyone else he deems necessary.

If the Rapporteur considers that there are additional grounds for complaint or that the charges concern persons other than the respondent, he submits a request to that effect to the Board. The Board acts on the Rapporteur's request in accordance with Article 18 of Decree 2003-1109 of 23 November 2003.

The Rapporteur draws up a report on the results of these proceedings and serves it on the respondent.

The respondent is ordered to appear before the Sanction Commission or one of its divisions within a period that may not be less than 30 days. The order informs the respondent that he has 15 days in which to submit written observations on the report.

The Sanction hearing is based on an adversarial procedure. The hearing may be held in public if the respondent so requests. However, the Chairman of the bench (i.e., the Commission or division) can conduct all or part of the proceedings *in camera* for the sake of public order or if a public hearing would comprise business secrecy or any other legally protected information.

First, the Rapporteur outlines the case. The Government Commissioner may also submit observations. The respondent and his adviser, if he has one, then present the arguments in defense. The Chairman of the bench can hear any person deemed necessary. The respondent and his adviser are entitled to have the last word. If the bench decides it does not have sufficient information, it instructs the Rapporteur to pursue his enquiries.

When the hearing is complete, the respondent, the Rapporteur, and the Government Commissioner leave the chamber and the bench deliberates and makes its decision.

The Secretary for the hearing draws up a report, which is signed by the

Chairman of the bench, the Rapporteur, and the Secretary before being forwarded to the members of the Sanction Commission and the Government Commissioner.

The Commission may impose sanctions or penalties on the following persons:

- Professional entities under the supervision of the AMF, for any breach of professional obligations established by law, regulations, or rules of professional conduct approved by the AMF
- Natural persons (individuals) under the authority of or acting on behalf of such entities
- Any other person whose practices violate legislative or regulatory provisions, when such practices infringe upon investors' rights or impair the orderly operation of markets

Professional entities may be subject to sanctions related to the conduct of their business activity (warning, reprimand, temporary or permanent prohibition on providing all or part of the services previously provided) as well as fines up to €1.5 million or 10 times the unlawful profits earned (five times when the professional in question is an individual, except in cases of market manipulation).

Other persons may be subject to fines not exceeding €1.5 million or 10 times the amount of profits earned. The amount of the fine is set based on the seriousness of the acts committed and in proportion to the profits made or other advantages gained by virtue of those acts. The Commission may make public its sanction decisions in any publications, journals, or reports that it chooses.

The decision is communicated to the Government Commissioner and to the Chairman of the AMF, who reports back to the Board. Where a sanction decision concerns an investment service provider other than a management company, it is also communicated to the industry oversight group (*Comité des établissements de crédit et des entreprises d'investissement*) and to the banking authorities (*Commission bancaire*).

The Sanction Commission can publicly disclose the sanction decision in the publications, journals, or reports of its choosing. An appeal can be lodged against any sanction decision within two months of the date of notification, for the persons sanctioned; and from the date of publication, for any other interested parties.

Appeals are heard by the Paris Appeals Court, except in the case of sanctions against industry professionals (ISPs, direct sellers, investment advisers, custodians, members of regulated markets, etc.), in which case the court of competent jurisdiction is the *Conseil d'Etat*.

Of all the market activities that fall within the purview of the AMF, perhaps the most important is the enforcement of the rules dealing with insider trading. Insider trading is a criminal offense codified in the French monetary and financial code (*Code Monétaire et Financier*), which also gives rise to disciplinary sanctions based on the General Rules (*Règlement Général*) of the AMF.

Pursuant to article L 465-1, subparagraph 1, of the French monetary and financial code, directors and officers of a company such as referred to in article L. 225-109 of Code de Commerce can risk up to two years of imprisonment and a fine from 1.5 million euros up to 10 times the profit realized, if they dispose, at the time of the performance of their profession or their duties, of privileged information on the prospects or the situation of an issuer whose securities are negotiated on a regulated market or the prospects for evolution of one financial instrument or to allow to realize, either directly or by related third party, one or more operations before the public is informed of this information.

These rules apply not only to directors and officers of the company, but also to anyone having privileged information (article L 465-1, 3rd paragraph, of the French monetary and financial code).

If the AMF decides to join the lawsuit brought before a criminal court in order to obtain civil damages, the AMF will not be able to exercise its power of sanction with regard to the same person and the same facts.

In addition to the commercial code sanctions, articles 622-1 and 622-2 of the AMF General Rules organize a parallel scheme of sanctions that apply to any person who holds privileged information due to: (1) membership in the bodies of administration, direction, management, or monitoring of the issuer; (2) ownership of shares of the issuer; (3) access to information based on a professional relationship with the issuer as well as its participation in the preparation and the execution of a financial transaction; (4) activities likely to be qualified as crimes or offenses; and (5) any other person holding privileged information and who should have known that this information is privileged. When the abovementioned person is a legal entity, these obligations of abstention also apply to the individuals who take part in the decision to proceed to the operation on behalf of the legal entity in question.

Such referred persons must abstain from using the privileged information that they hold while acquiring or while assigning such for their own account or the account of others, either directly or indirectly, the financial instruments to which such privileged information is referred or any related financial instruments.

Article 621-1 of the General Rules of AMF gives a definition of privileged information. This consists of precise information that was not made public, which concerns, directly or indirectly, one or more issuers of financial instruments, or one or more financial instruments, and which, if it were made public, would be likely to have a material effect on the price of such financial instruments or the price of related financial instruments.

Information is deemed to be precise if it mentions a set of circumstances or events that occurred or are likely to occur and if it is possible to draw a conclusion from them regarding the price of such financial instruments or related financial instruments.

Information, which if it were made public, would be likely to have a material effect on the price of such financial instruments or derivative financial instruments, is information that a reasonable investor would be likely to use in making an investment decisions.

DIRECTORS' AND OFFICERS' INSURANCE IN FRANCE

Directors and officers of a French company have not traditionally had access to professional liability insurance. This is due in large part to the French law approach, which treats directors and officers as the personification of the legal entity entrusted with full power to bind the company and thus personally responsible for their actions. The movement to introduce directors' and officers' (D&O) insurance was spearheaded by international groups of companies seeking to protect the local and group management structures.

The adoption of this practice has encountered some resistance. Many exclusions are still set out in the D&O contract. For example, the policy will usually not cover certain major risks like the court-ordered assumption of company debts by the officers and directors in case of bankruptcy (*action en comblement de passif*).

The use of D&O insurance has experienced rapid growth lately with the recent development of litigation pertaining to the disclosure of financial information (Les Echos 2002) in such a manner that certain new exclusions have been created. For example, D&O contracts may well exclude civil liability coverage of directors of the board of noncontrolled entities.

The payment of the policy by the company remains an important and intricate legal question in France.

The legal committee of the French national association of limited liability companies (*Association Nationale des Sociétés par Actions*, ANSA) has established the general position that is currently accepted as the market norm (*assurance responsabilité civile des administrateurs*, n°04-005, 1er octobre 2003, ANSA).

The company should bear the cost of the D&O insurance for the sake of its own directors: it is never considered as a misuse of the company's assets and goods. Indeed, as long as the director does not act on behalf of herself but on behalf of the company and in the company's interest, the director's fault should be regarded as the company's fault.

The civil liability incurred by the directors and officers toward third parties remains the only type of liability covered by a D&O insurance contract paid by the company. That contract should cover any fault in service (*faute de service*) and therefore should exclude any separable fault as discussed before.

The civil damages allocated in the course of a criminal law action should also be covered by the D&O insurance contract paid by the company, as long as the fault at stake is not a separable fault. This D&O insurance contract paid by the company will also be able to cover the fault performed during the director's time of presence in the company, who has left the company since then.

Also the ANSA's legal committee has adopted an innovative approach inasmuch as a company could certainly directly endorse the risks taken by a director of a company without the insurance company's aid.

However, the company could certainly extend its coverage against any action or liability brought against directors and officers that would not be insured by the D&O contract. The company can certainly take over from the insurance contract, be the amount of damage inferior to the insurance threshold or the amount of the damage superior to the assured risk.

CHAPTER 17

Independent Directorship Systems in Greater China

Margaret Wang

INTRODUCTION

The need for better corporate governance for public-listed companies had been a hot topic for discussion and debate around the globe over the past few years, particularly after the collapse of a number of well-known companies, such as Enron and WorldCom. One of the issues central to these debates had been the need for companies to appoint independent directors, which is based on the Anglo-American model of corporate governance. The roles of these independent directors are to monitor the conduct of the board of directors, the company's directing mind and will, to safeguard the interests of shareholders, and to ensure that the powers given to directors are not misused and/or abused.

Such a topic had also generated much discussion in Greater China, particularly after its accession to the World Trade Organization in December 2001. With the further opening of its markets to foreign capital and participation, Greater China (that is, People's Republic of China (*China* or *mainland*), Chinese Taipei (*Taiwan*) and Hong Kong—excluding Macau for now) had implemented various law and regulations requiring independent directors to be on the board of directors in publicly listed companies.

This chapter examines the legal and regulatory requirements of having independent directors on the board of directors in companies in these three regions in Greater China. It also explores the challenges encountered when the Middle Kingdom tried to adopt this western, and hence foreign, model of corporate governance to its corporations. The effectiveness of an alternative model of monitoring the conduct of directors, the use of a supervisory board based on the German model, which is also in place in some regions

359

in Greater China, will also be examined. Finally, the chapter will conclude with some suggestions on how some of these challenges may be overcome to ensure that adequate supervision of the board is in place so that the shareholders' interests may be safeguarded.

WHY DID THE MIDDLE KINGDOM ADOPT WESTERN CORPORATE GOVERNANCE PRACTICES?

Before embarking on the task of examining the detailed legal and regulatory requirements of having independent directors and supervisors, it is important to first ask the fundamental question of why the Middle Kingdom chose to adopt the western corporate governance practices, either the Anglo-American model or German model, or a combination of the two models. After all, people perceive the need for better corporate governance to be linked to better financial performance for companies, measured by means of better returns to shareholders, for example. For a nation, better corporate governance may be related to improving economic situation and growth. In the case of China, without much of a system of corporate governance in place in the late 1990s and early 2000s, it was already the second largest economy after the United States, measured by purchasing power parity, and had experienced one of the fastest industrializations in history (Plender 2003). Further, before the existence of any regulation dealing with any corporate governance practices, China was already very successful in attracting foreign capital by way of investment. By July 2000, foreign direct investment in China was more than US$327 billion, and more than 353,000 foreign-invested enterprises were established. In addition, from 1993 to 2000, China absorbed the largest amount of foreign investment of any developing country in the world. Of the 500 best-known multinational corporations, nearly 400 have made investments in China (Wang 2002). So, why did the Middle Kingdom choose to adopt a western model of corporate governance?

As an attempt to solve this puzzle, the Association of Chartered Certified Accountants (ACCA) conducted a survey and found that "China had a whopping 90% of their CFOs saying they had performed post-Enron formal reviews. The respondents from mainland China do see corporate governance as a business issue to attract capital markets" (Lin 2002). A similar view had been echoed by another observer, who commented that "in China, the new corporate governance rules and structures are highly impressive to foreign observers, in this case particularly from the foreign aid community and the international agencies" (Hutchinson 2002). While believing China's perception of a better corporate governance structure to be attributable to its ability to attract more foreign capital, Hutchinson also expressed another of his beliefs for such a decision: "China has 1160 publicly listed state-owned enterprises. . . . Currently, all of these 1160 companies are majority owned by the Chinese state. Hence, corporate governance, far from providing protection for minority shareholders, is in fact simply providing a mechanism whereby the state can prevent enterprise management from stealing from it" (Hutchinson 2002).

Regardless of the real reasons behind the Middle Kingdom's decision to adopt a western model of corporate governance, it is important to bear in mind that the existence of independent directors on the board may indeed be very valuable. It should be noted that independent directors can play an important role that may benefit a corporation as well as a country. At the corporation level, independent directors can be invaluable in transferring knowledge and experience and, at the country level, building constituencies for corporate governance reform.

IMPORTANCE OF AN INDEPENDENT DIRECTORSHIP SYSTEM

The concept of independent directorship originated from the Anglo-American model of corporate governance, in which the corporate governance structure had a unified board of directors. With only a single tier, as opposed to the two-tier board structure found in countries such as Germany, with no independent supervisory organization to monitor the conduct of this unified board, the concept of independent directorship was introduced to provide *checks and balances* to the conduct of the board.

The need for independent directors arises particularly where there is a separation between ownership and control of the corporation, as well as where there is a majority or controlling shareholder. In order to prevent those controlling the corporation (that is, directors and managers or majority shareholders) from acting for their own private benefit and at the expense of the company's owners (that is, the shareholders as a whole, including the minority shareholders), independent or *outside* directors were introduced as a means of providing a supervisory function over the executive directors who made up the board, who are the directing mind and will of the company. In addition, such positions are seen also to prevent majority shareholders from dominating the decision-making process of directors (by having the power to remove the directors in the event that they do not follow their instruction) and from abusing their power and position to the detriment of minority shareholders.

REQUIREMENT TO HAVE INDEPENDENT DIRECTORS

All of the three regions in Greater China (People's Republic of China (*China*), Chinese Taipei (*Taiwan*), and Hong Kong—excluding Macau for now) have regulatory requirements for publicly listed companies to have independent directors on their boards. However, each of these regions has different definitions as to what constitutes *independence* and the functions that these independent directors are expected to perform.

Definition of Independent Directors

China The two main codes dealing with corporate governance in China are "Code of Corporate Governance for Listed Companies in China" (Corporate Governance Code or China CG Code) issued in January 2001 and "Guidelines for Introducing Independent Directors to the Board of Directors in Listed Companies" (Guidelines for Independent Directors or Guidelines) issued in August 2001. Both of these codes were issued by China Securities and Regulatory Commission (CSRC), the body governing companies' affairs in China.

According to the Guidelines, independent directors are those "who hold no posts in the company other than the position of director, and who maintain no relations with the listed company and its major shareholder that might prevent them from making objective judgment independently" (Article I(1), Guidelines). Apart from meeting the definition of independent directors, the CSRC has also made an attempt to ensure the independence of these directors by stipulating in its Guidelines that a person may *not* hold the position of independent director in any of the following circumstances:

- The person holds a position in the listed company or its affiliated enterprises, or where their direct relatives and major social relations hold such position (Article III(1), Guidelines)
- The person holds more than 1% of the outstanding shares of the listed company, whether directly or indirectly, or the natural person shareholders of the 10 largest shareholders of the listed company, or such shareholder's direct relative (Article III(2), Guidelines)
- The person holds a position in a unit that holds more than 5% of the outstanding shares of the listed company directly or indirectly, or of the unit which ranks as one of the five largest shareholders of the listed company, or such employee's direct relative (Article III(3), Guidelines)
- The person meeting any of these three abovementioned conditions in the immediately preceding year (Article III(4), Guidelines)

- The person providing financial, legal, or consulting services to the listed company or its subsidiaries (Article III(5), Guidelines)
- The person stipulated in the articles of association (Article III(6), Guidelines)
- The person determined by the CSRC (Article III(7), Guidelines)

Taiwan   The main piece of regulation dealing with the area of corporate governance and independent directors is "Corporate Governance Best-Practice Principles for Taiwan Stock Exchange Corporation (TSEC)/GreTai Securities Market (GTSM, an Over the Counter Securities Market)," issued by Taiwan Stock Exchange in November 2002 (Taiwan CG Principles). These principles appear to be silent on the definition of independent directors and simply require companies to appoint independent directors.

Hong Kong   There are two main guidelines regulating corporate governance and independent directors in Hong Kong and both were issued by Hong Kong Institute of Directors. One is "Guidelines for Directors," issued in 1995, and the other is "Guidelines for Independent Non-Executive Directors" (HK Guidelines), issued in 2000. Hong Kong seems to have taken a more liberal approach, reflected by the fact that the abovementioned guidelines merely act as a "concise, user-friendly guidance" (Hong Kong Institute of Directors 2000), in contrast to the mainland's approach of mandatory compliance by all listed companies.

Supporting this point and on the issue of the definition of independence, the requirements of HK Guidelines appear to be purely subjective, as one Guideline states:

> *Independence is a state of mind and only you will know upon reflection in good faith whether you can or will act independently. At a minimum independent judgment is judgment formed after a fair consideration of all relevant information available and made free from the influence of your personal interests whether direct or indirect. You will need to be honest with yourself in answering whether motives of personal gain, no matter how derived or in what form, will interfere with the exercise of your judgment. (HK Guidelines: Guideline 4)*

Apart from the author's perception of the subjectivity of the definition of independence required under HK Guidelines, the Guidelines appear to be supporting the use of such a subjective test, as Guideline 4 states:

> *This subjective test if taken with the best of intention is probably the only real test of whether you are or will be actually independent. Of*

course, there are tests of independence which purport to be objective and are effective at dealing with the appearance of independence or lack of it. . . . These tests generally concern the existence of certain personal and professional relationships, direct and indirect interests in business related to the company on whose Board one sits, and the significance or importance of such interests to one's own business or situation.

While a subjective test is used by HK Guidelines to provide an interpretation of whether an independent nonexecutive director is independent, this method of determination may be questionable, as it is doubtful that every person in this role would be answering these questions with absolute honesty. Therefore, the Chinese tests for independence appear to be more straightforward and may provide a more accurate determination on the actual independence of independent directors.

Requirement to Have Independent Directors on the Board of Directors

China   The CSRC makes it clear in the early part of its Guidelines that it is mandatory for all publicly listed companies to comply, as the preliminary part of the Guidelines states "all listed companies are required to act in accordance with the Guidelines." In addition, a timeframe for compliance was also set: "by June 30th, 2002, at least two members of the board of directors shall be independent directors; and by June 30th, 2003, at least one third of the board shall be independent directors" (Article I(3), Guidelines). The Guidelines also prescribed the consequences of a failure to comply with these requirements by stating:

In case . . . the number of independent directors fails to reach the requirements stipulated in the Guidelines, the listed companies shall make up for the deficiency by electing new independent directors to the board in accordance with the requirements of the Guidelines. (Article I(4), Guidelines)

The CSRC further set out the qualifications that these directors are required to have by stipulating that "at least one of the independent directors should be an accounting professional" (Article I(3), Guidelines) and each independent director must meet the following basic requirements:

- Have qualifications required to be a director of listed companies according to the laws and regulations (Article II(1), Guidelines)

- Meet the independence requirements (Article II(2), Guidelines)
- Have basic knowledge regarding the operations of the listed company and be familiar with the relevant laws and regulations (Article II(3), Guidelines)
- Have more than five years' work experience in law, economics, or other fields that may be required by his or her performance of the duties of an independent director (Article II(4), Guidelines)
- Other requirements set forth in the articles of association (Article II(5), Guidelines)

Taiwan   The situation in Taiwan does not appear to be as rigid as China when it comes to the number of independent directors that must be appointed to sit on the board. Taiwan CG Principles seem to have given the listed companies the autonomy to choose the numbers, as it simply requires all Taiwan Stock Exchange Corporation (TSEC) or GreTai Securities Market (GTSM) listed companies to stipulate an appropriate number of independent directors to be elected in the shareholders' meeting (Article 24, Taiwan CG Principles). In the event of a shortfall of these required numbers, the company shall arrange an election of additional independent directors (Article 24, Taiwan CG Principles).

Even though the Taiwan CG Principles appear to be more flexible and have given the listed companies the freedom to choose the number of independent directors as they see appropriate, when compared with their mainland counterpart, there is one additional requirement which Taiwan has. In Taiwan, if a TSEC or GTSM listed company has managing directors, the Principles advise that there shall be one or more independent directors among them (Article 24, Taiwan CG Principles).

Hong Kong   Consistent with the perception that Hong Kong has taken a more liberal approach when it comes to regulating corporate governance, it is not surprising to see HK Guidelines, as a "user-friendly guidance," being silent on the requirement of having independent directors on the board of companies.

The Roles of Independent Directors

China   Apart from the duties akin to fiduciary duties imposed on directors in other common law countries (such as duties of good faith, care, and diligence), the CSRC's Guidelines have also prescribed the specific roles that independent directors of listed companies are required to perform and the *special powers* they possess, which may not have been given to other executive directors (Article V(1)). It is therefore stated that:

■ Major related-party transactions (that is, the transactions that the listed company intends to conclude with the related party and whose total value exceeds RMB 3 million or 5% of the company's net assets audited recently (Article V(1), Guidelines) should be approved by the independent directors before being submitted to the board of directors for discussion (Article V(1)(a), Guidelines).

■ Independent directors also have the power to:

  ■ Put forward proposals to the board relating to the appointment or removal of the accounting firm.
  ■ Propose to the board a calling of an interim shareholders' meeting.
  ■ Propose the calling of a meeting of the board.
  ■ Appoint an independent outside auditing or consulting organization.
  ■ Solicit proxies before convening the shareholders' meeting (Article V(1)(b)–(f), Guidelines).

It is important to note that if an independent director wishes to exercise any of the above powers, consent from over half of all the independent directors must be obtained (Article V(2), Guidelines).

Taiwan   In contrast to the mainland, Taiwan appears to have a more flexible approach when it comes to the roles independent directors are expected to play. The decision of what roles independent directors should be given to play appears to have been left to the individual company. According to Taiwan CG Principles, a TSEC or GTSM listed company shall stipulate expressly the scope of duties of the independent directors and empower them with staff-power and material support related to the exercise of their power (Article 25, Taiwan CG Principles). Having given this decision-making power to the companies, Taiwan CG Principles did, however, make it clear that "the company or other board members shall not restrict or obstruct the performance of duties by the independent directors" (Article 25, Taiwan CG Principles).

One concern the author has over this type of approach is that a listed company may simply take the easy way out of not expressly giving any power to its independent directors, thereby avoiding the risk of obstructing the performance of independent directors' duties. However, this would simply defeat the purpose of setting up the independent directorship system in the first place.

Hong Kong   Consistent with the Guidelines' approach to providing concise, user-friendly guidance, HK Guidelines state:

> *As an Independent Non-Executive Director, your role is or will be to supervise management, participate in the direction of the com-*

pany's business and affairs and speak out firmly and objectively on these and other issues that may come before the Board. (Guideline 1, HK Guidelines)

To ensure that people taking up the position as independent directors do not treat their roles lightly, the Guidelines state:

Before accepting an appointment to the Board, you must acquire a realistic appreciation of the time that will be necessary to devote to Board matters and then decide whether you will have sufficient time to meet your new responsibilities. (Guideline 2, HK Guidelines)

In addition, the Guidelines warn potential independent directors on the seriousness of their roles by stating, "On becoming a Director you are accepting significant legal responsibilities. Do not accept these lightly" (Guideline 3, HK Guidelines).

Having emphasized the importance of the functions of independent directors, the Guidelines state the need for independent directors to cooperate with other executive directors, as they state:

An independent attitude is not arrogance or a need to be different or to find divergence. It is not being uncooperative, disruptive or loud, and it is not being suspicious or critical for the sake of putting on a good show. One can be independent and remain a constructive member of the Board. (Introduction, HK Guidelines)

CHALLENGES WITH IMPLEMENTATION

While the regions in Greater China have made serious attempts to regulate corporate governance and to ensure that proper independent directorship systems are in place to monitor the executive directors, full and successful implementation of these practices has been fraught with tough challenges. Such a finding may not be surprising, given that, after all, the Middle Kingdom had (almost) always been used to doing things in its own way and, of course, a simple transplantation of foreign practices would be almost sure to be faced with enormous difficulties. Some of the major challenges identified include: the lack of qualified independent directors; the effect of state influence on company decisions; inability to introduce outside directors to sit on the boards of family companies; and independent directors being unable to perform their jobs properly. These problems will each be discussed below.

Lack of Independent Directors

For listed companies in China, there is a mandatory requirement that by June 30, 2003, at least one third of board members must be independent directors (Article I(3), Guidelines). This had put tremendous pressure on the large number of listed companies (in fact, over 1,200 by 2003) (Plender 2003) to find independent directors who are qualified according to the criteria set out in the Guidelines (in particular, Article II and I(3) of the Guidelines). Finding the required number was indeed a great challenge for most of these listed companies. In fact, in 2001, the CSRC intended to issue guidelines that would have the effect of requiring companies listed on domestic exchanges to have at least two independent directors as part of a sweeping campaign to improve corporate governance. However, this decision was delayed due to difficulties experienced by companies in finding enough qualified independent directors.

Apart from the fact that it was already very difficult for a large number of listed companies to recruit enough qualified independent directors to fill the numbers, the tough stance taken by CSRC in enforcing its Guidelines appears to have made this problem even more challenging. It was reported that:

> In September [2001] . . . CSRC fined an independent director for the first time. Lu Jiahao of Shanghai-listed store Zhengzhou Baiwen was fined RMB100,000 for failing to fulfil his fiduciary duties. More than 10 independent directors have resigned in the past year. (Li 2002)

The resignation of independent directors following the heavy sanctions imposed by CSRC is not surprising given that "most directors are paid less than RMB50,000 a year. None of these independent directors receive more than this amount" (*China Economic Review* 2002). As directors are not highly remunerated for their responsibilities, given the fact that the fine can be more than twice their maximum annual income, it is little wonder that people may be reluctant to take up such positions.

Having given the above example to demonstrate the challenges facing full implementation of the CSRC's Guidelines, it must be mentioned that the situation may slowly be changing. It was reported that regarding the department store in which Professor Lu was an independent director and was thus fined by the CSRC, Zhengzhou Baiwen, in June 2002, "25 shareholders, with 18.99% of Zhengzhou Baiwen shares between them, voted overwhelmingly to pay independent directors on its nine-member board well over 100,000 yuan a year" (Li 2002). Such increase in remuneration may presumably be aimed at attracting people to take up a position of independent director in order for the company to satisfy the mandatory quota requirement imposed by the CSRC.

On this note, many may question why people have taken up a position as independent director if they are not prepared to comply with CSRC's Guidelines, including the fulfillment of fiduciary duties to the company and its shareholders. To understand this, it is important to bear in mind that China is a country where businesses have until recently largely operated as state-owned-enterprises (SOEs) with no concept of shares, separate legal entity, and so on, let alone the notion of *independent directorship*. To this end, people who take up such posts quite understandably do not fully understand what is required of them. This can be clearly illustrated by the situation of Professor Lu in Zhengzhou Baiwen. Professor Lu was a retired English teacher and had served on the board of the department store as an independent director between 1995 and 2001. Lu had been reported to describe his role as "nominal and advisory, believing he was appointed to window-dress a board packed with secondary school graduates" (Hu 2002). Further, he said, "I always regard the independent director as a honorary title.... I couldn't understand a thing about the financial reports. And why would I bother to question them if the presiding accountants and the supervisory board had signed off?" (BBC Worldwide Monitoring 2002).

Professor Lu was reported to have appealed the CSRC's verdict and the imposition of the fine. However, he was not successful in the appeal (BBC Worldwide Monitoring 2002).

Perhaps due to having a longer history of private enterprise, and thus having a larger pool of people with business acumen, and the fact that the regulations do not specify the minimum number of independent directors on a board, Taiwan and Hong Kong companies do not appear to have faced the same problem as China when it comes to recruiting sufficient talent to take up such posts.

State Influence

Influence of the government over the listed companies seems to be the most prevalent in China when compared with Taiwan and Hong Kong. According to the findings of the World Bank and the International Finance Corporation, "local governments were responsible for selecting which companies were to be listed.... Thus the companies that are listed on China's stock exchanges are mostly SOEs. They have strong links with the government, especially local governments, and their boundaries with their parent groups are relatively new and often artificial" (Tenev and Zhang 2002).

The World Bank and the International Finance Corporation conducted a survey of 257 companies listed on the Shanghai Stock Exchange and found that "in more than 95% of cases, the state is directly or indirectly in control of listed companies" (Tenev and Zhang 2002). This extent of control may also be seen in the selection of directors and supervisors of listed companies, as shown in Table 17.1 (data sourced from Tenev and Zhang 2002).

Further, the survey also showed that most independent directors' former employers were government departments, government ministries, and SOEs; this finding thereby further raises the question of these outside nonexecutives' true independence. This may be seen from Table 17.2 (data sourced from Tenev and Zhang 2002).

From Tables 17.1 and 17.2, we can see that the state appears to control the vast majority of listed companies in China and has wide power over the selection of directors, including independent directors. This may also be illustrated with an example of a case where a Chinese public procurator was appointed as an independent director of a SOE. It was reported that Li Changsen, vice-director of the Anti-Corruption Bureau of the Tiexi District in Shenyang had been appointed the independent director of the board of a local SOE, the Shengyang Airblower Manufacturing Corp Ltd. (*People's Daily* 2000).

As a high majority of independent directors previously worked for the state, it is questionable whether they will ever have the independence required to perform their jobs properly according to the Guidelines.

TABLE 17.1 Selection of Directors and Supervisors of Listed Companies (Percent)

	Total	Executive Directors	Nonexecutive Directors	Supervisors
State shares (shares held by central and local governments)	28	36	16	25
State-owned legal person shares (shares held by domestic institutions)	45	44	54	44
Public legal person shares	18	13	27	12
Internal employee shares	3	3	1	11
Publicly circulating shares	6	5	2	7

TABLE 17.2   Company Directors' Former Employers (Percentage of Directors)

Employer	Executive Directors Appointed by Shareholders	Other Executive Directors	Nonexecutive Directors	Independent Directors
Macroeconomic government department	9	5	16	24
Government ministry	15	12	24	32
Research institute or university	15	9	15	33
Financial institution	3	1	13	24
SOE	76	73	73	43
Collectively owned enterprises	9	8	7	6
Private enterprise	6	5	8	4
Joint venture	11	6	10	4
Other listed Co.	2	1	6	2
Foreign Co.	0.4	1	4	2

Note: Number exceeds 100% because individuals can have different employers over the course of their career.

Family Companies

Family companies certainly play a very important part in many communities around the globe that have Chinese ancestry. The traditional family culture that runs in Chinese blood means that family businesses are guarded closely (Cheng and Firth 2005).

In Taiwan, regardless of the size, most Taiwanese companies are family owned and family controlled (Solomon, Lin, Norton, and Solomon 2003). With respect to listed companies, a recent study of 141 companies listed on the Taiwan Stock Exchange shows that 48% of these companies are controlled by family groups (Gulinello 2003). The study further finds that these family groups have a great deal of control over the boards of directors, often holding more than half of the board seats, and typically control the agenda for shareholder meetings (Gulinello 2003).

This situation is very similar in Hong Kong and most listed companies in Hong Kong appear to be controlled by families as well (Cheung 2002). There was a survey conducted by Hong Kong Society of Accountants in 1997, which examined the ownership structure of 553 listed companies in Hong Kong in 1995 and 1996. The survey found that 53% have one shareholder or one family group of shareholders owning more than half of the entire issued capital (Cheung 2002). It was also found that control by a single shareholder or family group extends to more than 35% of issued capital in 77% of the companies, and more than 25% of issued capital in 88% of the companies (Cheung 2002). These results demonstrate the dominance of family-owned and -controlled companies in Hong Kong.

In China, the situation is different. While there are a number of family-owned and -operated companies, by far, the state is still in direct or indirect control of companies listed on the stock exchange, as discussed above.

The concept of independent directorship is extremely difficult to implement in family companies. The main reason is simple—having an outside director in a family business telling how the family business ought to be run would be unthinkable! The reality with listed family companies is often that "family owners fail to understand that when they list the company it's no longer theirs" (Mitchell 2003).

Independent Directors Unable to Perform Their Jobs Properly

Like any independent director in the world, the independent directors in Greater China also face the challenge of not being able to perform their tasks set out by the regulatory requirements. This situation may be summed up by the following description:

> The NED [nonexecutive director] lives in a Jekyll-and-Hyde state. The paradox of being boardroom-friendly by day and a shareholders' informant by night suggests that the "experts" have misplaced faith in NED's ability to dissemble. Companies appear to expect NEDs to don both hats: that of the policeman and the golfing partner. (Ham 2003)

In addition, from the perspective of executive management and shareholders, independent directors are, in effect, outsiders to the company. As a result, they may rarely be given all of the relevant information about the company. This may be even more obvious in family companies, as "family entrepreneurs tend to keep four sets of books. One for the shareholders (lousy profits), one for the tax man (just over breakeven), one for the bank (great profits) and one for themselves (reality)" (Plender 2003). Therefore, as independent directors are outsiders to the company, it is possible to conclude that they would only be given the set of books that the directors would wish to disclose to shareholders—accounts that do not represent the reality. Without accurate information, it is hardly surprising that independent directors find it difficult to properly perform their jobs and the tasks set out by the various regulations.

ALTERNATIVE TO INDEPENDENT DIRECTORSHIP SYSTEM: SUPERVISORY BOARD

Given the tremendous challenges faced in full implementation of the independent directorship system in the three regions in Greater China, it is worthwhile to briefly examine the alternative system currently in place in both China and Taiwan, the supervisory board under the German corporate governance model.

In China, the requirement of having a supervisory board is contained in Code of Corporate Governance for Listed Companies in China (China CG Code) and while the code does not appear to specifically prescribe for the minimum number of supervisors a listed company must have (unlike the case of independent directors), the qualification and roles required of supervisors appear to be very similar to those of independent directors. According to article 64 of the code, "supervisors shall have professional knowledge or work experience in such areas as law and accounting." Further, they must ensure the board's capability to independently and efficiently conduct its supervision of directors, managers, and other senior management personnel and to supervise and examine the company's financial matters (Article 64, China CG Code).

As to the power of a supervisory board, it also seems very similar to the power possessed by independent directors, in which "the supervisory board may ask directors, managers and other senior management personnel, internal auditing personnel and external auditing personnel to attend the meetings of supervisory board and to answer the questions that the supervisory board is concerned with" (Article 67, China CG Code).

In relation to Taiwan, the requirements for having supervisors and independent supervisors appear to be very similar, if not identical, to the requirements for having independent directors. The wording of article 43 seems identical to that of article 24, as it states, "a TSEC/GTSM listed company shall . . . stipulate an appropriate number of independent supervisors to be elected in the shareholders meeting. In case of any shortfall, an election of additional independent supervisors shall be timely arranged." Having said that, there appears to be an additional requirement with respect to independent supervisors when compared with independent directors, that is, "an independent supervisor is advised to have a domicile within the territory of R.O.C. [Republic of China in Taiwan] in order to timely perform the supervisory functions" (Article 43, Taiwan CG Principles).

It appears that independent supervisors in Taiwan may be perceived to play a more important role when compared with independent supervisors. Apart from the additional residency requirement imposed on independent supervisors, as discussed above, there appear to be more duties being placed upon them. In contrast to independent directors, supervisors are required to be "familiar with the relevant laws and regulation, understand the rights, obligations, and duties of directors of the company and the functions, duties, and operation of each department, and frequently attend meetings of the board of directors to supervise the operations and to state his/her opinions when appropriate so as to control or discover any abnormal situation early on" (Article 45, Taiwan CG Principles). Further, they must "supervise the implementation of the operations of the company, and the performance of duties by directors and managers" (Article 46, Taiwan CG Principles).

While the alternative to the independent directorship system, that is, the supervisory board, exists in China and Taiwan, a very important question becomes: Would the supervisors be more effective, when compared with independent directors, in monitoring the board of directors of listed companies in these two regions? Further, are the challenges in implementation of an independent directorship system unique to that system? Would it be possible that these difficulties would still exist when putting in place an effective supervisory board?

It is believed that many of the challenges encountered in implementing an independent directorship system, discussed above, would also be felt by the supervisory boards. After all, in China, the government effectively controls the appointment of the Chairman and Deputy Chairman of Supervisory Boards (Dahya, Karbhari, Xiao, and Yang 2003). Therefore, like the independent directorship system, the independence of supervisory boards may still be questioned in China.

In the other regions of Greater China, due to the prevalence of family companies, the ability of supervisory boards to properly perform their function is still questioned. While the regulations may require the company to provide the books or documents that will be needed for the supervisor's review, the accuracy and contents of these may still be dubious. Therefore, it is believed that both the independent directorship system and the supervisory board system face similar cultural and institutional challenges when it comes to implementation.

CONCLUSION

The Middle Kingdom has come a long way to meet the west and in adopting a western style of corporate governance of its companies. It introduced the Anglo-American model of independent directorship as well as the German model of supervisory board to its state-owned-enterprises and family companies.

In relation to the transplantation of the Anglo-American model of independent directorship into Greater China, of the three regions therein, China appears to have the strictest and most detailed and onerous requirements regarding the requirements and appointment of independent directors. The number and minimum qualifications of independent directors were specified, as well as the specific tasks that they are required to perform. Hong Kong, in contrast, appears to have taken a much more liberal approach and treats the regulation as mere *concise and user-friendly guidelines*.

While the regulations in all of three regions appear to be well drafted, with many provisions resembling those in western regulations, the implementation of such foreign regulations has been fraught with enormous difficulties. First, the kingdom experienced difficulties in recruiting a sufficient number of qualified personnel to take up the posts of independent directors. Second, these *independent* directors found it hard to be truly independent. Particularly in the case of China, it appears that the state still has considerable influence over their decision making; and in Taiwan and Hong Kong, they are treated as *outsiders* of the family business, therefore unable to obtain sufficiently accurate information to carry out their tasks properly.

Perhaps foreseeing the potential challenges in implementing the Anglo-American independent directorship system in the Middle Kingdom, two of the three regions, namely China and Taiwan, have also transplanted the German system of the supervisory board into their regulations. However, the effective implementation of this supervisory system appears to have encountered similar cultural and institutional obstacles as the adoption of the independent directorship system.

Therefore, it may be concluded that, to fully and effectively transplant a foreign system into the Middle Kingdom, major changes to the way things are usually done, and the structures that were used to support this, may be required. However, if the culture of China is to be changed in order to have a foreign system in place, regardless of the perceived benefits to be gained, one needs to ask oneself—is this what the Middle Kingdom, with more than 5,000 years of its own unique history, really wants?

Responsibilities to Stakeholders and Other Emerging Trends in Corporate Governance

The Primary Stakeholder Relationships: Corporate Governance and Value Creation

Andrea Beretta Zanoni

INTRODUCTION

A firm is an *open system* in which the growing complexity of the times we live in is fully reflected. Today enterprises are exposed to more influences than they were in the past, with new interests and new requirements to satisfy. In this context, managing relationships with stakeholders has become a crucial element of modern corporate governance.

This chapter defines some economic principles for the management of the relationship with the primary stakeholders, both in a theoretical and in a practical perspective. It is possible to define the primary stakeholders as those who, voluntarily and knowingly, make some form of investment in the firm's activity (Clarkson 1994). Primary stakeholders typically include shareholders, employees, capital suppliers, other suppliers, customers, and public stakeholder groups (governments and communities that provide services and infrastructure and to whom taxes may be due) (Clarkson 1995).

This Chapter adopts some basic hypotheses:

■ The firm tends to survive through the maximization of the value created. The maximization of the income during the time, in general, the difference between the value of the resources produced and the value of the resources consumed by the firm, is the best indicator of the achievement of

Note: The author expresses his appreciation to Silvia Vernizzi for her scholarly support.

the firm's institutional goal. Furthermore, the value of the resources consumed represents the remuneration of all the production factors used by the firm, including the risk capital. The factors are acquired in competitive markets that indicate the minimum benchmark values.

- This means that, even if the firm lives in a complex and multirelational environment, it pursues objectives that are all referable to a unique objective function (an overriding goal): to maximize the flows in a lasting and increasing way and therefore to maximize at the moment t_0 the company's value.

- Given the growing complexity, both competitive and social, achievement of the previous objective requires paying attention to the management of the relationships with the different primary stakeholders (resources contributors), in a perspective that can be defined as *stakeholder value*.

STAKEHOLDER PROFIT AND LOSS (RELATIONAL PROFIT AND LOSS)

Between resource contributors and the firm there is established an exchange relationship, which is regulated by a price. According to microeconomics theory, the price derives from the opportunity cost of the production factor. It is possible to define the opportunity cost as the minimum price required for the resource contributors to undertake or continue the transaction with the firm (Charreaux and Desbrières 1998; Milgrom and Roberts 1992; Castanias and Helfat 1991).

In general terms, all the production factors are traded under this logic of value determination, but with a substantial difference between the risk capital and the other factors. For the risk capital (equity), in fact, the reward depends on the income that remains after having remunerated all the other factors of production. Therefore, this remuneration is totally subjected to the operating and financial risk of the firm. Since the shareholders are the exclusive residual claimants, they entirely receive the rent created by the firm.

The other contributors, instead, provide resources under different conditions: a contract regulates the trading price (related to the opportunity cost) and the firm normally pays that price, regardless of the results really obtained. However, the value of the trading takes shape in relation to the level of the opportunity cost both for the stakeholders and for the shareholders.

For prolonged periods of time the value really taken by the transaction (explicit cost) and its opportunity cost can be substantially different, in consequence of phenomena related, according to the traditional theory, to the informative asymmetries or to the contractual power of the agents. It is known that the economic profit consists exactly in this difference, or better, in the residual rent created by the firm, after having remunerated all the other factors of production, equity capital included. In other words, the economic profit is the margin that exceeds the normal-average conditions of the remuneration of the equity.

With the same logic, for the stakeholders that are different from the shareholders, it should be spoken of as relational profit when the explicit values received by the stakeholders exceed the opportunity values. Of course, there exists a direct link between the remuneration of the stakeholders and the economic profit that depends, in fact, also on the level of this remuneration. A numerical example will better explain the dynamic of the opportunity costs and the explicit costs. Take the case in Table 18.1.

The values in Table 18.1 are explicit and drive the firm to achieve an accounting profit of 200 that, in absence of taxation, is partially distributed to the shareholders (100).

Furthermore, suppose that equity capital is equal to 2.000 and that the rate of the expected return (opportunity cost) is equal to 5%. The economic profit would be equal to 100, that is:

$$\text{Economic profit} = 200 - (0.05 \times 2{,}000) = 100$$

Now, supposing a difference between explicit and opportunity values, for classes of stakeholders examined, the situation could be as shown in Table 18.2.

The difference between the opportunity values and the explicit values shows an advantage or a damaging position for the stakeholder in the sphere of the relationship with the firm. For example, the explicit cost of the suppliers, that is, the real price of the transaction, is higher than the opportunity cost. The suppliers obtain a relational profit (stakeholder

TABLE 18.1 Dynamic of Opportunity Costs

	Explicit Cost	Explicit Price
Clients		1,900
Suppliers	400	
Employees	1,000	
Financial creditors	300	
Total	1,700	1,900
Accounting profit	200	
Shareholder remuneration	100	

TABLE 18.2   Difference between Explicit and Opportunity Costs

	Explicit Cost	Explicit Price	Opportunity Cost	Opportunity Price	Stakeholder Profit/Loss
Clients		1,900		2,000	100
Suppliers	400		350		50
Employees	1,000		900		100
Financial creditors	300		250		50
Total	1,700	1,900	1,500	2,000	300
Accounting profit	200				
Shareholder remuneration	100		100		0

profit). In Table 18.2 that profit is equal to 50. The difference between the opportunity price to which the firm's supply is sold and the sum of all the opportunity costs (including the cost of the shareholder's remuneration) identifies the value created (that is, the global profit) and its distribution.

So, in the example the result is:

$$2000 \text{ (Opportunity price)} - 1600 \text{ (Sum of opportunity cost)}$$
$$= 400 \text{ (Global profit)}$$

The global profit, equal to 400, is shared in as follows:

Clients = 100

Suppliers = 50

Employee = 100

Financial creditors = 50

Shareholder = 0

Not shared = 100

In the example there is a surplus, equal to 100, available to the firm. It is a slack, not shared between the different stakeholders. Since it is supposed that the opportunity cost of the equity capital is equal to the value distributed to the shareholders, that is $0.05 \times 2,000 = 100$, the amount of profit not shared corresponds to the economic profit. If the relational profits of the stakeholders were reduced or driven to zero (explicit values equal to opportunity values), then, ceteris paribus, the economic profit would increase.

Once again, the numerical example can be useful to understand and simplify these relationships. Suppose the explicit values are brought to the level of the opportunity values, in order to bring to zero the relational profits, as represented in Table 18.3.

Compared with the economic profit calculated earlier and equal to 100, we would obtain a greater value of the accounting profit of 300, due to an increase of the returns by 100 and to a decrease in the costs of 200. Without changing the other variables (cost of the capital and amount of proprietary capital invested) we would obtain:

$$\text{Economic profit} = 500 - (0.05 \times 2{,}000) = 400$$

In the first case (explicit values different from opportunity values), we have:

Accounting profit = 200
Global profit = 400
Economic profit = not shared profit = 100

In the second case (explicit values equal to market conditions, that is, equal to opportunity values), we have:

Accounting profit = 500
Global profit = 400
Economic profit = not shared profit = 400

TABLE 18.3 Difference between Explicit Cost, Opportunity Cost, and Opportunity Price

	Explicit Cost	Explicit Price	Opportunity Cost	Opportunity Price	Stakeholder Profit
Clients		2,000		2,000	0
Suppliers	350		350		0
Employees	900		900		0
Financial creditors	250		250		0
Total	1,500	2,000	1,500	2,000	0
Accounting profit	500				
Shareholder remuneration	100		100		0

The value of the global profit doesn't change, because it is obtained from the difference between the opportunity price and the sum of the opportunity costs (both of them don't change during the passage from the first to the second hypothesis), but its destination changes: in the first case it increases the stakeholders' profits, while in the second case, it remains inside the firm, as economic profit.

THE "CONTRIBUTIONS–REWARDS" CURVE AND THE ECONOMIC PERSPECTIVE OF STAKEHOLDERS

The concepts examined in the previous paragraph can be further developed, by putting the analysis into the specific economic perspective of the stakeholder. During the relationship the stakeholder wants to receive some rewards whose value has to be proportional to the contributions he brings to the firm system (Halal 1997). In other words, it is possible to define the perceived value of the rewards expected by the stakeholders as a function of the perceived value of the contributions to the firm.

$$Vr = \int (Vc)$$
$$Vr = \text{value of rewards}$$
$$Vc = \text{value of contributions}$$

In this way, we determine the contributions–rewards curve represented in Figure 18.1. The curve represents the average positions (equilibrium positions) of the *contributions–rewards* ratio.

The contributions–rewards curve represents the opportunity costs of the specific relationship with the stakeholder, analyzed in relation to his contributions. Positions placed in the area under or over the curve represent situations that diverge from the average positions, to the firm advantage (point B) and to the stakeholder advantage (point A) respectively. The evaluation that stakeholders and firm give of rewards and contributions is a relative evaluation, depending on the state of other relationships. By other relationships we mean both the relationships that the same firm maintains with other stakeholders and the relationships that the same group of stakeholders maintains with other firms.

Moreover, it's important to remark that the evaluations are influenced by the widest cultural context, that is, made up of values, political trends, culture, economic policy, social trends, and so on. As in every other evaluation process, all the aspects tied to the way events are perceived assume a

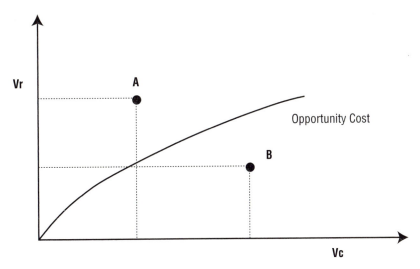

FIGURE 18.1   The Contributions–Rewards Curve

lot of significance. However, the significance of these elements changes in accordance with the nature of the relationship and, in real terms, in accordance with the object of the exchange, as stakeholders' competence, life cycle of the relationship, and so on.

If we consider the contributions–rewards curve in the stakeholders' perspective, it is clear that stakeholders would like:

- To not be damaged by the relationship, and so they would like to place themselves on the curve, or better in the area over the curve. In this case it would be possible to talk about relational profit, as we have seen before.
- To think that an improvement of the position is possible in the long run; so, assuming α as the positive relational profit at time t_0, it is necessary to foresee that:

$$\alpha 1 \geq \alpha + \Delta\,\alpha$$

where $\alpha 1$ represents the expected relational profit of period t_1 and $\Delta\alpha$ is the increase of the relational profit that the stakeholder values *fair* at time t_0 (Amaduzzi 1978).

RELATIONAL PROFIT AND LOSS IN THE REAL-TIME ECONOMIC SYSTEM

In the long run, the imperfections of the markets should be progressively absorbed and the explicit costs should tend to the opportunity costs' level. According to neoclassical economic theory, the result should be Pareto optimal (the resources are allocated to their best use). In reality the question is more complex, not only because of market failures. Two phenomena, in fact, have assumed a growing relevance.

First, there is a greater involvement of the stakeholders in the firm's activity, caused by the increasing role assumed by the firms in the economic and cultural organization of the society. In this way, firms tend to assume a higher responsibility toward the subjective aspirations (of the stakeholders), compared with the past. Actually, the contractualistic approach used to interpret the economic relationship between the different stakeholders and the firm can result in underestimation in respect of a wider social vision of the firm. According to some studies, the firm is not only a nexus of contracts but it is a dynamic system of relationships between moral actors (Hendry 2001; Roberts 1996). For years, such an approach has been developed in the institutional perspective of Italian and German business economics (Borgonovi 1991; Beretta Zanoni 2003).

Second, the greater involvement increases the risk level associated with the relationship by increasing the opportunity costs implicit in the relationship. Moreover, some stakeholders, such as workers and suppliers, can develop firm-specific skills, which are hardly transferable to other relations (Blair 1996). But, in this way also, the difficulties related to the opportunity costs' determination increase and, consequently, the difficulties in the formation of the explicit values that regulate the relationship. In this condition, the explicit costs have to be compared with the opportunity costs, keeping in mind two aspects that are quite new in regard to the traditional theoretical formulation.

The relationship is set in the real time and not in the abstract time of the neoclassical economics. The comparison between opportunity and explicit costs concerns a specific period of time, depending on the nature of the relationship. So, the time factor has to enter into the analysis. The management of the firm can decide to generate, coherently with a specific strategic plan, some rents for the stakeholders (stakeholders' profit), also for prolonged periods of time. This choice has to be seen not in contradiction to the objective of the maximization of the economic value of the firm's capital, but as subordinate (or functional) to it. These issues lead to modifying the traditional analytical methods. In particular, the outstanding value in the relationship firm–stakeholder is no longer only the relational profit (or relational loss), but also its projection in time, that is, its projection in the future (relational goodwill or relational badwill). This projection is not to be necessarily understood as allocative inefficiency, but as a possible strategic choice of the firm. The following discussion will attempt to clarify the concepts of relational goodwill and relational badwill and to define their determinants.

RELATIONAL GOODWILL AND RELATIONAL BADWILL: CONCEPTS AND DRIVERS

To introduce the concept of relational goodwill, it is possible to start by stating what the goodwill is. Projecting the economic profit into the time and discounting back the flows, it is possible to get the goodwill value, which is a part of the total company value.

In an equity side type evaluation logic (simplifing technical questions that are not of immediate interest) the value of the firm W is equal to:

$$W = K + \sum_{t=1}^{n} \frac{R_t - i \times K}{(1-i)^t}$$

where W = company value
       K = net rectified capital
       i = discount rate
       R_t = net income achieved in the t years

$$\sum_{t=1}^{n} \frac{R_t - i \times K}{(1-i)^t} = \text{goodwill}$$

This is an evaluation method based on the separate determination of the goodwill value, and on residual income approach (RIM). It is known that, under conditions related to the rates used, the formula based on the discounting back of the net benefits coincides with the formula obtainable from a residual income approach.

Now it is possible to move to the determination of relational goodwill. Relational goodwill, in fact, is a concept equivalent to goodwill understood in its strict sense. If we consider the whole duration of the relationship between the firm and a specific stakeholder, the value generated for her is equal to:

$$WR = \sum_{t=1}^{n} \frac{B_t - C_t}{(1-i)^t} \qquad (18.1)$$

where WR = value of the relationship
  B_t = benefits assured to the stakeholder during the year t
  C_t = contributions stakeholder is required to pay during the year t
  i = discount rate of the flow $(B_t - C_t)$
  n = duration of the relationship analyzed

The value of the relationship can be quantified also through an alternative method of evaluation, with distinct determination of the relational goodwill. So Formula 18.1 can be written in the following way:

$$WR = K + \sum_{t=1}^{n} \frac{(B_t - C_t) - i \times K}{(1-i)^t} \qquad (18.2)$$

where K = investments borne by stakeholders for the maintenance of the relationship

It is equivalent to the capitalization of the contributions C_t that the stakeholder is expected to give to the firm during the relationship.

$$\sum_{t=1}^{n} \frac{(B_t - C_t) - i \times K}{(1-i)^t} = \text{relational goodwill in the stakeholder perspective}$$

The equality between the two expressions is easily verifiable. To that end, the perpetuity formula is used, so that:

the $\sum_{t=1}^{n} \dfrac{B_t - C_t}{(1-i)^t}$ can be expressed as $\dfrac{B-C}{i}$

and the $K + \sum_{t=1}^{n} \dfrac{(B_t - C_t) - i \times K}{(1-i)^t}$ as $K + \dfrac{(B-C)-iK}{i}$

If $K = \dfrac{C}{i}$ then $\dfrac{C}{i} + \dfrac{B-C-C}{i} = \dfrac{B-C}{i}$

Compared with Formula (18.1), this last method underlines the value of the relational profit and the value of the relational goodwill. Moreover, through this method, the determinants of the relational goodwill come to light clearly, and its interpretation is made easier.

Since the net benefits' flow $(B_t - C_t)$ is the return of the invested capital (K), the relation at the numerator $(B_t - C_t) - i \times K$ (relational profit) can be represented in the following way (Copeland, Koller and Murrin 1996):

$$(r_t - i_t) \times K_{t-1} \tag{18.3}$$

where r_t = return of the invested capital at time t, obtained by the ratio

$$\frac{B_t - C_t}{K_{t-1}}$$

i_t = cost of the invested capital in year t, that is, the minimum expected return related to the risk of investment

$k_t - 1$ = invested capital at the beginning

Since the K value comes from the value of the contributions C_t that stakeholders are required to make during the relationship (to make it easier, C/i), formula 18.3 can be expressed also in the following way:

$$r_t \times K_{t-1} - i_t \times K_{t-1}$$
$$C \times \left(\frac{r_t}{i_t} - 1 \right) \tag{18.4}$$

So it is possible to say that the value of the relational profit and, consequently, the value of the relational goodwill depends on the dimensions of two variables:

1. The average value of the stakeholder contributions (C)
2. The value of the difference existing between the investment return r and the opportunity cost i (or normal return), which depends on the return of the alternative investments that the specific stakeholder could decide to make.

It is necessary to go into the concept of differential of return, starting from the concept of normal average return i. In the evaluations of the goodwill, the normality of the rate of return corresponds to the minimum level of return that justifies the investment (opportunity cost). So, in the specific relationship between firm and stakeholders, the i rate can be defined only through the analysis of the minimum conditions offered by the market for that specific relationship. The analysis has to be carried out referring to relational realities that are really comparable with the one we are examining, paying particular attention to the strategic business area and, if it is relevant, to the geographical area.

As has already been said, the level of the opportunity rate depends on the risk connected to the stakeholder's expected return. If we compare two relationships, value of investments (C_t) being equal, the relationship that presents a greater risk, that is, a greater uncertainty about the results of the investments has, from the stakeholder point of view, a smaller value. Once having determined the i rate, it is possible to compare it to r, that is, the return really expected from the relationship's investment from the stakeholder's point of view.

A MODEL OF ANALYSIS FOR THE MANAGEMENT OF THE STAKEHOLDER'S RELATIONSHIPS

So each stakeholder, in a specific moment, is theoretically in a position that is:

- Neutral
- Of relational goodwill
- Of relational badwill

The knowledge of this positioning is very important from the corporate governance point of view. For this reason, it is important to set the stakeholder positioning into a decisional process that allows the firms to manage the relationships with the stakeholders in an optimum way and to insert them in a wider governance system. This process could be logically articulated in the following way:

1. Identification of the existing relationships
2. Evaluation of the nature of the existing relationships
3. Evaluation of the relational positioning (goodwill, badwill)
4. Impacts of the different positionings on the firm's value (value of relationships and company value)
5. Consequent choices of the management approaches

Identification of the Primary Stakeholders

Legitimacy has to be understood as what enables a specific group of people to consider themselves stakeholders of the firm. So, legitimacy allows one to identify the relationships and to understand the essential features of the exchange.

Naturally, the problem consists in defining the source of the legitimacy, that, to go to the extremes, could have a formal-legal nature, for example, a property right, or a symbolic and cultural nature. In the development of the studies there have been different definitions of what legitimacy is: wide definitions (for example, the original definition of Freeman), and more restricted definitions, aimed at limiting the concept of stake.

Among these definitions we find those that are related to the concept of risk. Now, the total risk, besides theoretically quantifying the value of the rewards, qualifies the relationship, and justifies the existence of it: in fact, there is no investment without risk, and there is no kind of interest without some kind of investment (even unintentional). In other words, the origin of the interest's legitimacy is referable to the risk taken by the subject in relation to the investment made in the business (this investment could have a different nature; it can also be of a psychological nature), or in relation to the fact that the enterprise business creates for that specific subject a determined risk, also in absence of a voluntary investment.

Evaluation of the Nature of Existing Relationships

After having been identified, the relationships have to be evaluated, with regard to their nature (Figure 18.2). The evaluation depends on:

- The level of reactivity of the stakeholder in the relationship
- The strategic relevance of the stakeholder for the firm

The reactivity is the capability and the will of the stakeholder to react, positively or negatively, to his perceived positioning in the relationship. In its turn, the reactivity depends on the criticality assumed by the relationship for the stakeholder and on the power he has toward the firm. It is possible to trace the criticality that the relationship with the firm assumes for each stakeholder to the following two elements:

1. The significance, or relevance, of the interest that ties the stakeholder to the firm
2. The urgency of this interest's fulfillment, which inserts into the analysis the temporal constraint

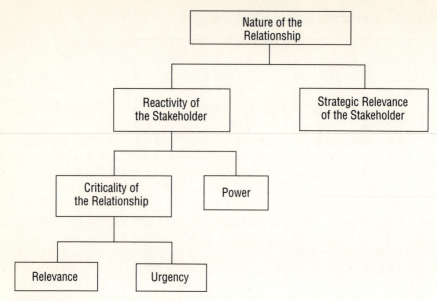

FIGURE 18.2   Evaluation of Relationships

The following elements can define the relevance of the interest, making more explicit the general concept of risk:

- High costs of exit from the relationship charged to the stakeholder, as in the case in which the stakeholder holds some form of asset that cannot be used or that can improbably be used in an other way;
- High level of expectation by the stakeholders of the benefits obtainable from the relationship with the firm, justified by the usage or by the specific hypothesis on the future
- The symbolic significance of the relationship

The power is here understood in the Weberian sense, as the ability to impose one's will on the sphere of a relationship. Of course, the power depends on the legitimacy, but its origins and manifestations are more complex. To make it easier, under the common legitimacy of the interests, some stakeholders have a lot of power in the firm system while others have less power or no power at all. There are a lot of power drivers: the level of organization of the stakeholder's group, the ease of access to the communication media, the knowledge of the business processes, the institutional support, and so on.

While the legitimacy is a source of power, the power is not a source of legitimacy. So, the power is not an element that allows the identification and the recognition of the relationship; the power is an element that only allows an evaluation of the relationship's functioning. After all we have said it is possible to use the following indicators to measure the reactivity:

- The level of expectations
- The level of the costs of exit from the relationship
- The level of the symbolic significance given to the relationship
- The level of urgency of the expectations' fulfillment
- The level of the stakeholder's power that in turn can be subdivided into his different determinants (media access, firm's knowledge, etc.)

The second step in the process of the relationship's evaluation is represented by the strategic relevance of the relationship. In this case, it is the role that each stakeholder assumes in the achievement of the firm's strategy to be estimated. The starting point is represented by the strategic framework chosen for the period in which the analysis is carried out and so, concretely, by the formulation of the existing strategic plan. In general terms, the strategic framework could be developed in the following way:

- Corporate strategy
- Financial and economic strategy
- Portfolio strategy (in the case of firms working in more than one strategic business area)
- Competitive strategy for each strategic business area (SBA)
- Activities strategy and social strategy

Each one of the strategic decision areas mentioned above answers to specific objectives and each group of stakeholders assumes a specific level of relevance in relation to the achievement of each of them.

If we join the reactivity of the stakeholder with his strategic importance, we obtain the following type-relationships:

- High reactivity and high strategic functionality
- High reactivity and low strategic functionality
- Low reactivity and low strategic functionality
- High strategic functionality and low reactivity

It is possible to point out the following considerations:

- The relationships of the first type require the highest attention by the firm, in terms of instruments for the management of the relationship.

- The relationships of the second type could be problematic, because of the discrepancy between the stakeholder's expectations and his real weight in the achievement of the firm's objectives.
- The relationships of the third and the fourth types, usually don't present, for different reasons, particularly critical elements.

Positioning of the Relationship (Relational Goodwill/Badwill)

In the third phase, we move on to the determination of the value assumed by the relationship for the stakeholder, in terms of relational goodwill or relational badwill. Passing from a theoretical analysis to a more practical one, it is necessary to admit that, at least for a great number of relationships between firms and stakeholders, firms don't have the necessary means to determine r (rate of return of the capital invested by the stakeholder) and, still fewer, to determine i (cost of the capital invested by the stakeholder).

The markets of the resources brought by the stakeholders are not clear and public enough to be able to provide believable information. More than this, contributions and rewards can be expressed in a monetary way only with a lot of difficulty and, furthermore, contributions and rewards can have different natures so that they can be difficult to compare (Luffman, Witt and Lister 1982).

Anyway, we can examine, during the time, the existing difference between what stakeholders really received and what would be offered to them in comparable situations, also through nonmonetary indicators. This is one way, even if less explicit, to measure the differential between r and i.

So, each relationship, after having been evaluated on the basis of its criticality, is once again evaluated. For each primary stakeholder it is possible to determine the value of the relationship, or the value of the relational goodwill or the differential between r and i, however expressed, also through specific indicators. The choice will depend on the information that is available.

The Value of the Relationship and the Company's Value

The value of the relationship expresses the result of an evaluation carried out from the stakeholder's perspective. This value doesn't explain a lot about the company's value, as an entity. The value of relationship, in fact, is a partial value that could satisfy some groups of stakeholders and damage the others or, even worse, that could satisfy certain groups of stakeholders but damage the whole firm system (Hillman and Keim 2001).

We need to pay attention to the following question: What impacts do the specific relationship positions (goodwill, badwill, neutral) have on the value of the firm (W)?

First of all, it is necessary to link together the analysis made up to this moment on the nature of the relationship and on the value of the relationship. For instance, relational goodwill obtained in a nonstrategic relationship will probably have little impact on the future results; on the contrary, badwill in a strategic relationship will certainly be very damaging (Slinger 1999; Kelly, Kelly. and Gamble 1997).

To make it easier, the economic capital value (company's value) can be expressed as:

$$W = \sum_{t=1}^{n} \frac{R_t}{(1-i)^t} \qquad (18.5)$$

where R represents the perspective net result in period n and i represents the discounting rate of the R flows. The net result R depends on:

Re = Revenues

Co = Costs

This formula underlines the main drivers that determine the value; that is,

Re = revenues

Co = costs

i = rate

n = time

With regard to these drivers, it is possible to go through the second step of the analysis process. We start the evaluation process of the company (W_0) by supposing that all the relationships with stakeholders (S_1, S_2, ... S_n) are in a neutral position, that is, with a goodwill equal to 0. So the W_0 is determined by supposing that none of the firm's stakeholders have an advantaged or a disadvantaged position.

Then the value of the economic capital (W_1) is calculated with regard to the real positions assumed by the relationships (S_1, . . . S_n). Globally, the difference between W_1 and W_0 represents the value of the relationships with the stakeholders, in the perspective of the company's value, that is, in the perspective of the firm system as an entity.

$$WR = W_1 - W_0 \qquad (18.6)$$

A numeric example could make it easier to clarify the concept. We can calculate the company's value under the neutral relationship hypothesis (W_0), and with the following data it determines a value equal to 118.64.

> Time = 5 years
>
> Rate = 9.5%
>
> Revenues and costs (see Table 18.4)

Now, we consider two significant relationships: the relationship with researchers/stakeholders (S_1), who work in the firm, and the relationship with banks/stakeholders (S_2), that assure financing. It is supposed that both the relationships are in a position of relational goodwill and that this has some impact on the variable considered in the evaluation of the economic capital in the following years. These impacts can lead to the following result.

The relational goodwill obtained by the researchers permits:

- Increasing the evaluation period by 1 year (from 5 to 6 years)
- Decreasing the discount rate by half a percentage point (from 9.5% to 9%)
- Increasing the revenues of the fifth and of the sixth year of evaluation by 10 (under the same costs)

The relational goodwill obtained by the banks permits:

- Decreasing by another 1% the discounting bank rate (from 9% to 8%)
- Decreasing by 5 the costs of the fourth and of the fifth year of evaluation

The effect of these variations raises the value of the economic capital. While under the neutrality of hypothesis, the value W_0 was equal to 118.64, inserting into the analysis the hypothesis related to the positioning

TABLE 18.4   Calculation of the Company's Value

Years	Revenues	Costs	Net Result
1	100	80	20
2	100	80	20
3	120	80	40
4	120	80	40
5	120	80	40

of two groups of stakeholders (S_1 and S_2), we obtain a W_1 value equal to 167.02, that is to say, 48.38 more than the starting W_0 value:

$$W_R = W_1 - W_0 = 167.02 - 118.64 = 48.38 \qquad (18.7)$$

Under the starting hypothesis, this increase (by about 40%) is completely due to the relational goodwills and therefore it represents the relational goodwills' value from the firm's system point of view. More than this, the value 48.38 is obtained from the two different stakeholders' groups, in different parts. To the relationship with the reasearchers is due 38.08 whereas to the relationship with the banks is due 10.3.

$$W_R = W_1 - W_0 = W_{R1} + W_{R2} = 38.08 + 10.3 = 48.38 \qquad (18.8)$$

The Value of the Relationship and Consequences for Corporate Governance

Relational goodwill and relational badwill are not exclusively caused by a temporary imperfection of the markets; they can also be the result of strategic choices. For this reason, the strategic management of the relationship with the stakeholders becomes an integral part of the corporate governance. In other words, the relationships have to be managed with suitable instruments and operating mechanisms that make it possible to achieve relational value.

In the United States and in Europe, the corporate governance issue rose to prominence in 1980s. Because of the strong activity of mergers and acquisitions (M&A) that took place in that decade, the attention was centered particularly on the responsibilities of the management toward the shareholders (Driver and Thompson 2002). However, in 1999, in a OECD working paper, there emerged a wider vision of the concept of corporate governance, which was extended also to relationships with the stakeholders (OECD 1999, 2004).

In this perspective, the corporate governance's instruments will be also turned to the maximization of the quality of the relationships with the stakeholders. It is possible to say that a relationship has a high quality in the measure in which its value is coherent within the strategic plan goals. In particular, we can see what could be the principal consequences of the relational evaluations in the corporate governance perspective.

- It will become necessary to identify in a systemic way the primary relationships and their nature.
- It will be necessary to quantify the value for the stakeholder, not only in terms of relational profit but also, for the reasons mentioned above, in terms of relational goodwill and relational badwill.

- The firm's management should consciously make the choices related to future positioning of the primary relationships coherently with the wider strategic choices assumed.
- The firm's management will need to provide suitable instruments of planning and controlling, designed in a specific way for the relationships with the primary stakeholders. In particular we refer to the budgeting and reporting instruments.
- It will be necessary to improve the accountability instruments toward the primary stakeholders, especially toward those that are characterized by a high reactivity (Logsdon and Lewellyn 2000). Furthermore, there appears to be growing evidence of a trade-off between the secrecy constraints on one hand and the communication and transparency opportunities on the other.
- The corporate governance mechanisms designed and used to safeguard the little shareholders, such as those referable to the independent administrator role, to the nomination commitee, to the remuneration commitee, to the audit commitee, etc., could be further improved with regard also to the exigency of safeguards expressed by the stakeholders.

In more general terms, different groups of stakeholders could play very important roles in the conditioning of the corporate governance system of the single firms and also at the level of public policy.

CONCLUSION

The quality of the relationships with the primary stakeholders has a great impact on the process of value creation and, consequently on the achievement of the institutional goal of the firm. Since these relationships have an articulated and complex nature, the firm is obliged to regulate the dynamic by using suitable instruments, especially concerning:

- The measurement of the value generated for the stakehoder, that is to say, the relational profit and the relational goodwill
- The measurement of the impacts that the relational strategies have on the firm's value
- The definition of the suitable mechanisms of corporate governance

CHAPTER 19

Family Ownership and Corporate Governance

María Sacristán-Navarro and Silvia Gómez-Ansón

INTRODUCTION

During the last few decades, ownership of firms and, in particular, family ownership has received increased attention among scholars. The prevalence of widely held corporations as described in the classic book by Berle and Means (1932) does not seem to be the image of reality. Different authors have questioned this idea of dispersed ownership and corporations run by managers (Demsetz 1983; Demsetz and Lehn 1985; Shleifer and Vishny 1996). Recently, the studies by La Porta et al. (1999a), Claessens et al. (2000), and Faccio and Lang (2002) demonstrate that ownership concentration is a common feature in many countries worldwide and that families and individuals play an important role as shareholders.

In this chapter we first review the empirical evidence concerning the importance of families and individuals as large shareholders worldwide, identifying factors that may influence the existence of family firms and groups, as well as the mechanisms that are employed by families to enhance their voting rights. Second, we analyze from a theoretical point of view the arguments that may link family ownership to firm performance, and third, we review the empirical evidence concerning the influence of families as large shareholders on firm value. The review highlights the importance of family ownership in some European, Latin American, and East Asian countries. Factors such as the countries' shareholder protection and firm size seem to influence the family's presence. In addition, the large number of empirical papers that analyze the relationship between family ownership, a firm's governance structure, and its value do not provide a conclusive image, but they do show that families as large shareholders influence firms' governance structures.

THE IMPORTANCE OF FAMILY OWNERSHIP

Traditionally, most corporate governance literature has focused on the classic conflicts of interests between managers and owners, assuming dispersed ownership (Jensen and Meckling 1976; Grossman and Hart 1980). But, except for the United States and some other Anglo-Saxon countries, ownership concentration is a fact all over the world (La Porta et al. 1999a), families and individuals being the most important type of large shareholders (La Porta et al. 1999a).

The study by La Porta et al. (1999a), using data of the 20 largest corporations in 27 wealthy economies, shows that the percentage of widely held firms, defined as those lacking a controlling shareholder whose voting rights (both direct and indirect) exceed 20%, amounts to 36.48% (see Table 19.1). Nevertheless, there are significant differences among countries, with corporations of Anglo-Saxon countries (that is, Australia, Canada, Ireland, U.K., or the United States) being mainly widely held, while in other countries (for example, Austria, Belgium, Israel, Hong Kong, or Singapore), widely held companies amount to no more than 15%. Actually, widely held corporations are more common among the countries showing good shareholder protection—mostly common law countries (47.92%)—than among the countries with low shareholder protection—mostly civil law countries (27.33%).

Among large shareholders, families and individuals are the predominant type of blockholders, with one third of the firms worldwide being family-controlled. Once again there are significant differences among countries, the importance of families being especially remarkable in countries showing low shareholder protection (34.33% of the corporations of the countries with low shareholder protection versus 24.58% of the corporations of the countries with high shareholder protection). Families control more than 50% of the corporations in some Latin American countries (i.e., Argentina and Mexico), some Asian countries (i.e., Hong Kong), and close to 50% of the corporations in some European countries (Belgium, Greece, Portugal, or Sweden).

When studying the ownership structure not only of the largest quoted corporations, but of the whole universe of listed firms in European countries, the proportion of widely held corporations decreases for some countries (Faccio and Lang 2002). Actually, while in the study by La Porta et al.

TABLE 19.1 Listed Companies Ownership around the World

				Percent			
	Number of Firms	Widely Held	Family	State	Widely Held Financial	Widely Held Corporation	Miscellaneous
Panel A: Control of Large Publicly Traded Firms							
Argentina	20	0	65	15	5	15	0
Australia	20	65	5	5	0	25	0
Canada	20	60	25	0	0	15	0
Hong Kong	20	10	70	5	5	0	10
Ireland	20	65	10	0	0	10	15
Japan	20	90	5	5	0	0	0
New Zealand	20	30	25	25	0	20	0
Norway	20	25	25	35	5	0	10
Singapore	20	15	30	45	5	5	0
Spain	20	35	15	30	10	10	0
U.K.	20	100	0	0	0	0	0
United States	20	80	20	0	0	0	0
High antidirector avg.		47.92	24.58	13.75	2.5	8.33	2.92
Austria	20	5	15	70	0	0	10
Belgium	20	5	50	5	30	0	10
Denmark	20	40	35	15	0	0	10
Finland	20	35	10	35	5	5	10
France	20	60	20	15	5	0	0
Germany	20	50	10	25	15	0	0
Greece	20	10	50	30	10	0	0

(Continued)

TABLE 19.1 (Continued)

	Number of Firms	Widely Held	Family	State	Widely Held Financial	Widely Held Corporation	Miscellaneous
					Percent		
Israel	20	5	50	40	0	5	0
Italy	20	20	15	40	5	10	10
South Korea	20	55	20	15	0	5	5
Mexico	20	0	100	0	0	0	0
Netherlands	20	30	20	5	0	10	35
Portugal	20	10	45	25	15	0	5
Sweden	20	25	45	10	15	0	5
Switzerland	20	60	30	0	5	0	5
Low antidirector avg.		27.33	34.33	22.00	7.00	2.33	7.00
Sample average		36.48	30.00	18.33	5.00	5.00	5.19
Panel B: Control of Western European Publicly Traded Firms							
Austria	99	11.11	52.86	15.32	8.59	0.00	11.11
Belgium	130	20.00	51.54	2.31	12.69	0.77	12.69
Finland	129	28.68	48.84	15.76	0.65	1.55	4.52
France	607	14.00	64.82	5.11	11.37	3.79	0.91
Germany	704	10.37	64.62	6.30	9.07	3.65	3.37
Ireland	69	62.32	24.63	1.45	4.35	2.17	5.07
Italy	208	12.98	59.61	10.34	12.26	2.88	1.20
Norway	155	36.77	38.55	13.09	4.46	0.32	4.54

Panel B: Control of Western European Publicly Traded Firms (Continued)

Portugal	87	21.84	60.34	5.75	4.60	0.57	6.90
Spain	632	26.42	55.79	4.11	11.51	1.64	0.47
Sweden	245	39.18	46.94	4.90	2.86	0.00	5.71
Switzerland	214	27.57	48.13	7.32	9.35	1.09	6.31
U.K.	1,953	63.08	23.68	0.08	8.94	0.76	3.46
Total Western Europe	5,232	36.93	44.69	4.14	9.03	1.68	3.43

Panel C: Control of East Asian Publicly Traded Firms

Hong Kong	330	7.0	66.7	1.4	5.2	19.8
Indonesia	178	5.1	71.5	8.2	2.0	12.2
Japan	1,240	79.8	9.7	0.8	6.5	3.2
Korea	345	43.2	48.4	1.6	0.7	6.1
Malaysia	238	10.3	67.2	13.4	2.3	6.7
Philippines	120	19.2	44.6	2.1	7.5	26.7
Singapore	221	5.4	55.4	23.5	4.1	11.5
Taiwan	141	26.2	48.2	2.8	5.3	17.4
Thailand	167	6.6	61.6	8.0	8.6	15.3

Data at the 20% cut-off.
Data for Panels A, B and C sourced from La Porta et al. (1999a), Faccio and Lang (2002), and Claessens et al. (2000) respectively.

(1999a) the proportion of widely held large corporations amounted to 100 in the U.K., this figure amounts only to 63.08% for Faccio and Lang (2002). Similar decreases in the proportion of widely held corporations are shown for France (from 60% to 14%), Germany (from 59% to 10.37%), or for Switzerland (from 60% to 27.57%). Overall, in Western Europe, according to Faccio and Lang (2002) the proportion of widely held corporations amounts, on the average, to 36.93%, being the Anglo-Saxon countries, that is, Ireland and the U.K., those that show a higher proportion of widely held companies (62.32% and 63.08% respectively). Faccio and Lang's (2002) figures also reinforce the importance of families as large shareholders in Western Europe. Families control 44.69% of Western European companies, controlling in Austria, Belgium, France, Germany, Italy, Portugal, and Spain more than 50% of the corporations.

For East Asian countries, the study by Claessens et al. (2000) also reveals the importance of families as large shareholders. Families control 66.7% of the corporations in Hong Kong, 71.5% of the corporations in Indonesia, 67.2% of the corporations in Malaysia, 55.4% of the corporations in Singapore, and 61.6% of the corporations in Thailand. Only in Japan do families control below 10% of the corporations.

These data reveal that families are the predominant type of controlling shareholder, controlling, on average, 25% of the value of the 20 largest companies, while a controlling family controls, on average, 1.33 of these firms. Moreover, the controlling power of these families seems to be very high, as the probability of the families being the only large shareholder in the firms they control is quite large, 71% (La Porta et al. 1999a). In addition, in East Asian countries, a significant share of firms' assets belong to a small number of families. For example, respectively, 16.6% and 17.1% of the value of listed corporate assets in Indonesia and the Philippines rest in the hands of a single family. Moreover, the 10 largest families in Indonesia, the Philippines, and Thailand control half of the listed corporate assets, and in Hong Kong and Korea the 10 largest families control one third of corporate assets (Claessens et al. 2000). In Western European countries, for 54.74% of the family-controlled firms, Faccio and Lang (2002) report that families stand as the only controlling owner.

Regarding family ownership, various questions may arise: What determines the differences in family control among countries? What other factors influence or drive family ownership? Do families use means to enhance their control?

Regarding the first question, the reasons for observing these sharp differences between family and individual ownership between countries, one of the factors seems to be shareholder protection. Widely held firms are more common in countries with good shareholder protection, while countries with poor shareholder protection have more firms with ultimate owners, among them, families (La Porta et al. 1999a). Moreover, the most corrupt countries poorly protect shareholders (La Porta et al. 1999b). In these countries, family control gives controlling shareholders autonomy in decision making and this may facilitate corruption. The economic development of a country may also influence the firm's ownership concentration and, thus, family corporate control. In this sense, the results of Claessens et al. (2000) show, for East Asian corporations, that Japan has the largest share of widely held firms, but also of family-controlled firms (see Table 19.1), while Indonesia and Thailand have the smallest share of widely held firms and also one of the highest shares of family-controlled firms.

In addition to the countries' regulations, law enforcement, and development, other factors influence the ownership held by families in corporations. Firm size is one of these factors. La Porta et al. (1999a) report that while 45.15% of the medium-sized publicly traded firms worldwide are owned by families, this figure amounts to 30% for large publicly traded firms (figures at the 20% threshold). Claessens et al. (2000) for East Asian corporations and Faccio and Lang (2002) for Western European countries both report that family ownership increases for smaller firms. Another factor that might influence family ownership could be firm age. Although, according to some authors (Black and Gilson 1998), younger companies would be the ones that more frequently show concentrated ownership, the results of Claessens et al. (2000) contradict this prediction. Actually, the latter authors find that older East Asian corporations are more likely family controlled.

How do families exercise their power? One way is by managing the firm. According to La Porta et al. (1999a), in 69% of family-controlled firms, families also participate in management; that is, a member of the controlling family is the CEO, the Chairman, the Honorary Chairman, or the Vice Chairman of the firm. Thus, there does not seem to be a problem of separation of ownership and control among these firms. Likewise, for Western European countries, Faccio and Lang (2002) report that in almost 70 percent of the family-controlled firms, the family is in management.

Pyramids are also usually used by families in order to enhance their voting power, to acquire power disproportionate to their cash flow rights (Wolfenzon 1999). Overall, and according to La Porta et al. (1999a), 27.36% of the time, families that control firms use pyramids to separate their cash flow ownership from their control rights. Similarly, Claessens et al. (2000) report that the ratio of cash flow to control rights is the highest among family-controlled East Asian corporations and conclude that firms controlled by families show the greatest separation of ownership and control. In Western European countries, pyramids are used in 13.81% of the family-controlled firms (Faccio and Lang 2002). Dual-class shares may also be employed by families to enhance their control. For instance, they are issued by 17.61% of family-controlled firms in Western European countries (Faccio and Lang 2002). Other means of enhancing control that may be used by families and large shareholders are holdings through multiple control chains, voting caps, or cross-shareholdings. Cross-shareholdings are present in 3.15% of the largest public companies worldwide (La Porta et al. 1999a), in 10% of East Asian corporations (Claessens et al. 2000), and in Western European companies (Faccio and Lang 2002). Overall, deviations from the one-share-one-vote rule tend to be small worldwide (La Porta et al. 1999) and this is also the case for family firms, for example, in Western European countries. The average minimum percent of the book value of equity required to control 20% of the votes of a company amounts, on average, to 18.64% (Faccio and Lang 2002).

THEORETICAL FOUNDATIONS CONCERNING THE INFLUENCE OF FAMILIES ON FIRM VALUE

Economic literature has claimed that concentrated family ownership as well as owner-management may influence a firm's performance. As suggested by Bearle and Means (1932) and Jensen and Meckling (1976), a firm's ownership concentration should have a positive effect on a firm's value because, due to the large shareholder's greater incentives to monitor managers, its presence will reduce managerial opportunistic behavior. Nevertheless, when the large shareholders are families or individuals, they may have incentives to extract private benefits at the expense of the minority shareholders, pursuing the family's interests and neglecting those of other shareholders. Moreover, the relationship between family members could also be more at odds than between nonfamily members, thus triggering agency problems and enhancing agency costs (Schulze et al. 2001).

Consequently, family ownership could have positive or negative effects on a firm's value. These effects are known as the monitoring (positive effect) and the expropriation (negative effect) hypotheses. We shall first refer to the monitoring hypothesis.

From a theoretical point of view, economic literature has claimed that concentrated family ownership may positively influence a firm's performance. Concentrated ownership would give the owners, for example, families and individuals, incentives to monitor managers and to assume the task of monitoring (Shleifer and Vishny 1997). In this sense, Pollack (1985) and Coleman (1990) argue that in family businesses the relations within the families, characterized by loyalty and trust, may promote flexibility in operations, ease decision making, and reduce shirking. Moreover, when monitoring requires knowledge of firm technology, families potentially provide superior oversight because their lengthy tenure allows them to move further along the firm's learning curve (Anderson and Reeb 2003b, 1305). The long time horizon that characterizes family firms may also affect a firm's efficiency. Family ownership may provide incentives for a firm to invest according to market rules (Anderson and Reeb 2003b) and could lead to lower debt financing costs (Anderson et al. 2003c).

Nevertheless, there are also theoretical arguments suggesting that family-owned firms may be less efficient than nonfamily firms. The concentration of ownership reduces the possible diversification of financial risk, increases the risk premium, and increases, consequently, the cost of capital (Demsetz and Lehn 1985). In addition, agency problems may also occur between family members (Schulze et al. 2001) and the presence of family groups, when firms obtain outside equity financing, may also trigger agency issues: "the use of pyramidal groups to separate ownership from control, the entrenchment of controlling families and non-arm's length transactions—tunnelling—between related companies" (Morck and Yeung 2003). Moreover, founding families may have the incentives and power to take action and adopt investment decisions that benefit them at the expense of other shareholders (Demsetz and Lehn 1985).

An important question that arises when analyzing the influence of families on firm value is their use of pyramids to channel family ownership (Claessens et al. 2002; La Porta et al. 1999a). Empirical evidence shows that the separation of ownership and control is more pronounced among family-controlled firms and among small firms and that the separation between voting and cash flow rights may have an influence on firm performance (Claessens et al. 2002).

The participation of the family in firm management may also increase a firm's value as owner-managers should tend to minimize agency costs arising from the separation of ownership and control. For instance, the need to monitor the behavior of family agents should decrease: "Family members have many dimensions of exchange with one another over a long horizon leading to advantages in monitoring and disciplining family-related decision agents" (Fama and Jensen 1983, 306). Moreover, kinship and altruism among family members will temper managers' self-interest and will provide incentives for family directors to adopt a long-term perspective and undertake investments that will benefit the next generations of owners (Schulze et al. 2003). However, owner-managed firms will also be particularly vulnerable to entrenchment, and there may also be agency threats under family contracting, as affective ties between the parties may reduce the presence of formal safeguards designed to mitigate possible threats to firm performance (Gómez-Mejía et al. 2001). For instance, several authors report that family firms CEOs hold an average tenure of 24 years (Beckhard and Dyer 1983), twice that observed in widely held firms (Hambrick and Fukutomi 1991). In addition, the choice of a top manager among a more restricted pool of talent, the family, may lead to a lower quality among owner-managers than among professional managers.

EMPIRICAL EVIDENCE CONCERNING THE RELATIONSHIP BETWEEN FAMILY OWNERSHIP AND FIRM VALUE

The relationship between family ownership and firm value has traditionally received quite a lot of theoretical and empirical attention among scholars from the very beginning of the research in family businesses (Chaganti and Damanpour 1991; Daily and Dollinger 1992). This is due to the fact that families are in an uncommon position to exert influence and control over a firm, which may potentially lead to differences in the firms' performance when comparing family and nonfamily firms (Anderson and Reeb, 2003b, 1304).

In this section we review the empirical literature that analyzes the link between family ownership, firm corporate governance structure, and firm value. The characteristics of the papers reviewed are summarized in Table 19.2. In this table we refer to the following characteristics of the papers: their authors, the aims of the papers, the samples used, the definitions of family ownership and family firms that were employed, the way performance was measured, and the main results of the papers. We will follow the structure of Table 19.2 in order to undertake the review. Consequently, we first refer to the aims of these papers; second, to the characteristics of the samples employed; third, to the different definitions of family ownership and family firms; fourth, to the way performance has been measured by the different studies; and finally, to the empirical evidence of the link between family ownership, family firm corporate governance structures, and firm value.

We conducted an ISI cross-search with the following terms: family business, family firm, family performance and family firm, firm value and family firm, corporate governance and family firm, family ownership, governance structure, family management and firm value, family control and performance, large shareholders and family firms. In the same way, we operated with EBSCO host and the term family firms. After revising the abstracts, we selected 27 papers. We considered only those empirical papers that explicitly refer to family firms. Results refer mainly to the last five years.

Issues Analyzed in the Empirical Papers Linking Family Ownership and Firm Value

Although some studies only refer to the relation between a family stake in a firm and its value (Galve and Salas 1996; Lauterbach and Vaninsky 1999; Sraer and Thersmar 2004), the papers that analyze the relationship between family ownership and firm value usually study, in addition, the relation between a family's ownership and a firm's corporate governance structure, attempting to derive implications concerning the relations, not only between a firm's ownership structure and its value, but also between a firm's ownership structure and its corporate governance structure and between a firm's corporate governance structure and its performance. In this context, one of the more frequently analyzed questions refers to the so-called *founder effect*. The authors try to explore the link between the presence of founders among the firm's managerial team and the firms' value (Anderson and Reeb 2003b; McConaughy et al. 2001; Mishra et al. 2000). Nevertheless, we must point out that the influence of the families' descendants on firm value is a question that remains understudied.

While some papers consider family influence on firm corporate governance structure by analyzing jointly the relationships between family ownership and family's participation in a firm's management or control and the firm value (Barth et al. 2005; Lee 2004; Randoy and Goel 2003; Van den Berghe and Carchon 2002; Villalonga and Amit 2004), other studies only analyze the relationship between firm management (and the presence of family members among the managerial team) and firm value (Gnan and Songini 2003). When studying the influence of the involvement of families in firm management on firm value, many authors take into consideration the identity of the managerial team. Adams et al. (2003) analyze the influence of founder CEOs on firm value, Daily and Near (2000) deal with the impact of CEO satisfaction, Lausten (2002) studies the influence of the replacement of CEOs on firm performance, Gómez-Mejía et al. (2003) analyze the impact of family compensation in family-controlled firms and firm value, Pérez-Gonzalez (2001) studies how inherited control affects firm performance, and Morck et al. (1988) analyze the influence of heirs on firm value. These studies mainly consider the issue of the identity of the CEO and whether he or she is the founder of the firm or has inherited the firm's control, while the presence of family members among the firms' directors and its influence on the firms' performance has received less attention in family firm literature (Anderson and Reeb 2004).

TABLE 19.2 Review of Empirical Papers Linking Family Ownership and Firm Value

Authors	Question	Firm's Characteristics and Country's Sample	Family Firm's Definition	Performance Measure	Results
Adams et al. (2003)	The relationship between founder-CEOs and performance	Fortune 500 American firms over the 1992–1999 period	Founder CEO: equal to one if any source explicitly named the current CEO as a founder or the main executive at any time the company began	Tobin's Q and ROA measures	Founder CEO status is endogenous in performance regressions After factoring out the effect of performance on founder-CEO status, they find a residual positive correlation between founder-CEO status and firm performance (+)
Anderson and Reeb (2003a)	Do founding family firms reduce firm-specific risk by influencing firm's diversification and capital structure decisions?	S&P 500 Industrial firms as of year-end 2002 (319 firms); United States	Fractional equity ownership of the founding family (binary variable that equals one when the founding family has an equity stake in the firm and zero otherwise)	Economic Value Added: (net operating profit after taxes) − (capital × cost of capital) Excess Value: (market value of equity + book value of debt) − book value of assets/book value of assets	Founding-family ownership is associated to less corporate diversification and has similar risk profiles to nonfamily firms Family firms are more valuable than nonfamily firms (+)
Anderson and Reeb (2003b)	The relationship between founding family ownership and firm performance	Large publicly traded U.S. firms, S&P 500 as of Dec. 1992 excluding banks and utilities	The fractional equity of the founding family and (or) the presence of family members on the board of directors	Tobin's Q (market value of total assets divided by the replacement cost of assets) and return on assets	Family firms perform better than nonfamily firms (+) The relation between family holdings and firm performance is nonlinear When family members serve as CEO performance is better than with outside CEOs.

Study	Research question	Sample	Measure	Results
Anderson and Reeb (2004)	How founding family board presence affects firm value	Publicly traded American S&P 500 firms (excluded banks and utilities), 403 firms, period 1992–1999	Publicly traded firms in which the founding family continues to have an ownership stake or maintain board seats	Tobin's Q and Sterns Stewart's economic value added (EVA)	Most valuable public firms are those in which the independent directors balance family board representation / A moderate family board presence provides substantial benefits to the firm
Barth et al. (2005)	Is family-owned firm equally productive as non-family-owned firm? How does it affect management regime?	438 firms associated with the Confederation of Norwegian Business and Industry; Norwegian Business Survey during 1996	Family owned firms: if at least 33% of the shares in the firm are owned by one person or one family / Family-owned firms run by a professional / Family owned firms run by a manager of the family	Cobb-Douglas production function	Family owned firms are less productive than non-family-owned firms (−) / Family-owned firms managed by a person hired outside the owner family are equally productive as non-family-owned firms (=) / Family-owned firms managed by a person from the owner family are significantly less productive (−)
Daily and Near (2000)	Does CEO satisfaction affect firm performance?	Sample: 221 American owner/managers of family-owned and -controlled automobile dealerships / Method of obtaining information: questionnaires	Those dealerships indicating that they were family businesses / Owner/manager and family equity holdings	Total sales revenues / Firm growth / Sales per full-time employee	No relation is found

(Continued)

411

TABLE 19.2 *(Continued)*

Authors	Question	Firm's Characteristics and Country's Sample	Family Firm's Definition	Performance Measure	Results
Ehrhardt et al. (2004)	The evolution of ownership, control, and performance in German family firms	German family-owned firms over the last century	When a dominant influence of the founding family is documented by a voting rights concentration of more than 50%	Return on assets and stock market performance	In this evolutionary study they document that family firms seem to perform significantly better than non-family firms with an all period average (median) return on assets
Galve and Salas (1996)	Relationship between ownership and performance	81 nonfinancial firms quoted on the Spanish stock market	Family controlled firms depend upon he shares owned by the largest shareholder group	Performance is measured in terms of both productive efficiency and profitability (rate of return)	Family and nonfamily firms have the same profitability but different productive efficiency and therefore the conclusion as to whether ownership influences performance depends on how we measure performance
Gnan and Songini (2003)	What is the relation between the professionalism of family firms and firm performance?	151 small and medium-sized Italian family manufacturing businesses, questionnaires	Family firm: a company both owned and managed by members of one or more families and is perceived as familiar	Sales growth, invested capital growth, net asset growth, return on sales, return on investment, and return on equity	Involvement of family members in the company management contributes to performance
Gómez-Mejía et al. (2003)	Determinants of executive compensation in family-controlled firms	253 family-controlled public firms included in the COMPUSTAT database	Family-controlled firm if two or more directors had family relationship and family members owned or controlled at least 5% of the voting stocks	CEO compensation (np)	CEOs of family-controlled firms receive lower total income than outsider CEOs, increasingly so as family ownership concentration increases

Gómez-Mejía et al. (2001)	What are the predictors of chief executive tenure when a firm's owners and its executive have family ties?	Spanish population of the 276 Spanish newspapers during the period 1966–1993	The presence or absence of family was determined separately for each CEO and editor. The CEO's last name was compared with the last name of the newspaper's owners. Idem with the editor	Performance trend (% change in the number of newspapers sold from the time the executive departed) Performance changes (% changes in the average number of newspapers sold between the tenure of a particular executive and the preceding executive)	Firm performance and business risk are much stronger predictors of chief executive tenure when a firm's owners and its executive have family ties Organizational consequences of CEO dismissal are more favorable when the replaced CEO is a member of the family owning the firm
Gugler (2003)	The relationship between dividends and the ownership and control structure of the firm	A panel of Austrian listed firms over the 1991–1999 period	Ultimate owners to find the family-controlled firms		State-controlled firms engage in dividends smoothing while family-controlled firms do not Family firms have lower payout ratios
Lausten (2002)	The relationship between the replacement of CEOs and corporate performance	A sample of Danish large and medium-sized firms in the period 1992–1995	Dummy for family ownership; dummy adopts one if the firm is family-controlled (CEO)	Pre-tax accounting profits, sales, rate of return on the firm's own capital	CEO turnover is inversely related to firm performance. The status of the chairman of the board and family ties within the management and ownership of the company strengthen the relationship between CEO turnover and firm performance

(Continued)

TABLE 19.2 *(Continued)*

Authors	Question	Firm's Characteristics and Country's Sample	Family Firm's Definition	Performance Measure	Results
Lauterbach and Vaninsky (1999)	How does ownership structure affect firm performance?	280 public companies traded on the Telavit Stock Exchange (TASE) during 1994; Israeli firms	Firms controlled by a family	Relative performance: Data Envelopment Analysis (DEA): actual net income of the firm divided by the optimal net income given the firm's inputs	Owner-manager firms are less efficient in generating net income than firms managed by a professional (not owner) manager (−)
Lee (2004)	How does family ownership and family management affect firm performance?	150 largest family firms in the United States in 2003	A single family controlled the firm ownership, the controlling family's members were active in top management, and the family was involved in the firm for at least two generations	Gross profit margin, net profit margins, return on equity, return on assets, and return on invested capital	Family ownership and control tend to enhance firm efficiency leading to a higher return on investment (+)
McConaughy et al. (2001)	Do founding family controlled firms have greater value than other firms?	Public firms, COMPUSTAT data base for 1986–1988 American firms	Public corporations whose CEOs are either the founder or a member of the founder's family	Market/equity to book equity (ME/BE) ratio and stock return	Firms controlled by the founding family have greater value, operate more efficiently, and carry less debt than other firms
Mishra et al. (2000)	Does founding family control add value to the firm? How does the founding family influence interact with other corporate governance mechanism to affect firm value?	120 Norwegian founding-family-controlled and nonfounding-family-controlled firms	Founding family control measured through a binary variable that equals one if the CEO is a founder or a relative of the founder The percentage of ownership by founding family	Q-value (market value to book value of total assets); market value is the sum of market value of equity and the book value of total liabilities	Founding-family controlled firms are more valuable and governed differently than firms without such influence (+) Founding family CEOs and firm value are stronger among younger firms, firms with smaller boards and with a single class of shares

Study	Research focus	Sample	Variables	Findings
Mishra et al. (2000) (*continued*)		The percentage of directors that are members of the founding family if the firm satisfies at least one of the indicators		The impact of founding family directors on firm value is not affected by firm age, board independence, and number of shares The relationship between founding family ownership and firm value is greater among older firms, firms with larger boards, and firms with multiple class of shares
Morck et al. (1998)	The effect of heir-controlled firms on firm performance	Heir-controlled Canadian firms extracted from the publicly traded firms among the largest 500 Canadian firms Firms controlled by descendants of their founders (over the 20% threshold)	Return on assets, return on sales, real growth in total sales, and growth in number of employees	Heir-controlled Canadian firms show low industry-adjusted financial performance, labor capital ratios, and R&D spending relative to other firms the same ages and sizes (−)
Pérez-Gonzalez (2001)	The impact of inherited control on firm's performance	U.S. publicly traded corporations using data from 335 management transitions In firms with concentrated ownership or founding family involvement	ROA and market to book ratios (M-B)	Firms where incoming CEOs are related by blood or marriage to a founder or a large shareholder of the corporation undergo large decreases in return on assets and market to book ratios that are not experienced by firms that promote unrelated CEOs

(*Continued*)

TABLE 19.2 *(Continued)*

Authors	Question	Firm's Characteristics and Country's Sample	Family Firm's Definition	Performance Measure	Results
Randoy and Goel (2003)	How does ownership structure affect firm performance in small- and medium-sized enterprises with and without founding family leadership?	Sample of 68 small and medium enterprises publicly traded in Norway from 1996, 1997, 1998	Founding family firms are defined as corporations in which the founder or a family member is the leader of the firm (either as a CEO or as Chair)	Market capitalization, book value of assets	Founding family leadership (CEO or Chair) moderates the relation between ownership structure and firm performance. Nonfounder firms benefit from a low level of board and inside ownership, a high level of block-holder ownership, and a high level of foreign ownership. Founding families benefit from a high level of insider ownership, a low level of blockholder ownership, and a low level of foreign ownership
Sraer and Thersmar (2004)	How do French family firms perform?	All firms listed on the French stock markets over the 1994–2000 period	They look at the main shareholders; when it was obvious that a single family controlled at least 20% of the shares, they labeled them family firms; they also distinguish between *founder controlled*, when the founder of the firm still holds the family block and is CEO; *heir managed*, when the founder no longer holds control over the firm	ROA and ROE, Ln (sales), Tobin's Q	Family firms outperform widely held corporations. (+) This result holds for founder-controlled firms as for heir-managed firms

Study	Objective	Sample/Method	Definition	Measure	Findings
Sraer and Thersmar *(continued)*			but heirs of the founder control the company votes; *family owned but professionally managed*, when the family holds the controlling group but the CEO position is held by an outsider		
Van den Berghe and Carchon (2002)	Differences between family business and nonfamily business in ownership structures, board, and management practices	Sample: 325 Belgian companies Method: survey	FF definition: if a firm fits at least one of the following criteria: One person or family owns more than 50 percent of the shares; One firm is capable of exercising considerable influence on the company's policy, or the company's management consist of one family		Family firms active keep control and management over the firm; FF and NFF have similar number of independent directors; FF have "paper board of directors" (no meetings at all)
Villaloga and Amit (2004)	Family ownership and firm value	Fortune 500 firms during 1994–2000	FF as those where the founder or a member of his or her family by either blood or marriage is an officer, a director, or a blockholder	Tobin's Q	Family ownership creates value only when the founder serves as the CEO of the family firm or as its Chairman with a hired CEO

Sample Characteristics of Family Firm Studies

Although there are papers analyzing the presence of the whole spectrum of family firms in a country's economy (Barth et al. 2005; Daily and Near 2000; Gnan and Songini 2003; Gómez-Mejía et al. 2003; Van den Berge and Carchon 2002), or the evolution of a country's firm ownership, management, and performance (Ehrhardt et al. 2004), most studies use samples of large family firms, especially family-listed firms (Mishra et al. 2000; McConaughy et al. 2001; Gugler 2003; Lauterbach and Vaninsky 1999; Sraer and Thesmar 2004; Anderson and Reeb 2003a; 2003b; 2004; Brunello 2003; Claessens et al. 2002; Demsetz and Villalonga 2002; Galve and Salas 1996; Randoy and Goel 2003). As can be observed in Table 19.2, only a minority of the papers refer to small and medium family firms; that is, to nonlisted family firms (Randoy and Goel 2003). This is probably due to the difficulty of obtaining the data for nonlisted firms.

Regarding the nationality of the sample firms, a significant part of them refers to the U.S. market (Adams et al. 2003; Anderson and Reeb 2003a; 2003b; 2004; Daily and Near 2000; Demsetz and Villalonga 2001; Gómez-Mejía et al. 2003; Lee 2004; McConaughy et al. 2001; Pérez-Gonzalez 2001; Villalonga and Amit 2004), to some European countries, such as Norway (Barth et al. 2005; Mishra et al. 2000; Randoy and Goel 2003), Italy (Brunello et al. 2003; Gnan and Songini 2003), Germany (Ehrhardt et al. 2004), Spain (Galve and Salas 1996; Gómez-Mejía et al. 2001), France (Sraer and Thermar 2004), Austria (Gugler 2003), Denmark (Lausten 2002), or Belgium (Van den Berghe and Carchon 2002), and to other industrialized countries, such as Israel (Lauterbach and Vaninsky 1999) or Canada (Morck et al. 1998). Among the studies referring to Asian countries, the study by Claessens et al. (2002) that analyzes listed firms of eight East Asian countries should be highlighted.

Regarding the sample period, most studies are cross-sectional; that is, they only take into consideration data for one year, although there are an increasing number of papers that employ longer periods of time (Adams et al. 2003; Anderson and Reeb 2004; Brunello et al. 2003; Gugler 2003; Gómez-Mejía et al. 2001; Lausten 2002; Randoy and Goel 2003; Sraer and Thersmar 2004; Villalonga and Amit 2004). Most studies also refer to nonfinancial firms, especially industrial firms (Anderson and Reeb 2003a; Gnan and Songini 2003; Barth et al. 2005; Daily and Near 2000).

What Is a Family Firm?

The definition of a firm as a family firm is one of the most troublesome issues in the research on the family business (Astrachan et al. 2002). This definition becomes especially important when one attempts to establish comparisons between the results of the family businesses of related papers. One may classify the definitions of family firms adopted in the literature in two categories: a broad one and a narrow one. Within the broad category we may include those definitions that categorize as family firms those in which a family is present, either as shareholder, as part of the managerial team, or as member of the Board of Directors, without requiring the family to hold any threshold of the firms' shares. In this sense Anderson and Reeb (2003a) consider as family firms those in which the founding family holds an equity stake in the firm, or holds seats on the Board of Directors (Anderson and Reeb 2003b; 2004), while other authors require that the CEO belongs to a family in order to consider a firm as a family firm. Examples of papers that use this broad definition of family firms are those by Daily and Near (2000); Gómez-Mejía et al. (2001); Lausten (2002); Lauterbach and Vanisky (1999); McConaughy et al. (2001); Mishra et al. (2000); Pérez-Gonzalez (2001); Randoy and Goel (2003); and Villalonga and Amit (2004).

The narrow definition of family firms, on the contrary, imposes more restrictions in order to consider a firm as a family firm. For example, it requires a minimum of family ownership (for example, at least 33% of the firms' shares must be owned by an individual or by a family; Barth et al. 2005). Some authors even add to the family's ownership restriction additional conditions: that the family participate in the firms' corporate governance structure, either as part of the Board of Directors or as part of the managerial team, mainly holding the post of the CEO (Gómez-Mejía et al. 2003; Morck et al. 1998; Sraer and Thermar 2004); or, for example, the need of being perceived as a family firm by the firm's owners (Gnan and Songini 2003), that different family generations are part of the firms' managerial team (Lee 2004), or that the family effectively influences the company's policy (Van den Berghe and Carchon 2002).

Performance Measures

The way the firms' performance is measured is also important when trying to compare the empirical results that link family ownership and firm value. As most of the papers use samples of listed firms, they usually employ market performance measures such as the Tobin's Q ratio, or the ratios of return on assets—ROA—or return on equity—ROE—(Adams et al. 2003; Anderson and Reeb 2003b; Brunello et al. 2003; McConaughy et al. 2001; Mishra et al. 2000; Pérez-Gonzalez 2001; Randoy and Goel 2003; Sraer and Thermar 2004; Villalonga and Amit 2004). Nevertheless, academics have also employed other measures of a firm's performance: the Economic Value Added (Anderson and Reeb 2003a, 2004), the firm's sales revenues, the firm's growth, the ratio of sales per employee (Daily and Near 2000), the growth in firm sales or in firm capital invested (Gnan and Songini 2003; Gómez-Mejía et al. 2001; Lausten 2002), the firm's gross profit margin (Lee 2004), the firm's real growth in total sales or in the number of employees (Morck et al. 1998). Some authors even employ more sophisticated performance measures like the Cobb-Douglas production function (Barth et al. 2005), productive efficiency (Galve and Salas 1996), or data enveloped analysis in order to measure the firm's relative performance (Lauterbach and Vaninsky 1999). Thus, given the different measures and ratios employed in the literature, one should be cautious when establishing comparisons among the empirical results of the studies that analyze the relationship between family ownership and firm value.

Empirical Evidence Concerning the Link between Family Ownership and Firm Value

Although the possible influence of family ownership on firm value has been extensively studied in economic literature, there is no conclusive evidence. Papers have explored the relationship between family ownership and firm value, the effect of a family CEO on firm value and the effect of family directors on firm value, as well as the combination of family directors and family CEOs on firm value. Among the authors that report a positive influence of family ownership on firm value we encounter Anderson and Reeb (2003a, 2003b), Lee (2004), and Sraer and Thersmar (2004). This positive influence is not homogeneous. In this sense, there is evidence concerning the nonlinear relationship between family holdings and firm performance (Anderson and Reeb 2003b). Anderson and Reeb (2003b) and Gnan and Songini (2003) find that family CEOs enhance firm value; but this relation is stronger for founding family CEOs among younger firms, firms with smaller boards, and firms with a single class of shares (Mishra et al. 2000). Anderson and Reeb (2004) report that the presence of family members among the firms' directors increases firm value and the results of Villalonga and Amit (2004) point to the beneficial effect on firm value of the existence of a founder Chairman along with a hired CEO.

Differences in performance are mixed with the founder effect. Therefore many papers distinguish between the family effect and the founder effect (Adams et al. 2003; Pérez-Gonzalez 2001; Sraer and Thersmar 2004). Because firms where the CEO is a founder are by definition family firms, these studies are related with the founder effect (Jayaraman et al. 2000). In this sense, some studies have reported the positive effect of a founder CEO on firm performance (Adams et al. 2003; McConaughy et al. 2001; Mishra et al. 2000; Sraer and Thersmar 2004; Villalonga and Amit 2004). The relationship between founding family ownership and firm value is greater among older firms, firms with larger boards, and firms with multiple classes of shares. There is also a positive impact of heir-managed firms on firm value (Sraer and Thersmar 2004).

Other authors find that family ownership has a negative impact on firm value. For instance, Barth et al. (2005) report that family-owned firms are less productive than nonfamily firms and Barth et al. (2005) and Lauterbach and Vaninsky (1999) find that family-owned firms that are managed by a person from the owner family are less productive; or the negative impact of heir-controlled Canadian firms on industry-adjusted financial performance (Morck et al. 1998), or the negative impact of incoming CEOs related by blood or marriage to a founder or a large shareholder in return for assets and market to book ratio (Pérez-Gonzalez 2001).

Some papers do not report significant differences between the firm value of family and nonfamily firms. In this sense, family-owned firms managed by a person hired outside the owner family are equally productive as non-family-owned firms (Barth et al. 2005); or family and non-family firms have the same profitability but different productive efficiency (Galve and Salas 1996); or they find no relationship (Daily and Near 2000).

CHAPTER 20

The European Social Model of Corporate Governance: Prospects for Success in an Enlarged Europe

Irene Lynch Fannon

> *The Lisbon strategy is even more urgent today as the growth gap with North America and Asia has widened, while Europe must meet the combined challenges of low population growth and ageing. Time is running out and there can be no room for complacency. Better implementation is needed to make up for lost time.*
> —Wim Kok quoted in European Commission 2005e

INTRODUCTION

This chapter will consider the competitiveness goal of the European Union as outlined at the Council Summit in Lisbon in 2000, summarized in the statement "that no one gets left behind as it strives to become the world's most competitive and dynamic knowledge-based economy." The express linking of competitiveness with employment, and social policies, a cornerstone of the Lisbon agenda or strategy, presents us with an imperative to consider simultaneously the issues of economic growth, employment and social policy from a number of different perspectives. This chapter will focus on European initiatives in company law and corporate governance and secondarily in labor market regulation as two areas that are fundamental to the advancement of the uniquely European approach. It is hoped that this will provide the reader with an initial understanding of where the European Union is seeking to place itself along a spectrum of potential approaches to these issues. Some issues regarding the effectiveness of the strategy will also be raised.

The first section will proffer a categorization of the European *social model of corporate governance* as compared with other governance systems, in particular the U.S. model, with the proviso that classification systems currently adopted by corporate governance scholars do not necessarily capture significant variations of type. The second section will consider continued development of European policies both before and after Lisbon in 2000, with particular emphasis on the mid-term review of Lisbon this year (2005) and on evidence of an intrainstitutional debate regarding the Lisbon goals. The third section will highlight the difficulties in establishing exact correlative connections and even more problematically actual causative connections between both corporate governance systems, elements of the Lisbon agenda, particularly those relating to labor market regulation and economic and social outcomes. Two particular issues of considerable concern to European policy makers will be considered: namely continued high unemployment rates and shrinking populations with a decline in the productive workforce. The fourth section will focus on particular challenges faced in the context of the 2004 enlargement to include 10 new eastern European states. Here regulatory harmonization of both company laws and social protection legislation presents acute problems, not only in relation to the existing body of community legislation (the *acquis communitaire*) but also in relation to future legislative planning. The conclusion will follow.

MODELS OF CORPORATE GOVERNANCE

De minimis classification of corporate governance systems would identify two categories of governance structures. The first, the *arm's-length financial model* of corporate governance, relies significantly on the capital markets as an accountability and monitoring device. This model is also described as an *outsider* model with the emphasis on shareholders, on the shareholder-management relationship, and on the market as a monitoring device (Fama 1980; 1991; Alchian and Demsetz 1972). This is the U.S. model. In the last decade or so, increased emphasis on shareholder wealth maximization has underlined an increasingly robust approach in the

United States to the resolution of conflicts between "other stakeholders" and shareholders in favor of the latter (Mitchell 2001; Millon 2002). In contrast there is the *relational finance* model relying on close internally constructed relationships between the corporation and the providers of capital, including both shareholders and bankers or other financial institutions. This model is also described as an *insider* model as it gives internal recognition through, for example, representative board membership, for stakeholders in addition to shareholders. Such stakeholders include creditors (financiers) and employees. This type of model is exemplified both by the Japanese experience (Gilson and Roe 1993; La Porta et al. 1999a) and in continental Europe. While many corporate governance scholars, particularly academics in the United States, describe the arm's-length financial model as being Anglo-American in character with the common law being identified as its legal progenitor, this classification ignores the significant shift in understanding of the appropriate corporate response to employees as stakeholders that has taken place in the United Kingdom and the British Isles since the beginning of the last century, and accelerated as a result of membership of the European Union since 1972 (Lynch Fannon 2004). Furthermore it underestimates significant local variations even in apparently similar corporate law rules governing, for example, the rights of minority shareholders (Lynch Fannon 2005; Nolan 2003). Similarly, within the broad category of *relational finance models* there are also significant local variations of these governance systems. This is true of continental European countries where differences are found as between member states of the European Union in relation to the recognition of workers' interests and rights, in relation to recognition of minority shareholder rights (COM (2003) 284/final); MARKT/13.05.2005), and in relation to the recognition of the rights of creditors (COM (2003) 284/final).

Nevertheless, in a comparative context, particularly in light of the transatlantic experience and in the context of the subject matter of this paper, the European social model of governance differs from the U.S. model of corporate governance in two fundamental and significant ways.

First, at a theoretical level, there is a completely different understanding of the relationship of the corporation to the state in terms of the achievement of what are considered to be broader policy goals, such as those outlined in considerable detail in the European Union's Lisbon Strategy. Under European policy the corporation is seen as the appropriate subject of state regulation, where the object of this regulation is to achieve broadbased social, employment, or economic policies as distinct from simply delivering an acceptable level of corporate behavior. Such policies and subsequent legislation can include legislation designed to facilitate investment in job creation and growth, legislation designed to assist in the elimination of social exclusion or poverty, such as legislation facilitating and supporting part-time workers to increase labor market participation (Directives 97/81/EC OJ (L 14) and 98/23/EC OJ (L 131) on Part-Time and Fixed Term Workers), initiatives to support a better work–life balance for employees (Directives 92/85/EC OJ (L 348) on Maternity Leave, Directive 96/34/EC OJ (L 145) on Parental Leave, and Directive 93/104/EC, the Organisation of Working Time Directive), or indeed legislation ensuring environmental protection and sustainable development. From the European perspective the corporation is seen as one of a number of *social partners*, all of whom have a role to play in contributing to the planning of both macroeconomic and social outcomes. In addition the European approach not only considers it appropriate to regulate external corporate relationships with stakeholders such as employees or the community (environment), but also considers it appropriate to regulate governance structures within the corporation, to reinforce recognition of stakeholders' rights specifically through mandated representation of stakeholders, creditors and/or employees, on boards of management (Directive 2001/86/ EC on worker representation on the board of the European company provided for under Council Regulation 2157/2001: the Statute for the European Company), the latter a feature of a number of continental European corporate governance structures (Dorresteijn et al. 1994).

Thus different divisions or Directorates within the European Commission such as the Internal Market Directorate, which deals with company law and corporate governance inter alia, and the Employment and Social Affairs Directorate, dealing with social protection, issue documents which resonate with similar assumptions regarding the interrelationship between corporations as the drivers of economic growth and others who may be the beneficiaries of broader societal goals. For example, the following is from Social Affairs:

> . . . *the Lisbon agenda must be owned by all stakeholders at EU, national, regional and local level; Member States, European citizens, parliaments, social partners and civil society and all Community institutions. They should all contribute to construct Europe's future. (COM (2005) 24/final)*

And this is from Internal Market:

> *An effective approach (to corporate governance) will foster the global efficiency and competitiveness of business in the EU. Well managed companies, with strong corporate governance records and sensitive social and environmental performance, outperform*

their competitors. Europe needs more of them to generate employment and higher long term sustainable growth. (COM (2003) 284/final)

In contrast in the United States this level of managed planning is not present. In addition, the *free market* ideal militates against regarding the corporation as some sort of tool of state or government planning. Furthermore the broader European concept of social partnership (inclusive of business and trade unions and other social groups) is completely lacking. In theoretical terms this has been described in earlier research as a contrasting view from both sides of the Atlantic of the corporation as a public or private actor and some examination of the significant philosophical and political theories underlying these particularly different approaches has been carried out (Lynch Fannon 2003). Interestingly it would seem that the theoretical view is probably overstated given the actual level of regulation of corporations in the United States, but nevertheless the ideological commitment to the corporation as a private actor in a relatively unregulated or free market is very influential. Many U.S. corporate governance scholars have claimed that the U.S. governance model represents the optimum model from an efficiency perspective having evolved over time in a relatively free market context (Friedman 1953; Alchian 1950; Easterbrook and Fischel 1991; Roe 1996; Hansmann and Kraakman 2001).

Second, this different European theoretical approach is given concrete pragmatic expression in extensive regulation of corporate activity—regulation that is not only directed toward normal or mainstream governance relationships between shareholders and management, but is also aimed at regulating the relationship of the corporation first, to its nonshareholding stakeholders, stakeholders that would be considered in the United States as external to the core activities of the corporation, and second, in its relationship to the state, in particular in the context of the Lisbon Agenda in relation to its role in contributing to the objectives. In the European Union the question is not *whether* the corporation should be regulated to achieve these goals, an issue which would still spark a pretty lively debate in the United States, but how and to what extent corporate activity should be regulated or corporations co-opted in the delivery of these important economic and social goals. Thus regulation is seen as a proper and appropriate area of enquiry in the context of the mid-term review of the Lisbon Agenda. Questions are raised as to the quality of the regulatory environment, the need to create appropriate "incentives for business, cutting unnecessary costs and removing obstacles to adaptability and innovation" (COM (2005) 24/final). Labor market regulation is a specific example of legislative activity central to some of the goals of the Lisbon Agenda, including the creation of more and better jobs and making Europe "a more attractive place to invest and work" (COM (2005) 24/final). Similarly a modernized system of company law is "essential for a modern, dynamic, interconnected industrialized society" (COM (2003) 284/final).

In conclusion therefore the European model of the relationship of the corporation to the state stands in stark contrast to the view of the appropriate corporation–state relationship in the United States. Policy documents and legislation influencing the domestic legislation of all member states, including the 10 new members since May 2004, has significantly altered the regulatory landscape, particularly in relation to employment and social protection and will continue to do so as the Lisbon Agenda is continued into the immediate future. Yet some corporate governance scholars have described this European model as a failed social model (Hansmann and Kraakman 2001) and it is timely to reflect on that diagnosis and consider what the issues are.

LISBON AND BEYOND

The period for achieving the ambitious Lisbon strategy described in the introduction to this chapter was the first decade of this century, concluding in 2010. This year (2005) has prompted much soul searching, research, and positioning as a mid-term review of the Lisbon Agenda was embarked upon. A number of key documents presented by the EU will be considered in this section including the Kok Report (European Commission 2003b), the High Level Group Report (European Commission 2004b), and most recently, in February and July 2005 respectively, communications from the President of the European Commission, President Barroso, and Communications from the Commission on the Social Agenda.

In its report on the future of European Social Policy in an enlarged Europe, the Commission-appointed High Level Group noted in keeping with the observations made in the first section of this chapter that "there is a distinct European social model" marked by "the consistency between economic efficiency and social progress." The Group identified three significant features of the social model, which are first a compromise between the state and the market, reflecting a theoretical opting for regulation as distinct from what a U.S. law and economics scholar would describe as a *free market approach*. Second, a compromise between labor and capital is accepted, and finally a compromise must be made between the welfare state and individual responsibility. In describing the social model in these terms the report notes that in the 1960s when the distinctively European approach was being developed by the original six member states the "conditions were excellent" with strong economic growth, low inflation, and confidence in public affairs as well as in individual rights. The report also notes that law and collective bargaining played a key role. However, these conditions no longer persist and this presents a challenge to adapt "the balance between economic efficiency and social progress" to take account of a changing economic environment and social context.

The High Level Group report reiterates a commitment to the three-pronged integrated approach to social, economic, and employment policy. It describes how from 1995 onward and toward Lisbon the EU and its member states "started revisiting their approach to social policy: affirmation of employment as an objective, and not only as an outcome of economic policy; increasing attention paid to social policy as an investment (and not only as a cost) and to the 'productive' role of social policy within the framework of a virtuous circle combining flexibility and security, adaptability and employability." The report emphasizes the importance of developments of the EU in this direction from the mid-1990s with the accession of Sweden and Finland, acknowledging the Scandinavian influence on thinking on these matters, on to Maastricht (1992) and the Social Charter and on to Amsterdam (1997) when the Maastricht Protocol was incorporated into the Treaty, and finally to Lisbon "with the affirmation of the integrated objectives and the launching of the open method of co-ordination as a new instrument to address social policy issues." (For a description of what is involved in the OMC, see the High Level Group Report 2004, 35, para. 2.2.2. In addition the OMC procedure will be included in the Constitution in relation to social policy under Article III-107 (High Level Group Report, 36). The relationship between reform of social protection and the introduction of OMC is considered in relation to legal and political challenges facing the Lisbon strategy in the fourth section of the chapter.)

The integrated approach, which was fully articulated at Lisbon, emphasizes an understanding that these objectives and policies are not in conflict but can reinforce each other.

By the mid-term review period of 2005, however, the statements as described in the Lisbon strategy seem less a reflection of reality and more a collection of noble theoretical assertions. Unemployment still remains a significant problem in the European Union averaging at 9%, compared with a much lower 4%–5% in the United States. Labor market participation figures compare unfavorably with the United States outside the core group of male workers of prime age (U.S., EU15, and EU25 figures for men of prime age between 25 and 54 are similar. See High Level Group Report 2004, 42 with figures from Eurostat, European Foundation for Living and Working Conditions, and OECD), and GDP growth has been lower than the projected annual rate of 3%, with figures for the U.S. being much healthier. In 2000 the Lisbon Agenda had stated that "an average economic growth rate of around 3% should be a realistic prospect for the coming years." Since 2001, the European Union growth rate, which was 3.5% in 2000, has been only 1.6% in 2001, 1.1% in 2002, and 1.3% in 2003. The forecast for 2004 was 2.3% (High Level Group Report 2004). The Report goes on to observe that 3% does not look like "a realistic prospect for the coming years." However, it is important to note that some differences in GDP growth as between the United States and EU can be explained by factors which are particular to the economic structures of both trading blocs (Gordon 2004a, 2004b). Yet despite these negative indicators and despite ominous statements from the Kok Report published in 2003 on the performance of the Lisbon Agenda in the context of enlargement, the Report of the High Level Group stated (in a surprisingly confident manner) that the first phase of the implementation of the Lisbon Strategy is now almost complete. It acknowledged, however, that "many actors stress the gap between statement and reality."

Table 20.1 is instructive (data sourced from Kok Report 2003, DGECFIN's Ameco database, Commission Service, latest updates to Commission's 2003 Spring Forecasts, Eurostat, and OECD for average hours worked).

The subsequent Communication from President Barroso acknowledged the difficult economic conditions which have occurred since Lisbon, but more significantly the President also noted that the failure of Lisbon to meet its mid-term goals could also be attributed to a "policy agenda which has become overloaded, failing co-ordination and sometimes conflicting priorities." In fact the Presidential address was quite overt in reflecting criticisms that had been leveled against the Lisbon Agenda regarding the burgeoning bureaucratic nature of the attempt to move Europe forward, the core objective of which had translated into 28 core objectives and 117 indicators. President Barroso clearly envisaged far greater focus than that

TABLE 20.1 GDP, Employment, Productivity Comparison EU15 and United States (Annual Average Change over the Periods Indicated in %)

	1991–1996		1997–2002	
	EU15	U.S.	EU15	U.S.
GDP	1.5	3.2	2.4	3.0
Employment	−0.3	1.7	1.4	1.0
Apparent labor productivity	1.9	1.4	1.0	1.9
Hourly labor productivity	2.2	1.4	1.5	2.2

achieved by the High Level Group. The group went well beyond the more focused goals as expressed by the President and included in an annex to the report a great number of matters and policy initiatives pursued under the umbrella of the Lisbon Agenda, ranging from Information Society initiatives, to Environmental initiatives, Education, and so on (European Commission 2004b, Annex 3). The Presidential address reiterated the main focus of Lisbon as being on *growth and jobs* and outlined three major strategies or goals going forward. These were to ensure that Europe is a more attractive place to invest and work; that knowledge and innovation are the heart of European growth; and to ensure that policies are developed which allow businesses to create more and better jobs. Similarly, the Communication from the Commission on the Social Agenda identified two priority areas:

1. Moving toward full employment, increasing the quality and productivity of work, and anticipating and managing change
2. A more cohesive society; equal opportunities for all

Putting Lisbon Back on Track

Although these documents try to identify cause-and-effect factors in attempts to reach solutions to the mid-term problems faced by Lisbon, it is not clear whether these cause-and-effect issues have been tested either on a statistical basis or an empirical basis. The yardstick against which the European Union measures itself tends to be the performance of other large economic blocks such as the United States and Japan, but even though some comparative figures are given there is little evidence of an attempt to understand the reality of these comparative figures or to question what these comparative figures might teach us. There does not seem to be any evidence of a sustained comparative analysis or indeed of a sustained internal analysis. That is not to say that supporting research has not been carried out, the criticism being more based on the fact that the reader cannot assess the potential impact of solutions proffered even where these are expressed in more than vague aspirational terms, because the articulation of the issues or the likely effect of proposed solutions is not precise. A further criticism is more substantive and that is that although the European policy makers are theoretically very confident of the European social model and its virtues, there seems to be a crisis of confidence when comparative economic figures are actually considered. This crisis of confidence is considered in this section in relation to the problem of unemployment, while the difficulties surrounding cause and effect between regulatory and other policies on the one hand and economic outcomes on the other will be returned to in the third section of this chapter.

High Unemployment

Further assessment of the position of Europe in Kok (2003, Annex 2) fore-casted an overall unemployment rate for EU15 of 8%, with some of the member states such as Ireland, Luxembourg, Sweden, U.K., Portugal, Austria, Netherlands, and Denmark in this group displaying lower than the average, and others, including the major economies of France, Germany, Greece, Spain, and Italy, displaying figures higher than this.

The High Level Group identified a number of factors contributing to the relatively high unemployment figures in the EU as compared with the United States. Thus low participation among younger people and comparatively (with U.S.) among women are identified as significant factors in contributing to an overall higher unemployment figure as compared with the United States. The report notes that for the core age group of 25 to 54 the figures as between EU15, EU25, and the United States, for percentages of population in employment are similar at around 95%–96%. For women in this age group the employment differential as between the United States and EU15 or EU25 seems to be at about 10%. However the biggest differential as between the United States and EU15 or EU 25 is in the age group of 15 to 24 where the employment differential is 13.4%. A similar differential is present in relation to workers aged 55 to 64.

Therefore it is proposed in the report to address the European high unemployment rate by increasing employment of young people aged 15 to 24, women generally, and older people aged 55 to 64. Proposed solutions for young people focus on matching skills with jobs, developing educational and workplace training in tandem, and encouraging "both public authorities and social partners (employer and unions amongst others) to foster a lasting integration of young people into the labour market." In relation to female participation, it is proposed to increase the availability of childcare and eldercare, to remove financial disincentives to women to participate in the labor market, and to improve on flexible working arrangements. Similarly in relation to the participation of older workers the report recommends decreasing of incentives in the social security systems for early retirement and promoting later retirement through pension reforms. Again the involvement of the social partners, and in particular (in the corporate governance context) corporate involvement, is invoked to "promote the implementation of lifelong learning for older workers," "to improve working conditions and to organise work structures differently," reiterating points made in the earlier part of this chapter regarding a different perspective on the role of the corporation in relation to social and economic planning as compared with the prevalent view in the United States.

In relation to youth participation in the labor market, there is no examination or analysis of what factors in the United States propel youthful labor market participation. To this writer's knowledge there is no managed planning in the United States involving "matching skills with jobs" or involving "local authorities and social partnership" (a concept that is alien in the United States) to foster lasting integration of young people into the market. Even if studies were to identify what causes American youth to work, the next question is whether Europeans are willing to actually take these on board. This brings us to the substantial criticism concerning the crisis of confidence in the European mission, the failure to resolve or address the acute tension between the requirements of Lisbon in terms of economic growth and the results of socially protective policies that have led to situations that are now considered to be problematic. A noted U.S. economist has described the nonparticipation of European youth in the labor market as the problem of the "lazy European youth," but the fact is that a stated European social goal is to ensure that young people stay in full-time education both at secondary and tertiary level. Where both high-quality secondary and tertiary education are publicly provided the financial incentive for young people to participate in the labor market is low, unlike in the United States where the cost of third-level education would certainly be prohibitive for most young people without some level of labor market participation. So we cannot fall into the temptation of explaining profoundly different outcomes by reference to easily constructed cultural stereotypes.

One of the core values of the European social model was to protect young people from having to work, to encourage young people to stay in full-time education, to facilitate that broad availability of state funded third-level education, and furthermore to ensure that young people, at least in some European countries, performed some kind of civic duty, traditionally military service but now different kinds of service, before taking up employment. No such centralized planning is present in the United States, particularly once high school graduation is completed. Participation in tertiary education, particularly high-quality tertiary education, is much more a function of the consumer operating in a free market for education, where the ability to purchase this good is a private choice, privately funded. In relation to high school completion, certainly a public good supported by all developed countries, the figures for the percentage of upper secondary graduates to the population as provided by the OECD for 2002 do indicate a differential between the United States, where the figure is 73%, and main European countries, where the figure ranges from 82% for Italy and France to as high as 100% in Denmark and 93%, 97% in Germany and Norway. This differential of almost 10% accounts for youthful participation differentials as far as 16-to-19-year-olds are concerned, leaving a much smaller differential to be concerned about in the overall bracket, regarding merely 19-to-24-year-olds.

Similarly in relation to older workers, it is not clear what specific type of reform of taxation or social security structures is envisaged. As regards the relationship between social protection systems and high unemployment, both the High Level Group and the later Commission Communication from President Barroso attempt to identify in better detail what is required. The High Level Group, however, has already pointed out a difficulty with this goal (generally acknowledged), which is that "within the EU competence for organising and financing social protection systems belongs to the Member states. Each Member State has a collective system which protects people against social risks thereby preventing and reducing poverty." The report diagnoses a broad problem experienced in many member states, specifically that the high cost of social security currently borne by employer and employee contributions deducted at source "negatively affects growth and employment creation and promotes the persistence of unemployment" by both creating a disincentive for employers to create jobs and creating a disincentive to work. The Presidential communication states, "Moving people from unemployment or inactivity back to employment and giving incentives to stay longer in the workforce all require the modernisation of social protection systems." It continues, "Member States should modernise social protection systems (most importantly pensions and health care systems) and strengthen their employment policies . . . [which] . . . should aim at attracting more people into employment (notably through tax and benefit reforms) to remove unemployment and wage traps, improved use of active labour market policies and active ageing strategies."

Moving forward in the next phase of the Lisbon Strategy from 2006 to 2010, the problem of conflict between social protection policies pursued throughout the union and the impetus toward employment is adumbrated. Unfortunately despite the diagnosis the problem is that essentially the devil is in the detail of social protection structures. This is also acknowledged at Commission level: "Conflict between employment and social protection often arises on account of the detailed features of policy. The switch from individual to family-based unemployment benefits, for example, has inadvertently caused a serious disincentive to work for the partners of unemployed person."

Yet, if the policy makers at the center are clear as to what needs to be done, it would have been helpful to facilitate reform with a clear identification from the highest level of particular features of each domestic tax or social security system which require reform or even to provide a state-to-state comparison as guidance. Perhaps the lack of detail is deliberate for the simple reason that if we consider what is being proposed for more than a moment, it is clear that a dismantling of what the European public consider to be the social model of Europe is intended. Political pragmatism overrides the need to be specifically critical of particular legislative supports, a pragmatism that has been more acutely felt since France and the Netherlands rejected the European Constitution in their referendums this year (2005). The adoption of OMC, or the open method of coordination of social policies envisaged in the Report, provides a neat if not entirely goal-centered political solution to these tensions. Given the public lack of willingness to grant further legislative competence to the European institutions as evidenced by the rejection of the European Constitution, OMC may be the only option at present in relation to harmonization of social protection measures.

Similarly in relation to female participation in the workplace, incentives to stay at home with children, which are both financial and legally supported (these are discussed in the next section) in the European Union yield results which are then considered to be alarming when it comes to considering labor market participation rates. It is argued here that concerns regarding the nonperformance of the Lisbon Agenda most importantly illustrate an internal intrainstitutional conflict between stated policy goals in some areas, monitored by one set of institutional players, and economic outcomes monitored by another. Despite the overt commitment to the Lisbon three-pronged approach, it is clear that the European Union must face and consider a difficult question. Either it takes the European social model seriously and lives with some of the consequences or it accepts that when it comes to employment rates we actually want to look more like the United States than we thought we did. Further analysis must take place to answer coherently several awkward questions. How do we really compare with the United States economically? What do GDP figures indicate? Is full employment a realistic or even desired goal? What about the interface between social protection measures and the operation of the labor market? What about the interface between publicly provided services such as education and health, which decreases the incentive to work, and the lack of full employment participation? Europe does not look like the United States, so why do we expect similar results when we look at one particular issue? In conclusion, policy choices made over the last 40 years throughout the member states (both original and recently acceding) have yielded particular results, but yet the alarms bells are ringing across Europe where the social policy goals have succeeded but the economic outcomes seem less palatable. In the United States some commentators are concerned with the reverse problem, the social costs of uneven economic success (Freeman 1996; Mitchell 1996; 2002; Millon 2002).

CAUSATIVE OR CORRELATIVE DETERMINATION BETWEEN REGULATION AND OUTCOMES

This section focuses on a more difficult question, the relationship between regulation and social and economic outcomes. In previous research regarding comparative distinctions between both U.S. and EU corporate governance models and U.S. and EU patterns of labor market regulation, it seemed clear that there are unresolved questions regarding the connectivity between structures and economic outcomes (Lynch Fannon 2003, 2004). Thus, for example, it cannot be assumed that a particular corporate governance structure delivers economic success or vice versa; nor can it be assumed that particular types of labor market regulation or deregulation have particular economic consequences in all cases. In fact most corporate governance scholarship is now concerned with the unusual rather than the usual. So, for example, why did Ireland's economic miracle happen against a backdrop of increased labor market regulation and indeed regulation of all kinds, including increased corporate regulation, environmental regulation, and so forth? Similarly, why is it that in some highly regulated European labor markets, most notably Sweden and in particular Norway, does economic success seem sustainable whereas this is not the case in others?

The conclusion seems to be that regulation is one, perhaps relatively insignificant factor in contributing to economic success. Furthermore, most corporate governance scholars now accept the path-dependency of corporate governance models and the proposition that there is no one-size-fits-all approach to corporate governance questions (La Porta et al. 1997, 1999a; Roe 2003a; Parkinson et al. 2000). In fact it seems to be the case that governance failures are present in many systems and that perhaps bad governance features are more readily identifiable rather than good governance features. Scandals such as WorldCom, Enron, Barings Bank, Tyco, and so forth have shaken confidence in the capital markets model of corporate governance.

At a recent UNECE Roundtable on Corporate Governance it was agreed by many contributors that different governance structures deliver different things and can be valued differently accordingly. It is much more complicated than we first thought to answer the question of what are the essential elements to a good governance structure rather than a bad. Nevertheless particular problems with corporate governance in Europe have been identified and European efforts to improve particular corporate governance elements will be considered in the next section. For the moment, in considering the relationship between regulation and outcomes one of Europe's biggest problems will be described together with legislation which has had a surprising effect on the issue.

The European Baby: A Near-Extinct Species?

> ... *Europe must address the challenge of ageing populations which in the long-run will result in a considerable shrinking of the working-age population while increasing the share of retired persons. Unless the decline in the size of the workforce is compensated by increases in labor productivity, potential growth will drop dramatically to around 1% by 2040. ... Such a decline in economic performance together with a rise in age-related expenditures would put the European social model under considerable stress. (COM (2005) 330/final)*

Despite the apparent support for families in the European model, the demographic figures belie the expected impact these initiatives have had on the birth rate. EU Directives impose significant burdens on corporate employers in facilitating leave for all employees in relation to maternity leave and parental leave. Harmonized standards across the EU ensure that these rights are available to all employees. However, in many European countries the harmonization of labor market regulation at EU level represents a *de minimis* situation where workers' rights and entitlements in many member states are significantly better than the minimum required under EC Directives. Furthermore Europeans enjoy mandated rights to four weeks' annual vacation and there is also considerable regulation of working hours at European level under the Organisation of Working Time Directive. On a national level considerable tax burdens are imposed on workers and business to finance family-friendly social protection initiatives.

Childcare provision is publicly funded and supported in Europe whereas in the United States a system of individually based tax credits seems to be the primary source of financial support for childcare. Typically the European countries have early school starting ages, much more so than in the United States. Yet, total fertility trends in the EU15 and EU25 show a similar decline from the 1970s to 2000 where the average birthrate for both groups has declined to 1.5 per woman during the 1990s and into 2000. This figure seems to be leveling off (High Level Group Report 2004). In the United States in contrast, where there is little or no support for many workers in terms of family leave (paid or unpaid) or vacation leave, the overall figure is much nearer 2 births per woman. The High Level Group report acknowledges that in this question there are broader social and cultural issues at play, but also notes that in surveys there is a gap between the actual number and the desired number of children women have.

Effectively despite considerable proactive positions in relation to protection against gender discrimination and the legalization of positive discrimination provisions in favor of women and despite generous mandated leave rights relating to birth, childcare, and annual leave, European women are choosing to stay at work and not have families. In the context of the EU as a whole it is instructive to consider Article 2(3) and Article 2(4) of the EC Directive 76/207 implementing equal treatment of men and women. These two provisions exempt both maternity provision and positive discrimination provisions from the principle of equal treatment. Decisions of the European Court of Justice have approved of positive discrimination measures in favor of working women adopted in some member states (Case-450/93, *Kalanke v. Freie Hanestadt Bremen* [1995] ECR I-3051, and Case C-409/95, *Hellmut Marschall v. Land Nordhein Westfalen* [1997] ECR I-6363). Furthermore the ECJ has approved favorable treatment granted to women workers in the context of maternity, where such favorable treatment is specifically exempted from the broader gender equality agenda (Case 184/83, *Hofman v. Barmer Ersatzkasse* [1984] ECR 3047) (Craig and de Burca 2003).

Older European women are choosing not to work at all. In this regard the policies and resulting legislation seem to have had no positive impact. When looked at in a comparative light the relationship between family-friendly policies, including legislation and other state-funded and voluntary initiatives, does not make any sense at all. The United States presents an entirely different picture, indeed a labor market that some have described as downright hostile to the family (Williams 2002) and certainly very little planned support, yet a higher birth rate. Similarly in both the U.K. and Ireland, the birth rate is higher than the European average despite de minimis support comparatively in Europe.

Nevertheless the solutions proposed by EU policy makers revert to the old belief that more regulation and more support will deliver, when already existing support has achieved very little. The experience of France in recent years and of the Nordic member countries are cited to support this approach, the report noting that "France and the Nordic member states have higher fertility rates because of better provisions for combining child care and work, and partly because of family friendly policies." Interestingly the Commission report shies away from pursuing what it describes as a *natalist policy*, although in some respects it seems that the relative success in France is as a result of certain policies giving significant financial support (in some cases an amount of almost 20,000 euros is available to support home care for children; this rate varies to this upward point from about 16,000 euros per annum) to parents for childcare.

The conclusion in this section is that attempts to tackle this big issue facing Europe again place faith in centralized managed planning, whether this is given expression in further regulation, adoption of further publicly funded social policies, or a mixture of both. The question raised is whether it is possible to deliver these outcomes in light of the social and cultural context and furthermore to ask whether imposing additional burdens on business and taxpayers can be justified in light of the doubts raised regarding correlation between regulation and outcome to date, particularly highlighted by the contrasting U.S. experience. It must also be pointed out that even where planning does seem to have effects, there seems to be a crisis of confidence, as there is regarding youthful abstention from the workplace, between the outcomes of social policies pursued over the last four decades and what is now considered to be desirable economically. Perhaps it is timely for those assessing the Lisbon Strategy to clearly articulate its vision for Europe without yielding to what seems to be an institutional case of profound ambivalence.

HARMONIZING THE REGULATORY LANDSCAPE IN THE CONTEXT OF ENLARGEMENT

Looking to the future and the impact of enlargement, the challenges facing the European social model of governance are threefold. First there is the problem of implementing the existing body of legislation, the *acquis communitaire*, and the costs that this will impose on emerging European economies. Second, there is the problem of lack of competence of the European institutions in relation to social protection provisions, which thus requires reliance on nonlegislative methods such as the open method of coordination (OMC), mentioned previously. Finally, going forward the challenges of harmonizing a complex body of legislation such as company law across a Europe of 25 nations cannot be underestimated.

The *Acquis Communitaire*

One of the most important of all the challenges and vital to the success of the enlargement is the problem of the *acquis* and the problem of regulatory competition or "race to the bottom," however illusory and illegal this may be. This is referred to in the Report of the High Level Group and a number of particular issues are identified. In particular from a lawyer's perspective there is a considerable challenge faced by all accession states in implementing the *acquis* and this must be distinguished from the more formulaic process of transposing the *acquis*. Particular areas of concern include implementation of health and safety standards, environmental standards and legislation on equal treatment as between men and women. Considerable difficulties will be faced both in terms of costs imposed on SMEs and costs generally in relation to modernizing an industrial infrastructure to meet current EU standards.

Beyond these particular problems the HLG report noted that there were several broad ranging issues facing implementation of the *acquis*, described as the problem of *the four gaps*. These are the difference between the broad integrated approach adopted in Lisbon and the more narrowly defined understanding of social policies adopted in the accession process; the problem that social dialogue structures will not be strong enough to support implementation of the social *acquis* in new member states, given what is expected of these structures, particularly from employers and particular sectors; the tension between the character of the social policies as developed from Amsterdam to Lisbon and beyond and "the trend to a liberal neglect of social policies in some new Member States in the recent past"; and finally a gap between "the strong egalitarian expectations of major parts of the population in the new Member States" and "the economic and political realities." These are effectively challenges to achieving a different balance between social protection and economic growth. There is also acknowledgment of the problems presented by lack of competence and doubts as to whether OMC can deliver.

Social Protection and Lack of Competence

In relation to OMC and social protection, the necessary reforms described by the Commission must take place on a state-by-state basis and this has been identified as a matter of urgency. The federal structure and the lack of competence, which the EU has in relation to these issues, raise questions about the ability of the EU to deliver. How can member states be persuaded to dismantle or at least reform certain aspects of social protection systems which have as their stated object creating incentives for people to return to work? Will this be politically acceptable in Europe? At some point it can be predicted that certain kinds of reforms which perhaps some would call for will be seen not only by the body politic but also by member state governments as a dismantling of social Europe. Will the OMC adopted in 2005 be successful in facilitating a creation of more modern social protection systems? The OMC was included in the European Constitution but this has now been rejected by both the French and Dutch public and its future is, at the time of writing, somewhat uncertain.

Harmonization of Company Law and Corporate Governance Models

When the High Level Group of Experts on Company Law issued its report in November 2002 (European Commission 2002b), some commentators were of the view that the group had espoused a more Anglo-American share-holder model as compared with the more continental stakeholder model as the future for Europe. However, this shift is not evident in the Commission's response and in its plan for harmonization of company law going forward (COM (2003) 284/final). It is interesting that in its report the Commission reiterates resistance to a deep-level approach to harmonization of European company law and corporate governance codes noting that there was no real perceived need for the latter, a point also made by the High Level Group. This seems to underline a resistance to convergence theories of corporate governance, recently popular among U.S. academics (Hansmann and Kraakman 2001; Bebchuk and Roe 1999; Gilson and Roe 1993). More profoundly a subtly described but significant emphasis on a stakeholder model is reiterated with a number of references to the improvement of governance for "shareholders *and third parties*" (author's emphasis). Third parties expressly includes creditors, reflecting the relational finance model prevalent in Germany and Italy. The Commission action plan calls for the modernization of protection of creditors with a view to "maintaining a high quality framework in relation for example to capital maintenance and alteration." Here there seems to be significant resistance to any further moves toward a liberal capital maintenance regime based on a par value, similar to that available in California and New York. Other creditor protection devices include the introduction of personal liability of directors for corporate failure, and director disqualification procedures. Further encroachment on an American shareholder model is evidenced in softer statements in the Commission document regarding the role of corporate governance in the overall European landscape:

> *An effective approach will help to strengthen shareholders rights and third parties protection. In particular, it will contribute to rebuilding European investor confidence in the wake of a wave of recent corporate governance scandals. The livelihood of millions of Europeans, their pensions, their investments are tied up in the proper, responsible performance and governance of listed companies in which they invest. (COM (2003) 284/final)*

In addition explicit reference is made to the Commission report on corporate social responsibility (COM (2002) 347/final) and to the Commission report on industrial policy in an enlarged Europe, which addresses the need for a more sustainable production structure as "a driver of growth and productivity" (COM (2002) 714/final). Finally in terms of specific reforms the Commission action plan confines itself to a relatively small number of specific issues, shareholder democracy, management compensation, management accountability for creditor loss and director disqualification, in addition to some initiatives to improve cross-border mobility, the latter being unquestionably important to the completion of the internal market. In conclusion therefore the Commission program for the reform of European corporate governance and company law is both conservative and realistic in its outlook recognizing the importance of flexibility of regulatory frameworks and the subsidiarity and proportionality principles of the EU Treaty, which supports the diversity of choice among member states of both regulatory framework and corporate form.

CONCLUSION

In terms of the newly revised and restated goals at the mid-term review point for Lisbon the European social model of corporate governance faces more difficulties than one would have first envisaged. Economic indicators have led to a crisis of confidence among the policy makers giving rise to tension between continued assertions of the core values of the Lisbon Agenda and goals which are identified as necessary to achieve in the next five years before 2010. This tension or conflict does not seem to have been resolved by the documents describing the strategy going forward. Furthermore correlation and in particular causative connections between proposed solutions and expected outcomes do not seem to be particularly well articulated in these review documents. This conflict is also reflected intrainstitutionally at Commission level. On the one hand, there is a willingness to be impressed by economic indicators from the United States without asking important questions regarding the underlying realities and without articulating substantially different contexts. Similarly those within the Commission who are solely concerned with economic or competitiveness matters espouse policies which are more reflective of U.S. theoretical and political policy approaches. This is indicated in the report of the High Level Group Report on Company Law. On the other hand, various parts of the Commission bureaucracy and perhaps a majority of the European body politic continue to place their faith in Europe's social model of governance and the integrated approach expressed in Lisbon to economic, employment, and social policies.

In relation to enlargement, the completion of a European regulatory landscape faces three particular difficulties. Whether the four gaps in relation to the *acquis* result in profound disagreement or rather simply a period of catchup played out by the new accession states is something one cannot accurately predict. In relation to all three categories of regulatory reform activity, the implementation of the *acquis* in new and indeed older states, social protection reform, and future harmonization, there is no reason to assume that this will be a passive process on the part of the accession states. On the contrary, it is entirely possible that some influence toward change may well be exerted by the accession countries and that the resultant Lisbon Agenda is changed from where it started in 2000. Although many documents have been prepared and considered it is clear that the stakes are very high not only for Europe but also globally. The following statement really underlines the importance of the project:

> . . . *we need to restore confidence in Europe's ability to create the conditions to meet its objectives. Europe can build on its rich tradition and diversity, its unique social model and draw from its recent enlargement which makes it the largest single market and biggest trading block in the world (European Commission 2004c).*

CHAPTER 21

Contract Negotiation and Internal Regulation Mechanisms in a Firm

Hubert de La Bruslerie

INTRODUCTION

The traditional stakeholders approach enlarges the view of the firm as a nexus of contract (Jensen and Meckling 1976). These contracts link managers, considered as operating representative of shareholders, with different other economic agents. The traditional agency relation between managers and shareholders is only one of them which has been privileged in literature. Many external stakeholders are identified: suppliers, consumers, clients, public authorities, government, lobbying groups (Charreaux and Desbrières 1998; Charreaux 2002a, 2002b). However, all these are not in the traditional focus of corporate governance. Internal stakeholders are different, for they set long-term relationships with the firm. They develop their economic exchange with the firm in a long-term partnership based on a contract. This is obviously the case for shareholders, executives, employees, and other suppliers of funds such as banks or public lenders (Dewatripont and Tirole 1994; Modigliani and Perotti 2000).

The necessity of considering economic relations with internal stakeholders as a negotiated contract satisfying both parties leads to an agency problem: stakeholders, as well as the firm, have different goals; they are risk averse in an uncertain economic world and experience information asymmetries. The design and the content of economic contracts between the firm and internal stakeholders are very different according to situations, but they all involve a certain or an uncertain transfer of wealth and/or economic resources. Moreover, they all have a deferred execution/payment aspect that involves the future. During the negotiation or at inception, they all involve an exchange of some elements of information either directly by disclosure of private information, or indirectly by using signals. Once agreed, an economic contract recognizes a complete set of rights and liabilities and each party becomes responsible for its execution. This responsibility is generally seen as a duty in the context of a legal environment where enforcement of contracts is possible. A third party, such as courts or public authorities, will guarantee the good execution of the contract (Jensen and Meckling 1976; Hayek 1973; Von Mises 1949). There also exist regulation procedures and social rules conditioning the contract.

This analysis is somewhat traditional and the link with the legal system or the sense of responsibility has been underlined by Von Mises (for instance, 1949). The idea is that an economic contract is not ex ante a fair game between two similar agents. Agents are free to contract, but not equal. Risk aversion exists and will condition the present utility of the future rights/liabilities in an uncertain economic world. Power relationships, and above all asymmetries of information, do exist and condition the process of contracting. Particularly, the creation of value ensuing from a contract is not equally shared. One can expect more than the other. But rational economic agents will not agree to contract if their present expected utility of monetary and nonmonetary proceeds from the contract is negative. The economic context means that agents are aware of the limited and uncertain quality of their information in their evaluation process. However, they can assess whether a choice is satisfactory. Law and the legal system are important only for contracts that have a legal existence. This status comes after negotiation, when the contract is "legally agreed and formally approved"; such contracts are explicit contracts and become objects in the legal system. The process of negotiation converges when an agreement is reached, but the outcome of explicit contract is not mandatory.

A specific category of economic contracts exists and should be pointed out: implicit contracts between two parties are economic contracts without a third party's eye. They have no legal existence, so they cannot be enforced. Such contracts organize a value creating activity or a reduction in opportunity costs, which profits are shared. They involve exchanges that can be explicit (payment) or implicit (private benefits). The negotiation process of implicit contracts is particularly refined. Implicit contract recalls that before being a system of rights/liabilities between two parties, an economic contract (1) results from a process of negotiation exchanging actual projects, hopes, and information and (2) exchanges future goods, economic resources, works, or incentive after an agreement is reached. The second step follows the first, which is particularly important for implicit contracts. These aim at organizing economic relationships between two stakeholders, at inducing behaviors, or at developing activities of control. They are very common in management situations.

Corporate governance perspective usually considers economic contracts globally. Corporate governance traditionally highlights external regulation by considering external authorities, by setting institutions, or by organizing procedures. External control by auditors, external control by the market, and external control by courts are presented as solutions to conflicts of interest (Shleifer and Vishny 1997; Stulz 1988). The first input for external control is transparency and disclosure of good-quality information. External regulations and rules is only one side of corporate governance. The basic problem is, upstream, to curb behaviors in such a way as to avoid conflicts of interest and undue appropriation. Corporate governance should also analyze the self-regulation procedures between stakeholders when they contract.

Contract negotiation is a learning school where internal stakeholders of the firm will exchange information and agree to self-regulate their behavior. This autolimitation process, when it leads to an agreement, introduces an economic relationship profitable for both parties. The traditional illustration is given by incentive contracts. Stock options, employees' ownership plans, or profit participation plans are explicit contracts based on the idea that one party is stimulated to undertake supplementary efforts from which will result a creation of value shared between both. These traditional incentive contracts are well identified in the literature (Grossman and Hart 1982; Grossman and Hart 1983; Holmstrom 1979; Holmstrom and Milgrom 1987; Laffont and Martimort 2002; Mehran 1992; 1995; Myerson 1979; Murphy 1999). But what is important is the contract design and the negotiation of its terms, in order to efficiently limit the conflicts of interest and organize the best creation of value. The process of negotiation itself creates value in two aspects: it leads to the partial delivery of private information, and it generates self-regulated behaviors allowing the convergence toward a joint equilibrium.

Implicit contracts are far more important in the corporate governance concern because they ensue from the fundamental conflict of interest in the firm between controlling and outside shareholders. An implicit contract of control is accepted by the so-called controlling group on behalf of the outside shareholders. The economic activity of control can create value for both parties and private benefits can be seen as the rent of control. The self-limitation in the process of implicit contract is not simple, because here the agreement is not formalized through the acceptance of terms, prices, and conditions. This is a situation agreed to by management. Even if negotiation does not occur, an equilibrium process exists, which limits the behavior of appropriation.

This chapter is structured in two sections. The first analyzes self-regulation in traditional incentive contracts. The second section presents the implicit contract of control. It underlines the role of debt. The information policy from the firm toward outside investors is then highlighted. A conclusion will follow.

SELF-REGULATION IN TRADITIONAL INCENTIVE CONTRACTS

We will look at two traditional incentive contracts with two major stakeholders: managers and employees. Stock options are frequently issued toward managers and top executives of the firm; employee stock ownership plans (ESOPs) are more broadly diffused to employees and middle executives. Even if the logic of these contracts is not the same, that is, award of options to buy stocks for the former, and direct purchase of subsidized stocks in the latter, the logic of the negotiation process is very similar. In both cases, there exists an asymmetry of information with one party knowing more about the firm and its true economic perspectives. In both cases, risk aversion will affect the behavior of the parties when negotiating.

Stock Option Contracts

Beyond the formal law regulation and tax rules conditioning the form, the length, and the characteristics of a stock options contract, we will consider here a stylized contract between shareholders and managers based on two key parameters. The first one is the exercise price E, which is supposed lower than the stock market price C_0. This initial discount premium is a strong incentive because, anything remaining equal, it will lead the managers to exercise the option. A discount is a potential wealth transfer that stockholders may want to limit. The second key parameter is α, the percentage of capital opened to the managers. These new potential shares will mechanically dilute the initial shareholders' wealth (Agrawal and Mandelkar 1987; Martin and Thomas 2003; Nohel and Todd 2002). The joint problem for both is to agree on two equilibrium values (E, α) defining an ex ante fair economic contract.

We call the equilibrium relationship between E and α from the shareholders' point of view *contract curve*. It can be an increasing or decreasing curve in the two-dimensional (E, α) plan. An increasing curve means a trade-off logic between the opening capital ratio and a discount in the subscription price. Shareholders will stimulate managers by giving them either a larger stake of capital or a larger discount in price, but not both at the same time. In a negatively sloped relation, the logic is not the same. The dilution effect is important and the managers' wealth itself becomes exposed to a dilution effect. Maintaining the stimulation pressure on weakly efficient managers will make the shareholders compensate dilution by offering larger discounts in exercise price. Then, a negative relation between α and E signals a possible entrenchment of managers looking at increasing their share of capital to settle their position in the firm (Berger et al. 1997; Jensen 1986; Morck et al. 1988).

The shareholders will consider the situation from outside and do not know in which framework they are. The slope and the sign of the contract curve depend on the effort function of the managers, which is private information. That function expresses the link between the efforts from stimulated managers and, as output, the increase in the firm's economic profit from which all shareholders will benefit. If possibilities of untapped profit and productivity improvement exist in the firm, or if a stronger incentive will result in better management decisions, the gains will be important. The effort function will then appear as very efficient. Conversely, it can be weakly productive if the firm is at its economic optimum with competitors and if possibilities of windfall profit from nature are negligible. Taking into account uncertainty will make things more complex. Moral hazard is possible. Will the managers undertake any effort? And if they do so, what is the exact slope of the effort function?

The design of an optimal contract between the two parties takes place in a situation of information asymmetry. Shareholders can only forecast the exact slope of the effort function and the real economic profit opportunities that only managers know exactly (or more precisely). Nevertheless, shareholders may be informed by managers, but this information can be inexact and deliberately biased. Managers can be boastful, displaying a probability of success in entering a new effort that is bigger than the real probability of realizing economic profits. Shareholders suffer from poor information, but they know that the probability of economic gain announced by managers in the negotiation of the stock option contract is flawed.

Risk aversion is also a dimension in the behavior of shareholders because they are exposed to a risk in the information quality. Shareholders ignore whether they are in a positive normal trade-off between E^* and α^*, or in a negative framework giving a rent to managers. Shareholders ignore the utility function and also the risk tolerance coefficient of managers. They cannot, in a first step, evaluate and set the best parameters for an optimal stock options contract in the sense of the best stimulation of managers and the best increase of the two parties' wealth. Besides the legal context where stock options are discretionarily awarded by shareholders who are the legal owners of the firm, to managers who are their agents, this situation initiates a process of negotiation. This process leads (or does not) to the joint setting of the two key parameters of the contract and conveys the partial delivery of private information.

Figure 21.1 illustrates the two possible situations for the contract curve according to the sign of the slope. If it is positive, there exists an infinity of optimal locus, that is, optimal contracts. In the situation of a negative slope, the set of possible contracts starts from the point $(C_0, 0)$. The only optimal contract for shareholders then is the one with an exercise price of $E^* = C_0$, which involves a zero value for α. This means that in fact no contract is agreed. Any other solution would imply a possible expropriation of the shareholders.

The Process of Negotiation   The process of negotiation will reveal to the shareholders the nature of the relationship between α^* and E^* they do not yet know and can only guess. Shareholders will try to make the managers deliver private information about the productivity of their efforts and the true possibility of their success in an uncertain economic context. Both parties know that the final setting of the percentage of capital awarded to managers is the shareholders' ultimate decision. The latter will begin to propose a first set of arbitrary values, α_0 and E_0, designing a contract that is not located on the optimal incentive curve based on the true economic information only known by managers. These will react because accepting a suboptimal contract, even if it is profitable for both parties, is unsatisfactory. Managers are drawn to signal an opportunity loss compared to an

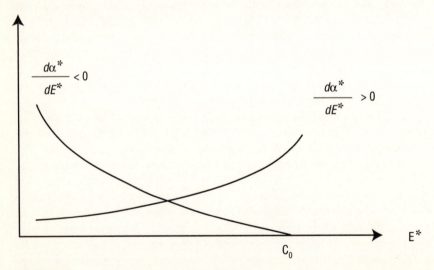

FIGURE 21.1   Relations between α^* and E^*

optimal contract to shareholders, because the managers' own behavior and future wealth will be increased in an optimal situation. The negotiation initiates explicitly or implicitly a process of exchange of information from one party to the other that creates wealth for both.

This process can be iterative and converges more or less easily toward the set of optimal incentive contracts. As an example, we can imagine the following step as the counterproposal by the managers of two possible contracts with the following set of parameters (α_1, E_1) and (α_1', E_1'). If $\alpha_1 > \alpha_1'$ and $E_1 > E_1'$, shareholders will infer that they stand in a framework of trade-off and that the equilibrium relation is positive. They are informed that the stock options are economically productive and that managers are aware that their efficient effort will enhance the future economic profit of the firm (see Figure 21.2a). Conversely, if the managers reply by proposing two contracts (α_1, E_1) and (α_1', E_1') with $\alpha_1 > \alpha_1'$ and $E_1 < E_1'$, we are in the opposite logic of weakly productive efforts leading to dilution of their wealth and entrenchment of managers (see Figure 21.2b)

We are led to a separative process of negotiation. The final outcome of the process depends on the sign of the relation $d\alpha^*/dE^*$. A positive sign will make the shareholders arbitrate between a discount in price and the share of capital proposed to managers. In the context of a negative relationship, the logic of proposing larger discounts in price and larger share of capital is nonsense for shareholders. They should limit the risk of a pure transfer of value. The only risk-safe solution then is the absence of stock options and the values $E = C_0$ and $\alpha = 0$ are the only joint optimal situation. The process of negotiation allows separating the frameworks and

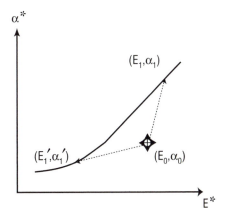

FIGURE 21.2a Positive Relation

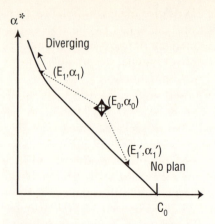

FIGURE 21.2b   Negative Relation

only productive stock option plans will appear. Three consequences can be drawn from this analysis:

1. The public announcement of a stock option plan is a priori good news as seen by the general investor in the market. Only efficient plans should appear; it is then normal that event studies will identify positive reaction on the stock market price (DeFusco et al. 1991; Desbrières 1997c; Yermack 1995, 1997).
2. Any regulation that will limit or constrain the negotiation process will entail difficulties in the process of separation between efficient and in-efficient effort functions and in the design of stock option plans. This is particularly true for tax rules, which in many European countries levy specific charges or costs on the discount. In France, a discount below 20% is practically forbidden.
3. Stock option plans with negative discounts (that is, stock exercise price at premium versus the stock market price) are possible and will illus-trate strongly efficient stock option plans.

The previous framework should be enlarged with the possibility of a common uncertainty for managers and shareholders. In the stock market, a white noise process exists that makes the stock price depart from its true economic value. This white noise is limited and known by managers who are aware from the inside of the economic value of the firm. These discrep-ancies are random and are either positive or negative. They are supposed to be small because arbitrage by managers buying or selling shares is possible. Such a bubble is a risk for managers because the true discount they obtain in a stock option plan refers to the true economic value, although shareholders will grant a discount based on the market value. In a situation with a positive (negative) bubble, the true discount is lower (larger) than the one negotiated with shareholders.

This source of uncertainty will affect their satisfaction as far as they are risk averse. A noise in the stock market is a fear for managers because a situation of overvaluated stock prices has a negative impact on the utility of the stock option plan as considered from their point of view. They fear plans that are awarded particularly in high-water market periods. The shareholders also are in a lower utility situation. They know that a possible and unknown bias exists in the observed stock price compared with the true economic value of the firm. They know that this uncertainty will modify the managers' behavior. The process of negotiation will then create value in itself for the two parties because of their common interest in delivering some private information. Managers are interested in signaling to shareholders situations where stock prices are overvalued. Of course, strategic poker games are possible (that is, assert that the market price is overvalued to ask for a larger discount). Nevertheless, a lower forecasted market noise (or a greater accuracy on the firm's true economic value) will enhance the situations of both managers and shareholders. The process of negotiation is a way and an occasion to disclose elements of private information on the under- or overvaluation of the market stock price. Reducing the information gap between the two parties will help the convergence of the process.

The Setting of an Optimal Contract A more complex situation where two sources of uncertainty cumulate will paradoxically lead to an easier convergence toward optimal contract equilibrium. The formal optimization program of the managers is then submitted to more constraints (La Bruslerie and Deffains-Crapsky 2001). Self-regulation makes them give less biased and more truthful information compared with the situation before negotiation. A joint equilibrium process means that they have to base their choice on economic optimal choices. Delivering private information nevertheless does not mean disclosing all private information or disclosing it perfectly. The dynamic of negotiation for a party is to influence the behavior of the other party by delivering exaggerated or biased information to make the latter's optimal choice converge with the former's optimal locus of optimality. A will to influence the wealth sharing in their favor leads each party to pull the contract curve in their own direction. The shareholders' curve is conditioned by their information level. Self-limitation exists because partial or exaggerated information entails a lack of credibility. A risk on the quality of the information delivered through the negotiation process makes the shareholders hesitate; a weak credibility results in no agreement. The analysis developed about contractual stock options negotiations between managers and shareholders may also apply mutatis mutandis when considering employees and shareholders in stock ownership plans.

Employee Stock Ownership Plans (ESOPs)

The formal and legal context of ownership plans is not privileged here, but we focus on the process of negotiation leading to an optimal creation of economic value through incentive. A joint equilibrium results from a set of parameters (1) leading to the larger value for both parties and (2) leading to the repartition of value which stimulates the employees at best (Chang and Mayers 1992). Such a joint Pareto equilibrium is not ex ante certain. The negotiation process can lead to a situation of second-best optimality where one party is not at its economic optimal situation and suffers an opportunity cost. Noneconomic considerations linked to power relationship, information conditioning, or contingencies, can lead to contracts resulting in an opportunity loss for one party and an improved profit for the other (Dhillon and Ramirez 1994; Gordon and Pound 1990; Pagano and Volpin 2002).

Similarly as with stock options, we are in a situation of an uncertain creation of value resulting from the incentive. If, by any chance, the firm is at its economic optimum, no value is created and an ESOP contract will induce a transfer of value to the employees who will profit from a discounted price at subscription. The ESOP contract differs from stock options in two ways:

1. Employees and other executives pay in cash for the new shares they subscribe. They risk their own savings. The concern is the reinvestment of these funds in the firm: What is the expected rate of return of the investment projects in the firm? Only managers and controlling shareholders know the exact answer (Hall and Murphy 2002).
2. A passive third party appears in the process: governments usually subsidize employee stock ownership plans. A tax-cut mechanism is often introduced to limit the cost of the discount given by the firm when it sells shares to its employees at a price below the market price. In France, for instance, the legal provision of the PERCO resulting from the 2001 law introduces a tax subsidy system representing up to 14% of the total amount of the shares sold to employees. So a discount of 14% will in fact cost the firm nothing.

A stylized analysis of the negotiation process outlines three major sources of information asymmetry:

1. First is the existence of a random white noise in the market price of stocks. Employees do not know the exact economic value of the firm. The real value of the discount is biased by the existence of possible bubbles in the stock market. Employees and middle executives do not know the true economic cash flow of the firm and can only observe the market price. Shareholders, in this framework, know it from the managers. But employees know that such a discrepancy exists and is limited around the true market value, otherwise shareholders will themselves arbitrage the market price. So, it is rational for employees to consider the market price of stocks with a zero expected white noise.
2. In the general situation, shareholders are facing imperfect information and a moral hazard situation from employees. They have an imperfect view of the probability of success of their effort and of the possible increase in economic cash flow resulting from it. Employees can send a biased message about the success of the incentive contract and dissimulate their opportunism behind optimistic and systematically biased information.
3. There is another source of information asymmetry penalizing employees: shareholders know the true profitability of the investments of the firm. They can announce expected returns to new investors that are optimistically biased to make them subscribe. To avoid dilution, they may choose to sell the new shares at a high price.

The process of negotiation appears complex here. It may converge toward a joint economic equilibrium and lead to the (partial) delivery of private information. The optimal equilibrium for employees doesn't depend on the information bias, on the probability of success of their effort, nor on the productivity of their effort. So, they can play with these variables to influence the shareholders and the setting of a contract. In this way, employees will condition the process of negotiation although the opening percentage of capital issued and the subscription price of stocks are shareholders' choices. But, too much boasting may affect the trustworthiness of information. Shareholders are aware that a bias exists in the information they are given in the process of negotiation. They forecast the average bias and can weight it by a variance measure corresponding to the quality of information. So, they can correct the forecasted new economic cash flow and estimate its true uncertain value (Beatty 1995). Because of risk aversion, employees are led to deliver better quality (but not totally unbiased) information on the true probability of improvement of cash flow resulting from their effort. This mechanism obeys the same logic as the one described above between managers and shareholders.

Shareholders have also in their hand a discretionary parameter: they know the true rate of return of the investment projects in the firm. They can modify the demand function for shares of the employees by issuing a biased good profitability. But too much exaggeration will mine the credibility of this information considered from the employees' point of view. Investing their own savings and being risk averse, they integrate a risk on the quality of information in their own calculus. Formalizing this problem is possible because employees can estimate an average exaggeration bias in the announced profitability weighted by a measure of quality such as the variance of the bias around its average.

Shareholders can also condition the convergence of the process of negotiation by using information on the true value of the firm compared to the market value. A better transparency on the true economic value will improve the expected utility of employees looking at buying shares. It may help to modify the equilibrium curve of employees' contracts and make it converge toward their own equilibrium curve.

In a global framework, it can be shown (La Bruslerie and Deffains-Crapsky 2003) that two economic key variables (profitability of the investment projects and probability of improvement of the economic cash flow) and three uncertainties resulting from asymmetries of information will condition the setting of a global equilibrium. With risk aversion, the interest of the two parties is to limit or to reduce (but not to cancel) the fuzziness of information added by possible bias. The process of negotiation does not converge systematically toward the delivery of unbiased and transparent information. The two parties will each limit the bias of optimism directed to the other and their attempt to manipulate the contract negotiation. Convergence means that the risk attached to a poor quality of information is self-limited by parties who are aware that a possible lack of confidence will result in a no-agreement situation. So, the partial delivery of private information coming from both sides will increase their expected utility and improve the economic equilibrium for both. This equilibrium is seen by the two parties as economically satisfying enough to share the profit of the incentive mechanism. However, it is not a Pareto-optimal equilibrium because strategic behaviors, moderately biased information, and power pressures still condition the convergence process. A minimal trustworthiness explains the convergence toward a joint contract that can mix economic and political logic (Pagano and Volpin 2000). In that sense, this joint contract is not Pareto optimal. But the convergence of a process of negotiation resulting in an agreement means that the sharing of the new value is not totally and strategically seized by one party. The basis for convergence is the logic of trustworthiness: as far as information is seen contaminated by an important bias, its quality gets lower and is put into question by rational and averse economic agents.

SELF-LIMITATION AND IMPLICIT CONTRACTS

The process of information exchange also occurs in contracts that are not formal contracts, but economically managed situations. There exists a category of economic contracts which are not formally legal contracts between two economic agents or bodies. They are called implicit contracts, and are common in a management situation. Implicit contracts are not enforceable by third parties or legal authorities. As economic contracts, they are supporting an economic choice and convey some information between two agents.

The Conflict of Interest between Controlling and Outside Investors

La Porta et al. (1999a, 2000) pointed out that controlling shareholders are very frequent in many developed countries, for instance, in Europe and Asia (Becht et al. 2003; Claessens et al. 2000; Faccio and Lang 2002; Klapper and Love 2002). Even in the United States (Fama and Jensen 1983; Gadhoum et al. 2005), the traditional view of generalized atomized shareholders is questioned. Considered from a theoretical point of view, the logic of concentration of ownership and power should be to improve the efficiency of the strategic control of the firm. If financial markets are weak, a better exercise of the control can be assumed by a group of shareholders. This activity implies time and expertise to monitor the management of the firm. The function of control is economically legitimate if it reduces management costs, improves economic efficiency, or improves information. The controlling shareholder bears some specific costs by assuming control of the firm's management. These costs will consist of lack of liquidity of their investment, which is blocked at a minimum control threshold, in implicit costs of underdiversification of their wealth, in personal involvement and work, in costs of strategic or audit consultancy. It seems fair that, as a counterpart to this activity, they earn a specific payment. This economic function of control is different from the function of investing in risky capital which is assumed by each shareholder. It is similar to entrepreneurship as described by Schumpeter, which is based on, at the same time, clairvoyance, a sense of innovation and assumption of some economic risk. The other shareholders appear as outside because they do not have access to the best economic information on the firm. Nevertheless, they have a legal right to the economic cash flow of the firm. Such a situation of apparent free riding finds a solution if we consider private benefits as a payment to the controlling shareholder (Grossman and Hart 1980).

The profit resulting from controlling the management will reward the work of the controlling group. This is done through a direct appropriation of the economic cash flow which is diverted by the controlling group (Bebchuk 1999; Dyck and Zingales 2002; La Porta et al. 1998, 2000). Means to appropriate are different: pyramidal structure of firms within a group (Attig et al. 2003; Bebchuk 1999), bilateral shareholding between two firms, and different classes of stocks (double voting right shares or nonvoting shares, Nenova 2003). The idea of *tunneling* refers to skill in manipulating the economic cash flow and diverting a part of it in order to create private benefits directed toward the controlling group and the managers (for example, Friedman et al. 2003; Johnson et al. 2000).

The economic debate on the rent of control is a question of relative sizes of the profit generated by this activity compared to the direct appropriation by the controlling shareholder. The answer is an implicit contract of delegation of control from outside shareholders to the controlling shareholder. Designing a fair contractual equilibrium is not explicitly possible because we face a political debate considering that a direct appropriation of a part of the economic cash flow induces an unequal treatment between categories of shareholders. Legal systems preclude or limit direct appropriation by a specified category of shareholders. Distinctions between cash flow rights and voting rights are frequent in the international context (Nenova 2003). Nevertheless, the global trend is protecting the outside shareholders and encouraging the one-share-one-vote principle (La Porta et al. 1998, 2000; Modigliani and Perotti 1997; Roe 2002b). In countries where legal systems and financial markets are weak, for instance, developing countries in Asia, the question of self-regulation doesn't appear because a political logic of pure expropriation may develop without any limit at the expense of outside shareholders. This is the idea behind predatory rent of control (Claessens et al. 2000; Guedes and Loureiro 2002; Klapper and Love 2002; Roe 2000).

The setting of an implicit contract involving a joint equilibrium may occur between these two polar situations. First, the existence of a legal system increases the cost of direct appropriation. We accept the idea that in many countries the risk and the cost (in terms of reputation, lawsuits, penalties, etc.) resulting from direct expropriation by the controlling shareholder will increase with the size of the diverted private benefits (Roe 2003b). Second, the uncertainty of the economic cash flow does not involve a guaranteed rent of control. Even if private benefits are diverted before public earnings, they remain uncertain and bear a financial risk linked to the financial structure of the firm. The design of that implicit contract is not formalized and does not proceed from an explicit process of negotiation. Implicit contracting means that equilibrium is possible, with the existence of self-limitation mechanisms conditioning the final equilibrium status.

That idea of implicit and contingent contracting equilibrium underlines the limit of the institutional external determinism of the legal system (La Porta et al. 2000; Roe 2003b). The overdetermination in term of cultural environment (ethical attitude), in terms of legal system (French civil law versus Anglo-Saxon common law systems), is limited because regulation should also recognize the contingent and idiosyncratic nature of internal regulation mechanisms.

The self-limitation process here involves a shared equilibrium based on the common signals evidencing an implicit contract between controlling shareholder and outside shareholders. They are (at least) two objective signals revealing the level of that equilibrium: the participation rate of the controlling group in the capital of the firm, α, and the debt leverage ratio, λ. The wished-for participation rate of the controlling group optimizing its global economic reward also refers to θ, the percentage of private benefits extracted from the raw economic cash flow. Profit can be taken either directly by expropriation, or through the sharing of public earnings. At equilibrium on the market, the wished-for participation rate of the controlling shareholder should be in line with the wished-for ownership from the outside shareholders $(1 - \alpha)$. An equilibrium situation means that the controlling group should act to influence and deliver information so that others will buy exactly the available fraction of capital $(1 - \alpha)$, knowing that an uncertain level of direct appropriation exists. If this equilibrium does not occur, the market price of stocks will reflect the imbalance and a control contest by a third party in the market can develop. Self-limitation appears because the behavior of the other party is integrated by the dominant shareholder. Even if outside investors are weak, even if they ignore the real expropriation rate θ, and as a consequence the real economic profitability of the firm, a process of implicit negotiation does exist because the demand functions for shares must be strictly opposite. The participation rate α is then an unambiguous signal. A process of convergence toward equilibrium should entail an exchange of information on a conditioning parameter which is asymmetrically shared: the forecasted economic return of the firm. Here again, we show the importance of a process of exchange information of which the quality is uncertain. Strategic behaviors may explain optimistic (or pessimistic) bias in the delivered information.

The Process of Exchanging Information and the Role of Debt Structure

We consider here that a controlling shareholder can follow two polar attitudes. In the first one (logic A), a self-regulated appropriation makes him optimize a trade-off between more direct private benefits and more standard payment ensuing from his rights to the public earnings. A limitation appears because the expropriation of the controlling shareholder should remain compatible with the demand of $(1 - \alpha)$ percent of the capital that he does not own. Conversely, in a logic of unlimited diversion (logic B), the controlling shareholder may be encouraged to increase both his private appropriation and his ownership of the firm's capital.

Expropriation through private benefits is feared by outside investors who a priori can only guess its level as a percentage of the raw economic cash flow. Let us imagine that a strong external regulation gives them perfect information on this amount which becomes publicly known. Such a situation does not converge toward a joint equilibrium because outside shareholders' participation is then totally determined by exogenous elements (required rate of return of the market, risk aversion). Nothing will cause their desired ownership to be coherent with the optimal ownership, α^*, of the controlling shareholders. One reason for that is the higher required rate of return for the controlling shareholder who will support a specific cost of underdiversification of their wealth and a cost of monitoring. That situation is not Pareto optimal because one party should leave its own optimum. The introduction of a minimum level of information asymmetry is needed to modify the locus of equilibrium of the outside investors and make them converge with the economic optimum of the controlling shareholders. The variables influencing the demand for shares by outside investors are:

- The forecasted expropriation rate, which is influenced by an exchange of information or by a communication policy of the controlling group. The probability p that expropriation occurs is subjective. It depends on the trustworthiness of the controlling group. A strong value of p means a lack of confidence. Expropriation is not certain, but random. The level of expropriation is also influenced by the legal system and the incurred risks. A good protection of minor investors will limit the absolute level of possible private benefits. We find here the conditioning role of the legal system as evidenced by La Porta et al. (1998, 2000), with Anglo-Saxon systems appearing more protective of minor investors.
- The bias in the announced future public economic profitability of the firm is a key variable for the outside investors. The controlling group

knows the true economic profitability of the firm, but they can announce biased perspectives of returns (Leuz et al. 2002; Liu and Lu 2002). This bias can be boastfulness (if positive) or modesty. A negative bias means a desire to move the outside investors out of the firm.

In any case, trustworthiness on the delivered information is of central importance. The outside investors appreciate the quality of the announcement by a measure of its possible dispersion around the true value (Bhattacharya et al. 2002 and Bhattacharya et al. 2003). The desired participation in capital by outside investors is a negative function of the perceived opacity of information about the economic profitability and a positive function of the credibility of the controlling group in not extracting private benefits. The controlling shareholder sets up an information policy whose elements are the bias in the announced economic results and the possibility of extracting private benefits. Trustworthiness covers at the same time confidence in no (or limited) expropriation and transparency (or limited bias) in the announcement of future returns. Manipulation of information is possible, but outside shareholders know that expropriation and bias do exist. A boastful behavior with abnormal profit announcement will cast doubt on information. Controlling shareholders ignore how their information is perceived by the outside ones. The probability p attached to their own behavior in terms of private benefits is private information of the outside shareholders. So, the controlling group cannot manipulate them without any limit because they ignore the way outside shareholders will react. If the information policy is considered trustworthy, an announced increase in economic results is a clear signal that will correspond to (1) a true change in the economic profitability of the firm, and/or (2) a will of the controlling shareholder to make the outside ones increase their share $(1 - \alpha)$ in the capital. It could mean, for instance, in a logic of trade-off (logic A), that the controlling shareholder looks for a lower participation in capital and a larger direct appropriation through private benefits. Conversely, such an announcement from an untrustworthy shareholder will raise doubts and result in a lower demand for stocks from outside shareholders, which is the opposite of what was looked for by the controlling shareholder. Distrust will lead outside investors to vote with their feet, which means, in the stock market, a drop in price.

The risk when a controlling shareholder chooses an information policy is that outside investors do not know if the controlling shareholder is following a behavior of self-limited appropriation (logic A) or a behavior of total diversion (logic B). The controlling shareholder does not know if he is perceived as trustworthy or not. A necessary period of information exchange occurs when, by a learning process, the controlling shareholder sees how the outside investors will interpret his information policy. This could explain:

- Why identical information policies between two firms may have opposite consequences regarding the participation of the outside investors in the capital. For some firms, a positive announcement will result in a higher demand of shares from trustful or credulous minor investors. In others, outside investors facing the same information will fear boastfulness. In the stock market, opposite reactions to the same information can be rational.
- Why investors may face erratic or variable information policies from the same firm, because the controlling shareholder tests how the outside shareholders filter information and react, and whether they are trustworthy. Learning is exchanging information and reaction. The result from this exchange of information is not a priori known by the two parties and reputation can play a role.
- Why a modification in the controlling group ownership may have no consequences in the stock market. In a perspective of fair and adequate information policy, a higher (or a lower) participation in capital can meet a symmetrical demand from outside investors who sell (or buy) shares in accordance with the new information they are delivered. We should then expect an increase in communication flow and better information around the period of change or modification in control.

The Role of Debt

In the previous analysis, outside shareholders only consider and observe α, the fraction of capital held by the controlling shareholder (and only on an ex post basis). Introducing debt will enlarge their analysis because debt leverage is another objective signal they can use to infer the behavior of the controlling shareholder (Brailsford et al. 2002).

In a context of private appropriation of profits, debt plays an important role because it helps to overcome the limit imposed by the amount of equity and the financing constraint of the controlling group (Faccio et al. 2001). We know from traditional agency analysis that debt is considered as a disciplinary tool in the manager–shareholder conflict (Harris and Ravis 1988, 1990; Heinrich 2000). Debt limits the discretionary behavior of managers; a similar analysis can be done considering controlling shareholders. Debt service is mandatory and is paid using the economic cash flow of the firm. Interest payments should be paid first. A controlling shareholder, with a long-term view of appropriation, wants to avoid bankruptcy and will expropriate private benefit only after the payment of debt interests. So, the signal given by the debt leverage ratio, λ, is of most importance for the outside investors. It appears as an element of the implicit contract of control (Zhang 1998).

In a situation with debt, the controlling shareholder has to optimize three key parameters: α, λ, and θ, respectively his ownership in capital, the debt ratio, and his direct appropriation of private benefits. Outside shareholders will only observe the first two and guess with some noise the third one. Nothing will insure that the two optimizations will result in a joint solution. Particularly, we get the same conclusion regarding the perfect information and pure transparency case: then best choices for each party are not compatible. The equilibrium in such a framework is not Pareto optimal when considering the economic situation of one of the two parties. Information asymmetry considering either the announced future return or the private appropriation eventuality, or both, is needed to restore a negotiation process and to converge toward a joint common equilibrium. The controlling investor should define an information policy, taking the risk of badly specified or untrustworthy communication. The set of information variables used is enlarged because he can play on the two equilibrium parameters α and λ to influence the outside shareholders. The conditioning variables for their equilibrium are the same as above:

- The future economic profitability of the firm announced with a possible bias of boastfulness or modesty
- The perceived probability regarding the eventuality of a direct expropriation through private benefits
- The trustworthiness or fuzziness around the estimated appropriation rate

The backward solution of the optimization program of the outside investors is done through manipulation and design of an information policy by the controlling group. But, the need of trustworthiness will limit information manipulation or exaggeration. Unreasonable or doubtful information will contaminate credibility, and outside investors will ask more to cover the risk linked to the information asymmetry. For instance, considering the adjacent problem of IPOs, Chen et al. (2001) or Labegorre and Broubaker (2005) show that a positive relation exists between the sizes of the optimistic biases in future announced earnings at the offer and the price decline in the market after the offer.

Considered from the outside investors' point of view, the information policy is global and covers several elements. There is a continuum between information regarding appropriation and a bias in the announced return. The first case is a cut in the economic cash flow due to an "organizational cost" ensuing from an implicit mandate of control. In the second one, boastfulness is an artificial increase in future earnings. In both cases the true net economic return of the firm is lower. To lie or to steal has the same consequence for outside investors when lying consists in overvaluing stock values, that is, to sell dreams. We get identical economic programs to solve between controlling and outside shareholders only when supposing perfect information, no private appropriation, and no specific costs for the controlling shareholders (that is, identical valuation rates). That situation corresponds to the traditional "Berle and Means situation" where the group of shareholders is homogeneous. The only remaining variable is the indebtedness and we collapse into the traditional agency conflict between a group of lenders and a (unified) group of shareholders.

The idea of control is linked with information asymmetry and the management of an information policy. Flexibility when using direct appropriation helps the controlling shareholder without making it necessary to manipulate information about the future expected earnings. He can deliver better information on the true economic return and the information becomes trustworthy. Conversely, we can imagine that a manipulated information policy takes place when the expropriation of private benefits is difficult. Greenspan (2002) pointed out that forecasts of earnings in the United States were systematically and optimistically biased. Considering the S&P 500 firms, the average expected increase in profits was 12% per year according to analysts, during the period 1985–2001. In fact, the real average increase covering this period was only 7%. We can hypothesize that the more constraints or limits on direct appropriation exist, the lower private benefits are and the more it becomes necessary to manipulate information announced to general investors about the future profitability of the firm. The analyses of La Porta et al. (1998, 2000), which underline a close relationship between legal and contractual systems and investors' protection, are partial. They should account for the level of trustworthiness and the average quality of information delivered by firms and diffused by financial intermediaries. Countries like Anglo-Saxon ones where the protection of outside investors is good may be those where information is systematically biased. The reason is the need to get an adjustment variable to influence the behavior of outside investors in the market. In countries where direct expropriation by a controlling shareholder is possible, an equivalent manipulation of information is not as much needed. Financial information and forecasts may be of better quality there (thief or liar, but not necessarily both).

CONCLUSION

Corporate governance aims at making explicit what is often implicit in the firm's management. To make explicit does not only mean implementing external regulation, imposing procedures, and reporting obligations. External regulation through third-party control gives a great importance to the formal existence of procedure and to the compliance with rules. The danger is pure formalism. Within firms, internal regulations and mechanisms will lead to disclosure of information and self-limitation of behaviors of stakeholders involved in long-term relationships. Designing economic contracts and accepted rules is a complex activity that needs to mix adequately incentives and penalties; negotiating the contractual commitments imposing these rules is part of the art of management.

This chapter has looked to highlight the place of the economic contractual process within the firm as a learning mechanism regulating the behavior of stakeholders. The process of negotiation regulates because it leads to self-limitation of pure opportunism and to the partial delivery of information as a common good. Total transparency is not possible because negotiation is a discovery process and both parties need to issue signals through objective variables. The internal regulation between inside stakeholders is pegged with the negotiation of incentive contracts. But it also exists when implicit contracts are involved, as we showed when considering the control activity delegated by outside shareholders to a controlling shareholder. These internal regulation mechanisms are at the heart of financial governance because self-limited equilibrium does curb behaviors even if we consider the possibility of private benefits. The negotiation process is in itself an economic good creating value, disclosing better information or helping the convergence toward an agreement. Future developments in this area can be twofold: the first one is the analysis of communication policy and trustworthiness; the second will privilege an empirical point of view to look at a possible link between the efficiency of protective legal systems and the overall quality of financial information toward outside investors.

CHAPTER 22

Prospects and Limits of Corporate Governance Codes

Björn Fasterling

INTRODUCTION

Following the publication of the Cadbury Report's "Code of Best Practices" in 1992, there has been a significant production of nonlegislative codes that deal with corporate governance issues. The pace of this development is astounding, even for those who have become used to the hastiness of our times. To illustrate, the most detailed comparative study that treats corporate governance codes in Europe (Weil, Gotshal, and Manges 2002) requires revision after only three years of being published, because the number of codes that the study identifies nearly doubled (if we apply the study's own definition of *corporate governance code*), and many of the existing codes the study mentions were amended. Also around the globe there is a burgeoning of codes that try to establish corporate governance standards. The web site of the European Corporate Governance Institute indexes codes throughout the world with easy accesses to the respective texts (http://www.ecgi.org/codes/all_codes.php), an impressive demonstration that the *code movement* has become a global phenomenon. The worldwide proliferation of the code idea caused some to speak of the "triumph of the code" (Monks and Minow 2004, 297).

All the same, the euphoria is tempered with question. Corporate governance codes are sometimes suspected of paying a partisan tribute to influential minority investors, whose relative powers grow as shareholdings disperse (see Convert 2003, 142 et seq., 251 et seq. with further references). A more pragmatic skepticism simply questions the effectiveness of voluntary corporate governance codes as disciplinary instruments (see, for example, Wymeersch 2004, 156–157).

The fact that corporate governance codes have been issued by different bodies aiming to serve a variety of purposes further poses the problem of a broad definition. A corporate governance code's defining features seem to be limited to (1) not being a law, and (2) providing for a systematic array of prospective norms concerning the institutional structure of a company's direction, control, and risk management.

Anybody could draft and publish such a text. For this reason it is worthwhile examining corporate governance codes by the manner they attract attention and claim normative authority (for one plausible classification see Weil, Gotshal, and Manges 2002, 13 et seq.). This approach, however, would require an empirically supported analysis of the factual effects of different types of corporate governance codes, which cannot be done in limited space.

The following will therefore confine itself to an argument that corporate governance codes create but modest incentives to adjust corporate governance practices to the norms a code proposes, but make an important contribution to the global exchange of ideas on how companies should be directed and controlled. In the following the term *normative authority* will be used to describe the extent to which a corporate governance code disciplines the behavior of companies.

The argument will be developed alongside the presentation of three functions of corporate governance codes, which will be referred to as *referential*, *metrical*, and *communicational*. In its referential function a corporate governance code helps to rationalize corporate governance reporting by providing a point of reference (in the second section of this chapter). The metrical function describes how corporate governance codes facilitate the measurement of corporate governance (in the third section). Finally, the communicational function stands for the opportunity of creating a corporate governance language that furthers a global exchange of ideas (in the fourth section).

REFERENTIAL FUNCTION

In its recent proposal to amend the fourth company law directive, the European Commission promulgates the idea that each listed company should be legally obliged to report on corporate governance using a corporate governance code as a *point of reference* (European Commission, COM (2004) 725 final of Oct. 27, 2004). According to Article 46a, the proposed directive text, a company may choose to refer to any corporate governance code it wishes to—as long as it is not subject to one certain code under the law. This proposal prompts a series of to-date unresolved questions, one being on the minimum quality a code needs to have in order to become an appropriate point of reference. However, the basic idea is clear and finds its equivalences also outside of the European Union: companies are required to report on corporate governance addressing the standards recommended by a nonlegislative best practices code.

This approach was inspired by the linking of the Cadbury Report's best practices code to U.K. financial regulation. The U.K. model was the first to combine an advisory code of best practices with a legally binding disclosure obligation. The hybrid of voluntary code compliance and mandatory disclosure is viewed as an optimal governance regime (see, for example, Anand 2005, 43 et seq.). As will be argued in the following, it may be a regime that facilitates corporate governance reporting, but it only moderately incites companies to observe the norms a referenced code recommends.

Comply or Explain

The Cadbury Report attained its prominent position in the U.K. because the London Stock Exchange, at that time in its function as U.K. Listing Authority, was willing to integrate the Cadbury Report's best practices code in its admission to listing process on the basis of a disclosure regime, to which we refer today under the name *comply-or-explain* principle. Under this principle, listed companies are required to publicly declare whether they comply with the norms the code recommends and, as may be the case, explain deviations of their practices from a code's recommendations. Today, U.K. financial regulation refers to the present successor of the Cadbury Report's best practices code, the Combined Code on Corporate Governance that was drafted and is regularly revised by the U.K. Financial Reporting Council (FRC). Paragraph 12.43A of the U.K. Listing Rules, now adopted by the U.K. Financial Services Authority, contains a comply-or-explain obligation for listed companies. The text of the Combined Code does not form part of the Listing Rules, but is appended to them.

With the comply-or-explain obligation that refers to a best practices code, the U.K. Listing Rules assume quite a different approach from the listing requirements of the New York Stock Exchange (NYSE), which directly prescribes certain corporate governance standards (see NYSE, Corporate Governance Rules in 303A of the Listed Companies Manual).

Implicit in the comply-or-explain principle is a two-tier order of compliance, the first tier relating to a voluntary compliance with a code's prospective norms, and the second tier, the compliance with the comply-or-explain principle, to the fulfilment of a legal disclosure obligation.

The Dutch example provides an even better illustration for the two-tier order of compliance than its U.K. model. In the Netherlands, a governmental order that implements a Dutch civil code provision (see Art. 2:391 para. 4 Dutch Civil Code and Order of Dec. 23, 2004, Staatsblad 2004/747) mandates corporate governance disclosure by reference to the Dutch corporate governance code. Interestingly, the Dutch code's preamble uses the expression *pas toe of leg uit*, which literally translates into *apply or explain*. Commentators point out that the literal translation is also the most appropriate one (Huizink et al. 2004, 429). Under apply or explain, *explanation* is not an alternative to (legal) *compliance*. This clarifies that only the compliance with the disclosure obligation is legally relevant, which, for example, helps lawyers to confirm under the current rule 303.00 of the New York Stock Exchange's Listed Company Manual that a Dutch company listed on the NYSE *complies* with its home country's laws and rules.

Other examples, where a law or a governmental order contains an obligation for listed companies to refer to a certain corporate governance code, are Germany (see para. 161 Stock Company Act), Spain (see Art 116(4)(f) of the Spanish Security Markets Law), and Portugal (Art. 1(1a) of CMVM regulation No. 7/2001).

In many countries the comply-or-explain or similarly labeled obligation is not an element of governmental regulation or legislation but a matter of self-regulation. Often the comply-or-explain requirement is incorporated into the listing rules of a stock exchange. By this means the comply-or-explain or similarly labeled principle becomes an integral part of the listing agreement between two private persons, namely the stock exchange and the issuer. Examples where a stock exchange's listing rule obliges companies to disclose on corporate governance by referring to a code can be found in Australia, Canada, Finland, Hungary, Ireland, Italy, or Singapore. India provides a slightly different approach. Here the regulatory authority, the Security Exchange Board of India (SEBI), is empowered by the law to draft provisions of the Listing Agreement that Indian stock exchanges must use. The SEBI introduced a clause 49 to this Listing Agreement, which contains corporate governance provisions and an obligation for listed companies to report on corporate governance—including a statement on the level of compliance with clause 49 provisions (see SEBI circular SEBI/MRD/SE/31 of August 26, 2003). The SEBI was guided by a corporate governance report that an SEBI-appointed expert committee (chaired by Shri Kumar Manglam Birla) published in 2000.

Disclosure under the comply-or-explain principle, if legally mandatory, seeks to reverse the sense of a company's public declaration on corporate governance. Without a legal obligation to comply or explain, a company could send a positive signal to the public by voluntarily stating its compliance with a well-reputed code, whereas under a legal comply-or-explain obligation a company must publish a declaration to avoid a negative signal, which ultimately places the company on the defense.

With the adoption of corporate governance codes and the integration of the comply-or-explain principle into a legally binding disclosure regime, we can say that securities regulation is permeating areas traditionally governed by company law. The capital markets are being used as the lever to change company law standards—at least with regard to companies that seek financing on public markets. This might be explained by the relative power of institutional investors, who can more effectively influence the rule-making of securities regulation than in the field of company law, where rules are in most cases changed following a parliamentary procedure, which involves the participation of many different actors (Davies 2003, 277).

Where there is a legal obligation to report on corporate governance under a comply-or-explain principle, the question arises as to how this obligation can be enforced and by whom.

Enforcement Difficulties

A stock exchange remains relatively independent in enforcing the comply-or-explain obligation. It can refuse a company's admission to listing. In cases where companies are already listed, a stock exchange could impose financial sanctions or even de-list a company. An exchange can also confine itself to publicly censuring a company for its nonobservance. If a stock exchange is under commercial pressure, there is a risk that it refrains from enforcing any kind of sanctions at all.

The latter problem could be solved by having enforcement powers vested in an independent or governmental financial authority. Even then problems remain. Inaccurate corporate governance disclosures are difficult to detect, and where disclosures are accurate, they may have hidden implications that are difficult to uncover (see Kraakman 2004, 106). For this reason, even if an independent or governmental authority were given the power to initiate investigations, report irregularities, and impose sanctions, it would still need to be endowed with sufficient financial means and a highly trained staff to carry out its tasks. It deserves questioning as to whether the costs of effective enforcement would ever justify the benefits of accurate corporate governance disclosures. The legally binding comply-or-explain mechanism has been in place in the U.K. for over 10 years, but the FSA makes no judgment on the accuracy or adequacy of compliance statements, leaving these matters for the judgment of directors and shareholders (see FRC 2003c, 6).

Matters are further complicated by the fact that inaccurate disclosures could often occur involuntarily, since companies cannot benefit from a judicial interpretation of code provisions or legal disclosure obligations. This problem cannot be resolved unless an authoritative body has the occasion and power to interpret provisions of a corporate governance code in individual disputed cases. Without authoritative interpretation, compliance statements risk becoming incorrect where code provisions are ambiguous. Experiences in the U.K. provide an illustration for different perceptions regarding compliance: There is considerable divergence between the percentage of companies who consider themselves to be fully compliant with the Combined Code (47%) and the percentage of companies that Pensions Investment Research Consultants Ltd. (PIRC) regards as being fully compliant (34%) (PIRC 2004, 9). Without authoritative interpretation, also noncompliance explanations risk becoming insignificant, brief, or uninformative because there is no guidance regarding the minimum quality required for such explanations. PIRC comments in its 2004 annual review that noncompliance explanations often "represent little more than a statement of the board's disagreement with a provision's appropriateness for the company" (PIRC 2004, 9). Obviously, such statements do not fulfill the objective of comply or explain, which is to allow investors to make an informed assessment of whether noncompliance is justified in the particular circumstances. In view of the practical difficulties experienced in the U.K., paragraph 161 of the German Stock Company Act seems to provide a more rationalized solution by requiring only a statement of noncompliance rather than an explanation for deviating practices.

Maybe also because of the apparent enforcement difficulties we find many examples for corporate governance codes that aspire after a nationwide application and invoke a comply-or-explain-like principle *without* being a point of reference of a legal disclosure obligation. Examples may be found in Austria, Brazil, Denmark, or in Russia. In these cases both tiers of compliance are voluntary, which avoids the subject of enforcement of legal disclosure obligations. Of course, *purely voluntary* codes offer no cure for the lack of normative authority of corporate governance codes described above. Companies will follow code recommendations and report accurately on corporate governance, solely if it is in their own interest.

Where legal enforcement is weak or absent, the comply-or-explain principle will not be able to back up the normative authority of an advisory corporate governance code. The normative authority of a referential code still benefits from a different source, which will be examined in the following.

Reliance on Market Forces and Public Opinion

Companies are free to implement code provisions. Still, a corporate governance code will usually prospect for a wider application of the standards it recommends. The conjunction of voluntary compliance with prospective standards and corporate governance disclosure (legally binding or not) offers companies a certain degree of flexibility, but at the same time is designed to place companies on the defense by making them report deviations. The rationale underlying this structure is that market mechanisms will cause firms to adopt a code's best practices recommendations, which would result in a high rate of compliance at low enforcement costs. One could ask at this point, how market forces will lead companies to adopt best practices if they are already unable to compel companies to choose the appropriate amount of disclosure.

The implementation of a voluntary code of best practices, as it is well expressed by the Cadbury Report, relies on *climate of opinion* that pressurizes a company to adhere to the code's proposed standards (Cadbury 1992, 18). Now the *public opinion* offers a rather diffuse source of authority. This makes it difficult, if not impossible, for companies to rationally decide whether to implement the standards of one or the other corporate governance code.

Companies will most likely orientate themselves toward code texts that receive widespread attention. A code's prominence will be determined by various factors: by the code's integration into a legal framework, by its governmental endorsement, by its endorsement through a stock exchange or other influential organization, by the reputation of the code-issuing body, by the manner institutional investors and rating services measure compliance with a certain code text, by a code's coverage in the financial media, or even by academic research on corporate governance codes. The popularity of a code is the motivation for a number of companies to declare their adherence, inflicting adverse publicity on companies that do not. A code's *informal* authority therefore grows as more companies are willing to follow its recommendations. One could say that companies decide to comply for the fear of being sorted out as a negative example. There are publications that amplify this mechanism by regularly reporting the level of compliance with certain code provisions (for the U.K., see PIRC 2004; for a German example, see von Werder et al. 2003).

However, if public opinion focused too much on compliance rates, companies could also become encouraged to go along with a custom of stating compliance without analysis and questioning, which would increase incentives to produce unreliable corporate governance information. A company might prefer risking false disclosure to accuracy, or mounting a façade of compliance rather than true compliance. This phenomenon is often portrayed as *ticking the boxes* and is virulent where verification systems are weak or absent. Over time a compliance statement might not be perceived as a positive signal any more, but could become comparable to copying an empty ritual that is published in an etiquette book (on the adverse normative effects of etiquette books see Posner 2002, 27). Compliance with corporate governance codes risks being reduced to a display of compliance.

Finally, by relying on the threat of adverse publicity, the normative claim of a corporate governance code faces up to a different, less visible challenge: A sound level of public scrutiny toward corporate governance practices might be difficult to sustain. Corporate governance codes have attracted much attention in recent years, but it is not certain whether this attention will remain unchanged, especially once public confidence in the functioning of capital markets is widely restored. Bad usages that a corporate governance code seeks to prevent have flourished in good times. The excesses that led to the U.S. corporate scandals were based on behavior patterns that developed during the bull market of the 1990s. Despite the fact that U.S. securities law, already before the adoption of the Sarbanes-Oxley Act, imposed numerous disclosure obligations on companies regarding governance issues, public attention at that time was absorbed by other pressing matters. This lesson tells us that reliance on disclosures and a *climate of opinion* could become detrimental to the well-functioning of a best practices code in times when authoritative measures of restraint would be most needed.

False Notion of Flexibility

The combination of a voluntary corporate governance code with a legal disclosure obligation that names a code as a point of reference has been celebrated as a new, hybrid regulatory technique that harmonizes seemingly incompatible objectives: It pressurizes companies to improve their governance practices on the one side while offering them sufficient *flexibility* on the other.

It is true that the combination of advisory best practices code with a disclosure regime offers a certain degree of flexibility to companies, when they make their governance choices. The flexibility argument, however, becomes flawed when it is used to contrast corporate governance codes with laws (see, for example, Coombes and Chiu-Yin Wong 2004, 227). Laws are not necessarily mandatory and can offer as much flexibility with regard to compliance as voluntary schemes. A corporate governance code could be integrated into company or securities law as a set of default rules that would be open to disapplication through a shareholders' resolution. Alternatively, one could also adopt a voluntary best practices norm as a non-mandatory law and combine it with a disclosure obligation.

Section 406(c) of the Sarbanes-Oxley Act provides a parallel example for the last-mentioned technique as regards the adoption of ethics codes: The law requires public companies to disclose *codes of ethics* for senior financial officers or explain why they have not adopted such codes. Here, the voluntary norm that is combined with a legal disclosure obligation is the adoption of a code of ethics for senior financial officers. The difference to the code mechanism is that the voluntary norm is incorporated into a statutory law enacted by a parliament after a legislative process, whereas in the case of corporate governance codes, the voluntary norm is usually issued by a nonlegislative and informally composed body of experts. Drafting and amending a corporate governance code is easier and quicker than enacting or amending a law, mainly because a code-issuing body does not have to compromise with the numerous interests that are involved in a legislative process. Therein lies the flexibility.

We can summarize that the flexibility argument, when used to compare codes with laws, confuses the flexibility of norm observance with the flexibility of norm creation.

Facilitation of Corporate Governance Reporting

The foregoing has argued that the aspiration of corporate governance codes to influence governance practices in companies is undermined by an ineffective enforcement of disclosure obligations and an unstable basis of normative authority. The flexibility advantage of corporate governance codes compared to laws lies in their creation and further development, but not in the choices they offer to companies.

Despite these shortcomings, corporate governance codes in their referential function could provide a good service by facilitating corporate governance reporting.

If a law or listing rule obliges a company to report on its governance, the company will face the practical problem of how to structure the report, and of what subjects to address. A referential corporate governance code offers a template and helps shorten the report's contents, because a company only has to report on practices that deviate from the standards a code proposes. For the rest, a company may declare that it implements the practices described in a code. The value of the referential use of a code is well illustrated by the reporting practice in France: French listed companies must by law publish a corporate governance report, but also a description of internal control procedures. As regards the corporate governance report, the French financial authority (AMF) advises companies to make reference to the consolidated corporate governance recommendations prepared by two French business associations (MEDEF/AFEP 2003). Contrarily, as regards the description of internal control procedures, companies are left without any guidance. The AMF publishes an annual survey of the corporate governance and internal control reports that listed companies are required to publish. The AMF's 2004 survey reveals a heterogeneous landscape of corporate governance practice in France. Interestingly, the survey notes that the quality of corporate governance reports of companies benefited from existing standards, to which companies could compare their own practices, whereas the quality of reports on internal controls suffered from a missing point of reference (see AMF 2005, 25).

By providing a template for corporate governance reports and ensuring their brevity a referential code could also help investors efficiently gain information on the corporate governance of a company. An investor can in a short time receive a first impression of a company's corporate governance by studying the referenced code and the areas where a company stated or explained its noncompliance. However, the risks of inaccurate or insignificant corporate governance disclosures that result from weak enforcement and verification mechanisms (see above) calls this advantage of a code's referential function into question. Investors might turn their attention away from corporate governance codes to corporate governance measurement services when assessing a company's corporate governance.

METRICAL FUNCTION

Corporate governance measurement has left the exclusive realm of academic research and become a flourishing services industry. Today, numerous organizations offer corporate governance rating services that attribute a certain score to the corporate governance of companies (for a list of prominent organizations see Viner 2004b, 2004c), or that assess corporate governance as an element of credit rating. This development has been set in motion in the wake of the corporate failures in the U.K. in the late 1980s and in the United States in the late 1990s, from where corporate governance emerged as a standard risk factor. Investors and analysts see a need to be able to assess and compare corporate governance practices between companies on an international level and to draw conclusions about governance as a *risk factor* in individual companies (for details see Dallas 2004, 2–15). Corporate governance ratings respond to the demand for the quantification of financial risks related to poor corporate governance practices.

Some rating services further justify the need for corporate governance measurement with the argument that corporate governance has a positive linkage to financial performance or firm value (see for example FTSE ISS 2005, 4). Research results about this question are divided. While some see a positive relation between certain governance practices and financial performance (examples: Bebchuk et al. 2004; Brown and Caylor 2004; Gompers et al. 2003), others do not find any significant link (examples: Coles et al. 2001; Tosi et al. 2000). Examining Canadian figures, Jog and Dutta conclude that the link between good governance and good performance is "so elusive that we would be better off searching for a unicorn" (2004, 33). All the same, with regard to the linkage between governance and performance of stock prices, assertive studies that are issued by well-reputed organizations such as McKinsey (McKinsey & Company, 2002) or Hermes (Hermes Pensions Management 2005) tend to be self-fulfilling.

Corporate governance rating services are not indifferent to corporate governance codes. First, codes have influenced the establishment of criteria of rating services' methodologies (under the next subheading below). And second, criteria and methodology of a rating service can mutate into a corporate governance code that aspires after normative authority of its own (under second subheading below). In these two aspects lies the metrical function of corporate governance codes.

The Influence of Corporate Governance Codes on Corporate Governance Rating

Corporate governance rating services have been trying to establish a practice of global benchmarking. Global benchmarking in this context means that the rating service develops a methodology that is designed to enable comparisons and assess corporate governance practices from "one firm to another and from one country to another" (Dallas and Bradley 2004, 160). Corporate governance codes, by prospecting for standards that are universally comprehensible, have paved the way for rating services to heave corporate governance out of its national context onto an international stage. Rating services have been inspired by corporate governance codes of national ambit, because such codes provide the link between a national regulatory infrastructure and desired international standard. Rating methodologies also draw on codes of international organizations, the most reputed code being the OECD Principles of Corporate Governance that was revised in April 2004, because such codes already provide a set of internationally desired corporate governance standards (for more details on the influence of codes on rating methodologies see Dallas 2004, 20 et seq. and FTSE ISS 2005, 6).

Rating services seek to base their assessments on overarching governance principles that surpass the national context. The code movement has provided aid to rating services by formulating these overarching principles and drawing widespread attention to them. However, rating services do not simply apply the norms of existing corporate governance codes. Instead, they pick their own criteria and develop sophisticated weighting methodologies. At this point a rating service can introduce its own preferences.

Rating Criteria and Methodology Mutating into Corporate Governance Codes

Rating criteria and methodology could match the definition of a corporate governance code that was formulated above (in the first section of this chapter). They, too, could propound a "systematic array of prospective norms concerning the institutional structure of a company's direction, control, and risk management," if we view rating criteria as norms and rating methodology as an appliance for norm enforcement.

The Managing Director and Global Practice Leader for Standard & Poor's Governance Services, George Dallas, seems to agree, when he writes, "In behavioural science as in the physical sciences, the act of measurement can have an effect on that which is being measured. Applied to the area of corporate governance, this suggests the potential for an effective governance rating system to serve as a positive discipline and incentive for improvement" (Dallas 2004, 6). This citation reveals that rating services are aware of the rating mechanism's potential for normative authority. The abovementioned difficulties regarding the normative authority of referential codes and the enforcement of the comply-or-explain principle (in the second section of this chapter) could make rating criteria and methodology appear as a more effective instrument to influence governance practices in companies.

Corporate governance rating criteria can become norms to the extent that corporate governance rating services publish their criteria and explain the methodology of how the criteria are applied. Despite the fact that rating services seldom uncover details on how exactly they calculate their ratings, they do indicate what kind of corporate governance practice will lead to a positive or a negative assessment. The advantage of corporate governance ratings with regard to normative authority is that a rating provides not only a set of norms by which companies can abide, but also an instant application of these norms that, in the case of some rating services, results in a corporate governance *score*, indeed a highly condensed final judgment. In other words, corporate governance ratings, unlike other code texts, are enforced, because the very act of measuring becomes equal to norm enforcement. Sanctions and rewards appear in the form of negative and positive scores.

The normative pressure that a corporate governance rating can exert depends largely on the reputation of the organization behind the rating service. Often these organizations are commercial enterprises. It will be the business strategy of any such enterprise to have its ratings become an important decision-making tool for managers, boards, insurance underwriters, shareholders, and other investors. The business success of a corporate governance rating service coincides with the rise of the normative authority of its ratings. This may be criticized by those who argue that normative authority should coincide with legitimacy.

Since rating services gain their information from publicly available sources or through voluntary cooperation with the senior management of rated companies, the abovementioned risk of inaccurate disclosures equally becomes a problem for corporate governance ratings. Even if a good rating service will have the chance to unveil contradictions and poorly disclosed information, it will not always be able to deal with outright dishonesty and the mounting of façades that create an appearance of norm compliance.

Ratings and Objectivity

By attributing corporate governance scores a rating service delivers opinions about certain corporate governance practices in companies. These opinions are based on the rating company's policy choices expressed in the rating criteria. However, some rating services claim to give *objective* assessments (see, for example, Standard & Poor's 2004, 4). The fact that an opinion is given in the form of a *number* furthers the appearance of objectivity. Nevertheless, corporate governance ratings should not be discarded because of the claim of offering objectivity where (objectively) there is none.

The purpose of a corporate governance rating is mainly to provide an assessment on corporate governance being a risk factor for certain financial stakeholders, most often investors that seek minority shareholdings. Many other imaginable goals of good corporate governance are eliminated from the list. It is easier to develop an objective method if the method is concentrated on a single (subjectively defined) goal.

Objectivity could therefore be related to the process of norm application: Even where a rating company promotes selected norms, and thereby seeks to serve particular interests, once the policy choices have been taken, the application of these norms follows a methodology that invokes objective rules of scientific logic. Some might conclude that the relationship between rating criteria and methodology resembles the relationship between legislation and legal method. It will be interesting, however, to see how corporate governance ratings deal with circumstances that do not fit into preconceived schemes, with ambiguous terms, with contradictory results, in short, the whole battery of problematic cases, for which legal method has already developed sophisticated techniques.

COMMUNICATIONAL FUNCTION

Corporate governance codes are vehicles that, despite many differences in detail, have transported a remarkably uniform perception of organization, direction, and control in companies. The convergence of prospected standards expressed in code texts is contrasted by a divergent landscape of corporate governance practices that is determined by various factors. Such factors are not only different company and security laws and their enforcement mechanisms, but also varying socioeconomic determinants such as ownership structures and cultural perceptions of business organization. Further, there is no common understanding on the theoretical basis of corporate governance. To illustrate, French company law—at least in the books—puts the common interest of the company (*l'intérêt social*) in the forefront, whereas shareholder interests or the interests of financial stakeholders play a secondary role. This is one reason why in France the notion of corporate governance, awkwardly translated into *gouvernement d'entreprise* (note that there is neither a literal translation for *corporate* nor for *governance* into French language), is still by many regarded with wary eyes as an Anglo-Saxon import (for references, see Convert 2003, 142 et seq.).

Divergent practices are not inconsistent with a convergence of standards (Millstein 2000, 27–28). Corporate governance codes respond to factual commercial pressures, notably a global competition for capital that does not halt at national borders. Influential institutional investors such as CalPERS or Hermes can therefore promote their own corporate governance standards with success. It would not be correct to speak of a convergence of corporate governance systems, but we can at least assert a convergence of challenges that the divergent systems have to face.

Here corporate governance codes play an important role by providing a source of inspiration for future legislation (under the first subheading below), explaining distinct national features to an international public (under the second subheading below), and establishing a language that enables an international exchange of ideas (under the third subheading below).

Source of Inspiration for Future Legislation

The OECD Principles of Corporate Governance are mainly addressed to governments, providing them with a source of inspiration for future legislation (see preamble to the OECD Principles, OECD 2004, 11). The World Bank, closely involved in the development of the OECD Principles, launched the "Reports on the Observance of Standards and Codes" initiative (ROSC), an organization that assists governments on the shape of corporate governance regulatory framework on the basis of the principles promulgated by the OECD.

Also other code texts, including rating criteria and methodology, seek to influence future regulation pertaining to corporate governance issues. Recently adopted changes to company law have been drawing on existing corporate governance codes. For example, recent French law that introduced the alternative to split the functions of the board chairman and the chief executive officer (see Art. L 225-51-1 French Commercial Code) was favored by an analogous recommendation provided by the Vienot report of 1999 (MEDEF 1999, 6 et seq.).

Finally, it is often the threat of legislation that spurs a stronger commitment of the business community to adopt, either by itself or in collaboration with governments, more effective codes that operate outside of the law. Thus, we can speak of an interrelation between self-commitment and legislative threat, which is a phenomenon that typically materializes in almost any matter of self-regulation. Following the logic of this interrelation, legislation is introduced when a code building on informal deterrence is viewed as an insufficient measure. Germany might provide a future example for this phenomenon. The German government announced that it would adopt a law that makes the publication of details of individual executive remuneration mandatory. The disclosure of individual executive remuneration is already a recommendation of the German corporate governance code but apparently—in the eyes of the legislator—it has not been applied with satisfactory results (Government Commission on the German Corporate Governance Code 2005a). On the other side, a well-functioning code mechanism can provide a good argument against legislation. Regulation by a code can appease a legislator that needs to react to public calls for more stringent rules (for Australian experiences, see Hill 2004, 235).

Explanatory Codes

Corporate governance codes that have received direct or indirect support from national governments (by setting up an expert committee or by endorsing the work of an expert committee that drafted a code text) can aim at explaining special features of a national legal system of company and securities law to an international public. Such explanatory codes formulate principles that summarily describe existing rights and obligations under the laws of a country.

Next to giving best practices recommendations, the German corporate governance code recites certain contents of German company law. The foreword of the German code reads, "The Code aims at making the German Corporate Governance system transparent and understandable. Its purpose is to promote the trust of international and national investors, customers, employees and the general public in the management and supervision of listed German stock corporations" (Government Commission on the German Corporate Governance Code 2005b, 1). The explanatory approach has the advantage that it can signal to an international community to what extent internationally desired standards of corporate governance are implanted into a national system of company law. In this sense a corporate governance code operates as a communicational bridge between a national legislation and the international community that drives the corporate governance movement.

The China Securities Regulatory Commission's Code of Corporate Governance for Listed Companies in China (Jan. 7, 2001) could also be reviewed in this light. At first sight, the Chinese code echoes the language that is used in other code texts. A closer look at the code reveals discrepancies between expectations of good corporate governance and the reality of shareholder and investor protection in China. The code uses vague formulations (see, for example, sections 12 to 14 on related party transactions), contains unspecified references to the law (see, for example, section 1 on shareholder rights), or implicitly reveals the limits of shareholder rights (see, for example, section 4 on shareholder suits). No foreign investor will have rejoiced because of the adoption of a corporate governance code by the Chinese Securities Regulation Commission (see Viner 2004a, 154). However, the Chinese corporate governance initiative should not be discarded as the construction of a mere façade. The code deserves acknowledgment because it facilitates the communication on corporate governance. It enables foreign investors to demonstrate gaps between international expectations and domestic reality by referring to an official text that was prepared by a Chinese authority. This will not improve investor protection in China overnight, but might have long-term effects generated by a soft but constant pressure of investor demand.

The Chinese corporate code helps in making comparisons between the Chinese and other corporate governance systems. This leads us to the final aspect of a corporate governance code's communicational function.

A Comparative Basis for an International Exchange of Ideas

In a dinner speech to the 2004 annual meeting of the Transatlantic Corporate Governance Dialogue, Frits Bolkestein, at that time European commissioner for the internal market, said that an agreement on the equivalence of approaches to corporate governance would in some cases be more important than taking identical approaches (see Bolkestein 2004). Certainly meant as a reference to the debated issue, whether corporate governance structures and practices of large corporations are converging or should converge (for an overview to the discussion and a critical view, see Branson 2001, 321 et seq.), the citation points out the value of creating a common reference for corporate governance.

The corporate governance code movement has established a comparative basis for diverging corporate governance practices throughout the world. Corporate governance codes and reporting mechanisms have smoothed the progress of one of the most difficult issues of any comparative exercise, which is to formulate a globally unified language on the issues that require comparison. Corporate governance codes enable us to extract certain terms and concepts out of their particular national context. For example, the practical differences between one-tier and two-tier board models have become more discernible, since different codes prompted a common discussion about the role of nonexecutive directors. This is well demonstrated by a recent recommendation of the European Commission on "The role of non-executive or supervisory directors of listed companies and on the committees of the (supervisory) board," that, as the title already suggests, adopted a unitary approach (European Commission 2005c).

CONCLUSION

Corporate governance codes prospect to become widely accepted norms. A code's normative strength depends on its popularity, which is but an unstable basis for authority. Mandatory legal disclosure regimes that guarantee a prominent place for a code text by making it a point of reference do not cure the normative weaknesses of a code, because legal disclosure rules still lack efficient enforcement mechanisms that can verify accuracy and provide interpretational guidance on the contents of corporate governance disclosures.

The weak normative authority of corporate governance codes is contrasted by their communicational virtue. Corporate governance codes have aided in providing an international language of corporate governance and thereby changed the way we perceive organizational and control structures within companies. Any legal reform of company or securities law will at least take notice of, if not be inspired by, the norms that the international corporate governance movement has been promulgating through code texts.

Asked whether corporate governance codes can prevent the kind of abuses that have spurred widespread attention to corporate governance issues, the answer is no. Corporate governance codes, however, can contribute to an elimination of bad usages, in which abuses flourish.

CHAPTER 23

Assessing the Effectiveness of Boards of Directors and Individual Directors

Richard Leblanc

INTRODUCTION

Recent high-profile corporate failures, scandals, and, in some cases, executive corruption have focused international regulatory and public attention on the need for having appropriate corporate governance standards and practices. Canada, the United States, United Kingdom, Australia, New Zealand, and other countries have enacted corporate governance rules, codes, and guidelines of varying types for publicly traded companies. These guidelines address the issue of *governance assessments*, that is, the requirement/recommendation that the effectiveness of boards of directors, committees of boards, and individual directors, as the case may be, be assessed on a regular basis.

This chapter will respond to practitioners' legitimate objections and concerns and offer guidance on how to conduct assessments, based on the qualitative research experience of the author.

Note: This chapter is an expanded and modified version of a booklet produced by the author for the Canadian Institute of Chartered Accountants (CICA), forthcoming (permission granted). Some select excerpts may also have originated from Leblanc and Gillies, *Inside the Boardroom* (John Wiley & Sons, Toronto, 2005). Qualitative data herein originate from the author's doctoral study, as well as ongoing research work with boards of directors.

In assessing board effectiveness, guidelines for the United States, United Kingdom, Australia and New Zealand read as follows:

> *The board should conduct a self-evaluation at least annually to determine whether it and its committees are functioning effectively. (Final NYSE Corporate Governance Rules, codified in Section 303A of the NYSE's Listed Company Manual Commentary to Rule 9)*

The NYSE also has separate rules that the nominating/corporate governance committee, audit committee, and compensation committee have written charters that address annual performance evaluations, at Rules 4, 5, and 7 respectively.

> *The board should undertake a formal and rigorous annual evaluation of its own performance and that of its committees and individual directors. (Financial Reporting Council 2003b: Main Principle A.6)*

> *The performance of the board and key executives should be reviewed regularly against both measurable and qualitative indicators. (Australian Stock Exchange Corporate Governance Council 2003, 8.1)*

The ASX governance Principles go on to read, within its guidance section, that the following should be made publicly available: "a description of the process for performance evaluation of the board, its committees and individual directors, and key executives."

> *The board should have rigorous, formal processes for evaluating its performance, along with that of board committees and individual directors. The chairperson should be responsible to lead these processes. (New Zealand Securities Commission 2004: 2.10)*

In Canada, in December 1994, the Toronto Stock Exchange Committee on Corporate Governance published "Where Were the Directors: Guidelines for Improved Corporate Governance in Canada" (the "Dey Report") to assist Toronto Stock Exchange (TSX)-listed companies in their approach to corporate governance. Subsequently, in 1995, the TSX adopted the Dey Report's 14 guidelines as *best practice guidelines* for its listed companies; that is, they were not intended to be mandatory. Guideline 5 reads as follows:

> *Every board of directors should implement a process to be carried out by the nominating committee or other appropriate committee for assessing the effectiveness of the board as a whole, the committees of the board and the contribution of individual directors.*

There have been major initiatives following up from the Dey Report since 1994, notably (1) the report entitled "Five Years to the Dey," sponsored by the Institute of Corporate Directors and the TSX, which evaluated how Canadian companies were complying with the Dey Report's best practice guidelines, and (2) the Joint Committee on Corporate Governance (the "Saucier Committee"), whose final report, released in November 2001, recommended that the TSX amend its corporate governance guidelines in a number of respects. In April 2002, the TSX proposed changes to its guidelines in response to the Saucier Committee's recommendations.

On April 15, 2005, members of the Canadian Securities Administrators (CSA) published two initiatives requiring reporting issuers to provide greater disclosure about their corporate governance practices: National Policy 58-201 Corporate Governance Guidelines (the "Policy") and National Instrument 58-101 Disclosure of Corporate Governance Practices (the "Instrument"). At that time, and at the time of writing this publication, the CSA, subject to receiving all necessary Commission and ministerial approvals, intended that the Policy and the Instrument would come into force in Canadian jurisdictions on June 30, 2005. The Instrument would apply to information circulars or annual information forms, as the case may be, which are filed following financial years ending on or after June 30, 2005.

Section 3.18 of the Policy, entitled "Regular Board Assessments," reads as follows:

> *The board, its committees and each individual director should be regularly assessed regarding his, her or its effectiveness and contribution. An assessment should consider (a) in the case of the board or a board committee, its mandate or charter, and (b) in the case of an individual director, the applicable position description(s), as well as the competencies and skills each individual director is expected to bring to the board [emphasis added].*

Implicit in this regulatory attention to governance assessments is the belief that (1) such assessments enhance the effectiveness of boards, committees, and individual directors, and (2) more effective boards, committees, and directors are in the best interests of corporations and contribute positively to their continued performance and success.

TYPES OF GOVERNANCE ASSESSMENTS

Each evaluation process should be tailored to meet the needs of the individual company.
    —National Association of Corporate Directors 2005, 18

Other than the assessment of the chief executive officer or other members of management, which are beyond the scope of this chapter, there are four main types of governance assessments. They are:

1. *Board assessments.* This is the type most frequently practiced and involves the board assessing its own effectiveness, typically against its mandate and via a self-administered, written questionnaire.
2. *Committee assessments.* These assessments are similar to board assessments but occur at the committee level. They typically involve a committee of the board, for example, the audit committee, the compensation committee, and the nominating/corporate governance committee, assessing its own effectiveness against their respective written charters.
3. *Individual director assessment—self.* This type of assessment involves individual directors assessing their own effectiveness, either in writing, for example, questionnaire, or in a discussion with the chair of the board, either in an open-ended fashion or against specific criteria. If the self-assessment occurs in writing, directors may retain the questionnaire themselves, choose to submit it, or use it as the basis for a discussion with the chair of the board to discuss that director's individual effectiveness. Directors may also submit the questionnaire to a member of management, for example, the corporate secretary, to be kept on file. The benefits of this type of assessment are that (1) it allows an opportunity for self-reflection on one's performance and how it might be enhanced; (2) the data sharing is confined primarily to the individual director, and therefore may be more self-critical and candid; (3) the self-assessment provides a convenient step before proceeding to the fourth type of assessment, for those boards wishing to do to.
4. *Individual director assessment—peer.* This is the least-widely practiced and most challenging form of assessment and involves directors assessing one another on a number of performance dimensions. The

data produced include what a director's colleagues' views are on the effectiveness and contribution of that director, on an individual basis. The raw data on a particular director's effectiveness made by other board members are typically not shared collectively with all other directors, other than in aggregate form. The chair of the board may see more than the aggregate data, depending on the preferences of the board and the individual director. The chief benefits of a director peer assessment are that (1) it allows for collegial feedback on one's own performance as a director, and in this sense may be more objective than a self assessment; (2) depending on how widely the data are shared, the peer assessment provides for collective focal points of discussion for key issues surrounding the effectiveness of individual directors, for example, the effectiveness of the chair of the board, the chairs of committees, and individual directors. There may be a greater tendency to act on data that are collectively shared. It is, however, critical that a board contemplating conducting a peer assessment for individual directors be ready to do so. *Readiness* may involve (1) proceeding through director, committee and self assessments; (2) a collective commitment by all directors to the peer assessment, including the criteria for individual director assessment, how the peer assessment process will work, how the data will be managed, and how feedback will be provided; and (3) effective board leadership in overseeing and managing the overall process.

Two general points are important when discussing the above governance assessments.

First, the lines among these four types of assessments may blur. For example, a board assessment might involve canvassing directors on their views of executive compensation oversight, which may fall under the initial purview of the charter of the compensation committee. A board or committee assessment may canvass members' views on the effectiveness of the chair of the board or the chair of the respective committee, and, in doing so, incorporate the assessment of those individual directors, and so on.

Second, and more importantly, the above four types of assessments are not meant to convey a mechanistic approach or a hierarchical progression. For example, it is not inevitable that a director peer assessment should follow—or is superior to—a director self-assessment. Governance assessment processes depend on the unique circumstances, individual personalities, and trust levels for a particular board. For example, a director self-assessment, as the basis of a discussion with a strong and engaged chair of a board, addressing key performance issues of that director in a candid and highly constructive manner, would be productive.

How Common Are Governance Assessments?

> *Nearly half the leading companies in the English-speaking world
> now carry out some type of board performance reviews . . . As
> positive as that seems, the fact remains that most of these reviews
> focus on the board, and not on individual directors. . . .
> Performance appraisal for individual directors, as well as boards,
> is an idea whose time has come.*
>   —Carter and Lorsch 2004, 125 (footnote omitted)

> *It is impossible to learn without feedback from the environment
> on our success, and yet many in top management and half of all
> boards do not provide performance appraisals. Everyone else in
> the enterprise can be assessed, but somehow the more senior
> players find excuses to not collect this often discomforting
> information.*
>   —Gandossy and Sonnenfeld 2004, 20–21

Why some boards do not assess their own effectiveness, including the
effectiveness and contribution of board committees and individual directors, when (1) presumably they are in the assessment business—one of
their responsibilities is constantly to assess management, (2) those boards
that do conduct regular assessments find them very valuable, and (3)
boards are requested to do so within corporate governance guidelines, is an
interesting question.

> *First, this is new. Second, directors are uncomfortable being criti-
> cal of their colleagues. It's okay for management to be evaluated
> but there's ego and fear for directors being judged by their fellows.
> My own view is that this can be done so that it is tasteful, thought-
> ful and rigorous. Sacking under-performing directors is the stick.
> Some positives are that assessing other directors is not necessarily
> not of value—it can enhance director performance. You can iden-
> tify individual performance that can be corrected. (Chair of a gov-
> ernance committee)*

> *Directors are reluctant to pass judgment on their peers. (Regulator)*

The reason may well be that the process of undertaking assessments is
much easier said than done. Directors may not think they are necessary.
They may not be comfortable with the prospect of being assessed or of assessing their fellow directors. And directors may have concerns about what

assessments might disclose and who will be privy to that information. These are legitimate concerns that this chapter will address.

THE RATIONALE FOR ASSESSING BOARD AND INDIVIDUAL DIRECTOR EFFECTIVENESS

An increasing percentage of boards evaluate the CEO, themselves and their individual members. Of the three practices, two (board and member evaluations) have been found to be related to board effectiveness. . . . Boards that assess their members and themselves tend to be more effective than those that don't.
—Lawler and Finegold 2005, 70

As evaluation progresses, it must serve one clear objective: to provide guidance that creates superior long-term value.
—National Association of Corporate Directors 2001, 5

To begin with, why should a board assess its own effectiveness? The simple answer to this question—and indeed the primary purpose of assessments— is to enhance board and individual director effectiveness and thereby contribute to the success of the corporation and the long-term enhancement of shareholder value.

The assessment process provides a number of benefits. First, boards that conduct rigorous formal reviews of board and director effectiveness find the process valuable. They find that it is a healthy discipline whereby the board leads by example. A board assessment compels the chair of the board (or, if the chair and CEO positions are combined, the lead director or the equivalent), chair of the governance/nominating committee, and other directors to look inward to assess what factors are relevant for superior board performance and how they should be measured, for example, the adequacy of the information that board members receive, the appropriateness of the agendas, the effectiveness of committee operations and reporting, the achievement of the board's mandate, and so on.

Second, conducting assessments also enables board members to consider how well the board is dealing with its strategic tasks, how well it is making decisions, the state of the company's relationship with its stakeholders, and so on. Assessments are not simply meaningless acts with no operational substance. They bring about tangible enhancements of overall board operations and process, which, of course, is what they are designed to do.

Third, the boards that engage in assessments find that it increases the level of dialogue about governance, encourages opinions to be shared by all directors—both orally and in writing—and enables attention to be paid to specific governance issues that might otherwise have been neglected.

Fourth, when a board of directors makes its expectations explicit in the form of written mandates and position descriptions and subjects itself to internal review, doing so signals to shareholders, management, and other corporate stakeholders that the board is an active and engaged one and that it has set explicit internal goals and priorities for which it is responsible.

In short, boards that have conducted assessments found the benefits to be substantial and that it was the right thing to do. As one director remarked early on in that board's assessment process:

> *I learned early in my career that if something is important, it must be measured, measured, measured. To that end, all . . . directors complete confidential questionnaires on every aspect of board conduct, and the various committees. In addition, we have designed a peer evaluation process. . . . Each director completes his or her assessment of every other director, again by completing a confidential questionnaire. These reviews are sent to an outside consultant, who writes to each director, suggesting areas for improvement as provided by fellow directors. . . . Personally, I have learned that a strong and effective board is an enormous asset to a CEO. (Chair and CEO)*

There are also negative consequences that a board may encounter if it chooses not to conduct governance assessments in some form. As best practices continue to develop in this area, boards of directors that choose not to conduct assessments, or do so in a superficial manner, might find that if corporate performance or governance difficulties subsequently ensue, the board might not have the time to react, or, worse yet, might not have the standards and processes in place to react. Directors might be subsequently questioned in various fora, for example, media, professional bodies, court, and so on, as to why they did not assess themselves when they had the opportunity and were urged by regulatory authorities and experts to do so.

And so, it is also becoming increasingly difficult to disclose to shareholders why a particular board or set of directors is immune from some form of internal review. Given the experience of boards that have begun to assess the effectiveness of the board and its individual directors in a regular, systematic, and rigorous manner, there appear to be no insurmountable reasons why boards of directors should not assess their effectiveness as well as that of their directors.

Objections to Assessing Board and Individual Director Effectiveness

Nevertheless, some boards are reluctant to embark on assessments and may choose not to do so. The answers offered by directors for not undertaking self-assessments of the quality of the board's performance and their own individual contributions include: (1) concern that there is a general lack of criteria for conducting assessments, (2) uneasiness about the manner in which the information collected may be interpreted and administered, (3) fear of the potential damage that assessment may have on the chemistry of the board, (4) concern about the confidentiality of results, and (5) worry that results might be used by the attorneys of plaintiffs in suits against directors.

Underlying these objections are that governance assessments, at least at the outset, may make directors feel uncomfortable; directors may not think they need them; and directors may have concerns about what assessments might imply or disclose about their own performance. Directors may be of the view that *ad hoc* discussions between a nonexecutive chair or lead director and other directors is all that is needed to assure that the board and individual directors are performing well. A formal process of review, such directors believe, may simply be unnecessary.

However, these types of views increasingly appear to be a minority position and may be addressed and in many cases overcome. As best practices continue to emerge in the area of governance assessments, it is inevitable that standards and practices will heighten and become more robust and rigorous. For example, director industry associations and regulators are increasingly acknowledging that (1) governance assessments should include the assessment of individual directors' effectiveness and contributions and that (2) expectations for individual director performance—including position descriptions for key board positions—ought to be made more explicit. In Canada, the Canadian Securities Administrators' new Policy places an emphasis on position descriptions (§ 3.5), *competencies and skills* of individual directors (§§ 3.12 and 3.14), and states that assessments, in the case of an individual director, should consider "the applicable position description(s), as well as the competencies and skills each individual director is expected to bring to the board" (§ 3.18)

However, the emphasis on the identification and assessment of explicit individual director performance criteria, particularly the competencies and skills of directors on an individual as opposed to a collective basis, is not without risks—and notably legal and reputational risks for individual directors. This is particularly true for directors self-assessing their own performance as well as assessing one another's performance, for example, peer assessment. Two directors offered acute views:

> *Evaluation of the board? What about litigation? You want me to serve a personal evaluation? You're nuts! (Director)*

> *The peer appraisal is a smoking gun on both sides. (Director)*

There are two legal concerns about individual director assessments. The first is that once the competencies and skills of directors begin to be assessed on an individual basis, lawyers for the plaintiff's bar may attempt to obtain and utilize such individual director reviews, assuming they can establish relevance, as evidence that a director or group of directors possessed or lacked the appropriate standard of care required. There is concern in particular with director peer assessments that, if they are completed, the records of them and their conclusions will be disclosed in legal actions brought against the company, its officers, and directors. This fear leads people to believe they should as a general practice discard all records and keep records of discussions to a minimum. It also leads directors to be wary of having assessments done of individual director performance. If done, there is a desire to have such assessments privileged or shielded from subsequent discovery (disclosure) in the event that a board of directors is sued.

Second, assuming relevancy can be established and such individual director assessments are ultimately disclosed in a court proceeding, there is also the concern that an individual director with a particular competency or skill (as further evidenced by the assessment document itself, for example, the views of his or her colleagues in a peer review, working notes taken by directors during a self-assessment, etc.) may be subsequently found by a court to be more or less liable than his or her colleagues, depending on what circumstances may have transpired with the company and the role (impact) of that particular director's expertise—hence the smoking gun on the part of the individual director, referred to in the quotation by the second director immediately above.

Similarly, if an individual director's competencies and skills were found as a result of a director assessment review to be lacking, then this may be evidence that may expose the company and its management (as well as the individual director) to liability as well, in that the company knew this director's (s') competencies or skills were found to be wanting, by virtue of the assessment, and may have chosen not to act on this knowledge. For instance, company officers or executive directors knew that Director X, for example, chaired or sat on the compensation committee of the board, or the risk management committee, and so on, and was found by fellow directors or committee members not to possess sufficient compensation literacy, or lacked sufficient knowledge of the risks of the business, and so on. (And therefore the company would be wise to act on the data from such an assessment, for example, director development and education, asking the director to step down, etc.).

The capacity of individual director assessments, therefore, given the movement to competencies and skills in the governance field, to expose a director or the company and its management to additional liability is cause for concern, on the basis of (1) the subsequent disclosure of the assessment documents themselves in the event of litigation, and (2) the possibility of enhanced liability of individual directors and the company based on the results of the assessment.

Boards of directors should therefore seek the advice of experienced counsel in this area when undertaking individual director assessments.

Overcoming Objections to Assessing Board and Individual Director Effectiveness

To address and (attempt to) overcome objections to assessments such as those cited above, the following is suggested:

- *Board leadership.* There should be an independent leader on the board with the internal credibility and authority to lead the assessment, for example, the non-executive chair of the board or chair of the corporate governance or nominating committee.
- *Rationale for the assessment and generation of board buy-in.* This independent leader should articulate to the board why the assessment is being contemplated and what is hoped to be accomplished. The board needs to understand that an appropriate assessment will lead to increased dialogue, recommendations, action, and ultimately more effective corporate governance. Otherwise, skepticism will prevail. Buy-in by the entire board—every director—is an absolute necessity for assessment success.
- *Addressing director concerns.* There should be appropriate assurances of confidentiality and confidence in the data compilation, interpretation, and feedback provided to individual directors. These issues will be addressed in later questions.
- *Addressing the legal concerns.* The two legal concerns with director assessments and peer assessments in particular—disclosure of the assessment document itself and enhanced liability for directors—will now be addressed.

First, in most jurisdictions and certainly throughout Canada, a party is only required to disclose records that are in some way relevant to the factual and legal issues raised in an action. If the action deals with allegations that the board failed to ensure some fact or conduct were disclosed, the findings in a peer assessment simply may not be relevant to the issue of whether a fact or some conduct were material and ought to have been disclosed. Under such circumstances, the assessment therefore would not be disclosed in the action.

Assuming relevance can be established, individual director evaluations prepared internally or by an outside expert are likely to be discoverable unless the company can establish that such assessments were prepared for the dominant purpose of reasonably contemplated litigation, that is, they were *privileged*, which would generally not be the case in routine individual director assessments. There may be greater chances of obtaining privilege protection if the director assessments were conducted and organized by counsel for the purpose of providing legal advice to the board, that is, a true attorney–client communication; for example, director assessments would be undertaken for the purpose of ensuring that the board and its members are prepared to deal with anticipated legal actions.

For example, the peer assessment could be done as part of an effort to ensure the board was fulfilling its duty to exercise reasonable business judgment. If a peer review were done in this fashion, the claim could be made that the peer assessments are privileged and therefore not producible to a party in a civil action. This approach has never been tested but the justification for maintaining privilege is consistent with the legal authorities, according to one litigation lawyer with experience in director and officer liability. Privilege could be asserted against any outsider to the company. But, if there is an oppression claim brought against directors by shareholders, the privilege would not apply. Instead, one would focus on whether anything in the assessments was relevant to the oppression claim. The general view appears to be, however, that routine director assessments may not be covered by attorney–client privilege and hence may be discoverable in the event of litigation.

Second, as jurisprudence continues to develop in the area of director liability, it may be the case that directors who possess "specialized expertise and knowledge" (and individual director assessments may provide further evidence of this) may have enhanced liability exposure (see, for example, a recent Delaware case, *In re Emerging Communications, Inc.*, No. CIV.A. 16415, Del. Ch. May 3, 2004), depending on whether a legislative *safe harbor* exists to insulate specialized directors from enhanced liability. For example, the Securities and Exchange Commission's rule under the Sarbanes-Oxley Act that requires public companies to disclose whether they have a financial expert on their audit committee contains a specific safe harbor for financial experts that is meant to protect such directors from additional liability under federal securities laws.

It would be prudent therefore for boards of directors to seek experienced counsel when undertaking individual director assessments and that counsel would provide advice given the factual circumstances of a particular board.

However, notwithstanding the legitimate legal concerns and litigation risks expressed by directors, these concerns should be balanced with the risk of *not* acting in the areas of board, committee, and individual director assessments, when boards had the opportunity to act and were urged to conduct such assessments by regulatory and best practice authorities. A board of directors that decides against taking action on problems that could have been identified, in a manner that at least addresses the litigation risks above, might ultimately expose the board and individual directors to greater liability for not acting when it could or should have.

WHEN A BOARD OF DIRECTORS SHOULD PROCEED WITH THE ASSESSMENT PROCESS

Depending on the director or committee who is ultimately responsible for leading and conducting a particular governance assessment—for example, the chair of the board, chair of a committee, or the nominating or governance committee as a whole—a board of directors should proceed with an assessment only after all directors have heard an explanation of the rationale for doing so, have had an opportunity to express their views, and the board collectively has agreed on an optimal process for doing so. Boards should progress deliberately, especially in assessing the effectiveness of individual directors, and resist any temptation or pressure to act prematurely. Undue haste could cause irreparable harm to board dynamics. A board would know that it is ready to proceed with a rigorous assessment process once it has collectively agreed, under the leadership of an independent director, on (1) what is being assessed, (2) how the data will be managed, and (3) how the overall self-assessment process is expected to play out.

Board assessments should be undertaken before assessing the effectiveness of committees of the board and certainly before assessing the effectiveness and contribution of individual directors. A time gap is necessary for boards to get comfortable in assessing their own effectiveness before turning their attention to assessing individual members.

As well, new directors should be given time to get up-to-speed before they become involved in any assessments. Experienced directors suggest that most new directors require time to become proficient on the board, especially if they are not experienced in the company's particular industry sector.

> *Directors need to thoroughly understand the nature of the business and businesses. Each new director should have a substantive written briefing on the business, its nature, and over the first year it's best to schedule to spend half a day at each of the major manufacturing sites to get up to speed. You need to develop an understanding then through osmosis and put significant time into it. Get external information as well, from third parties and analysts. Management has a strategic plan, but it helps to have third party assessments. (Director)*

WHO SHOULD LEAD THE ASSESSMENT OF THE BOARD OF DIRECTORS AND COMMITTEES OF THE BOARD?

> *Research on corporate boards and board reform efforts alike have been dominated by a concern for board independence and its effect on the monitoring of the CEO. However, attention to what we call the "usual suspects"—the number of outsiders on boards, director shareholdings, board size, and whether the CEO also holds the Chair position (CEO duality)—does not yield either strong research results or more robust corporate governance in practice.*
>
> —Finkelstein and Mooney 2003, 101

> *For director evaluations, the two questions are "on what basis?" and "by whom?"*
>
> —Director

Board Assessments

Under section 3.18 of the Policy, the board should regularly assess its own effectiveness and contribution and the assessment should consider the board's written mandate. The person most often considered appropriate to do so is the nonexecutive chair of the board. If the chair and CEO roles are combined, it should be the lead director or the chair of a committee of the board, for example, the governance committee, or another independent director, on behalf of the board. The independent board leader chosen to lead and conduct the board assessment should have the trust, confidence, and respect of all directors and should solicit their input as part of the assessment. Another model is that the chair of the board and chair of the governance or nominating committee may co-lead the board assessment. Regardless of the person or persons chosen, the board as a whole or a committee of the board should ultimately be responsible, through its mandate or charter, for ensuring that the board regularly assesses its own effectiveness and that the data are acted upon.

Management may also play a supportive and facilitative role in the assessment, for example, the corporate secretary in administering questionnaires, and so on, as may an external expert, but it is important that ultimate authority for leading and conducting the assessment rest with the independent board leader.

Committee Assessments

Under section 3.18 of the Policy, committees of the board should regularly assess their effectiveness and contribution and such assessments should consider the charter of each respective board committee. The person considered appropriate to lead and conduct a committee assessment is the chair of that respective committee, that is, the chair of the audit committee leads the audit committee assessment, the chair of the compensation committee leads the compensation committee assessment, and so on.

A committee assessment should solicit the input of committee members as part of the assessment. The Policy reads that the "board, its committees and each individual director" should be regularly assessed regarding "his, her or its effectiveness and *contribution*" (author's emphasis)—as opposed to the NYSE guidelines, whereby committees must have a written charter that "addresses . . . an annual performance evaluation of the [nominating/corporate governance, compensation and audit] committee." An earlier iteration of this Policy read that the "board should regularly assess . . . the effectiveness and contribution of each board committee."

The final wording by the Canadian Securities Administrators would seem to imply, or at least leave open the possibility, that a committee assessment, along with soliciting the input of individual committee members who sit on the committee, might also solicit the input of other directors who may not sit on a particular committee, yet have views on that committee's effectiveness and *contribution* (again, author's emphasis). In other words, directors who do not sit on the compensation committee, for example, would be able to offer their views on how well the compensation committee fulfills the terms of its charter.

Soliciting the views of noncommittee members, acknowledging that they may lack committee expertise and exposure, incorporates members' views on committee reporting and issues that members feel may fall under that committee's charter, but that the committee may be doing a better job at addressing, for example, risk management, executive compensation, governance, and so on, thus stimulating a possible wider board discussion. Soliciting the views of noncommittee members may be accomplished constructively without signaling a lack of confidence in colleagues.

In addition, executive officers who regularly interact with a particular committee may also be solicited on their views of the effectiveness of a particular committee, in the discretion of the committee chair or the committee. Outside experts who provide assistance to the committee may be asked as well, as appropriate.

Each committee of the board should ultimately be responsible, through its charter, for ensuring that the committee regularly assesses the effectiveness and contribution of that committee, that the results are reported to the board, that the data are acted upon, and that the committee is held accountable for doing so as part of its work plan.

Who or What Committee Should Lead the Assessment of the Effectiveness and Contribution of Individual Directors?

The chair of the board, on behalf of the board, may be the person who assesses the effectiveness of an individual director, during an oral discussion or in-person meeting with the chair. As well, the effectiveness of the chair may be assessed by the chair of the nominating or governance committee, also during an interactive discussion. While these are certainly viable models of assessing individual director effectiveness that have been used in the past, the Policy is moving toward consideration of clear position descriptions and consideration of competencies and skills each individual director is expected to bring to the board, as well as a greater involvement by the nominating committee.

Under section 3.18 of the Policy, each individual director should be regularly assessed regarding his or her effectiveness and contribution. The assessment should consider the position description(s), as well as the competencies and skills each individual director is expected to bring to the board. The board should develop clear position descriptions for the chair of the board and the chair of each board committee (§ 5). Section 12 of the Policy sets out a two-step process for nominating or appointing individuals as directors, which involves assessing the competency and skills each existing director possesses as the second step. A previous iteration of the Policy also suggested that a position description be developed for *directors*, including the chair of the board and the chair of each board committee. (Emphasis added. In other words, there exist three possibilities for position descriptions: the chair of the board, the chair of board committees, and individual directors. See Leblanc and Gillies 2005, for these best practice position descriptions, as well as the CEO and corporate secretary.)

Individual Director Assessment Considering "The Applicable Position Description(s)"　　The chair of the board, on behalf of the board, may be the person who assesses the effectiveness and contribution of directors who chair committees of the board and other individual directors as well, considering the position description(s) applicable to each director. For example, (1) the chair of the board would assess the effectiveness and contribution of a committee chair, for example, the chair of the audit committee, considering the audit committee chair's position description and as well the position description for individual directors of that board (if the latter position description existed; it is not suggested in the final wording of the Policy that a position description exist for individual directors); and (2) the chair would assess other individual directors also considering the position description for directors generally, if such a position description existed.

For the assessment of the effectiveness and contribution of the chair of the board, the chair of the nominating or governance committee, on behalf of the board, may be the person who conducts the assessment, considering the position description for the chair of the board, that is, assessing the chair's performance against this position description.

While this is certainly a beneficial assessment model—for example, the chair assessing individual directors and the chair being assessed by another director—an alternative model would be that *who* does the assessing could be made to be more collective in nature. In other words, (1) the opinions of all directors would be solicited for an assessment of the effectiveness and contribution of the chair of the board, considering the position description of the chair of the board. Similarly, (2) the opinions of all committee members (and possibly noncommittee members and members of management, as appropriate) should be solicited for an assessment of the effectiveness and contribution of a chair of a committee of the board, for example, members of the audit committee would offer their views on the effectiveness of the chair of the audit committee, considering the position description, and so on. Similarly, (3) directors collectively would assess one another based on the position description for individual directors, for example, a peer assessment whereby directors assess one another's effectiveness.

There are various models that can be used so far as *who* does the assessing, but the Policy is recommending that an assessment of an individual director "should consider . . . the applicable position description(s)."

Individual Director Assessment Considering "The Competencies and Skills Each Individual Director Is Expected to Bring to the Board"   Under section 3.12 of the Policy, the board should "adopt a process involving the following steps: (A) Consider what competencies and skills the board, as a whole, should possess" and "(B) Assess what competencies and skills each existing director possesses." Step (B) goes on to read, "Attention should also be paid to the personality and other qualities of each director, as these may ultimately determine the boardroom dynamic." This two-step nominating procedure appears to go beyond governance guidelines in other jurisdictions, for example, United States, United Kingdom, Australia, and so on, and explicitly acknowledges the impact that competencies and behaviors of directors have on boardroom decision making and governance effectiveness.

The Policy goes on to read, "In carrying out these functions, the board should consider the advice and input of the nominating committee." In addition, section 3.14 reads that "the nominating committee should consider (a) the competencies and skills that the board considers to be necessary for the board, as a whole, to possess; (b) the competencies and skills that the board considers each existing director to possess; and (c) the competencies and skills each new nominee will bring to the boardroom."

Essentially, what sections 3.12 and 3.14 mean is that —as part of *who* is responsible for assessing the competency and skills of individual directors—the nominating committee would advise and provide input to the board and would now have the primary responsibility for undertaking a competency and skills gap assessment of the existing board. A model or way for a nominating committee to approach this would be in the form of a sequential Competency and Skills Matrix Analysis, as follows:

1. Determining the competencies and skills the board should have, given the company, its industry, its strategic environment, and its CEO, for example, say along a vertical axis
2. Assessing which competencies and skills are possessed by which incumbent directors, for example, say along the horizontal axis, checking off or rating which directors possess which competencies and skills
3. Having the competencies and skills gap drive the selection of new directors

Under the Instrument (*Disclosure of Corporate Governance Practices*), "the process by which the board identifies new candidates for board nomination" would have to be described (§ 6).

In determining what competencies and skills the board should possess, together with which directors possess which competencies and skills, members of the nominating committee under the leadership of the chair might wish to design an inclusive process for the board to adopt that might incorporate the views of individual directors and other parties, for example, (1) the chair of the board; (2) the chief executive officer (who may have input into the strategic skills needed by the directors); (3) individual directors who do not sit on the nominating committee (who may have views on competencies and skills that the board should possess, as well as views on their own competencies and skills); (4) outside advisers, for example, director search firms; and (5) members of management as appropriate. Care should be exercised by the nominating committee in identifying and assessing particular competencies that a certain director(s) might be expected to bring to the board as well as the manner in which directors contribute such competencies.

> *For instance, some directors perform in committee. Some directors perform more one-on-one. Some directors use their outside expertise. Some directors are active in the community. So effectiveness measurements should measure the different ways the directors contribute. (Director)*

CRITERIA FOR ASSESSING BOARD AND COMMITTEE EFFECTIVENESS AND CONTRIBUTION

> *Research by ... shows that a majority of FTSE 100 companies prefer self-assessment. . . . The preference for self-assessment is problematic—not least because it may prove to be a warm, self-congratulatory pat on the boardroom back.*
> —Plender 2005

There is presently no generally accepted definition of *board effectiveness*. One could say in general terms that such a definition would encompass the elements necessary to enable a board to discharge its responsibilities owed to the corporation and its shareholders as required by legislation or regulation. The first step in assessing its effectiveness is for the board of directors to identify and describe its specific responsibilities. These responsibilities should be reflected in a comprehensive, up-to-date mandate for the board, charters for the principal committees of the board—for example, the audit committee, the compensation committee, and the nominating and corporate governance committee—and position descriptions for individual directors, for example, the chair of the board, the chairs of each board committee, individual directors, and the CEO.

Section 3.18 of the Policy reads that the board and its committees, in assessing their effectiveness and contribution, should consider the mandate of the board and charters of committees, respectively. Section 3.4 of the Policy refers to the mandate of the board and other sections of the Policy refer to responsibilities of specific committees, for example, the compensation and nominating committees. In assessing audit committee effectiveness, other Multilateral Instruments (including one proposed) refer to responsibilities regarding audit committees and financial reporting, for example, "Certification of Disclosure in Issuers' Annual and Interim Filings," "Audit Committees," and "Reporting on Internal Control over Financial Reporting." These regulatory requirements should be incorporated into assessing whether a board of directors and committees of the board are effective.

For example, when assessing the effectiveness of a board of directors, directors should be canvassed as to whether the mandate of the board is being fulfilled. Section 3.4 of the Policy refers to the mandate of the board, building on the Dey guidelines, and reads as follows:

The board should adopt a written mandate in which it explicitly acknowledges responsibility for the stewardship of the issuer, including responsibility for:

(a) to the extent feasible, satisfying itself as to the integrity of the chief executive officer (the CEO) and other executive officers and that the CEO and other executive officers create a culture of integrity throughout the organization;

(b) adopting a strategic planning process and approving, on at least an annual basis, a strategic plan which takes into account, among other things, the opportunities and risks of the business;

(c) the identification of the principal risks of the issuer's business, and ensuring the implementation of appropriate systems to manage these risks;

(d) succession planning (including appointing, training and monitoring senior management);

(e) adopting a communication policy for the issuer;

(f) the issuer's internal control and management information systems; and

(g) developing the issuer's approach to corporate governance, including developing a set of corporate governance principles and guidelines that are specifically applicable to the issuer.

The written mandate of the board should also set out:

(i) measures for receiving feedback from stakeholders (e.g., the board may wish to establish a process to permit stakeholders to directly contact the independent directors), and
(ii) expectations and responsibilities of directors, including basic duties and responsibilities with respect to attendance at board meetings and advance review of meeting materials. . . .

At a minimum, when assessing the effectiveness of a board, the board's effectiveness as measured against the above mandate should be assessed. Since boards tend not to share the details of the basis on which they assess their effectiveness, it is difficult to determine how reliable assessments may be—they could consist of a simple self-evaluation checklist or questionnaire. See, for example, Stuart and the Rotman School of Management (2003, 7): "The current nature of evaluations raises some important issues. Performance evaluations are useful only if they are conducted objectively and provide constructive feedback to directors. Based on survey responses, the most common method of conducting evaluations is a written questionnaire followed by interviews or meetings among directors. Since companies tend not to share details of how these evaluations are conducted, this raises questions as to how effective they are."

When assessing whether the board fulfills each of the above responsibilities, however, it is important that this undertaking not be regarded merely as a generic, high-level, check-the-box undertaking, whereby the board and its committees simply assesses whether they have adequately fulfilled each of the responsibilities in their mandate or charter. The underlying robustness of the above responsibilities, including the drivers and interdependencies, should be adequately canvassed in order to maximize the value inherent in the assessment undertaking. If the right subquestions in an assessment are not asked, tailored to a particular board and consistent with leading practices, then the answers and dialogue will not follow. Therefore, the opportunities in an assessment process may be lost and the board, ultimately, will not address key issues that may be affecting its effectiveness. The opportunity to enhance shareholder value will be missed.

Other Elements of Board Effectiveness that Should Be Assessed

> *The key to better corporate governance lies in the working relationships between boards and managers, in the social dynamics of board interaction, and in the competence, integrity and constructive involvement of individual directors.*
>
> —Nadler 2004, 102

> *At least as important are the human dynamics of boards as social systems where leadership character, individual values, decision making processes, conflict management, and strategic thinking will truly differentiate a firm's governance. Can fellow directors be trusted? Does management provide the full story? Is there enough time for advanced reading and full discussion of materials? Is dissent encouraged? Are people well prepared? Does management allow themselves to be vulnerable? How are board members kept accountable for their preparation and decisions? How is assessment conducted so board members can learn and improve?*
>
> —Sonnenfeld 2004, 112

> *[F]or a board of directors to be effective at accomplishing the tasks assigned to it, it needs to have the right board structure, supported by the right board membership, and engaged in the right board processes.*
>
> —Leblanc and Gillies 2003, 9

Board process refers to how directors make decisions. Boards of directors, like most groups, are made up of diverse individuals, all of whom have different behavioral patterns that govern their actions. Board process should be an important part of any board or committee assessment.

Broadly speaking, board process includes the following elements:

- Board leadership effectiveness, that is, the independence of mind, competencies, and behaviors of the chair of the board and chairs of board committees
- The *hard* components, including:
  - Information (for example, quantity, quality, timeliness, source, and format)
  - Setting of board and committee agendas, work plans, calendars of responsibilities, etc.

- Length, frequency, and location of board and committee meetings
- Management resources and support provided to the board and committees
- The *soft* components, including:
  - The operation of board and committee meetings
  - The quality of board discussions and the overall decision-making effectiveness
  - Executive sessions (for example, with independent directors only; with the CEO as the only executive director; and with independent advisers in the absence of management)
  - The balance of director behavioral characteristics that the board, as a whole, should possess to ensure a healthy dynamic and effective decision making
  - The behavioral posture of the CEO toward governance and the relationship between the CEO and the board
  - Exposure to and relationship with the CEO's direct reports and the board
  - Exposure to and relationship with independent advisers and the board
  - The quality of management presentations to the board and committees
  - Committee reporting to the board and delegation from the board to committees
  - Informal board processes such as board dinners, offline communications, strategic retreats etc.
- The identification of problem areas for the board

A lack of attention to board process during a board effectiveness assessment means ignoring an important reality—it is the behavior of directors, and the mix of behavioral characteristics of directors, that really determine the decision-making effectiveness of the board.

Criteria for Assessing the Effectiveness and Contribution of an Individual Director

The assessment needs to recognize the distinctive set of competencies that each director brings to the boardroom. At the same time, there should be a set of general dimensions that describe what is expected from every director irrespective of his or her expertise.

—Conger and Lawler 2003, 3

The National Association of Corporate Directors (NACD), in its Report of the NACD Blue Ribbon Commission on Director Professionalism—2005 Edition, set out five "guidelines [to] help boards select qualified director candidates for board membership" (2005, 9), including (1) personal characteristics, (2 core competencies, (3) independence, (4) level of commitment, and (5) team and company considerations. In speaking to "personal characteristics," the Report goes on to address "integrity and accountability," "informed judgment," "financial literacy," "mature confidence" and "high performance standards." In speaking to "core competencies of the board," the Report goes on to address "accounting and finance," "business judgment," "management," "crisis response," "industry knowledge," "international markets," "leadership," and "strategy/vision," and so on. In an earlier Report of the NACD Blue Ribbon Commission on Board Leadership (2004), the NACD included position descriptions for the nonexecutive chairman, CEO, and lead director and remarked, "Selection of board leaders should be based on performance, and leaders should be evaluated regularly" (2004, 5).

The Canadian Policy, released April 2005, is recommending that an assessment of an individual director should consider "the applicable position description(s), as well as the competencies and skills each individual director is expected to bring to the board." Both of these items will be discussed at greater length in turn.

The "Applicable Position Description(s)"   In a previous iteration of the Instrument ("Proposed Multilateral Instrument 58-101: Disclosure of Corporate Governance Practices," January 16, 2004, at § 3), if companies did not have position descriptions for the roles of (1) chair, (2) chair of each board committee, and (3) director, they would have had to explain how the board assesses the performance of the individuals who occupy these roles. In the final Instrument, companies will have to disclose whether the board has developed written position descriptions for the chair of the board and chair of each board committee, that is, not individual directors, and the Policy recommends that the assessment *consider* the position description(s) applicable to the individual director. In other words, as iterations of the Policy and Instrument developed, there is not a formal requirement for position descriptions for individual directors (there is, however, for the chair of the board and committee chairs) and it is not recommended that individual directors be assessed against the position description(s) that applies to them, only that the assessment of an individual director consider the applicable position description(s).

There are many important reasons why the preparation and adoption of position descriptions are essential for any board that aspires to operate efficiently and to provide good corporate governance, but two are overwhelming—first, it is the only way to ensure that all the elements essential for the proper operation of a board of directors are being dealt with; and second, without specific, explicit performance requirements, it is unlikely, or at least highly difficult, to make sound judgments about the effectiveness of various people involved in, and activities associated with, the board's functions.

"The Competencies and Skills Each Individual Director Is Expected to Bring to the Board"   A major condition for board success is the presence of directors on the board with the competencies needed to assure the company can achieve its goals. Director competencies may be defined broadly as the knowledge, experience, education, and training that a director brings to the boardroom. Competencies may be classified as generic or core competencies, required of all directors, for example, business judgment, but include more specific competencies that are aligned with the company's business, circumstances, and strategic environment.

Defining, and more importantly assessing in a rigorous manner, very precise, specific competencies that individual directors possess may be difficult for many boards to do, but such an exercise must be undertaken if the board is to have the right directors serving on it. The first step in determining that the board collectively has the appropriate competencies to fulfill its responsibilities is the creation by the chair of the nominating committee, in consultation with the chair of the board and other directors, of a Director Competency Matrix Analysis, as the Policy is recommending. Once such a matrix is prepared, the gaps between the board and the necessary competencies can be readily identified.

In addition, it is the appropriate combination of the varying behavior characteristics of such directors (that is, the *chemistry* among them) that also determines whether the board will operate effectively. Individually, you can be independent and competent as a director, but if you do not behave in a certain way, you will not be effective. Therefore, the softer skills of directors should also form part of this assessment. In the words of the CSA's Policy, "Attention should also be paid to the personality and other qualities of each director, as these may ultimately determine the boardroom dynamic" (at § 3.12). It is the behavior of directors, and the mix of behavioral characteristics of directors, that really determine the effectiveness of the board.

METHODS IN CONDUCTING GOVERNANCE ASSESSMENTS

Governance assessment criteria need to be applied, measured, and interpreted in meaningful and constructive ways, ensuring as much as possible that bias and subjectivity are removed from the assessment process. There are different approaches and methods possible, and they can be summarized under the broad headings of *quantitative* and *qualitative*.

Quantitative Analysis

A questionnaire or survey is a preferred method. Questions should address depth, rather than merely canvassing scope. They should contain a combination of quantitative scoring metrics as well as qualitative, for example, verbal commentary enabling directors to write in a more open-ended fashion. Responding in a more open-ended fashion provides context and color to quantitative ratings. Questions can also be structured in a more closed-ended fashion, for example, using scales such as binary, Likert, semantic differential, numerical, ordinal word, and ranking (Australian Institute of Company Directors 2003).

A difficulty with questionnaires is asking the right questions for a particular board, consistent with best practices, in order to surface key issues that contribute to board and individual director effectiveness.

The questionnaires are then collected and the data are compiled and analyzed, with recommendations for improvement that may accompany the analysis.

Having Management Participate in the Questionnaire as Appropriate

If board members are comfortable doing so, members of management may also participate in a particular questionnaire or governance assessment, in a so-called 360-degree feedback method. A disadvantage to this method is that it might confuse accountability in that management is accountable to the board. An advantage to this approach is that management may also offer valid, constructive feedback on the effectiveness of the board, committee, or individual directors in certain instances. For example, a CEO may offer constructive views on how a director can more effectively understand the key drivers of the business, and in doing so, improve that director's effectiveness at providing strategic input to the CEO and management team. The CFO could offer constructive suggestions to members of the audit committee; the chief risk officer might offer similar suggestions to members of a risk management committee; the chief human resources officer vis-à-vis the compensation committee, and so on.

Qualitative Analysis

The two approaches here are interviews and direct observations, the former being far more prevalent. An interview can be structured or more unstructured and free-flowing, and can create a powerful dynamic if done properly. An interview can be between the director and the chairman of the board, the chair of a particular committee, or a governance adviser. A major advantage of an interview, depending on the skill of the interviewer and how confidentiality and trust is handled, is that it may provide greater candor and be more effective in addressing sensitive issues and key points that may not surface in a (mechanistic) questionnaire.

An interview, however, is time-intensive. An interview can also be more collective in nature, with varying degrees of participation, for example, a facilitated group discussion. A governance assessment model can be designed so that the questionnaire—canvassing a wider scope and identification of key issues—can precede a more qualitative, in-depth interview, where deep dives and key insights are possible.

The second qualitative method is direct observation of a board of directors and committees in action. This is not an option for the vast majority of boards because of confidentiality concerns, culture, past practices, and so forth. However, unobtrusive observation by a trained qualitative researcher provides robust data on board and individual director effectiveness. Depending on the comfort level of directors, direct observation of the board as a group in real time can be designed to round out a quantitative questionnaire and interviews with individual directors.

External Assistance with Governance Assessments

> *There is so much pride and ego with high rollers that it is worse than death to be embarrassed or lose face in front of their peers. So you must manage the process of board and peer assessments so there is no war path or sabotage.*
> —Professional adviser

An advantage that a board of directors has in conducting an internal self-assessment, with the administrative support from management as appropriate, is that, providing there is candor on the part of directors, the board is presumably most informed and able to judge whether the board, committees of the board, and individual directors are effective. Directors have an intimate knowledge of the board's inner-workings, including decision-making dynamics, processes, and the skills, competencies, and personalities of their colleagues. The board also (presumably) understands and knows the business and the industry in which it operates and has regular exposure to the management team. This knowledge is important when it comes to assessing the board's own performance in overseeing strategic planning, management succession planning, risk management, and oversight of and relations with the CEO and other senior officers.

However, some disadvantages of a board conducting its own internal review, depending on the board makeup, include the following:

- The board may not possess the knowledge of leading assessment practices or may lack experience in conducting the review.
- The board may lack sufficient objectivity, as directors are ultimately assessing themselves.
- The board, as any small group, may be vulnerable to subtle political or interpersonal agendas and relations.
- Directors may simply lack the time and resources to conduct a thorough review.

Most importantly, however, depending on who sees the data and how the data are managed, the assessment may result in a lack of candor on the part of directors. As an almost entirely closed decision-making body, a board lacking in leadership may not have a *catalyst* for generating critical momentum and necessary buy-in to conduct the assessment, particularly if it is doing so for the first time or there is strong resistance from an influential director or a majority shareholder. Ultimately, directors may simply lack a comfort level and not know how to proceed. As a result, self-assessments by boards might default into informal discussions with the chair, result in pro-forma check-the-box surveys of some sort, of a few pages or so, or, worst yet, not occur at all.

A source of assistance and support to the board is an external adviser or service provider who specializes in advising boards and has the experience and expertise in conducting board reviews. Governance advisors— who are accountable to the board rather than management—will bring a level of objectivity and independence to the process that, from the start, contributes to board buy-in and provides the needed comfort level, especially to skeptical directors, that the criteria for the assessment and the assessment process itself have integrity. Independent advisers also assist boards, committees, and directors in compiling the data and providing feedback and recommendations to the board and to individual directors in a credible, constructive, and meaningful way. Although external experts may lack the full industry and firm-specific knowledge that directors possess, those who are quick studies and methodologically trained may come up to speed quickly in working with the chair of the board or chair of the governance committee in enhancing the value of the assessment process.

This said, however, the board as a whole must own the entire assessment process and be completely comfortable with it. An expert brings expertise, but may never fully appreciate the complex subtleties, alliances, dynamics, and the historical and political landscape within a given boardroom.

Boards contemplating assessments, or improving upon those they have already conducted, therefore, should obtain external advice, including (1) canvassing director-colleagues who have used assessment models and processes on other boards on which they serve, (2) talking to management such as the Corporate Secretary and General Counsel, and (3) speaking to outside advisers to the board. Publications from director associations may provide useful guidance. Management may also provide assistance, including obtaining suggestions and expertise from professional and industry associations to which they belong. Management may also play a facilitative and coordinating role, providing resources and administrative support, under the leadership of the board.

THE INFORMATION PRODUCED BY THE GOVERNANCE ASSESSMENT

> *How will the feedback be handled? This is probably the single most important component of the entire process. Deciding who will share the feedback with whom, in what settings, under what conditions and employing what steps to turn feedback into action—those are the choices that may ultimately determine whether the assessment is a success or a failure.*
>
> —Nadler 2003, 14

Directors do express concern about how the data emerging from governance assessments are managed and who would see them. There therefore need to be appropriate assurances of confidentiality and confidence in the data compilation and interpretation and the provision of feedback to individual directors. That said, there are various possibilities for carrying this out, and best practices are continuing to emerge. Directors need to be comfortable with the process and tailor it to suit their circumstances.

In general terms:

1. The data from the board assessment are disclosed to, and discussed by, the entire board in aggregate form.

2. The chair of the board could be assessed as part of the board assessment, with the data from the chair's assessment being provided to all directors. Alternatively, the chair of the board could have a separate assessment with the aggregate data being provided to one or more directors, a committee of the board, or the entire board, depending on preferences of the individuals involved.

3. The data from a committee assessment are shared with all committee members, as well as with the full board, that is, all directors.

4. The chair of a committee of the board could be assessed as part of the committee assessment, with the data from the committee chair's assessment provided to committee members and the chair of the board or the full board. Alternatively, the chair of a committee could have a separate assessment with the aggregate data provided to one or more directors, the committee of which the director is chair, or the entire board, depending on the preferences of the individuals involved.

5. The data, and/or recommendations flowing from the data in the first and fourth items above, are shared with members of management in addition to the CEO, as appropriate and in the discretion of the individuals involved, for feedback and remediation purposes; for example, the board is not receiving appropriate information from management, the working relationship between the chair of the risk committee and the chief risk officer may be impaired, and so on.

6. For director self-assessments, the nonexecutive chair or lead director may see the data under appropriate circumstances, that is, with consent of the director, as may a trusted corporate secretary for data compilation or filing purposes.

7. The data from an individual director peer assessment—that is, directors all assessing one another—are provided to the individual director to whom the assessment applies, but are not shared with other directors. In other words, directors see their own individual results but not the results of their colleagues. These data could consist of anonymous commentary in order to provide candor, for example, written qualitative responses without individual directors being identified. Quantitative scores could also be used.

8. However, a summary of the aggregate data of a peer assessment may be presented to the chair of the board, corporate governance committee, and/or the board without individual directors being identified.

9. The raw data from an individual director's peer assessment may be shared with the chair of the board for feedback and remediation purposes, if the director being assessed is comfortable doing so.

Over time, as boards and directors become more comfortable with assessments, there may be an increasing likelihood that assessment data will be shared more broadly with other directors, as appropriate and in a constructive, enabling manner. In other words, the data from an assessment of the chair of the board may be shared with all directors; the data from an assessment of the chair of committees may be shared with all directors; and the data from individual director peer assessments may be shared with all directors. It is important, however, to remember that boards should design a process with which they are comfortable, to suit their circumstances and at their stage in the assessment cycle, as there are different models and approaches that are possible.

DIRECTOR CONCERNS WITH GOVERNANCE ASSESSMENT CONFIDENTIALITY VERSUS SHAREHOLDER DISCLOSURE

So far, reporting on board evaluation in the annual report tends to be bland, with little information on responses to findings.
—Plender, 2005

Shareholders' understanding of board and director assessment processes and criteria is indispensable to both board credibility and shareholders' ability to appraise the board's recommended resolutions and proposed slate of directors. Boards should disclose evaluation procedures to shareholders in the proxy statement or other shareholder communication. Board disclosure of procedures is distinct from sharing the substance of such deliberations, which should be confidential.
—Report of the NACD Blue Ribbon Commission on Director Professionalism—2005 Edition, 19

There needs to be a balance between disclosure to shareholders about governance assessment criteria and processes and the legitimate need to have a *zone of privilege* surrounding assessments in order to promote the disclosure of candid, meaningful data by directors. This is not unlike other forms of privilege, for example, solicitor–client, doctor–patient, and so on. One would be considerably more reluctant to be candid and therefore obtain the best professional advice if it were possible that sensitive information about an individual could be disclosed to third parties who did not have a legitimate right to know, for example, the government, a regulator, the other side in a court case, and so on. This concern with confidentiality does not necessarily imply that boards or directors have anything in particular to hide, only that such concerns are quite legitimate and must be respected in order for the governance assessment process to work and have integrity.

Therefore, the data from governance assessments must be confidential and not disclosed to outsiders without full board approval. Otherwise, directors will be deterred from being candid and the assessment process will not work.

The fact that a board engages in an assessment (and perhaps the criteria being assessed, for example, board mandate, committee charters, position descriptions, if these documents are used as a basis for board, committee, and director assessments, respectively) ought to be disclosed to shareholders, but such disclosure should not include any specific results. Those boards who see fit to do so may also wish to disclose the competencies and skills that the board as a whole should possess or that individual directors are expected to bring to the board, but such disclosure should not include any individual director assessment results of competencies and skills.

The National Instrument 58-101 Disclosure of Corporate Governance Practices sets out corporate governance disclosure in the areas of the board of directors, the board mandate, position descriptions, orientation and continuing education, ethical business conduct, the nomination of directors, compensation, other board committees, and finally, assessments. Reporting issuers to which the Instrument applies will be required to disclose whether the board, its committees, and individual directors are regularly assessed with respect to their effectiveness and contribution. If assessments are conducted, the process will need to be described. If the board does not conduct governance assessments, it will need to justify this decision. This will be increasingly difficult to do.

ACTING ON THE RESULTS OF THE GOVERNANCE ASSESSMENT

> *An evaluation process is only as effective as the decisions and action plans that come out of it.*
>
> —Kiel 2004

> *The problem is that the information isn't acted upon, other than the individual director initiative—where you stand in relation to the average. Directors aren't acting upon the data. There's no 360-degree mechanism for feedback.*
>
> —Director

Assessments offer the opportunity for boards to set internal performance benchmarks, assess their own effectiveness, and focus on opportunities for development, with the objective of remediation and self-improvement. From the outset of a board assessment, there needs to be a commitment from the board, its committees, and individual directors to be receptive to and act on the resulting data.

It is important that the board prioritize opportunities for improvement and not try to do too much too soon or, worse yet, avoid acting on the data. The board could commit to collectively selecting three or four key issues and working on those for the next year, or until the next assessment. Boards should therefore take assessments one step at a time, have a work plan to address the issues, act on the data, and be held accountable collectively as peers for doing so. Otherwise, the assessment process will lack credibility and directors may become cynical if their comments are not followed up on. In setting such priorities, leadership by the chair or lead director is essential.

> *That's why it's so important to have a regular performance process, for everyone to see, with objective data. The better job the board does at a performance management system, the better it will detect performance problems and then have to deal with them. For example, "here are the five objectives that we have not accomplished." (Director)*

The feedback and remediation plans for a committee assessment are similar. Once the data from the committee assessment (for example, the audit committee) are tabulated, analyzed, and reported back to committee members and the rest of the board, the chair of the committee should take ownership of the results and fashion an action plan on a going-forward basis that addresses the assessment, incorporating the findings into the committee's calendar of responsibilities. The governance committee (or its equivalent, the board as a whole or the chair of the board) may be the focal point of holding individual committees accountable for acting on their assessments. The chair of the board or chair of the governance committee should communicate with other committee chairs as he or she deems appropriate. In other words, committee chairs should be accountable for ensuring that committee assessments are addressed and the resulting recommendations are implemented in a timely fashion. In summary, the results of the committee assessments must be owned by all committee members and integrated into the committee's work plan, under the leadership of the committee chair.

Concerted efforts should be made at closing the loop on individual feedback and remediation as well so that development opportunities can be provided to directors. A one-on-one meeting between the director and the chair of the board may be the most appropriate forum for this debriefing. At this meeting, the director should be encouraged to share his or her assessment with the chair, as a basis for a candid discussion. If warranted, the chair and the individual director should sculpt out a developmental path for the director based on the director's assessment (self or peer). Often the data are sufficient as a prompt for remediation, but an effective chair will ensure that the director gets any assistance he or she needs. This might include courses, outside assistance, tutorials, and talking with the chair about how that director might shift or modify his or her behavior to become more effective in the eyes of colleagues.

For feedback and remediation for the chair of the board assessment, the sit-down should occur between the chair of the board (as recipient of the feedback) and the chair of the corporate governance committee, or its equivalent, using a similar approach.

The assessments should be developmental as opposed to judgmental. (Director)

THE NONPERFORMING CHAIR OF THE BOARD

Although board chairmen have no statutory position, the choice of who is to fill that post is crucial to board effectiveness. Broadening the point, when we attend a meeting of any kind, we can sense almost from the start whether the chairman is competent or not. Providing he or she is, the meeting will serve its purpose. If the chairman is not up to the task, it is improbable that the meeting will achieve anything but frustration and waste of that most precious of resources—time.

—Cadbury 2002

[Only] 16% of Boards with a non-executive Chair specified they had a process for evaluating the Chair's performance. . . .
—Patrick O'Callaghan & Associates 2004

The Blue Ribbon Commission Report on Board Leadership (2004), of the National Institute of Directors, advocates "not one or two leaders, but a system of leadership." (The Report was released by the NACD (National Association of Corporate Directors), Washington, DC, October 2004. The Commission's Co-Chairs were Professor Jay W. Lorsch and Dr. David A. Nadler.) "[W]e view leadership as a complex issue. Our perspective is that the requirements for leadership in boards are changing, but that structural solutions alone do not help boards become more effective in their primary purpose of ensuring the long-term health of the enterprise on behalf of stakeholders, including shareholders" (National Association of Corporate Directors 2004, 3–4).

The leadership of the board—namely the independence of mind, competence and behaviors of the chair of the board—is perhaps the single most important factor impacting effective board process, optimal decision making, and overall board effectiveness. The board should develop a clear position description for the chair of the board. The position description should be comprehensive and conform to best practices, as well as perhaps be tailored to any unique circumstances present.

> *There should be a special course for how to be a chairman. Training for chairmen. The right chairman creates the right atmosphere. With the wrong chairman, it's completely different. (Director)*

As is the case with other directors, the chair should be assessed based on the applicable position description, should receive appropriate feedback on performance and should have an opportunity for remediation to improve his or her effectiveness, if warranted. If it is deemed that a nonperforming chair cannot improve his or her effectiveness, then the chair should be asked to leave the board or step down as chair.

THE NONPERFORMING DIRECTOR

> *Although advocates of corporate governance plead for a formal board and director evaluation, this is still a bridge too far for most boards. Only a small number of companies evaluate the performance of the entire board. Individual director evaluation is also exceptional and occurs mainly if a director stands for re-election.*
>
> —Van den Berghe and Levrau 2004, 470–471

> *Boards should require that all directors submit for consideration a resignation as a matter of course if evaluation indicates that they are not meeting standards established by the board, if their actions reflect poorly upon the board and the company (e.g., scandal, indictment), or if poor health or new and pressing commitments prevent effective functioning. If, through the evaluation process or otherwise, it becomes apparent that a director is not meeting the standards established by the board*

(including ethical standards), where appropriate the governance committee should provide the director with feedback, additional education, or other reasonable means of guidance. If such attempts are either inappropriate or unsuccessful, the director's resignation should be accepted.
                              —Report of the NACD Blue Ribbon Commission
                              on Director Professionalism—2005 Edition, 20

In a similar manner, counseling ineffective directors off the board cannot be done unless there is a fair and equitable manner for assessment of the directors' effectiveness and, in any event, should only be done after concerted efforts have been undertaken to remediate identified areas of improvement resulting from the assessment.

The peer appraisal was effective for one director. He said to the board, "I realize no one wants me on this board." But he stayed and his performance increased significantly. (CEO)

From a competency and behavioral standpoint, the task of improving the effectiveness of a particular director may be a difficult undertaking. Behavioral characteristics especially may be well-ingrained. Competency augmentation requires time and effort. The director may not recognize the need to improve. And if the director does, he or she may not reach out to colleagues or obtain external assistance.

Counseling ineffective directors off a board requires effective board leadership. The cost of not doing so is resentment by fellow directors, the use of a valuable board seat, and an overall decline in the effectiveness of the board.

LINKING INDIVIDUAL DIRECTOR ASSESSMENT AND CONTINUED SERVICE ON THE BOARD

Sixty-nine percent of directors in the Americas stated their Boards have mandatory retirement ages. We anticipate that retirement age policies are going to become a topic of debate as Boards become more effective in annually reviewing their compositions.
                              —Patrick O'Callaghan & Associates 2004, 44

Interestingly, the most popular practice having to do with membership—enforcing an age limit for board members—is not significantly related to board effectiveness. This observation raises the interesting question of whether this practice should be in place at all, particularly given concerns about age discrimination. The same may be true of term limits, which have become increasingly popular even though they are not related to board effectiveness.
—Lawler and Finegold 2005, 69–70)

As evaluation gains favour, tenure limits and mandatory retirement are becoming less attractive.
—Report of the NACD Blue Ribbon Commission on Director Professionalism—2005 Edition, 26 fn 27

The majority of boards have some type of formal or informal retirement plan—including chronological age, tenure in years, geographical restrictions, change-in-principal-occupation restrictions, or restrictions on the number of external directorships. Part of the rationale for these types of policies is that they provide transparency and remove the perception or possibility of inconsistent or arbitrary treatment of directors. These types of policies do have a downside, however, as directors have pointed out, the most important of which is that these types of measurements, for example, age, tenure, and so forth, may not be indicative of the effectiveness of a particular director.

I don't see the need for tenure. Both age 70 and tenure are mechanisms to deal with the issue of non-performers. Otherwise, why participate and have an age of 70? Really as a board it's a real loss [in losing an effective director because of a fixed retirement age] and others we couldn't wait and should strike them at age 66. Tenure is designed to avoid dealing with performance. (Director)

The fuzzy [stuff] about lowering the retirement age, tenure—it all comes down, as non-executive chairman, you tap old Charlie, the nonperformer, on the shoulder, after you've talked to others, and say he has no time if he's young, or tell him "don't stand for re-election." So fire me if I'm not doing my job. Don't use tenure or retirement. They're excuses for non-performers. (Chair)

Professor Jeffrey Sonnenfeld, in "Good Governance and the Misleading Myths of Bad Metrics" (*Academy of Management Executive*, February 2004), addresses the corporate governance myths of age, split CEO/board chairman, director equity, former CEO, independent board, and outmoded standards of attendance, size, and others, and the lack of empirical support for many of these items. The age of a director, tenure on a board, number of shares a director owns, strict attendance measures, number of other boards on which a director serves, formal independence standards, and so on may have a limited relationship as to whether a particular director is effective or not within a boardroom. Empirical literature supports the lack of a settled relationship between these types of board structure variables and board effectiveness or corporate performance. (See, for example, "The Directors' Consortium" Questionnaire, a working paper canvassing some of the empirical literature, presented by the author at the University of Chicago, August 24, 2005.) While these types of governance metrics are relatively easy to measure, a problem with such metrics is that what can be readily measured may matter less in determining good corporate governance than the competency and behavioral characteristics of the board members, which are very difficult to measure, but nonetheless may impact board and individual director effectiveness.

The implication of all this for the assessment of individual director effectiveness is that, as assessments become *de rigueur* over the next several years, and assessments of individual directors in particular, tenure on a board should instead be based on, or at least incorporate the data from, director effectiveness assessments: As a director, you continue to serve on a board as long as you remain effective in the eyes of those who know your performance most—your board colleagues. Shareholders should thus insist that this link be made more explicit by corporate boards, namely the link between director effectiveness and director tenure, as opposed to using arbitrary measures which may or may not reflect actual director effectiveness.

For boards themselves, this may mean moving from a succession policy based on attrition to one that has as its foundation individual director effectiveness. In the short to medium term, this might involve progressing with a hybrid policy of (1) external limitors, for example, chronological age or tenure, coupled with (2) internal robustness, for example, director assessments. Making such a policy change would require two actions: (1) the actual assessment of individual directors, and (2) the association of the resulting assessment data with continued tenure by that director, that is, acting on the data obtained through effective board leadership. More boards may choose to revise their tenure policies as the emphasis on assessing individual directors continues, particularly if rating agencies begin to focus on individual director effectiveness assessments as well.

FREQUENCY OF GOVERNANCE ASSESSMENTS

> *[W]e don't believe that boards need to evaluate their performance annually. Every two years is about right. Boards don't meet that often, and annual reviews tend to run into one another and to absorb too much of the board's time. A new cycle begins as soon as last year's effort is finished. This can become tiresome, and people will begin to see evaluation as an endless process, which erodes its effectiveness.*
>
> —Carter and Lorsch 2004, 125

Once board, committee, and individual director assessments are underway, they should be continued on a regular basis. Doing so provides numerous advantages:

- Assessments will become formally established as a continuing activity of the board.
- Assessment questionnaires and criteria may continue to be refined as the board becomes comfortable with the self-assessment process.
- Assessment tools and formats may expand, for example, more fulsome questionnaires, face-to-face interviews, observation of the board, fillable on-line forms, use of the Internet, etc.
- The board may experiment with the frequency of assessments, for example, a biannual review or a more comprehensive review might be undertaken in alternate years or every three years.
- Assessment data may be compared to those of a previous assessment, that is, across assessment cycles, thus providing trendlines, patterns, and a context so boards can track their improvement between assessments.
- Priorities can be established over time and the board can specifically address strengths, opportunities for improvement, and future challenges relating to board/committee and director performance and the link to shareholder value.
- The data obtained from ongoing assessments can be benchmarked against best practices, providing useful comparisons for directors on

how the board's effectiveness compares to that of other similar boards on a variety of performance criteria.

- A culture of continuous governance improvement can be instituted.

CONCLUSION

In summary, while assessments of the board and individual directors are often controversial and can raise many sensitive and legitimate issues and concerns, they are nevertheless well worth the undertaking. Assessments are an important investment in board effectiveness and experience shows that they can be accomplished with very positive results.

References

Accountancy Ireland. 2004. US oversight of Irish firms. *Accountancy Ireland* (December).

Adams, R. B., H. Almeida, and D. Ferreira. 2003. Understanding the relationship between founder-CEOs and firm performance. Working paper, Stockholm School of Economics.

Agrawal, A., and C. R. Knoeber. 1996. Firm performance and mechanisms to control agency problems between managers and shareholders. *Journal of Financial and Quantitative Analysis* 31 (3):377–398.

Agrawal, A., and G. Mandelkar. 1987. Managerial incentives and corporate investment and financing decisions. *Journal of Finance* 42 (4):823–838.

Albert, M. R. 1999. The future of death futures: Why viatical settlements must be classified as securities. *Pace Law Review* 19:345–430.

Alchian, A. A. 1950. Uncertainty, evolution and economic theory. *Journal of Political Economy* 58 (3):211–221.

Alchian, A. A., and H. Demsetz. 1972. Production, information, costs and economic organisation. *American Economic Review* 62 (5):777–795.

Ali, P. U., and M. Gold. 2002. Analysing the cost of ethical investment. *Journal of the Securities Institute of Australia* (3):9–14.

Ali, P. U., and J. J. de Vries Robbé. 2003. *Synthetic, insurance and hedge fund securitisations.* Sydney: Thomson.

Ali, P. U., G. P. Stapledon, and M. Gold. 2003. *Corporate governance and investment fiduciaries.* Rozelle, New South Wales: Lawbook Company.

Allen, F., and G. Gorton. 1993. Churning bubbles. *Review of Economic Studies* 60 (4):813–836.

Allen, J. W., and G. M. Phillips. 2000. Corporate equity ownership, strategic alliances, and product market relationships. *Journal of Finance* 55 (6):2791–2814.

Amaduzzi, A. 1978. *L'azienda nel suo sistema e nei suoi principi.* Torino: Utet.

Amin, G., and H. Kat. 2002. Welcome to the dark side: Hedge fund attrition and survivorship bias over the period 1994–2001. Working paper, ISMA Centre, University of Reading.

Anand, A. 2005. Voluntary vs. mandatory corporate governance towards an optimal regulatory framework. Working paper, Berkeley Electronic Press.

Anderson, R., and D. S. Lee. 1997. Ownership studies: The data source does matter. *Journal of Financial and Quantitative Analysis* 16 (3):311–329.

Anderson, R. C., S. A. Mansi, and D. M. Reeb. 2003. Founding family ownership and the agency cost of debt. *Journal of Financial Economics* 68 (2):263–285.

Anderson, R. C., and D. M. Reeb. 2003a. Founding-family ownership, corporate diversification and firm leverage. *Journal of Law and Economics* 46 (2):653–684.

Anderson, R. C., and D. M. Reeb. 2003b. Founding-family ownership and firm performance: Evidence from the S&P 500. *Journal of Finance* 58 (3):1301–1328.

Anderson, R. C., and D. M. Reeb. 2003c. Who monitors the family? Working paper, Kogod School of Business, American University.

Anderson, R. C., and D. M. Reeb. 2004. Board composition: Balancing family influence in S&P 500 firms. *Administrative Science Quarterly* 49 (2):209–237.

Asquith, P. 1983. Merger bids, uncertainty and stockholder returns. *Journal of Financial Economics* 11 (1):51–83.

Astrachan, J., S. Klein and K. Smyrnios. 2002. The F-PEC scale of family influence: A proposal for solving the family business definition problem. *Family Business Review* 15 (1):45–58.

Atkins, P. 2005. Speech by SEC commissioner: Remarks before the Charles Hamilton Houston Lecture. Washington, DC., April 4.

Attig, N., F. Klaus, and Y. Gadhoum. 2003. On the determinants, costs and benefits of pyramidal ownership: Evidence on dilution of minority interest. Working paper, EFA Maastricht.

Australian Council of Superannuation Investors. 2003. Corporate governance guidelines for superannuation trustees and corporations. Melbourne: Australian Council of Superannuation Investors.

Australian Financial Review. 2005a. Beware Big Brother. *Australian Financial Review* (April 13):38.

Australian Financial Review. 2005b. Putting a price on a founder's control. *Australian Financial Review* (April 13):29.

Australian Institute of Company Directors. 2003. Results of an AICD survey of directors of Australian listed companies on the ASX Corporate Governance Council, September 25.

Australian Law Reform Commission. 1982. *Insurance contracts.* ALRC Report No. 20. Canberra: Australian Law Reform Commission.

Australian Securities and Investments Commission. 2003. Section 1013DA disclosure guidelines: ASIC guidelines to product issuers for disclosure about labour standards or environmental, social and ethical considerations in product disclosure statements. Sydney: Australian Securities and Investments Commission.

Australian Stock Exchange Corporate Governance Council. 2003. *Principles of good corporate governance and best practice recommendations.* Sydney: Australian Stock Exchange.

Automatic Data Processing (ADP) Investor Communication Services. 2005. 2005 proxy season key statistics and performance ratings.

Autorité des Marchés Financiers (AMF). 2005. *RAPPORT AMF 2004 sur les informations publiées par les émetteurs faisant appel public à l'épargne relatives aux conditions de préparation et d'organisation des travaux du conseil d'administration ou de surveillance ainsi qu'aux procédures de contrôle interne.* Paris: Autorité des Marchés Financiers.

Badreshia, S., V. Bansal, P. S. Houts, and N. Ballentine. 2002. Viatical settlements: Effects on terminally ill patients. *Cancer Practice* 10 (6):293–296.

Bakan, J. 2004. *The corporation: The pathological pursuit of profit and power.* London: Constable and Robinson.

Baker, G. P., M. C. Jensen, and K. J. Murphy. 1988. Compensation and incentives: Practice vs. theory. *Journal of Finance* 43 (3):593–615.

Baliga, B. R., R. C. Moyer, and R. S. Rao. 1996. CEO duality and firm performance: What's the fuss? *Strategic Management Journal* 17 (1):41–53.

Bancel, F. 1997. *La gouvernance des entreprises.* Paris: Economica.

Banzhaf, J. F. 1965. Weighted Voting Doesn't Work: A Mathematical Analysis. *Rutgers Law Review* (19):317–343.

Barca, F., and M. Becht, eds. 2001. *The control of corporate Europe.* Oxford: Oxford University Press.

Barth, E., T. Gulbrandsen and P. Schone. 2005. Family ownership and productivity: The role of owner management. *Journal of Corporate Finance* 11 (1):107–127.

Bauer, R., N. Guenster, and R. Otten. 2004. Empirical evidence on corporate governance in Europe: The effect on stock returns, firm value and performance. *Journal of Asset Management* 5 (2):91–104.

Bauer, R., R. Otten, and A. T. Rad. 2004. Ethical investing in Australia: Is there a financial penalty? Working paper, Limburg Institute of Financial Economics, University of Maastricht.

Baum, T. 2000. General meetings in listed companies—New challenges and opportunities. Conference paper, Organisation for Economic Co-operation and Development.

Baumol, W. 1959. *Business behaviour, value and growth.* New York: Macmillan.

Baysinger, B., and H. Butler. 1985. Corporate governance and the board of directors: Performance effects of change in board composition. *Journal of Law, Economics and Organization* 1 (1):101–124.

BBC Worldwide Monitoring. 2002. Chinese board director loses appeal against securities commission verdict. *BBC Worldwide Monitoring*, August 16.

Beatty, A. 1995. The cash-flow and informational effect of employee stock ownership plans. *Journal of Financial Economics* 38 (2):211–240.

Bebchuk, L. A. 1982. The case for facilitating competing tender offers. *Harvard Law Review* (95):1028–1056.

Bebchuk, L. A. 1985. Towards undistorted choice and equal treatment in corporate takeovers. *Harvard Law Review* 98:1693–1808.

Bebchuk, L. A. 1989. Takeover bids below the expected value of minority shares. *Journal of Financial and Quantitative Analysis* 24 (2):171–184.

Bebchuk, L. A. 1999. A rent protection theory of corporate ownership and control. Working paper, National Bureau of Economic Research, Cambridge, MA.

Bebchuk, L. A. 2003a. The case for shareholder access to the ballot. Working paper, John M. Olin Center for Law, Economics and Business, Harvard Law School.

Bebchuk, L. A., ed. 2003b. Symposium on corporate elections. John M. Olin Center for Law, Economics and Business, Harvard Law School.

Bebchuk, L. A. 2003c. Why firms adopt anti-takeover arrangements. *University of Pennsylvania Law Review* 152:713–753.

Bebchuk, L. A. 2004a. Designing a shareholder access rule. Working paper, John M. Olin Center for Law, Economics and Business, Harvard Law School.

Bebchuk, L. A. 2005. The case for increasing shareholder power. *Harvard Law Review* 118:833–914.

Bebchuk, L. A., J. C. Coates, and G. Subramanian. 2001. The effect of takeover defenses on bid outcomes and bid incidence. Working paper, John M. Olin Center for Law, Economics and Business, Harvard Law School.

Bebchuk, L. A., J. C. Coates, and G. Subramanian. 2002. The powerful anti-takeover force of staggered boards: Theory, evidence and policy. *Stanford Law Review* 54:887–951.

Bebchuk, L. A., J. C. Coates, and G. Subramanian. 2003. The power of takeover defenses. Working paper, National Bureau of Economic Research, Cambridge, MA.

Bebchuk, L. A., and A. Cohen. 2004. The costs of entrenched boards. Working paper, John M. Olin Center for Law, Economics and Business, Harvard Law School.

Bebchuk, L. A., A. Cohen, and A. Ferrell. 2004. What matters in corporate governance? Working paper, John M. Olin Center for Law, Economics and Business, Harvard Law School.

Bebchuk, L. A., and O. Hart. 2001. Takeover bids vs. proxy fights in contests for corporate control. Working paper, Harvard Law School.

Bebchuk, L. A., and M. J. Roe. 1999. A theory of path dependence in corporate ownership and governance. *Stanford Law Review* 52:775–808.

Becht, M. 2003. Reciprocity in takeovers. Working paper, European Corporate Governance Institute.

Becht, M., P. Bolton, and A. Roell. 2003. Corporate governance and control. In *Handbook of the economics of finance*, ed. G. M. Constantinides, M. Harris, and R. M. Stulz. Amsterdam: Elsevier.

Beckhard, R., and G. Dyer. 1983. Managing continuity in the F-owned business. *Organizational Dynamics*, 5–12.

Belgian Banking and Finance Commission. 1998. Recommendations of the Belgian Banking and Finance Commission.

Belgian Commission for Corporate Governance. 2004. *Projet de code de Gouvernance d'entreprise.*

Belkaoui, A., and E. Pavlik. 1992. The effects of ownership structure and diversification strategy on performance. *Managerial and Decision Economics* 13 (3):343–353.

Benfari, R. C., H. E. Wilkinson, and C. D. Orth. 1986. The effective use of power. *Business Horizons* 29:12–16.

Bennedsen, M., and K. Nielsen. 2002. The impact of a break-through rule on European firms. Working paper, Copenhagen Business School.

Bennedsen, M., and D. Wolfenzon. 2000. The balance of power in closely held corporations. *Journal of Financial Economics* 58 (1):113–139.

Beretta Zanoni, A. 2003. Genesis of entity theory: An analysis of the scientific context in the United States of America at the beginning of the XX century. Working paper, Graduate College Santa Chiara di Siena.

Berger, P., E. Ofek, and D. Yermak. 1997. Managerial entrenchment and capital structure decision. *Journal of Finance* 52 (4):1411–1438.

Berglof, E., and M. Burkart. 2003. European takeover regulation. *Economic Policy* 36 (18):172–213.

Berglof, E., and S. Claessens. 2004. Enforcement of corporate governance. Working paper, Stockholm School of Economics.

Berkovitch, E., and M. Narayanan. (1993). Motives for takeovers: An empirical investigation. *Journal of Financial and Quantitative Analysis* 28 (3):347–362.

Berman, P. S. 2005. From international law to law of globalization. *Columbia Journal of Transnational Law* 43:485–556.

Berle, A. A., and G. C. Means. 1932. *The modern corporation and private property*. New York: Macmillan.

Bertrand, M., and S. Mullainathan. 1999a. Corporate governance and executive pay: Evidence from takeover legislation. Working paper, Sloan School, MIT, Cambridge, MA.

Bertrand, M., and S. Mullainathan. 1999b. Is there discretion in wage setting? A test using takeover legislation. *Rand Journal of Economics* 30 (3):535–554.

Bertrand, M., and S. Mullainathan. 2000. Enjoying the quiet life? Managerial behavior following anti-takeover legislation. Working paper, Sloan School, MIT, Cambridge, MA.

Bessiere, V., and L. Thomas. 1999. Stock options and managerial incentive. Working paper, L'Association Française de Finance.

Bhagat, S., and B. S. Black. 1998. The uncertain relationship between board composition and firm performance. In *Corporate governance: The state of the art and emerging research*, ed. K. J. Hopt, M. J. Roe, and E. Wymeersch. Oxford: Oxford University Press.

Bhagat, S., and B. S. Black. 2002. The non-correlation between board independence and long-term firm performance. *Journal of Corporation Law* 27:231–273.

Bhagat, S., J. Brickley, and R. Lease. 1985. The impact of long range managerial compensation plans on shareholder wealth. *Journal of Accounting and Economics* 7 (1):115–129.

Bhagat, S., and R. H. Jefferis. 2002. *The econometrics of corporate governance studies*. Cambridge, MA: MIT Press.

Bhattacharya, U., H. Daouk, and M. Welker. 2003. The world price of earning opacity. *Accounting Review* 78 (3):641–678.

Bhattacharya, U., P. Grosnik, and B. Haslem. 2002. Is CEO certification of earnings numbers relevant? Working paper, Kelley School of Business, Indiana University.

Bizjak, J., A. Brickley, and J. Coles. 1993. Stock based incentives compensation and investment behavior. *Journal of Accounting and Economics* 16 (1):349–372.

Bines, H. E., and S. Thel. 2004. *Investment management law and regulation*. 2nd ed. New York: Aspen.

Black, B. S., and R. J. Gilson. 1998. Does venture capital require an active stock market? *Journal of Financial Economics* 47 (3):243–277.

Black, B. S., R. R. Kraakman, and A. S. Tarrassova. 1998. *Guide to Russian law on joint stock companies.* The Hague: Kluwer Law International.

Blair, M. M., ed. 1996. *Wealth creation and wealth sharing: A colloquium on corporate governance and investment in human capital.* Washington, DC: Brookings Institution.

Blair, M. M. 2001. Corporate governance. In *International encyclopedia of the social and behavioral sciences*, ed. N. J. Smelser and P. B. Baltes. Amsterdam: Elsevier.

Blanchard, O. J., and M. W. Watson. 1982. Bubbles, rational expectations and financial markets. In *Crises in the economic and financial structure*, ed. P. Wachtel. Lexington, MA: Lexington Books.

Bliss, D. R. 1992. Strategic choice: Engaging the executive team in collaborative strategy planning. In *Organizational architecture, designs for changing organizations*, ed. D. A. Nadler, M. S. Gerstein, and R. B. Shaw. San Francisco: Jossey-Bass.

Bloch, F., and U. Hege. 2001. Multiple shareholders and control contests. Discussion paper, Université Aix-Marseille and HEC School of Management.

Boardman, A. E., and A. R. Vining. 1989. Ownership and performance in competitive environments: A comparison of the performance of private, mixed, and state-owned enterprises. *Journal of Law and Economics* 32:1–33.

Bobo, L. J. 1984. Nontraditional investments of fiduciaries: Re-examining the prudent investor rule. *Emory Law Journal* 33:1067–1102.

Bøhren, Ø., and B. A. Ødegaard. 2000. The ownership structure of Norwegian firms: Characteristics of an outlier. Research report, Norwegian School of Management.

Bøhren, Ø., and B. A. Ødegaard. 2001. Patterns of corporate ownership: Insights from a unique data set. *Nordic Journal of Political Economy* 27:57–88.

Bolkestein, F. 2004. Dinner speech to the transatlantic corporate governance dialogue on 12 July 2004. European Corporate Governance Institute.

Bollerslev, T. 1986. Generalized autoregressive conditional heteroscedasticity. *Journal of Econometrics* 31 (3):307–327.

Borgonovi, E. 1991. The importance of the concept of institution for concern economics. *Economia Aziendale* 10 (2):247.

Borokhovich, K., K. Brunarski, and R. Parrino. 1997. CEO contracting and anti-takeover amendments. *Journal of Finance* 52 (4):1495–1517.

Bott, C. 2002. *Aktionärsstruktur, Kontrolle und Erfolg von Unternehmen.* Wiesbaden:Deutscher Universitäts Verlag.

Boyson, N. M. 2002. How are hedge fund manager characteristics related to performance, volatility and survival? Working paper, Fisher College of Business, Ohio State University.

Bradley, M. H., A. Desai, and E. Kim (1988). Synergistic gains from corporate acquisitions and their division between the stockholders of target and acquiring firms. *Journal of Financial Economics* 21 (1):3–40.

Bradley, M. H., and A. Sundaram. 2004. Do acquisitions drive performance or does performance drive acquisitions? Working paper, Fuqua School of Business, Duke University.

Brailsford, T., B. Oliver, and S. Pua. 2002. On the relationship between ownership and capital structure. *Accounting and Finance* 42 (1):1–26.

Braithwaite, J., and P. Drahos. 2001. *Global business regulation.* Cambridge: Cambridge University Press.

Brancato, C. K., and C. Wilde. 2004. The future of the annual general meeting. Global Corporate Governance Research Center, The Conference Board.

Branson, D. 2001. The very uncertain prospects of "Global" Convergence in Corporate Governance. *Cornell International Law Journal* 34:321–362.

Bratton, W. W., and J. A. McCahery. 1999. Comparative corporate governance and the theory of the firm: The case against global cross reference. *Columbia Journal of Transnational Law* 38:213–297.

Brennan, M. J., and H. H. Cao. 1997. International portfolio investment flows. *Journal of Finance* 52 (5):1851–1880.

Brennan, M. J., and A. Subrahmanyam. 1996. Market microstructure and asset pricing: On the compensation for illiquidity in stock returns. *Journal of Financial Economics* 41 (3):341–364.

Brent, A. 2002. Some funds try shareholder activism. *Mutual Fund Market News* (10):1.

Brickley, J., J. Coles, and G. Jarrell. 1997. Leadership structure: Separating the CEO and chairman of the board. *Journal of Corporation Finance* 3 (3):189–220.

Brickley, J., R. Lease, and C. Smith. (1988). Ownership structure and voting on antitakeover amendments. *Journal of Financial Economics* 20 (1):267–291.

Brown, L. D., and M. L. Caylor. 2004. Corporate governance and firm performance. Working paper, School of Accountancy, Georgia State University.

Brown, S. J., W. N. Goetzmann, and J. Park. 2001. Careers and survival: Competition and risk in the hedge fund and CTA industry. *Journal of Finance* 56 (5):1869–1886.

Brown, S. J., and J. B. Warner. 1985. Using daily stock returns: The case of event studies. *Journal of Financial Economics* 14 (1):3–31.

Bruck, C. 1989. *The Predators Ball.* New York: Penguin.

Brunello, G., C. Graciano, and B. M. Parigi. 2003. CEO turnover in insider-dominated boards: The Italian case. *Journal of Banking and Finance* 27 (6):1027–1051.

Brussels Stock Exchange. 1998. Report of the Belgian Commission on Corporate Governance (Cardon Report).

Burkart, M. 1995. Initial shareholdings and overbidding in takeover contests. *Journal of Finance* 50 (5):1491–1515.

Burkart, M., D. Gromb, and F. Panunzi. 1997. Large shareholders, monitoring, and the value of the firm. *Quarterly Journal of Economics* 112 (3):693–728.

Burkart, M., F. Punanzi, and A. Shliefer. 2003. Family firms. *Journal of Finance* 58 (5):2167–2201.

Business Line. 2003. The sweatshop of the world. *Business Line*, May 16.

Cadbury, A. 1992. *The report of the Committee on the Financial Aspects of Corporate Governance, Cadbury Report.* London: Gee Publishing.

Cadbury, A. 2002. *Corporate governance and chairmanship: A personal view.* Oxford: Oxford University Press.

Calomiris, C. 2005. A reply to O'Brien. In *The structure of financial regulation*, ed. D. Mayes and G. Wood. London: Routledge.

Camara, K. A. D. 2005. Classifying institutional investors. *Journal of Corporation Law* 30:219–253.

Campbell, C. J., S. L. Gillan, and C. M. Niden. 1999. Current perspectives on shareholder proposals: Lessons from the 1997 proxy season. *Financial Management* 28 (1):89–98.

Campos, R. C. 2005. Speech by SEC Commissioner Campos: The SEC's shareholder access proposal. Securities and Exchange Commission.

Carleton, W. T., J. M. Nelson, and M. S. Weisbach. 1998. The influence of institutions on corporate governance through private negotiations: Evidence from TIAA-CREF. *Journal of Finance* 53 (4):1335–1362.

Carter, C. B., and J. W. Lorsch. 2004. *Back to the drawing board: Designing corporate boards for a complex world.* Boston: Harvard Business School Press.

Carver, J. 2002. *On board leadership.* San Francisco: Jossey-Bass.

Castanias, R., and C. E. Helfat. 1991. Management resources and rents. *Journal of Management* 17 (1):155–171.

Chaganti, R., and F. Damanpour. 1991. Institutional ownership, capital structure, and firm performance. *Strategic Management Journal* 12 (7):479–492.

Chandler, W., and L. Strine. 2003. The new federalism of the American corporate governance system: Preliminary reflections of two residents of one small state. *University of Pennsylvania Law Review* 152 (2):954–1005.

Chang, S., and D. Mayers. 1992. Management vote ownership and shareholder wealth: Evidence from employee stock ownership plans. *Journal of Financial Economics* 32 (1):103–131.

Charreaux, G. 2002a. Au delà de l'approche juridico-financière: Le rôle cognitif des actionnaires sur l'analyse de la structure de la propriété et la gouvernance. Working paper, IAE Université de Bourgogne.

Charreaux, G. 2002b. Variation sur le thème: A la recherche de nouvelles fondations pour la finance et la gouvernance d'entreprise. *Finance-Contrôle-Stratégie* 5 (3):5–68.

Charreaux, G., and P. Desbrières. 1998. Gouvernance des entreprises: Valeur partenariale contre valeur actionnariale. *Finance-Contrôle-Stratégie* 1 (2):57–88.

Charreaux, G., and D. Philippe. 2001. Corporate governance: Stakeholder value versus shareholder value. *Journal of Management and Governance* (5):107–128.

Chemla, G., M. Habib, and A. Ljungqvist. 2004. An analysis of shareholders agreements. Working paper, Centre de Recherches sur la Gestion (CEREG), University Paris IX Dauphine.

Chen, G., M. Firth, and G. Krishnan. 2001. Earning forecast errors in IPO propectuses and their association with initial stock return. *Journal of Multinational Financial Management* 11 (2):225–240.

Cheng, S., and M. Firth. 2005. Ownership, corporate governance and top management pay in Hong Kong. *Corporate Governance* 13 (2):291–302.

Cheung, Y. L. 2002. Corporate governance in Hong Kong, China: Rising to the challenge of globalization. Asian Development Bank.

China Economic Review. 2002. Corporate governance: A question of control. *China Economic Review* (August 23).

China Securities and Regulatory Commission. 2001. Guidelines for introducing independent directors to the board of directors in listed companies.

China Securities and Regulatory Commission and State Economic and Trade Commission. 2001. Code of corporate governance for listed companies in China.

Chiplin, B., and M. Wright. 1987. *The logic of mergers*. London: Institute of Economic Affairs.

Cho, M. H. 1998. Ownership structure, investment and the corporate value: An empirical analysis. *Journal of Financial Economics* 47 (1):103–121.

Chordia, T., A. Subrahmanyam, and V. R. Anshuman. 2001. Trading activity and expected stock returns. *Journal of Financial Economics* 59 (1):3–32.

Choy, J. 2000. Japanese corporate governance continues to evolve. *Japan Economic Institute Weekly Review*, 27.

Chung, K. H., and J.-K. Kim. 1999. Corporate ownership and the value of a vote in an emerging market. *Journal of Corporate Finance* 5 (1):35–54.

Claessens, S., S. Djankov, J. P. H. Fan, and L. H. P. Lang. 2002. Disentangling the incentive and entrenchment effects of large shareholdings. *Journal of Finance* 57 (6):2741–2771.

Claessens, S., S. Djankov, and L. H. P. Lang. 2000. The separation of ownership and control in East Asian corporations. *Journal of Financial Economics* 58 (1):81–112.

Clark, G. 1999. *Betting on lives: The culture of life insurance in England 1695–1775*. Manchester: Manchester University Press.

Clark, R. (1981). The four stages of capitalism: Reflections on investment management treatises. *Harvard Law Review* 94:561–582.

Clarke, M. 2004. Hamstrung or properly calibrated? Federalism and the appropriate role of government in the post-Sarbanes-Oxley world. *International Journal of Disclosure and Governance*. 1 (4):385–412.

Clarke, T. 2004. *Theories of corporate governance*. Abingdon: Routledge.

Clarkson, M. 1994. A risk based model of stakeholder theory. Conference paper, Centre for Corporate Social Performance and Ethics, University of Toronto.

Clarkson, M. 1995. A stakeholder framework for analyzing and evaluating corporate social performance. *Academy of Management Review* 20 (1):92–117.

CNN. 1997. "Sokaiya" scams hit Japan. CNNfn, December 19.

CNN. 2002. Vivendi: Hackers wrecked vote. CNN.com, April 29.

Coale, A. J. 1992. Age of entry into marriage and date of initiation of voluntary birth control. *Demorgraph* 29:333–342.

Coase, R. H. 1937. The nature of the firm. *Economica* 4 (16):386–405.

Coates, J. 1999. The contestability of corporate control: A critique of the scientific evidence on takeover defences. Working paper, John M. Olin Center for Law, Economics and Business, Harvard Law School.

Cobbaut, R. 1997. *Théorie financière*. 4th ed. Paris: Economica.

Coffee, J. C. 1984. Regulating the market for corporate control: A critical assessment of the tender offer's role in corporate governance. *Columbia Law Review* 84:1145–1296.

Coffee, J. C. 1986. Shareholders versus managers: Strains in the corporate web. *Michigan Law Review* 85:1–108.

Coffee, J. C. 2004a. What caused Enron. In *Theories of corporate governance*, ed. T. Clarke. London: Routledge.

Coffee, J. C. 2004b. What caused Enron? A capsule social and economic history of the 1990s. *Cornell Law Review* 89:269–309.

Cohen, A,. and D. Brodsky. 2004. The US Sarbanes-Oxley Act of 2002: What audit committees of non-US issuers need to know. *International Journal of Disclosure and Governance* 1 (4):313–323.

Coleman, J. S. 1990. *Foundations of social theory.* Cambridge, MA: Belknap Press.

Coles, J. L., F. Meschke and M. Lemmon. 2003. Structural models and endogeneity in corporate finance: The link between managerial ownership and corporate performance. Working paper, Finance Department, Arizona State University.

Coles, J. W., V. B. McWilliams, and N. Sen. 2001. An examination of the relationship of governance mechanisms to performance. *Journal of Management* 27 (1):23–50.

Comment, R., and G. Schwert. 1995. Poison or placebo? Evidence on the deterrence and wealth effects of modern anti-takeover measures. *Journal of Financial Economics* 39 (1):3–43.

Committee on Corporate Laws, ABA Section of Business Law. 2004. Corporate director's guidebook, fourth edition. *Business Lawyer* 59 (3):1057–1120.

Company Law Review Steering Group. 2000. Modern company law for a competitive environment: Completing the structure. Department of Trade and Industry, United Kingdom.

Confederation of British Industry. 1995. Greenbury Report/Study Group on Directors' Remuneration. United Kingdom.

Conger, J. A., and E. E. Lawler. 2003. Individual director evaluations: The next step in boardroom effectiveness. *Ivey Business Journal* (September/October):3.

Convert, L. 2003. *L'impératif et le supplétif dans le droit des sociétés.* Paris: Librairie Générale de Droit et de Jurisprudence.

Conyon, M., and A. Florou. 2002. Top executive dismissal, ownership and corporate performance. Working paper, London Business School.

Conyon, M., and K. J. Murphy. 2000. The prince and the pauper? CEO pay in the United States and the United Kingdom. *Economic Journal* 110 (469):640–671.

Coombes, P., and S. Chiu-Yin Wong. 2004. Why codes of governance work. *McKinsey Quarterly* (2):225–230.

Coopers & Lybrand. 1989. Barriers to takeovers in the European community. Department of Trade and Industry, United Kingdom.

Copeland, T., T. Koller, and J. Murrin. 1996. *Valuation, measuring and managing the value of companies.* New York: John Wiley & Sons.

Costa, L. 2005. Terms of art: The perfect pill. SharkRepellent.net.

Cotter, J., and M. Zenner. 1994. How managerial wealth affects the tender offer process. *Journal of Financial Economics* 35 (1):63–97.

Coulton, J., and S. Taylor. 2004. Directors' duties and corporate governance: Have we gone too far? *Australian Accounting Review* 14 (1):17–24.

Council of Institutional Investors. 2004. Submission to SEC of Sara Teslik, Executive Director of the Council of Institutional Investors regarding shareholder access.

Cowley, A., and J. D. Cummins. 2005. Securitization of life insurance assets and liabilities. *Journal of Risk and Insurance* 72 (2):193–226.

Cowling, K. 1980. *Mergers and economic performance.* Cambridge: Cambridge University Press.

Craig, P., and G. de Burca. 2003. *EU law: Text, cases and materials.* Oxford: Oxford University Press.

Crama, Y., L. Leruth, L. Renneboog, and J.-P. Urbain. 2003. Corporate control concentration measurement and firm performance. *Social Responsibility* 17:123–149.

Craswell, A. T., S. L. Taylor, and R. A. Saywell. 1997. Ownership structure and corporate performance: Australian evidence. *Pacific-Basin Finance Journal* 5 (3):301–323.

Crespi, R., M. A. Garcìa-Cestona, and V. Salas. 2004. Governance mechanisms in Spanish banks: Does ownership matter? *Journal of Banking and Finance* 28 (10):2311–2330.

Crespi-Cladera, R., and L. Renneboog. 2003. Corporate monitoring by shareholder coalitions in the UK. Discussion paper, European Corporate Governance Institute.

Crites-Leoni, A., and A. S. Chen. 1997. Money for life: Regulating the viatical settlement industry. *Journal of Legal Medicine* 18:63–91.

Cubbin, J., and D. Leech. 1983. The effect of shareholding dispersion on the degree of control in British companies: Theory and measurement. *Economic Journal* 93 (370):351–369.

Cunningham, L. 2002. The Sarbanes-Oxley yawn: Heavy rhetoric, light reform (and it might just work). Working paper, Boston College Law School.

Dahl, R. A. 1957. The concept of power. *Behavioural Science* 2:201–215.

Dahya, J., Y. Karbhari, J. Xiao, and M. Yang. 2003. The usefulness of the supervisory board report in China. *Corporate Governance* 11 (4):308–321.

Daily, C. M., and M. Dollinger. 1992. An empirical examination of ownership structure in family and professionally managed firms. *Family Business Review* 5 (2):237–250.

Daily, C. M., J. L. Johnson, A. E. Ellstrand, and D. R. Dalton. 1996. Institutional investor activism: Follow the leaders? Working paper, Krannert Graduate School of Management, Purdue University.

Daily, C. M., and J. P. Near. 2000. CEO satisfaction and firm performance in family firms: Divergence between theory and practice. *Social Indicators Research* 51 (2):125–170.

Dallas, G. 2004. *Governance and risk.* New York: McGraw-Hill.

Dallas, G., and N. Bradley. 2004. Calibrating corporate governance practices—Corporate governance scores. In *International corporate governance.* ed. J. C. Lufkin. London: 2nd ed., Euromoney.

Dallas, L. L. 1996. The relational board: Three theories of corporate boards of directors. *Journal of Corporation Law* 22:1–25.

Dann, L., and H. DeAngelo. (1988). Corporate financial policy and corporate control. *Journal of Financial Economics* 20 (1):87–127.

Dauner-Lieb, B., and M. Lamandini. 2002. The new proposal of a directive on company law concerning takeover bids and the achievement of a level playing field. Working paper, Director-General for Research, European Parliament.

Davidson, R., and J. G. MacKinnon. 1993. *Estimation and inference in econometrics.* Oxford:Oxford University Press.

Davies, P. 2003. Shareholder value, company law, and securities markets law: A British view. In *Capital markets and company law*, ed. K. J. Hopt and E. Wymeersch. Oxford: Oxford University Press.

Davies, P., and K. J. Hopt. 2004. Control transactions. In *The anatomy of corporate law*, ed. R. R. Kraakman, P. Davies, H. Hansmann, G. Hertig, K. J. Hopt, H. Kanda, and E. B. Rock. Oxford: Oxford University Press.

Dedman, E. 2002. The Cadbury Committee recommendations on corporate governance—A review of compliance and performance impacts. *International Journal of Management Reviews* 4 (4):335–352.

Dedman, E., and S. Lin. 2002. Shareholder wealth effects of CEO departures: Evidence from the UK. *Journal of Corporate Finance* 8 (3):189–220.

DeFusco, R. A., R. R. Johnson, and T. S. Zorn. 1990. The effect of executive stock option plans on stockholders and bondholders. *Journal of Finance* 45 (2):617–627.

DeFusco, R. A., R. R. Johnson, and T. S. Zorn. 1991. The association between executive stock option plan changes and managerial decision making. *Financial Management* 20 (1):36–43.

De Jong, A., G. Mertens, and P. Roosenboom. 2004. Shareholders' voting at general meetings: Evidence from the Netherlands. Working paper, Erasmus Research Institute of Management.

Demirag, I., and J. O'Brien. 2004. Conflicting and conflating interests in the regulation and governance of the financial markets in the United States. *Journal of Corporate Citizenship* 15 (1):111–119.

Demsetz, H. 1983. The structure of ownership and the theory of the firm. *Journal of Law and Economics* (26):375–390.

Demsetz, H., and K. Lehn. 1985. The structure of corporate ownership: Causes and consequences. *Journal of Political Economy* 93 (6):1155–1177.

Demsetz, H., and B. Villalonga. 2002. Ownership structure and corporate performance. *Journal of Corporate Finance* 7 (3):209–233.

Deni Green Consulting Services. 2004. Socially responsible investment in Australia—2004. Sydney: Ethical Investment Association.

Department of Trade and Industry. 2003. Review of the role and effectiveness of non-executive directors. (Higgs Report), United Kingdom.

Desbrières, P. 1991. *Participation financière, stock-options et rachat d'entreprise par les salariés.* Paris: Economica.

Desbrières, P. 1997a. La participation financière des salariés et ses incidences sur la performance et l'organisation interne de l'entreprise. In *Le gouvernement des entreprises*, ed. G. Charreaux. Paris: Economica.

Desbrières, P. 1997b. Le rôle de l'actionnariat des salariés non-dirigeants dans le système de gouvernement d'entreprise. In *Le gouvernement des entreprises*, ed. G. Charreaux. Paris: Economica.

Desbrières, P. 1997c. Stock-options et signalisation. In *Le gouvernement des entreprises*, ed. G. Charreaux. Paris: Economica.

Deutsche Schutzvereinigung fur Wertpapierbesitz (DSW). 2004. AGM turnouts of the DAX-30 companies.

Dewatripont M., and J. Tirole. 1994. A theory of debt and equity: Diversity of securities and manager-shareholder congruence. *Quarterly Journal of Economics* 109 (4):1027–1054.

Dewey, D. 1961. Mergers and cartels: Some reservations about policy. *American Economic Review* 51 (2):255–262.

Dhillon, U., and G. Ramirez. 1994. Employee ownership and corporate control: An empirical study. *Journal of Banking and Finance* 18 (1):9–26.

Dittmer, L. 1977. Political culture and political symbolism: Towards a theoretical synthesis. *World Politics* 29 (4):552–583.

Djurasovic, G. 1997. The regulation of socially responsible mutual funds. *Journal of Corporation Law* 22:257–294.

Dodd, P. 1980. Merger proposals, management discretion and stockholder wealth. *Journal of Financial Economics* 8 (2):105–137.

Dodd, P., and R. Ruback. 1977. Tender offers and stockholder returns: An empirical analysis. *Journal of Financial Economics* 5 (3):351–373.

Doherty, N. A., and H. J. Singer. 2003. The benefits of a secondary market for life insurance policies. *Real Property, Probate and Trust Journal* 38:449–478.

Donaldson, L., and J. H. Davis. 1994. Boards and company performance—Research challenges the conventional wisdom. *Corporate Governance* 2(2):151–160.

Donaldson, W. 2004. Chairman of the Securities and Exchange Commission speech to business roundtable. Washington, DC, October 14.

Donaldson, W. 2005. Chairman of the Securities and Exchange Commission speech to London School of Economics. London, January 25.

Dorresteijn, A., I. Kuiper, and G. Morse. 1994. *European company law.* Deventer, The Netherlands: Kluwer Law and Taxation.

Doukas, J., M. Holmen, and N. Travlos. 2002. Diversification, ownership and control of Swedish corporations. *European Financial Management* 8 (3):281–314.

Drew, E. 2000. *The corruption of American politics.* New York: Overlook Press.

Driver, C., and G. Thompson. 2002. Corporate governance and democracy: The stakeholder debate revisited. *Journal of Management and Governance* (6):111–130.

Drucker, P. F. 1976. *The unseen revolution: How pension fund socialism came to America.* London: Heinemann.

Dual Code of the Brussels Stock Exchange and the Belgian Banking and Finance Commission. 1998. Corporate governance for Belgian listed companies.

Dubey, P., and L. Shapley. 1979. Mathematical properties of the Banzhaf power index. *Mathematics of Operations Research* 4 (1):99–131.

Dyck, A., and L. Zingales. 2002. Private benefits of control: An international comparison. Working paper, National Bureau of Economic Research, Cambridge, MA.

Dyck, A., and L. Zingales. 2003. The bubble and the media. In *Corporate governance and capital flows in a global economy*, ed. P. Cornelius and B. Kogut. New York: Oxford University Press.

Easterbrook, F. H. 1984. Two agency-cost explanations of dividends. *American Economic Review* 74 (4):650–659.

Easterbrook, F. H., and D. R. Fischel. 1981. The proper role of a target's management in responding to a tender offer. *Harvard Law Review* 94:1161–1204.

Easterbrook, F. H., and D. R. Fischel. 1982. Auctions and sunk costs in tender offers. *Stanford Law Review* 35:1–21.

Easterbrook, F. H., and D. R. Fischel. 1991. *The economic structure of corporate law.* Cambridge, MA: Harvard University Press.

Easterbrook, F. H., and G. Jarrell. 1984. Do targets gain from defeating tender offers? *New York University Law Review* 59:277–299.

Edelman, L., C. Uggen, and H. Erlanger. 1999. The endogeneity of legal regulation: Grievance procedures as rational myth. *American Journal of Sociology* 105 (2):404–454.

Edelman, M. 1960. Symbols and political quiescence. *American Political Science Review* 54 (3):695–704.

Edelman, M. 1964. *The symbolic uses of politics.* Urbana: University of Illinois Press.

Edelman, M. 1988. *Constructing the political spectacle.* Chicago: University of Chicago Press.

Edwards, J. S. S., and A. J. Weichenrieder. 2004. How weak is the weakest-link principle? On the measurement of firm owners' control rights. Working paper, Center for Economic Studies and Ifo Institute for Economic Research (CESifo).

Ehrhardt, O., E. Nowak, and F.-M. Weber. 2004. The evolution of ownership, control and performance in German family-owned firms 1903–2003. Working paper, Center for Economic Policy Research.

Elston, J. A., and L. G. Goldberg. 2003. Executive compensation and agency costs in Germany. *Journal of Banking and Finance* 27 (7):1391–1410.

ESS Technology Inc. 2005. Proxy statement for annual meeting of shareholders to be held June 16, 2005.

European Association for Securities Dealers. 2000. Corporate governance: Principles and recommendations.

European Commission. 1993. European social policy: Options for the Union. COM (93) 551.

European Commission. 1993. White paper on growth, competitiveness and employment. Supplement 6/93, European Commission Bulletin.

European Commission. 1994. European social policy: A way forward for the Union. COM (94) 333.

European Commission. 1999. Implementing the framework for the financial markets: Action plan. COM (1999) 232.

European Commission. 2000. Communication from the Commission to the Council, the European Parliament, the Economic and Social Committee and the Committee of the Regions on the social policy agenda. COM (2000) 379.

European Commission. 2001a. Communication from the Commission to the Council, the European Parliament, the Economic and Social Committee and the Committee of the Regions on employment and social policies: A framework for investing in quality. COM (2001) 313.

European Commission. 2001b. Communication from the commission to the council, the European Parliament, the Economic and Social Committee and the Committee of the Regions on promoting core labour standards and improving social governance in the context of globalisation. COM (2001) 416.

European Commission. 2001c. Corporate social responsibility. COM (2001) 366.

European Commission. 2002a. Comparative study of corporate governance codes relevant to the European Union and its member states. Final Report, March 27.

European Commission. 2002b. Report of the high level group of company law experts on a modern regulatory framework for company law in Europe, November 4.

European Commission. 2002c. Report of the high level group of company law experts on issues related to takeover bids, January 10.

European Commission. 2003a. Communication from the Commission to the Council and the European Parliament: Modernising company law and enhancing corporate governance in the European Union—A plan to move forward. COM (2003) 284.

European Commission. 2003b. Facing the challenge: The Lisbon strategy for growth and employment, November. (Kok Report).

European Commission. 2004a. Fostering an appropriate regime for shareholders' rights. Consultation document, MARKT/16.09.2004.

European Commission. 2004b. Report of the high-level group on the future of social policy in an enlarged European Union. May.

European Commission. 2004c. The social situation in the European Union 2004 Overview.

European Commission. 2005a. Communication from the Commission to the Council and the European Parliament: Common actions for growth and employment: The Community Lisbon programme. COM (2005) 330.

European Commission. 2005b. Fostering an appropriate regime for shareholders' rights. Second Consultation Document, MARKT/13.05.2005.

European Commission. 2005c. Recommendation of 15 February 2005. 2005/162/EC, *Official Journal of the European Union* L52:51–63.

European Commission. 2005d. The 2005 review of the EU sustainable development strategy: Initial stocktaking and future orientations. COM (2005) 33.

European Commission. 2005e. Working together for growth and jobs: A new start for the Lisbon strategy; Communication from President Barroso in agreement with the Vice-President Verheugen. COM (2005) 24 final.

European Shareholders' Group (Euroshareholders). 2000. Euroshareholders corporate governance guidelines 2000.

Faccio, M., and L. H. P. Lang. 2002. The ultimate ownership of Western European corporations. *Journal of Financial Economics* 65 (3):365–395.

Faccio, M., L. H. P. Lang, and L. Young. 2001. Debt and expropriation. Working paper, European Financial Management and Marketing Association (EFMA).

Faccio, M., and M. A. Lasfer. 2000. Do occupational pension funds monitor companies in which they hold large stakes? *Journal of Corporate Finance* 6 (1):71–110.

Fama, E. F. 1970. Efficient capital markets: A review of theory and empirical work. *Journal of Finance* 25 (2):383–417.

Fama, E. F. 1980. Agency problems and the theory of the firm. *Journal of Political Economy* 88 (2):288–307.

Fama, E. F. 1991. Efficient capital markets. *Journal of Finance* 46 (5):1575–1617.

Fama, E. F., and M. C. Jensen. 1983. Separation of ownership and control. *Journal of Law and Economics* 26:301–325.

Fama, E. F., and M. C. Jensen. 1985. Organizational forms and investment decisions. *Journal of Financial Economics* 14 (1):101–119.

Fannon, I. Lynch. 2003. *Working within two kinds of capitalism.* Oxford: Hart.

Fannon, I. Lynch. 2004. Employees as corporate stakeholders: Theory and reality in a transatlantic context. *Journal of Corporate Law Studies* 4:155–186.

Fannon, I. Lynch. 2005. A transatlantic case: The derivative action as a corporate governance device. *Dublin University Law Journal* 27:1–27.

Favre, L., and J. A. Galeano. 2002. Mean-modified value-at-risk optimization with hedge funds. *Journal of Alternative Investments* 5 (2):21–25.

Federation of Enterprises in Belgium. 1998. Corporate governance—recommendations.

Felsenthal, D., M. Machover, and W. Zwicker. 1998. The bicameral postulates and indices of a priori voting power. *Theory and Decision* 44:83–116.

Filatotchev, I., and T. Miekiewicz. 2001. Ownership concentration, private benefits of control and debt financing. Working paper, Centre for the Study of Economic and Social Change in Europe, University College, London.

Financial Reporting Council. 2003a. Audit committees—combined code guidance (Smith Report), London.

Financial Reporting Council. 2003b. The combined code on corporate governance. London.

Financial Reporting Council. 2003c. Regulatory impact assessment combined code on corporate governance. London.

Financial Reporting Council and London Stock Exchange. 1992. The financial aspects of corporate governance (Cadbury Report), London.

Finkelstein, S., and A. C. Mooney. 2003. Not the usual suspects: How to use board process to make boards better. *Academy of Management Executive* 17 (2):101–113.

Firth, M. 1979. The profitability of takeovers and mergers. *Economic Journal* 89 (354):316–328.

Firth, M. 1980. Takeovers, shareholder returns and the theory of the firm. *Quantitative Journal of Economics* 94 (2):235–260.

Fletcher, W. M. 1917. *Cylopedia of the law of private corporations.* New York: West.

Fondation des Administrateurs. 2000. The directors' charter. Belgium.

Fox, M. B. 1998. Required disclosure and corporate governance. In *Comparative corporate governance,* ed. K. J. Hopt, H. Kanada, M. J. Roe, E. Wymeersch, and S. Prigge. Oxford: Oxford University Press.

Franks, J., M. Harris, and C. Mayer. 1988. The role of medium of exchanges in the US and the UK. In *Corporate takeovers: Causes and consequences,* ed. A. Auerbach. Chicago: University of Chicago Press.

Franks, J., and C. Mayer. 1996. Hostile takeovers and the correction of managerial failure. *Journal of Financial Economics* 40 (1):163–181.

Franks, J., C. Mayer, and L. Renneboog. 2001. Who disciplines management of poorly performing companies? *Journal of Financial Intermediation* 10 (3):209–248.

Franks, J., C. Mayer, and S. Rossi. 2004. Spending less time with the family: The decline of family ownership in the UK. Working paper, European Corporate Governance Institute.

Fraser, S. 2005. *Wall Street: A cultural history.* London: Faber and Faber.

Freeman, R. 1996. Towards an apartheid economy. *Harvard Business Review* 74 (5):114–121.

Freeman, R. E. 1984. *Strategic management: A stakeholder approach.* Boston: Pitman.

French, J. R. P., and B. H. Raven. 1959. The bases of social power. In *Studies in social power,* ed. D. Cartwright. Ann Arbor, MI: Institute for Social Research.

Friedman, E., S. Jonhion, and T. Milton. 2003. Propping and tunnelling. Working paper, National Bureau of Economic Research, Cambridge, MA.

Friedman, M. 1953. The methodology of positive economics. In *Essays in positive economics,* ed. M. Friedman. Chicago: Chicago University Press.

FTSE ISS. 2005. FTSE ISS corporate governance rating and index series—Measuring the impact of corporate governance on global portfolios. Research report, London.

Gadhoum, Y. 1998. Corporate governance and top managers: Potential sources of sustainable competitive advantage. Asian-Pacific Interdisciplinary Research in Accounting Conference Program, Osaka, Japan.

Gadhoum, Y., L. H. P. Lang, and L. Young. 2005. Who controls US? *European Financial Management* 11 (3):339–363.

Galbraith, J. K. 1967. A review of a review. *The Public Interest* 9 (4):109–117.

Galbraith, J. K. 1997. *The Great Crash 1929.* Reprint, New York: Houghton Mifflin.

Galve, C., and V. Salas. 1996. Ownership structure and firm performance: Some empirical evidence from Spain. *Managerial and Decision Economics* 17 (6):575–586.

Gandossy, R., and J. A. Sonnenfeld, eds. 2004. *Leadership and governance from the inside out.* Hoboken, NJ: John Wiley & Sons.

Garvey, G., and G. Hanka. 1999. Capital structure and corporate control: The effect of takeover statutes on firm leverage. *Journal of Finance* 54 (2):519–546.

General Accounting Office. 2003. Investment banks, the role of firms and their analysts with Enron and Global Crossing. GAO-030511, March.

General Motors. 2001. 2001 proxy statement.

George, W. W. 2002. Imbalance of power. *Harvard Business Review* 80 (7):22–23.

Gillan, S. L., and L. T. Starks. 2000. Corporate governance proposals and shareholder activism: The role of institutional investors. *Journal of Financial Economics* 57 (2):275–305.

Gillan, S. L., and L. T. Starks. 2003. Corporate governance, corporate ownership, and the role of institutional investors: A global perspective. *Journal of Applied Finance* 13 (2):4–22.

Gilson, R. J. 1982. Seeking competitive bids versus pure passivity in tender offer defense. *Stanford Law Review* 35:51–66.

Gilson, R. J., and M. J. Roe. 1993. Understanding the Japanese keiretsu: Overlaps between corporate governance and industrial organisation. *Yale Law Journal* 102:871–905.

Gilson, R. J, and M. J. Roe. 1999. Lifetime employment labour peace and the evolution of Japanese corporate governance. *Columbia Law Review* 99:508–540.

Glosten, L., R. Jagannathan, and D. Runkle. 1993. On the relation between expected value and the volatility of the nominal excess returns on stocks. *Journal of Finance* 48 (5):1779–1801.

Gnan, L., and L. Songini. 2003. The professionalization of family firms: The role of agency cost control mechanisms. Working paper, Scuola di Direzione Aziendale dell'Università Bocconi.

Goergen, M., and L. Renneboog. 2004. Shareholder wealth effects of European domestic and cross-border takeover bids. *European Financial Management* 10 (1):9–46.

Gold, M. 2004. Investing in pseudo-science: The active versus passive debate. *Journal of the Securities Institute of Australia* (3):2–6.

Goldstein, M. 2004a. The colorful palette of Japan's proxy season. Institutional Shareholder Services, Japan.

Goldstein, M. 2004b. Japanese proxy season 2004—Guidelines for Japanese meetings of shareholders. Institutional Shareholder Services, Japan.

Gómez-Mejía, L. R., M. Larraza-Quintana, and M. Makri. 2003. The determinants of executive compensation in family-controlled public corporations. *Academy of Management Journal* 46 (2):226–237.

Gómez-Mejía, L. R., M. Nuñez-Nickel, and I. Gutierrez. 2001. The role of family ties in agency contracts. *Academy of Management Journal* 44 (1):81–95.

Gompers, P., J. Ishii, and A. Metrick. 2003. Corporate governance and equity prices. *Quarterly Journal of Economics* 118 (1):107–156.

Gordon, J. N. 1994. Institutions as relational investors: A new look at cumulative voting. *Columbia Law Review* 94:124–180.

Gordon, J. N. 1997. The puzzling persistence of the constrained prudent investor rule. *New York University Law Review* 62:52–114.

Gordon L., and J. Pound. 1990. ESOPs and corporate control. *Journal of Financial Economics* 27 (2):525–555.

Gordon, R. J. 2004a. Two centuries of economic growth: Europe chasing the American frontier. Working paper, Department of Economics, Northwestern University.

Gordon, R. J. 2004b. Why Europe was left at the station when America's productivity locomotive departed? Working paper, National Bureau of Economic Research, Cambridge, MA.

Gorton, G., and F. A. Schmid. 2000. Universal banking and the performance of German firms. *Journal of Financial Economics* 58 (1):29–80.

Government Commission on the German Corporate Governance Code. 2005a. Press release. Berlin Center of Corporate Governance (March 11).

Government Commission on the German Corporate Governance Code. 2005b. German corporate governance code. Berlin: Government Commission on the German Corporate Governance Code.

Green, R. 1993. Shareholders as stakeholders: Changing metaphors of corporate governance. *Washington and Lee Law Review* 50:1409–1421.

Greenspan, A. 2002. Corporate governance. Presentation, Stern School of Business, New York University.

Gregoriou, G. N. 2002. Hedge fund survival lifetimes. *Journal of Asset Management* 3 (3):237–252.

Gregoriou, G. N., and W. Kelting. 2003. The billion dollar hedge fund fraud. Working paper, School of Business and Economics, State University of New York.

Gregory, A. 1997. An examination of the long-run performance of UK acquiring firms. *Journal of Business Finance and Accounting* 24 (7):971–1002.

Grossman, S. J., and O. D. Hart. 1980. Takeover bids, the free-rider problem and the theory of the corporation. *Bell Journal of Economics* 11 (1):42–64.

Grossman, S. J., and O. D. Hart. 1982. Corporate financial structure and managerial incentives. In *The economics of information and uncertainty*, ed. J. J. McCall. Chicago: University of Chicago Press.

Grossman, S. J., and O. D. Hart. 1983. An analysis of the principal-agent problem. *Econometrica* 51 (1):7–45.

Grossman, S. J., and O. D. Hart. 1988. One share–one vote and the market for corporate control. *Journal of Financial Economics* 20 (1):175–202.

Grullon, G., and G. Kanatas. 2001. Managerial incentives, capital structure and firm value: Evidence from dual-class stocks. Working paper, Jesse H. Jones Graduate School of Management, Rice University.

Guedes, J. C., and G. Loureiro. 2001. Are European corporations fleecing minority shareholders? Results from a new empirical approach. Working paper, European Financial Management and Marketing Association (EFMA).

Guedes, J. C., and G. Loureiro. 2002. Are European corporations fleecing minority shareholders? Discussion paper, Universidade Católica Portugesa and Universidade do Minho.

Gugler, K. 2001. *Corporate covernance and economic performance.* Oxford: Oxford University Press.

Gugler, K. 2003. Corporate governance, dividend payout policy, and the interrelation between dividends, R&D, and capital investment. *Journal of Banking and Finance* 27 (7):1297–1321.

Gugler, K., and B. B. Yurtoglu. 2003. Corporate governance and dividend pay-out policy in Germany. *European Economic Review* 47 (4):731–758.

Gulinello, C. 2003. The revision of Taiwan's company law: The struggle toward a shareholder-oriented model in one corner of East Asia. *Delaware Journal of Corporate Law* 28:75–127.

Haberer, T. 2003. *Corporate governance.* Vienna: Manz.

Hagaman, T. C. 1995. Reflections on the annual meeting season. *Management Accounting* 77 (1):16.

Halal, W. E. 1997. A return-on-resource model of corporate performance. *California Management Review* 19 (4):23–26.

Hall, B., and B. Liebman. 1998. Are CEOs really paid like bureaucrats? *Quarterly Journal of Economics* 103 (3):653–691.

Hall, B., and K. Murphy. 2002. Stock options for undiversified executives. *Journal of Accounting and Economics* 33 (1):3–42.

Hall, B., and K. Murphy. 2003. The trouble with stock options. Working paper, National Bureau of Economic Research, Cambridge, MA.

Hallerbach, W., H. Ning, A. Soppe, and J. Spronk. 2004. A framework for managing a portfolio of socially responsible investments. *European Journal of Operational Research* 153:517–529.

Halpern, P. 1973. Empirical estimates of the amount and distribution of gains to companies in mergers. *Journal of Business* 46 (4):554–575.

Ham, P. 2003. Wary watchdog is just what boards need—Corporate governance: Business survey series. *The Australian* (May 23):14.

Hambrick, D. C., and G. Fukutomi. 1991. The seasons of a CEO's tenure. *Academy of Management Review* 16 (4):719–744.

Hamilton, W. D. 1964. The genetic evolution of social behaviour. *Journal of Theoretical Biology* 7:1–52.

Hampel Report. 1998. National Association of Pension Funds, London Stock Exchange, Confederation of British Industry, Institute of Directors, Consultative Committee of Accountancy Bodies, Association of British Insurers, United Kingdom.

Hansmann, H. 1996. *The ownership of enterprise.* Cambridge, MA: Harvard University Press.

Hansmann, H., and R. R. Kraakman 2001. The end of history for corporate law. *Georgetown Law Journal* 89:439–467.

Hansmann, H., and R. R. Kraakman. 2004. Agency problems and legal strategies. In *The anatomy of corporate law,* ed. R. R. Kraakman, P. Davies, H. Hansmann, G. Hertig, K. J. Hopt, H. Kanda, and E. B. Rock. Oxford: Oxford University Press.

Harris, M., and A. Raviv. 1979. Optimal incentive contracts with imperfect information. *Journal of Economic Theory* 20 (2):231–259.

Harris, M., and A. Raviv. 1988a. Corporate control contests and capital structure. *Journal of Financial Economics* 20 (1):55–86.

Harris, M., and A. Raviv. 1988b. Corporate governance: Voting rights and majority rules. *Journal of Financial Economics* 20 (1):203–235.

Harris, M., and A. Raviv. 1990. Capital structure and the informational role of debt. *Journal of Finance* 45 (2):321–350.

Hart, J. 1995. President Clinton and the politics of symbolism: Cutting the White House staff. *Political Science Quarterly* 10 (3):385–403.

Hart, O. 1995. *Firms, Contracts and financial structure*. Oxford: Oxford University Press.

Hart, O., and B. Holmström. 1987. The theory of contracts. In *Advances in econometrics*, ed. T. F. Bewley. Cambridge: Cambridge University Press.

Hartzell, J., E. Ofek, and D. Yermack. 2004. What's in it for me? CEOs whose firms are acquired. *Review of Financial Studies* 17 (1):37–61.

Harvey, S. J. 1999. Owner as manager, extended horizons and the family firm. *International Journal of the Economics of Business* 6 (1):41–55.

Hawawini, G., and D. B. Keim. 2000. The cross-section of common stock returns: A synthesis of the evidence and explanations. In *Security market imperfections in worldwide equity markets*, ed. D. B. Keim and W. Ziemba. Cambridge: Cambridge University Press.

Hawley, J. P., and A. T. Williams. 1997. The emergence of fiduciary capitalism. *Corporate Governance* 5 (4):206–213.

Hawley, J. P., and A. T. Williams. 2003. Shifting ground: Emerging global corporate governance standards and the rise of fiduciary capitalism. Working paper, Center for the Study of Fiduciary Capitalism, Saint Mary's College of California.

Hebb, T. 2003. Emerging trends in corporate engagement by public pension funds. *Employee Benefits Journal*, 28 (1):13–15.

Heinrich, R. 2000. Complementarities in corporate governance: Ownership concentration, capital structure, monitoring and pecuniary incentives. Working paper, Kiel Institute of World Economics.

Hellwig, M. 2000. On the cconomics and politics of corporate finance and corporate control. In *Corporate governance: Theoretical and empirical perspectives*. ed. X. Vives. Cambridge: Cambridge University Press.

Hendry, J. 2001. Economic contacts versus social relationship as a foundation for normative stakeholder theory. *Business Ethics* 10 (3):223–232.

Hermalin, B. E., and M. S. Weisbach. 2003. Boards of directors as an endogenously determined institution: A survey of the economic literature. *Economic Policy Review—Federal Reserve Bank of New York* 9 (1):7–26.

Herman, E., and L. Lowenstein. 1988. The efficiency effects of hostile takeovers. In *Knights, raiders and targets, the impact of the hostile takeover*, ed. J. C. Coffee, L. Lowenstein, and S. Rose-Ackerman. New York: Oxford University Press.

Hermes Pensions Management Ltd. 2005. Corporate governance and performance. London.

Heron, R., and E. Lie. 2006. On the use of poison pills and defensive payouts by takeover targets. *Journal of Business*, forthcoming.

Hertig, G., R. R. Kraakman, and E. B. Rock. 2004. Issuers and investor protection. In *The anatomy of corporate law*, ed. R. R. Kraakman, P. Davies, H. Hansmann, G. Hertig, K. J. Hopt, H. Kanda and E. B. Rock. Oxford: Oxford University Press.

Hertig, G., and J. McCahery. 2003. Company and takeover law reforms in Europe: Misguided harmonization efforts or regulatory competition. *European Business Organization Law Review* 4:179–211.

Higgs, D. 2003. Review of the role and effectiveness of non-executive directors. Department of Trade and Industry, United Kingdom.

Hill, J. 2004. Corporate scandals across the globe: Regulating the role of the director. In *Reforming company and takeover law in Europe*, ed. G. Ferrarini, K. J. Hopt, J. Winter, and E. Wymeersch. Oxford: Oxford University Press.

Hillman, A. J., and G. D. Keim. 2001. Shareholder value, stakeholder management and social issues: What's the bottom line? *Strategic Management Journal* 22 (2):2–125.

Himmelberg, C. P., R. G. Hubbard, and D. N. Palia. 1999. Understanding the determinants of managerial ownership and the link between ownership and performance. *Journal of Financial Economics* 53 (3):353–384.

Hirschey, M. 1986. Mergers, buyouts and fakeouts. *American Economic Review* 76 (2):317–322.

Hirschman, A. O. 1970. *Exit, voice and loyalty.* Cambridge: Cambridge University Press.

Holderness, C. G. 2003. A survey of blockholders and corporate control. *Economic Policy Review—Federal Reserve Bank of New York* 9 (1):51–63.

Holderness, C. G., R. S. Kroszner, and D. P. Sheenan. 1999. Were the good old days that good? Changes in managerial ownership since the Great Depression. *Journal of Finance* 54 (2):435–470.

Holler, M. J., and G. Illing. 2000. *Einführung in die Spieltheorie.* 4th ed. Berlin: Springer.

Holmstrom, B. 1979. Moral hazard and observability. *Bell Journal of Economics* 10 (1):74–91.

Holmstrom, B., and P. Milgrom. 1987. Aggregation and linearity in the provision of intertemporal incentives. *Econometrica* 55 (2):303–328.

Holmstrom, B., and J. Tirole. 1993. Market liquidity and performance monitoring. *Journal of Political Economy* 101 (4):678–709.

Hommelhoff, P., and M. Schwab. 2003. Regelungsquellen und Regelungsebenen der corporate governance: Gesetz, Satzung, codices, unternehmensinterne Grundsätze. In *Handbuch corporate governance*, ed. P. Hommelhoff, K. J. Hopt, and A. v. Werder. Cologne: Dr. Otto Schmidt Verlag.

Hong Kong Institute of Directors. 2000. Guide for independent non-executive directors.

Hood, C., H. Rothstein, and R. Baldwin. 2004. *The government of risk.* Oxford: Oxford University Press.

Hopt, K. J. 2001. Disclosure rules as a primary tool for fostering party autonomy—Observations from a functional and comparative legal perspective. In *Party autonomy and the role of information in the internal market*, ed. S. Grundmann, W. Kerber, and S. Weatherill. Berlin: de Gruyter.

Hopt, K. J. 2002. Takeover regulation in Europe—The battle for the 13th directive on takeovers. *Australian Journal of Corporate Law* 15:1–18.

Hopt, K. J., M. J. Roe, and E. Wymeersch, eds. 1998. *Corporate governance: The state of the art and emerging research.* Oxford: Oxford University Press.

Hopt, K. J., and E. Wymeersch. 2003. *European company and financial law.* Oxford: Oxford University Press.

Horngren, C. T., S. G. Foster, and M. Datar. 2000. *Cost accounting: A managerial emphasis*. Upper Saddle River, NJ: Prentice-Hall.

House of Commons. 2002. Appendix 12: Memorandum by Brewin Dolphin Securities Ltd. United Kingdom Parliament.

Hu, B. 2002. Former Zhengzhou director sues CSRC; First independent board member to seek withdrawal of penalty imposed over retailer's financial wrongdoings. *South China Morning Post (Business Post)* (June 8):3.

Huddart, S. 1993. The effect of large shareholders on corporate value. *Management Science* 39 (11):1407–1421.

Huddart, S. 1994. Employee stock options. *Journal of Accounting and Economics* 18 (1):207–231.

Huddart, S., and M. Lang. 1996. Employee stock option exercise, an empirical analysis. *Journal of Accounting and Economics* 21 (1):5–43.

Huizink, J. B., A. J. M. Klein-Wassink, and S. E. Zijlstra. 2004. De Nederlandse corporate governance code in de wet: Statisch, dynamisch of problematisch. *Nederlands Juristenblad*: 425–430.

Huson, M., R. Parrino, and L. Starks. 2001. Internal monitoring mechanisms and CEO turnover: A long term perspective. *Journal of Finance* 56 (6): 2265–2297.

Hutchinson, J. D., and C. G. Cole. 1980. Legal standards governing investment of pension assets for social and political goals. *University of Pennsylvania Law Review* 128:1340–1388.

Hutchinson, M. 2002. The bear's lair: Do we need governance? United Press International, March 4.

Institute of Chartered Accountants in England and Wales. 1999. Internal control: Guidance for directors on the combined code (Turnbull Report), London.

International Association of Insurance Supervisors. 2003. Issues paper on life insurance securitisation. Issues Paper.

International Corporate Governance Network. 1999. Statement on global corporate governance principles.

International Finance Corporation. 2004. *The Russia corporate governance manual*. Moscow: International Finance Corporation/The World Bank.

International Shareholder Services. 2003. ISS viewpoint: SEC shareholder access proposal.

Investment and Financial Services Association. 2003. *Shareholder activism among fund managers: Policy and practice*. 5th ed. Sydney: Investment and Financial Services Association.

Investment and Financial Services Association. 2004. *Corporate governance: A guide for fund managers and corporations—blue book*. 5th ed. Sydney: Investment and Financial Services Association.

Investor Responsibility Research Center (IRRC). 2003. Corporate governance service 2003 background report F: Confidential and cumulative voting.

Iskander, M. R., and N. Chamlou. 2000. *Corporate governance: A framework for implementation*. Washington, DC: The World Bank.

Jacquemin, A., and E. de Ghellinck. 1980. Familial control, size and performance in the largest French firms. *European Economic Review* 13 (1):81–91.

Jarrell, G., and A. Poulsen. 1987. Shark repellents and stock prices: The effects of antitakeover amendments since 1980. *Journal of Financial Economics* 19 (1):127–168.

Jayaraman, N., A. Khorana, E. Nelling, and J. Covin. 2000. CEO founder status and firm financial performance. *Strategic Management Journal* 21 (12):1215–1224.

Jenkinson, T. and C. Mayer. 1994. *Hostile takeovers.* London: McGraw-Hill.

Jensen, M. C. 1986. Agency costs of free cash flow, corporate finance and takeovers. *American Economic Review* 76 (2):323–329.

Jensen, M. C. 1991. Corporate control and the policy of finance. *Journal of Applied Corporate Finance* 4 (2):13–33.

Jensen, M. C. 1993. The modern industrial revolution, exit, and the failure of internal control systems. *Journal of Finance* 48 (3):831–880.

Jensen, M. C. 2001. Value maximization, stakeholder theory and the corporate objective function. *European Financial Management* 7 (3):297–317.

Jensen, M. C. 2004. Agency costs of overvalued equity. Working paper, Harvard Business School.

Jensen, M. C., and W. H. Meckling. 1976. Theory of the firm: Managerial behavior, agency costs and ownership structure. *Journal of Financial Economics* 3 (4):305–360.

Jensen, M. C., and K. Murphy. 1990a. CEO incentives—It's not how much you pay, but how. *Harvard Business Review* 68 (3):138–153.

Jensen, M. C., and K. Murphy. 1990b. Performance pay and top-management incentives. *Journal of Political Economy* 98 (2):225–264.

Jensen, M. C., K. Murphy, and E. Wruck. 2004. Remuneration: Where we've been, how we got to here, what are the problems, and how to fix them. Working paper, European Corporate Governance Institute.

Jensen, M. C., and R. Ruback. 1983. The market for corporate control: The scientific evidence. *Journal of Financial Economics* 11 (1):5–50.

Jesover, F. 2001. Corporate governance in the Russian Federation: The relevance of the OECD principles on shareholder rights and equitable treatment. *Corporate Governance* 9 (2):79–88.

Jessop, B. 2003. *The future of the capitalist state.* Oxford: Blackwell Publishing.

Jog, V., and S. Dutta. 2004. Searching for the governance grail. *Canadian Investment Review* 33–43.

Johnson, C. 2005. Cox vows vigilance on fraud. *Washington Post* (July 27).

Johnson, L. 2002. Reclaiming an ethic of corporate responsibility. *George Washington Law Review* (70):957–967.

Johnson, S., R. La Porta, F. Lopez-de Silanes, and A. Shleifer. 2000. Tunneling. *American Economic Review* 90 (2):22–27.

Kang, J. K., and R. M. Stulz. 1994. Why is there a home bias? An analysis of foreign portfolio equity ownership in Japan. *Journal of Financial Economics* 46 (1):3–28.

Kant, I. 1993. *Grounding for the metaphysics of morals.* Indianapolis, IN: Hackett Publishing Co.

Karpoff, J. M. 1998. Does shareholder activism work? A survey of empirical findings. Working paper, University of Washington Business School.

Karpoff, J. M. 2001. The impact of shareholder activism on target companies: A survey of empirical findings. Working paper, University of Washington Business School.

Karpoff, J., and P. Malatesta. 1989. The wealth effects of second generation state takeover legislation. *Journal of Financial Economics* 25 (2):291–322.

Karpoff, J. M., P. H. Malatesta, and R. A. Walkling. 1996. Corporate governance and shareholder initiatives: Empirical evidence. *Journal of Financial Economics* 42 (3):365–395.

Keasey, K., and L. McGuiness. 1991. Prospectuses, earnings forecasts and the pricing of new issues on the unlisted securities market. *Accounting and Business Research* 21 (1):33–145.

Kehren, S. 2005. Paketaktionäre, Macht und Unternehmenserfolg. Dissertation, University of Hamburg.

Keim, D. B., and W. Ziemba, eds. 2000. *Security market imperfections in worldwide equity markets.* Cambridge: Cambridge University Press.

Kelly, G., D. Kelly, and A. Gamble, eds. 1997. *Stakeholder capitalism.* London: Macmillan.

Kelman, M. 1979. Consumption theory, production theory and ideology in the Coase theorem. *Southern California Law Review* 52:669–698.

Kershaw, D. 2002. No end in sight for the history of corporate law: The case of employee participation in corporate governance. *Journal of Corporate Law Studies* 2:34–81.

Keutgen, G., and C. Darville. 1998. Le corporate governance, une perspective nouvelle pour les sociétés. *Journal des Tribunaux*, 365–376.

Khachaturyan, A. 2005. Can Bolkestein finally break the takeover directive deadlock? Commentary, Centre for European Policy Studies.

Khatri, Y., L. Leruth, and J. Piesse. 2001. Corporate performance and governance: A stochastic frontier approach to measuring and explaining inefficiency in the Malaysian corporate sector. Discussion paper, International Monetary Fund and Birkbeck College, University of London.

Kiel, G. C. 2004. Effective board assessment: Practices, opportunities and issues. Conference paper, Henley Management College.

Kiel, G. C., G. J. Nicholson, and M. A. Barclay. 2005. *Board, director and CEO evaluation.* Sydney: McGraw-Hill.

Kim, W., and E. Sorensen. 1986. Evidence of the impact of agency costs of debt in corporate debt policy. *Journal of Financial and Quantitative Analysis* 21 (2):131–144.

Kirshner, J. 2003. The inescapable politics of money. In *Monetary orders: Ambiguous economics, ubiquitous politics,* ed. J. Kirshner. Ithaca: Cornell University Press.

Klapper, L., and I. Love. 2002. Corporate governance, investor protection and performance in emerging markets. Working paper, The World Bank.

Knoeber, C. 1986. Golden parachutes, shark repellents and hostile offers. *American Economic Review* 76 (1):155–167.

Köke, J. 2001. New evidence on ownership structures in Germany. *Kredit und Kapital* 34:257–292.

Köke, J. 2002. *Corporate governance in Germany: An empirical investigation.* Heidelberg: Physica.

Kole, S. R., and J. H. Mulherin. 1997. The government as a shareholder: A case from the United States. *Journal of Law and Economics* 40:1–22.

Kooiman, J. 2003. *Governing as governance.* Beverly Hills, CA: Sage.

Koppes, R. H. and M.L. Reilly. 1995. An ounce of prevention: Meeting the fiduciary duty to monitor an index fund through relationship investing. *Journal of Corporation Law* 20:413–449.

Kowalski, A. 1990. *Der Ersatz von Gesellschafts-und Gesellschafterschaden.* Cologne: Schmidt.

Koziol, H., and B. C. Steininger. 2004. *European tort law 2003.* Vienna: Springer.

KPMG. 2004. Early reporting trends: A survey of early reporting trends under the ASX corporate governance council guidelines.

KPMG. 2005. Reporting against ASX corporate governance council guidelines.

Kraakman, R. R. 2004. Disclosure and corporate governance. In *Reforming company and takeover law in Europe,* ed. G. Ferrarini, K. J. Hopt, J. Winter, and E. Wymeersch. Oxford: Oxford University Press.

Kroll, M. S. 1999. Socially responsible investment and modern financial markets. Working paper, The Wharton School, University of Pennsylvania.

Kuehn, D. 1975. *Takeovers and the theory of the firm.* London: Macmillan.

Kummer, D., and J. Hoffmeister. 1978. Valuation consequences of cash tender offers. *Journal of Finance* 33 (2):505–516.

Labegorre, F., and S. Boubaker. 2005. Publication volontaire de prévisions et rentabilités initiales: Le cas des admissions à la cote du second marché. *Banque et Marchés* (77):35–46.

La Bruslerie, H. de. 2003. Contrôle, bénéfices privés et endettement. Working paper, L'Association Française de Finance.

La Bruslerie, H. de, and C. Deffains-Crapsky. 2001. Stock-options et equilibre incitatif dirigeant-actionnaires: Le cas Français. In *Finance d'entreprise,* ed. H. La Bruslerie. Paris: Economica.

La Bruslerie, H. de, and C. Deffains-Crapsky. 2003. Contrat optimal d'actionnariat salarié et asymétrie d'information. *Finance* 24:113–142.

La Bruslerie, H. de, and C. Deffains-Crapsky. 2005. Takeover bids, unconditional offer price and investor protection. *Review of Financial Economics* 14 (2):103–126.

Laertius, D. 1925. *Lives of eminent philosophers.* Cambridge, MA: Harvard University Press.

Laffont, J. J., and D. Martimort. 2002. *The theory of incentives.* Princeton: Princeton University Press.

Lane, B. J. 1999. Views into the crystal ball. Speech to Committee on Federal Regulation of Securities. American Bar Association, November 13.

Langetieg, T. 1978. An application of a three-factor performance index to measure stockholder gains from merger. *Journal of Financial Economics* 6 (4):365–383.

La Porta, R., F. Lopez–de Silanes, and A. Shleifer. 1999. Corporate ownership around the world. *Journal of Finance* 54 (2):471–517.

La Porta, R., F. Lopez–de Silanes, A. Shleifer, and R. W. Vishny. 1997. Legal determinants of external finance. *Journal of Finance* 52 (3):1131–1150.

La Porta, R., F. Lopez–de Silanes, A. Shleifer, and R. W. Vishny. 1998. Law and finance. *Journal of Political Economy* 106 (6):1113–1155.

La Porta, R., F. Lopez–de Silanes, A. Shleifer, and R. W. Vishny. 1999. The quality of goverment. *Journal of Law, Economics and Organization* 15 (1):222–279.

La Porta, R., F. Lopez–de Silanes, A. Shleifer, and R. W. Vishny. 2000. Investor protection and corporate governance. *Journal of Financial Economics* 58 (1):3–28.

Latham, M. 2005. Vote your stock. Working paper, Corporate Monitor.

Lausten, M. 2002. CEO turnover, firm performance and corporate governance: Empirical evidence on Danish firms. *International Journal of Industrial Organization* 20 (3):391–414.

Lauterbach, B., and A. Vaninsky. 1999. Ownership structure and firm performance: Evidence from Israel. *Journal of Management and Governance* 3 (2):189–201.

Lawler, E. E., and D. L. Finegold. 2005. The changing face of corporate boards. *MIT Sloan Management Review* 43 (2):92–116.

Lawrence, J., and G. P. Stapledon. 1999. Is board composition important? A study of listed Australian companies. Working paper, Centre for Corporate Law and Securities Regulation, University of Melbourne.

Lawrence, P. 1967. *Organization and environment: Managing differentiation and integration.* Cambridge, MA: Harvard Business School Press.

Leblanc, R., and J. Gillies. 2003. The coming revolution in corporate governance. *Ivey Business Journal* 68 (1):9–20.

Leblanc, R., and J. Gilles. 2005. *Inside the boardroom: How boards really work and the coming revolution in corporate governance.* Toronto: John Wiley & Sons.

Lee, J. 2004. The effects of family ownership and management on firm performance. *SAM Advanced Management Journal* 69 (4):46–50.

Leech, D. 2000. Shareholder power and corporate governance. Warwick Economic Research Paper.

Leech, D. 2002a. Computation of power indices. Warwick Economic Research Paper.

Leech, D. 2002b. An empirical comparison of the performance of classical power indices. *Political Studies* 50:1–22.

Leech, D., and J. Leahy. 1991. Ownership structure, control type classifications and the performance of large British companies. *Economic Journal* 101 (409):1418–1437.

Leech, D., and M. C. Manjón. 2003. Corporate governance and game theoretic analyses of shareholder power: The case of Spain. *Applied Economics* 35 (7):847–858.

Lehmann, E., and J. Weigand. 2000. Does the governed corporation perform better? Governance structures and corporate performance in Germany. *European Finance Review* 4 (2):157–195.

Lehne, K. H. 2002. Working document on the proposal for a directive of the European Parliament and of the Council on Takeover Bids. European Parliament, Committee on Legal Affairs and the Internal Market, DT\419152EN.doc.

Leiserson, M. 1968. Factions and coalitions in one-party Japan: An interpretation based on the theory of games. *American Political Science Review* 62:770–787.

Leland, H., and D. Pyle. 1977. Informational asymmetries, financial structure and financial intermediation. *Journal of Finance* 32 (2):371–387.

Les Echos. (2002). Communication financière: les compagnies d'assurance vigilantes. *Les Echos*, August 20.

Letreguilly, H. 2004. La responsabilité des Émetteurs en matière d'information financière. *Revue de Droit Bancaire et Financier* 6 (November/December):448.

Leuz, C., D. Nanda, and P. Wysocki. 2002. Investor protection and earning management: An international comparison. Working paper, Sloan School, MIT, Cambridge, MA.

Lev, B., and A. Schwartz. 1971. On the use of economic concept of human capital in financial statement. *Accounting Review* 46 (1):103–112.

Levitt, A. 2003. *Take on the Street.* New York: Pantheon Books.

Levitt, A. 2004. Corporate governance and the culture of seduction. In *Leadership and governance from the inside out*, ed. R. Gandossy, and J. Sonnenfield. Hoboken, NJ: John Wiley & Sons.

Li, C. 2002. Independent directors quit as CSRC gets tough. *South China Morning Post (Business Post)* (June 26):4.

Liang, B. 1999. On the performance of hedge funds. *Financial Analysts Journal* 55 (4):72–85.

Lin, L. 2002. Management: NEDs need to play larger role. *The Edge Malaysia* (December 16).

Lin, Y., and S. H. Cox. 2005. Securitization of mortality risks in life annuities. *Journal of Risk and Insurance* 72 (2):227–252.

Linden, P., and Z. Matolcsy. 2004. Corporate governance scoring systems: What do they tell us? *Australian Accounting Review* 14 (1):9–16.

Lintner, J. 1954. Effect of corporate taxation on real investment. *American Economic Review* 44 (2):522–534.

Lipton, M. 1979. Takeover bids in the target's boardroom. *Business Lawyer* 35 (1):101–134.

Lipton, M., and P. Rowe. 2002. Pills, polls and professors: A reply to Professor Gilson. *Delaware Journal of Corporate Law* 27:1–34.

Liu, Q., and J. Lu. 2002. Earning management: Evidence from China's listed companies. Working paper, University of Hong Kong.

Lochner, P. R., and R. H. Koppes. 1994. Stop us before we meet again. *Wall Street Journal* (March 18).

Loderer, C., and K. Martin. 1997. Executive stock ownership and performance: Tracking faint traces. *Journal of Financial Economics* 45 (2):223–255.

Logsdon, J. M., and P. G. Lewellyn. 2000. Expanding accountability to stakeholder: Trends and predictions. *Business and Society Review* 105 (4):419–435.

Lowenstein, L. 1999. Corporate governance and the voice of the paparazzi. Working paper, Center for Law and Economic Studies, Columbia Law School.

Lowenstein, R. 2004. *Origins of the Crash.* New York: Penguin Press.

Luffman, G. A., S. F. Witt, and S. Lister. 1982. A quantitative approach to stakeholder interests. *Managerial and Decision Economics* 3 (2):70–78.

Maassen, G. F., F. A. J. van den Bosch, and H. Volberda. 2004. The importance of disclosure in corporate governance self-regulation across Europe: A review of the Winter report and the EU action plan. *International Journal of Disclosure and Governance* 1 (2):146–159.

Maassen, G. F., and D. Brown. 2005. The election of directors with cumulative voting. Working paper, Rotterdam School of Management, Erasmus University.

MacAvoy, P., and I. Millstein. 2003. *The recurrent crisis in corporate governance.* New York: Palgrave Macmillan.

Macey, J. R. 1998. Institutional investors and corporate monitoring. In *Comparative corporate governance*, ed. K. J. Hopt, H. Kanada, M. J. Roe, E. Wymeersch, and S. Prigge. Oxford: Oxford University Press.

MacNeil, I., and X. Li. 2005. Comply or explain: Market discipline and non-compliance with the combined code. Working paper, University of Glasgow School of Law.

Malatesta, P., and R. Walking. 1988. Poison pill securities. *Journal of Financial Economics* 20 (1):347–376.

Mallin, C. A. 2004. *Corporate governance.* Oxford: Oxford University Press.

Mandelker, G. 1974. Risk and return: The case of merging firms. *Journal of Financial Economics* 1 (4):303–335.

Manne, H. G. 1965. Mergers and the market for corporate control. *Journal of Political Economy* 73 (2):110–120.

Manne, H. G. 1966. In defense of insider trading. *Harvard Business Review* 44 (6):113–122.

Manville, B. and J. Ober. 2003. *A company of citizens: What the world's first democracy teaches leaders about creating great organisations.* Boston: Harvard Business School Press.

Marris, R. 1964. *The economic theory of managerial capitalism.* London: Macmillan.

Martin, J. E. 2001. *Hanbury and Martin's modern equity.* 16th ed. London: Sweet & Maxwell.

Martin, K., and R. Thomas. 2003. When is enough, enough? Market reaction to highly dilutive stock option plan and the subsequent impact on CEO compensation. *Journal of Corporate Finance* 11 (1):61–83.

Masulis, R., C. Wang, and F. Xie. 2005. Corporate governance and acquirer returns. Working paper, Owen Graduate School of Management, Vanderbilt University.

Mathiesen, H. 2002. Managerial ownership and financial performance. PhD dissertation, Copenhagen Business School, Denmark.

Mattout, J.-P. 2004. Information financière et responsabilité des dirigeants. *Revue de droit bancaire et financier* 6 (November/December):454.

Maug, E., and K. Rydqvist. 2001. What is the function of the shareholders meeting? Evidence from the US proxy voting process. Working paper, Norwegian School of Management.

Maw, N. G. 1994. *Corporate governance.* Aldershot, UK: Dartmouth.

McBarnet, D. 2005. After Enron: Corporate governance, creative accounting and the uses of corporate social responsibility. In *Governing the corporation: Regulation and corporate governance in an age of scandal and global markets*, ed. J. O'Brien. Chichester: John Wiley & Sons.

McCahery, J., L. Renneboog, P. Ritter, and S. Haller. 2003. The economics of the proposed takeover directive. Working paper, Centre for European Policy Studies.

McChesney, F. 1997. *Money for nothing: Politicians, rent extraction and political extortion.* Cambridge, MA: Harvard University Press.

McConaughy, D. L., C. H. Matthews, and A. S. Fialko. 2001. Founding family controlled firms: Performance, risk and value. *Journal of Small Business Management* 39 (1):31–49.

McConnell, J. J., and H. Servaes. 1990. Additional evidence on equity ownership and corporate value. *Journal of Financial Economics* 27 (2):595–612.

McCraw, T. 1984. *Prophets of regulation.* Cambridge, MA: Harvard University Press.

McDonough, W. 2005. Accountability in an age of global markets. In *Governing the corporation*, ed. J. O'Brien. Chichester: John Wiley & Sons.

McKinsey & Company. 2002. Global investor opinion survey.

McLean, B., and P. Elkind. 2003. *The smartest guys in the room.* New York: Penguin Viking.

McNulty, T., J. Roberts, and P. Stiles. 2003. Creating accountability within the board: The work of the effective non-executive director. Department of Trade and Industry, United Kingdom.

MEDEF/Association Françaises des Entreprises Privées (AFEP). 2003. Principes de gouvernement d'entreprise résultant de la consolidation des rapports conjoints de l'AFEP et du MEDEF de 1995, 1999 et 2002. MEDEF, Paris.

Meeks, G. 1977. *Disappointing marriage: A study of the gains from merger.* New York: Cambridge University Press.

Mehran, H. 1992. Executive incentive plans, corporate control and capital structure. *Journal of Financial and Quantitative Analysis* 27 (4):539–560.

Mehran, H. 1995. Executive compensation structure, ownership and firm performance. *Journal of Financial Economics* 38 (2):163–184.

Merino, B. 2003. Financial reporting in the 1930s in the United States. *Accounting Forum* 27 (3):270–290.

Merkt, H. 2001. Disclosure rules as a primary tool for fostering party autonomy. In *Party autonomy and the role of information in the internal market*, ed. S. Grundmann, W. Kerber, and S. Weatherill. Berlin: de Gruyter.

Miguel, A. De, J. Pindado, and Ch. de la Torre. 2004. Ownership structure and firm value: New evidence from Spain. *Strategic Management Journal* 25 (12):1199–1208.

Milgrom, P., and J. Roberts. 1992. *Economics, organization and management.* Englewood Cliffs, NJ: Prentice-Hall.

Millon, D. 2002. Why is corporate management obsessed with quarterly earnings and what should be done about it? *George Washington Law Review* 70:890–920.

Millstein, I. 2000. Corporate governance: The role of market forces. *OECD Observer* (221/222):27–28.

Mishra, C., T. Randøy, and J. I. Jenssen. 2000. The effects of founding family influence on firm value and corporate governance: A study of Norwegian firms. *Journal of International Financial Management and Accounting* 12 (3):235–259.

Mitchell, L. E. 1996. *Progressive corporate law.* Boulder, CO: Westview Press.

Mitchell, L. E. 2001. *Corporate irresponsibility: America's newest export.* New Haven: Yale University Press.

Mitchell, R. K., B. R. Agle, and D. J. Wood. 1997. Toward a theory of stakeholder identification and salience: Defining the principle of who and what really counts. *Academy of Management Review* 22 (4):853–886.

Mitchell, T. 2003. Tales from the Asian dark side: Writer Michael Backman says little has changed in corporate governance since the 1997–98 regional financial crisis. *South China Morning Post (Business Post)* (May 5):16.

Modigliani, F., and E. Perotti. 1997. Protection of minority interest and the development of security markets. *Managerial and Decision Economics* 18 (7):519–528.

Modigliani, F., and E. Perotti. 2000. Security versus bank finance: The importance of a proper enforcement of legal rules. Working paper, Sloan School, MIT.

Moeller, R. R. 2004. *Sarbanes-Oxley and the new internal auditing rules.* Hoboken, NJ: John Wiley & Sons.

Moeller, T. 2004. Let's make a deal! How shareholder control impacts merger payoffs. Working paper, Jesse H. Jones Graduate School of Management, Rice University.

Monks, R. A. G., and N. Minow. 1996. *Watching the watchers: Corporate governance for the 21st century.* Oxford: Blackwell.

Monks, R. A. G., and N. Minow. 2004. *Corporate governance.* 3rd ed. Malden, MA: Blackwell.

Moran, M. 1991. *The politics of the financial services revolution,* London: Macmillan.

Moran, M. 2003. *The British regulatory state.* Oxford: Oxford University Press.

Morck, R., A. Shleifer, and R. W. Vishny. 1989. Alternative mechanisms for corporate control. *American Economic Review* 79 (4):842–852.

Morck, R., A. Shleifer, and R. W. Vishny. 1998. Management ownership and market valuation: An empirical analysis. *Journal of Financial Economics* 20 (1):3–24.

Morck, R., D. A. Strangeland, and B. Yeung. 1988. Inherited wealth, corporate control, and the economic growth: The Canadian disease? Working paper, National Bureau of Economic Research, Cambridge, MA.

Morck, R., and B. Yeung. 2003. Agency problems in large family groups. *Entrepreneurship Theory and Practice* 27 (4):367–382.

Morishita, K. 1997. Scandals put corporate culture on trial. *Nikkei Weekly* (June 23):4.

Mouvement des entreprises de France (MEDEF). 1999. Rapport du comité sur le gouvernement d'entreprise présidé par M Marc Vienot. European Corporate Governance Institute.

Mueller, D. 1985. Mergers and market shares. *Review of Economics and Statistics* 67 (2):259–267.

Mueller, D., and M. Sirower. 1998. The causes of mergers: Tests based on the gains to acquiring firms' shareholders and the size of premia. Working paper, Economic and Social Research Council (ESRC) Centre for Business Research.

Mulbert, P. 2004. Make it or break it. In *Reforming company and takeover law in Europe*, ed. G. Ferrarini, K. J. Hopt, J. Winter, and E. Wymeersch. Oxford: Oxford University Press.

Murphy, K. 1999. Executive compensation. In *Handbook of labor economics*, ed. O. Ashenfelter and D. Card. Amsterdam: North Holland.

Myers, S., and N. Majluf. 1984. Corporate financing and investment decisions when firms have information that investors do not have. *Journal of Financial Economics* 13 (2):187–221.

Myerson, R. 1979. Incentive compatibility and the bargaining problem. *Econometrica* 47 (1):61–73.

Nadler, D. A. 2003. Minefields in the boardroom. *Chief Executive* (July):14.

Nadler, D. A. 2004. Building better boards. *Harvard Business Review* 82 (5):102.

Nadler, D. A. 2005. What's the board's role in strategy development? "Engaging the Board in Corporate Strategy." *Strategy and Leadership* 32 (5):25–33.

Nagy, M. 2002. Canadian hedge watch proposes a new performance compensation structure for Canadian hedge funds. Unpublished paper.

National Association of Corporate Directors. 2001. Report of the NACD Blue Ribbon Commission on Board Evaluation: Improving director effectiveness. Washington, DC.

National Association of Corporate Directors. 2004. Report of the NACD Blue Ribbon Commission on Board Leadership. Washington, DC.

National Association of Corporate Directors. 2005. Report of the NACD Blue Ribbon Commission on Director Professionalism—2005 Edition. Washington, DC.

Nenova, T. 2003. The value of corporate voting rights and control: A cross-country analysis. *Journal of Financial Economics* 68 (3):325–351.

Nestor, S. 2002. *International efforts to improve corporate governance: Why and how?* Paris: Organisation for Economic Co-operation and Development.

Newbould, G. 1970. *Management and merger activity.* Liverpool: Gusthead.

New Zealand Securities Commission. 2004. *Corporate governance in New Zealand: Principles and guidelines.* Wellington, New Zealand.

Nicholls of Birkenhead, Lord. 1995. Trustees and their broader community: Where duty, morality and ethics converge. *Trust Law International* 9:71–75.

Nicodano, G., and A. Sembenelli. 2004. Private benefits, block transaction premiums and ownership structure. *International Review of Financial Analysis* 13:227–244.

Nilsen, A. 2004. The EU takeover directive and the competitiveness of European industry. Oxford Council on Good Governance Economy Analysis.

Noe, T. 2002. Institutional activism and financial market structure. *Review of Financial Studies* 15 (1):289–318.

Nofsinger J., and K. Kim. 2003. *Infectious greed.* Englewood Cliffs, NJ: Prentice-Hall.

Nohel, T., and S. Todd. 2002. Stock options and managerial incentives to invest. Working paper, Loyola University of Chicago.

Nolan, R. 2003. Indirect investors: A greater say in the company? *Journal of Corporate Law Studies* 3:73–121.

O'Brien, J. 2003. *Wall Street on trial.* Chichester: John Wiley & Sons.

O'Brien, J. 2004a. Beyond compliance: Testing the limits of reforming the governance of Wall Street. *International Journal of Business Governance and Ethics* 1 (2):162–174.

O'Brien, J. 2004b. Ethics probity and the changing governance of Wall Street: Cure or remission. *Public Integrity* 7 (1):43–56.

O'Brien, J., ed. 2005a. *Governing the corporation: Regulation and corporate governance in an age of scandal and global markets.* Chichester: John Wiley & Sons.

O'Brien, J. 2005b. The politics of enforcement: Eliot Spitzer, State-Federal Relations and the Redesign of Financial Regulation. *Publius: The Journal of Federalism* 35(3):449–466.

O'Brien, J. 2005c. Transcending compliance in an age of scandal. In *The structure of financial regulation,* ed. D. Mayes and G. Wood. London: Routledge.

O'Dell, E. 2000. Incapacity. In *Lessons of the swaps litigation,* ed. P. B. H. Birks, and F. Rose. London: Mansfield Press.

O'Rourke, A. 2003. The message and methods of ethical investment. *Journal of Cleaner Production* 11:683–693.

Ontario Securities Commission. 2004. Proposed National Policy 58–201 Corporate Governance Guidelines and Proposed National Instrument 58–101 Disclosure of Corporate Governance Practices. 27 OSCB 8825–8858.

Organisation for Economic Co-operation and Development Ad Hoc Task Force on Corporate Governance. 1999. *OECD principles of corporate governance.* Paris: Organisation for Economic Co-operation and Development.

Organisation for Economic Co-operation and Development Steering Group on Corporate Governance. 2001. *Corporate governance in OECD member countries: Recent developments and trends.* Paris: Organisation for Economic Co-operation and Development.

Organisation for Economic Co-operation and Development. 2004. *OECD principles of corporate governance.* Paris: Organisation for Economic Co-operation and Development.

Oyer, P. 2003. Why do firms use incentives that have no incentive effects? *Journal of Finance* 59 (4):1619–1650.

Oyer, P., and S. Schaefer. 2004. Why do firms give stock options to all employees?: An empirical examination of alternative theories. Working paper, National Bureau of Economic Research, Cambridge, MA.

Pagano, M., and P. Volpin. 2000. The political economy of corporate governance. Working paper, Corporate Social Responsibility Forum (CSRF).

Pagano, M., and P. Volpin. 2002. Managers, workers and corporate control. Working paper, Faculty of Economics, University of Naples Federico II.

Palepu, K. 1986. Predicting takeover offerees: A methodological and empirical analysis. *Journal of Accounting and Economics* 8 (1):3–35.

Palia, D., and F. Lichtenberg. 1999. Managerial ownership and firm performance: A re-examination using productivity measurement. *Journal of Corporate Finance* 5 (4):323–339.

Palmer, J. 1973. The profit-performance effects of the separation of ownership from control in large US industrial corporations. *Bell Journal of Economics and Management Science* 4 (1):293–303.

Park, S., and M. Song. 1995. Employee stock ownership plans, firm performance and monitoring by outside blockholders. *Financial Management* 24 (1):52–65.

Parkinson, J. 2003. Preface. In *Working within two kinds of capitalism*, ed. I. Lynch Fannon. Oxford: Hart.

Parkinson, J., A. Gamble, and G. Kelly. 2000. *The political economy of the company*. Oxford: Hart.

Patrick O'Callaghan & Associates and Korn/Ferry International. 2004. Corporate board governance and director compensation in Canada, a review of 2004. Vancouver: Patrick O'Callaghan & Associates.

Paul, J. 1992. On the efficiency of stock-based compensation. *Review of Financial Studies* 5 (3):471–502.

Pensions Investment Research Consultants. 2004. Corporate governance annual review 2004. Pensions Investment Research Consultants, London.

People's Daily. 2000. Chinese public procurator appointed as independent director of SOE. *People's Daily* (November 27).

Perez, J. M. 2002. You can bet your life on it! Regulating senior settlements to be a financial alternative for the elderly. *Elder Law Journal* 10:425–452.

Pérez-Gonzalez, F. 2001. Inherited control and firm performance. Working paper, Columbia Business School.

Perino, M. 2002. Enron's legislative aftermath: Some reflections on the deterrence aspects of the Sarbanes-Oxley Act of 2002. *St John's Law Review* 76:676–689.

Pettigrew, A. N., and T. McNulty. 1995. Power and influence in and around the boardroom. *Human Relations* 48 (8):845–873.

Pettigrew, A. N., and T. McNulty. 1998. Sources and uses of power in the boardroom. *European Journal of Work and Organisational Psychology* 7 (2):197–214.

Pfeffer, J. 1981. *Power in organisations*. Boston: Pitman.

Pfeffer, J. 1992. *Managing with power*. Boston: Harvard Business School Press.

Pierce, C., ed. 2001. *The effective director: The essential guide to director & board development*. London: Kogan Page.

Plender, J. 2003. Capitalism, Higgs and the China syndrome: Home thoughts, oriental habits. *Financial Times* (January 27):24.

Plender, J. 2005. Managing the board, Part II: Evaluating performance: How to bring the board to book. *Financial Times* (January 20):8.

Pohjola, M. 1988. Concentration of shareholder voting power in Finnish industrial companies. *Scandinavian Journal of Economics* 90:245–253.

Pollack, R. A. 1985. A transaction cost approach to families and households. *Journal of Economic Literature* 23 (2):581–608.

Porter, M.E. 1997. Capital choices: Changing the way America invests in industry. In *Studies in international corporate finance and governance systems: A com-*

parison of the US, Japan, and Europe, ed. D. H. Chew. New York: Oxford University Press.

Posner, E. 2002. Law and social norms. Cambridge, MA: Harvard University Press.

Pound, J. 1988. Proxy contests and the efficiency of shareholder oversight. *Journal of Financial Economics* 20 (1):237–265.

Preda Report. 1999. Report & code of conduct. Committee for the Corporate Governance of Listed Companies.

Prigge, S. 1998. A survey of German corporate governance. In *Corporate governance: The state of the art and emerging research*, ed. K. J. Hopt, M. J. Roe, and E. Wymeersch. Oxford: Oxford University Press.

Provost, C. 2003. State attorneys general, entrepreneurship, and consumer protection in the New Federalism. *Publius: The Journal of Federalism* 33 (2):37–53.

Randoy, T., and S. Goel. 2003. Ownership structure, founder leadership, and performance in Norwegian SMEs: Implications for financing entrepreneurial opportunities. *Journal of Business Venturing* 18 (5):619–637.

Ravenscraft, D., and F. Scherer. 1987. Life after takeover. *Journal of Industrial Economics* 36 (2):147–156.

Rawls, J. 1999. *A theory of justice*. Cambridge, MA: Belknap Press.

Rechner, P. L., and D. R. Dalton. 1991. CEO duality and organizational performance: A longitudinal analysis. *Strategic Management Journal* 12 (2):155–160.

Ribstein, L. 2002. Market vs. regulatory responses to corporate governance fraud: A critique of the Sarbanes-Oxley Act of 2002. Research paper, University of Illinois Law and Economics.

Rickford, J. 2003. Do good governance recommendations change the rules for the board of directors? In *Capital markets and company law*, ed. K. J. Hopt and E. Wymeersch. Oxford: Oxford University Press.

Riker, W.H. 1962. *The theory of political coalitions*. New Haven: Yale University Press.

Roberts, J. M. 1996. Corporate governance: A systemic view. Seminar paper, University of Cambridge Judge Institute of Management Studies.

Roe, M. J. 1996. Chaos and evolution in law and economics. *Harvard Law Review* 109:641–667.

Roe, M. J. 2000. Rents and their corporate consequences. *Stanford Law Review* 53:1463–1494.

Roe, M. J. 2002a. Can culture constrain the economic model of corporate law? *University of Chicago Law Review* 69:1251–1269.

Roe, M. J. 2002b. Corporate law's limits. *Journal of Legal Studies* 31:233–271.

Roe, M. J. 2003a. *The political determinants of corporate governance*. Oxford: Oxford University Press.

Roe, M. J. 2003b. Rôle de l'actionnaire et système politique. *Revue Française de Gestion*: 305–345.

Romano, R. 1993. Competition for corporate charters and the lesson of takeover statutes. *Fordham Law Review* 61:843–864.

Romano, R. 1998. Empowering investors: A market approach to securities regulation. In *Comparative corporate governance*, ed. K. J. Hopt, H. Kanada, M. J. Roe, E. Wymeersch, and S. Prigge. Oxford: Oxford University Press.

Romano, R. 2000. Less is more: Making institutional investor activism a valuable mechanism of corporate governance. Working paper, Yale Law School.

Romano, R. 2002. *The advantage of competitive federalism for securities regulation*. Washington, DC: American Enterprise Institute.

Romano, R. 2004. The Sarbanes-Oxley Act and the making of quack corporate governance. Working paper, European Corporate Governance Institute.

Ross, S. 2004. Compensation incentives and the duality of risk aversion and riskiness. *Journal of Finance* 59 (1):207–225.

Ruback, R. 1988. Do target shareholders lose in unsuccessful control contests? In *Corporate takeovers: Causes and consequences*, ed. A. Auerbach. Chicago: University of Chicago Press.

Rydqvist, K. 1987. *The pricing of shares with different voting power and the theory of oceanic games*. Stockholm: Stockholm School of Economics.

Ryngaert, M. 1988. The effect of poison pill securities on shareholder wealth. *Journal of Financial Economics* 20 (1):377–417.

Scharfstein, D. 1988. The disciplinary role of takeovers. *Review of Economic Studies* 55 (182):185–200.

Scholes, M., and M. Wolfson. 1990. ESOPs and corporate restructuring: Myth and realities. *Financial Management* 19 (1):12–28.

Schulze, W., M. Lubatkin, and R. Dino. 2003. Toward a theory of agency and altruism in family firms. *Journal of Business Venturing* 18 (4):473–490.

Schulze, W., M. Lubatkin, R. Dino, and A. Buchhaltz. 2001. Agency relationships in family firms: Theory and evidence. *Organization Science* 12 (1):99–116.

Scott, C. 2000. Accountability in the regulatory state. *Journal of Law and Society* 27 (1):38–60.

Securities and Exchange Commission. 1998. Amendments to rules on shareholder proposals. Final Rule, Release No. 34-40018.

Securities and Exchange Commission. 2003. Security holder director nominations. Proposed Rule, Release No. 34-48626.

Securities and Exchange Commission. 2004. Summary of comments: In response to the commission's proposed rules relating to security holder director nominations. Release No. 34-48626.

Seligman, J. 2003a. Cautious evolution or perennial irresolution: Self-regulation and market structure during the first seventy years of the Securities and Exchange Commission. Paper presented at Global Capital Markets Center-NYSE Conference on Current Issue in Institutional Equities Trading, West Palm Beach, FL, December 13.

Seligman, J. 2003b. *The transformation of Wall Street: A history of the securities and exchange commission and modern corporate finance*. New York: Aspen.

Senate Governmental Affairs Committee. 2002. Financial oversight of Enron: The SEC and private sector watchdogs. October 8.

Shapley, L. S. 1953. A value for n-person games. *Annals of Mathematical Studies* 28:307–317.

Shapley, L. S., and M. Shubik. 1954. A method for evaluating the distribution of the power in a committee system. *American Political Science Review* 48 (3):787–792.

Shleifer, A., and L. Summers. 1998. Breach of trust in hostile takeovers. In *Corporate takeovers: Causes and consequences*, ed. A. Auerbach. Chicago: University of Chicago Press.

Shleifer, A., and R. W. Vishny. 1996. Large shareholders and corporate control. *Journal of Political Economy* 95 (3):461–488.

Shleifer, A., and R. W. Vishny. 1997. A survey of corporate governance. *Journal of Finance* 52 (2):737–783.

Short, H. 1994. Ownership, control, financial structure and the performance of firms. *Journal of Economic Surveys* 8 (3):203–249.

Short, H., and K. Keasey. 1997. Institutional shareholders and corporate governance in the United Kingdom. In *Corporate governance: Economic, management, and financial issues*, ed. K. S. Keasy, S. Thomson, and M. Wright. Oxford: Oxford University Press.

Singh, A. 1971. *Takeovers, their relevance to the stock market and their theory of the firm*. Cambridge: Cambridge University Press.

Skeel, D. 2005. *Icarus in the boardroom*. New York: Oxford University Press.

Skog, R. 2004. The takeover directive—a breakthrough? Conference paper, British Institute of International and Comparative Law.

Slinger, G. 1999. Spanning the gap: The theoretical principles that connect stakeholder policies to business performance. *Corporate Governance* 7 (2):136–151.

Smiley, R. 1976. Tender offers, transaction costs and the firm. *Review of Economics and Statistics* 58 (1):22–32.

Smith, M. P. 1996. Shareholder activism by institutional investors: Evidence from CalPERS. *Journal of Finance* 51 (1):227–252.

Sonnenfeld, J. A. 2002. What makes great boards great. *Harvard Business Review* 80 (9):106–113.

Sonnenfeld, J. A. 2004. Good governance and the misleading myths of bad metrics. *Academy of Management Executive* 18 (1):108–113.

Snoy, J.-C. 2001. La corporate governance et la place qu'elle donne à l'information en Belgique. Unpublished paper.

Solomon, J., S. Lin, S. Norton, and A. Solomon. 2003. Corporate governance in Taiwan: Empirical evidence from Taiwanese company directors. *Corporate Governance* 11 (3):235–248.

Song, W., and S. H. Szewczyk. 2003. Does coordinated institutional investor activism reverse the fortunes of underperforming firms? *Journal of Financial and Quantitative Analysis* 38 (2):317–336.

Spencer, P. 2000. *The structure and regulation of financial markets*. Oxford: Oxford University Press.

Sraer, D., and D. Thesmar. 2004. Performance and behaviour of family firms: Evidence from the French stock market. Working paper, Centre de Recherche en Economie et Statistique (CREST-INSEE), Toulouse.

Standard & Poor's. 2004. Corporate governance scores and evaluations, criteria, methodology and definitions. New York: McGraw-Hill.

Standard & Poor's Governance Services. 2002. Standard & Poor's corporate governance scores: Criteria, methodology and definitions. New York: McGraw-Hill.

Stapledon, G.P. 1996. *Institutional shareholders and corporate governance*. Oxford: Clarendon Press.

Stein, J. 1997. Internal capital markets and the competition for corporate resources. *Journal of Finance* 52 (1):111–133.

Sternberg, E. 2003. Competition in company control: A shareholder-driven alternative to the Higgs proposals on non-executive directors. Imediacopy.

Stiglitz, J. 2003. *The roaring nineties*. New York: Norton.

Strätling, R. 2003. General meetings: A dispensable tool for corporate governance of listed companies? *Corporate Governance*, 11 (1):74–82.

Streeck, W., and P. Schmitter. 1985. Community, market, state and associations? The prospective contribution of interest governance to social order. In *Private Interest Government*, ed. W. Streeck, and P. Schmitter. Beverly Hills, CA: Sage.

Strine, L. 2002. Derivative impact: Some early reflections on the corporation law implications of the Enron debacle. *Business Lawyer* 57 (4):1371–1402.

Stuart, S., and the Rotman School of Management. 2003. *Canadian board trends and practices at leading Canadian companies*. Toronto.

Stulz, R. M. 1988. Managerial control of voting rights: Financing policies and the market for corporate control. *Journal of Financial Economics* 20 (1):25–54.

Subramanian, G. 2001. The influence of anti-takeover statutes on incorporation choice: Evidence on the 'race' debate and anti-takeover overreaching, negotiations, organizations and markets. Working paper, Harvard Law School.

Swisher, P. N. 2005. The insurable interest requirement for life insurance: A critical assessment. *Drake Law Review* 53:477–543.

Taiwan Stock Exchange. 2002. Corporate governance best-practice principles for Taiwan Stock Exchange Corporation (TSEC)/GreTai Securities Market (GTSM) listed companies.

Telus Corporation. 2005. Notice of annual and special meetings and class meetings information circular.

Tenev, S., and C. Zhang. (2002). Corporate governance and enterprise reform in China: Building the institutions of modern markets. World Bank and the International Finance Corporation.

Teske, P. 2004. *Regulating the states*. Washington, DC: Brookings Institution.

Thomas, G. 1998. *Powers*. London: Sweet & Maxwell.

Tirole, J. 2001. Corporate governance. *Econometrica* 69 (1):1–35.

Tosi, H. L., S. Werner, J. P. Katz, and L. R. Gómez-Mejía. 2000. How much does performance matter? A meta-analysis of CEO pay studies. *Journal of Management* 26 (2):301–339.

Tricker, R. I. 2003. *The essential director: An* Economist *guide*. London: Economist Books.

Vafeas, N., and E. Theodorou. 1998. The relationship between board structure and firm performance in the UK. *British Accounting Review* 30:383–407.

van Boom, W. H. 2004. Pure economic loss: A comparative perspective. In *Pure economic loss*, ed. W. H. van Boom, H. Koziol, and C. A. Witting. Vienna: Springer.

van Boom, W. H., H. Koziol, and C. A. Witting. 2004. Outlook. In *Pure economic loss*, ed. W. H. van Boom, H. Koziol, and C. A. Witting.

Van den Berghe, L. A. A., and S. Carchon. 2002. Corporate governance practices in Flemish family businesses. *Corporate Governance—An International Review* 10 (3):225–245.

Van den Berghe, L. A. A., and A. Levrau. 2003. Measuring the quality of corporate governance: In search of a tailormade approach? *Journal of General Management* 28 (3):71–83.

Van den Berghe, L. A. A., and A. Levrau. 2004. Evaluating boards of directors: What constitutes a good corporate board? *Corporate Governance: An International Review* 12(4):461–478.

Van Duzer, A. J. 2003. *The law of partnerships and corporations.* 2nd ed. Toronto: Irwin.

Varaiya, N., and K. Ferris. 1987. Overpaying in corporate takeovers: The winner's curse. *Financial Analysts Journal* 43 (3):64–70.

Villalonga, B., and R. Amit. 2004. How do family ownership, control and management affect firm value? Working paper, Harvard Business School.

Viner, A. C. 2004a. Corporate governance in China. In *International corporate governance*, ed. J. C. Lufkin, 2nd ed. London: Euromoney.

Viner, A. C. 2004b. The international corporate governance revolution. In *International corporate governance*, ed. J. C. Lufkin, 2nd ed. London: Euromoney.

Viner, A. C. 2004c. Some practical resources for corporate governance specialists. In *International corporate governance*, ed. J. C. Lufkin, 2nd ed. London: Euromoney.

Vivendi Universal. 2003. Form 20–F-2002.

Vives, X., (ed.). 2000. *Corporate governance: Theoretical and empirical perspectives.* Cambridge: Cambridge University Press.

Völkl, C. R. 2004. *Corporate governance enforcement.* Vienna: Manz.

von Bar, C., and U. Drobnig. 2004. *The interaction of contract law and tort and property law in Europe.* Munich: Sellier.

von Hayek, F. A. 1973. *Law, legislation and liberty*, Vol. I: *Rules and order.* London: Routledge and Kegan Paul.

von Mises, L. 1949. *Human action: A theory on economics.* New Haven: Yale University Press.

Von Werder, A., T. Talaulicar, and G. L. Kolat. 2003. Kodex report 2003: Die Akzeptanz der Empfehlungen des Deutschen Corporate Governance Kodex. *Der Betrieb* 56 (34):1857–1863.

Vries Robbé, J. J. de, and P. U. Ali. 2005. *Securitisation of derivatives and alternative asset classes.* London and The Hague: Kluwer Law International.

Wahal, S. 1996. Pension fund activism and firm performance. *Journal of Financial Economics* 31 (1):1–23.

Walker, D. 2005. Restoring trust after recent accountability failures. In *Governing the corporation regulation and corporate governance in an age of scandal and global markets*, ed. J. O'Brien. Chichester: John Wiley & Sons.

Walking, R., and M. Long. 1984. Agency theory, managerial welfare and takeover bid resistance. *Rand Journal of Economics* 15 (1):54–68.

Wang, X. 2002. The prospect of antimonopoly legislation in China. *Washington University Global Studies Law Review* 1:201–230.

Ward, R. D. 2003. *Saving the corporate board: Why boards fail and how to fix them.* Hoboken, NJ: John Wiley & Sons.

Warner, J., R. Watts, and K. Wruck. 1988. Stock prices and top management changes. *Journal of Financial Economics* 20 (1):461–492.

Waring, K., and C. Pierce (eds.). 2005. *The handbook of international corporate governance: A definitive guide.* London: Kogan Page.

Weihrich, H., and H. Koontz. 1994. *Management: A global perspective.* New York: McGraw-Hill.

Weil, Gotshal & Manges. 2002. Comparative study of corporate governance codes relevant to the European Union and its member states. European Corporate Governance Institute.

Wenger, E., and C. Kaserer. 1998. German banks and corporate governance: A critical view. In *Corporate governance: The state of the art and emerging research*, ed. K. J. Hopt, M. J. Roe, and E. Wymeersch. Oxford: Oxford University Press.

Werner, W. 1981. Corporation law in search of its future. *Columbia Law Review* 81:1611–1666.

Weynand, W., and O. Lemaire. 2004. Gouvernement d'entreprise: L'importance des administrateurs indépendants au sein du conseil et de ses sous-comités. Luxembourg: Ernst & Young.

Williams, J. 2005. Reflections in the private versus public policing of economic crime. *British Journal of Criminology* 45 (3):316–339.

Williams, J. C. 2002. The family-hostile corporation. *George Washington Law Review* 70:921–930.

Winter, J. 2004. EU company law at the cross-roads. In *Reforming company and takeover law in Europe*, ed. G. Ferrarini, K. J. Hopt, J. Winter, and E. Wymeersch. Oxford: Oxford University Press.

Wired News. (2002). Vivendi votes hacked? Ha: Experts. *Wired News*, 29 April.

Wolfenzon, D. 1999. A theory of pyramidal structures. Working paper, Stern School of Business, New York University.

Wong, T. K. H. (1989) An application of game theory to corporate governance. *Omega (An International Journal of Management Science)* 17:59–67.

Wu, X., and Z. Wang. 2003. Equity financing in a Myers-Majluf framework with private benefits of control. Working paper, City University of Hong Kong.

Wulf, J. 2004. Do CEOs in mergers trade power for premium? Evidence from "mergers of equals." *Journal of Law, Economics, and Organization* 20 (1):60–101.

Wymeersch, E. 2004. About techniques of regulating companies in the European Union. In *Reforming company and takeover law in Europe*, ed. G. Ferrarini, K. J. Hopt, J. Winter, and E. Wymeersch. Oxford: Oxford University Press.

Yermack, D. (1995) Do corporations award CEO stock options effectively? *Journal of Financial Economics* 39 (2):237–269.

Yermack, D. 1996. Higher market valuation of companies with a small board of directors. *Journal of Financial Economics* 40 (2):185–211.

Yermack, D. 1997. Good timing: CEO stock option awards and company news announcements. *Journal of Finance* 52 (2):449–476.

Zeff, S. 2003. How the US accounting profession got where it is today. *Accounting Horizons* 17 (4):67–286.

Zellner, A. (1962) An efficient method of estimating seemingly unrelated regressions and tests for aggregation bias. *Journal of American Statistical Association* 57:348–368.

Zhang, G. 1998. Ownership concentration, risk aversion and the effect of financial structure on investment decisions. *European Economic Review* 42 (9):1751–1778.

Zingales, L. 1994. The value of the voting right: A study of the Milan Stock Exchange experience. *Review of Financial Studies* 7 (1):125–148.

Index

A

Accountancy profession, 19–20, 20–23, 82–83
ACSI guidelines, 140–142, 143
Activism of institutional investors, 146–148, 224–228, 265
Administration processes, 68–69
Adopting financial reports, 83
ADP, 232
Agency relationship:
  in Australia, 143–144
  between managers and shareholders, 96, 445
  problems with, 267
Agency theory:
  board as monitoring device and, 312
  hedge funds and, 131–132
  overview of, 96
  owner type and, 30–31
  single-equation models and, 63
  See also Principal agent theory
AMF (Autorité des Marchés Financiers):
  annual survey by, 475–476
  damages allowed by, 345
  development of enforcement by, 351–356
  power of, 346

Anti-takeover measures:
  in European Union, 259–262
  evidence on, 282
  managerial welfare hypothesis and, 279–282
  shareholder's welfare hypothesis and, 277–279
  staggered board structure and, 262–263
  in United States, 255–258, 284–285
  See also Takeover Directive (EU); Takeovers
Application of financial reporting standards, 80
Apria Healthcare, 264
Arm's-length financial model of corporate governance, 424–425
Armstrong v. Jackson, 174
Arthur Andersen, 20–21
Assessment:
  of effectiveness of board, 503–507
  of effectiveness of directors, 507–509
  by ratings services, 476–480
  See also Governance assessments
Assignment of life insurance policies, 191–192
Atkins, Paul, 19–20

Germany:
  corporate governance code in,
    482
  investor empowerment in, 180,
    181, 182–183
  publication of remuneration in,
    481
  shareholder structure in,
    219–221
Glass-Steagall Act, 17
Global benchmarking,
  477–478
Global equilibrium, 456–457
Goldschmidt, Harvey, 19
Governance advisers, 512–513
Governance assessments:
  acting on results of, 516–518
  of board effectiveness,
    503–507
  confidentiality *vs.* disclosure and,
    515–516
  definition of, 485
  of director effectiveness,
    507–509
  external assistance with,
    511–513
  frequency of, 523–524
  information produced by,
    513–515
  leadership of, 498–503
  linking with continued service on
    board, 520–523
  methods of conducting,
    509–513
  nonperforming chairman of
    board and, 518–519
  nonperforming director and,
    519–520
  objections to, 493–495
  overcoming objections to,
    495–497
  prevalence of, 490–491

proceeding with process of,
  497–498
rationale for, 491–492
types of, 488–491

H

Hamilton's Rule, 6
HealthSouth, 19, 24
Hedge funds:
  agency theory and, 131–132
  corporate governance and,
    134–135
  literature review on, 130–131
  overview of, 129–130
  performance fees and,
    132
  regulation of, 133–134
  structure of, 135
Herfindahl index, 202–203
Hermes, 480
Higgs Report, 300, 305, 306,
    307–308, 315–316
High Level Group Report,
    428–429, 430, 434
HIH Insurance, 162
Hollinger, 24
Hong Kong, *see* China
Horizontal ownership structure:
  Banzhaf index and,
    205–206
  coalitions between shareholders
    and, 206–207
  incomplete data and, 207–210
  index preference and,
    210–211
  measures of, 201–203
  overview of, 200
  power index and, 211–215
  Shapley-Shubik index and,
    203–205

Volkswagen AG, 229
Voluntary code of best practices,
    472–474
Voting:
    cross-border proxy, 231–232
    electronic, in Europe,
        232–233
    proxy, 142–143, 231–232
Voting guidelines of institutional
    investors, 226–227

W

Walden Asset Management, 227
Weakest link principle, 218
Weak ownership rule, 219
White noise, 452–453, 455
Whole of life policy, 188
Whole-of-portfolio approach, 168,
    169
Williams, Harold, 11
Winter, Jaap, 283

Winter Report:
    on bids, 287
    breakthrough rule and, 288–289,
        292
    on cross-border voting, 232
    market for corporate control
        and, 283, 284–285
WorldCom, 10, 17, 20, 131

Y

Youth participation in labor
    market, 432–433

Z

Zero exercise price options,
    329–330
Zero social discount rate, 5
Zhengzhou Baiwen, 368–369
Zone of privilege, 515–516